The Art of Living to God

A Study of Method and Piety in the
Theoretico-practica theologia *of*
Petrus van Mastricht (1630-1706)

Adriaan C. Neele

The Art of Living to God

A Study of Method and Piety in the *Theoretico-practica theologia* of Petrus van Mastricht (1630-1706)

Een onderzoek naar de methode en vroomheid in de *Theoretico-practica theologia* van Petrus van Mastricht (1630-1706)

(Met een samenvatting in het Nederlands)

PROEFSCHRIFT

Ter verkrijging van de graad van doctor aan de Universiteit te Utrecht op gezag van de rector magnificus, Prof. Dr. W. H. Gispen ingevolge van het besluit van het College voor Promoties in het openbaar te verdedigen op maandag 3 October 2005 des ochtends te 10:30 uur

DOOR

ADRIAAN CORNELIS NEELE

Geboren op 14 oktober 1960 te Rotterdam

Promotor: Prof. Dr. A. de Reuver (Faculteit der Godgeleerdheid)
Co-promotors: Dr. W. J. van Asselt (Faculteit der Godgeleerdheid)
                Dr. R. A. Muller (Calvin Theological Seminary, USA)

This study was printed with support of the Oikonomos foundation.

CONTENTS

Acknowledgments

Obschon seine [Petrus van Mastricht 1630-1706] Arbeit wenig geachtet wird, lässet er sich doch solches nicht irren, sondern bleibet bey seiner Meynung, welche hie und da ihr Liebhaber noch finden.[1]

This study represents an introduction to the life and work of the successor of Gisbertus Voetius (1589-1676). This study, furthermore, attempts to demonstrate the relationship between exegesis, doctrine, elenctic, and *praxis* in the doctrine of God in Mastricht's *Theoretico-practica theologia*, a work characterized by Jonathan Edwards (1703-1758) "as much better than Turretin or any other book in the world, excepting the Bible." In particular my interest is in the relationship between method and piety as found in Mastricht's work.

My first debt of gratefulness is to Prof. Dr. Arie de Reuver: advisor of this doctoral thesis at the University of Utrecht. I was privileged to benefit from his scholarly erudition and pastoral mentoring. Further, I thank my co-advisors Dr. Willem J. van Asselt (University of Utrecht) and Prof. Dr. Richard A. Muller (Calvin Theological Seminary, Grand Rapids: my *alma mater*) for their continuing support, encouragement, and guidance of this project. Words of thanks are also extended to the readers of the manuscript Prof. Dr. W. Otten (University of Utrecht), Prof. Dr. Carl Trueman (Westminster Theological Seminary, Philadelphia, USA) and Prof. Dr. James DeJong (president-emeritus of Calvin Theological Seminary). Without the gracious help of the librarians of the University of Utrecht, Hekman Library, Grand Rapids, and the University libraries of Duisburg, Frankfurt an der Oder, Harvard, Pittsburgh Seminary, Princeton, Rostock, and Yale, this work would not have been what it is. I also extend my thanks to Drs. Ton Bolland for obtaining Mastricht's *magnum opus*, Mr. Jarl Waggoner for editing my writing and Dr. C.A de Niet and Drs. G. van den Brink for their expertise of the Latin language. The Reverend Cornelis van de Berg—pastor and missionary—is thanked for his enduring friendschip in the years past. Without the assistance of Prof. Dr. J.W Hofmeyr, University of Pretoria, South Africa, colleague and friend and the Oikonomos foundation this study was not printed.

Finally, this work I offer to my wife, Kornelia *sine qua non*, and our children Ruth, Matthew, Hadassah, Deborah, Joël and Salóme for their unwavering support.

Soli Deo Gloria
Adriaan C. Neele

1. Heinrich L. Benthem, *Holländischer Kirchen- und Schulen-Staat* (Frankfurt an der Oder: Förster, 1698), 2:460

Introduction

This study deals with the post-Reformation Reformed concern for right doctrine and piety. In respect to the former, scholarship has tended to appraise the theology of the seventeenth-century Reformed orthodox era, which includes the *Nadere Reformatie*, Puritanism and Pietism, as rigid and polemic; i.e. an abstract doctrine with little or no regard for practical significance. Consequently, the concern for orthodox doctrine has been seen as stalling the biblical exegesis of that era. In particular such exegesis has been critiqued for serving only to proof-text dogmatic and polemic works. Furthermore, the concern for doctrine has been regarded as leading to the relapse to Scholasticism and the neglect of the vitality of the Reformers' humanism. This argument in particular is applicable to the study of the doctrine of God of the seventeenth-century post-Reformation period, which is appraised as merely a doctrinal, intellectual, static, or abstract truth with also no practical importance. In respect to piety or *praxis pietatis*, which is a distinct feature of the seventeenth-century Reformed thought, scholarship has often negatively appraised its subjectivism, mysticism, and pietism, which deviated from Scripture. In addition, piety usually is described in opposition of the post-Reformation Reformed (Scholastic) orthodoxy. Contrary to these two emerging perspectives, more recent scholarship recognizes that piety is a working out of the theology of the seventeenth-century Reformed orthodoxy, which includes methodological aspects of scholasticism and Renaissance humanism.

This author asserts, however, that the appraisals of the post-Reformation Reformed concern for right doctrine and piety are often deficient in demonstrating a possible correlation of Scripture, doctrine, and *praxis*. The method of exegesis, the formulation of doctrine, and its practical implications are often disregarded. Furthermore, such studies fail to consider seventeenth-century Reformed theology as a living theology and dialogue of divine revelation and salvation. It is from this perspective that this study will examine and evaluate the doctrine of God in the *Theoretico-practica theologia* of Petrus van Mastricht (1630-1706) and shall consider the question of whether Mastricht's approach was, in fact, successful, thus legitimatizing the above-mentioned criticism.

The State of Research

The state of research, or secondary literature, will be examined in four distinguished parts: (1) the life and work of Mastricht, (2) the intellectual thought of his time, (3) the study of the doctrine of God, and (4) piety of the seventeenth-century Reformed orthodoxy. The first section will be extensive, because this study is the first monograph on the life and work of Mastricht. Contrary to the extensive treatment of section one, sections two to four, will outline various scholarly opinions.

Life and Work of Petrus van Mastricht

The life and work of Petrus van Mastricht has remained relatively unknown. This is in contrast to his immediate predecessors, such as William Ames (1576-1633), Gisbertus Voetius (1589-1676), and Johannes Cocceius (1603-1669) and contemporaries, such as Simon Oomius (1630-1706), Wilhelmus à Brakel (1635-1711), Theodor Undereyck (1635-1693), and Herman Witsius (1636-1708), who have been the subject of dissertations[1] and many publications.[2] Nonetheless, some theologians and historians of America, Germany, the Netherlands, and Scotland have commented on the life and work of Mastricht with diverse enunciations and conclusions. In respect to his life B. Glasius, C. Sepp, S. van der Linde, H. Kaajan, W. J. van Asselt, A. Goudriaan, and others provide concise biographical information,[3] which primarily originates from H.

---

1. F. J. Los, *Wilhelmus à Brakel* (Leiden: Brill, 1892); A. C. Duker, *Gisbertus Voetius*, 3 vol. (Leiden: Brill, 1897-1915); Keith L. Sprunger, *The Learned Doctor William Ames* (Chicago: University of Illinois Press, 1972); W. J. van Asselt, *Amicitia Dei, een onderzoek naar de structuur van de theologie van Johannes Cocceius (1603-1669)* (Ede: Grafische vormgeving ADC, 1988); idem, *Johannes Cocceius, Portret van een zeventiende-eeuws theoloog op oude en nieuwe wegen* (Heerenveen: Groen, 1997); idem, *The Federal Theology of Johannes Cocceius* (Leiden, New York: Brill, 2001); Do-Hong Jou, *Theodor Undereyck und die Anfänge des reformierten Pietismus* (Diss., Bochum, 1993); J. van Genderen, *Herman Witsius, bijdrage tot de kennis der Gereformeerde theologie* ('s-Gravenhage: Guido de Bres, 1953); Jan van Vliet, *William Ames: Marrow of the Theology and Piety of the Reformed Tradition* (Ph.D. diss., Westminster Theological Seminary, 2002); Gregory D. Schuringa, *Embracing* Leer *and* Leven: *The Theology of Simon Oomius in Context of* Nadere Reformatie *Orthodoxy* (Ph.D. diss., Calvin Theological Seminary, 2003).

2. F. W. Huisman, *Bibliografie van het gereformeerde Piëtisme in Nederland to 1800* (Woudenberg: Uitgeverij Op Hoope, 2001); See for Ames, Voetius, Cocceius, and Undereyck also *Biographisch-Bibliographisch Kirchenlexikon* (Bremen: Bautz, 2000).

3. B. Glasius, *Godgeleerd Nederland, Biographisch Woordenboek van Nederlandsche Godgeleerden*, vol. 2 (s-Hertogenbosch: Gebr. Muller, 1853), 470; C. Sepp, *Het Godgeleerd Onderwijs in Nederland gedurende de 16e en 17e eeuw* (Leiden: De Breuk en Smits, 1873-1874), 2:346; S. van der Linde, "Mastricht, Petrus van," in *Christelijke Encyclopaedie voor het Nederlansche volk*, vol. 4, ed. F. W. Grosheide (Kampen: Kok, 1956), 250; H. Kaajan, "Mastricht (Petrus van)," in *Christelijke Encyclopaedie voor het Nederlansche volk*, 2d revised edition, vol. 4, ed. F. W. Grosheide (Kampen: Kok, 1959), 252; W. J. van Asselt, "Petrus van Mastricht," in *Biographisch Lexicon voor de geschiedenis van het Nederlands Protestantisme* (Kampen: Kok, 2001), 360; A. Goudriaan, "Petrus van Mastrigt," *The Dictionary of Seventeenth and Eighteenth-Century Dutch Philosophers*, (Bristol: Thoemmes Continuum, 2003), 2:340. See also, *Allgemeines Gelehrten-Lexicon*, ed. Christian Gottlieb Jöcher (Leipzig: Gleditsch, 1750-1751; reprint, Hildesheim: Olms, 1960); Jean Noël Paquot, *Mémoires pour servir à l'histoire littéraire des dix-sept provinces des Pays-Bas, de la principauté de Liége, et de quelques contrées voisines* (Louvain: de l'Imprimerie académique, 1765); Jacobus Kok, *Vaderlandsch woordenboek* (Amsterdam: Johannes Allart, 1785-1799); *Historisch-literarisches Handbuch berühmter und denkwürdiger Personen, welche in dem 18. Jahrhundert gestorben sind*, ed. F. C. G Hirsching (Leipzig: 1794-1815); *Allgemeine Deutsche Biographie* (Leipzig: Duncker und Humblot, 1875-1912); Abraham Jacob van der Aa, *Biographisch woordenboek: bevattend levensbeschrijvingen van zoodanige personen, die zich op eenigerlei wijze in ons vaderland hebben vermaard gemaakt* (1852-1878; reprint, Amsterdam: Israël, 1969); G. J. Loncq, *Historische schets der Utrechtsche Hoogeschool tot hare verheffing in 1815* (Utrecht: Beijers en Van Boekhoven, 1886); *Kerk en Maatschappij in verleden en heden*, ed. J. C. Rullmann (Amsterdam: N. V. Uitgevers-Maatschappij Enum, 1934); *Encyclopedia of the Reformed Faith*, ed. Donald K. McKim (Louisville: Westminster, John Knox Press, 1992).

Pontanus (1652-1714)[4] and C. Burman (1696-1755).[5] In respect to Mastricht's work, the interpretation of his theological thought is mainly restricted to the *Theoretico-practica theologia* (hereafter cited as *TPT*), and its significance for the history of theology is incoherent. Systematic theologians such as K. Barth, H. Bavinck, L. Berkhof, E. C. Gravemeijer, H. Hoeksema, H. Heppe, and H. Kersten,[6] cite the *TPT* favorably, for example in the doctrine of God, but usually limit their references to footnotes. Preceding these systematic theologians is B. de Moor (1710-1765), who cites not the *TPT* but primarily the *Novitatum Cartesianarum Gangræna* of Mastricht.[7] Those with a historical-theological interest in the *Nadere Reformatie* such as J. Beeke, T. Brienen, B. Elshout, K. Exalto, A. de Reuver, and W. van 't Spijker demonstrate an awareness of Mastricht but do not elaborate on his theological thought.[8]

4. Henricus Pontanus, *Laudatio Funebris In excessum Doctissimi Et Sanctissimi Senis, Petri van Mastrigt, S. S. Theol. Doctoris & Professoris: Quam jussu amplissimi Senatus Academici D. XXIV. Februarii / postridie sepulturæ dixit Henricus Pontanus* (Rotterdam: van Veen, 1706); idem, *Liick En Lof-Reden Op het Afsterven van den Hooghgeleerden en seer Godsaligen Ouden Man, Petrus van Maastricht, Doctor en Hoogleermeester der H. Godtsgeleertheyt. Welke wyt last van de Hooghaensienlijke Raad der Academie op den 24. van Sprockelmaand des Jaars 1706. 's anderen daags na de Begraeffenis, gedaen heeft Henricus Pontanus,* trans. C. T. V. D. M. (Leyden: Jan Van Damme, [ca. 1706]); idem, "Lyk-enLof-Reede over het Afsterven van Petrus van Mastricht," in Petrus van Mastricht, *Beschouwende en Praktikale Godgeleerdheyt: waarin, door alle godgeleerde hoofdstukken henen, het Bijbelverklarende, Leerstellige, Wederleggende, en Praktikale deel, door eenen onafgebroken schakel onderscheidendlyk samengevoegt, voorgestelt word* (Rotterdam: Hendrik van Pelt, Utrecht: Jan Jacob van Poolsum, 1749-1753).

5. Caspar Burman, *Trajectum eruditum, virorum doctrina inlustrium, qui in urbe Trajecto et regione Trajectensi nati sunt sive ibi habitarunt, vitas, fata et scripta exhibens* (Utrecht: Padenburg, 1738), 212.

6. Karl Barth, *Die Kirchliche Dogmatik* (Zürich: EVZ-Verlag, 1970) I/1:5, 199; I/2:310; II/1: 369f., 373, 404, 508, 516, 592, 601, 646, 731f.; II/2:83, 122, 142, 150, 371; III/2:456; III/3:72, 75, 107, 118, 178, 186, 333; IV/2:115; IV/3:17. N.B. Those works with no reference index will be cited with page number; Herman Bavinck, *Gereformeerde Dogmatiek* (Kampen: Kok, 1921); Louis Berkhof, *Systematic Theology,* with a new preface by Richard A. Muller (Grand Rapids: Eerdmans, 1996); E. C. Gravemeijer, *Leesboek over de Gereformeerde Geloofsleer* (Utrecht: H. Ten Hove, 1896), 1:118, 194, 254, 256, 263, 283, 293, 319, 334, 338, 342, 344, 349, 351, 362, 368, 370, 374, 376 ,379, 393, 402, 408, 410, 414, 421, 422, 455; Herman Hoeksema, *Reformed Dogmatics* (Grand Rapids: Reformed Free Publishing Association, 1966), 61, 287, 447; Heinrich Heppe, *Reformed Dogmatics,* trans. G. T. Thomson (London: Allen&Unwin, 1950) ,12, 20, 62, 81, 83, 91, 92, 93, 95, 96, 99, 108, 152, 196, 220, 226, 229, 236, 240, 266, 270, 308, 317, 351, 361, 366, 367, 375, 381, 385, 493, 510, 546 [The majority of citations are found in the doctrine of God); Hendrik Kersten, *De Gereformeerde Dogmatiek* (Utrecht: De Banier, 1988, zesde druk), I:15, 25, 43, 94, 96, 97, 100, 110, 148, 150, 164, 179, 197, 207, 216, 228, 230, 244, 251, 326, 394, 412, 415; II:5, 11, 13, 14, 16, 19, 25, 26, 28, 29, 34, 39, 42, 45, 56, 237, 255, 301, 346.

7. Bernardus de Moor, *Commentarius perpetuus in Johannis Marckii Compendium Theologiæ Christianæ didactico-elencticum* (Leiden: Johannes Hasebroek, 1761). Except the reference to the *Theoretico-practica theologia,* I:796, all other references are made to the *Novitatum Cartesianarum Gangræna,* I:49, 53, 70 (2x), 90, 318, 321(3x), 322, 410, 414, 416, 436, 468(2x), 589, 590, 591, 600, 601, 603, 630, 657, 672, 714, 796, 833, 883, 889.

8. Joel R. Beeke, *Assurance of Faith, Calvin, English Puritanism and the Dutch Second Reformation* (New York: Peter Lang, 1991); T. Brienen, *De prediking van de Nadere Reformatie* (Amsterdam: Ton Bolland, 1981); Bartel Elshout, *The Pastoral and Practical Theology of Wilhelmus à Brakel* (Grand Rapids: Reformation Heritage Books, 1997); T. Brienen *et al., Theologische aspecten van de Nadere Reformatie* (Zoetermeer:

The portrait of Mastricht's life and work that is rendered in European continental scholarship, however, is related to: (1) practical theology and Pietism, (2) Voetianism, Scholasticism and Cocceianism, (3) William Ames, (4) Cartesianism, (5) chiliasm, lapsarianism, and laypeople. In addition, English (American, Scottish) scholarship contributes, primarily in the context of Jonathan Edwards, to Masricht's description of life and work.

Practical Theology and Pietism. Pontanus mentions Mastricht's unique position among Reformed theologians, having the title "professor of practical divinity,"[9] while De Moor recommends the reading of Mastricht for practical theology.[10] Heppe typifies Mastricht as pietistic because of the warm recommendation of J. Hondius's pietistic works,[11] and M.J.A. de Vrijer reads Mastricht's pietistic inclination in his last will, which stated that the will-benefited students must be

> Geneegen en sich obligeerende particulierlijk tot het studeeren in de practycale Godtsgeleerdtheit en dies te bequamer te worden Godt in sijn kerke dienst te doen.[12]

For J. van Genderen, Mastricht was a practical *systematicus*, one who paved no new ways but was a man of thesis contrary to H. Witsius (1636-1708) (synthesis) and M. Leydekker (1642-1721) (antithesis).[13] In summary, Mastricht was a pietistic and practical theologian. This emphasis on *praxis* is balanced by Johannes d'Outrein (1662-1722), who notes that Mastricht combines the *theologia theoretica* and *theologia practica* of theology.[14] This thought is echoed by J. F. Buddeus (1667-1729) of the Lutheran University of Jena, Germany, who argues that the *TPT* of Mastricht is a laudable work that brings together

Boekencentrum, 1993); Aza Goudriaan, *Philosophische Gotteserkenntnis bei Suárez und Descartes, im Zusammenhang mit der niederländischen reformierten Theologie und Philosophie des 17 Jahrhunderts* (Leiden: Brill, 1999).

9. Pontanus, *Laudatio Funebris*, 20: "Unicus est inter Reformatos Doctores, quos novi, qui nomine et titulo Professoris Theologiæ Practicæ est insignitus."

10. This citation also attests that Mastricht still was known in the latter half of the eighteenth century.

11. H. Heppe, *Geschichte des Pietismus und der Mystik in der Reformirten Kirche* (Leiden: Brill, 1879), 164. Heppe refers to Hondius's *Swart register van duijsent sonden* (1679) and *Register van veelerlij vertroostingen* (1685).

12. M. J. A. de Vrijer, *Ds. Bernardus Smytegelt en zijn "Gekrookte Riet"* (Vianen: De Banier, 1968), 10.

13. Van Genderen, *Herman Witsius, bijdrage tot de kennis der Gereformeerde theologie*, 68 and 69.

14. Johannes D'Outrein, *De Droefheid die naar God is, werkende een Onberouwelijke Bekeeringe tot Zaligheid. Mitsgaders de ware Selfs-Verloochening* (Amsterdam: Jacobus Borstius, 1710), Æn den Leeser, 5. Johannes d'Outrein is lauded that he followed not only the English and Scottish but also the Dutch theologians such as Ames, Voetius, Mastricht, Witsius, and others in the *theologia theoretica* and *theologia practica*.

theology as *theoretico-practica, ascetica,* and *moralis.*[15] Finally, W. Geesink identifies the *TPT* as a thetical and antithetical dogmatic work combined with *praxis.*[16] In summary, Mastricht was not only a practical theologian but also one who brought theory and *praxis* together.

Voetian, Scholasticism, and Cocceianism. Heppe identifies Mastricht as one of the most important opponents of the Cocceians.[17] L. Diestel, W. Ring, A. Ritschl, and C. Graafland[18] restrict this identification to the doctrine of the covenant, while B. Loonstra places Mastricht in the same category of covenant theologians as Witsius and F. Turretin (1623-1687).[19] A. Ypey described Mastricht as a Voetian who used the "scholastic method very cautiously"[20] and was acquainted with the Cocceians. G. van der Zee amends this observation by writing that Mastricht "did not lose sight of Cocceius' valuable work."[21] C. Steenblok asserts that Mastricht followed Voetius in his ethics.[23] In respect to the scholastic notion, Graafland assesses him as an anti-*scholasticus,*[24] while E. Böhl refers to Mastricht as a "typical Reformed medieval" theologian.[25] P. H. Roessingh notes Mastricht is one of the dogmatic-scholastic theologians "from abroad" who opposed the thought of the biblical theologian Jacobus Alting.[26]

15. J. F. Buddeus, *Isagoge Historico-Theologica ad Theologiam universam* (Lipsea: Thomas Fritschi, 1730) 1:595, 596. Cf. C. van der Kemp, voorrede, in Petrus van Mastricht, *Beschouwende en Praktikale Godgeleerdheit,* ***3.

16. W. Geesink, *De Ethiek in de Gereformeerde Theologie* (Amsterdam: W. Kirchner, 1897), 55.

17. Heppe, *Geschichte des Pietismus und der Mystik in der Reformirten Kirche,* 225, "Als einer der bedeutendsten Gegner derselben [Cocceians] war der Utrechter Professor Peter van Mastricht."

18. L. Diestel, *Studien zur Föderaltheologie, Jahrbücher für deutsche Theologie,* 10 (1865): 209-276; W. Ring, *Geschichte der Universität Duisburg* (Duisburg: Stadtarchiv, 1920), 137; A. Ritschl, *Geschichte des Pietismus* (Bonn: Marcus, 1880-1886), 3:451; C. Graafland, "Johannes Coccejus" in Brienen *et al., Theologische aspecten van de Nadere Reformatie,* 69.

19. B. Loonstra, *Verkiezing, verzoening, verbond: beschrijving en beoordeling van de leer van het "pactum salutis" in de gereformeerde theologie* ('s-Gravenhage: Boekencentrum, 1990), 109. Loonstra argues that Mastricht, Witsius and Turretin are in line with the covenant theology of Johannes Cloppenburgh.

20. A. Ypey, *Algemeene Kerkelijke Geschiedenis* (Haarlem: F. Bohn, 1816), 25:170.

21. G. van der Zee, *Vaderlandse Kerkgeschiedenis van de Hervorming tot heden,* (J. H. Kok: Kampen, 1930), 3:142.

23. C. Steenblok, *Voetius en de Sabbat* (Gouda: Gereformeerde Pers, 1975), 24.

24. C. Graafland, "Gereformeerde Scholastiek VI," in *Theologia Reformata,* XXX, no. 2, (1987): 323.

25. Eduard Böhl, *Von der Rechtfertigung Durch den Glauben. Ein Beitrag zur Rettung des Protestantischen Cardinaldogmas* (Leipzig: K. Gustorff, 1890), 55.

26. P. H. Roessingh, *Jacobus Alting, een Bijbelsch Godgeleerde uit het midden der 17e eeuw* (Groningen: van Zweeden, 1864), 160. Roessingh argues that Alting, being professor of oriental languages, opposed the dogmatic-scholastic direction of his time, building, with the help of philology, a theology based on Scripture (34, 41). Note: thesis one of this work reads: "Onder degene die de dogmatische-scholastiek

Ames. W. Goeters notes that Mastricht in his *TPT* obviously is dependent on Ames,[27] a thought that is echoed by K. Reuter, who notes that Mastricht is Ames' commentator.[28]   H. Visscher[29] and W. Prins[30] argue that Ames influenced structurally and materially the theological thought of Mastricht. Van 't Spijker notes that the mainline of Reformed theology did not seem to pay attention to Ames, except Mastricht,[31] of whom Graafland asserts that he merged of the theological thought of Ames and Voetius.[32]

Cartesianism. E. Bizer argues that Mastricht was, with Melchior Leydekker, a main opponent of Cartesianism but concludes that "the orthodox were bound to confuse their outmoded worldview with their faith [and] their concept of truth was closer to the 'new philosophy' than it suspected."[33] Goudriaan nuances this view and notes that Mastricht, among others, questioned the Cartesian philosophy.[34]

The Last Days (Chiliasm), Lapsarianism, and Laypeople. W. Rutgers argues, in his historical discussion on premillennialism in America, that seventeenth and eighteenth-century Dutch theologians show a "divergence of opinions"[35] on chiliasm and, like

theologie, welke in het midden der 17e eeuw in Nederland algemeen heerschte, met vrucht bestreden hebben, bekleedt Jacobus Alting eene eerste plaats."

27. W. Goeters, *Die Vorbereitung des Pietismus in der Reformierten Kirche der Niederlande bis zur Labadistischen Krisis 1670* (Leipzig: J. C. Hinrich, 1911), 56: "in seiner Theoretico-practica theologia ist die Abhängigkeit von Ames offensichtlich."

28. K. Reuter, *Wilhelm Amesius, der führende Theologe des erwachenden reformierten Pietismus* (C. Brugle: Ansbach, 1940), 35. See also Sprunger, *The Learned Doctor William Ames*, 260: "Ames's posthumous influence remained in pietistic and precisanist corners of Dutch theology, in Voetius, Nethenus, Anna Maria van Schurman, Jodocus van Lodenstein, and Peter van Mastricht. Mastricht in his famous practical divinity, *Theoretico-practica theologia* (1655) professed to follow the Amesian methodology."

29. H. Visscher, *Guilielmus Ames* (Haarlem: J. M. Stap, 1894), 212. The assertion of Visscher that Mastricht is a proof of Nethenus' recommendation of the works of Ames is probably unfounded. M. Nethenus served at the University of Utrecht from 1653 - 1662.

30. W. Prins, *Het Geweten. Een Exegetisch-Historisch-Dogmatisch Onderzoek* (Delft: W. D. Meinema, 1937), 287-92.

31. W. van 't Spijker, "Guilelmus Ames (1576-1633)," in Brienen *et al.*, *De Nadere Reformatie en het Gereformeerd Piëtisme*, 54.

32. C. Graafland, "Petrus van Mastricht," in Brienen *et al.*, *Theologische aspecten van de Nadere Reformatie*, 61. The dichotomy between Ames and Voetius may be less than is suggested by Graafland.

33. Ernst Bizer, "Die reformierte Orthodoxie und der Cartesianimus," in *Zeitschrift für Theologie und Kirche*, 3 (55)1958; Cf. Ernst Bizer, *Reformed Orthodoxy and Cartesianism*, trans. C. MacCormick, in Rudolf Boltman *et al.*, *Translating Theology into the Modern Age* (New York: Harper Torchbooks, 1960), 81, 82. Note, Bizer donated Mastricht's *Novitatum Cartesianarum Gangræna* to the Theological faculty of Duisburg University, Germany. C. Sepp, *Het Godgeleerd Onderwijs*, 2:346 writes, "Of lag zijne aanbeveling [to succeed Voetius at Utrecht University] daarin, dat hij van Coccejanisme en Cartesianisme een heftig tegenstander was."

34. Goudriaan, *Philosophische Gotteserkenntnis*, 6.

35. William H. Rutgers, *Premillennialism in America* (Goes: Oosterbaan & Le Cointre, 1930), 78. Rutgers notes that Voetius, Witsius, Brakel, and Marck were inclined towards chiliast ideas.

18

Hoekstra,[36] classifies Mastricht as anti-chiliastic and rejecting the application of the promises of salvation (heilsbeloften) for national Israel. However, K. Dijk asserts that Mastricht "judges that, in respect to Revelation twenty the millennium lies in the past"[37]; thereby, Dijk continues, Mastricht followed Calvin in his exegesis on Romans 11 but believed that the last times would be a time of great prosperity and that many Jews would be converted and gathered into the spiritual kingdom of God. Moreover, Dijk, with others, asserts Mastricht's mediating position between supra- and infralapsarianism.[38] Last but not least, the laypeople of the Dutch Reformed congregations read Mastricht's Beschouwende en praktikale godgeleerdheit, as the sixty-five-year-old Pieter Morilyon Jacobszoon exemplifies in his daily journal on June 15, 1769:

> Ik hebbe uit vele, veel nut mogen genieten, bijzonder uit de oude godgeleerde, zo wel in Frankrijk, Engeland, Schotland, als in Nederland. De Schriften van latere Godgeleerde, als die van...Mastricht,...en vele andere zijn mij zeer nuttig geweest[39]

Concentrating on the English-speaking world, C. Bogue, C. Harinck, A. Guelzo, P. Miller, A. Morimoto, W. van Vlastuin, B. Withrow, and T. Schafer imply the possible influence of Mastricht on eighteenth-century Scottish and American Reformed theology, particularly on Jonathan Edwards (1703-1758).[40] In respect to Scotland, the "Marrow-

36. H. Hoekstra, Bijdrage tot de kennis en de beoordeling van het Chiliasme (Kampen: Kok, 1903), 39-48; G. P. van Itterzon, Het gereformeerde leerboek der 17ᵉ eeuw "Synopsis Purioris Theolgiæ" ('s-Gravenhage, 1931), 82.

37. K. Dijk, Het Rijk der Duizend Jaren (Kampen: J. H. Kok, 1933), 83.

38. Ibid., De strijd over Infra-en Supralapsarisme in de Gereformeerde Kerken van Nederland (Kampen: J. H. Kok, 1912), 48; ibid., Om 't Eeuwig Welbehagen, De Leer der Praedestinatie (Amsterdam: De Standaard, tweede druk, 1925), 404. Note, in the latter book Dijk identifies Mastricht with an infralapsarian position, while in the former he argues that Mastricht with Trigland, Voetius, and Hoornbeeck made an attempt to mediate between supra- and infralapsarism (406); Hendrik Kersten, De Gereformeerde Dogmatiek, 1:179; Loonstra, Verkiezing, verzoening, verbond: beschrijving en beoordeling van de leer van het "pactum salutis" in de gereformeerde theologie, 51.

39. Middelburg, The Netherlands, Regional Archive Zeeland, archive Steenbakker, number 3. With thanks to S. Post (personal communication June 2001). W. van 't Spijker indicated that Mastrichts's work was also read by the people of the Afscheiding (personal communication July 2000).

40. Carl W. Bogue, Jonathan Edwards and the Covenant of Grace (Cherry Hill, NJ: Mack Publishing Co.,1975); C. Harinck, De Schotse Verbondsleer, van Robert Rollock tot Thomas Boston (Utrecht: De Banier, 1986), 88 and 91-94; Allen C. Guelzo, Edwards on the Will (Middletown, CT: Wesleyan University Press, 1989), 3 and 4; Perry Miller, the New England Mind, the Seventeenth Century (Cambridge, MA; Harvard University Press,1939), 96, 105, 224; Anri Morimoto, Jonathan Edwards and the Catholic Vision of Salvation (University Park, PA, Pennsylvania State University Press, 1995), 18-20, 26, 34, 45, 51, 63, 87, 106, 109, 116, 142; W. van Vlastuin, De Geest van Opwekking. Een onderzoek naar de leer van de Heilige Geest in de opwekkingstheologie van Jonathan Edwards (1703-1758) (Heerenveen: Groen, 2001), 92; Adriaan C. Neele, The History of the Work of Redemption: a Reappraisal. Mastricht's covenant theology foundational for Edwards' theology (unpublished article: Calvin Theological Seminary, 2001);The works of Jonathan Edwards, ed. John E. Smith, vol. 13, idem, The Miscellanies, ed. Thomas A. Schafer (New Haven, London: Yale University Press, 1994), 319, fn. 2; Petrus van Mastricht, A Treatise on Regeneration, ed. Brandon Withrow (Morgan: Soli Deo Gloria Publications, 2002), viii.

men,"[41] such as Ralph Erskine (1685-1752)[42] and John Brown (1722-1787),[43] were favorable towards Mastricht's thought on the doctrine of the covenant, as D. Lachman[44] attests of this probable influence on James Hog (c. 1658-1734). The Scottish interest continued into the nineteenth century as testified by D. Fraser's notes to his English translation of the *Apostles' Creed* of Herman Witsius.[45] In respect to America, the eighteenth-century theologians of New England were deeply acquainted with Mastricht's work. Cotton Mather (1663-1728) recommended the *TPT* to ministerial students,[46] and

41. John Macleod, *Scottish Theology. In relation to Church History* (Edinburgh: Knox Press, 1974), 152.

42. Ralph Erskine, *Faith no fancy, or, A treatise of mental images: discovering the vain philosophy and vile divinity of a late pamphlet entitled [sic] Mr. Robe's fourth letter to Mr. Fisher, and showing that an imaginary idea of Christ as man (when supposed to belong to saving faith, whether in its act or object), imports nothing but ignorance, atheism, idolatry, great falsehood, and gross delusion* (Philadelphia: William M'Culloch, 1805), 31. See for the theological relationship between seventeenth and eighteenth century Scotland and the Netherlands Robert H. Story, ed., *The Church of Scotland, past and present: its history, its relation to the law and the state, its doctrine, ritual, discipline, and patrimony* (London: William Mackenzie, 1890), 216: "... a deeper study of the Covenant theology which had been imported from Holland, and was destined to occupy a prominent place in the orthodox school in Scotland"; John Kennedy, *The Days of the Fathers in Ross-shire* (Inverness: Christian Focus Publications, 1979), 134: "They [the Ross-shire fathers] had no difficulty in regarding the Sacrament of the Supper, as intended by the Lord, specially to seal something other and higher than that which is specially sealed by baptism. They called it, with Mastricht, "sacramentum nutritionis", Cf. L. J. van Valen, *Gelijk de Dauw van Hermon* (Zwijndrecht: Het Anker, tweede druk, 1982), 476; Keith L. Sprunger, *Dutch Puritanism: A History of English and Scottish Churches of the Netherlands in the Sixteenth and Seventeenth Centuries* (Leiden: E. J. Brill, 1982), 435, "At Utrecht Voetius, Nethenus, and van Mastricht showed favor to Scottish Presbyterians, and van Mastricht went so far as to praise the discipline of the Church of Scotland as 'the purest that had been since the apostles' days'."

43. John Brown, *The Systematic Theology*, introduced by Joel R. Beeke, and Randall J. Pederson (Grand Rapids: Reformation Heritage Books, 2002), [j].

44. David C. Lachman, *The Marrow Controversy* (Edinburgh: Rutherford House, 1988), 125, 126.

45. H. Witsius, *The Apostles' Creed*, translated from the Latin and followed with notes, critical and explanatory by Donald Fraser (1823; reprint, Escondido: The den Dulk Christian Foundation, 1993), I:379: "See also some short historical notes on the Arminian controversy in that truly valuable work, *Theol. Pet. Van Masticht*, lib. viii. Cap.3. sect. xliii. P.1152, et seq.;" idem, I:441: "Calvin, Mastricht, Guthrie and many other excellent Divines have styled faith the condition of the covenant;" idem, I:455: "The judicious *Mastricht* may be mentioned as furnishing another [after discussing Witsius' position, AN] example of the unfavorable sentiments with which even well-informed Christians at first regarded the system maintained by the celebrated Newton (who, by the way, was a decided believer of the Scriptures) with his predecessors and followers. That excellent Theologian, when taking notice of the system of the world, has the following observation; 'The Reformed ascribe the lowest place to this earth, which according to the uniform tenor of sacred writ, is contradistinguished from the heavens and stars, and which beginning in a manner the centre of the universe, remains unmovable, Eccles i.4, *Theol. Lib.iii. cap. vi. Sect. 19;*' idem, II:551: "The reader who is disposed to study this subject [the argument for the divinity of the Spirit, AN] may consult...Owen's Exposition of the Hebrews, Ch. vi.4-6. x.26-29, and Maestricht's Theology, lib.iv.cap.3.sect.16, 17;" idem, II:554: "On the reality, nature, and importance of the unions between Christ and believers, the reader may consult Maestricht, Theolog. lib.vi.cap.5." Note, Mastricht is missing in the "index of authors quoted by Witsius," idem, II:598-628.

46. Cotton Mather, *Manuductio Ad Ministerium, Directions for a Candidate of the Ministry* (Boston: Thomas H (...) eck, 1726), 85: "I hope, you will next unto the Sacred Scripture make a Mastricht the

Jonathan Edwards, frequently refers[47] to the *TPT* in his reflections on the Sabbath, fall, predestination, Trinity,[48] humility,[49] sin, and Christ's ascension.[50] Edwards's appreciation[51] of Mastricht's work, to which he was introduced by his wife Sarah,[52] is best summarized when he wrote to Bellamy:

> But take Mastricht for divinity in general, doctrine, practice and controversy; or as an universal system of divinity; and it is much better than Turretin or any other book in the world, excepting the Bible, in my opinion.[53]

This thought is echoed by Samuel Hopkins in a treatise on saving faith:

> That great, learned, and accurate Dutch divine, Van Mastricht, whose body of divinity perhaps excels all others that have yet been written, and is, in my opinion, richly worth the repeated perusal of every one.[54]

storehouse to which you may resort continually, for in it the minister will find everything." See for the sources and structures of Mather's Theology, Richard F. Lovelace, *The American Pietism of Cotton Mather: Origins of American Evangelism* (Grand Rapids: Christian University Press, 1979), 35-37.

47. The *TPT* heads (the second part of) Edwards's catalogue and was his chief book in systematic theology, as Poole was his favorite biblical commentator. Cf. William S. Morris, *The Young Jonathan Edwards* (Brooklyn: Carlson Publishing, 1991), 299. Morris also contends that Edwards's *Miscellanies* are "thoroughly theological. This is a common place of 'Divinity.' Theology, for Edwards as for Maastricht, had a four-fold part: exegetical, dogmatic (i.e., that which is derived and deduced as a consequence from Scriptures); theoretical, in which reason depends and contends for the dogmatic truths of the faith, using all the reason, philosophy, and theology that it can muster, and arguing the case for faith in the light of a full, accurate, and critical knowledge of 'the state of the question'; and last, practical, in which the theoretical truths of faith found their immediate practical explication and application" (464).

48. *The works of Jonathan Edwards*, ed. John E. Smith, vol. 13, *The Miscellanies*, ed. Thomas A. Schafer (New Haven, London: Yale University Press, 1994), 319 (Sabbath), 382 (fall), 384 (predestination), 524 (Trinity).

49. Ibid., vol. 2, *Religious Affections*, ed. John E. Smith (New Haven, London: Yale University Press, 1994), 337.

50. Ibid., vol. 15, *Notes on Scriptures*, ed. Stephen J. Stein (New Haven, London: Yale University Press, 1998), 298.

51. See for the covenant theology of J. Edwards and Reformed thought: Bogue, *Jonathan Edwards and the Covenant of Grace.*

52. Elisabeth D. Dodds, *Marriage to a Difficult Man. The Uncommon Union of Jonathan and Sarah Edwards* (Philadelphia: Westminster Press, 1971; reprint, Laurel: Audobon Press, 2003), 21. Mrs. Lia Veldman-van Dijk is acknowledged.

53. *The works of Jonathan Edwards*, ed. John E. Smith, vol. 16, *Letters and Personal writings*, ed. Georges S. Claghorn (New Haven, London: Yale University Press, 1998), 217.

54. Samuel Hopkins, *The system of doctrines: contained in divine revelation, explained and defended: showing their consistence and connection with each other: to which is added, A treatise on the millennium* (Boston: Isaiah Thomas and Ebenezer T. Andrews, 1793), 769.

Furthermore, the translator of Mastricht's chapter *De redimendorum Regeneratione* of the *TPT*, published in New England,[55] notes that Edwards in *Enquiry into the Freedom of Will* had a similar understanding of the will as Mastricht but hopes primarily that the *Treatise on Regeneration* will

> put a stop to the controversy, which seems to be growing among us, relative to regeneration; whether it be wrought by the immediate influences of the divine Spirit, or by light [of reason] as the means? And happily to unite us in the truth.[56]

D.J. Elwood[57] argues that probably the most singular influence, apart from the Bible, in Edwards's conviction of divine immediacy in the soul was the *TPT*. The link, then, between Edwards and Mastricht is succinctly recognized by G.R. McDermott when he writes,

> But we have better evidence of the possibility of Dutch influence on Edwards's eschatology. [...] Van Mastricht's view on the dispensation of the covenant of grace section teaches a progressive view of history in which the covenant of grace is "renewed and widened" through time, though not without waxing and waning.[58]

55. Petrus van Mastricht, *Treatise on Regeneration, Extracted from His System of Divinity, Called Theologia theoretico-practica*, trans. unknown (New Haven: Thomas and Samuel Green, in the Old Council Chamber, 1770), 39. I am indebted to Dr. Stephen Crocco and the Rev. William Harris of Princeton Theological Seminary and Spier Library for their generous assistance in making this treatise available to me. Note: Norman S. Fiering, "Will and Intellect in the New England Mind," *The William and Mary Quarterly*, vol. xxxix, no. 4 (1972), comments on this treatise on 552, "it is remarkable how close the correspondence is between the seventeenth-century Augustian voluntaristic position and the ideas of Jonathan Edwards, and the seventeenth-century intellectualist position and the ideas, for example, of Edwards's opponent Charles Chauncy." Fierling asserts then that Edwards's familiarity with Ames and Mastricht contributed to his understanding of the will. On 553 Fierling writes, "In 1770 in the midst of the controversy over the Edwardsean theology in America this section of Mastricht on the topic of regeneration was published. A good part of this small volume, which contains a valuable appendix of statements from various authorities (Charnock, Twisse, Flavel, Witsius, Ames and Rutherford) before and after Van Mastricht who shared his views, concerns the relation of will and intellect, and particularly the questions of whether divine regeneration is a physical process in the will or simply a matter of intellectual illuminations and moral suasion. Van Mastricht emphasizes that it is the whole man that is regenerated—intellect, will and affections—but the point at issue is whether there is a supernatural physical change in the will." Cf. W. van 't Spijker, "Teellincks opvatting van de menschelijke wil," *Theologia Reformata* VII, no. 3 (1964).

56. Petrus van Mastricht, *Treatise on Regeneration*, preface. The translator further argues that both parties "manifest their entire approbation of, and concurrence with van Mastricht." Another New England acquaintance with Mastricht is also noted on the title page of the anonymous work, *Some occasional Thoughts on the Influence of the Spirit, with seasonable cautions against mistakes and abuses* (Boston: S. Kneeland and T. Green, 1742).

57. Douglas J. Elwood, *The Philosophical Theology of Jonathan Edwards* (New York, Columbia University Press, 1960), 121.

58. Gerald R. McDermott, *One Holy and Happy Society, the Public Theology of Jonathan Edwards* (University Park: Pennsylvania State University Press, 1992), 79. Cf. Petrus van Mastricht, *Beschouwende en Praktikale Godgeleerdheit*, 3:709-10; 4:481.

In respect to the theme of covenant, John D. Eusden asserts that Edwards's favorite, Mastricht, continued to insist on the covenant ideas of Ames and Cocceius in a time of great theological change.[59] However, D. Visser asserts that Mastricht polemicized against Cocceius and that the *TPT* reflects his pastoral experience and the Voetian emphasis on pastoral as opposed to a primarily systematic theology.[60] Finally, Richard A. Muller notes in his discussion of the *Duplex cognitio dei* in early Reformed orthodoxy that Mastricht, among others, unifies the non-soteriological knowledge of God under the perception of God as Judge rather than—as in Calvin's *Institutes* of 1559—the sense of God as Creator.[61] Moreover, Muller identifies the "perfect balance of Mastricht's scholasticism: exegetical, dogmatic, historical-polemical and practical"[62] and notes that this "finely balanced method"[63] was a central concern of orthodoxy in the seventeenth century.

In conclusion, Mastricht's portrait is primarily formed by two different emerging perspectives. On one hand scholars of the European continent have assessed him, in the context of the *Nadere Reformatie*, as a Voetian (anti-)scholastic, anti-Cocceian, anti-Cartesian, anti-chiliastic, dogmatic-scholastic, covenant, and pietistic or practical theologian, who is an expositor of Ames's work. This appraisal is dominated by a dogmatic and practical notion. On the other hand, scholars of the English-speaking world praise his mediating, balanced, and scholastic work, though primarily assessed in an Edwardsean context. These points of view underscores the fact that the European continental scholarship, restricted to Mastricht, reinforces the doctrinal and practical interpretation of seventeenth-century Reformed theology, which differs from the American scholarship that notes a continuity of Scholasticism in the intellectual thought of that era.

The Intellectual Thought of the Seventeenth-century Reformed Orthodoxy

This study is neither directly involved in the debate over the continuity and discontinuity of intellectual thought of the seventeenth-century Reformed orthodoxy nor does it provide a sketch of the seventeenth-century post-Reformation in general or the *Nadere Reformatie* in particular. However, the following assessment of scholarship suffices to identify the intellectual thought of Mastricht's time.[64] First, the amount of

59. William Ames, *The Marrow of Theology*, ed. John D. Eusden (Grand Rapids: Baker Books, 1997), 65.

60. Derk Visser, "Petrus van Mastricht," *Encyclopedia of the Reformed Faith*, 383.

61. Richard A. Muller, "*Duplex cognitio dei* in the Theology of Early Reformed Orthodoxy," *Sixteenth Century Journal*, x. 2 (1979): 60.

62. Ibid., "Giving Direction to Theology: The Scholastic Dimension," *Journal of Evangelical Theological Studies*, 28/2 (1985): 191.

63. Ibid., *Post-Reformation Reformed Dogmatics* (Grand Rapids: Baker Academic, 2003) 1:218.

64. In respect to the translation of the term *Nadere Reformatie*, one notes that Muller includes representatives of seventeenth-century Dutch theologians in his discussion of Protestant orthodoxy or Protestant Scholasticism (Richard A. Muller, *Christ and the Decree*, [Durham, NC: The Labyrinth Press,

scholarly literature on the seventeenth-century post-Reformation has, contrary to Mastricht scholarship, increased significantly over the last two decades.[65] The attention given to this period originated in Germany (M. Goebel, 1849, A. Tholuck, 1854, and Heppe, 1879)[66] and culminated in the Netherlands (from the late nineteenth century[67]

1986], 11) or Reformed orthodoxy (idem, "The Covenant of Works and the Stability of Divine Law in Seventeenth-Century Reformed Orthodoxy: a study in the theology of Herman Witsius and Wilhelmus à Brakel," *Calvin Theological Journal*, 29, no. 1 (1994): 75. These representatives are described by others as theologians of the *Nadere Reformatie* or Closer Reformation (Thomas A. McHagen, *Cartesianism in the Netherlands, 1639-1676; The New Science and the Calvinistic Counter-Reformation* [Ph.D. diss., University of Pennsylvania, 1976], 9) or Second Reformation (J. W. Hofmeyr, *Johannes Hoornbeeck as Polemikus* [Kampen: Kok, 1975], 219) or Dutch Second Reformation (Joel R. Beeke, "The *Nadere Reformatie*" *Personal assurance of Faith: English Puritanism and the Dutch "Nadere Reformatie;" from Westminster to Alexander Comrie [1640-1760]* [Ann Arbor: UMI, 1988]; idem, "The Dutch Second Reformation," *Calvin Theological Journal*, 28, no. 2 (1993):298-327). Specifically, Beeke points out that the translation of the term poses problems. According to Beeke, *nadere* ("nearer, more intimate, more precise") does not have standard English translation. Further, he notes that other attempts such as Dutch Precisianism, Dutch Pietism or Puritanism causes more problems than they solve. Therefore, he argues that "Second Reformation" or "Dutch Second Reformation" is a weak translation and "misses the Dutch terms" emphasis on continuity, although it has a long pedigree and appears to be gaining [unfortunately, AN] acceptance among scholars.

65. F. W. Huisman, *Bibliografie van het gereformeerde Pietisme in Nederland*; B. G. Armstrong, *Calvinism and the Amyraut Heresy: Protestant Scholasticism and Humanism in Seventeenth-century France* (Milwaukee, University of Wisconsin Press, 1969); W. J. van Asselt and E. Dekker, eds., *De Scholastieke Voetius, een luisteroefening aan de hand van Voetius' Disputationes Selectæ* (Zoetermeer: Boekencentrum, 1995); idem, *Johannes Coccejus*; idem, *The Federal Theology of Johannes Coccejus*; idem, "Protestant Scholasticism: Some Methodological Considerations in the Study of its Development," *Nederlands Archief voor Kerkgeschiedenis*, 81, no. 3 (2001); W. J. Asselt and E. Dekker, eds., *Reformation and Scholasticism: An Ecumenical Enterprise, Texts and Studies in Reformation & Post-Reformation Thought* (Grand Rapids, Baker Books, 2001); Joel R. Beeke, *Assurance of Faith, Calvin, English Puritanism and the Dutch Second Reformation* (New York: Peter Lang, 1991); idem, "The Dutch Second Reformation," Calvin Theological Journal, vol. 28, no. 2 (1993); Bartel Elshout, *The Pastoral and Practical Theology of Wilhelmus à Brakel* (Grand Rapids: Reformation Heritage Books, 1997); O. Fatio, *Méthod et Théologie. Lambert Daneau et les débuts de la scolastique réformée* (Geneva: University Press, 1976); Richard A. Muller, *Post-Reformation Reformed Dogmatics* (Grand Rapids: Baker Academic, 2003), vols.1-4; idem, "Giving Direction to Theology: The Scholastic Dimension," *Journal of Evangelical Theological Studies* (June 1985); idem, "The Covenant of Works and the Stability of Divine Law in Seventeenth-Century Reformed Orthodoxy: A Study in the Theology of Herman Witsius and Wilhelmus à Brakel," *Calvin Theological Journal*, 29, no. 1 (1994); H. A. Oberman, *The Dawn of the Reformation* (Edinburgh: T & T Clark, 1986); idem, *The Impact of the Reformation* (Grand Rapids: W. B. Eerdmans, 1994); W. Otten, "Medieval Scholasticism: Past, Present and Future," *Nederlands Archief voor Kerkgeschiedenis*, 81, no.3 (2001); A. de Reuver, *Verborgen omgang, Sporen van Spiritualiteit in Middeleeuwen en Nadere Reformatie* (Zoetermeer: Boekencentrum, 2002); Henry M. Knapp, *Understanding the Mind of God: John Owen and Seventeenth-Century Exegetical Methodology* (Ph.D diss., Calvin Theological Seminary, 2002).

66. M. F. W. Goebel, *Geschichte des christichen Lebens in der rheinisch-westphalischen evangelishen Kirchen* (Koblenz: Badeker, 1849), particularly 140-47 (G. Voet), 147-160 (J. Koch), 160-180 (J. von Lodenstein); A. Tholuck, *Das akademische Leben des siebzehnten Jahrhunderts mit besondere Beziehung auf die protestantisch-theologischen Fakultäten Deutschlands* (Halle: E. Anton, 1854), 204-245 and 377-381(Utrecht University); H. Heppe, *Geschichte des Pietismus und der Mystik in der reformirten Kirche, namentlich der Niederlande* (Leiden: Brill, 1879).

and into the twentieth century with scholars such as Van der Linde, Graafland, van Asselt, and de Reuver.)[68] Furthermore it expanded internationally (South Africa: Hofmeyr, Raath,[69] USA: Muller, Beeke, and England: Trueman)[70] and widened, particular with Dutch scholarship, the scope from theology to other areas of interest such as philosophy,[71] literature[72] and printing of books.[73] Second, it could be argued that this period of Protestant orthodoxy can be divided into an early (ca. 1565-1640), middle or high (ca. 1640-1700), and late part (ca. 1700-1750).[74] Third, in respect to its assessment, older post-Reformation scholarship observed distinct movements such as the sixteenth-century Reformation, the *Nadere Reformatie*, Pietism, and Puritanism and noted a discontinuity of the theological thought from the latter three to the former. In

67. F. J. Los, *Wilhelmus à Brakel*; A. F. Krull, *Jacobus Koelman* (Sneek: Campen, 1901); H. Visscher, *Guilielmus Ames*; P. Proost, *J. van Lodenstein* (Amsterdam: Brandt, 1880).

68. S. van der Linde, "De antropologie der Nadere Reformatie," in *Waarheid, wijsheid en leven* (Kampen: Kok, 1956); idem, "Betekenis van de Nadere Reformatie," in *Kerk en Theologie*, 5 (1954), 215-225. See also F. H. Huisman, *Bibliografie van het gereformeerde Pietisme in Nederland*, 44, 45, 83 and 84; C. Graafland, *De zekerheid van het geloof* (Wageningen: Veenman, 1961); W.J. van Asselt, *The Federal Theology of Johannes Cocceius*; A. de Reuver, *Bedelen bij de Bron. Kohlbrugge's geloofsopvatting vergeleken met Reformatie en Nadere Reformatie*.

69. J. W. Hofmeyr, *Johannes Hoornbeeck as Polemikus* (Kampen: J. H. Kok, 1975); ibid., *Nederlandse Nadere Reformasie en sy invloed op twee kontinente: vergelyking van die invloed en deurwerking van enkele aspekte van die Nederlandse Nadere Reformasie in die Suid-Afrikaanse en Noord-Amerikaanse kontekste* (Pretoria: UNISA, 1988); A. W. G Raath, "Wilhelmus à Brakel se werk oor die redelike Godsdiens,"in *Konteks*, 3 (2000), 36-37; ibid., "Jacobus Trigland en die aanloop tot die Sinode van Dordt," in *Konteks*, 6 (2000), 36-37; ibid., "Abraham Hellenbroek se werke," in *Konteks*, 5 (2001), 34-35; ibid., "Bevinding en geestelike verlating op die limiete: Die historiese en teologiese kontekstualisering van die pioniersvrou Hester Venter (c. 1750-c. 1830) se ondervindelike bekeersweg," in *Hervormde Teologiese Studies*,4 (2004), 1449-1489.

70. Carl R. Trueman, *The Claims of Truth: John Owen's Trinitarian Theology* (Carlisle: Paternoster Press, 1998); Carl R. Trueman, and R. Scott Clark, eds., *Protestant Scholasticism: Essays in Reassessment*, (Carlisle: Paternoster, 1999).

71. Paul Dibon, *La philosphie Néerlandaise au siècle d'or. Tome I: L'Enseignement philosophique dans les Universités néerlandaises à l'époque précartesienne (1575-1650)* (Amsterdam: Elsevier, 1954); Th. H. M. Verbeek, "Descartes and the problem of atheism: the Utrecht Crisis," in *Nederlands archief voor kerkgeschiedenis*, 71 (1991): 211-223; idem, "J. Koelman en de filosofie zijner dagen," *Documentatieblad Nadere Reformatie*, 20 (1996), 62-71; A. Vos, "Voetius als reformatorisch wijsgeer," in *De onbekende Voetius*, ed. J. van Oort, (Kampen: Kok, 1989), 220-241; Goudriaan, *Philosophische Gotteserkenntnis*.

72. S. D. Post, *Pieter Boddaert en Rutger Schutte, Piëtistische dichters in de achttiende eeuw* (Houten: Den Hertog, 1995); L. Strengholt, *Bloemen in Gethsemane. Verzamelde studies over de dichter Revius* (T. Bolland: Amsterdam, 1976).

73. J. Verkruijsse, "Holland 'gedecideerd'. Boekopdrachten in Holland in de 17e eeuw," in *Holland regionaal-historisch tijdschrift*, 23 (1991): 225-42; C. Traas, *Het leven en werk van Abraham Boekholt (1664-1709). Boekenverkoper te Amsterdam*, (Amsterdam: VU, 1987).

74. Muller, *Post-Reformation Reformed Dogmatics* (1987), 1:42-49; idem, (2003), 1:60-83. Muller details in the latter his earlier periodization 'Early Orthodoxy ca. 1565-1640' to 'ca.1565-1618-1640,' 'High Orthodoxy ca. 1640-1700' to 'ca. 1640-1685-1725' and 'Late Orthodoxy ca. 1700-1790' to '1725-.'

particular the *Nadere Reformatie* is depicted as either radical[75] or reactionary.[76] However, more recent literature assessed the period of Protestant orthodoxy as a doctrinal and methodological, scholastic continuity of preceding periods,[77] where for example the *Nadere Reformatie* is a subcategory of seventeenth-century confessional orthodoxy with a strong notion of piety. In respect to the issue of continuity of scholasticism, one should be alert that this scholarship[78] understands scholasticism of seventeenth-century Protestant orthodoxy not as theological content but as an internationally used academic method.[79] For example, van Asselt[80] notes that Cocceius, like his contemporaries, used the characteristic medieval scholastic technique of *disputatio* and *quæstio* but had modified Thomistic theological positions.[81] Nonetheless one should avoid the conclusion that these assessments advocate that the intellectual thought of seventeenth-century Reformed orthodoxy is either a simplistic continuity or a discontinuity of the sixteenth-century Protestant Reformation.[82] Van Asselt observes that such an appraisal

75. S. van der Linde, "De betekenis van de Nadere Reformatie," 215-25, "De radikale, gereformeerde reformatie, die preciesheid wenst in plaats van vrome (onvrome) algemeenheden, een piëtisme dus, een bewust wijden van het hele leven aan God."

76. C. Graafland, W.J. op 't Hof, F.A. van Lieburg, "Nadere Reformatie: opnieuw een poging tot begripsbepaling," in *Documentatieblad Nadere Reformatie* 19:2 (1995): 108 "De Nadere Reformatie is die beweging binnen de Nederlandse Gereformeerde Kerk in de zeventiende en achttiende eeuw, die in reactie op de verflauwing van of een gebrek aan levend geloof de persoonlijke geloofsbeleving en godsvrucht centraal stelde en van hieruit inhoudelijke en procedurele reformatieprogramma's opstelde, bij de bevoegde kerkelijke, politieke en maatschappelijke organen indiende en/of in aansluiting hierbij zelf een verdere hervorming van kerk, samenleving en staat in woord en daad nastreefde."

77. Muller, *Post-Reformation Reformed Dogmatics*, 1:31, argues that it "represents a still broader theological synthesis than early orthodoxy: it rests upon a confessional summation of the faith, has a somewhat sharper and more codified polemic against its doctrinal adversaries, and possesses a broader and more explicit grasp of the tradition, particularly of the contribution of the Middle Ages."

78. See for example, Trueman and Clark, *Protestant Scholasticism*; Richard A. Muller, "Giving Direction to Theology," 183-93; idem, "The Problem of Protestant Scholasticism—A Review and Definition," in *Reformation and Scholasticism: An Ecumenical Enterprise, Texts and Studies in Reformation & Post-Reformation Thought*, eds., W. J. van Asselt and E. Dekker (Grand Rapids: Baker Academic, 2001), 45-64; idem, *Christ and the Decree*; idem, *Post-Reformation Reformed Dogmatics*, 1:35.

79. W. J. van Asselt, L. Rouwendal, eds., *Inleiding in de Gereformeerde Scholastiek* (Zoetermeer: Boekencentrum, 1998), 98-102, 127-33, 150-55; Otten, "Medieval Scholasticism, 275: "I tend to see scholasticism as referring to what is essentially a 'school practice' rather than the embodiment of a well-defined doctrine;" Muller, *Post-Reformation Reformed Dogmatics*, 1:37, 66

80. Van Asselt and Rouwendal, *Inleiding in de Gereformeerde Scholastiek*, 122.

81. Van Asselt, *The Federal Theology of Johannes Cocceius*, 61-71.

82. The main contention, among others, is that the seventeenth-century Protestant orthodoxy has scholastic influences on the theology, which was not or was barely present in John Calvin and others of the Protestant Reformation. For example O. Fatio, argues in *Méthod et Théologie. Lambert Daneau et les débuts de la scolastique réformée*, 16, that those who contrast Reformation and orthodoxy in this way, see this as a process of deterioration. He writes, "Le passage de la doctrine réformée à la dogmatique orthodoxe est un processus d'objectivation croissante des découvertes existentielles du début de la Reformeé... Ces auteurs opposent dynamisme à statisme, créativité à redite, règne de la grâce à

is no longer justifiable and argues in favor of an "interdisciplinary approach" in contrast to the older research, which was characterized by "a dogmatic approach."[83] Moreover, such an interdisciplinary approach requires taking the genre and structure of primary sources, such as dogmatic, exegetical, catechetical, polemical, and academic material, into consideration.[84]

Finally, in respect to these different appraisals of the intellectual thought of Mastricht's time, two comments are in order. First, this study does not minimize the contributions of older research but concurs for the most part with the evaluation of recent scholarship. Second, this study argues that the latter, addressing methodology and doctrine, is often deficient in appraising the exegetical labors and discussion of piety of the studied seventeenth-century sources. The next section demonstrates this deficiency, particularly as it relates to the studies on the doctrine of God.

The Doctrine of God of the Seventeenth-century Reformed Orthodoxy

The appraisal of the doctrine of God of the seventeenth-century post-Reformation has been limited to aspects of the divine efficiency, such as predestination, decree and covenant,[85] and has in general restricted the study on the divine sufficiency, to the divine attributes.[86] Concentrating on the divine sufficiency, these studies omit the examination

---

ontologisation de la connaissance de Dieu et à systématisation de l'Ecriture, pour qualifier la différence entre la périod précédant la mort de Calvin et celle qui la suit."

83. Van Asselt, "Protestant Scholasticism," 268.

84. For example of a study on *Disputationes* see Van Asselt and Dekker, *De Scholastieke Voetius*.

85. Jürgen Moltmann, *Pradestination und Perseveranz : Geschichte und Bedeutung der reformierten Lehre* "de perseverantia sanctorum" (Neukirchen: Kreis Moers, Neukirchener Verlag, 1961); C. Graafland, *De Zekerheid van het geloof*; G. Schrenk, *Gottesreich und Bund im Älteren Protestantismus vornehmlich bei Johannes Coccejus* (Darmstadt: Wissenschaftliche Buchgesellschaft, 1967); Dewey D. Wallace, *Puritans and Predestination: Grace in English Protestant Theology, 1525-1695* (Chapel Hill: University of North Carolina Press, 1982); Michæl D. Bell, *Propter potestatem, scientiam, ac beneplacitum Dei: The Doctrine of the Object of Predestination in the Theology of Johannes Maccovius* (Th.D. diss., Westminster Theological Seminary, 1986); James E. Williams Jr., *An evaluation of William Perkins' Docrtine of Predestination in the Light of John Calvin's Writings* (Th.M. thesis, Dallas Theolgical Seminary, 1986); Muller, *Christ and the Decree*; C. Graafland, *Van Calvijn tot Barth, oorsprong en ontwikkeling van de leer der verkiezing in het Gereformeerd Protestantisme* ('s-Gravenhage: Boekencentrum, 1987; idem, *Van Calvijn tot Comrie, oorspong en ontwikkeling van de leer van het verbond in het Gereformeerd Protestantisme* (Zoetermeer: Boekencentrum, 1996); B. Loonstra, *Verkiezing, verzoening, verbond : beschrijving en beoordeling van de leer van het "pactum salutis" in de gereformeerde theologie*; John V. Fesko, *Diversity within the reformed tradition : supra- and infralapsarianism in Calvin, Dort, and Westminster* (Ph.D. diss., University of Aberdeen, 1999); Frederic J. Koning, *The Doctrine of Predestination in Scholastic Calvinism: an Evaluation of the Muller Thesis* (Th.M. thesis, Regent College, 1999).

86. J. J. Grandia, *Immutabilitas, necessitas et contingentia : speurtocht naar de structuur in de theologie van de vermaarde, godzalige, hoogh-geleerde heer, d'hr. Melchior Leydecker, S.S. Theol. Doctor en Professor tot Utrecht* (Master Thesis: Faculty of Theology of University of Utrecht, 1990); For an introduction on the divine attributes from a philosophical-theological perspective see G. van den Brink and M. Sarot eds., *Hoe is Uw Naam? opstellen over de eigenschappen van God* (Kampen: Kok, 1995), translated as *Understanding the Attributes of God* (New York: Peter Lang Publishing, 1999). The authors write that in recent years, God's nature and attributes have been the center of numerous attempts at conceptual clarification and critical

of a possible relationship of exegesis, doctrine, elenctics and *praxis* [87] and restrict the assessment primarily to doctrine and polemic.[88] This observation is supported by a review of general studies and those addressing the structure and content, certain features of the doctrine, and philosophical-theological reflections on the doctrine of God. Muller provides a cross-section study of the doctrine of God, touching on many representatives of the seventeenth-century post-Reformation.[89] Although this work may possibly become a standard work for post-Reformation Reformed studies, it also invites for a more detailed study on relationship, if any, between exegesis, doctrine and piety. Loonstra observes that the doctrinal and theological reflection on the doctrine of God did not appear to be a high priority for the '*practikaal georiënteerde*' movement of the *Nadere Reformatie.*[90] His thesis, which is echoed by Graafland,[91] is that the orthodox doctrine of God of the *Nadere Reformatie* is controlled by static thinking about eternity; that God cannot communicate directly with humanity. In other words, experiences, spiritual impressions, and subjective affections are the effect of God's eternal and constant activity but are not a real personal meeting with God. De Reuver[92] praises Loonstra's attempt but notes that the pneumatological element is lacking in the

reflection. This volume contains, besides an introduction to the method of philosophical theology, essays on God's love, immutability, omnipresence, omniscience, simplicity, (im)passibility and omnipotence. *Understanding the Attributes of God* is not only a highly readable survey of recent developments in philosophical theology but also aims at making a distinctive contribution. The authors all belong to the so-called "Utrecht school" in philosophical theology, whose approach is characterized by the cross-fertilization of Anglo-Saxon and continental philosophical and theological, traditional and recent thinking. The book offers a programmatic sample of their work and is well documented with secondary literature on the study of the divine attributes in general. See also, Vincent Brummer, *Over een persoolijke God gesproken* (Kampen: Kok, 1988); G. Immink, *Divine Simplicty* (Kampen: Kok, 1987); Marcel Sarot, *God, Passibility and Corporeality* (Kampen: Kok, 1992); A. Vos, *Kennis en Noodzakelijheid* (Kampen: Kok, 1981); Gijsbert van den Brink, *Almighty God. A Study of the Doctrine of Divine Omnipotence* (Kampen: Kok Pharos, 1993).

87. The scholarly literature for each individual topic is discussed in part III and IV of this study.

88. Studies on exegesis of the seventeenth-century Protestant orthodoxy in general and the doctrine of God in particular are not yet on par with the emerging efforts on sixteenth-century exegesis. Cf. Richard A. Muller, "Biblical Interpretations in the 16th & 17th Centuries," in *Historical Handbook of Major Biblical Interpretations*, ed. Donald K. McKim (Downers Grove: InterVarsity Press, 1998), 135-52.

89. Muller, *Post-Reformation Reformed Dogmatics*, vol.3, *The Divine Essence and Attributes*, and vol. 4, *The Triunity of God*.

90. B. Loonstra, "De leer van God en Christus in de *Nadere Reformatie*" in Brienen, *et al.*, *Theologische aspecten van de* Nadere Reformatie, 99-150. Here the author notes that a specific study has not been published on the relationship of the development of the doctrine of God and the *Nadere Reformatie*.

91. C. Graafland, *Bijbels en daarom Gereformeerd* (Kampen: Groot Gouderiaan, 2001). Graafland argues that Reformed orthodoxy in its scholastic form is a closed system and does not allow for further theological development. Particularly, according to Graafland, the doctrine of God of the seventeenth and eighteenth-century is an abstract notion.

92. A. de Reuver, "Wat is het eigene van de Nadere Reformatie?" *Documentieblad Nadere Reformatie*, XVIII (1994): 149-53.

development of his thesis. He also questions Loonstra's negative evaluation of representatives of the *Nadere Reformatie* in regard to the experiential aspect of the doctrine of God. Van Asselt provides an in-depth introduction of Cocceius's structure and content of the doctrine of God.[93] Though the central aim of his study is not the examination of relationship of exegesis, doctrine and practice in Cocceius' work, the study provide an ample stimulant to study this aspect in Cocceius's theology.[94] Other studies, reviewed Voetius's *Disputationes Selectæ* in respect to his understanding of God's knowledge, will and power.[95] The authors, here, note Voetius's diversion of Boethius and Aquinas, and indicate he probably followed Scotus's understanding that the underpinning of the divine knowledge of future contingencies is the divine will and not predestined knowledge. Further, the authors point to Voetius's ontological definition and adherence to the Augustinian formulation of the divine will. Finally, in respect to the *potentia absoluta* and *potentia ordinata*, the authors argue that Voetius brings together the Reformed and the earlier and later scholastic traditions, and presents a modified Thomastic interpretation. A. Beck's reconstruction of Voetius's doctrine of God is focused on the relationship between the divine essence and attributes. He notes that Voetius believed that the question *An sit Deus*, "whether God exists," is a preliminary one of which its affirmative answer directs the main question, *Quid sit Deus*. Voetius, according to Beck, asserts that in "asking 'what God is'—asking for God's 'whatness' (*quidditas*) or essence—we are dependent on the names and attributes by which God has revealed himself." Thus, he asserts the proper name *par excellence* is the tetragrammaton יהוה (Exod. 3:14) denoting, for Voetius, "the primary, eternal and immutable essence of God in an exclusive way. "[97] Although both analyses provide a valuable introduction to Voetius's thought, it does not address how these aspects of the doctrine of God are exegetically understood or how they are part of practical theology.[98] Finally, studies of T. Verbeek, T. McGahagen, and Goudriaan[99] describe the philosophical-theological

93. Van Asselt, *The Federal Theology of Johannes Cocceius*, 139-192.

94. Seven of the ten volumes of Cocceius's *Opera Omnia* are exegetical works. In addition, Van Asselt explains that Cocceius's theology was a result of his exegetical labors. Cf. Van Asselt, *The Federal Theology of Johannes Cocceius*, 139. Johannes Cocceius, *Opera Omnia Theologica, Exegetica, Didactica, Polemica, Philologica* (Amsterdam: P&J Blaev, 1701), vol. 7, 3, § 1, "Theologia est doctrina secundum veram pietatem."

95. Van Asselt and Dekker, *De Scholastieke Voetius*, 34-54 and 55-85.

97. Andreas Beck, "Gisbertus Voetius (1589-1676): Basic Features of His Doctrine of God," in *Reformation and Scholasticism: An Ecumenical Enterprise, Texts and Studies in Reformation & Post-Reformation Thought*, eds., W. J. van Asselt and E. Dekker, (Grand Rapids: Baker Academic, 2001), 212.

98. W. van 't Spijker, "Voetius practicus," in *De onbekende Voetius*, ed. J. van Oort, (Kampen: Kok, 1989).

99. Thomas A. McGahagen, *Cartesianism in the Netherlands, 1639-1676: The New Science and the Calvinistic Counter-Reformation* (Ph.D. diss., University of Pennsylvania,1976); Theo Verbeek, *Descartes and the Dutch* (Carbondale, Il: Southern Illinois University Press, 1992); Goudriaan, *Philosophische Gotteserkenntnis*.

developments of the seventeenth century in general and the early reactions of the Dutch theologians to Cartesian philosophy during the seventeenth century. In particular Goudriaan deals with questions regarding the philosophical knowledge of God according to Suárez and Descartes, two very different but historically linked early-modern philosophers. He asserts both critical and positive reactions to these philosophers on the part of seventeenth-century Dutch Reformed theologians, including Petrus van Mastricht. Opposing Descartes, Mastricht asserted that "the knowledge of God is a (knowledge) worked by the Spirit."[100]

In conclusion, the secondary literature on the doctrine of God[101] depicts the primary seventeenth-century Reformed sources as theology that has been formulated dogmatically, rather than exegetically and practically. Accordingly, the doctrine of God has been primarily evaluated by older scholarship on a doctrinal basis independent of exegesis and other considerations. However, recent scholarship identifies in the formulation of the post-Reformation doctrine of God philosophical considerations and the use of scholastic methodology.

The Practical Theology of the Seventeenth-century Reformed Orthodoxy

Mastricht distinguishes between *pars practica*, as part of his fourfold approach to systematic theology, and *praxis pietatis*, as part of the *theologia ascetica*. When one asserts both terms as piety, or *beoefende vroomheid*, the assessment of the practical theology of the seventeenth-century Reformed orthodoxy can be reiterated with distinct appraisals, which are linked by the quest of origin.[102] Furthermore, these appraisals have a

---

100. Goudriaan, *Philosophische Gotteserkenntnis*, 57: "der vollkommenste Gottesbegriff der des *Spiritus a seipso vivens*." Cf. Petrus van Mastricht, *Gangræna*, 227: "...quasi balbutiendo nobiscum, seipsum [Deus] describit: *Spiritum a seipso viventem*, Joh. 4:24."

101. Loonstra, "De leer van God en Christus in de *Nadere Reformatie*" in Brienen, *et al.*, *Theologische aspecten van de* Nadere Reformatie, 99-150; C. Graafland, *Bijbels en daarom Gereformeerd*. See also, L. Berkhof, *Principles of Biblical Interpretation* (Grand Rapids: Baker Books, 1950), 29; K. O'Dell Bullock, "Post-Reformation Protestant Hermeneutics," in *Biblical Hermeneutics: A Comprehensive Introduction to Interpreting Scripture*, ed. Bruce Corley, Steve Lemke, Grant Lovejoy, 2d ed. (Nashville: Broadman & Holman Publishers, 2002), 129.

102. The relationship and origin of English Puritanism, *Nadere Reformatie*, and (German) Pietism is much debated. German Pietism was rooted in English Puritaism (Heppe) or, with the *Nadere Reformatie*, was a continuity of medieval notions of spirituality (Ritschl). The *Nadere Reformatie* is thereby an ecclesiastical reformation movement, rooted in (Heppe) or associated with English Puritanism (Graafland, op 't Hof) and to be understood against the background of the synod of Dordrecht 1618-1619 (Goeters). On the other hand Stoeffler argues that these three movements are in essence a single expression of post-Reformation evangelical pietism, a thought that is not shared in general by the study group *Documentatieblad Nadere Reformatie*. Cf. H. Heppe, *Geschichte des Pietismus und der Mystik in der Reformirten Kirche* (Leiden: Brill, 1879); A. Ritschl, *Geschichte des Pietismus* (Bonn: Marcus, 1880-1886); W. Goeters, *Die Vorbereitung des Pietismus* (Leipzig: J. C. Hinrich, 1911); F. Ernest Stoeffler, *The Rise of Evangelical Pietism* (Leiden: Brill, 1971); W. J. op 't Hof, *Engelse piëtistische geschriften in het Nederlands*, 1598-1622 (Rotterdam: Lindenberg, 1987). For a recent summary of these issues, see Ian S. Maclean, "The First Pietist: Jodocus van Lodensteyn," (American Society of Church History, 2002), X.1-3. See further for the different appraisals part III, chapter 4, Introduction and Statement of the Problem, of this study.

common tendency: piety is a result of external factors—ecclesiastical (Labadism), doctrinal, and medieval spirituality—or is an expression of living faith in communion with God in Christ by Word and Spirit. The former prompts the question that the formulation of doctrine became prevalent over exegesis and served as basis for the expression of piety or that practical theology is founded upon different presuppositions. The latter stimulates the inquiry of the relationship between Scripture, exegesis, doctrine, and *praxis*.

Statement of the Problem and the Methodology of This Study

This review of the state of research on the life and work of Mastricht, the intellectual thought of his time, the study of the doctrine of God, and piety of the seventeenth-century post-Reformation, identifies several predicaments. First, the twofold emerged portrait of Mastricht and various interpretations of his time demands an additional examination of his life and work in the context of his time. Second, the theology of the seventeenth-century Reformed orthodoxy emerged as either dogmatic or practical—whereby, for both, the relationship to Scripture and its exegesis is overlooked or implicitly assumed. This is particularly evident in literature on the doctrine of God. In summary, a description of the theology of the seventeenth-century Reformed orthodoxy raises the question of how systematic and practical theology was formulated. One of the debates inherited by the Protestant scholastics from medieval theology concerns the character and purpose of the discipline as theoretical or practical.[103] Like the medieval doctors, the Protestant orthodox argued the question of whether theology was theoretical or practical or, if a "mixed" (*theoretico*-practical) discipline, whether it was more theoretical or more practical. The answer to this question is reflected in many seventeenth-century Reformed orthodox systems and designs of theology.[104] Moreover, like the question itself, the meaning of the terms arose out of the medieval theological tradition, and not merely out the tradition of the scholastic system but also out of the tradition of piety and mysticism. One of the issues that remain to be resolved is, according to Muller, the balance of the theory and practice in the *theoretico-practica* paradigm. Although explicit discussion of this point has disappeared from modern theological systems, the issue remains as an undercurrent in all discussion of the purpose and, indeed, the reason for theology as a discipline.[105] It is against this background that an examination of the *TPT* of Mastricht is of interest. Both, the conjunction of theory and *praxis* in the title of Mastricht's *magnum opus* and his fourfold exposition of each of the *loci*: exegetical, doctrinal, elenctic, and practical, are unique for a seventeenth-century

103. *Theoria* may be defined as a teaching (*doctrina*) known in and for itself and *praxis* as a teaching known for the sake of the end toward which it directs the knower. Cf. Muller, *Post-Reformation Reformed Dogmatics*, 1:341.

104. W. Geesink, *De Ethiek in de Gereformeerde Theologie* (Amsterdam: W. Kitchner, 1897), 29-45; Muller, *Post-Reformation Reformed Dogmatics*, 1:343-346.

105. Richard A. Muller, *The Study of Theology: From Biblical Interpretation to Contemporary Formulation* (Foundations of Contemporary Interpretation 7; Grand Rapids: Zondervan, 1991), 42.

system of theology. This observation does not ignore the fact that these systems of theology contain elements of theory and *praxis* as well as aspects of exegesis, doctrine, and polemic. However, the observation accentuates the fact that all foresaid elements are integral and distinctly present in Mastricht's system of theology, which combines both the tradition of the scholastic system and *praxis pietatis*.

Therefore, the central concern of this study is the understanding of Mastricht's formulation of theology, the quest for method and piety. Our examination is restricted to the doctrine of God for two reasons: because the doctrine of God is foundational for Mastricht to the broader scope of his theology, and because the neglect or enhancement of seventeenth-century post-Reformation studies on this doctrine.

The methodology followed in this examination is a descriptive-analytical study of historical theology.[106] Moreover, the examination is fourfold. Part one provides a more detailed account of the life and work of Mastricht in the context of his time, and part two describes premises of the *TPT*. Parts three and four offer a matrix examination of the doctrine of God as found in the *TPT*; the former presents a cross sectional assessment, and the latter provides an in-depth analysis of Mastricht's exegesis, doctrinal formulation, elenctic reflection, and practical implications. The concern of the cross-section examination is to probe Mastricht's way of formulating theology, the quest of method. The concern of the in-depth analysis is to examine, with the results of the preceding examination, the relationship, if any between exegesis, doctrine, elenctic and *praxis*. The study concludes with a reappraisal of the statement of the problem in light of our examination.

Sources

Our examination is primarily confined to *TPT*. However, this will not exclude consideration of Mastricht's own intellectual trajectory and that of his time. In respect to the first, we must include other relevant documents of Mastricht related to the subject matter. In respect to the latter, in parts two and four of this study we examine, though not with the aim of presenting a broad historical-theological study, material of some of Mastricht's contemporaries in order to evaluate his thought.

---

106. This understanding of historical theology can be found in Trueman, and Clark, *Protestant Scholasticism: Essays in Reassessment*, xi-xix.

Part 1

The Life and Work of Petrus van Mastricht in the Context of His Time

Chapter 1
The Life of Petrus van Mastricht

Introduction and Statement of the Problem

The question of who Petrus van Mastricht was[1] has resulted in various sketchy and incoherent biographic and bibliographic representations in the secondary scholarly literature.[2] The former is primarily placed in the context of the *Nadere Reformatie*. This Dutch churchly movement is appraised having a strong emphasis on *praxis* and opposing various divergent views of Reformed orthodoxy. Its theology is evaluated as "dogmatic," and negatively assessed as "scholastic." The bibliographic depiction of Mastricht is mainly restricted to his *Theoretico-practica theologia* (*TPT*). Such presentations lack an examination of Mastricht's place of birth, study, pastorate, and professorate in various parts of Germany before his move to Utrecht, the Netherlands.[3] In addition, such presentations are deficient in the assessment of Mastricht's intellectual trajectory and the historical, philosophical, and theological context of his total œuvre. Moreover, Visser notes that no modern treatment of Mastricht exists.[4] Therefore, this chapter offers an initial but more detailed and cohesive portrait of Mastricht than previously has been presented.

Cologne and Study: 1630-1652

Petrus van Mastricht[5] was born in November 1630 and baptized[6] on December 23 at Cologne, as the son of Thomas of Mastricht and Jeanne de la Planque.[7] Thomas's

---

1. Petrus van Mastricht, *A Treatise on Regeneration*, ed. Brandon Withrow (Morgan: Soli Deo Gloria Publications, 2002), viii.

2. See the introduction chapter of this study, paragraph "Life and Work of Petrus van Mastricht."

3. Germany of the seventeenth century consisted of several counties, ruled by an elector or mark. The Netherlands of that time consisted of several provinces.

4. Derk Visser, "Van Mastricht, Petrus (1630-1706)," in *Encyclopedia of the Reformed Faith*, ed. Donald K. McKim (Louisville: Westminster/John Knox Press, 1992), 383.

5. He is also known as Cephas Scheunenus, Petri van Mastricht, Petrus van Mastrigt, Pieter van Maestricht, Petro von Mastricht, Petrus van Maestricht, Peter (van) Mastricht, Petrus van Maastricht, and Petrus (van) Mastricht the Elder or the theologian. The latter is to distinguish him from his nephew Petrus van Mastricht (1685-1721) the jurist.

6. A. E. van Tellingen, *Het leven en enige aspecten uit de theologie van Petrus van Mastricht (1630-1706)* (Master Thesis: Faculty of Theology of University of Utrecht, 2003), 8. Van Tellingen writes that the baptism register mentions: Pieter van Maestricht "Den 23 December 1630 is door onsen ordinarien dienaer gedoopt het kindt van Thomas van Maestricht ende Janneken la Planck. Is ghenaemt Pieter. Getuygen syn geweest Jan [Faffen] in plaetse van syn soon Pieter [Faffen], Daniel van Hamele in plaetse van Pieter Buyssen, . . .sel Maria Erber in plaetse van Maria Slechtendale tot Hessen. Kercken weges tegenwoordich geweest C[ornelis] v[an] M[aestricht] den ouden." In addition, Mastricht was most probably baptized by Rev. Wilhelm Damen, who served the congregation from 1627-1635. Cf. Rudolf

father, Cornelius Sc(h)oning, fled during the reign of Alva with his family from Mastricht to Cologne.[8] Here, he took the family name "van Mastricht." The family Mastricht[9] belonged to the Dutch Reformed (refugee) congregation of Cologne, where Petrus's grandfather and father served as elders.[10] The congregation was internationally oriented, with contacts to Utrecht.[11] In this congregation "under the cross,"[12] Petrus van Mastricht received catechism lessons from Johannes Hoornbeeck (1617-1666) who served the congregation from 1639-1643.[13] For his studies Mastricht went to the Latin school in Duisburg, where he had Theodor Undereyck (1635-1693) as a fellow student.[14]

Löhr and Jan Pieter van Doorn, *Protokolle der Niederländisch-Reformierten Gemeinde in Köln von 1651-1803* (Köln: Rheinland Verlag Düsseldorf, 1971), 1:xiii.

7. Her father, Nicolas de la Planque, from Aath by Antwerp, served the Reformed congregation at Cologne from 1613-1619. Cf. Löhr and van Doorn, *Protokolle*, 1:xiii.

8. His wife was Magdalena Voss and their children were Thomas and Elisabeth. Cf. Löhr and van Doorn, *Protokolle*, 2:419; H. Heppe, *Geschichte des Pietismus und der Mystik in der Reformirten Kirche* (Leiden: Brill, 1879), 465 and 466 notes that Dutch (refugee) families settled in the second part of the sixteenth century in the Lower Rhine area.

9. The children of Thomas and Jeanne, Petrus, Magdalena, Johannes and Gerhardus, married, with the exception of Petrus, members of the congregation; Magdalena married David Behagel, Johannes, who was in Amsterdam from April 1653 to January 1656, married Anna Behagel, and Dr. Gerardus married Magdalena le Brun. Cf. Löhr and van Doorn, *Protokolle*, 2:419. Van Tellingen suggests that Petrus had five brothers and four and sisters (*Het leven en enige aspecten*, 10).

10. Cornelius served from 1651-1655 and died in November 1658. Thomas, succeeding his father, served from 1655-1663 and died in August, 1667. Cf. Löhr and van Doorn, *Protokolle*, vol.1.

11. Ibid., vols. 1 and 2. The minutes of the consistory of the Dutch Reformed church at Cologne show that (1) the consistory had regular meetings with the German and France (Huguenot) members; (2) ecclesiastical attestations were received and provided for members of Dutch refugee congregations of London and Utrecht; (3) collections were held for the Reformed congregation in Straßburg; (4) correspondence was held with G. Voetius and J. Bogaert; (5) A. Essensius was considered to be called from Utrecht; (6) marriages where solemnized for Frederic Spanheim, doctor of theology and professor at Heidelberg, and Lucretia Elisabeth van Bilderbeck on May 21, 1657, and for Johan Ludwick Fabricius, professor *der heilige theologie* at Heidelberg, and Agnes Sibylle de Bilderbeck on January 31, 1669; (7) members of the consistory and congregation traveled internationally and visited annually the Frankfurter Messe. In addition, the Reformed congregations of Cologne and Mühlheim am Rhein worked closely together.

12. Petrus van Mastricht, *Theoretico-practica theologia qua, per singula capita theologica, pars exegetica, dogmatica, elenchtica et practica, perpetua successione conjugantur; accedunt historia ecclesiastica, plena quidem, sed compendiosa, idea theologiæ moralis, hypotyposis theologiæ asceticæ etc. proin opus quasi novum* (Utrecht: Thomas Appels, 1699), 1059: "(43) Johannes Hoornbeeck...Ecclesiastes primò sub cruce apud Coloniam Agrippinensem." J. A. Cramer in *De Theologische Faculteit te Utrecht ten tijde van Voetius* (Utrecht: Kemink en Zoon, 1932), 18, fn.2, incorrectly notes that Hoornbeeck served not in Cologne but Mühlheim am Rhein.

13. Mastricht, *Theoretico-practica theologia*, 1059: "(43) Johannes Hoornbeeck. . . à quo prima Religiones rudimenta Catechetica;" Löhr and van Doorn, *Protokolle*, 1:xiii.

14. W. Raup, in *Biographisch-Bibliographisch Kirchenlexikon* (Bremen: Bautz, 2000), 17:1439 mentions about Theodor Undereyck, "Begründer des kirchlichen Pietismus in der Deutsch reformierten Kirche, *

Following school in Duisburg, he came to Utrecht in 1647 to be treated for a foot handicap and to study at the academy with the well-known professors Gisbertus Voetius (1589-1676), Carolus de Maets (1597-1651) and his catechism teacher. [15] For the latter Mastricht defended the theological disputation *De esu sanguinis et suffocati ad Act. XV* in 1650.[16] The theology professors de Maets and Hoornbeeck taught respectively New Testament and Old Testament.[17] Under Voetius, Mastricht received a thorough education: didactic-dogmatic theology, which included the *loci communes* as presented in the Leiden *Synopsis purioris theologiæ*; an introduction to the *Summa Theologia* of Thomas Aquinas; and an acquaintance with the scholastic *disputationes* of Voetius's Saturday morning teachings. In summary, he received a scholastic methodological schooling, including the knowledge of the medieval scholastic definitions and distinctions.[18]

Voetius's program resulted in 1644 in the publication *Exercitia et bibliotheca studiosi theologæ*, a comprehensive 700-page introduction to theological literature and a four-year program of theology. Its theme is one with his overall vision: theology must be known and practiced.[19] Thus, Mastricht came to Utrecht for his "voet" and came under the

---

15.6. 1635 in Altstaden bei Duisburg als Sohn des wohlhabenden Kaufmanns Gerhard Undereyck († 1636) und dessen Frau Sara, geb. Salanger († 1636), † 1.1. 1693 Bremen. - Als Waise bei seinem Onkel aufgewachsen, studierte U. Theologie in Utrecht, Duisburg und Leiden (1653-58). Seine konträr zueinander stehenden ref.-orth. Lehrer waren bedeutende Wegbereiter des Pietismus: Gisbert Voetius (s.d.), eine führende Gestalt der niederländisch-calvinistischen Reformbewegung der "*Nadere Reformatie*," und Johannes Coccejus." See also Johannes Wallmann, *Der Pietismus*, (Göttingen: Vandehoeck & Ruprecht, 1990), 26-28. In addtion, H. Heppe in *Geschichte des Pietismus*, 470 notes that Undereyck studied from 1654-1657 in Utrecht, and from 1657-1658 studied at Duisburg having as teachers "die Coccejanischen Professoren Hund und Clauberg." Finally, James Tanis in *Dutch Calvinistic Pietism in the Middle Colonies, A Study in the Life and Theology of Theodorus Jacobus Frelinghuysen* (The Hague: M. Nijhoff, 1967), 19 notes that Dutch pietism on the Lower Rhine had its first outspoken advocate in Theodor Undereyck and Samuel Nethenus. Undereyck, the more important theologian of the two, was deeply influenced by his studies in Utrecht with Voetius, Essenius, and Matthias Nethenus (older brother of Samuel).

15. *Album Studiosorum Academiæ Rheno-Trajectinæ 1636-1886* (Utrecht: Beijers en Van Boekhoven, 1886), 15. The student register shows students primarily from Zeeland, Amsterdam and Utrecht but also from Hungary, Poland, England and Germany. Fellow students included Simon Simonides (1629-1675), Jacobus Hondius, and Stephanus Kapossi.

16. J. Hoornbeeck, *De esu sanguinis et suffocati ad Act. XV*, resp. Van Maestricht, (Utrecht: Henricus Versteeg, 1650). Cf. J. W. Hofmeyr, *Johannes Hoornbeeck as Polemikus* (Kampen: J. H. Kok, 1975), 227.

17. G. W. Kernkamp, *De Utrechtsche Universiteit 1637-1936*, vol I, *De Utrechtsche Academie 1636-1815* (Utrecht: A. Oosterhoek's Uitgevers Maatschappij, 1936), 239.

18. Ibid., 1:233; Richard A. Muller, *After Calvin. Studies in the Development of a Theological Tradition* (Oxford: Oxford University Press, 2003), 110-16.

19. Joel R. Beeke, "Gisbertus Voetius: Toward a Reformed Marriage of Knowledge and Piety," in *Protestant Scholasticism, Essays in Reassessment*, ed. Carl R. Trueman and R. S. Clark (Carlisle: Paternoster Press, 1999), 232. See also, Gisbertus Voetius, "*Reedenwoeringe van de Nuttigheit der Akademien en Schoolen, mitsgaders der Wetenschappen en Konsten*," in Isaac le Long, *Hondert-Jaarige Jubel-Gedachtenisse der Academie van Utrecht* (Utrecht: M. Visch, 1736).

teaching of Voet-(ius). Both Voetius's and Hoornbeeck's emphasis on *theologia practica*[20] would contribute to Mastricht's theological formation. In 1651, during Mastricht's study, de Maets passed away, and the academy attempted to call Samuel Rutherford (1600-1661). However, Rutherford remained in Scotland and recommended Andreas Essenius (1618-1677), minister at Utrecht.[21] According to Pontanus, Mastricht probably obtained additional instruction during his Utrecht academy years at the Universities of Leiden and Heidelberg. He also traveled briefly to England "for language and practical or Christian moral study."[22] Nevertheless, with these possible visits abroad, Mastricht went back to Utrecht and completed his study of divinity. And so, he left the academy of Utrecht, the European axis of *pietatis cum scientia* and the summit of Reformed orthodoxy and Protestant Scholasticism, which often disagreed with the content of medieval Scholasticism but expediently used its methodological structure.[23] He returned to Cologne and brought his church membership papers to the consistory on August 5, 1652.[24]

We can conclude, then, that the period 1630-1652 of Mastricht's life formed him catechetically and academically in Reformed orthoxy and vital piety.

20. Joel R. Beeke, "Gisbertus Voetius, 232. See also Johannes Hoornbeeck, *Theologia practica* (Utrecht: Johannes & Guiljelmus van de Water, 1689).

21. Kernkamp, *De Utrechtsche Universiteit*, 1:239; idem, *Acta et Decreta Senatus* (Utrecht: Broekhoff, 1936), 1:264. Rutherford's *Examen Arminianismi* was published for the benefit of divinity students in Utrecht and received the imprimatur of Voetius and Essenius. Cf. P. G. Ryken, "Scottish Reformed Scholasticism," in *Protestant Scholasticism, Essays in Reassessment*, 202. Essenius was called in December 1652, after Mastricht had left Utrecht.

22. Henricus Pontanus, *Laudatio Funebris In excessum Doctissimi et Sanctissimi Senis, Petri van Mastrigt, S. S. Theol. Doctoris & Professoris: Quam jussu amplissimi Senatus Academici D. XXIV. Februarii, postridie sepulturæ dixit Henricus Pontanus* (Rotterdam: Petrus van Veen, 1706). The suggestion of Van Tellingen that Mastricht could have met John Owen (1616-1683) is speculative. Cf. Van Tellingen, *Het leven en enige aspecten*, 12, 119. This author could not verify Van Asselt's indication of Oxford as a study location. Cf. W. J. van Asselt, P. L. Rouwendal, *Inleiding in de gereformeerde scholastiek* (Zoetermeer: Boekencentrum, 1998), 129. Mastricht's going to Leiden during his study of Utrecht is probable. Many students from the Lower Rhine studied at Leiden University during Cocceius's professorate (1650-1669) (See footnote 26 of this chapter). However, that Mastricht went to Heidelberg in the period 1647-1652 is contentious, bearing in mind that the university was closed between September 1631 and November 1652. He is not listed in the student records of the theological and philosophical faculty of Heidelberg University (personal communication August, 2002). See also Van Tellingen, *Het leven en enige aspecten*, 11.

23. Richard A. Muller, *Christ and the Decree* (Durham, NC: The Labyrinth Press, 1986); idem, *Post-Reformation Reformed Dogmatics* (Grand Rapids: Baker Academic, 2003), vols. 1-4. Cf. Martin I. Klauber, "Continuity and Discontinuity in post-Reformation Reformed Theology: An Evaluation of the Muller Thesis," *Journal of Evangelical Theological Society* 33 (1990): 467; Willem J. van Asselt, "Herwaardering van de gereformeerde scholastiek," *Kerktijd* 7 (1995), 1-12.

24. Löhr and van Doorn, *Protokolle*, 1:18: "Behoorlijke attestatie van de gemeynte van Utrecht ingelevert sijnde voor Petrus Mastricht, soo is deselve tot litmaat deser gemeynte op en aangenomen."

Germany: Cologne, Xanten, Glückstadt, Frankfurt an der Oder, and Duisburg: 1652-1677

The twenty-five-year "German" period (1652-1677) following his study of divinity can be divided into four parts: (1) Cologne and Xanten (Cleve) from 1652 to 1662, (2) Glückstadt (Schleswig-Holstein) from 1662 to 1667, (3) Frankfurt an der Oder (Brandenburg) from 1667 to 1670 and (4) Duisburg from 1670 to 1677.

1652-1662

In 1652, while a ministerial candidate, Mastricht received a call from Xanten. He accepted the call and began working as *vicarus* in early 1653.[25] The congregation of Xanten belonged to the predominantly Cocceian classis of Cleve.[26] In respect to the Cocceians, Mastricht writes later that particularly after the death of J. Cocceius (1603-1669) the contention with the Voetians was greater than was necessary.[27] While at Xanten, Mastricht kept his membership at the Cologne congregation.[28] This period of his life, however, is clouded with unknowns. We know, however, that he attended as witness[29] in 1658 the baptism of a child of his sister Magdalena and her husband Daniel Behaeghel.[30] Moreover, the consistory of Cologne recommends on August 9, 1655 to

25. Mastricht was deputy-vicar for a couple months, according to Jürgen Rosen of the Evangelische Kirchengemeinde Xanten-Mötmter (personal communication in October 2002). Cf. Walter Bösken, *Geschichte der Evangelischen Kirchengemeinde* (Magdeburg: Heinrichshofen, 1900), 53. Thus, he did not become minister of the Reformed church at Wesel in 1652 as mentioned by Van Vliet. See Jan van Vliet, *William Ames: Marrow of the Theology and Piety of the Reformed Tradition* (Ph.D. diss., Westminster Theological Seminary, 2002), 346. Van Tellingen notes that Mastricht begun at January 20, 1653. Cf. Van Tellingen, *Het leven en enige aspecten*, 13, 14.

26. Jonathan I. Israel, *The Dutch Republic, Its Rise, Greatness, and Fall 1466-1806* (Oxford: Oxford University Press, 1998), 665, mentions that the German Reformed consistories in the Lower Rhine and its Synod of Cleve, to which Xanten belonged, were mainly Cocceian. The Synod of Cleve, which followed the church order of Dordrecht (1578) and Middelburg (1581), was for a long time part of the Dutch general synod. In addition to the ecclesiastical link, there were academic connections among the universities of Utrecht, Leiden, Hardewijk and Duisburg. Many ministers of the Synod of Cleve were trained, prior to the founding of the Duisburg University in 1655, at the Dutch universities and in particular at Leiden University, having among others, Cocceius as professor.

27. Petrus van Mastricht, *Theoretico-practica theologia*, 1074: "...nata sunt nomina *Coccejanorum & Voetianorum*, quæ utinam audita nunquam fuissent. Hinc, comprimis post decessum Celeb.Coccei A 1658 [1669, AN] ex contentionibus major concitata est animorum συρραξις quam res exigebat."

28. Löhr and van Doorn, *Protokolle*, 2:419, implies a membership from 1652 to 1671.

29. Ibid., 1:100. In addition, on October 14, 1669 Petrus van Mastricht, addressed in the minutes of the consistory as *dominus*, was witness-in-absentia for the baptism of Anna Maria, daughter of Dr. Gerardus van Mastricht and his wife Magdalena le Brun (261). In the same capacity he serves, with his sister-in-law Magdalena, for a baptism of De Wreed(t) family on December 6, 1671 (291).

30. This baptism was administered by Petrus Montanus, who was called on November 14, 1653, with the particular approval of the French members and was present for the first time at the consistory meeting of April 15, 1654. Cf. ibid., 1:35, 37. In addition, Petrus Montanus served later the Reformed congregation of Schellingwoude, classis Amsterdam, the Netherlands.

the congregation of Mühlheim am Rhein to call Mastricht, who is *"sacrosanctæ theologiæ candidatus* van seer goede gaven en stichtelijke van leven sijnde."[31] This call was not accepted by Mastricht. Meanwhile he proved "not to be an indifferent spectator of his time."[32] Christopher Wittichus (1625-1687)[33] was appointed at the newly established (1655) theological faculty of Duisburg University and as preacher at the Reformed church of Duisburg, classis of Cleve.[34] Wittichus published a *disputatio* in 1655, revealing his appreciation of Descartes's philosophical thought.[35] He probably never intended to weaken the hegemony of theology to the extent that it occurred later that century. Nevertheless, that same year Wittichus's Cartesianism was opposed by Mastricht's first publication: *Vindicæ veritatis et autoritatis sacræ scripturæ...adversus dissertationes Chr. Wittichii.*[36] According to Israel, Wittichus argued that the scriptural passages Voetians referred to as incompatible with Cartesianism should not be construed literally,[37] a point Mastricht vehemently opposed.

The period 1652-1662 of Mastricht's life thus took place in a predominantly Cocceian churchly environment, in which his first philosophical-theological (anti-Cartesian) treatise was published.

31. Ibid., 1:58 (minutes 39.1).

32. B. Glasius, *Godgeleerd Nederland, Biographisch Woordenboek van Nederlandsche Godgeleerden* ('s-Hertogenbosch: Gebr. Muller, 1853), 2:471.

33. Wittichus was, according to Jonathan Israel, a leading Cartisio-Cocceian and champion of philosophical reason, whose life and work spanned both the Lower Rhine and the Dutch Republic. He held that "what we know from within, by means of pure reason, we must deem to be revealed to us by God." Jonathan I. Israel, *Radical Enlightenment, Philosophy and the Making of Modernity 1650-1750* (Oxford: Oxford University Press, 2001), 25, 26; W. J. van Asselt, "Petrus van Mastricht," in *Biographisch Lexicon voor de geschiedenis van het Nederlands Protestantisme* (Kampen:Kok, 2001), 360.

34. Günter von Roden, *Die Universität Duisburg* (Duisburg: Walter Braun Verlag, 1968), 240.

35. Christoph Wittich, *Disputatio Theologica de Stylo Scripturæ Quem adhibet cum de rebus naturalibus sermonem instituit* (Duisburg: Ravins, 1655). See also, Christoph Wittich, *Annotationes ad Renati Descartes Meditationes* (Dordrecht: Casparus, 1685). Jonathan Israel characterizes the mid-seventeenth century, with the rise of Cartesianism, the 'Crisis of the European Mind.' Cf. Israel, *Radical Enlightenment*, 14. Furthermore, he argues that this intellectual turmoil developed first in the Dutch Republic and Calvinist states of Germany (24).

36. Petrus van Mastricht, *Vindicæ veritatis et autoritatis sacræ scripturæ in rebus Philosophicis adversus dissertationes D. Christophori Wittichii* (Utrecht: J. à Waesberge, 1655). Mastricht's work was an early Reformed response to Wittichus. Van Tellingen mentions (incorrectly, AN) that this work was written in Glückstadt in the period 1661/1662-1667. In addition, Van Tellingen indicates (probably incorrectly, AN) an additional publication date of this work of 1659. Cf. Van Tellingen, *Het leven en enige aspecten*, 15. See for the Cartesian issues in relation to the seventeenth-century Dutch Reformed, including the less favorable reception of the Cartesians at the Duisburg Synod, Thomas A. McGahagen, *Cartesianism in the Netherlands, 1639-1676: The New Science and the Calvinistic Counter-Reformation* (Ph.D. diss., University of Pennsylvania, 1976).

37. Israel, *The Dutch Republic*, 890, 892. See for a brief discussion on the content of Mastricht's *Vindicæ veritatis* Rienk Vermeij, *The Calvinist Copernicans. The reception of the new astronomy in the Dutch Republic 1575-1750* (Amsterdam: KNAW, 2002), 260, 261.

1662-1667

In 1662 Mastricht moved to Glückstadt (Schleswig-Holstein) to serve the Reformed congregation, which belonged to the classis Hamburg.[38] At that time the city was an international business center and served with Copenhagen as a Danish royal city. Furthermore, the city, which was located at the end of the Elbe, was strategic for the Brandenburg constituency. The ecclesiastical situation of Glückstadt, with a significant Dutch presence, was known to be "ecumenical and tolerant," a place where Portuguese-Dutch Jews, Remonstrants, Contra-Remonstrants, and Mennonites cooperated.[39] In this international and ecumenical environment, Mastricht published in 1666 the *Theologiæ didactico-elenchtico-practicæ prodromus*.[40] This forerunner of the *TPT* is a threefold work that deals respectively with (1) the creation of man, (2) humility and arrogance in respect to God, and (3) the walk with God.[41] Each chapter has a fourfold division: exegesis, doctrine, elenctic, and practice. The *Prodromus* is dedicated to his father[42] and the consistory of the Reformed church at Hamburg.[43] The latter was instrumental in

---

38. The year of Mastricht's move to Glückstadt is 1661 or 1662. Cf. Van Tellingen, *Het leven en enige aspecten*, 14, fn. 46. In addition, since 1649 Glückstadt had been the capital of Schleswig-Holstein and the royal governmental seat of Frederik III, king of Denmark. The Reformed church was a gift of Danish king Christian IV, who died in 1648 at Copenhagen. During Mastricht's pastorate Charlotte Amalie, queen of Denmark, attended the congregation in the summer. Cf. Pontanus, *Laudatio*, 10. Students of divinity from Schleswig-Holstein and Hamburg, like those from the Lower Rhine area, studied, during the first part of the seventeenth century, at the University of Leiden. Cf. H. Schneppen, *Niederländische Universitäten und Deutsches Geistesleben von der Gründung der Universität Leiden bis ins späte 18. Jahrhundert* (Münster: Aschendorfsche Verlagsbuchhandlung, 1960), 23-26. The (ecclesiastical) link, if any, between the Reformed congregations of Xanten and Glückstadt needs more study, which could contribute to more understanding of how Mastricht was known in the Danish, and thus outside the Brandenburg, consituency.

39. Karl Rasmussen, *Glückstadt im Wandel der Zeiten* (Glückstadt: Augustin, 1966), 2:169-71. Prior to Mastricht's arrival, the Reformed, Remonstrants, and Mennonites operated together an elementary school and shared a church building. However, the city and church archives of Glückstadt, Schleswig, and Copenhagen do not provide information regarding the Reformed church of Glückstadt, as most records have been lost. Mrs. Tatjana Ceynowa, Glückstadt Museum und Archive and Mr. Robert Knull, Landesarchive Schleswig-Holstein are acknowledged.

40. Petrus van Mastricht, *Theologiæ didactico-elenchtico-practicæ Prodromus tribus speciminibus* (Amsterdam: Johannes van Someren, 1666). Hereafter called *Prodromus*. The university library of Röstock, Germany is acknowledged for making a copy available to me.

41. In chapter 2 we evaluate and assess that the structure and content are a precursor of the *Theoretico-practica theologia*.

42. His mother died in January, 1656 and in October, 1657 Thomas van Mastricht married Elisabeth Bouls, widow of Jacob Agache. Cf. Löhr and van Doorn, *Protokolle*, 1:64, 93. Van Tellingen notes that Thomas van Mastricht died in the fall of 1666 (*Het leven en enige aspecten*, 17, fn. 58). However, Petrus van Mastricht's father died in August 1667. See footnote 10 of this chapter.

43. This included the ministers (Daniel Sachsio and Andreas de la Fontaine), elders, and deacons. Cf. Mastricht, *Prodromus*, titlepage. Van Tellingen discusses succinctly the tension between Mastricht and the Glückstadt congregation and mentions that the arbitrage between Mastricht and the congregation took place in February 1667. Cf. Van Tellingen, *Het leven en enige aspecten*, 17, 18. The arbitrage date is

resolving the strained relationship between Mastricht and the "happy city" (Tychopolis), the Glückstadt congregation. The *Prodromus* was written upon advice of Voetius and Hoornbeeck[44] and has the "Nazarenes"—the divinity students—in mind. Simon Oomius (1630-1706) wishes in 1672 that Mastricht would be able to complete this work of practical theology.[45]

We can conclude, then, that the Glückstadt period of Mastricht's life (1662-1667) took place in an ecumenical churchly environment, in which his first theological work was published.

1667-1770

In 1667 Fredrick Wilhelm (1620-1688), the elector of Brandenburg, who had contact with the city of Glückstadt,[46] offered Mastricht a professorate in Hebrew and practical theology at the University of Frankfurt an der Oder.[47] Mastricht accepted, thereby declining a ministerial call from Copenhagen, Denmark.[48]

interesting considering the date of dedication and preface of the *Prodromus* are respectively November 16 and 17, 1665.

44. Petrus van Mastricht, *Theoretico-practica theologia: qua, per capita theologica, pars dogmatica, elenchtica et practica, perpetua sumbibasei conjugantur; præcedunt in usum operis, paraleipomena, seu sceleton de optima concionandi methodo* (Amsterdam: Henricus et Vidua Theodori Boom, 1682), præfatio, "Sisto tandem Theologiæ Theoretico-Practicæ, diu promissæ Tomum-primum cujus jam tum a MDCLXV (cum, consilio Celebb. Theologorum Voetii & Hoornbeeckii, ejus prodiret PRODROMUS)."

45. S. Oomius, *Disseratie van de Onderwijsingen in de Practycke der Godgeleerdheid* (Bolsward: Samuel van Haringhouk, 1672), 388. Oomius discusses published works on the practical theology, and notes those who published parts of practical theology (e.g., Voetius, *Ascetica, Politica Ecclesiastica, Disputationes*), and those who published a whole body of such theology (e.g., A. Cocquius, *Theologiæ praxis, de ware practycque der godt-geleertheit* (Utrecht: Simon de Vries, 1658). He then writes, "Petrus van Mastricht, die in den jære 1665 heeft uytgegeven zijn *Theologiæ Didactico-Elenchtico-Practicæ Prodromus*, in drie preuven, van de Scheppinge des menschen, van de Ootmoedigheydt en Hoogmoedigheydt nevens Godt, en van de Wandel met God; welcken arbeydt ick van herten wensche volmaekct te sien."

46. Karl Rasmussen, *Glückstadt im Wandel der Zeiten*, 2:193.

47. The University of Frankfurt an der Oder was at that time the only Brandenburg University. It became reformed in the 1610s with the appointment of three Reformed theologians, Johann Peter Bergius (1587-1658), Wolfgang Crell († 1664), the father of C. F. Crell, professor at Duisburg (1658-1700), and Gregor Franckius († 1651). See for Brandenburg (politics, church, and university) in the seventeenth century: Richard L. Gawthrop, *Pietism and the Making of Eighteenth-century Prussia* (Cambridge, UK: Cambridge University Press, 1993); Bodo Nischan *Prince, People, and Confession: The Second Reformation in Brandenburg* (Philadelphia: University of Pennsylvania Press, 1994). In 1667, Johannes F. Rhetius (1633-1717) was rector of the university, and Mastricht is listed in the university register as "Petrus von Mastricht Coloniensis Ubius." Mr. Ralf-Ruediger Targiel, Stadtarchiv Frankfurt an der Oder is acknowledged. The reference to Cologne probably is due to the fact that Mastricht tranferred his church membership papers in 1667 from Cologne—thus not from Glückstadt—to Frankfurt an der Oder. Cf. Löhr and van Doorn, 1:123.

48. J. Koelman (1631-1695) served from 1657-58(?) as embassy minister at Copenhagen for the Dutch ambassadors van Beuningen, van Amerongen, and van Viersen. Cf. A. F. Krull, *Jacobus Koelman* (Amsterdam: Ton Bolland, 1972), 12.

The history of the University of Frankfurt an der Oder leading up to Mastricht's arrival is a composite of theological and philosophical developments. In respect to the former, Mühlpfordt asserts that the teaching at the university during the period 1506-1537 can be characterized as "catholic high-humanism or pre-reformed humanism" and during the Lutheran period of 1537-1616 as a "replacement of Wittenberg."[49] From 1616-1656 the university became known as the "easternmost bastion of Calvinism,"[50] and a "second Heidelberg."[51]

During this time the ruler of Brandenburg created a union of the Lutheran and Reformed churches. The formed congregation was made up of Huguenot refugees, other immigrants, university students, and local people.[52] The church and university of Frankfurt an der Oder, though, were known as *irenisch-unionistisch.*[53] The university intended, according to Nischan, not only to educate new Reformed leaders but also to help stem the tide of Lutheran criticism that J. Sigismund of Brandenburg's (1572-1619) reform had precipitated.[54] The elector of Brandenburg instructed the university, also known as the *Toleranz-Universität*, to appoint only irenic professors. They were to be "*moderat und nicht zancksüchtig* and *furnehme gelerte leutte.*"[55] In respect to philosophical and other developments, it can be noted that the influx of people from England and France imported respectively piety and Ramism.[56]

49. G. Mühlpfordt, "Die Oder-Universität 1506-1811," in *Die Oder-Universität Frankfurt: Beiträge zu ihrer Geschichte*, ed. M. Knäbke, R. Kusch, R. R. Targiel (Weimar: Hermann Böhlaus Nachfolge, 1983), 19: "Ersatz-Wittenberg."

50. Nischan, *Prince, People and Confession*, 129.

51. Mühlpfordt, "Die Oder-Universität," 19.

52. Gawthrop, *Pietism and the Making of Eighteenth-century Prussia*, 45. Gawthrop notes that the elector of Brandenburg sought to build a strong Reformed presence by promoting every possible means for immigration of Calvinistic refugees into Brandenburg. The immigrants consisted mostly of wealthy, well-educated individuals, who came from France, Scotland, and Silesia. See also, Martin Preetz, *Die Deutsche Hugenottenkolonien: Ein Experiment des Merkantilismus* (Ph.D diss., Jena 1930). Jonathan Israel notes that the elector of Brandenburg had a tolerant outlook in theological and intellectual matters. Pointing out his ecumenical approach to the Lutheran and Calvinist confessional blocs in Brandenburg, Israel asserts (surprisingly?, AN) that the elector was inclined toward the Cartesian-Coccesians rather than Voetian-style Calvinist orthodoxy. See Israel, *Radical Enlightenment*, 30.

53. O. Feyl, "Die Viandrina und das östliche Europa," in *Die Oder-Universität Frankfurt*, 116.

54. Nischan, *Prince, People, and Confession*, 129.

55. Gerd Heinrich, "Frankfurt an der Oder," in *Theologische Realenzyklopadie*, ed. Gerhard Muller (Berlin, New York: de Gruyter, 1977, 1988), 339. According to Heinrich the university can be characterized as tolerant and poly-confessional. Jonathan Israel asserts that the Dutch Republic, Brandenburg, and Poland until the mid-seventeenth century, embraced a broader, more formal toleration of confessions. Cf. Israel, *Radical Enlightenment*, 23.

56. Mühlpfordt, "Die Oder-Universität 1506-1811," 55-57. In this contribution Mühlpfordt argues also that the Dutch immigrants imported at that time Cartesianism. This is *contra* Israel, who states that "despite rumours that the Cartesians predominated at Frankfurt an der Oder as early as 1656, there is no firm evidence of Cartesian hegomony in Frankfurt until the 1680's" (Israel, *Radical Enlightenment*, 31).

In this pro-Calvinistic, confessional hybrid state of Brandenburg, with its mediating environment, Mastricht succeeded the Old Testament scholar and Hebraïcus Gregor Frankius († 1651).[57] With full academic ornate—from which he abstained the rest of his life[58]— he accepted, at the age of thirthy-six, his Hebrew and theology professorate. The inaugural address was on the correlation of *praxis* and theory in theology,[59] a theme that was already familiar to him during his study at Utrecht. Upon Mastricht's arrival at Frankfurt an der Oder, the university entered the second generation of Calvinistic teachers and a period of consolidation. He served on the faculty of theology with Johann Christoph Bec(k)mann (1641-1717), who was approving of the theology of Ames.[60] The Hebrew faculty was a leading European center in Hebraic studies[61] and had a renowned press for oriental and Hebrew language publications, including the Babylonian Talmud.[62] Both the faculty of theology and the faculty of Hebrew studies, probably as a result of Renaissance humanism, attracted students from Poland, Hungary, Lithuania, and Bohemia.[63]

Although not much is known of Mastricht's labors at Frankfurt an der Oder,[64] he most probably published the *Methodus Concionandi*, a preaching method for students of the ministry. [65] In it Mastricht stresses the need for a fourfold approach—exegesis, doctrine, elenctic and *praxis*—and illustrates this with the biblical text of Colossians 3:1. Further, in 1669 he obtained at the University of Duisburg the degree of *artium liberalium magister et theologiæ doctor*[66] after a public defense of the disputation *De Natura Theologiæ* and an oration *De Nomine et Omine doctoris Theologi*.[67] However, the University

57. Heinrich, "Frankfurt an der Oder," 338.

58. Pontanus, *Laudatio Funebris*, 11: "...quas phaleras fortean usque ad suprema sata sprevisset, si salvo ordine & legibus Academicis illis potuisset abstinere."

59. Petrus van Mastricht, *Perpetua praxeos cum theoria in theologicis pariter et theologis Συμβίβασις, oratione inaugurali lectionibus Hebræo-theologicis præmissa...accedit...programma invitatorium* (Frankfurt an der Oder: M. Hübner, 1668). Van Asselt mentions that the inaugural address was on the meaning of the name of 'theologian' and the calling of theology and science. Cf. W. J. van Asselt, "Petrus van Mastricht," 360.

60. Feyl, "Die Viandrina und das östliche Europa," 121.

61. G. Mühlpfordt, "Die Oder-Universität 1506-1811," 71.

62. Heinrich, "Frankfurt an der Oder," 340.

63. Feyl, "Die Viandrina und das östliche Europa," 109.

64. Most records of the university were lost in World War II, as Frankfurt an der Oder is located 50 miles west of Berlin on the Polish border. A rare surviving record indicates that the university had at that time professors from Hungary and other parts of Germany. Mr. Ralf-Ruediger Targiel, Stadtarchiv Frankfurt an der Oder is acknowledged.

65. Petrus van Mastricht, *Methodus Concionandi* (Frankfurt an der Oder: M. Hübner, undated).

66. Glasius, *Godgeleerd Nederland*, 2:471.

67. H. Kaajan, "Mastricht (Petrus van)," in *Christelijke Encyclopaedie voor het Nederlansche volk*, ed. F. W. Grosheide and G. P. van Itterzon, 2d revised edition (Kampen: Kok, 1959), 4:252.

of Frankfurt an der Oder continued to develop during the second half of the seventeenth century and it became the "Amsterdam des Ostens."[68] During that time Mastricht was called to the (Brandenburg) University of Duisburg.

The Brandenburg period of Mastricht's life at Frankfurt an der Oder (1667-1670) thus took place in a Reformed-Lutheran church and university environment. He advanced his studies to the doctor's degree and published a theological (homiletic) work. Thereby, his professorate at the Hebrew faculty in relationship to (Christian) Hebraism should not go unnoticed.

1670-1677

Having just received his doctorate, Mastricht moved to the Duisburg University in 1670.[69] The Duisburg University was founded by the elector of Brandenburg in 1655, for the expansion of the Reformed teaching, for the training of jurists for the Brandenburg cities, and for its geographic position between the Jesuit schools of Emmerich and Düsseldorf.[70]

Mastricht inaugurated his professorate with an address on the obligation of the academic oath, a subject that most likely was influenced by his younger brother Gerhardus van Mastricht (1639-1721), who had taught jurisprudence in Duisburg since 1669.[71] Petrus van Mastricht served from 1670 to 1677 on the theological as well as the

68. Mühlpfordt, "Die Oder-Universität 1506-1811," 53. Mühlpfordt calls the period 1652-1727 the *morgenrot der Aufklärung.*

69. The universities of Duisburg, Frankfurt an der Oder, and Halle belonged to the elector of Brandenburg.

70. Roden, *Die Universität Duisburg*, 61. See for the Duisburg University also, W. Ring, *Geschichte der Universität* (Duisburg: Stadtarchiv, 1920); Joseph Milz, *Die Universität Duisburg 1655-1818* (Duisburg: Buschmann, 1980); Gernot Born and Frank Kopatschek, *Die Alte Universität Duisburg 1655-1818* (Duisburg: Mercator Verlag, 1992). These four (authoritave) books on the history of the Duisburg University discuss Petrus van Mastricht, which is omitted in most books on the history of the Utrecht University. See for example, J. A. Cramer, *De Theologische Faculteit te Utrecht in de 19e Eeuw* (Utrecht: Broekhof, 1936) and Aart de Groot en Otto J. de Jong eds., *Vier eeuwen Theologie in Utrecht* (Zoetermeer: Meinema, 2001). In respect to the Jesuit schools, it should be noted that the strong Catholic anti-Cartesianism resulted in Cartesianism penetrating later in Catholic circles than in Reformed. Cf. Israel, *Radical Enlightenment*, 33.

71. Gerhardus van Mastricht was born on September 25, 1639 at Cologne (the *Allgemeinen Deutschen Biographie* [München: Leipzig, 1912), 20:579] notes that he is a son of the local Reformed pastor Thomas von Mastricht and of Johanna de Plancq—a note that can not be confirmed) and did confession of faith on November 27, 1655 at Cologne Reformed congregation. He obtained in 1665 his jurisprudence doctorate in Basel with the *Disputatio Juridica Inauguralis de Adulteriis* (Basel: Decker, 1665) and became professor of history and Greek in 1669, rector in 1670, and served until 1688 at Duisburg University. He then became Syndikus in Bremen, where he lived until his death January 22, 1722. In the Bremen period, he published a critical edition of the Greek New Testament and was, according to Goeters, a *Laienpiëtist*. Cf. Johann F. G. Goeters, "Der reformierte Pietismus in Bremen und am Niederrhein im 18. Jahrhundert," in *Der Pietismus im achtzehnten Jahrhundert*, ed. M. Brecht, K. Depperman (Göttingen: Vandenhoeck & Ruprecht, 1995) 2: 249. In Bremen he attended the St. Stephani church, whose pastor, Friedrich Adolf Lampe (1709-1720), had served the congregations of Weeze (classis Cleve, 1703-1706) and Duisburg (1706-1709). At Bremen, Gerhardus functioned on a

philosophical faculty. At the latter he taught Hebrew and oriental languages. In 1673 he became *rector-magnificus*.[72] At the theological faculty he worked with Christoph F. Crell (1626-1700)[73] and the cocceian Johann H. Hugenpoth (1634-1675), who succeeded Martinus Hundius (1624-1666).[74] In respect to theology and church, Hugenpoth, on the one hand, continued Hundius's advocacy of the cocceian covenant theology. On the other hand, Crell was against any form of ecclesiastical separatism, thereby opposing the Labadists, and the influence of Theodorus Untereyck. Untereyck had studied at Duisburg under Clauberg and Hundius and served a congregation at Mühlheim am Ruhr (1667-1671), while promoting the conventicler's, the *kleine Kirche*.[75] Furthermore, the churches of the entire Lower Rhine area leaned towards the *praxis der Gottseligkeit*.[76]

regular basis as diplomat for the city council. Moreover, in 1719 he compiled a catalogue of his massive book collection, *Catalogus Bibliothecæ Gerh. V. Mastricht* (Bremen: Herman Braueri, 1719). Gerhardus's *Historia Juris Ecclesiastici* (Halle: Christopher A. Zeitleri, 1705), which is dedicated to the elector of Brandenburg, is considered his most important work in the field of ecclesiastical jurisprudence. This work became enlisted since 1718 at the pontifical *index librorum prohibitorum*. Gerhardus Mastricht married Magdalena le Brun (Cf. Gerhard von Mastricht, *Gedicht op het Bruylofs-Feest van den Heer G. Mastricht en de Juffrouw Magdalena le Bruns gehouden binnen Ceulen den 17 April 1678*, Cologne: 1678) a sister of Johann le Brun (1644-1717), who, also born at Cologne, was involved in William Penn's Pennsylvanischer Companie in Frankfurt am Main. Cf. C. Owens Peare, *William Penn: A Biography* (Philadelphia: J. B. Lippincott Co., 1957). Gerard and Magdalena had four children, Anna, Magdalena, Gerhardus Jr., and Petrus (1682-1711, Cf. Petrus van Mastricht, the Younger, *Brüderliche Ehren-Pflicht auff die ehliche Verknüpfung des Herrn J. L. Meinertzhagen mit der Jungfrauen Saren Magdalenen von Mastricht...am 23 Mai/2 Junnij 1693*, Bremen, 1693). Gerhardus's brother Petrus attests in his dedication of the TPT (1699), fol. 637, of the warm relationship with his brother Gerhard and mentions his works, including *De Susceptore*—about the Surety. One notes the remarkable parallels in the lives of the brothers Mastricht and Johannes Cocceius, oriental Hebrew linguistic and theologian, and his brother Gerhardus, a jurist and diplomat. See on the brothers Cocceius, Willem J. van Asselt, *Amicitia Dei, een onderzoek naar de structuur van de theologie van Johannes Coccejus (1603-1669)* (Ede: Grafische vormgeving: ADC, 1988), 10.

72. Roden, *Die Universität Duisburg*, 283 (faculty of philosophy) and 378 (rector); Matrikel Duisburg Universität 1655-1818, 106, "Decimo octavo rectore, Petro von Mastricht, S.S.Theol. et philosophiae doctore ac theologiae iuxta et Hebraeae linguae professore ordinario, a die 20 Octobris 1673 nomina sua huic albo commiserunt."

73. Son of professor Wolfgang Crell of Frankfurt an der Oder. Christoph F. Crell succeeded Johannus Clauberg, the first rector of the University of Duisburg and served from 1658-1700. The last professor of theology at Duisburg University served in 1807 was Friederich A. Krummacher.

74. Martinus Hundius served the theological faculty from 1655-1666. He was a brother-in-law of Johannes Cocceius and admired his covenant theology. Cf. Heiner Faulenbach, "Johannes Coccejus," in *Orthodoxie und Pietismus*, ed. Martin Greschat (Stuttgart: W. Kohlhammer, 1982), 168. Petrus van Mastricht did not succeed Martinus Hundius, as is suggested by Pontanus, *Laudatio Funebris*, 12. Cf. Van Asselt ("Petrus van Mastricht," 360). Hundius, who died in the pest in 1666, was succeeded by Hugenpoth. Cf. Roden, *Die Universität Duisburg*, 242.

75. Wallmann, *Der Pietismus*, 26; Schneppen, *Niederländische Universitäten*, 90, 91.

76. Heppe, *Geschichte des Pietismus und der Mystik in der reformirten Kirche, namentlich der Niederlande*, 483, 485.

In this ecclesiastical context, the faculty of the University of Duisburg favored biblical exegesis over the traditional dogmatic theology.[77] In respect to philosophy, the attentiveness to Cartesianism initiated by J. Clauberg (1622-1665) and Wittichus [78] continued at the time of Mastricht.[79] In respect to the confessional stand, the Cleve church order demanded that each professor of the Duisburg theological faculty ascribe to a *rechtgläubigen reformierten* confession of faith,[80] the Heidelberg Catechism,[81] and preach under the supervision of the classis.[82] This also applied to Mastricht, who preached for the Duisburg congregation beginning November 22, 1676.[83] Politically the university and its faculty were under the jurisdiction of the elector of Brandenburg. The dual relationship of the professors to the church and the court of Brandenburg was a point of contention at the classis of Cleve. Though most professors were not interested in a new *Geistesrichtung*,[84] according to Bredt some did not always teach in accordance with the "confession of faith or the Belgic Confession."[85]

In this setting of philosophy, theology, and church policy, Mastricht continued his labors. The philosophical context of the Duisburg University may have contributed to the publication of his *Novitatum cartesianarum gangræna...seu theologia cartesiana detecta*.[86]

77. Schneppen, *Niederländische Universitäten*, 88.

78. According to Feyl, Johannes Clauberg was the first German Cartesian. Cf. Feyl, "Die Viandrina und das östliche Europa," 123. See also about J. Clauberg, Roden, *Die Universität Duisburg*; H. Schneppen, *Niederländische Universitäten*, 77, 78, 90; Israel, *Radical Enlightenment*, 30, 31, 35. Israel notes that contrary to Frankfurt an der Oder, Cartesianism became dominant at Duisburg as early as 1651. In addition, Cartesianism penetrated Sweden under the leadership of Petrus Hoffvenius (1630-1682), who published his *Synopsis physica* in 1678, a compendium based chiefly on Clauberg's work.

79. Wolfgang Petri comments on the minutes of the Cleve provincial synod of June 22-24, 1677, that Mastricht opposed the Cartesian teaching of Clauberg and Wittichus. Cf. Wolfgang Petri, *Die Reformierten Klevischen Synoden im 17. Jahrhundert*, vol. 3: 1673-1700 (Rheinlag-Verlag: Cologne, 1981), 54.

80. Joh. Victor Bredt, *Die Verfassung der reformierten Kirche in Cleve-Jülich-Berg-Mark* (Ansbach: C. Brügel, 1938), 2:145.

81. Roden, *Die Universität Duisburg*, 163.

82. The Jülich-Berg church order instructed that no one *von seiner Classe oder Theologischen Facultät* could preach without an examination and approval of the classis. Bredt asserts that this specifically was written with the Duisburg theological faculty in mind. Cf. Bredt, *Die Verfassung der reformierten Kirche in Cleve-Jülich-Berg-Mark*, 2:108. Moreover, the Jülich-Berg classis—not the classis of Cleve—condemned the theology of Cocceius as unorthodox. Cf. Roden, *Die Universität Duisburg*, 163

83. Van Tellingen, *Het leven en enige aspecten*, 22.

84. Roden, *Die Universität Duisburg*, 163.

85. Bredt, *Die Verfassung der reformierten Kirche in Cleve-Jülich-Berg-Mark*, 2:144: "*Confession de Foi oder der Confessio Belgia*." The Reformed churches of Jülich, Berg, Cleve, and Mark opposed Labadism in 1674. Cf. Heppe, *Geschichte des Pietismus und der Mystik in der reformirten Kirche, namentlich der Niederlande*, 484, 487.

86. Petrus van Mastricht, *Novitatum Cartesianarum Gangræna, Nobiliores plerasque Corporis Theologici Partes arrodens et exedens. Seu Theologia Cartesiana detecta* (Amsterdam: Jansson, 1677). This work (hereafter called, *Gangræna*) was reprinted in 1678 and 1716. Cf. Petrus van Mastricht, *Theologia Cartesiana detecta,*

Mastricht deals in the *Gangræna* particularly and in an elaborate way with Cartesianism and theology, and argues strongly against the ideas of Descartes. This work, according to Israel, became the most influential of all late seventeenth-century academic assaults on Cartesianism.[87] Not only the Reformed but also Lutherans and Catholics appealed to the *Gangræna*. The faculty of theology at Uppsala looked to him as their principal authority to persuade the Swedish crown to condemn Cartesianism in 1687, and the Jesuit (sic!) Giovanni B. De Benedictis (1622-1706) excessively approved Mastricht's view against the new philosophy.[88] The Dutch Reformed pastor Jacobus Fruytier (1659-1731) writes about the *Gangræna*:

> De godvruchtige Maastricht he(e)ft in zijn leven een boek uitgegeven, getiteld: *Gangræna Philosophiæ Cartesianæ*: daar heeft hij vele dingen in ondekt en voorzegd, die uit die wijsbegeerte zullen voortvloeien; doch daarop is geen acht geslagen, men wilde dat boek niet eens lezen, omdat het geen man van den nieuwe tijd was.[89]

It was Michael Foertstius (1654-1724), the colleague of Johann F. Buddeus (1667-1729) at Jena University, who, in his survey of theological-philosophical debates of the

---

seu gangræna Cartesiana: nobiliores plerasque corporis theologici partes arrodens et exedens (Deventer: Daniel Schutten, 1716). In the elenctical parts of the *TPT* (1682, 1687, and 1699) Mastricht deals, according to Goudriaan, less extensive with (recent) Cartesianism than in the *Gangræna* (personal communication Dr. Aza Goudriaan, October, 2002).

87. Israel, *Radical Enlightenment*, 215: "The *Novitatum Cartesianarum Gangræna* (1677), written by Petrus van Mastricht whilst teaching at Duisburg in Cleves—albeit dedicated to William III and published in Amsterdam—reserves some of its most vehement passages for the *Philosophia* (S. Scripturæ Interpres of Lodewijk Meyer [1629-1681], AN) and the Wolzogen affair. Its chief aim—ironically also one of Spinoza's objectives, advancing from the other side—is to ruin the project of Wittichus and his followers to reconcile theology and philosophy (including Galilean science) by means of Cartesianism. Unlike Maresius, but like Voetius, Mastricht judges Descartes' entire system, beginning with his procedural principle of 'universal doubt'—the 'primum Cartesianismi fundamentum'—a catastrophe for mankind and the Reformed Church, which had destroyed the traditional role of philosophy as a handmaiden to theology and foisted the godless and arrogant ' magistracy' of philosophy on theology. Everywhere one encountered furious disapproval of the *Philosophia*. But had not Wittichus, Velthuysen, Burman, and Wolzogen—Van Mastricht's four *bêtes noirs*—while not going as far as the author of that execrable text, or expressing themselves as impudently, nevertheless also, like him, proclaimed 'reason and philosophy' instead of Holy Writ the true and divine Revelation, the only sources of absolute certainty? Van Mastricht considers the *Philosophia* and the writings of Spinoza, 'atheus quidem sed Cartesianus' (an atheist certainly, but a Cartesian) the most dangerous and pernicious of all intellectual threats to mankind."

88. Giovanni B. De Benedictis, *Difesa della terza lettera apologetica di Benedetto Aletino, divisa in tre discussioni, una teologia, l'altra filosofica della filosofia cartesiana, la terza critica* (Rome: Antonio DeRossi, 1705), 45, 46; Sten Lindroth, *A History of Uppsala University, 1477-1977* (Stockholm: Almqvist & Wiksell international, 1976), 73.

89. Jacobus Fruytier, *Sion's Worstelingen of historische samenspraken over de verscheide en zeer bittere wederwaardigheden van Christus Kerke, met openbare en verborgene vyanden: in de reformatie, ten tyde der Remonstranten, in deze onze dagen* (Rotterdam: Johan van Doesburg, 1715), 659.

century, identifies Mastricht as the most commanding critic of the "detestable" Cartesianism.[90]

Contrary to Mastricht's opposition to Cartesianism his position on the Labadists was far less opposing than Crell. During Mastricht's Duisburg period, the Labadistic movement made inroads[91] in the Reformed congregations of Duisburg and the Lower Rhine area.[92] In 1671 Pierre Yvon (1646-1707), the emerging leader of the Labadists and *separatistischer reformierter Pietist*,[93] was on his way to visit the Lower Rhineland. Mastricht met him at Cologne[94] and discussed important Christian doctrines and his view on the kingdom of God.[95] This meeting may have resulted in an extensive preamble to *De fide salvifica syntagma theoretico-practicum*,[96] which was published that same year. In the preface, entitled *de membris ecclesiæ visibilis*, he contested the separatist movement influenced by Jean de Labadie (1610-1674). Over against the subjectivism of this movement, Mastricht placed the objective character of Reformed doctrine. Despite his disagreement with the Labadists, he discussed the central question—church or separation?—in an irenic way. [97]

90. Michael Foertstius, *Selectorum theologorum breviarum, id est discussio principalium punctorum theologicorum nostro tempore maxime controversorum* (Jena: Lager, 1708), 32.

91. Roden, *Die Universität Duisburg*, 164: "In den Glaubensgewohnheiten der evangelischen Kirche machte sich am Ende des 17. Jahrhunderts eine neue Strömung bemerkbar, die die Geschlossenheit der Gemeinden zwar gefährdete, viele tief religiöse Menschen jedoch stark ergriff. Es war die Bewegung der sogenannten 'Seperatisten' oder des Labadismus." In addition, Pierre Yvon visited the Lower Rhine area several times. In 1669, the Labadist's conventiclers gave the congregation of Wesel enough reasons to appeal to the synod of Cleve, which passed the task to the classis of Duisburg. Cf. T. S. Saxby, *The Quest for the New Jerusalem, Jean de Labadie and the Labadists, 1610-1744* (Dordrecht, Boston: M. Nijhoff Publishers, 1987), 193; Aart De Groot, "Jean de Labadie," in *Orthodoxie und Pietismus*, 199.

92. The Reformed congregation of Duisburg consisted mainly of trading people, with international, including Dutch, backgrounds. Cf. Milz, *Die Universität Duisburg*, 35.

93. Andreas Plagge, "YVON, Pierre" in *Bautz Biographisch-Bibliographischen Kirchenlexikons*, Band XXII (2003), http://www.bautz.de/bbkl/y/yvon_p.shtml, accessed October 5, 2003.

94. Saxby, *The Quest for the New Jerusalem*, 175. Saxby also mentions that Yvon, starting from Utrecht, where he met with G. Voetius, met at Duisburg the secretary of the elector of Brandenburg, and at Mülheim am Ruhr some people of the congregation of Theodorus Untereyck. The meeting of Mastricht and Yvon in also mentioned by H. Faulenbach. Cf. H. Faulenbach, "Die Anfänge der Pietismus bei den Reformierten in Deutschland," in *Pietismus und Neuzeit: ein Jahrbuch zur Geschichte des neueren Protestantismus* (Göttingen : Vandenhoeck & Ruprecht, 1979), 4:222.

95. Max Goebel, *Geschichte des Christlichen Lebens in der Rheinisch-westphælischen evangelischen Kirche* (Koblenz: Bädeker, 1849), 232: "in Köln besprach er [Yvon] sich mit dem dortiger niederländischen Prediger Peter von Mastricht...über die wichtigsten Wahrheiten des Christenthums und Reiches Gottes."

96. Petrus van Mastricht, *De fide salvifica syntagma theoretico-practicum: in quo fidei salvificæ tum natura, tum praxis universa, luculenter exponitur; cum præf. de membris Ecclesiæ visibilis seu admittendis, seu rejiciendis, oborienti scismati moderno applicanda* (Duisburg: Franc. Sas, 1671).

97. The *Allgemeinen Deutschen Biographie* (München: Leipzig, 1912), 20:580 mentions that this is one of the best works addressing the question: church or separation? "In höchst irenischem Tone behandelt er in demselben die Gründe der damals unter den sogenannten Labadisten entstandenen seperatistischen Bewegung am Niederrhein. Dem Subjectivismis derselben setzt er in geschicktester Weise den Objectivismus der reformierten Kirche in Lehre und Verfassung entgegen, wodurch er jenem

In such a context of church and theology Mastricht wrote *De fide salvifica*, a work about saving faith, biblically exegetically expounded, doctrinally formulated, and practically applied.[98]

In addition, his academic work continued at Duisburg and included a contribution to a work of Hugenpoth[99] and two disputations.[100] One of the disputations about *De Existentia et Cognitione Dei*[101] indicates that Mastricht was working at that time on the doctrine of God. This disputation also has a fourfold division: exegesis, doctrine, elenctic, and practice. In the meantime Mastricht's publications had reached the Netherlands,[102] and the theological faculty at Franeker nominated him for professor in 1675. Two possible factors could have contributed to his nomination by the University of Franeker: Hebraism and Ames. In respect to the former, Johannes Drusius (1550-1616) had laid a foundation for the philological study of the Hebrew Bible since his arrival at the Franeker academy in 1585. For Drusius the prerequisite of theology remained philology.[103] This view on theology was continued by Sixtinus Amama (1593-1629), who was a noted philologist and defender of the study of Hebrew as the proper

Seperatismus vielen Abbruch tat." Cf. Ring, *Geschichte der Universität Duisburg*, 136. Roden's citation calls for "ironische" instead of "irenischem," and notes, "Gegen Seperatismus und Labadismus nahm er [van Mastricht] Stellung. Er zeigte sich in seinen Schriften als entschiedener und starrer Vertreter des alten System." Cf. Roden, *Die Universität Duisburg*, 165. See also W. Goeters, *Die Vorbereitung des Pietismus* (Leipzig: J. C. Hinrichs'sche Buchhandlung, 1911), 282, fn. 2: "Ganz milde ist auch das Urteil [about Labadism, AN] des Peter van Mastricht, in seiner Schrift *De fide salvifica*, Duisburg, 1670. Our research differs with Van Vliet's assessment of Mastricht's view on the Labadists. He writes, "His [Mastricht, AN] polemic against the Labadists of the day and their subjectivism and separatist tendencies was grounded in the objective character of Reformed doctrine and its corresponding idea of the church. This developing thought became *the basis* [italic, AN] for his *magnus opus, Theoretico-practica theologia* ..." See Van Vliet, *William Ames*, 346, 347.

98. The chapter on saving faith in the *TPT* is similar, although summarized, in structure, and content as *De fide salvifica*. See further part II, chapter 2 of this study.

99. Petrus van Mastricht, *Vita viatoris quasi transitus*, in Johann Hermann Hugenpoth, *Lachrymæ Academiæ Duisburgensis* (Duisburg: Franc. Sas 1676).

100. Petrus van Mastricht, *Diatribe Theologica...De Casu Conscientiæ: An Viduus Uxoris Novercam, Salva Conscientia, Ducere possit?: An saltem non sit dispensabile, tale Matrimonium? Immo &, si partibus de eo convenerit, per Magistratum dispensandum?* Pars 1 et 2, Johannes Adolphus Eylerdt (Duisburg: Franc. Sas, 1676); idem *Theologiæ Theoretico-Practicæ Disputatio Quinta, De Existentia Et Cognitione Dei*, Wilhelmus Mercamp (Duisburg: Franc. Sas, 1677).

101. The discussion of a topic of the doctrine of God was not unique to Mastricht. His colleague at Duisburg, Johann Hermann Hugenpoth wrote *Dissertatio Theologica Continens Aliquot Positiones De Actione Dei Circa Indurationem Cordis Humani*, resp. Joannes Theodor Helmius (Duisburg: Franc. Sas, 1670). His later colleague, F. Burman at Utrecht in the spring of 1676 defended a *disputatio* on the divine omnipresence. Cf. M. J. A. de Vrijer, *Henricus Regius, een 'Cartesiaansch' hoogleeraar aan de Utrechtsche Hoogeschool* ('s-Gravenhage: M. Nijhoff, 1917), 83.

102. See fn. 45 and 89 of this chapter.

103. Aaron L. Katchen, *Christian Hebraist and Dutch Rabbis. Seventeenth Century Apologetics and the Study of Maimonides' Mishneh Torah* (Cambridge, MA: Harvard University Press, 1984), 32.

foundation for theology. This intellectual trajectory can be extended to (the philologist-exegete) Johannes Cocceius' presence at Franeker (1626 study, and 1643-1650 professor of theology). His teacher, Ames, taught biblical exegesis at Franeker (1622-1633)[104] and produced his major writings there, the *Medulla theologia* and *De Conscientia*: two works appreciated by Mastricht. Nevertheless, Mastricht was not appointed: the University of Franeker chose Herman Witsius.[105]

At the same time, the situation at Duisburg between faculty of the university and synod of the church became strenuous. This also affected Mastricht, particularly after the synod of June 1677 commented on Mastricht's *ärgerlichen* Pentecost sermon.[106] Mastricht had preached on John 16:8-11 and had noted that the prince of this world is Christ. The affair reached a culmination when Mastricht did not receive the deputies of the synod, replying that "the Synod has nothing to do with it," because of the jurisdiction of Brandenburg over the university.[107] Nevertheless, the same month the parties restored peace and, or because, Mastricht received a call from his *alma mater*.[108]

Mastricht's time in Duisburg (1670-1677) shows continuity in his work: the Hebrew teaching, the theological publications in the form of a book and disputations, both characterized by his fourfold approach (exegesis, doctrine, elenctic, and practice), and a major philosophical work against Cartesianism.

Finally, we end the "German" period of the life and work of Mastricht with a threefold observation. First, in respect to the work localities, Mastricht was participant

---

104. Keith L. Sprunger, *The Learned Doctor William Ames* (Chicago: University of Illinois Press, 1972), 76, 77.

105. J. van Genderen, *Herman Witsius, bijdrage tot de kennis der Gereformeerde theologie* ('s-Gravenhage: Guido de Bres, 1953), 50: "In de eerste week van het jaar 1675 deden Curatoren aan Gedeputeerde Staten, die het benoemingsrecht hadden, een nieuwe voordracht toekomen. P. van Mastricht, professor te Duisburg, stond als eerste op de nominatie, H. Witsius, predikant te Leeuwarden, als tweede, en Ph. Tilemann, hofprediker van Brunswijk-Lünenburg, als derde. Met algemene stemmen werd Witsius gekozen."

106. Petri, *Die Reformierten Klevischen Synoden*, 55.

107. Goebel, *Geschichte des Christlichen*, 111: "in 1677 ließ die general Synod den sonst sehr recht gläubigen, und berühmten Prof. Petrus van Mastricht, wegen seiner 'fremden und ärgerlichen Auslegung von Joh. 16, 8-11,' wonach Christus selber 'der gerichtete Fürst der Welt' sein sollte, zur Rede stellen; Mastricht empfing die Deputirten aber gar nicht als solche, 'weil die Synod ihm nichts verzuschreiben haben'." Here, we note that Mastricht followed the elector of Brandenburg, Friedrich Wilhelm, who ruled that university professors were accountable only to him and not to the ecclesiastical authorities. Cf. Israel, *Radical Enlightenment*, 31.

108. Ring, *Geschichte der Universität Duisburg*, 137: "dem Rufe nach Utrecht der im Jahre 1677 an ihn erging folgte er um so williger, als er in Duisburg wegen seiner Ansicht, dass der 'Fürst dieser Welt' (Joh. 16, vers 11) Jesus Christus sei, in unangenehme Konflikte mit den Predigern und der Generalsynode gekommen war. Obgleich er die Generalsynode, die eine Widerlegung seines Standpunktes drucken ließ, für sich als Universitätslehrer nicht als vorgeseßte Behörde anerkannte, entzog er sich doch gerne durch die Annahme der Utrechter Profesor weiterer Streitigkeiten."

and (paid) "devoted servant"[109] of the Brandenburg (academic) expansion. Second, Mastricht's work in Xanten, Glückstadt, Frankfurt an der Oder, and Duisburg reflects an interaction with the theological, philosophical, and ecclesiastical issues of his time. In respect to philosophy, his negative evaluation of Cartesianism grew from a humble but certain beginning in 1655 (*Vindicæ veritatis ... adversus dissertationes D. Christophori Wittichii*) to immense and influencial scope in 1677 (*Grangæna*). Here, Mastricht emerges as a vehement polemic in regard to one extraecclesiastical issue: Cartesianism. In respect to theology, his publications in Glückstadt (*Prodromus*), Frankfurt an der Oder (*Methodus Concionandi*), and Duisburg (*De Fide Salvifica* and disputations on the doctrine of God) provide the contours of a systematic theology and are characterized by a fourfold approach: exegesis, doctrine, elenctic, and *praxis*. Here, Mastricht emerges as a mediating person to two interecclesiastical issues: the intellectual thought of Cocceius and the Labadism.

The Netherlands

The period of Mastricht in the Netherlands parallels the latter part of high-orthodoxy[110] and half the *Nadere Reformatie* period.[111] The Dutch orthodox churchly movement has been described in several ways.[112] In summary, the definitions and appraisals characterize the *Nadere Reformatie* as a Dutch movement with strong emphasis

109. Petrus van Mastricht, *Theoretico-practica theologia* (1682). The dedicatio ends with "Devotissimus servus."

110. Richard A. Muller, *Post-Reformation Reformed Dogmatics* (Grand Rapids: Baker Academic, 2003), 1:31, 73.

111. See also footnote 64 of the introduction of this study. For "Second Reformation," a term that gained acceptance, see for example, J. W. Hofmeyr, *Johannes Hoornbeeck*, 219. However, this term is used also to identify the period of 1638-1648 in English church history. Cf. Andrew Symongton, *Introductory Lecture on the Principles of the Second Reformation*, (Glasgow: Henderson, 1841), 2. Therefore, it is advisable to use the term *Nadere Reformatie* in non-Dutch publications. This suggestion is not only for linguistic reasons but in particular for historical reasons. Namely, the term was used by participants of the movement. See for example, *Concept van nader reformatie in de leer, ordre en zeden*, (Utrecht: Willem Clerck, 1682); J. Koelman, *Reformatie Nodigh omtrent de Feest-dagen, Naaktelijk vertoont ende bewezen*, (Rotterdam: H.Goddaeus, 1665); idem, *De Pointen van Nodige Reformatie*, (Rotterdam: de Wilde, 1678); Cf. F. A. van Lieburg, *De Nadere Reformatie in Utrecht ten tijde van Voetius. Sporen in de gereformeerde kerkeraadsacta* (Rotterdam: Lindenberg, 1989), 35, 45, 144.

112. S. van der Linde, "De betekenis van de Nadere Reformatie voor Kerk en Theologie," in *Kerk en Theologie* 5 (1) (1954): 215-25. De radikale, gereformeerde reformatie, die preciesheid' wenst in plaats van vrome (onvrome) algemeenheden, een piëtisme dus, een bewust wijden van het hele leven aan God; T. Brienen, L. F. Groenendijk, W. J. op 't Hof, C. J. Meeuse, "Nadere Reformatie, een poging tot begripsbepaling," in *Documentatieblad Nadere Reformatie*, VII (1983), 109-116. Definition: De Nadere Reformatie is de beweging binnen de Nederduits Gereformeerde Kerk die, zich tegen algemeen verbreide wantoestanden en misvattingen kerend, alsmede de verdieping en de verbreding van de doorwerking van de zestiende-eeuwse Hervorming beogend, met profetische bezieling aandringt op en ijvert voor zowel de innerlijke doorleving van de gereformeerde leer en de persoonlijke levensheiliging alsmede de radicale en totale heiliging van alle terreinen des levens." For a revised definition see footnote 76 of the introdcution of this study.

on piety and a theological diversion of the sixteenth-century Protestant Reformation, partly due to Protestant Scholasticism.[113] The last and Dutch period of Mastricht's life and work can be divided the into four parts, of which the first three parts are end-marked by a major publication of the *TPT*: (1) 1677-1682 (books I-IV), (2) 1683-1687 (books V-VIII), (3) 1688-1699 (final edition), and (4) 1700 to his death in 1706.

1677-1682

The first generation of teachers at the Utrecht academy passed away, and in June of 1677 Mastricht was called to Utrecht to succeed Essenius[114] († May 18, 1677, professor of theology) and Voetius[115] († November 1, 1676, professor of theology and Hebrew). A succinct reconstruction of events may clarify the succession.[116] Voetius's position was not filled when the *vroedschap*, the mayor and city council, of Utrecht requested the academy on May 28, 1677 to search for a qualified person because of the death of Essenius. They responded fifteen days later identifying several persons who could fulfill the function of professor of theology, but they recommended "professor Maestricht of Duisburg." The *vroedschap*, accepting the recommendation, unanimously called Mastricht on June 18 with an offer of an annual compensation of one thousand guilders. Eleven days later the *vroedschap* received a letter from Mastricht, in which he accepted the position. Then, by the middle of August, Mayor Strick contacted the former mayor of Utrecht, Van Hoolck, now a member of the *Staten Generaal*, requesting passport and transportation for Mastricht. Hoolck responded that Mastricht would be moved under the same terms and

---

113. See for example, S. van der Linde, *Opgang en Voortgang der Reformatie* (Amsterdam: Ton Bolland, 1976), 164; T. Brienen, *De Prediking van de Nadere Reformatie* (Amsterdam: T. Bolland, 1981); C. Graafland, "Jodocus van Lodenstein (1620-1676)" in *De Nadere Reformatie, beschrijving van haar voornaamste vertegenwoordigers*, ('s-Gravenhage: Boekencentrum, 1986), 101; W. Verboom, *De catechese van de Reformatie en de Nadere Reformatie*, (Amsterdam: Buijten & Schipperheijn, 1986); C. Graafland, "Gereformeerde Scholastiek VI, De invloed van de Scholastiek op de *Nadere Reformatie*," in *Theologia Reformata*, XXX, no.4, (1987); M. van Campen, "Het verbond en Israel bij Calvijn en de Nadere Reformatie," in *Het joodse volk en het verbond* ed. C. Boer ('s-Gravanhage: Boekencentrum, 1988), 150-175; K. Exalto, "Genade en heilsweg," in T. Brienen *et al.*, *Theologische Aspecten van de Nadere Reformatie*, (Zoetermeer: Boekencentrum, 1993), 182. I have noted before that Mastricht has been identified as a representative of the *Nadere Reformatie*. However, it is too early, at this point in this study of Mastricht's life and work to affirm such.

114. Kaajan, "Mastricht (Petrus van)," 252: "Den 12den Juni 1677 werd hij te Utrecht tot opvolger van de den 18den Mei van dit jaar overleden professor Essenius benoemd (Notulen der Vroedschap van Utrecht)"; G. Van der Zee, *Vaderlansche Kerkgeschiedenis van de Hervormde Kerk* (J. H. Kok: Kampen, 19xx), 3:142.

115. Pontanus, *Laudatio Funebris*, 12: "Ideo cum post Gallicam captivitatem Academia esset instauranda, & de successore Magni Voetii ageretur;" Caspar Burman, *Trajectum eruditum, virorum doctrina inlustrium, qui in urbe Trajecto et regione Trajectensi nati sunt sive ibi habitarunt, vitas, fata et scripta exhibens* (Utrecht: Padenburg, 1738), 212; Glasius, *Godgeleerd Nederland*, 2:471; Kernkamp, *De Utrechtsche Universiteit*, 1:51; H. Knipscheer, "Mastricht," in *Christelijke Encyclopaedie*, ed. F. W. Grosheide and G. P. van Itterzon (J. Kok: Kampen, 1959), 4:591; Visser, "Van Mastricht, Petrus," 383.

116. This reconstruction is based on Kernkamp, *Acta et Decreta Senatus*, 2:33, 34 (*vroedschap*), and 31, 32 (*senaat*).

conditions as those of Professor Le Moine, who came in 1676 from France to Leiden. These terms included a passport, a *vrijgeleide* of the *Staten Generaal*, and moving of all furniture and books. On September 7 Mastricht inaugurated his professorate with the succinct oration *De Academicæ Ultrajectinæ voto symbolico: sol justitæ illustra nos*.[117] Thus, prompted by the death of Essenius, one of the two vacancies at the theological faculty was filled by Mastricht, who wrote later that he succeeded his teacher.[118] Kernkamp notes that Mastricht, as successor of Voetius, "was zijn gelijke in rechtzinnigheid, maar overigens niet zijn evenknie."[119]

Immediately upon arrival, Mastricht took up his work on the doctrine of God, which he had started at Duisburg. Theodorus Groen defended the disputation *De omnisufficientia Dei*,[120] and Baldiunus Drywegen and Jacobus de Clyver, both from Zeeland, defended the *disputatio De essentia, nominibus et attributis Dei in genere*, a theme that Mastricht continued until the spring of 1678.[121] That year he was elected as elder[122] of the Reformed congregation of Utrecht, in which he also preached.[123] From his arrival at Utrecht until 1698, a flow of publications materialized in the form of disputations

117. Ibid., 2:31: "Clariss. vir D. Petrus van Mastricht, theol. Professor, in Curiam civitatis vocatus atque inde per ampliss. viros Consulares DD. Booth et Nellensteyn primum in conclave academicum ac porro in cathedram deductus, orationem inauguralem recitavit 'de sole justitiæ.' Hinc iterum in conclave ac deinceps a Collegis Professoribus domum reductus et salutationibus ac gratulationibis singulorum exceptus est honorifice." For the theological faculty this was only Franciscus Burmannus (1628-1679). Having now two professors, shortly a third was added, namely, in 1678, Melchior Leydecker (1642-1721). Probably the Gerardus de Vries, professor of philosophy, also attended the inauguration. Sepp praises the succinctness of the oration but is less favorable to its content, particular about Mastricht's assessment of his contemporaries and himself. Cf. C. Sepp, *Het Godgeleerd Onderwijs in Nederland gedurende de 16e en 17e eeuw* (Leiden: De Breuk en Smits, 1873-1874), 2:346 The "*sol justitæ illustra nos*" in the title of Mastricht's sixteen pages inaugural adress refers to the logo of the Univeristy of Utrecht. Cf. Roelof van den Broek, *Hy leeret ende beschuttet: over het wapen en de zinspreuk van de Universiteit Utrecht* (Diesrede Utrecht, 1995).

118. Petrus van Mastricht, *Theoretico-practica theologia*, 1059: "Gisbertus Voetius...cui ego successi in professione." Mastricht held in Duisburg the same position as Voetius held in Utrecht, namely professor of theology and Hebrew.

119. Kernkamp, *De Utrechtsche Universiteit*, 1: 275. C. Sepp, *Het Godgeleerd Onderwijs*, 2:346 writes, "al had Mastricht, te Keulen geboren, te Utrecht gestudeerd, al telde hij seven-en-veertig jaren, al had hij aan de hogescholen van Frankfurt a/d Oder en Duisburg gedoceerd, al was hij een zeer bemiddeld man, deze titels gaven nog geen regt op den rang, om Voetius ten opvolger te zijn."

120. Petrus van Mastricht, *De omnisufficientia Dei*, pars prior Theologiæ theoretico-practicæ disputatio sexta Theodorus Groen (Utrecht: Meinardus à Dreunen, 1677)

121. Petrus van Mastricht, *Theologiæ theoretico-practicæ disputatio septima De essentia, nominibus et atributis Dei in genere*, Pars 2, Balduinus Drywegen (Utrecht: Meinardus à Dreunen, 1677); idem, *Theologiæ theoretico-practicæ disputatio septima De essentia, nominibus et attributis Dei in genere*, Pars 3, Jacobus de Clyver (Utecht: Meinardus à Dreunen, 1677); idem, *Theologiæ theoretico-practicæ disputatio septima De essentia, nominibus et attributis Dei in genere*, Pars 4, Isaacus Ravensbergius (Utrecht: Meinardus à Dreunen, 1678).

122. Lieburg, *De Nadere Reformatie in Utrecht*, 156.

123. Petrus van Mastricht, *Theoretico-practica theologia* (1699), 1225: "Auditores palam profiterentur, se tantundem saltem utilitatis, percipere ex istis repetitionibus, ac ex ipsis concionibus."

and major works. Analyzing these publications, one notes that from 1678 until 1680 he paid attention to the assurance of salvation[124] and the nature of theology.[125] In 1680 he reviewed some Roman Catholic teachings.[126] Interesting to note is that some of the disputations were attended by students of other faculties and countries and ministers. Illustrative is the defense of James Hog, who defended on March 20, 1680 the disputation about the assurance of salvation[127] in the presence of other Scottish students: Thomas Hog, Jacob Kirton, Donald Cargill, and John Dickson, who studied at Leiden, and probably the ministers Jacobus Borstius (1612-1680) of Rotterdam and Jacobus Koelman (1632-1695).[128] The same year Herman Witsius succeeded Franz Burman († November 12, 1679) on April 29, while Mastricht concentrated his teaching on dogmatics, ethics, and church history.[129] It is also in 1680 that Mastricht, under the name Cephas Scheunenus, opposes the Cartesian views of Petrus Allinga (?- 1692).[130] At

124. Petrus van Mastricht, *Disputationum practicarum prima de certitudine salutis ejusque natura*, Johannes Kamerling (Utrecht: Meinardus à Dreunen, 1678); idem, *Disputationum practicarum tertia de certitudine salutis, eique opposita præsumptione seu securitate carnali*, pars prima, David de Volder (Utrecht: Meinardus à Dreunen, 1679); idem, *Disputationum practicarum tertia, de certitudine salutis, eique opposita præsumptione seu securitate carnali*, pars secunda, Jacobus Hoog (Utrecht: Meinardus à Dreunen, 1680).

125. Petrus van Mastricht, *Theologiæ theoretico-practicæ, sub velo sudantis, specimen de natura theologiæ primum*, Petrus Dix (Utrecht: Meinardus à Dreunen, 1680); idem, *Theologiæ theoretico-practicæ specimen, de natura theologiæ secundum*, Hugo Fittz (Utrecht: Meinardus à Dreunen, 1680); idem, *Theologiæ theoretico-practicæ specimen de natura theologiæ tertium*, Johannes Best (Utrecht: Meinardus à Dreunen, 1680); idem, *Theologiæ theoretico-practicæ specimen de natura theologiæ quartum*, Johannes Kelfkens (Utrecht: Meinardus à Dreunen, 1680). The defense of Fittz and Best was also attended by Guiljelmus Saldenus.

126. Petrus van Mastricht, *Ad illust. episcopi Condomensis expositionem doctrinæ, quam vocat, Catholicæ*, diatribe prima *de consilio auctoris*, Rutgerus van Bemmel (Utrecht: Meinardus à Dreunen, 1680); idem, *Ad illust. episcopi Condomensis expositionem doctrinæ quam vocat Catholicæ*, diatribe tertia *de adoratione creaturarum*, Petrus Westwoude (Utrecht: Meinardus à Dreunen, 1680); idem, *Ad illustr. episcopi Condomensis expositionem doctrinæ quam vocat Catholicæ*, diatribe quinta *de invocatione sanctorum*, Petrus Lastdrager (Utrecht: Meinardus à Dreunen, 1680); idem, *Ad illustr. episcopi Condomensis expositionem doctrinæ quam vocat Catholicæ*, diatribe septima *de cultu imaginum et reliquiarum*, Johannes Rodenborgh (Utrecht: Meinardus à Dreunen, 1680).

127. Petrus van Mastricht, *Disputationum practicarum tertia, de certitudine salutis, eique opposita præsumptione seu securitate carnali*, pars secunda, Jacobus Hoog (Utrecht: Meinardus à Dreunen, 1680). James Hog was "exalted" in the student records of Utrecht from Hog to (Jacobus) Hoog. He was considered as "one of the holiest ministers in the kingdom [of England and Scotland] having published or recommended the celebrated and edifying tract of the Cromwellian age, called *The Marrow of Modern Divinity*." Cf. Edward Fisher, *The Marrow of Modern Divinity*, with notes by Thomas Boston (reprint, Seoul, New York: Westminster Publishing House,), 344; James Hog, *Wet en Evangelie*, trans. E. Kuyk (Amsterdam: Kuyk, 1947), 5.

128. See title page of the disputation. J. Borstius died the following July 1, 1680 at the age of 68. J. van der Haar, "Jacobus Bortius," in *Het Blijvende Woord*, ed., J. van der Haar (Dordrecht: Gereformeerde Bijbelstichting, 1985), 35. J. Koelman was at that time in North Holland, Cf. Krull, *Jacobus Koelman*, 92.

129. Van Genderen correctly notes that each of the professors Mastricht, Leydekker, and Witsius, understood the whole of theology as their work field. Cf. Genderen, *Herman Witsius*, 79.

the same time he continued his theological project and introduced it with the 1681 disputation *De optima concionandi methodo paraleipomena*,[131] a slightly modified version of the *Methodus Concionandi*. The disputation was used to instruct the students in how to make use of his soon-to-be-published work, the *TPT*.[132]

The year 1682 was a busy one for Mastricht, although he almost died from an intestinal disease.[133] Beginning on March 16, 1682, he functioned for one year as *rector magnificus* of the university, with Lucas van de Poll, Jacobus Vallan, and Johann George Graevius[134] as assessors.[135] A day after his installation as rector, he welcomed Prince Ludwig of Brandenburg on behalf of the city of Utrecht.[136] The Brandenburg connection, cemented at Frankfurt an der Oder and Duisburg, continued. More

130. Cephas Scheunenus, *Cartesianismi Gangræna insanabilis. Duodecim erotematum illustrium decadibus, frustra curata per P. Allingham, pastorem...enneade erotematum vulgarium, demonstrata à C Scheuneno* (Utrecht: Meinardus à Dreunen, 1680). Here, Mastricht uses his original family name Sc(h)oning. Thus, Cephas (Peter) Scheunenus (Sc(h)oning). Mastricht's treatise was probably against Petrus Allinga, *Cartesiaensche waerheyt, tegen de valsche thien staeltjes Renatus Des Cartes en syn navolgers tegenwoordigh opgedight* (Enkhuizen: Neynert Mul, 1674).

131. Petrus van Mastricht, *De optima concionandi methodo παραλειπομενα: in usum theologiæ theoretico-practicæ*, Henricus Wagardus (Utrecht: Meinardus à Dreunen, 1681).

132. This differs from Van Vliet who asserts, most probably based on the location of *Nagedachten over de beste Predik-Wyze* in the *Beschouwende en praktikale godgeleerdheit*, that "it is entirely appropriate that van Mastricht, teacher, *ends* [italic, AN] his over 3,000 page work with a brief user's manual, as it were, of his entire work." See Van Vliet, *William Ames*, 2002), 351.

133. Pontanus, *Laudatio Funebris*, 22.

134. Kernkamp, *Acta et Decreta Senatus*, 2:65: "De leden van de Vroedschap . . .hebben P. Van Mæstricht tot Rector geproclameerd . . ." This differs with Van Vliet's assessment that Mastricht was vice-chancellor. See Van Vliet, *William Ames*, 347. Johann George Graevius (1632-1703) served the Duisburg University from 1656-1658 as librarian and professor of philosophy. He accepted a professorate at Utrecht, in 1661 for rhetoric and in 1667 for history and politics. He remained in Utrecht until his death on January 11, 1703. Cf. Roden, *Die Universität Duisburg*, 271. See for Graevius's Cartesian inclination, Israel, *Radical Enlightenment*, 33. See for Graevius's appreciation of the *Synopsis* of Franciscus Burmannus, *Synopsis Theologiæ & speciatim Oeconomiæ Fœderum Dei* (Utrecht: C. J. Noenardus, 1671), vol. 1, ad eundem.

135. Petrus Mastricht served as assessor during the academic years, which began mid-March, 1681-82, 1683-84, and 1704-05. Cf. Kernkamp, *Acta et Decreta Senatus*, 2:60, 73, 188.

136. Kernkamp, *Acta et Decreta Senatus*, 3:65. The senate, the rector, and assessors greeted the prince. The connection of Brandenburg-Utrecht-Frankfurt an der Oder was not restricted to Mastricht only. In 1689 the Brandenburg connection, and in particular with Utrecht-Frankfurt an der Oder, resurfaces, as Henricus Cocceius (1644-1719), coming from Heidelberg, was appointed at the Utrecht faculty of law. However, on 8 September 1690 Mr. de Reuver, secretary of the *vroedschap*, visits Cocceius to get a clarification of their understanding that the elector of Brandenburg called him to the University of Frankfurt an der Oder. Later that month Cocceius accepts the position and moves to Frankfurt. Kernkamp notes a letter exchange between Utrecht and Frankfurt an der Oder on March 10, 1706. Cf. Kernkamp, *Acta et Decreta Senatus*, 2:202. At Frankfurt an der Oder, Cocceius has Petrus van Mastricht (the Jurist) as a student, the nephew of Petrus van Mastricht. Cf. Petrus von Mastricht, *Dissertatio inauguralis juridica de antidotis*, praeside Henrico Coccejo (Frankfurt an der Oder, 1708).

importantly, however, was the publication of the first four books of the *TPT* (1682). Well-timed or not, the work was dedicated to Ludwig's father, Frederick Wilhelm of Brandenburg. This work is a significant milestone for Mastricht's intellectual trajectory, beginning at Glückstadt and continuing with several disputations held at Duisburg and Utrecht. Mastricht argued that the *TPT* was to be used in the preparation of preaching.[137] Though reaching this milestone, Mastricht already was working on chapters 1 and 2 of book V *De Redemptione Christi* of the *TPT*, dealing with the covenant of grace.[138] Besides his teaching and writing as *rector-magnificus*, Mastricht was involved in the church's question regarding the value of the *colloquia* and *testimonia* of the students at the Utrecht academy.[139] In addition, on August 29, 1682 Mastricht proposed a doctorate *honoris causa* for Franciscus Ridderus (1620-1683)[140] and Guiljelmus Saldenus (1627-1694),[141] which took place on December 4, 1682.

1683-1687

Meanwhile Mastricht did not forget Duisburg either. In 1683 he sent a substantial gift of "300 Talern" to the theological faculty of the University.[142] The same year he focused on the notion of spiritual desertion,[143] a theme that he started on in 1680. In addition to his teaching and writing, Mastricht wrote an approbation of Thomas Sheppard's (1605-1649) *De Gezonde Geloovige* in 1685.[144] Though he was involved in

---

137. Petrus van Mastricht, *Theoretico-practica theologia* (1682), ***.

138. Petrus van Mastricht, *De Foedere Gratiæ, pars prima, ex theologiæ theoretico-practicæ libro quinto, caput primum*, Hemmo Hovius (Utrecht: Meinardus à Dreunen, 1682); idem, *De mediatore foederis gratiæ, pars tertia, ex theologiæ theoretico-practicæ libro quinto, caput secundum*, Theodorus van Breen (Utrecht: Meinardus à Dreunen, 1682).

139. Kernkamp, *Acta et Decreta Senatus*, 2:69.

140. F. Ridderus (1620-1683) thus received a doctorate approximately a year before he died.

141. Kernkamp, *Acta et Decreta Senatus*, 2:70: "Convocato Senatui...proposuit Rector [Mastricht, AN]...D. Francisco Riddero...D. Guilielmo Saldeno...multis nominibus meritissimis, summos in Theologia honores decernere modo extraordinario..." This differs with Cramer, *De Theologische Faculteit*, 376, who writes that Witsius proposed the promotion. Cf. Genderen, *Herman Witsius*, 70, fn. 32.

142. Roden, *Die Universität Duisburg*, 116. A similar amount was granted by the elector.

143. Petrus van Mastricht, *Disputationum practicarum de desertione spirituali*, prima, eruditorum crisi subjicit Henricus Nahuys (Ultrajecti: Meinardus à Dreunen, 1680); idem, *Disputationum practicarum de desertione spirituali*, secunda, eruditorum crisi subjicit Daniel Bongart (Utrecht: Meinardus à Dreunen, 1680); idem, *Disputationum practicarum de desertione spirituali*, tertia, publice tueri conabitur Daniel le Roy (Utrecht: Meinardus à Dreunen, 1683); idem, *Disputationum practicarum de desertione spirituali*, quarta, publice tueri conabitur Samuel Kaposi (Utrecht: Meinardus à Dreunen, 1683).

144. Thomas Sheppard, *De Gezonde Geloovige* (Amsterdam: Joannes Boekholt, 1686). This approbation, written with Leydecker, Witsius, and Van Halen, was an ecclesiastical requirement but also indicates that the theology of New England was known at Utrecht. Other works that were translated to Dutch from New England ministers are, for example, Thomas Hooker, *De ware zielsvernedring en heilzame wanhoop*, trans. J. Koelman, (Amsterdam: J. Wasteliers, 1678); idem, *De arme twijfelende Christen, genadert tot Christus*, trans. J. Koelman (Amsterdam: J. Wasteliers, undated) and probably Salomo Stoddard, *Een leidsman tot Christus*, (Leiden: Buurman & De Kler, undated).

other New England contacts,[145] he could not have envisioned the favorable reception of his *magnum opus* in the New World. In 1687 books V to VIII of the *TPT* became available and were dedicated to Carolo of Hesse, the mark of Hirschfeld.

1688-1699

In 1689 Mastricht bought a house on the west side of the Oudegracht, close to the academy and church.[146] Meanwhile, his academic and ecclesiastical work continued. In respect to the former, he approbated the Dutch translation of *Der Närrische Atheist* of his former classmate Theodor Undereyck.[147] In respect to the Dutch Reformed Church, it appears that his preaching took him outside Utrecht, as he preached regularly at the congregation of Schellingwoude (classis Amsterdam).[148] At least this could serve (partly) as an explanation of his assistance to the classis of Amsterdam in 1692.[149] While Baltasar Bekker (1634-1698) made waves in Europe with his publications, including *De Betoverde Weereld*,[150] Mastricht supplied the classis Amsterdam with his *Contra Beckerum*. His main

145. Kernkamp notes that on January 12, 1687 professor Leusden presents the senate with a *Biblia in Americanam linguam translata* and to the library a gift with the inscription *Bibliothecam celeberrimæ apud Utrajectinos Academiæ hac sacrorum Bibliorum versione Indicadonat Crescentius Mathœus, Collegii Harvardini apud Cantabrigienses in Nova Anglia Præses pro tempore*. Leusden is requested to thank Mather. Cf. Kernkamp, *Acta et Decreta Senatus*, 2:90.

146. Somewhere between the Romerburger bridge, now the Hamburger bridge, and the Gaard bridge. G.J. Röhner, Utrechts Archief is acknowledged. See also http://www. hetutrechtsarchief.nl/ archieven, transactions: inv.nr.U93a33, akte nr. 56, d.d. 01-12-1697, inv.nr.U174a2, akte nr. 146, d.d. 23-09-1728, inv.nr.U217a6, akte nr. 231, d.d. 28-10-1760, accessed October 5, 2003.

147. Theodor Undereyck, *Der Närrische Atheist/ Entdeckt und seiner Thorheit überzeuget/ In Zwey Theilen In dem Ersten/ Als ein solcher/ der da wissentlich willens und vorsetzlich/ ihme selbst und anderen/ die Gedancken/ welche sie von Gott haben/ nehmen wil. In dem Zweyten/ Als ein solcher/ der da unwissend und ungemerckt/ auch unter dem Schein des wahren Christenthums/ ohne Gott in der Welt lebet* (Bremen: Herman Brauer 1689); Theodor Undereyck, *De dwaase atheist: ontdekt en van sijn dwaasheyd overtuygd*, trans. Jodocus Fridericus Rappardus (Amsterdam: Jan Groenwoud, 1702). The Dutch edition was approbated in 1689 by the theological faculty of Duisburg University, Marburg, and Franeker, and in 1690 by the theological faculty of Utrecht University. The latter included only those "who were learned in the German language and piety." See on *Der Närrische Atheist*, Israel, *Radical Enlightenment*, 89, 90, 300.

148. Löhr and van Doorn, *Protokolle*, 2:419. Petrus Montanus served the Reformed congregation of Schellingwoude and formerly the Reformed congregation at Cologne, in which Mastricht was born. Cf. Löhr and van Doorn, *Protokolle*, 1:35, 37.

149. This assistance probably attests more for Mastricht's continuing distaste of the philosophy of Descartes than an ecclesiastical contribution. Others, such as Mastricht's colleague Melchior Leydekker (1642-1721), also published against Bekker. Melchior Leydekker, *Historische en theologische redeneringe, over het onlangs uitgegeve boek van den seer vermaarden Balthasar Bekker, strekkende tot bevestinge der waarheit en authoriteit van de H. Schriftuur* (Utrecht: weduwe van Willem Clerck, 1692); Jacobus Koelman, *Eenige originele brieven geschreven aan Do. Balthasar Bekker, over sijn boek de Betoverde werelt* (Amsterdam: Daniel van den Dalen, 1692); idem, *Het vergift van de Cartesiaansche philosophie: grondig ontdekt en meest historischer wijze, uit de schriften van des Cartes zelfs, en van andere schrijvers, zo voor als tegen hem, getrouwelijk aangeweezen* (Amsterdam: Johannes Boekholt, 1692). See on Gerardus de Vries's position on Cartesianism, Israel, *Radical Enlightenment*, 479, 480.

150. Baltasar Bekker, *Naakte uitbeeldinge van alle de vier boeken der Betoverde weereld, vertonende het oogmerk van den schryver tot wechneeminge van vooroordeelen en een kort begryp des ganschen werx* (Amsterdam: Daniel van den

concern in this publication was Bekker's Cartesianism. Mastricht argued that Bekker placed philosophy above Scripture and that theology was being relinquished to the axiom "philosophy is the infallible interpreter of Scripture."[151]

In the meantime, and besides his work at the academy and church, Mastricht continued working on his *magnum opus*. In 1698, the final edition of the *TPT*[152] was published, a revised edition of the previous 1682 and 1687 editions[153] with the addition of the *Idea theologiæ moralis* and *Hypotyposis theologiæ asceticæ*. Mastricht received three hundred fifteen guilders from the *vroedschap* of Utrecht, because the work was dedicated on February 15, 1698 to the *Ed. Achtbare Heeren Borgermeesteren en Vroedschap deser Stad*.[154] His work, which began in Glückstadt, was finished and immediate reprinted in 1699.[155] It should be noted that the number of disputations decreased significantly after his rectorate, with two exceptions. In 1690 Arnoldus de Blankendæl defended *Diatribe theologica de æterna Christi sponsione*.[156] This disputation may have contributed to the only

Dalen, 1693). Bekker argued in four volumes his Cartesian philosophical and scriptural objections to ideas such as magic, Satan, spirits, and witchcraft. The book was immediately translated into English, German, and France. The consistory of Amsterdam condemned the book, and the regional synod of Alkmaar decided in 1692 to remove Bekker from office. Cf. R. B. Evenhuis, *Ook dat was Amsterdam* (Amsterdam: Ten Have, 1971), 3:258-305; Israel, *Radical Enlightenment*, 378-405.

151. Petrus van Mastricht, *Ad Virum Clariss. D. Balthasarem Beckerum, Epanorthosis gratulatoria occasione articulorum, quos venerandæ Classi Amstelodamensi exhibuit, die 22 Janu. 1692*, (Utrecht: Anthonius Schouten, 1692), 25: "...qui Religionem Reformatam profitentur, cum *Philosophiam infallibilem Scripturarum interpretem* proclamarent..."

152. Petrus van Mastricht, *Theoretico-practica theologia: qua, per singula capita theologica, pars exegetica, dogmatica, elenchtica et practica, perpetua successione conjugantur; accedunt historia ecclesiastica, plena quidem, sed compendiosa, idea theologiæ moralis, hypotyposis theologiæ asceticæ etc. proin opus quasi novum* (Utrecht: Gerardus Muntendam, 1698); idem, *Theoretico-practica theologia* (1699). The edition of 1698 is a very rare available print. Because the 1698 and 1699 editions are identical, including the repeated pagination of 325-424, the more accessible edition of 1699 is used in this study. See on the 1699 edition part I, chapter 2 of this study. The note that the *Theoretico-practica theologia* was published in 1655 is inaccurate. See for example, Van der Linde, "Mastricht, Petrus van," in *Christelijke Encyclopaedie*; Visser, "Van Mastricht, Petrus," 383; Sprunger, *The Learned Doctor William*, 260; Sepp, *Het Godgeleerd Onderwijs*, 2:348.

153. Books I – IV and V-VIII had been published respectively in 1682 and 1687. Petrus van Mastricht, *Theoretico-practica theologia: qua, per capita theologica, pars dogmatica, elenchtica et practica, perpetua sumbibasei conjugantur; præcedunt in usum operis, paraleipomena, seu sceleton de optima concionandi methodo* (Amsterdam: Henricus et Vidua Theodori Boom, 1682-1687).

154. Kernkamp refers to the *vroedschap* minutes of March 7, 1698. Kernkamp, *Acta et Decreta Senatus*, 2:160: "De vroedschap heeft de Heer Petrus Mastricht, SS Theol. Professor, vereerd met de somme van drie honderd vijftien gulden voor de dedicatie van zijn boek, geïntituleerd: Theologia Theoretico-practica."

155. Simon Oomius's wish of 1672 was fulfilled. However, Oomius's *Institutiones Theologiæ Practicæ* remained unfinished. Cf. Gregory Schuringa, *Embracing* Leer and Leven: *The Theology of Simon Oomius in the Context of* Nadere Reformatie Orthodoxy (Ph.D. diss., Calvin Theological Seminary, 2003), 13.

156. Petrus van Mastricht, *Diatribe theologica de æterna Christi sponsione*, Arnoldus de Blankendael (Utrecht: Franciscus Halma, 1690).

modification of the 1687 and 1698 editions.[157] Furthermore, Mastricht returned to primary Old Testament expositions with his students.[158] The possible decrease of dispuations may be the result of Mastricht's preparation of the final edition of the *TPT*. This work is notably diminutive on autobiographic material, with few references to earlier works, such as the *Prodromus* and *De fide Salvifica*, the exception being the *Gangræna*.

1700-1706

In 1700[159] Henricus Pontanus (1652-1714)[160] succeeded Herman Witsius at the faculty of theology, and Mastricht limited his own teaching to his home, due to physical weakness, and held public lectures only on Monday and Tuesday afternoons.[161] He continued to be involved in the affairs of the university,[162] and so he was called with his colleagues, Leydekker and Pontanus, before the *vroedschap* of Utrecht. They were asked to live in "peace and friendship" with the controversial appointed theology professor Herman A. Röell (1653-1718).[163] After a prolific life of teaching, writing, and preaching,[164] Mastricht died on February 9, 1706, due to a wound on his crippled foot,

157. The chapters *De Foedere Gratiæ* and *De Mediatore Foederis gratiæ* have been modified between 1682 and 1698.

158. Petrus van Mastricht, *Exercitationum analyticarum exegeticarumque, in caput Jesaiæ quinquagesimum-tertium*, prima, resp. Henricus Revius (Utrecht: Franciscus Halma, 1693); idem, *Exercitationum analyticarum exegeticarumque, in caput Jesaiæ quinquagesimum-tertium*, secunda & tertia, resp. Lambertus Wagardus (Utrecht: Franciscus Halma, 1693); idem, *Exercitationum analyticarum exegeticarumque, in caput Jesaiæ quinquagesimum-tertium*, quarta & quinta, resp. Theodorus Hagendyck (Utrecht: Franciscus Halma, 1694); idem, *Exercitationum analyticarum exegeticarumque, in caput Jesaiæ quinquagesimum-tertium*, sexta & septima, resp. Laurentius Le Brun (Utrecht: Franciscus Halma, 1694); idem, *Dissertationis historicophilologicotheologicæ, tremendum vindictæ divinæ monumentum, in perennem memoriam, Ananiæ et Sapphiræ Actor. Cap. V. vs. 1-12. miraculose erectum exhibentis*, pars prior, resp. Johannes Pelsöczi (Utrecht: Franciscus Halma, 1699).

159. In Utrecht on December 12, 1700 a new (Gregorian) calendar was introduced.

160. Pontanus, was in 1678 appointed by King William III of the Netherlands to the pastorate of the Reformed church in Lingen. On September 14, 1697, at the palace *Het Loo*, the king signed the papers for the establishment of an Academy of Lingen. With Pontanus as professor, the faculty was, according to Tanis, in the hands of the Voetians. Although moving to Utrecht, Pontanus remained involved in the affairs of the academy of Lingen, as he was appointed, while *Rector magnificus* at Utrecht, as curator of the academy of Lingen. Cf. Tanis, *Dutch Calvinistic Pietism in the Middle Colonies*, 26. It is interesting to note that Theodorus Frelinghuysen (1691-1747), also called the forerunner of the American Great Awakening, was born and raised in the "Cocceian" classis of Cleve and studied at the Academy of Lingen.

161. From November 11, 1700 onwards, Mastricht held public lectures twice a week. Cf. Kernkamp, *Acta et Decreta Senatus*, 2:176.

162. As assessor of the senate in 1704-05. Cf. Kernkamp, *Acta et Decreta Senatus*, 2:188.

163. Jacob van Sluis, *Herman Alexander Röell*, (Leeuwarden: Fryske Akademy, 1988); idem, "De Cartesiaanse Theologie van Herman Alexander Röell," in *Vier eeuwen Theologie in Utrecht*, 141-50; Cramer, *De Theologische Faculteit*, 18*; Cf. Kernkamp, *Acta et Decreta Senatus*, 2:199.

164. See Appendix I.1.1, "Works of Petrus van Mastricht."

which was caused by a fall from a kitchen step.[165] The funeral oration was given by Pontanus and was attended by Mastricht's fellow professors and ministers and the Utrecht magistrate. Also were present, coming from Bremen, his brother Gerardus, with his son Petrus.[166] Mastricht was buried on February 24 in the Catharine church, the resting place of his teacher Gisbertus Voetius, his colleague and friend Gerhardus de Vries, and his acquaintance Jacobus Koelman.[167] Oomius notes that not many ministers were, like him and Mastricht, given a long life.[168]

Mastricht remained unmarried and must have been wealthy. He left 500 Carolus guilders for the Utrecht deaconate and 24,000 guilders[169] in his oleographic will[170] for Reformed theology students.[171] Despite Mastricht's beneficence and academic attentiveness to his international group of students of divinity, they seemed not to remember their teacher. In the Netherlands, three students from Zeeland, Drywegen, De

---

165. Pontanus, *Laudatio Funebris*, 21. The same month the University of Frankfurt an der Oder commemorated her two hundred year anniversary. Cf. R. R. Targiel, "Nachbetrachtung einer Austellung," in *Die Oder-Universität Frankfurt*, 282.

166. Kernkamp, *Acta et Decreta Senatus*, 2:207 notes that the vroedschap places on March 15 and 22, 1707 a "Verbod aan de boekverkoper Van de Water om de lijkrede (van Prof. Pontanus) op Van Mastricht te verkoopen of te verspreiden, omdat deze is opgedragen aan Gerhard van Mastricht, Syndicus der stad Bremen, wien de titels worden gegeven, die alleen aan H. Ed. Achtb. toekomen; de reeds verspreide exemplaren moeten worden opgehaald (15 Maart); mededeeling, dat prof. Pontanus te goeder trouw heeft gehandeld en zijn excuses heeft aangeboden." Gerard van Mastricht inherited, according to Van Tellingen, his brothers' home. Cf. Van Tellingen, *Het leven en enige aspecten*, 35.

167. Mastricht is registred on March 1, 1706 in the list of deceased persons. Van Tellingen, *Het leven en enige aspecten*, 33: "Ænbracht den 1 Maert 1706 d'Heer Professor Petrus van Mastri[ch]t, bejaerd Heer...." See for De Vries, Pontanus, *Laudatio Funebris*, 5. Petrus Mastricht is burried next to Gerardus de Vries (1648-1705). For Koelman see Krull, *Jacobus Koelman*, 102, who mentions February 6, 1695.

168. S. Oomius, *Cierlijke Kroon des Grysen Ouderdoms* (Leiden: Daniel van den Dalen, 1707), 336: "Op den eersten Maart [1706] nu aanstaande, sal ik treden, soo het den Hemel behaagt, uit mijn leven seven en seventigste jaar; van deese hebb' ik op den Predik-Stoel mijne Stemme doen hooren. In den Kerkelyken dienst nu in de vier en vyftig jaren, een weldaad seeker, welke de Heere aan weinige bewijst. Hij heeft met deselve begunsigt dese Vermaarde Mannen, Petrus van Mastrigt (die agt maanden en vier dagen jonger was doe hy onlangs stierf als ik), Witsius, Joh. Vollenhovius..."

169. Isaac le Long, *Hondert-Jaarige Jubel-Gedachtenisse der Academie van Utrecht* (Utrecht: M. Visch, 1736), xii. The following works mention 20,000 guilders: *Biographisch Lexicon voor de geschiedenis von het Nederlands Protestantisme*, vol. 5 (Kampen, 2001, 362); Kernkamp, *De Utrechtsche Universiteit*, 1:175.

170. De Vrijer writes, "P. à Mastricht overleed in 1706 op vij en zeventigjarigen leeftijd. Op 31 December 1701 had hij zijn oleographisch testament opgesteld. Daarin legateerde hij o.a. vijfhonderd carolus guldens aan de armen; vier en twintig duizend bestemde hij voor een studie-fonds ten bate van Utrechtsche studenten in de Theologie. Curatoren daarover moesten zijn twee Theologische hoogleeraren (één er van wilde hij, dat zijn collega Gerardus de Vries, de theoloog-philosooph, zoude zijn) en twee leden van den kerkeraad. Zijn "hoogste eynde" hierbij zoo schreef hij, "was de verheerlijkinge van Godt en de stichtinge van sijn Kerk." M. J. A. de Vrijer, *Ds. Bernardus Smytegelt en zijn "Gekrookte Riet"* (Vianen: De Banier, 1968), 9, 10. Van der Zee, *Vaderlandse Kerkgeschiedenis van de Hervormde Kerk*, 3:142, mentions also 24,000 guilders.

171. Van der Linde, "Mastricht, Petrus van," in *Christelijke Encyclopaedie*, 4:250: "waaruit nog steeds studenten in de theologie te Utrecht een welkome ondersteuning in hun studie ontvangen."

Clyver,[172] and Bernardus Smytegelt (1665-1739)[173] seem not to remember him. Like Henricus Nahuys, the father of Petrus Nahuys (1692-1766), they seem to keep primarily in mind Herman Witsius, as does another student, Petrus Dinant (1663-1724).[174] It also seems that Mastricht's Hungarian students, such as Samuel Kaposki and Johannes Pelsöczi[175] as well as his Scottish students, did not recall him. An exception to the latter group is James Hog, who appealed to his teacher during the *Marrow controversy*.[176] Nevertheless, Pontanus mentions the great loss of Mastricht for the Utrecht academy, that took the *vroedschap* nine years to fill the vacancy.[177]

We can conclude, then, that Mastricht's time in Utrecht, or his "Dutch" period, as professor from 1677 to his death in 1706 shows continuity in his work. Three observations can be made. First, in respect to his academic life, the period in Utrecht was a productive time. His work begun at Xanten, Glückstadt, Frankfurt an der Oder, and Duisburg continued with theological disputations and other publications that ultimately contributed to his *magnum opus*: the *TPT*. Moreover, his (theological) academic work is strongly characterized with a particular methodology: exegesis, doctrine, elenctic, and *praxis*. Second, in respect to the church, his academic work was integrated with the life of the church. In that way, Mastricht continued his teaching of students of divinity and also continued his opposition to Cartesiansim (*Contra Beckerum*). Contrary to his colleagues Witsius and Leydekker or his acquaintance Koelman, Mastricht's academic and ecclesiastical work does not show a particular attention to the cause of the *Nadere Reformatie*. Finally, though his works seem to have been known in the Netherlands and abroad, Mastricht was mostly forgotten by his

172. De Cluyver came from the congregation of Wemeldinge, which was later served by Wilhelmus Eversdijk (1653-1729). Eversdijk also studied, partly, with Mastricht from 1675 to 1681 at Utrecht and served the Wemeldinge congregation from 1681-1684. Moreover, Eversdijk and Dinant, also a student of Mastricht, were friends. Cf. J. van der Haar, "Wilhelmus Eversdijk," in *Het Blijvende Woord*, 64.

173. Smytegelt came in 1683 to Utrecht, the year Mastricht was rector. Smytegelt defended for his cousin Melchior Leydekker in November 1686 a number of propositions of Augustine's *De unitate ecclesiæ*. Cf. Vrijer, *Ds. Bernardus Smytegelt*, 10; S. D. Post, *Bernardus Smijtegelt dienstknecht van God* (Houten: Den Hertog, 2001), 25, 29.

174. Tj. De Jong, "Petrus Dinant," in *Het Blijvende Woord 2*, ed. J. van der Haar (Leerdam: Gereformeerde Bijbelstichting, 1991), 67. According to De Jong, Petrus Dinant was a Cocceian. See also, Petrus Dinant, *De Brief van de H. Apostel Paulus aan die van Efeze*, 2d ed. (Rotterdam: Jan Daniel Beman, 1726), vol.1, preface (3): "Herm. Witsius, weleer myn hoog geachte Meester in de Akademie te Utrecht." See also preface (7), (9), (12), (17). The following persons were probably taught by Mastricht: Jacobus Fruytier from 1678-1681, Petrus Immens from 1683-1686 and Adrianus Reland (1690-1693).

175. Petrus van Mastricht, *Disputationum practicarum de desertione spirituali*, pars quarta, Samuel Kaposi (Utrecht: Meinardus à Dreunen, 1683); idem, *Dissertationis historico-philologico-theologicæ, tremendum vindictæ divinæ monumentum, in perennem memoriam, Ananiæ et Sapphiræ Actor. Cap V. vs. 1-12. miraculose erectum exhibentis*, pars prior, Johannes Pelsöczi (Utrecht: Franciscus Halma, 1699).

176. Fischer, *The Marrow of Modern Divinity*, 346.

177. Pontanus, *Laudatio Funebris*, 23. On the succession of Mastricht, see Van Tellingen, *Het leven en enige aspecten*, 36.

(international) students. On the other hand, Mastricht did not forget the Brandenburg family, the Universities of Duisburg and Utrecht and their students.

Retrospect

In retrospect our emerging portrait of Mastricht contains three main and consistent characteristics: theology, Hebrew, and anti-Cartesianism. In respect to theology, Mastricht's theological formation from catechism class to his graduation from the University of Utrecht consisted of a thorough Reformed orthodox and Protestant scholastic training, joined with piety. Both theory and practice—of theology and of the theologian—became a central theme of Mastricht's intellectual development. The "Utrecht emphasis" on *theologia practica* was advanced and codified by Mastricht with the *TPT*, a pinnacle of Protestant scholastic theology; exegetical, doctrinal, elenctical, and practical. In respect to Hebrew, Mastricht's teaching of Hebrew cannot be seen independently of the Renaissance humanist concern for the study of original languages. Furthermore, his acquaintance with the rabbinic literature provided him with a solid linguistic foundation and exegetical aids for theology. In respect to anti-Cartesianism, Mastricht was very attentive to the philosophical developments of his time. His reputation in this field was renowned throughout Europe.

In addition, this emerging portrait of Mastricht, formed by theology, Hebrew, and certain concerns of philosophy, contains two additional elements. First, the social and ecclesiastical context of his life and work was mostly international and ecumenically oriented. It was international in that it included French Huguenots, English Reformed and Presbyterians, and the Dutch Reformed church. The ecumenical aspect, although gradual, is most prominent in the union of Lutherans and Reformed at Frankfurt an der Oder. Moreover, his presence in the predominantly Cocceian classis of Cleve should not to be ignored. These aspects of his life in the Reformed church in Germany and the Netherlands suggests that he cannot be categorized exclusively as a figure of the *Nadere Reformatie*. The second permanent element in Mastricht's life is his concern for the students of divinity or ministry. This concern was expressed in the *Prodromus* and repeated in the *Methodus* and *TPT*, which were meant to be used for preaching.

In summary, we conclude that the influence of Protestant Scholasticism and Renaissance humanism contributed to Mastricht's status as a seventeenth-century post-Reformation Reformed theologian, Christian Hebraist, and philosopher. Mastricht's personal motto, ὅταν γὰρ ἀσθενῶ τότε δυνατός εἰμί and the deficiency of autobiographical material in his works reinforces the belief that his "true image is revealed when one lives by his book."[178]

---

178. Cf. Petrus van Mastricht, *Beschouwende en praktikale godgeleerdheit*, op de afbeeldinge. The motto is 2 Corinthians 12:10b, "for when I am weak, then I am strong."

Chapter 2
Mastricht's Work: The *Theoretico-Practica Theologia*

Introduction and Statement of the Problem

This chapter serves as a bridge between the preceding chapter and subsequent chapters. For the latter it serves as background, and for the former it sheds additional light on the work of Mastricht. Furthermore, although the *Theoretico-practica theologia* (*TPT*) has been distributed widely throughout Europe[1] and North America,[2] neither a representative overview nor an assessment has been provided.[3] Therefore, we will review the work in general and book II, *De Fide in Deum triunum*, or the doctrine of God, in particular. This general assessment will include an examination of the development, and structure of the *TPT* (1699). In respect to its development, we will examine which works of Mastricht may have contributed to the final edition. Finally, a brief overview of translations and reprints of the *TPT* is provided. The assessment of book II, the doctrine of God, includes an analysis of its structure, sources, and premises (part 2).

Theoretico-practica theologia: Development

Development

The *TPT* is a result of a lifelong labor of Mastricht. Therefore this section examines chronologically those works of Mastricht that were involved in the composition of the 1682-1687 and 1698 edition.

The Prodromus. This work, written at Glückstadt, was Mastricht's first major theological publication. The title indicates a threefold work concerning *De creatione*

---

1. The edition of 1698 seldom present in libraries. The distribution of the 1699, 1715, and 1724 edition is noted in (academic) libraries of England, Germany, the Netherlands, Scotland and Switzerland. Collectively over two hundred copies have been identified, excluding the Dutch translation *Beschouwende en praktikale godgeleerdheit*.

2. The distribution of the work is noted primarily in (academic) libraries of the east coast of the United States of America, including, Massachusetts, New York, and Pennsylvania. The libraries of Pittsburgh Theological Seminary, Pittsburgh and Calvin Theological Seminary each have a 1682-1687 edition. In addition, Jonathan Edwards's correspondence indicates that the 1699 edition was distributed from London, England to New England. Cf. Jonathan Edwards, *Letters and Personal writings*, The Works of Jonathan Edwards, vol. 16, ed., George S. Claghorn (New Haven, London: Yale University Press, 1998), 216, 217.

3. Miller, Kennedy, and Van Vliet provide a succinct overview of the structure of the *Theoretico-practica theologia*, or *Beschouwende en praktikale godgeleerdheit*. However, their analysis is primarily limited to their subject of research. Cf. Perry Miller, *The New England Mind, The Seventeenth Century* (Cambridge, MA: Harvard Univeristy Press, 1982), 96; James C. Kennedy, *Jonathan Edwards in a Dutch context: History and Prophecy in 17th Century Holland*, unpublished article, 1988; Jan van Vliet, *William Ames: Marrow of the Theology and Piety of the Reformed Tradition* (Ph.D. diss., Westminster Theological Seminary, 2002), 348-69.

Hominis, De humilitate et superbia erga Deum, and *De conversatione cum Deo*,[4] discussed didactically,[5] elenctically and practically. A closer look reveals that Mastricht begins each chapter with the exegesis of a biblical text in the original language, from which he infers doctrine, elenctic, and practical considerations. This fourfold structure of a *locus* became Mastricht's trademark in later theological publications, including his *disputationes*.[6] In addition to the structure of the *locus*, the content of the first chapter of the *Prodromus*, which deals with the creation of humankind, was largely used in the *TPT* edition (1682) of book III, *De operationibus Dei*, and in chapter nine *De homine et imagine Dei*.[7] Furthermore, the content of chapters two and three of the *Prodromus*, subsequently addressing the obedience and exercise of faith, to some extent have found their way into, respectively, the *Idea theologiæ moralis*[8] and *Hypotyposis theologiæ asceticæ*[9] of the *TPT* edition (1698). Therefore, we see that the *Prodromus* outlined Mastricht's lifelong program of theology: on a macro level it contains the contours of the systematic theology, the *Idea theologiæ moralis* and *Hypotyposis theologiæ asceticæ*, and on a micro level its exegetical, didactical or doctrinal, elenctical, and practical sections or divisions. Moreover, the significant use of chapter I of the *Prodromus* in the *TPT* edition (1682) alludes to the stability of Mastricht's intellectual thought.

Methodus Concionandi. This undated publication, published at Frankfurt an der Oder, is assigned to the late 1660s for the following reasons: (1) the letter type of the publication is used in the mid-seventeenth century, (2) the text is almost identical but different in layout from Mastricht's 1681 disputation *De optima concionandi methodo paraleipomena: in usum theologiæ theoretico-practicæ*, and (3) Mastricht 's reference that he

---

4. Petrus van Mastricht, *Theologiæ didactico-elenchtico-practicæ, prodromus tribus* (Amsterdam: Johannes van Someren, 1666).

5. One should note that this work usually uses *didactica*, whereas in the *TPT* editions the word *dogmatica* is used, with the exception of II.3.xiii, where didactica is used.

6. This differs with Van Vliet's assessment of a fivefold division. Cf. Van Vliet, *William Ames*, 350. He writes, "First, presentation of text; second an explanatory or expository (*verklarende*) section; third, a doctrinal (*leerstukkig*); fourth, a polemic "argumentative" (*wederleggende*,) section in which objections are posed and rebutted; and fifthly, a practical (*betrachtende*) section in which the uses of the scriptural teaching under consideration are brought forward." Following Vliet's Dutch translation, one notes a fourfold division.

7. The exegesis, based on the same biblical text (Gen. 1:26-30) is similar but more concise present in the *TPT* (1682). So are the doctrinal, elenctic, and practical sections. Cf. Mastricht, *Prodromus*, 30, observatio quarta, *De Corpore Humano*; and Petrus van Mastricht, *Theoretico-practica theologia* (1682), 580, quarto, *Efformatio corporis*.

8. Ibid., *De humilitate et superbia erga Deum*. Cf. Mastricht, *Theoretico-practica theologia* (1699), Idea theologiæ moralis, I.5, 1105. The latter has the same heading as book II of the *Prodromus* and is a summary using the same main points.

9. Mastricht, *Prodromus, De conversatione cum Deo*. Cf. idem, *Theoretico-practica theologia* (1699), Hypotyposis theologiæ asceticæ, III.7.iii, 1194. The latter, with surrounding chapters, resembles the same theme as book III of the *Prodromus* and uses similar Scriptural text references.

used the *Methodus* in his seventeen years of preaching, thus from 1652-1669.[10] The *Methodus* provides an outline or method for preaching and discusses a fourfold approach, illustrated by the text of Colossians 3:1: exegetical, didactical or doctrinal, elenctical, and practical.[11] From this, it can be concluded that Mastricht's fourfold approach to the *locus* of theology did not differ from his homiletic method.

De fide salvifica. The *De fide salvifica* was published during the Duisburg period and is an extensive and *theoretico*-practical exposition of saving faith, based on the text of John 1:11, 12.[12] Again, Mastricht elucidates the biblical text from an exegetical, doctrinal, elenctical, and practical perspective. In summarized version this work is used verbatim in the chapter on faith in the *TPT*.[13] Noteworthy is that the definition of saving faith remained equivalent in both works.[14] Therefore, this leads to the conclusion that Mastricht's approach—*theoretico*-practical and the fourfold division: exegesis, doctrine, elenctic, and *praxis*—and the verbatim use of previous publications contribute to the stability and continuity of his intellectual thought.

The Doctrine of God, the Nature of Theology, and Covenant Theology. Mastricht's *disputationes* in Duisburg, *De Existentia et Cognitione Dei*,[15] and those in Utrecht, *De Essentia, Nominibus et Atrributis Dei in genere*,[16] on the nature of theology[17]

10. Mastricht, *Theoretico-practica theologia* (1699), 1225.

11. Mastricht, *Methodus Concionandi* (Frankfurt an der Oder: M. Hübner, undated). The integral use of the *Methodus* in a 1681 disputation and its relation to the *TPT* will be examined below.

12. Mastricht, *De fide salvifica syntagma theoretico-practicum: in quo fidei salvificæ tum natura, tum praxis universa, luculenter exponitur; cum præf. de membris Ecclesiæ visibilis seu admittendis, seu rejiciendis, oborienti scismati moderno applicanda* (Duisburg: Franc. Sas, 1671).

13. Mastricht, *Theoretico-practica theologia* (1682), II.1, 91-122. Cf. II.1, 50-65.

14. Mastricht, *Theoretico-practica theologia* (1682, 1699): "Fides salvifica nihil aliud sit, quam actus totius animæ rationalis, *quo Deum accipit, quà summum finem*; & Christum, quà unicum Mediatorem, ad hoc, ut cum eo uniamur, & uniti, communionem consequamur, omnium ejus beneficiorum;" Cf. idem, *De fide salvifica syntagma theoretico-practicum*: "Fides salvifica nihil aliud sit, quam actus totius animæ rationalis, *recipientis, Deum quidem pro summo suo sine; Christus vero pro unico Mediatore*, ad hoc, ut cum eo uniamur, & uniti, communionem consequamur, omnium ejus beneficiorum." (The italic part of the definition is the textual difference, AN).

15. Mastricht, *Theologiæ Theoretico-Practicæ disputatio quinta, De Existentia Et Cognitione Dei*, resp. Wilhelmus Mercamp (Duisburg: Franc. Sas, 1677).

16. Mastricht, *Theologiæ theoretico-practicæ disputatio septima De Essentia, Nominibus et Atrributis Dei in genere*, Pars 2, resp. Balduinus Drywegen (Utrecht: Meinardus à Dreunen, 1677); idem, *Theologiæ theoretico-practicæ disputatio septima De Essentia, Nominibus et Atrributis Dei in genere*, Pars 3, resp. Jacobus de Clyver (Utecht: Meinardus à Dreunen, 1677); idem, *Theologiæ theoretico-practicæ disputatio septima De Essentia, Nominibus et Atrributis Dei in genere*, Pars 4, resp. Isaacus Ravensbergius (Utrecht: Meinardus à Dreunen, 1678); idem, *De dispensatione foederis gratiæ sub Patriarchis, Ex Theologiæ Theoretico-Practicæ propediem ex ituræ libro octavo caput primum*, resp. Nicolaus de Goyer (Utrecht: Meinardus à Dreunen, 1686); idem, *De dispensatione foederis gratiæ, sub æternitate, Ex Theologiæ theoretico-practicæ, parte posteriore, jam exituræ, caput postremum*, resp. Johannes Georgius Barovius (Utrecht: Meinardus à Dreunen, 1686).

17. Mastricht, *Theologiæ theoretico-practicæ, sub relo sudantis, specimen de natura theologiæ primum*, resp. Petrus Dix (Utrecht: Meinardus à Dreunen, 1680); idem, *Theologiæ theoretico-practicæ specimen, de natura*

and on the covenant[18] became an integral part of the *TPT* (1682, 1687).[19] In these disputations one notes the similar fourfold approach of the *locus* of theology. Not only did these disputations contribute to the formation of the *TPT*, but they also demonstrate again Mastricht's consistent thought on these issues.

De optima concionandi methodo paraleipomena. The disputation *De optima concionandi methodo* was held immediately prior to the publication of the first part of the *TPT* (1682).[20] The text of the disputation is verbatim like the *Methodus* published at Franfort an der Oder.[21] Moreover, the importance of this disputation, and therefore the *Methodus*, should not be overlooked. It provides the homiletic context and aim of the *TPT*, as the subtitle of the disputation indicates: the *TPT* is to be used for preaching. For Mastricht the discipline of theology was an academic and integral part of the training of the students of divinity—the homileticians of the church. For Mastricht, theology and preaching are distinct but not separable.

Theoretico-practica theologia: Structure

Mastricht's *magnum opus*[22] consists of two parts. Mastricht himself argues the "art of living to God" consists of two aspects: how one is made spiritually alive and, being alive, how one lives unto God (*Deo vivere*).[23] The first part comprises eight books, which could

---

theologiæ secundum, resp. Hugo Fittz (Utrecht: Meinardus à Dreunen, 1680); idem, *Theologiæ theoretico-practicæ specimen de natura theologiæ tertium*, resp. Johannes Best (Utrecht: Meinardus à Dreunen, 1680): idem, *Theologiæ theoretico-practicæ specimen de natura theologiæ quartum*, resp. Johannes Kelfkens (Utrecht: Meinardus à Dreunen, 1680).

18. Mastricht, *de Foedere Gratiæ, pars prima, Ex theologiæ theoretico-practicæ libro quinto caput primum*, resp. Hemmo Hovius (Utrecht: Meinardus à Dreunen, 1682); idem, *De mediatore foederis gratiæ, pars tertia, Ex theologiæ theoretico-practicæ libro quinto, caput secundum*, resp. Theodorus van Breen (Utrecht: Meinardus à Dreunen, 1682).

19. Comparing the documents indicate, in some cases, a rearrangement or combination of paragraphs.

20. Mastricht, *De optima concionandi methodo paraleipomena: in usum theologiæ theoretico-practicæ*, resp. Henricus Wagardus (Utrecht: Meinardus à Dreunen, 1681). The disputation was held on December 7, 1681.

· 21. Mastricht adds in 1681, that exegesis should be "[3] Ab extrinsecis textui, tum philologicis, tum philosophicis, tum historicis." This line is absent in the *Methodus*. Cf. Mastricht, *De optima concionandi methodo paraleipomena: in usum theologiæ theoretico-practicæ*, Henricus Wagardus (Utrecht: Meinardus à Dreunen, 1681); idem, *Theoretico-practica theologia* (1682, 1699), 1228. Compare with *Methodus Concionandi*, 13. Note, that the disputation is placed after the preface of the 1682 edition, and at the end of the 1699 edition.

. 22. The identical structure of the first (1682-1687) and final edition (1698), is like the *TPT* edition of 1699.

23. Petrus van Mastricht, *Theoretico-practica theologia* (1699), 1102, prologue of the *Idea Theologia Moralis*. Cf. *Theoretico-practica theologia*, I.i, 1: "Theologia...est doctrina deo vivendi per Christum," and William Ames, *Medulla*, I.i.1, 2: "Theologia est doctrina deo vivendi." Cf. William Ames, *The Marrow of Theology*, ed. John D. Eusden (Grand Rapids: Baker Books, 1997), 47. The definition of theology as *bene vivendi* is according to Sprunger, the kernel of theology influenced by Peter Ramus (1515-1572). Cf. Keith

be described as systematic theology, or as Mastricht states, it addresses the nature of faith.[24] Book I, which could be described as prolegomena, consists of three chapters that define, respectively, the nature, *principium*—Scripture—and division of theology.[25] The prolegomena, or premise, is followed by *De fide in Deum triunum* (book II), which deals with the doctrine of God.[26] The remainder of the work contains books III to VIII. These books treat the various Reformed *loci*, and include the eighth book *De dispensatione foederis gratiæ*. The latter comprises a historical-theological account from Adam to Mastricht's own time and attests of a broad international and up-to-date interest in historical, philosophical, and theological publications.[27] This book is an overview of the covenant history of the church throughout four dispensations, which cover Old and New Testament church history, including Mastricht's own time, and the eternal dispensation.[28] The latter could be taken as Mastricht's *locus* on eschatology but it should be noted that he does not have a distinct chapter—common for seventeenth-century Reformed systems of theology—on the last things.

In summary, one finds in the *TPT* an exposition of faith—God, the divine works, the apostasy of humanity, and the redemptive work of Christ and its application to the elect,

L. Sprunger, "Ames, Ramus, and the Method of Puritan Theology," *Harvard Theological Review*, 59 (Apr., 1966), 148-51. On the trajectory of this definition see, Richard A. Muller, *Post-Reformation Reformed Dogmatics* (Grand Rapids: Baker Academic, 2003), 1:154-158.

24. Mastricht, *Theoretico-practica theologia*, 1102: "Fidei naturam, octo libris hactenus expedivimus."

25. Ibid., index capitum, de præcognitis Theologiæ: (1) De Theologiâ, (2) De Scriptura, and (3) De distributione Theologiæ.

26. Ibid., index capitum, *De fide in Deum triunum*: (1) *De fide salvifica*, (2) *De existentia & cognitione Dei*, (3) *De essentia & independentiâ*, (4) *De nominibus Dei*, (5) *De attributis Dei in genere*, (6) *De spiritualitate & simplicitate Dei*, (7) *De immutabilitate Dei*, (8) *De unitate Dei*, (9) *De infinitate & magnitudine Dei*, (10) *De immensitate & omnipræsentiâ Dei*, (11) *De æternitate Dei*, (12) *De vita & immortalitate Dei*, (13) *De intellectu, scientia & sapientia Dei*, (14) *De veracitate & fide Dei*, (15) *De voluntate & affectibus Dei*, (16) *De bonitate Dei*, (17) *De amore, gratiâ, misericordiâ, longanimitate & clementiâ Dei*, (18) *De justitiâ Dei*, (19) *De sanctitate Dei*, (20) *De potestate & potentiâ Dei*, (21) *De omnisufficientia & perfectione Dei*, (22) *De majestate & gloriâ Dei*, (23) *De beatitudine Dei*, (24) *De SS. Trinitate*, (25) *De Deo Patre*, (26) *De Deo Filio*, and (27) *De Deo Spiritu S.*

27. Most likely Mastricht did not teach church history, as this subject was taught since October 16, 1686 by Paulus Bauldri. Cf. Kernkamp, *Acta et Decreta Senatus*, 2:90; idem, *De Utrechtsche Universiteit*, 1: 288.

28. Mastricht, *Theoretico-practica theologia*, VIII (1) *De dispensatione sub Patriarchis*, (2) *De dispensatione sub Mose*, (3) *De dispensatione sub Christo*, and (4) *De dispensatione sub æternitate*. Based on Van Asselt's assessment of Cocceius's concept of the dispensations within the covenant of grace, it could be argued that Mastricht resembles Cocceius's overall division but that Mastricht's OT subdivision is like Witsius's. Cf. Willem J. van Asselt, *The Federal Theology of Johannes Cocceius* (Leiden-New York: Brill, 2001), 294-95; Herman Witsius, *De oeconomia Foederum Dei cum hominibus* (Herborn, Nassau: Johannes Nicolai Andreas, 1712), 283-85. Moreover, this division is not restricted to theologians in the Netherlands. See for example, John Owen, *Theologoumena pantodapa : sive, De natura, ortu, progressu, et studio veræ theologiæ, libri sex : quibus etiam origines & processus veri & falsi cultus religiosi, casus & instaurationes ecclesiæ illustiores ab ipsis rerum primordiis, enarrantur* (Oxford: Hen. Hall, 1661). Mastricht disbanded the plan to write a separate church history, because of his age. Cf. Mastricht, *Theoretico-practica theologia* (1699), præfatio.

who are gathered to the church throughout the dispensations of the covenant of grace.[29]
The overall structure of the eight books is further distinguished by the fact that each
book contains several chapters.[30] As we have identified before, each chapter or individual
locus or topic of theology is divided into the characteristic approach: exegesis, doctrine,
elenctic,[31] and *praxis*.

The systematic part of the *TPT* is followed by the second major section, which
presents an outline of moral theology and *theologia ascetica*. Both these sections are
sketches compared with the size and structure of the *TPT*. It is noteworthy to mention
that the structure of each chapter of the *Idea Theologiæ moralis* and *Hypotyposis Theologiæ
asceticæ* differ with all other theological works of Mastricht; the characteristic fourfold
division is absent. Here, Mastricht acknowledged that for both outlines he used Ames'
Medulla and *De casibus conscientiæ*.[32] Moreover, in the second part of the *TPT*, which
contains the *Idea Theologiæ moralis*, Mastricht notes that the preceding eight books of the
TPT addressed the nature of faith, while the moral theology addresses the obedience of
faith.[33] The *Idea Theologiæ moralis* is divided into three sections: (1) Christian obedience
in general, (2) religion, i.e., the obedience in relationship to God, and (3) justice, i.e., the
obedience in relationship to one's neighbor.[34] The third and final part of the *TPT*
contains the *Hypotyposis Theologiæ asceticæ*. Referring to L. Bayly's *The Practise of Piety*, W.

29. Books III–VIII: (III) *De operationibus Dei*, (IV) *De hominis apostasiâ à Deo*, (V) *De redemptione
Christi*, (VI) *De redemptionis applicatione*, (VII) *De ecclesiâ & ecclesiasticalibus* and (VIII) *De dispensatione
fœderis gratiæ*. Book III deals with the works of God in decree, predestination, election, reprobation,
creation in general, world, angels, and humanity, general and special providence, and covenant of works.
Book IV deals with the fall of humanity and addresses the transgression of the covenant of works,
original and actual sin and its punishment and guilt. The redemption in Christ (book V) begins with the
discussion of the covenant of grace, and Mastricht covers in eighteen chapters the person and work of
the Mediator. This is followed with book VI, the application of redemption which in nine chapters
discusses respectively, the nature of the application, calling, regeneration, union with Christ, justification,
sanctification, and glorification. Book VII discusses the doctrine of the church, sacraments, and
ecclesiastical matters. The work is concluded with book VIII, dealing with the dispensations of the
covenant of grace. Here in four chapters, Mastricht discusses this covenant in relation to the patriarchs,
Moses, Christ, and eternity.

30. See Appendix I.2.1.

31. Alternatives are "*historio*-polemic" or "argumentative." Cf. Petrus van Mastricht, *A Treatise on
Regeneration, Extracted from His System of Divinity, called Theologia theoretico-practica*, trans. unknown (New-
Haven: Thomas and Samuel Green, 1770). We render "elenchtica" in English with "elenctic" and not
"polemic." The refutation of opponents includes, for Mastricht, an historic overview of the issue and
identification of the divergent view, leading his argument toward a positive (Reformed) statement. Cf.
Richard A. Muller, *Dictionary of Latin and Greek Theological Terms, Drawn Principally from Protestant
Scholastic Theology* (Grand Rapids: Baker Books, 1985), "elencticus," 101.

32. Mastricht, *Theoretico-practica theologia, præfatio*. Here, we agree overall with Van Vliet's assessment
of Mastricht's indebtness to Ames's work and thought. Cf. Van Vliet, *William Ames*, 360-64.

33. Mastricht, *Theoretico-practica theologia*, 1102.

34. Ibid., Idea Theologiæ moralis, 1003-1117-*De Observantiâ fidei in genere*; 1119-40-*De Religione*; 1143-
57-*De justitiâ & injuriâ versus proximum*.

Teellinck's *De præcipuis exercitiis Christianis*, J. Gerhardt's *Exercitium pietatis*,[35] and G. Voetius's *Ascetica*, the author notes that to know moral theology is not sufficient; in practice it must be exercised. These works by Presbyterian, Reformed, and Lutheran authors have in common the emphasis that doctrine should be "used."

Finally, the *Theologiæ asceticæ* or *Plichtvermanende Godgeleerdheit* is divided into four parts: (1) the *praxis pietatis* in general, (2) its relation to God, (3) one's neighbor, and (4) oneself.[36] Last but not least, the publisher of the 1699 edition incorporated after the last part the outline Mastricht's "best" preaching method.[37]

Theoretico-practica theologia : Editions, Reprints, and Translations

Editions. The 1682 edition, which includes books I to IV,[38] was followed by the 1687 publication of books V to VIII.[39] Each book contains a number of chapters, which are headed by a biblical text and divided in the characteristic fourfold approach.[40] Moreover, the title indicates that Mastricht perceived this fourfold approach as a unified, uninterrupted chain.[41] Thus, for Mastricht, exegesis, doctrine, elenctic, and *praxis* are

35. Gritsch asserts that "the chief voice of [Lutheran, AN] orthodoxy in Jena, intimately linked to Wittenberg theology, was John Gerhard (1582-1637). He was an admirer of the popular writer John Arndt, who had ministered to him when he was seriously ill at age fifteen. As president and dean of Wittenberg University, Gerhard had great influence in Germany. His work is best summarized in nine volumes, titled *Loci theologici*, 1610-1622. It is the magnum opus of Lutheran orthodoxy, contending on every page that pure doctrine is derived from biblical revelation and explicates the unconditional authority of Jesus Christ. Moreover, Gerhard also added a Christian ethics [*Exercitium pietatis*, AN] showing how doctrine is to be 'used' (in Latin *de usu*)" (Eric W. Gritsch, *A History of Lutheranism* [Minneapolis: Fortress Press, 2002], 118, 119).

36. Mastricht, *Theoretico-practica theologia*, Hypotyposis Theologiæ asceticæ, 1160-63-*De praxi pietatis in genere*; 1164-79-*De praxi pietatis erga Deum*; 1181-96-*De praxi pietatis versus proximum*; 1200-1222-*De praxi pietatis versus semetipsum*.

37. The *De optima concionandi methodo paraleipomena* is discussed above. In the preface Mastricht notes that others such as Perkins, Ames, Bowles, Saldenus, and Hoornbeeck have published eminent material on this topic but that his method was widely used in the Utrecht congregations.

38. Mastricht, *Theoretico-practica theologia: qua, per capita theologica, pars dogmatica, elenchtica et practica, perpetua sumbibasei conjugantur; præcedunt in usum operis, paraleipomena, seu sceleton de optima concionandi methodo* (Amsterdam: Henricus et Vidua Theodori Boom, 1682), (1) De præcognitis Theologiæ, (2) De fide in Deum triunum, (3) De operationibus Dei, and (4) De hominis Apostasiâ à Deo.

39. Petrus van Mastricht, *Theoretico-practica theologia: qua, per singula capita theologica, pars exegetica, dogmatica, elenchtica et practica, perpetua successione conjugantur* (1687) (5) De redemptione Christi, (6) De redemptionis applicatione, (7) De ecclesia & ecclesiasticalibus and (8) De dispensatione fœderis gratiæ.

40. The characteristic fourfold division of the *loci* in the *TPT* or its translation *Beschouwende en praktikale godgeleerdheit* is noted for example by J. van Genderen, *Herman Witsius* ('s-Gravenhage: Uitg. Guido de Bres, 1953), 68; Richard A. Muller, "Giving Direction to Theology: The Scholastic Dimension," *Journal of Evangelical Theological Studies* (June 1985), 21; idem, *Post-Reformation Reformed Dogmatics* (Grand Rapids: Baker Academic, 2003), 1:219; idem, *After Calvin*, 58.

41. "perpetua sumbibasei conjugantur" (1682) and "perpetua successione conjugantur" (1687, 1699). Cf. Petrus van Mastricht, *Theoretico-practica theologia* (1682, 1687, and 1699).

linked together. The structure of the final and combined edition of 1698 is identical with the preceding editions (1682-1687) but expanded with *Idea theologiæ moralis* and *Hypotyposis theologiæ asceticæ.*[42] The content of both editions is identical, with the exception of the chapters related to *fidejussio* and *expromissio* of Christ.[43]

Reprints and Translations. The Latin edition of the *TPT* was reprinted, after Mastricht's death in 1706, 1715 and 1724.[44] The 1724 edition served for the translation in Dutch, which came available in 1749-1753 with the title *Beschouwende en praktikale godgeleerdheit.*[45] Cornelius van der Kemp (1702-1772) praised the work as a "complete

42. See Appendix I.2.1.

43. Although the following observation falls outside the scope of this study, we note a remarkable modification of content of one (and only) chapter of the 1682-1687 and 1698 (=1699) editions. In the preceding chapter, we noted that the number of disputations decreased significantly after 1687, with the exception of *De æterna Christi sponsione* in 1690. The modification of content is found in chapters, and in particular those passages, related to the suretyship (*borgtocht*) of Christ (book V chapter 1 *De Foedere Gratiæ* and 2 *De Mediatore foederis gratiæ*). An initial examination shows that Mastricht attempts to clarify a number of passages, and it appears that he seeks a middle way in respect to the definition of *fidejussio* and *expromissio* of Christ. The clarification rests herein, that Mastricht perceives Christ's *borgtocht* as *expromissio* and not *fidejussio*. Further, he notes the exceptionality of this *expromissio* (*Theoretico-practica theologia* [1699], 412, V.2.ix) and describes the *fidejussio* as conditional and absolute (*Theoretico-practica theologia* [1699], 395, V.1.ix: "Idque non sub *conditione* aliquâ, si peccator restituendus non posset præstanda præstare; sed *absolutè*, ibid., & Psal. 40:9."). Cf. B. Loonstra, *Verkiezing, verzoening, verbond: beschrijving en beoordeling van de leer van het "pactum salutis" in de gereformeerde theologie* ('s-Gravenhage: Boekencentrum, 1990), 135. Mastricht's conditionality of the *fidejussio* appears in our observation more significant than Loonstra notes. In addition, Mastricht's brother Gerard published in 1681 a disputation on *De Expromissione* (Gerhardo von Mastricht, Disputatio Juridica *De Expromissione*, resp. Anthonius Ther-Schmitten [Duisburg: Francisci Sas, 1681]). Although this disputation is in the sphere of jurisprudence and not theology, the different forms of *expromissio* are discussed. Moreover, Mastricht attests of Gerard's publication *De Susceptore* (*Borgtocht opnemer*). Cf. *TPT* (1699), fol. 637 and *Beschouwende en praktikale godgeleerdheit*, vol. 1, *Opdracht*. We identify that this only modification—which is an exception to Mastricht's consistent intellectual thought—in content needs further study. Several questions need to be addressed, such as, What prompted Mastricht to hold the disputation *De æterna Christi sponsione*? Why did he make the identified changes? Did he move from a more Cocceian position to a Voetian position, or as is more characteristic for Mastricht, did he take a middle position?

44. Petrus van Mastricht, *Theoretico-practica theologica: qua per singula capita theologica, pars exegetica, dogmatica, elenchtica et practica, perpetua successione conjugantur. Ed. nova, priori multo emendatior, et tertia saltem parte auctior, accedunt Historia ecclesiastica plena ferè, quanquam compendiosa, idea theologiæ moralis, hypotyposis theologiæ asceticæ, huic novæ editione adjecta est auctoris vita a Pontano descripta* (Utrecht: Sumptibus Societatis, 1715); idem, *Theoretico-practica theologia: qua, per singula capita theologica, pars exegetica, dogmatica, elenchtica et practica, perpetua successione conjugantur; accedunt Historia ecclesiastica plena ferè, quanquam compendiosa, idea theologiæ moralis, hypotyposis theologiæ asceticæ. Ed. Nova, accedunt Historia ecclesiastica plena ferè, quanquam compendiosa, idea theologiæ moralis, hypotyposis theologiæ asceticæ* (Utrecht: W. van de Water, J. v. Poolsum, J. Wagens, G. v. Paddenburg, 1724). The repeated pagination (325-424) of the 1698 and 1699 edition has been corrected in the identical reprints.

45. Petrus van Mastricht, *Beschouwende en praktikale godgeleerdheit: waarin, door alle de godgeleerde hoofdstukken henen, het bybelverklarende, leerstellige, wederleggende, en praktikale deel door eenen onafgebroken schakel, onderscheidenlyk samengevoegt, voorgestelt word; hierby komt een volledig kort-begrip der kerklyke geschiedenisse, een vertoog der zedelyke, en een schets der plichtvermenende godgeleerdheit, enz. ; in het Latyn beschreven; naar den laatsten druk in het Nederduitsch vertaalt, benevens de lykrede van den vermaarden hoogleeraar*

synthesis of Holy Theology, a treasure, a storehouse of all kinds of divine matters."[46] Van der Kemp continues that those who are ignorant of the Latin language will make their mouth water (*watertanden*) with the Dutch translation. Despite some claims,[47] the translator(s) is (are) unknown, but his or her (their) work overall conscientiously follows the Latin edition.[48] Besides the Dutch translation of the entire work, the chapter on *Regeneration* has been translated into English. The English translation, also by an unknown translator, was published, including footnotes, in response to a controversy in New England on the work of the Holy Spirit. The translator expressed the hope that the

Henricus Pontanus, over het afsterven van den hoogwaardigen autheur, met eene voorrede van den heer Cornelius van der Kemp, 4 vols. (Rotterdam: Hendrik van Pelt; Utrecht: Jan Jacob van Poolsum, 1749-1753). In 1756 A. Comrie and N. Holtius assume that Mastricht's work is in the hands of the readers of their *Examen van het ontwerp van tolerantie*. Cf. Alexander Comrie and Nicolaas Holtius, *Examen van het ontwerp van tolerantie, om de leere in de Dordrechtse Synode Anno 1619 vastgesteld met de veroordeelde leere der Remonstranten te verenigen: voorgesteld in eenige samenspraken, door een genootschap van voorstanders der Nederlandse formulieren van eenigheid geschreven, tot versterking van de liefhebbers der waarheid* (Amsterdam: Nicolaas Bijl, 1753-1759), sevende samenspraak over de prædestinatie, 409.

46. Petrus van Mastricht, *Beschouwende en praktikale godgeleerdheit*, vol.1, voorrede, ***3, "De voornaamste deelen der Theologie worden hier by een gevoegt op eene wys, waar van men nergens eenige weerga zal kunnen aantoonen: waarom dit boek een VOLKOMEN SAMENSTEL DER HEILIGE GODGELEERDHEIT genoemt, ja voor een Schatboek, en Voorraadhuis van allerlei Godlyke zaken gehouden mag worden." Cornelis van der Kemp was the son of Johannes van der Kemp (1664-1718), minister at Dirksland and author of the well-known- to those who value the *Nadere Reformatie*- commentary on the Heidelberg Catechism.

47. The translation is, incorrectly, assigned to Pontanus. Cf. Van Vliet, *William Ames*, 347. The reading on the Dutch title page is, "Naar den laatsten Druk in het Nederduitsch vertaalt, benevens de *Lykrede* van den vermaarden Hoogleraar Henricus Pontanus, over het Afsterven van den Hoogwaardigen Autheur." (In English: "Translated in Dutch after the last edition, including the funeral oration of the famous professor Henricus Pontanus, about the death of the highly respected author," transl., AN).

48. Exceptions in book II, include (1) translation: for example, *Deus* is rendered in *Opperwezen* (Mastricht, *Beschouwende en praktikale godgeleerdheit*, 1:164, II.2.ii: "Vermits er, zonder kennisse en erkentenisse van een Opperwezen, gene liefde....;" idem, *Theoretico-practica theologia*, II.2.ii.2, 66: "*Quatenus, absque agnitione numinis, nullus ejus amor...*"; (2) additions: "in 't Duitsch, Denkbeeld," (*Beschouwende en praktikale godgeleerdheit*, 1:178, II.2.xxii. Cf. *Theoretico-practica theologia*, 71, II.2.xxii) and "in 't Duitsch, God" (*Beschouwende en praktikale godgeleerdheit*, II.4.xv, 222. Cf. *Theoretico-practica theologia*, II.4.xv, 89.); (3) explanation: "de langen a" for Hebrew vowel point qametz. (*Beschouwende en praktikale godgeleerdheit* vol.1, 218, II.4.xi. Cf. *Theoretico-practica theologia*, II.4.xi, 88; (4) missing sentence: "Cum nec Angelorum, nec animæ propriæ essentiam, tali modo assequi valeamus." (*Beschouwende en praktikale godgeleerdheit*, 1:192, II.3.vi. Cf. *Theoretico-practica theologia*, II.3.vi, 77.).

exposition by Mastricht, who is respected by both parties, will bring reconciliation.[49] Finally, both the Dutch and English translations have recently been reprinted.[50]

In summary, the *TPT* was shaped over a period of thirty-two years (1666-1698).[51] The work is composed of *disputationes* and *loci communes*, an arrangement or system of theology, and other theological publications.[52] The work was written by a pastor and professor for students of divinity, and was meant for homiletic use. The consistency of Mastricht's intellectual thought is particularly noted in the continuity of his methodology, approach, and content. The methodology of fourfold division, the approach of *theoretico-practica*, and content—the nature, obedience, and exercise of faith—presents theology as an enterprise of exegesis, doctrine, elenctic, and *praxis*.

De Fide in Deum triunum

Structure

The doctrine of God, or *De Fide in Deum triunum*, is located between the prolegomena (book I) and the *locus* on the divine works (book III). The importance of book II is emphasized by the multiple references throughout the *TPT* to various chapters of *De Fide in Deum triunum*. More than any other book in the *TPT*, the chapters on the doctrine of God point to as foundational of Mastricht's theology.[53] In respect to its composition, book II is structured into twenty-seven chapters and opens with an exposition of faith, similar to Ames's *Marrow*, Essenius's *Compendium*, and Witsius's *Symbolum*.[54] Yet Mastricht differs from most of his contemporaries, who positioned the

49. Petrus van Mastricht, *Treatise on Regeneration, Extracted from His System of Divinity, Called Theologia theoretico-practica*, trans. unknown (New Haven: Thomas and Samuel Green, in the Old Council Chamber, 1770), v, vi. The English translation of the chapter on regeneration is probably part of a body of material related to a debate on the work of the Holy Spirit in eighteenth-century New England that has not yet been studied.

50. Mastricht, *Beschouwende en praktikale godgeleerdheit* (reprint, F.N. Snoek: Ermelo, 2003); Peter van Mastricht, *A Treatise on Regeneration*, ed. Brandon Withrow (Morgan: Soli Deo Gloria Publications, 2002).

51. This period enhances Van Vliet's notion that "Van Mastricht worked on his masterpiece, *Praktikale Godgeleerdheit*, for more than twenty years." Cf. Van Vliet, *William Ames*, 347. See Appendix I.2.2 for an overview of how Mastricht's publications contributed to the *Theoretico-practica theologia*.

52. See Appendix I.2.3.

53. Petrus van Mastricht, *Theoretico-practica theologica*, III.4.xvii; III.4.xviii; III.5.xxii; III.6.iii; III.6.xx (printed as xix); III.6.l; III.7.ix; III.7.xxvi; III.7.xxx; III.8.xxi; III.9.xxvii; III.10.ii; III.10.xxxvi; III.11.xiii; III.11.xiv; III.12.ii; IV.4.xxx; V.1.viii; V.1.xx; V.1.xxxvi; V.1.xlvii; V.2.xix; V.2.xxiii; V.2.xxxiii; V.3.xxv; V.3.xxx; V.4.xiv; V.4.xxviii; V.6.xi; V.6.xi; V.8.xii; V.9.xi; V.10.ii; V.10.xix; V.11.ii; V.11.xxxi; V.11.xxxiv; V.12.i; V.12.ii; V.12.xxiii; V.12.xxvi; V.13.xiii; V.13.xix; V.16.xiii; V.17.xxi; V.18.xli [xlii (Dutch edition]; VI.1.xvi; VI.1.xxvi; VI.1.xxvi; VI.4.xv; VI.4.xxvii; VI.5; VI.6; VI.6.xxvii; VI.6.xxix; VI.6.xxix; VI.8.vi; VI.9.ix; VII.1.xxv; VII.3.ii/ii.2.

54. William Ames, *Marrow of Sacred Divinity* (London: Edwards Griffin, 1642); Andreas Essenius, *Compendium theologiæ dogmaticum: ubi præter explicationes theticas, & assertiones scripturarias, in controversiis vera sententia passim confirmatur argumentis, ad certas & paucas classes revocatis: præcipuæ adversariorum*

discussion of faith in the soteriological *loci*.[55] Although the location of chapters is not always significant in relation to the actual identification of the topic,[56] it raises the question of what motivated the author to place the chapter on faith at the beginning of his discussion on the doctrine of God. Mastricht argues that to desire and seek after God by saving faith, one needs to be "convinced and assured"[57] that God is, and that He is and communicates His all-sufficiency. With this point of departure and perspective on faith as the *principium cognoscendi internum*, Mastricht goes on to describe the object of faith: God in His sufficiency and efficiency. The latter is discussed in book III, *De operationibus Dei*. The divine sufficiency is discussed in book II, and distinguished in (1) *Existentia & cognitione Dei*; (2) *Essentia Dei*: the divine names and attributes; and (3) *Subsistentia Dei*: the Trinity and divine Persons.[58]

In addition to the distinctive entry to the doctrine of God, Mastricht differs also with his contemporaries by dividing the divine attributes into the sections: *Quid sit Deus*,[59] *Quantus sit Deus*,[60] and *Qualis sit Deus*.[61] This particular (rhetorical) distinction

---

exceptiones atque objectiones clare proponuntur, & solvuntur: usus autem practici suis locis etiam adscribuntur (Utrecht: Meinardus à Dreunen, 1669); Herman Witsius, *Exercitationes Sacræ in Symbolum quod Apostolorum dicitur*, ed. sec., (Franeker: Johannes Gyselaar, 1689).

55. This observation is nuanced when one considers that the overall structure (Book I-VII) of the *TPT* parallels other continental seventeenth-century works of reformed systematic theology, such as, J. Polyander, A. Rivetus, A. Walaeus, A. Thysius, *Synopsis purioris theologiæ* (Leiden: J. & D. Elsevier, 1625); Cf. sixth edition, H. Bavinck (Leiden: D. Donner, 1881); Samuel Maresius, *Collegium Theologicum sive Systema Breve Universæ Theologiæ* (Groningen: Franciscus Bronchorstius, 1656); Johannes Maccovius, *Loci communes theologici* (Franeker: Johannes Arcerius, 1650); Franciscus Burmannus, *Synopsis Theologiæ & speciatim Oeconomiæ Fœderum Dei* (Utrecht: C. J. Noenardus, 1671); Simon Oomius, *Institutiones Theologiæ Practicæ* (Samuel Haringhouk, 1676); Theodor Undereyck, *Halleluja, das ist, Gott in dem Sünder verkläret oder Des sünders Wanderstab zur Erkäntnüs, Geniessung und Verklärung Gottes, alß des höchsten Gutes* (Bremen: H. Brauer, 1678); Johannes Hoornbeeck, *Theologiæ practicæ* (Frankfurt: Ernst Claudium Bailliar, 1680); Johannes Cloppenburgh, *Theologica Opera Omnia* (Amsterdam: Gerardus Borstius, 1684); Franciscus Turrettini, *Institutio theologiæ elencticæ* (Geneva: Samuelis de Tournes, 1679-1685) NB. Turretin places the topic of faith between Christology and justification; Abraham Heidanus, *Corpus Theologiæ Christianæ in Quindecim Locos* (Leiden: Johannem de Vivie & Jordanus Luchtmans, 1686); Wilhelmus à Brakel, *ΛΟΓΙΚΗ ΛΑΤΡΕΙΑ, dat is Redelijke Godtsdienst in welken de Goddelijke Waerheden van het Genade-Verbondts worden verklaert, tegen partyen beschermt, en tot de practyke aengedrongen* (Rotterdam: Reynier van Doesburgh, 1700); Herman Witsius, *De oeconomia Fœderum Dei cum hominibus* (Herborne, Nassau: Johannes Nicolai Andreas, 1712); idem, *Oefeningen over de Grondstukken van het Algemeyne Christelyke Geloove en het Gebed des Heeren* (Rotterdam: Daniel Beman, 1699); Johann Heinrich Heidegger, *Corpus theologiæ christianæ* (Zürich: David Gessner, 1700).

56. Richard A. Muller, *The Unaccommodated Calvin* (Oxford, New York: Oxford University Press, 2000), 186, § 6.

57. Mastricht, *Theoretico-practica theologia*, 65, II.ii.1.

58. Ibid. See Appendix I.2.3 for an overview of the structure of book II, the doctrine of God.

59. "Quid sit Deus" includes *De spiritualitate et simplicitate Dei* and *De immutabilitate Dei*.

60. "Quantus sit Deus" includes *De unitate Dei, De infinitate et magnitudine, De immensitate et omnipræsentiâ Dei*, and *De æternitate Dei*.

unites Mastricht's methodology with that of medieval thinkers such as Lombard, Acquinas, Scotus, and other Protestant "Scholastics" such as Beze, Zanchi, Gerhard, and Perkins. All of them, Muller argues, establish the order of argument with such basic questions as "Does it exist (*An sit*)?" "What is it (*Quid sit*)?" and "Of what sort is it (*Qualis sit*)?" Mastricht difference is further expressed by the fact that the divine attributes discussed in the section '*Quid*' and '*Quantus*' are combined and that the '*Qualis*' patterns after the Lutheran classification. Thus the *attributa negativa* (*Quid* and *Quantus*) and *attributa positiva* (*Qualis*) are corresponding to the two ways of denominating divine attributes: the *via negativa* and *via eminentiæ*.[62] Moreover, it is clear that Mastricht follows a similar pattern, moving from God's existence to His essence and essential properties and then to the divine attributes in a broad sense and finally to the doctrine of the Trinity specifically considered.[63] These "scholastic" divisions are not absent in other seventeenth-century systems of theology, but Mastricht is unique in that he explicitly uses these devices to divide his treatment of the doctrine of God. Finally, the concluding chapter of the *Subsistentia Dei*, on the Holy Spirit, reaches back, in our opinion, to the pneumatological character of the opening chapter of *De fide in Deum triunum*.

In conclusion, the structure of the doctrine of God in the *TPT* is relatively unique for a seventeenth-century theologian. It is relative, in the sense that other Protestant "Scholastics," like Mastricht, have made use of the (rhetorical) devices in their works. However, it is unique that Mastricht is more precise, probably in order to achieve (more) clarity. This clarity and uniqueness is heightened by the fourfold division—exegesis, doctrine, elenctic, and *praxis*—of each chapter of the *De fide in Deum triunum*.[64]

Sources

Two motifs prompts the examination of the sources that Mastricht used in book II of the *TPT*. First and foremost, it assists in understanding what intellectual trajectories may have contributed to Mastricht's *magnum opus* and in particular his doctrine of God. Second, the *TPT* has been assessed by others as a commentary on Ames's *Medulla*, or *Marrow of Sacred Divinity*. Therefore, an examination of the underlying sources of the *De fide in Deum triunum* helps us to identify the (historical) intellectual trajectories of the *TPT* and to evaluate former appraisals of it.

An examination of book II of the *TPT* reveals immediately the extensive array of its sources.[65] In this book Mastricht refers to 170 different authors, which include forty-five citations of authors, seventy references to authors and their works, and fifty-five author-

---

61. "Qualis sit Deus" includes *De vita et immortalitate Dei, De intellectu, scientia et sapientia Dei, voluntate Dei* (which includes: *bonitate Dei, amore, gratiâ, misericordiâ, longanimitate et clementiâ Dei, justitiâ Dei, sanctitate Dei*) and *De potestate et potentiâ Dei*.

62. Muller, *Dictionary of Latin and Greek Theological Terms*, 50. Muller also notes, here, the Lutheran orthodoxy position of the division of divine attributes.

63. Muller, *After Calvin*, 28: "What unites these thinkers is...a common method."

64. Part III of this study provides a detailed examination of the fourfold division.

65. See Appendix I.2.4.

name references. Analysis of these combined references is revealing. First, it shows the distribution of these references throughout the four-fold division of a chapter. Second, it reveals the leading authors and opponents. In respect to the former, the distribution of these combined references are sixty percent in the elenctic sections, twenty-one percent in the doctrinal sections, eleven percent in the practical sections, and eight percent in the exegetical sections of the *De fide in Deum triunum*. Furthermore, twenty percent of the references are citations, and the rest are equally divided between being a reference to an author and his work and an author reference only.

In respect to leading authors, the most frequently and positively referenced author is Augustine (twenty-two percent of the citations). Further analysis shows that half of these sixteen citations[66] are in the doctrinal sections, followed by thirty-eight percent in the practical and twelve percent in the elenctic sections. In the latter section, Mastricht refers to this church father for (historical) support of his (Reformed) position. Moreover, the cited works of Augustine include: *De Civitate Dei* (3x), *De Trinitate* (3x), *Enarrationes in Psalmos* (7x), *Collatio cum Maximino Arianorum episcopo*, *Confessiones*, and *De Fide*. Moreover *De Civitate Dei* and *De Trinitate* are referenced solely in the elenctic (ninety-percent) and doctrinal (ten percent) sections. Finally, in the exegetical section of both chapter 5 (*On the attributes of God in general*) and chapter 16 (*On the goodness of God*), there are references to his name. Next to the bishop of Hippo, Bernardus (1090-1153) and the Calvinistic[67] Cartesian theologian Wittichius (1625-1687) are the most cited authors in book II. Bernardus is primarily quoted in the practical sections and always in the context of the *theologia practica*. In addition, when one considers the aspects of the piety of Bernardus such as, the love of God, Christ-meditation, *brautmystik* and communion with God, we observe that Mastricht's work echo's Bernardus' spirituality.[68] Wittichius is mentioned only in the elenctic sections. In the latter, Mastricht refutes the Cartesian position of Wittichius's *Theologia Pacifica* (1671).[69] Thus, the most important orientation,

66. Mastricht, *Theoretico-practica theologia*, II.ii, vi, vii, x(2x), xi(2x), xii, xiii, xv, xvi(3x), xx(2x), xxiii.

67. Thomas A. McGahagen, *Cartesianism in the Netherlands, 1639-1676: The New Science and the Calvinistic Counter-Reformation* (Ph.D. diss., University of Pennsylvania, 1976), 11.

68. For the practical sections see Mastricht, *Theoretico-practica theologia*, II.4.viii, 87; II.10.viii, 123; II.12.xxiv, 141; II.16.xxii, 177. On the four aspects of Bernardus' piety see A. de Reuver, *Verborgen omgang, Sporen van Spiritualiteit in Middeleeuwen en Nadere Reformatie* (Zoetermeer: Boekencentrum, 2002), 30-51, cf. K. Ruh, *Geschichte der abendländischen Mystik.Erster Band. Die Grundlegung durch die Kirchenväter und die Mönchstheologie des 12. Jahrhunderts* (München, 1990), 229-275; Ray C. Petry (ed.), *Late Medieval Mysticism* (Philadelphia: Westminster Press, 1957), 47-53; *Bernard of Clairvaux Selected Works*, transl. by G.R. Evans, introd. by Jean Leclerq, (New York: Paulist Press, 1987), 35-53; Mastricht, *Theoretico-practica theologia*, I.1.xlix, 15, I.2.lxxii, 44, I.1.ii, 51, I.1.xii, 52, I.1.xxv, 56, I.1.lv, 64, II.4.viii, 87, II.8.iii, 112, II.10.viii, 123, II.12.xxiii, 141, IV.30.xxxiv, 371, V.3.xxix, 430, V.3.xxxiv, 432, V.3.xxxv, 448, V.15.xxii, 584, VI.2.vi, 649, VI.15.692, VI.15.xxv, 697, VI.8.xxvii, 745. It is noteworthy that a majority of these references make mention of the Song of Songs.

69. It is noteworthy that all citations and references point to different chapters of Wittichius's work and are used diversely. Mastricht, *Theoretico-practica theologia*, II.v-Attributes of God in General; II.xi-Eternity of God; II.xii-Immortality of God; II.xiii-Intellect, Knowledge, and Wisdom of God' II.xiv-Veracity of God; and II.xv-Power of God. Further it is noteworthy that, in this context, Mastricht refers to

outside that of Scripture, in the doctrinal sections of book II of the *TPT* is Augustine. For the *theologia practica* this is Bernardus, and for the elenctical sections this is directed against Wittichius.

Further analysis reveals two other intellectual threads: patristic and rabbinic literature. References to patristic works include those of Athanasius, Irenæus, Cyrillus, and Nazianzenus, and they are primarily used in the doctrinal sections. The references to rabbinic works include those of Maimonides, Hakkadosch, Jarchi, and Kimchi, which are predominantly used in an exegetical context.

In summary, we observe, then, that the main sources (patristic, rabbinic, Augustine, Bernardus, and Wittichius) in book II of the *TPT*, *De fide in Deum triunum*, coincide with Mastricht's study and work: theology, Hebrew, and anti-Cartesianism. In contrast to these findings the citations and references to Ames' works are not dominant present.

We conclude, this chapter, then, by a remark in respect to the *TPT* in general and book two, *De Fide in Deum triunum* or the doctrine of God, in particular.

In respect to the former, the *TPT* is a lifelong project of Mastricht. Many of his publications contributed to the writing of the *TPT*: an arrangement or system of theology to be used in the preaching ministry. Further, though the structure of the *TPT* is similar to other works of contemporaries in respect to the *loci* of Reformed theology, there is a significant difference: the *locus* of eschatology is treated as part of book VIII on the dispensations of the covenant of grace. In addition, Mastricht's fourfold approach to the *loci* is unique and represents a culmination and codification of the exegetical, doctrinal, elenctic or polemical, and practical thought of seventeenth-century post-Reformation Reformed orthodoxy. Finally, the study of the *TPT* has been largely ignored over the centuries. Among several possible reasons is that the Latin edition was accessible primarily to academically trained readers, which accounts for the international recognition of the work in the eighteenth century and its subsequent fall into obscurity. In addition, the Dutch translation was probably overshadowed by the tremendous success of works such as *De Redelijke Godtsdienst* by Wilhelmus à Brakel and the *Hallelujah* by Theodor Untereyck.

In respect to book II of the *TPT*, *De Fide in Deum triunum*, Mastricht differs with his contemporaries by placing his discussion on faith in the first chapter of the book on the doctrine of God, while others put this topic in the context of the so-called *ordo salutis*. Furthermore, Mastricht's employment of the particular (rhetorical) distinction of *Quid sit, Quantus sit* and *Qualis sit* unites his methodology with that of medieval thinkers and other Protestant "Scholastics." This continuity in respect to methodology is also identified by the diverse and frequent references to patristic, rabbinic, and medieval sources in book II. These sources, in addition to Scripture as the primary basis, have shaped Mastricht's theological work and testify to a continuation of the orthodox

---

his own works in no less than twenty-five percent of the citations, notably to the *Gangræna* and one time to his *Prodromus* in the practical section dealing with the omnipresence of God.

theological tradition. Thus, contrary to the assessments of the secondary literature,[70] the characterization of the *TPT* as a commentary on Ames' works cannot be exclusively justified. The focus on Ames in respect to the *TPT*, has, in our opinion, led scholarship to ignore the diversity and riches of Mastricht's resources. In summary, the varied sources of the *TPT*, its structure and theology, its differences from and similarities to other seventeenth-century post-Reformation works, and the broad international interest in his work in Mastricht 's own time, as well as in eighteenth-century New England, warrant the study of this monumental work of Reformed theology.

---

70. W. Goeters, *Die Vorbereitung des Pietismus*; K. Reuter, *Wilhelm Amesius, der führende Theologe des erwachenden reformierten Pietismus*; C. Graafland, "Gereformeerde Scholastiek VI, De invloed van de Scholastiek op de *Nadere Reformatie*," in *Theologia Reformatica*, XXX, no.4, (1987).

Part 2

The Premises of the *Theoretico-practica theologica*

Chapter 1
Prolegomena

Introduction and Statement of the Problem

An accurate construct of Mastricht's theology, and in particular the doctrine of God, requires an examination of the premises of his theology. Furthermore, such assessment is necessitated by the different results of scholarship on post-Reformation Reformed orthodoxy. These differences concern (1) the nature of post-Reformation Reformed theology—including central dogmas such as predestination and covenant and the influence of rationalism in particular on the doctrine of God;[1] (2) the impact of Scholasticism and Aristotelianism—including the negative, theologized appraisal of "Scholasticism"; and (3) sources of knowledge—a bifurcation of natural theology and Scripture; the development of a positive *locus* of natural theology independent from Scripture and soteriology and complementary to special revelation.[2] Of course, some of the results of older scholarly literature have extensive implications for our interpretative framework. However, here our concern is to examine Mastricht's own position on the nature of theology, Scholasticism, Aristotelianism, Scripture, faith, and reason (*ratio*).

Therefore, we will examine Mastricht's premises leading up to the exposition of the divine existence and essence and Holy Trinity. Chapter 1 focuses on Mastricht's prolegomena, which includes the nature of theology—the method, description and definition of theology,— and Scripture. Chapter 2 focuses on Mastricht's exposition of faith. Our examination of this *locus* includes a review of its location in the *Theoretico-practica theologia* (*TPT*) and its content.

1. A. Tholuck, *Vorgeschichte des Rationalismus* (Berlin: E. Anton, 1861); idem, *Geschichte des Rationalismus: Erste Abteilung, Geschichte des Pietismus und des ersten Stadium der Aufklärung* (Berlin: E. Anton, 1865); P. Althaus, *Die Prinzipien der deutschen reformierten Dogmatik im Zeitalter der aristotelischen Scholastik* (Leipzig: A. Deichertsche Verlagsbuchhandlung Werner Scholl, 1914); H. E. Weber, *Reformation, Orthodoxie und Rationalismus*, 3 vol. (Gütersloh: Bertelsmann, 1937-1951); E. Bizer, *Frühorthodoxie und Rationalismus* (Zürich: EVZ Verlag, 1963).

2. See for an overview of different approaches of older and recent scholarship, Richard A. Muller, *After Calvin. Studies in the Development of a Theological Tradition* (Oxford: Oxford University Press, 2003), 63-80. On the relationship of Aristotelianism and Scholasticism, see Paul Oskar Kristeller, *Renaissance Thought and its Sources* (New York: Columbia University Press, 1979). On Ramus see W. J. Ong, *Ramus. Method and Decay of Dialogue: From the Art of Discourse to the Art of Reason* (Cambridge, MA: Harvard University Press, 1958).

The Nature of Theology

Mastricht opens the first chapter of the *TPT* with an exegesis and scope of 1 Tim. 6:2-3 [3] as the biblical foundation for his explanation of the nature of theology, which is divided in a discussion of the method, the description and definition of theology. [4]

Method of Theology

In respect to method, Mastricht argues that order is important in a system of theology.[5] First, he affirms this importance by testimonies of Holy Scripture (1 Tim. 6:2, 3; 2 Sam. 23:5; 2 Tim. 2:15; Rom.12:1), creeds, patristic fathers, medieval doctors and sixteenth-century reformers.[6] In particular, Mastricht notes that theology should be taught in accordance with 1 Timothy 6:2-3 and should be ordered after the covenant of grace, according to 2 Samuel 23:5: both these thoughts are reflected in Cocceius' theology.[7] Moreover, theology should be constructed rightly, according to 2 Timothy 2:15, because it is a "*redelijke Godtsdienst*"[8] (Rom. 12:1), a thought reflected in the title of Wilhelmus à Brakel's (1635-1711) work.[9] Second, he argues that such an order is also

3. Petrus van Mastricht, *Theoretico-practica theologia qua, per singula capita theologica, pars exegetica, dogmatica, elenchtica et practica, perpetua successione conjugantur; accedunt historia ecclesiastica, plena quidem, sed compendiosa, idea theologiæ moralis, hypotyposis theologiæ asceticæ etc. proin opus quasi novum* (Utrecht: Thomas Appels, 1699), I.1, 1. Mastricht renders 1 Timothy 6:2-3 in Latin as follows, "Ista doce & exhortare. Si quis diversam doctrinam, neque accedit sanis sermonibus, Domini nostri Jesu Christi, & ei quæ secundum pietatem est doctrinæ; is turget nihil sciens &c." "These things teach and exhort. If any man teach otherwise, and consent not to wholesome words, even the words of our Lord Jesus Christ, and to the doctrine which is according to godliness" (King James Version).

4. Ibid., I.1.iii, 2, *De Methodo Theologiæ*; I.1.ix, 4, *De Definito Theologiæ*; and I.1.xxxvi, 12, *De Definitione Theologiæ*. Each section contains a doctrinal, elenctical and practical part.

5. Ibid., I.1.iii, 2: "Jam è dictis, præliminariter emergit, quod *Theologia, certa sit tradenda methodo* . . ."

6. Ibid., I.1.iii, 2, 3. The creeds: Apostolic, Nicea, Ephesus, Chalcedon; the patristic fathers: Clement of Alexandria (*Stromaton*), Origenes (*Peri Archon*), Lactantius (*Institutionum divinarum*), Gregory of Nazianzi (*De Theologia*), Augustine (*De Doctrina Christiana, Encheidirion ad Laurentium*), Ruffinus (*Expositio Symboli*), Theodoretus (*Epitome divinorum dogmatum*), Prosper (*Sententiae*), Damascenus (*De Orthodoxa fide*); the medieval doctors: Lombardus (*Sententiae*), Albert Magnus, Thomas Aquinas (*Summa Theologiæ*), Scotus, Bonaventura; and the sixteenth-century reformers: Zwingli, Luther, Melanchton, Calvin, Bullinger, Musculus, Aretius, Martyr, Ursinus and Zanchius.

7. Johannes Cocceius, *Opera Omina Theologica* (Amsterdam: P&J Blaev, 1701), vol. 7, *Aphorismi per universam Theologiam*, 3, § 1: "Theologia est doctrina secundum veram pietatem;" ibid., *De Foedere Dei in Genere*, 45, § 3: "Sic 2 Sam. 23:5, *Nam non est recta domus mea cum Deo, sed fœdus æternum* (promissionem æternum) *posuit mihi...*;" ibid., *Summa Theologiæ*, 134, § 8: "...sit Theologi cognitio; & quam vocat *doctrinam secundum pietatem*, hoc est, ad pietatem efficiendam idoneam ea sit doctrina Theologi, Tit. 1:1, 1 Tim. 6:3;" idem, vol. 6, *Commentarius in Epist. I ad Timotheum*, 190, § 14: "*Doctrina secundum pietatem* est doctrina & institutio accommodata ad ingenerandam animo *pietatem*."

8. Petrus van Mastricht, *Theoretico-practica theologia*, I.1.iii, 2. Cf. Idem, *Beschouwende en praktikale godgeleerdheit*, I.1.iii, 4.

9. Wilhelmus à Brakel, *ΛΟΓΙΚΗ ΛΑΤΡΕΙΑ, dat is Redelyke Godtsdienst, in welken de Goddelijke Waerheden des Genaden-Verbondts worden verklaert, tegen partyen beschermt, en tot de practyke aengedrongen*, 2 vols. (Rotterdam: Reynier van Doesburgh, 1700).

derived from (1) the nature of God (God and his manifest order), (2) the nature of theology (doctrines are dispersed but related throughout Scripture), and (3) the benefits of a method (issues are clarified and facilitate the memory and strengthen the argument).[10] These two main arguments for order leads Mastricht to organize theology distinctly, based on Scripture, and to divide it into *pars exegetica* and *pars dogmatica* or *didactica*,[11] *pars elenctica*, and *pars practica*.[12] For Mastricht, then, theology begins with an analysis of the biblical text, presenting the scope and explicating doctrinal, elenctic, and practical issues. With this emphasis on the need of a (orderly) theological method, he yet warns against both excesses and defects. According to Mastricht, the latter is characteristic of "Anabaptist, Fanatics, and Enthusiasts,"[13] including "some Reformed theologians," who in their ignorance and opposition to philosophy eliminate any method of theology. In respect to the excess of method and order in theology, Mastricht is thinking of the philosophical "schoolmen." That is to say, the critique of these "schoolmen" diminished the simplicity of theology. This assertion is refuted by Mastricht's argument that the excesses may diffuse the theology but not the method itself.[14] This (orderly) method of theology, then, is employed by Mastricht in the organization of the theological *loci*.[15]

Mastricht concludes his reflection on the *methodus* of theology with some practical observations. First, one should be motivated to use a method of theology. The proper use of such a method avoids confusion in teaching and preaching. Explications that have no relation to a subject of theology can be eliminated by the proper use of method.[16] Moreover, he infers from the biblical text (1 Tim. 6:2) that it is better to follow the methodological advice of the apostle Paul: first teach and then admonish. Second, he recommends that the *modus* of the method consent with the subject of theology and

10. See below for this possible Ramist notion.

11. The title of the *Prodromus* does not mention *exegetica* but is more extensive in its exegesis than later works, while most of his publications mentions "didactico" instead of "dogmatica" except the *Theoretico-practica theologia* (1699).

12. Mastricht, *Theoretico-practica theologia*, I.1.v, 3: "Articulatius dicam quod optem ac sectabor ξὺν θεῳ pro virili. Nempe ut capita theologica 1. *positivè* probentur Scripturis...2.*elencticè* vindicentur...3. *practicè* applicentur..." Cf. idem, *Theologiæ didactico-elenchtico-practicæ prodromus tribus speciminibus* (Amsterdam: Johannes van Someren, 1666), *præfatio*.

13. Ibid., I.1.vi, 3.

14. Ibid., I.1.vi, 3, 4: "Quod 3. *Simplicitati Theologiæ deroget methodus & artificii logici subtilitas. Resp.* 1. Expugnat hoc quidem *excessum* Scholasticorum; non autem methodem θεολουμένοις naturalem. Tum 2. Falsum est: neque enim ordo rem ordinatam variat, aut ejus perfectioni quicquam detrahit. Et si Theologiæ deroget: non vitio methodi derogat; sed imperitia artificis, Theologiam torquentis, ad perversas suas regulas; nec methodum, Theologiæ prudenter adaptantis."

15. Ibid., title page: "*qua, per singula capita theologica, pars exegetica, dogmatica, elenchtica et practica, perpetuâ successione conjugantur.*" The individual sections—exegesis, doctrine, elenctic, and practical—are discussed in part IV of this study.

16. Ibid., I.1.vii, 4. NB. The proper use of method to avoid confusion in teaching is the entire genuine issue of scholasticism in theology.

the comprehension of the hearer.[17] In respect to the latter, Mastricht recommends use of catechetical instruction for beginners and for the more advanced ones a systematic method that includes partly definitions, divisions, principles, and arguments and partly refutations. Further, one should use for the adults exegesis and exposition of the biblical text so that the catechetical instruction and systematic method can be applied. Finally, the *modus* of the method should be utilized for piety, because "all scripture is inspired by God and profitable for teaching, for reproof, for correction, and for training in righteousness (2 Tim. 3:16)." [18] Mastricht, then, is concerned with a proper method of theology. It is a concern that dominates his *magnum opus* and its fourfold model—exegesis, doctrine, elenctic, and *praxis*.

Description of theology

In the second part of chapter 1 of the *TPT*, Mastricht focuses on the description of theology. He includes aspects such as etymological concerns, the archetypal-ectypal distinction, natural theology, the *theoretico-practica* paradigm, and Scholasticism.

Etymology and Archetypal-Ectypal Theology. Like other post-Reformation Reformed orthodox theologians,[19] Mastricht argues that the word *theology* originates from non-Christians. However, although it cannot be found in Scripture, it is not an unscriptural word.[20] With John Owen (1616-1683), he agrees that theology is speaking about God and proceeds from God. Moreover, Mastricht acknowledges that though the word *theology* is not used in Scripture, synonyms are used in the Old Testament (חכמה האלהים—the *sapientia Dei*; הידיעת התוריית—the *scientia legalis*; and תורה תלמוד—the *studium legis*) and the New Testament (λογια τῶ Θεῶ, Rom. 3:2; 1 Pet. 4:11; εὐσέβεια, 1 Tim. 3:16; 1 Tim. 6:3) or both (דרך or ὁδός-the way).[21] Following the discussion on etymology and synonyms, Mastricht also asserts that the word "theology" has an archetypal and

---

17. Ibid., I.1.viii (modus), 4: "Et, quo methodum rectius sectentur; tria suaserim observanda, ut methodus congruat 1. cum *re tractanda*...2. cum *captu* auditorum..."

18. Ibid.: "3. Cum *utilitate* ac pietate qua cuncta traducantur ad *praxin* & in ea substistatur, 2 Tim. 3:16."

19. Johannem Polyandrum *et al.*, *Synopsis purioris theologiæ* (Leiden: Elsevier, 1625), Disp. I, 1; Samuel Maresius, *Collegium Theologicum sive Systema breve universæ Theologiæ* (Groningen: Franciscus Bornchorstius, 1656), 1; Johannes Cloppenburgh, *Theologica Opera Omnia* (Amsterdam: Gerardus Borstius, 1684), 1:697; Simon Oomius, *Dissertatie van de Onderwijsingen in de Practycke der Godgeleerdheid* (Bolsward: Samuel van Haringhouk, 1672), 4; Franciscus Burmannus, *Synopsis Theologiæ & speciatim Oeconomiæ Foederum Dei* (Utrecht: C. J. Noenardus, 1671), 1:9; cf. Richard A. Muller, *Post-Reformation Reformed Dogmatics* (Grand Rapids: Baker Academic, 2003), 1:152-55.

20. Mastricht, *Theoretico-practica theologia*, I.1.xiii, 5: "Quantum ad vocis originem, ea procul dubio Ethnicis debetur...Quicquid sit, vox saltem Scripturis ἄγραφος est, nec αὐτολεξει, nec κατ' ἀναλογίαν, ibidem exstans." In this paragraph Mastricht questions the canonicity of the inscription in the book of Revelation, which contains the word *theology*.

21. In addition, Mastricht notes the Latin term *religio*, "which is derived from *relegendo* or *religando*" (Ibid., I.1.xiv, 5).

ectypal meaning.[22] Archetypal theology notes the divine self-knowledge, and ectypal theology is a human reflection resting on the former.[23] Moreover, ectypal theology should be distinguished, according to Mastricht, in a theology for those who are in *patria* and heaven and in a theology of the pilgrims on earth or the *theologia viatorum*.[24] In addition, Mastricht notes that ectypal theology is distinguished in natural or revealed theology.[25] The use of the language by Mastricht of *in via* and *in patria* points to a teleological and eschatological orientation. Theology here on earth is always a theology of pilgrims. Again, Mastricht's explication of theology and its distinctions are in agreement with other post-Reformation Reformed orthodox theologians.[26]

Natural theology. In the context of his description of theology, Mastricht touches also on the issues of natural theology. First, he notes that special revelation does not exclude natural theology because "natural theology has nothing that Scripture does not have."[27] Further, special revelation is directed to that which one believes and does, while natural theology consists of science, resting partly in the intellect and partly in the will. Moreover, Mastricht argues that natural theology, as distinct from false theology, does have its use, *contra* the Socinians.[28] First, in respect to God, it holds the ungodly without

22. Petrus van Mastricht, *Theoretico-practica theologia*, I.1.xv, 5. The scholastic language of archetype and ectype is further noted in Mastricht's treatment on the covenant of grace, where he distinguishes between prototypal and ectypal, that of eternity and temporal. Ibid., V.1.vii, 393.

23. On this (Scotist) distinction, see W. J. van Asselt, "The Fundamental meaning of Theology: Archetypal and Ectypal Theology in Seventeenth-century Reformed Thought," *Westminster Theological Journal* 64 (2002):322.

24. Mastricht, *Theoretico-practica theologia*, I.1.xv, 5: "Interim *Theologiæ* vox, non uni subest homonymiæ, quatenus jam *archetypam* notat Dei ipsius, de seipso cognitionem; jam *ectypam* prioris qualecunque apographum. Hanc rursus dispescunt, in *comprehensorum* qui sunt in patria, in cœlo; & *viatorum* , qui in terris." On the definitions of *theologia*, *archetypa*, and *ectypa*, see Richard A. Muller, *Dictionary of Latin and Greek Theological Terms, Drawn Principally from Protestant Scholastic Theology* (Grand Rapids: Baker Books, 1985), 299, 300. See also Van Asselt, "Archetypal and Ectypal Theology," 332; Muller, *Post-Reformation Reformed Dogmatics*, 1:225-228.

25. Mastricht, *Theoretico-practica theologia*, I.1.xv, 5: "Theologia, vel *naturalis* est; vel *revelata*. De quibus obviæ sunt, Locorum communium observationes."

26. Van Asselt, "Archetypal and Ectypal Theology"; Muller, *Post-Reformation Reformed Dogmatics*, 1:229-38.

27. Mastricht, *Theoretico-practica theologia*, I.1.xvi, 5: "Neque enim Theologia *naturalis*, quicquam habet quod non habeat *Scriptura*."

28. Mastricht raises the question of whether natural theology is innate or can be acquired. On the one hand, he opposes the excesses of the medieval theologians who use philosophy to support doctrines such as transubstantiation. On the other hand, he disagrees with those who are in defect, such as the Socinians, who deny any form of natural theology. Mastricht refutes the latter by noting that natural theology is found in Scripture (Rom. 1:19, 20; Ps. 19:2; Ps. 104; Acts 14:15), attested in the conscience, which bears witness, and with their thoughts either accuses or else excuses individuals (Rom. 2:15). The Reformed, according to Mastricht acknowledge that natural theology is innate and can be acquired, not by everyone, and is not sufficient for salvation. Cf. ibid., I.1.xxiii, 7: "Refellit negantes *naturalem* istam Theologiam 1. *Scriptura*...2. *Conscientia*...3. *Gentium consensus*...4. *Experientia*...."

excuse (Rom. 1:20), and second, in convinces the "heathens and atheist" (Acts 17:24, 25, 26, Ps. 8:2, 5, Matt. 6:26). Third, in respect to mankind, special revelation is confirmed by natural theology as the latter consents with the former. Fourth, Mastricht asserts that the use of natural theology invites those who acknowledge the revealed truth to pursue the highest good, which is confirmed in the natural world.[29] Contrary to the proper use of natural theology, Mastricht points also to a threefold abuse of natural theology. This is the case when, first, natural theology is used as foundation and norm for special revelation; second, when it is claimed to be sufficient for salvation; and, third, when it is a common theology, whereby one can be saved by reason from nature and without and outside Christ.[30] Thus, for Mastricht *theologia naturalis* can present knowledge of God, but this knowledge is insufficient for human salvation though sufficient to leave humanity without excuse in their sin. Natural theology is, according to Mastricht, not an independent issue but part of special revelation: it is not a separate source of knowledge.[31] Natural theology is, moreover, for Mastricht, not the foundation upon which revealed theology can be built.

Scholasticism. Recent scholarship has observed that it is correct to let the Protestant "Scholastics" themselves define Scholasticism.[32] This observation gives an opportunity to present Mastricht's own thought on the subject and to examine the incongruity of describing Mastricht as an (anti-)Scholastic.[33] Moreover, the examination of this issue may contribute to our main concern of this thesis: the relationship of Protestant Scholasticism to method and piety. Mastricht addresses the issue of Scholasticism in the context of his description of theology. Further, beyond this context, the *TPT* attests to other scholastic issues such as definitions, distinctions, and sources. Therefore, while focusing on book II of the *TPT*, the doctrine of God, we will also examine "scholasticism" in this entire work. Already on the opening pages of the *TPT*, Mastricht writes that theology should be taught in a certain order as is found in the works of Petrus Lombard (approx. 1100-1160), Albertus Magnus (1206-1280), Thomas Aquinas (1225-

29. Ibid., I.1.xviii, 5: "*Naturalis* usus, *quadruplex* potissimum observatur: quorum *primus*, Deum respicit, qui ejus ope, impios reddit ἀναπολογήτους, Rom. 1:20, *secundus*, Gentiles & Atheos, qui ejus operâ validissime convincuntur Act 17:24-26, Ps. 8:2,3, Matth. 6:26, *tertius*, Theologiam revelatum, quæ, saltem respectu nostri, egregie confirmatur, deprehensa, ex asse consentire, cum Theologia naturali: *quartus*, denique nosmetipsos, qui plurimum radicamur, in *agnitione veri* revelati, si deprehendamus, ipsam naturam ei applaudere."

30. Ibid., I.1.xxiv, 7: "sed ad salutum *sufficere*, nullo modo ferunt [the Reformed, AN]. Eo quod; 1. ad *justificationem* requiratur, cognitio Christi (Isa.53:10), item 2. ad *vitam æternam* (Joh. 17:3), adeo 3. ut extra Christum, *nulla* supersit *salus* (Acts 4:12, Joh. 14:6)...."

31. Cf. Van Asselt, "Archetypal and Ectypal Theology," 333.

32. W. J. van Asselt and E. Dekker, eds., *Reformation and Scholasticism: An Ecumenical Enterprise, Texts and Studies in Reformation & Post-Reformation Thought* (Grand Rapids: Baker Academic, 2001), 39; Muller, *After Calvin*, 63-102.

33. C. Graafland, "Gereformeerde Scholastiek VI," *Theologia Reformata*, XXX, no. 2 (1987):323. The appraisals on Mastricht range from a negative (anti-Scholastic) to a positive valuation of Scholasticism in his theology.

1274), Duns Scotus (1265-1308), and Bonaventura (1221-1264).[34] Mastricht's acquaintance with the *theologia scholastica* is further and frequently attested throughout the *TPT*, including book II on the doctrine of God.[35] This raises the question, then, of what Mastricht thought of scholastic theology that relates the theology of revelation to the method and arguments derived from natural theology.[36]

First, he clarifies, that scholastic theology should be understood as a philosophical theology. The latter is used at the papal schools in order to uphold certain doctrines such as transubstantiation.[37] Contrary to this, Mastricht understands scholastic theology as method, in the sense of Alsted's scholastic theology.[38] Thus, Mastricht is not discussing the method of scholastic theology but argues against the Roman Catholic theological content founded upon philosophical arguments. Nevertheless, as we have pointed out, Mastricht's warning against an unwarranted use of method in theology remains. Thus, for Mastricht, scholastic method in theology should be used properly, avoiding insufficient and excessive use. Mastricht underscores this position when he states that in general the Reformed, and some "excellent" Roman Catholics, such as Erasmus (1469-1536), Cano (1509-1560), and Petavius (1583-1652), tried to exclude scholastic theology. However, Mastricht agrees mainly with those who "follow a middle way."[39] This middle way, according to Mastricht, offers the advantage of using the scholastic method in (1) debating with the Roman Catholics, (2) convincing non-

---

34. Mastricht, *Theoretico-practica theologia*, I.1.iii, 2: "Jam è dictis, præliminariter emergit, quod *Theologia, certa sit tradenda methodo*...(1) Apostolus Timotheum omnia Theologiæ capita, *doceat pariter & exhortetur*:...(2) 2. Sam. 23:5 *Fœdus ordinatum in omnibus* ברית עולם בכל ...(8) a primis statim, Ecclesiæ Christianæ incunabilis...Prout apparet, non tantum in illustrioribus Symbolis: Apostolico, Niceno...sed & in privatis, primorum Patrum scriptis.... & quæ in hos libros commentati sunt: Albertus Magnus, Thomas Aquinas, Scotus, Bonaventura aliique; Thomæ Aquinatis *Summa Theologiæ*."

35. See Appendix I.2.4.

36. Mastricht, *Theoretico-practica theologia*, I.1.xxv, 8: "Quid statuendum, de Theologia Scholastica, mediâ inter naturalem & revelatam, quod revelata tradat, modo & argumentis naturalibus?"

37. Ibid., I.1.xxv, 8. Mastricht notes a development beginning with the Lanfranc-Berengarus debate, when the former lacked the evidence of Scripture and used Augustine to support his doctrine of transubstantiation by appealing to philosophical subtleties. This appeal increased in Lombard's Sentences, Magnus, and his student Aquinas. The latter incorporated rational arguments from Aristotle and Averroes.

38. Ibid., I.1.xxv, 8: "Per Scholasticam, hîc non intelligimus, revelatam, quatenus traditur modo scholis familiari, quo sensu, suam Theologiam Scholasticam edidit Alstedius noster: sed Theologiam illam Philosophicam, quæ obtinet in scholis Pontificiorum." With Alsted, Mastricht apparently shared not only a similar concern for method of theology but also his view on scholastic theology. Cf. Muller, *Post-Reformation Reformed Dogmatics*, 1:194 fn. 72.

39. Mastricht, *Theoretico-practica theologia*, I.1.xxv, 8: "Nec tamen desunt è Reformatis, qui via media, censent incedendum: nec omnino servari; nec omnino eliminari debere; sed purgari a suis nævis debere, tum servari posse." In respect to the Reformed who excluded the Scholastic theology, Mastricht does not provide names.

Christians, and (3) confirming the theology of revelation. In particular (4) the scholastic method is useful for questions comprising aspects of theology and philosophy.[40]

If Mastricht is receptive to the use of the scholastic method how, then, does he employ it? Our examination points to a discerned use of the medieval scholastic method and schoolmen by Mastricht, including their definitions and distinctions. A few examples may illumine his position. First, in his exposition of the character of theology, he proposes to "accept" Scotus's view that theology is mere practical enterprise.[41] In this context, he is less favorable to Aquinas, who stated, according to Mastricht, that "our salvation consists in a perfect contemplation of God."[42] On the other hand, Mastricht positively identifies with Aquinas, who, according to Mastricht, opposed those Scholastics who attempted to obtain knowledge of the Trinity by reason alone, thereby diminishing the importance of faith.[43] In this context he is less inclined to Scotus's view on the possibility of a rational understanding of the Trinity.[44] In this context, neither Scotus nor Aquinas seems to have his preference; both are used in a critical way by Mastricht. This critical and positive use of the schoolmen is also noticed when Mastricht cites Anselm (1033-1109),[45] Bonaventura (ca. 1217-1274), and Gabriel Biel (1425-1495)[46] but especially when he refers to Bernardus (1090-1153).[47] Contrary to this, Mastricht is rarely negative towards the schoolmen—the doctrine of transubstantiation excluded.[48]

40. Ibid., I.1.xxv, 8: "Quod usum habeat 1. In contentionibus cum Pontificiis, quippe cum quibus, parum solide ac feliciter congredieris si stylum, artes & dumeta eorum ignores. 2. In convincendis Gentilibus & Atheis. 3. In confirmandis circa ipsam veritatem revelatam, animis Potissimum 4. In his quæstionibus, quarum terminus alter est theologicus, alter philosophicus."

41. Ibid., I.1.xlviii, 15, "Sunt ex adverso, qui mere *practicum* malunt, prout Scotus cum suis, quam, sano sensu, & nos recipiemus."

42. Ibid., I.1.xvliii, 15: "Sunt hîc, qui merè *theoreticam* volunt, sic Aquinas cum suis, quod in perfectissima contemplatione Dei, vertatur salus nostra Joh. 17:3, 1 Cor. 13:13."

43. Ibid., II.24.xxi, 243: "Thomas Aquinas *Summæ* suæ part.1, Quæst.32, art.1. Scholasticis obstrepit statuendo, conatum istum. non uno modo derogare *fidei.*" In respect to Mastricht's view on Aquinas, we note a nuanced (Scotist?) position when Mastricht initially follows but modifies "Aquinas's proofs" for the divine existence.

44. Ibid., II.24.xxi, 242: "An dogma de *Trinitate*, obtineri queat ope rationis? . . . Alii apud eosdem (Scholastici, AN), ut Scotus, ad lib. 1 Sentent. Distinct. 2.9&10. Trinitatem conantur evincere, ex productione, hoc modo, *producere* est perfectio quædam, quæ nihil implicat imperfectionis, ergo enti perfectissimo competit;...Thomas Aquinas *Summa* suæ part. 1. quæst. 32. art. 1. Scholasticis obstrepit, statuendo, conatum istum, non uno modo derogare *fidei.*"

43. Ibid., II.17.xxi (doctrinal), 182: "Quod scitè Anselmus *Prosol, cap.8. Es misericors, o Deus...*," and II.16.xvi (practical), 174, "*Ama* (inquit Anselmus in *Prosol., cap.25) unum bonum in quo sunt omnia bona & sufficiet tibi.*"

46. Ibid., II.24.xxi, 243; III.7.xxxi, 348.

47. Ibid., II.4.viii, 87; II.10.viii, 123; II.12.xxiv, 141; II.16.xxii, 177.

48. For a negative assessment by Mastricht see, for example, Ibid., I.1.xxiii, 7: "Aberrant hîc, in *excessu...*Pontificiorum Scholastici...ad sustinendam suam transubstantiationem, aliasque superstitiones;" and III.7.xxx, (objectiones) 348: "Nec pro se habent, hujus ordinis patroni [order of angels, AN]...B.

Thus, Mastricht attests to a vast reservoir of medieval scholastic works, which he uses according to the "middle way" of his scholastic method.

Second, Mastricht employs scholastic definitions and distinctions in order to present a precise division and description of the *loci* of theology. In this context, we refer to the useful distinction of three levels in scholastic method, as employed in the post-Reformation period: a *micro-*, *meso-* and *macro* level.[49] The micro level includes definitions, distinctions, and the use of rhetoric. The latter is employed, for example, as we have seen, when Mastricht structures his discussion of the divine attributes with the help of the distinctions between *Quid sit Deus*, *Quantus sit Deus*, and *Qualis sit Deus*. In respect to the scholastic distinctions, Mastricht uses in the *TPT* distinctions such as *actus-habitus, credere Deum-credere in Deum, distinctio realis-distinctio formalis, esse-ens, fides qua creditur-fides quæ creditur, in abstracto-in concreto, potentia absoluta-potentia ordinata,* and *theoretica-practica.*[50] Sometimes Mastricht explains such a distinction, like the *theoretico-practica.*

Like the medieval doctors, Mastricht addressed the question of whether theology was (more) theoretical or (more) practical or a "mixed" (*theoretico*-practical) discipline.[51] Moreover, like the question itself, the meaning of the terms originated from the medieval scholastic and piety or mysticism tradition. It is against this background that the conjunction of theory and *praxis* in the title of his *magnum opus* and his explicit discussion of this conjunction are of interest. In respect to the former, Mastricht differs from most of his contemporaries, who entitled their works as "*theologia practica.*"[52] In

Rationes à congruentiis de quibus Scholastici ad Lomb. *Sent.lib.ii.Dist.ix* tam jejunas, ut non mereantur refutationem occupare."

49. Here, we follow Van Asselt and Rouwendal in W. J. van Asselt and P. L. Rouwendal, eds., *Inleiding in de Gereformeerde Scholastiek* (Zoetermeer: Boekencentrum, 1998), 88, 89.

50. Mastricht, *Theoretico-practica theologia,* II.1 (actus-habitus, credere Deum-credere in Deum, fides qua creditur-fides quæ creditur); II.2; II.3 (esse-ens); II.5 (distinctio realis-dictinctio formalis, in abstracto-in concreto); II.15 (potentia absoluta-potentia ordinata); and title page, I.1. (theoretica-practica). We have noted that the paradigm, *theoretica-practica,* is one of the debates inherited by the Protestant Scholastics from medieval theology concerning the character and purpose of the discipline of theology.

51. Ibid., I.1.xx, 6: "[Theologia est] *Theoretico-Practica,* h.e. nec *Theoretica* tantum, quæ in veritatis qualicunque contemplatione *quiescat*: nec *Practica* tantum, quæ veritatis *cognitionem,* susque deque habeat (quam Sociniani vellent & Arminiani...);" and I.1.xlviii, 15: "sitne habitus *theoreticus?* an *practicus?* an *theoretico-practicus?*"

52. For example, the following post-Reformation Reformed publications: Christopher Love, *Theologia practica, dat is: Alle de theologische wercken,* trans. C. van Diemerbroeck (Utrecht: Hermannus Ribbius, 1657); Johannes Hoornbeeck, *Disputatio theologica practica, de devotione,* resp. Daniel Radæus (Leiden: Elsevier, 1659); idem, *Disputatio theologica, practica, de mundo,* resp. Jacobus Corf (Leiden: Elsevier, 1659); idem, *Theologia practica,* 2 vols. (Utrecht: Henricus Versteegh, 1663-1666); Simon Oomius, *Institutiones theologiæ practicæ, ofte onderwysingen in de practycke der godtgeleertheydt: eerste tractaet des tweeden boeck's van het eerste deel, vervattende de verhandelinge der theologia didactica* (Bolsward: Wed. Van Samuel Haringhouk, 1676); Jacobi Alting, *Opera omnia theologica, analytica, exegetica, practica, problematica & philologica,* 5 vols. (Amsterdam: Gerardus Bortius, 1687); Matthew Henry, *An Exposition of the Old and New Testaments: Wherein Each Chapter is Summed Up as to Its Contents...with Practical Remarks and Observations* (London: Patridge and Oakey, 1706); Herman Witsius, *Theologiæ practicæ: quo veri ac interioris*

respect to the discussion of this issue, it should be noticed that the *TPT* opens with an explanation of the term "*Theologia theoretico-practica.*"[53] Mastricht emphasizes that the study of theology in particular thrusts one into a *theoretico*-practical science.[54] In discussing this issue, he presents four possibilities. First is the Thomistic position, which implies that theology is only a theoretical or contemplative science. Second is the Scotist position, which implies that theology is a mere practical enterprise. Mastricht agrees with this position by writing "*sano sensu & nos recipiemus.*" Third, there are those who, according to Mastricht, advocate neither a contemplative or speculative nor practical attitude but love and affection. Finally, he states that there is the position of *theologia theoretica* **and** *theologia practica*. The former is restricted to the *credenda*: God, Trinity, and the two natures of Christ. The latter is applied to the *facienda* of all other doctrines.[55] Mastricht then concludes that theology is not only theoretical but more practical. The *praxis* is defined as *doctrina* (teaching) known for the sake of the end toward which it directs the knower.[56] Mastricht thus has, in our opinion, a modified Scotist position. He does not reject Aquinas's position altogether but follows, according to Muller, the Augustian alternative of Thomas of Strasbourg († 1357), which sees theology as more practical than speculative.[57] Nevertheless, Mastricht's explicit statement concerning the conjunction *theoretico-practica* is a relatively unique feature for a Reformed orthodox system of theology. The description of such scholastic distinction results most probably contributed to Mastricht's fourfold approach to (the *loci* of) theology: as (1) explicative or exegetical study, (2) *theoretica* or contemplative-doctrinal study, (3) elenctic study, and (4)

christianismi genuinum exercitium (Groningen: Jacobus Sipkes, 1729); idem, *Practicale godgeleertheid, of algemeene pligten der christenen ten opzigte van Godt, van Christus, van zich zelven en zyn naasten*, trans. from Latin, 2d. ed. (Rotterdam: Nicolaas Topyn, 1732); Thomas Goodwin, *Opera, ofte alle de theologische werken: meest betreffende de practyke der godzaligheid en den wandel van een christen in de plichten nevens God en zyne even-naasten*, tran. Jacobus Koelman, 3d ed. (Amsterdam: Adrianus Douci, 1749). It is noteworthy that a student of Utrecht (and of Mastricht?) published a commentary on the Heidelberg Catechism entitled *Theoretico-practica.* Cf. Hermannus Glaserus, *Catechesis theoretico-practica. Dat is een eenvoudige verklaringe van de voornaamste hoofd-stukken onses catechismus* (Amsterdam: H. Burgers, 1729). G. Voetius introduced *theologia practica* as an academic discipline. Cf. C. A. De Niet, *Gisbertus Voetius, De Praktijk der Godzaligheid* (Utrecht: De Banier, 1996), 1:xxvii; Van Asselt and Rouwendal, *Inleiding in de Gereformeerde Scholastiek*, 87; A. de Reuver, *Verborgen omgang, Sporen van spiritualiteit in Middeleeuwen en Nadere Reformatie* (Zoetermeer: Boekencentrum, 2002), 12, 13; Muller, *After Calvin*, 120-21.

53. Mastricht, *Theoretico-practica theologia*, I.1.i, 1: "*Theologiam Theoretico-practicam* pro natura cujusvis disciplinæ, duobus concludemus: Præcognitis & Systemate."

55. Ibid., I.1.xlviii, 15: ". . . Sunt tandem, qui & theoreticam, & practicam, determinant; quod altera sui parte, scil. quod *credenda*, de Deo, Trinitate, unione personali duarum in Christo naturum, sit theoretica tantum; altera de *faciendis*, mere practica. Sed minus accuratè."

56. Ibid., I.1.xx, 6, and I.1.xlviii, 15: "(c) nihil in Theologia occurrat, quin habeat, seu finis, seu *mediorum* rationem, cujus generis omnia practica sunt."

57. Muller, *Post-Reformation Reformed Dogmatics*, 1:351.

praxis or goal-oriented study.[58] This understanding of *theoretico-practica* parallels probably Mastricht's unstated double understanding of *habitus* of theology. The term theology carried from the Pastristic Fathers onwards the basic idea of a *habitus*, or inward disposition, which permitted for a dual significance.[59] The primary meaning, termed as practical *habitus*, refered to, in so far as it concerned practical salvation-oriented knowledge of God united to the life of faith and the longing for God, whose end is eternal happiness with God. The other connotation, termed as cognitive *habitus*, refered to, in so far as it concerned self-consious scholarly quest, a discipline whose locus was ussualy a pedagogical setting. The setting, that corresponds to the efforts of discerning and setting forth in writing, truth revealed by God throught Christ. The latter meaning paralles Mastricht's aim of the *TPT*, the former understanding points to Mastricht's definition of theology. This double meaning of *habitus*, then, seem to be an early beginning of the *theoretico-practica* paradigm of Mastricht's theological enterprise. In addition to the *micro* level, Mastricht also employs the *meso* level of the scholastic method. This is most vividly present in the elenctic sections of the *TPT* in his use of *quæstio* technique. The scholastic structure of the *quæstiones* is used by Mastricht to articulate more precisely the *status questionis*, *objectiones*, *responsiones*, and the *fontes solutionum*.[60] Finally, we point to Mastricht's use of the *macro* level of the scholastic method in the combined analytical-synthetical method of theology and the order of the *loci communes*: the connection of exegesis, doctrine, and *praxis* with the loci of Reformed theology.[61]

Definition of theology

Mastricht defines theology as a doctrine of living to God through Christ and, secondly, as a doctrine that accords with piety (1Tim. 6:3).[62] This basic definition of

---

58. Cf. Van Asselt and Rouwendal, *Inleiding in de Gereformeerde Scholastiek*, 129.

59. Here we follow, Victor Babajide Cole, *Training of the Ministry* (Bangelor, India: Theological Book Trust, 2001), 5-10.

60. An examination of the marginal notes of the elenctic sections of the *TPT* reveals in general the structure (1) *Quæstio*, (2) *Sententia* or *Argumenta Orthodoxa (Reformed)*, (3) *Objectiones* and (4) *Conclusio*. Cf. L. M. de Rijk, *Middeleeuwse wijsbegeerte, Traditie en vernieuwing* (Assen/Amsterdam: Van Gorcum, 1977), 129; Van Asselt and Rouwendal, *Inleiding in de Gereformeerde Scholastiek*, 58. See further on Mastricht's use of the *quæstio* method, part III, chapter 3 of this study.

61. Mastricht, *Prodromus*, præfatio. In addition, most of the *Theoretico-practica theologia* is composed of *disputationes*. See part I, chapter 2 of this study. Moreover, if Van 't Spijker is correct on Melanchthon's separation of exegesis and *loci communes*, then Mastricht differs. Cf. W. van 't Spijker, "Orthodoxie en Nadere Reformatie," in *Theologische aspecten van de Nadere Reformatie*, ed. T. Brienen, *et al.* (Zoetermeer: Boekencentrum, 1993), 14: "Melanchthon was de eerste die de *loci communes*, de gemeenplaatsen, niet meer rechtstreeks met de exegese verbond. Hij gaf een voorbeeld dat vrij spoedig navolging vond. De dogmatiek kwam zo naast de exegese te staan."

62. Mastricht, *Theoretico-practica theologia*, I.1.xxxvi, 12: "Theologia ista Christiana, theoretico-practica, non est, nisi *doctrina vivendi Deo per Christum*; seu *doctrina, quæ est secundum pietatem* (1 Tim. 6:3)." Cf. William Ames, *Medulla*, I.i.1, 2: "Theologia est doctrina deo vivendi."

theology stands, according to Muller, in "continuity with the Ramist and with the Scotist or nominalist tendencies of the early orthodox Protestantism" of Mastricht's time.[63] Petrus Ramus (1515-1572), whose definitions and logic offered much of the framework for early orthodox Reformed thought, had defined theology as *doctrina bene vivendi*, "the doctrine of living well," a definition followed explicitly by Perkins and Ames. [64] This definition was carried forward in the Dutch theological tradition in general but expanded by Mastricht.[65] Further, he explicates each part of the definition.[66] The first part pertains, according to Mastricht, to the right teaching to live directed to God (*Godewaarts*).[67] However, he asserts that such is not sufficient unless such living is through Christ. The christological expansion of the definition prompts Mastricht to note that (*nostra*) theology, through Christ, differs from (1) the theology of the first created man, and (2) natural and false theology.[68] He asserts that outside Christ no one can live to God. Moreover, it is union with Christ through faith that gives and sustains spiritual life,

63. Richard A. Muller, *God, Creation, and Providence in the Thought of Jacobus Arminius. Sources and Directions of Scholastic Protestantism in the Era of Early Orthodoxy* (Grand Rapids: Baker Books, 1991), 63; idem, *Post-Reformation Reformed Dogmatics*, 1:169, 345, 351.

64. Petrus Ramus, *Commentariorum de religione Christiana libri quatuor* (Frankfurt: Andreas Wechel, 1576), I.1, 3. See on also, James V. Skalnik, *Ramus and Reform: University and Church at the End of the Renaissance* (Kirksville, MO: Truman State Univ. Press, 2002); Mordechai Feingold, ed., *The Influence of Petrus Ramus: Studies in Sixteenth and Seventeenth Century Philosophy and Sciences* (Basel: Schwabe, 2001); Donald K. McKim *Ramism in William Perkins' theology* (New York: Lang, 1987); W. J. Ong, *Ramus. Method and Decay of Dialogue: From the Art of Discourse to the Art of Reason* (Cambridge, MA: Harvard University Press, 1958); William Perkins, *The Workes of Mr. William Perkins, A Golden Chaine*, vol.1, mcol.1, 11; William Ames, *Marrow of Sacred Divinity*, I.1, 3, "Divinity is the doctrine of living to God." Cf. Muller, *Post-Reformation Reformed Dogmatics*, 1:156.

65. Cf. Muller, *God, Creation, and Providence*, 64. Another possible Ramist notion is Mastricht's view on the benefits of a method: "The issues are clarified, and facilitate the memory and strengthen the argument." See Petrus Ramus, *Commentariorum de Religione Christiana*, 3. Cf. Keith L. Sprunger, *The Learned Doctor William Ames* (Chicago: University of Illinois Press, 1972), 131, "The person who will have first applied this method to organization of theology will bring an extraordinary light to illuminate all the parts of theology clearly and brightly." This notion is absent in Ames's works.

66. Petrus van Mastricht, *Theoretico-practica theologia* (1699), 12, 13

I.1.xxxvi	Doctrina vivendi Deo per Christum
I.1.xxxviii	Doctrina
I.1.xxxix	vivendi Deo
I.1.xl	Deo
I.1.xli	vivendi (natura, gratia, gloria)
I.1.xlii	per Christum

67. Petrus van Mastricht, *Beschouwende en praktikale godgeleerdheit*, vol.1, I.1.xl, 33; idem, *Theoretico-practica theologia* (1699), I.1.xl, 13: "Vita enim nostra, cum *Deum* versus, dirigi necessario debeat, ut supremum & ultimum finem."

68. Mastricht, *Theoretico-practica theologia*, I.1.xlii, 13: "1. Theologia nostra, distat à Theologia *protoplastorum* cum primum essent creati: item à Theologia *naturali*; & à ψευδονύμω quavis..."

so that Christ is manifested in one's life.[69] True theology, he argues, is not enough for a theologian to know, "as Bernardus says 'one has the words of the saints but not their life.'"[70] This, then, brings Mastricht to the last part of his exposition of the definition: Christ-like living is directed to God.[71] Therefore, theology, according to Mastricht, is a means to the end of living well and blessedness.[72]

In the context of defining theology as a living to God through Christ, Mastricht raises the question of whether theology can make use of the Aristotelian *habitus* categories; thus that theology is *sapientia* or *prudentia*.[73] Using Aristotle's five basic ways of knowing (*intelligentia, scientia, ars, prudentia, and sapientia*), Mastricht responds with a middle position. Theology he asserts, like Junius and others before him, is unlike *intelligentia*, since *intelligentia* is identified as apprehension of principles but not of conclusion; theology consists both in principles and conclusions drawn from them. Nor can theology be identified with *scientia* or drawing conclusions; nor is theology identical with *ars*, which proceeds from *intelligentia* and *scientia* and intends to conclude in some external work. He then asserts "that *formaliter* it is the best to take the middle position"[74] Thus, Mastricht views theology as *sapientia*, i.e., wisdom in the sense of gathering of all theoretical and moral dispositions or capacities. This example and other references book II of the TPT—the consistent use of the *principium contradictionis*, the use of the distinctions such as, *potentia* and *actus* and *essentia* and *accidentia* to solve theological issues, the use of categories for the precise definition of theology, and the limited use of

69. Ibid., I.1.xlii, 14: "(c) Christus fide nobiscum unitus in nobis vivit...vitaque Christi, omni ista ratione, *manifesta* in nobis fiat, 2 Cor. 4:11." Mastricht's expansion is also defined in the prologue of the *Idea Theologia Moralis* that the "art of living to God" consist of two aspects: "how we are made alive from spiritual dead and, now being alive, *Deo vivamus.*" Cf. Ibid., *Theoretico-practica theologia*, 1102.

70. Ibid., I.1.xlix, 15: "Proinde *primo*, nec vera *Theologia* est nec verus *Theologus*,...*qui verba Sanctorum habet, non vitam*, ut alicubi Bernardus."

71. Ibid., I.1.lii 16: "1. *scopum* vitæ nostræ..."; and Ibid., liii, 16, "2. *vitam Christi*...quam ipse in exemplum nobis commendat Matth. 11:29."

72. Ibid., I.1.xliii, 14: "...Deo vivere duo complectatur...: *bene* vivere & *beate.*"

73. Ibid., I.1.xlvi, 14: "An de Theologia usurpari possit, unus aliquis ex habitibus intellectualibus Aristotelis ad Nicomach. *Ethic. Lib. VI.* seu, an Theologia dici debeat *sapientia* potius, an *prudentia?*"

74. Ibid., I.1.xlvi, 14: "...sunt, qui *omnes* habitus Aristotelis, ei convenire statuunt; eo quod Theologia sit *intelligentia*, quatenus in principia fertur, simplici apprehensione: *scientia*, quatenus ex principiis educit conclusiones, ratiocinando: *sapientia*, quatenus principia construit cum conclusionibus, modo perfectissimo: *prudentia*, quatenus sua dirigit, ad actionem *immanentem*: & *ars*, quatenus ad *transeuntem*. Tutissime medium dixeris, scil. *nullum formaliter*, ita loquar, ut excludat alios; *omnes eminenter*, quod omnium perfectiones absorbeat." Van Asselt, "Archetypal and Ectypal Theology," 326. Cf. idem, "Natuurlijke theologie als uitleg van openbaring? Ectypische versus archetypische theologie in de zeventiende-eeuwse gereformeerde dogmatiek," in *Nederlands Theologisch Tijdschrift* 57 (April, 2003), 143. Van Asselt notes the continuity of intellectual thought: "From the early thirteenth century onward the medieval doctors assimilated this paradigm and used it in their discussion of the *genus* of theology. Because it was not specifically addressed in the theology of the Reformers, the Reformed scholastics drew upon this Aristotelian classification in order to identify their view of the *genus* of theology."

syllogism[75]—attest to Mastricht's discerned reliance on the Western Aristotelian tradition, including Boethius and Avicenna.[76] Here, like Mastricht's Scholasticism, we note a discerned use of method and vocabulary. However, the content of Mastricht's theology was not defined by Aristotle but shaped by Scripture and the intellectual heritage of Augustine and Bernardus.[77]

We can conclude from this examination that method is important to Mastricht. His view of theology stands clearly in continuity with the "medieval prolegomena," not only in its emphasis on *nostra theologia* as a theology of the *viator* but also in its distinction between the two *modi* of knowing revelation and vision, as characteristic of our theology in this life (*in via*) and of our theology in its heavenly fulfillment (*in patria*). In respect to scholastic theology, we noted that Mastricht prefers a *via media* rather than embracing it fully and without discernment. For him the use of the scholastic method in its various forms and application is in particular useful in debating with the Roman Catholics and in the elenctical part. Mastricht's words are contrary to the assessment that he was an anti-Scholastic. In addition, we note that Mastricht's goal-directed disposition of theology points to a somewhat different conclusion than that reached by those who view theology not as a contemplative or speculative discipline but rather as a practical discipline.[78] Theology for Mastricht is *theoretico-practica*. However, his leaning toward the *theologia practica* stands in continuity with earlier Reformed orthodox thought, as expressed by Perkins, Ames, Keckerman, and Cocceius.

75. We note particularly in the practical sections of the *TPT* a limited use of syllogism. K. Barth observes that Mastricht, with F. Turretini, the *Leiden Synopsis*, A. Heidanus and F. Burman, avoid to make use—contrary to W. Ames, who, according Barth, had a major influence on the development and use— of the *syllogismus practicus*. Cf. Karl Barth, *Die Kirchliche Dogmatik* (Zürich: EVZ-Verlag, 1970), II.2, 370,371. See also Nico T. Bakker, *Miskende Gratie van Calvijn tot Witsius* (Kampen: J.H. Kok, 1991), 29.

76. See Appendix I.2.4. See, for, example, Mastricht's discerned use of (western) Aristotelianism; Mastricht, *Theoretico-practica theologia*, III.6.xxv, 327 (negative); IV.1.ii, 328 (neutral); IV.3.xxii, 367 (positive). The attention to Aristotelianism was not exclusive to the Reformed orthodox but also included Lutherans. Cf. E. W. Gritsch, *A History of Lutheranism* (Minneapolis: Fortress Press, 2002), 115. See also, C. H. Ratschow, *Lutherische Dogmatik zwischen Reformation und Aufklärung*, 2 vol., (Gütersloher Verlaghaus: Gütersloher, 1964-66). Furthermore, the influence of Raminism as a revision, not a repudiation, of Aristotelianism should not be discounted. Cf. K. L Sprunger, "Ames, Ramus and the Method of Puritan Theology,"in *Harvard Theological Journal* 59 (1966): 133-51; W. M. Kneale and J. Kneale, *The Development of Logic* (Oxford: Clarendon, 1962), 301.

77. See Appendix I.2.4.

78. Petrus van Mastricht, *Theoretico-practica theologia*, I.1.xl, 13; and ibid., xli, 13: "Est autem vita, quam Deum versus dirigit, triplex est: 1. *Naturæ*...2.*Gratiæ*...3.*Gloriæ*... vita *gloriæ*, tota pendet ex directione Theologiæ..."

Scripture

Introduction and Statement of the problem

Mastricht's doctrine of Scripture has received some attention in contributions of Heppe, Graafland, and Muller.[79] They have, each in their own way, situated Mastricht's view of *de Sacra Scriptura* in the context of seventeenth-century post-Reformation Reformed dogmatics. Moreover, they have, in this context, assessed the overall conformity of Mastricht's explication of the doctrine of Scripture with his contemporaries.[80] However, they also have pointed to some peculiarities. Heppe mentions that Mastricht is quite unique in constructing the concept of the inspiration of Scripture by linking up the concept of divine canonization with the revelation of the biblical books.[81] Both, Heppe and Muller note that the Reformed orthodox discussed various attributes of Scripture—*auctoritas*, *necessitas* and *perspicuitas*—but it is Mastricht who identified no less then eight incidental properties.[82] Graafland assesses two issues that require our attention. First, he notes the independence of the *locus* of Scripture prior to systematic theology, and, second, he notes Mastricht's emphasis on the *ratio* in the explication of the doctrine of Scripture in conformity with Voetian orthodoxy.[83] In respect to the latter, Graafland asserts an ambivalence between the indispensable and important function of reason and the necessity of the Holy Spirit in the understanding of Scripture. The other assessment of Graafland has, in our opinion, implications on the structure and method of the doctrine of Scripture in relationship to the system of doctrine.[84] These two concerns, then, will be the focus of our examination. Thus

79. H. Heppe and E. Bizer, eds., *Reformed Dogmatics*, trans. G. T. Thomson (London: The Wakeman Trust), chapter 2; C. Graafland, "Schriftleer en Schriftverstaan in de Nadere Reformatie," in Brienen et al., *Theologische aspecten van de Nadere Reformatie*, 61-68; Muller, *Post-Reformation Reformed Dogmatics*, vol. 2.

80. Mastricht and his contemporaries are in basic agreement regarding Scripture as Word of God (*principium cognoscendi*), the divinity and description of attributes of Scripture, the canon, and authentic and vernacular editions of Scripture.

81. Heppe and Bizer, *Reformed Dogmatics*, 20. Cf. Mastricht, *Theoretico practica theologia*, I.2.xiii, 21: "Condidit autem Deus Scripturam: partim *revelatione*...partim *Canonizatione*, qua, inspiratione scripta, Ecclesiæ fuit tradita Deut. 31:9, Ps. 147:19, Rom. 3:2 et obsignata."

82. Heppe and Bizer, *Reformed Dogmatics*, 22; Muller, *Post-Reformation Reformed Dogmatics*, 2:339. Cf. Mastricht, *Theoretico practica theologia*, I.2.xiv-xxi, 21-23. Mastricht notes the following properties of Scripture: *auctoritas, veritas, integritas, sanctitas, perspicuitas, perfectio, necessitas,* and *efficacia*.

83. On (1) see Graafland, "Schriftleer en Schriftverstaan," 36, 63, 84, which is in basic agreement with the assesment of C. Sepp, *Het Godgeleerd Onderwijs in Nederland gedurende de 16e en 17e eeuw* (Leiden: De Breuk en Smits, 1873-1874), 2:348; on (2) Ibid., 31. In addition, older scholarship has viewed the seventeenth-century Reformed orthodoxy as employing rationalistic development of doctrine, with the doctrine of God being the prime example of the rationalistic formulations. Cf. Tholuck, *Vorgeschichte des Rationalismus*; idem, *Geschichte des Rationalismus*; Althaus, *Die Prinzipien der deutschen reformierten Dogmatik*; Weber, *Reformation, Orthodoxie und Rationalismus*; Bizer, *Frühorthodoxie und Rationalismus*.

84. Although not irrelevant, but outside the scope of this study, we note Graafland's assessment of Mastricht's doctrine of Scripture as a combination of the thought of Ames and Voetius. The influence of the former is noted, according to Graafland, in Mastricht's definition of the doctrine of Scripture and

Mastricht's attention to hermeneutics requires examination in the context of his exegesis of the biblical text.

Locus de Sacra Scriptura: location and structure

The chapter on the doctrine of Scripture follows the discussion on the nature of theology. Moreover, it stands prior to chapters on the distribution of theology and the doctrine of God, which open with a chapter on faith. Subsequent reading of these chapters shows a continuation and interrelatedness of Mastricht's thought. First, Mastricht's definition of theology—from Scripture, as a doctrine of living to God through Christ—is further explicated in the definition of Scripture. Mastricht defines Scripture as a perfect rule or norm for living to God, in as far as such is described and contained in Scripture.[85] He then notes that Scripture is the norm for faith and obedience: the distribution of theology.[86] Thus, Scripture is the norm for a living to God in faith and obedience through Christ. The relationship of Scripture and faith is further noted, as Mastricht identifies Scripture as *principium*, received inwardly by faith at the inception of spiritual life.[87] Moreover, this relationship is noted in Mastricht's definition of the *scopus* or aim, purpose, goal, and center of Scripture. In the exegetical section of the doctrine of Scripture, Mastricht identifies the *scopus* as the *finis Scripturæ sacræ*. It is the goal of Scripture that believers be perfected before God and perfectly instructed in all good works. Therefore, Scripture has, according to Mastricht, a twofold *scopus* or *finis*. First, it has a *finis cui*, a goal to which it is directed in a material sense, which is the believer. Second, it has a *finis cuius*, a goal of which it enables the believer to partake formally as

---

his view on inspiration of Scripture and Bible translations. The Voetian line is noted in his Scholasticism and rationalistic character of truth. Cf. Graafland, "Schriftleer en Schriftverstaan," 61, 64, 65. In addition, Graafland asserts there is possibly less contradiction between Cocceius's and Mastricht's understanding of Scripture, especially since both follow Ames's teaching on the inspiration of Scripture as both a verbal and a historic "organic" inspiration (Ibid., 70, fn.70).

85. Mastricht, *Theoretico practica theologi*, I.1.xxxvi, 12; and, ibid., I.2.iii, 19, "Patet itaque, *sacram Scripturam, perfectam esse Deo vivendi regulam*;" and, ibid., I.2.vi, 19, "Sacrâ autem Scriptura, nil aliud intelligimus, quam *doctrinam vivendi Deo, quatenus illa literis continetur descripta*." Mastricht expounds that such rule requires that it is prescribed by God, be known, consistant, adequate, and public. Cf. Mastricht, *Theoretico practica theologia* I.2.v, 19: "In quo magis etiam confirmamur, eo quod, natura & *requisita Regulæ* in eam solam, quam exactissimè quadrent. *Primò*, enim regula *vivendi Deo*, procul dubio, à *Deo solo* debet esse præscripta...*Secundò*, regula debet esse *nota*, clara & perspicua...*Tertiò*, regula debet esse *constans* & immota...*Quartò*, regula debet esse *adæquata* regulando...*Denique*, regula debet esse *recepta* ac *publica*...." See also Muller, *Post-Reformation Reformed Dogmatics*, 2:360.

86. Ibid., I.3.i, 47: "Artificium istud vivendi Deo, cujus *norma* est Scriptura; certis *partibus* repræsentare...verbis præfixis (2 Tim. 1:13)." See also, Ibid., II.1.i, 50: "Vita illa *Dei*, cujus *normam* præstat Scriptura, perinde ut *naturalis*, duos actus concludit: *primum*, quo *possumus* operari spiritualiter, quem præstat *fides*...secundos, quos fides producit, actus scil. *observantiæ*...;" idem, *Theoretico-practica theologia*, 1102 (*Idea Theologiæ Moralis*).

87. Mastricht, *Theoretico-practica theologia*, I.2.i, 17: "[Scriptura]...quo nomine Theologiæ *principium* indigitatur." Cf. Ibid., II.1.i, 50. See for the distinction of *principium cognoscendi* and *essendi*, Muller, *Post-Reformation Reformed Dogmatics*, 1:194.

an outcome, which is the perfection or blessedness of the believer.[88] Second the structure of the *locus de Sacra Scriptura* attests to a scholastic pattern of argumentation, similar to Mastricht's division of divine attributes. That Scripture exists (*an sit*), no one denies, so Mastricht proceeds with the question, *Quid sit?*—What is it? Mastricht's answer to this question is the definition of Scripture. Furthermore, this question is answered in the scholastic discussion of Scripture according to its essence or *quidditas*: the *principium* and norm of spiritual life. Mastricht continues, then, to discuss the problem of description, that is, the question, *Qualis sit?*—which is to say, the discussion of the attributes of Scripture.[89]

The structure or method of argumentation points to two aspects of Mastricht's approach. First, the presentation of different *loci*, and in the case of the divine attributes, the differentiation of the *locus*, is enriched in clarity through the utilization of a scholastic method of argumentation. Second, there is an analogic relationship between the attributes of God and Scripture—presenting the properties of Scripture as the marks of the divine architecture and, central to Mastricht, the divine authority of the revelation of Scripture. Therefore, contrary to the assessment of Graafland, for Mastricht, Scripture is a foundational and interrelated part and not independent of Mastricht's theology in structure and method.[90]

Reason

Mastricht raises the question of human reason as a norm to interpret Scripture.[91] The question is not only important to Mastricht or post-Reformation scholarship but also forced by the frequent references to the *rationes* in the *TPT*. Structurally, the appeal to reason is located primarily in the doctrinal sections of book II, following immediately Scriptural testimonies.[92] Was reason, then, another source of knowledge, besides

88. Mastricht, *Theoretico-practica theologia*, I.2.ii, 18: "*Quibus Apostolus* [2 Tim.3:16, 17, Timotheo] promit...*Scripturæ* commendationem. *In qua duo prostant*: 1. Subjectum *commendatum*: tota Scriptura...2. Prædicatum, *seu argumentum commendationis, quod tria repræsentat*...α Originem...β utilitatem...γ Finem *ac* Scopum...1. *Finis* cui...2. *Finis* cujus...." We followed the translated summary of Muller in *Post-Reformation Reformed Dogmatics*, 2:221. Muller's discussion of the foundation and scope of Scripture could lead to the conclusion that Mastricht is silent, which he is in his chapter *De Sacra Scriptura*, on the Christological aspect compared to other Reformed orthodox, such as Perkins and Witsius.

89. Mastricht, *Theoretico-practica theologia*, I.2.iii-xiii (Quid sit), 19-21, I.2.xiv-xxi, 21-23 (Qualis sit). In addition, the question *An sit?* is discussed as the first elenctic question, "*An detur aliquod verbum Dei scriptum?*" (I.2.xxii, 23).

90. This is further noted in our discussion of Mastricht's hermeneutics in the context of biblical exegesis. See part III, chapter 1 of this study. See also on the use of reason for the interpretation of Scripture, Muller, *Post-Reformation Reformed Dogmatics*, 2:497-500.

91. Mastricht, *Theoretico-practica theologia*, I.2.xxxiv, 31: "Quæritur, an ratio humana sit norma infallibilis, exponendi Scripturas?"

92. Ibid., I.1.iii, 3; I.1.ix, 4; I.1.xxxvii, 12; I.2.iii, 19; I.3.iv, 48; and book II (Doctrine of God), II.2.iv, 66; II.3.xv, 80; II.6.iv, 99; II.7.iv, 108; II.9.iv, 118; II.10.v, 122; II.11.iv, 119; II.12.xix, 140; II.13.iv, 144; II.14.iv, 153; II.16.iv, 171; II.18.iv, 179; II.18.iii, 193; II.19.iv, 202; II.20.iv, 209; II.21.iv, 220; II.22.iv, 226; II.23.iv, 232. It is not found in the chapters II.1, *De Fide salvifica*; II.4, *De Nominibus Dei*; II.5, *De Attributis*

Scripture, for Mastricht? This question is answered by Mastricht's threefold response to the question of reason's relationship to Scripture. First, he refutes those are in defect: the Roman Catholics and Lutherans. The former acknowledge the papal and ecclesiastical authority, and the latter do not allow reason in the mysteries of theology. Second, he opposes those who are in excess: the Socinians and Cartesian philosophers. In respect to the latter, Mastricht linked Bekker to Spinoza and also the furore over Meyer's *Philosophia*. The true meaning of the uproar was, according to Mastricht, that it proved that "in matters of salvation" Bekker places philosophy above Scripture and that theology was being sacrificed to the axiom "philosophy is the infallible interpreter of Scripture." Do not Bekker's assertions prove that in everything not directly relating to salvation he ranks philosophy above theology? Israel asserts, "Undoubtedly, Mastricht had a point."[93] Mastricht's concern was, in a broader context, whether Scripture yielded to philosophy or the latter to the former. Either Scripture is the eternal, true, and authentic Word of God, held Mastricht, or the world will be overrun by philosophy, skepticism, and atheism.[94] These two refutations led Mastricht to the third, Reformed part, of the answer. The Reformed, according to Mastricht, hold reason as an instrument and argument but not as the norm. The instrumental use of reason is necessitated in the inquiries of matters of veracity, Scripture included. The argumentative use is useful for the confirmation of issues present and arising out the *principio Scriptura*.[95] Reason, Mastricht argues, is subjected to Scripture, because the *ratio* is blind (1 Cor. 2:14), obscure (John 1:5), fallible (Rom. 1:21), and imperfect (Rom. 1:19; cf. 1 Cor. 2:12). Moreover, the spiritual matters of true religion transcend reason; otherwise the Holy Spirit and Scripture and from both of these, faith, would be subjected to reason. In addition, Mastricht continues, Christ, the prophets, and apostles never remitted to

---

Dei in genere; II.8, *De Unitate Dei*; II.15, *De Voluntate & Affectibus Dei*; II.24, *De SS. Trinitate*; II.25, *De Deo Patre*; II.26, *De Deo Filio*; II.27, *De Deo Spiritu S*. This observation of the use of reason (restricted) in doctrinal formulation can be extended to the remainder of the *TPT*.

93. Petrus van Mastricht, *Ad virum clariss. Balthasarem Beckerum epanorthosis gratulatoria occasione articulorum*, quos venerandæ Classi Amstelodamensi exhibuit, die 22 Janu. 1692 (Utrecht: Anthonius Schouten, 1692), 25, 26; Cf. Jonathan I. Israel, *Radical Enlightenment, Philosophy and the Making of Modernity 1650-1750* (Oxford: Oxford University Press, 2001), 385.

94. Mastricht, *Ad virum clariss*, 52, 73, 76; idem, *Theoretico-practica theologia*, I.2.xxxiv, 31: "Eisdem omnio hypothesibus, nuper apud nos nati Theologi Rationalistæ, existimant, ipsius Scripturæ divinam auctoritatem, *aliunde* demonstrari non posse, quam *ex ratione*, & si contentio videatur existere, inter Scripturam & rationem; tum rationem potius audiendam esse, quam Scriptutam; idem, *Novitatum Cartesianarum Gangræna* (Amsterdam: Jansson, 1677), 34-39, 62-73, 96-105. Cf. Israel, *Radical Enlightenment*, 26.

95. Mastricht, *Theoretico-practica theologia*, I.2.xxxiv, 31: "Reformati, *rationem* cogitant; vel ut *instrumentum*, vel ut *argumentum*, vel ut *normam* & principium: ut *instrumentum*, statuunt ejus usum necessarium esse, in quavis inquisitione veritatis, ejus etiam, quæ circa Scripturam occupatur; ut *argumentum*, ejus usum esse *utilem*, nim. ut veritatem, ex Scriptura, tanquam ex primo & unico suo principio haustam, rationibus etiam naturalibis confirmemus; sed, ut *normam*...nequaquam admittunt."

reason but always to Scripture, which "commonly oblique reason."[96] God is known by his Word—and not another source—as "the Sun is known by its light."[97] Thus, Mastricht is open to the use of reason, but contra Cartesian philosophy, he vehemently retained the independence of theology from philosophical speculation. Mastricht, like other Protestant Scholastics, Muller argues, perceived and enunciated the use of instrumental and argumentative reason as a tool in the construction of his theological system. Certainly, he does not desire to create a synthesis of theology and philosophy.[98]

In conclusion, Graafland's observation regarding the independent character of the locus *de Sacra Scriptura* in the context of the (Voetian) system of doctrine and Mastricht's emphasis on the *ratio* in his doctrine of Scripture is contrary to our assessment. First, for Mastricht the doctrine of Scripture is foundational and interrelated to the definition of theology and locus *De fide salvifica*. This notion is underscored in method and content. Second, for Mastricht reason is subservient to Scripture. Thus, the presence of *rationes* in the doctrine of God does not imply rationalism on Mastricht's part. His understanding of reason and the pneumatological factor of the understanding of Scripture are not in ambivalency but culminated in one word: faith-the topic to which we turn in the next chapter.

---

96. Ibid., I.2.xxxiv, 31: "(2) Capita Religionis *rationem transcendunt*...a. quia *mysteria*...b. *paradoxa*...c. *spiritualia*...."

97. Ibid.: "3. Characteres divinitatis, ex quibus demonstratur Scripturæ divinitatis; sunt rationis, Resp. Characteres illi, ipsa sunt Scriptura, ut Scriptura agnoscatur divina, ex se, non ex ratione: sicut Sol agnoscatur ex propria luce, non aliunde."

98. Muller, *Post-Reformation Reformed Dogmatics*, 1:398-402.

Chapter 2
Faith

Introduction and Statement of the Problem

Commonly, in seventeenth-century Reformed orthodox systems of theology the doctrine of Scripture (*principium cognoscendi*) is immediately followed by the doctrine of God (*principium essendi*). This, then, raises a question about the location of the chapter *De Fide salvifica* of the *Theoretico-practica theologia* (*TPT*), which is the pivot between the two *principia* of theology. Although the order of the chapters is, according to Muller, not always significant as it relates to the actual identification of the topic,[1] the question remains why Mastricht placed the chapter on faith at the beginning of the doctrine of God, preceding the remainder of his theological enterprise. The second concern of our chapter regards the content or description of the *locus* of faith of the *TPT*. For this, firstly, we provide a historical-theological context of the topic of faith. Although it is not our intent to provide a full description of the understanding of the *locus* of faith of seventeenth-century Reformed theologians, in order to appreciate Mastricht's method of exposition and description of this locus, we will sketch a brief context in this chapter. Against this background, or in this context, we examine, secondly, Mastricht's method of explicating the *locus* and definition of faith. We examine, thereby, the relationship, if any, between exegesis, doctrine, and *praxis* and, in respect to the elenctic part, the use of a scholastic method. Parallel to this question, we will evaluate the critique of the Reformed description of faith in the seventeenth century, namely that it lost the "*blijde toon*" of the sixteenth-century Reformation and changed it with the language of "*onzekerheid en vreeze*,"[2] thereby altering the explication of the essence and assurance of faith.[3]

---

1. Richard A. Muller, "Calvin and the Calvinists: Assessing Continuities and Discontinuities between Reformation and Orthodoxy," in part 1 and 2, *Calvin Theological Journal* 30 (1995), 345-375; 31 (1996):125-60; Cf. W. J. van Asselt and E. Dekker, eds., *Reformation and Scholasticism: An Ecumenical Enterprise, Texts and Studies in Reformation & Post-Reformation Thought* (Grand Rapids: Baker Academic, 2001), 39.

2. H. Bavinck, *De Zekerheid des Geloofs* (Kampen: J. H. Kok, 1918), 44. See also K. Exalto, "Genadeleer en heilsleer" in *Theologische aspecten van de Nadere Reformatie*, ed. T. Brienen *et al.* (Zoetermeer: Boekencentrum, 1993), 182, 187.

3. See for example, selected discussions of this subject in H. Bavinck, *De zekerheid des geloofs*; idem, *Gereformeerde Dogmatiek* (Kampen: Kok, 1921), 4:103, 104; C. Graafland, *De zekerheid van het geloof* (Wageningen: Veenman, 1961), 88 (Gomarus), 152 (Voetius); Joel R. Beeke, *Personal Assurance of Faith: English Puritanism and the Dutch "Nadere Reformatie": from Westminster to Alexander Comrie (1640-1760)* (Ph.D. diss., Westminster Theological Seminary, 1988), 28; A. de Reuver, *Bedelen bij de Bron. Kohlbrugge's geloofsopvatting vergeleken met Reformatie en Nadere Reformatie* (Zoetermeer: Boekencentrum, 1992), 121, 124; Exalto, "Genadeleer en heilsweg," 179-89 and discusses W. à Brakel, J. Koelman, A. Comrie and Th. van der Groe; William Ames, *Marrow of Theology*, ed. John D. Eusden (Grand Rapids: Baker Books, 1997), 47-51.

Location

The doctrine of God in the *TPT* begins, as we have noted, with an exposition on saving faith. As such, Mastricht thus is unique among the Reformed theologians of his time. The *locus* of faith was commonly discussed either as a disputation[4] or in the *loci* of soteriology.[5] In addition, one finds the discussion on faith in the context of commentaries on the Heidelberg Catechism[6] and the Apostles' Creed.[7]

Mastricht, however, contributed in his own right to the discussion of *locus* of faith. He had, after all, dealt with the topic of faith in a separate book, unique for his time,[8] and in several disputations[9] prior to the publication of the *TPT* in 1682 and 1698. From

4. Johannes Cloppenburgh, *Theologica Opera Omnia* (Amsterdam: Gerardus Borstius, 1684), vol. 1, Exercitationes super Locos Communes Theologicos, XII.2, 1041-1051; and vol. 2, *Anti-Smalcius de Divinitate Jesu Christi*, XXIV, 902-908; G. Voetius, *De praxi fidei*, in *Disputationes Selectæ* (Utrecht, 1642) II:496-511.

5. J. Polyander, A. Rivetus, A. Walaeus, A. Thysius, *Synopsis purioris theologiæ, disputationibus 52 comprehensa, ac conscripta*, editio sexta H. Bavinck (Leiden: D. Donner, 1889), 31, 301-314; J. Hoornbeeck, *Theologiæ practicæ* (Frankfurt: Ernst Claudium Bailliar, 1680), *editio tertia*, VII.2, 245-254; Abraham Heidanus, *Corpus theologiæ christianæ in quindecim locos* (Leiden: Jordanus Luchtmans & Johannes Vivie, 1686), 133-298; Franciscus Burmannus, *Synopsis Theologiæ & speciatim Oeconomiæ Foederum Dei* (Amsterdam: Joannes Wolters, 1699), 2:VI.4, 182-194; Th. Undereyck, *Halleluja, das ist, Gott in dem Sünder verkläret*. (Bremen: H. Brauer, 1678), XVIII-XL, 116-390; Herman Witsius, *De oeconomia Foederum Dei cum hominibus* (Herborne, Nassau: Johannes N. Andreas, 1712), III.7, 345-363; Wilhelmus à Brakel, *ΛΟΓΙΚΗ ΛΑΤΡΕΙΑ, dat is Redelyke Godtsdienst in welken de goddelijke Waerheden van het Genade-Verbondts worden verklaert* (Rotterdam: Reynier van Doesburgh, 1700), I:32-33, 762-829; Johannes à Marck, *Compendium Theologiæ Christianæ didactico-elencticum* (Amsterdam: R. & G. Wetstenius, 1722), XXII, 446-468; Note, Heidanus discusses faith not as an individual locus but embeds this in the chapters on calling and justification, respectively locus X and XI, and Hoornbeeck does not follow the *ordo salutis* in a strict sense.

6. J. Cocceius, *Opera Omnia Theologica* (Amsterdam: P & J Blaev, 1701), vol. 7, *Explicatio Catecheseos Heidelbergensis*, 14, quæstio xx. Other commentaries on the Heidelberg Catechism also include discussions on faith. See for example, F. Ridderus, *Sevenvoudige Oeffeningen over de Catechismus zijnde, ziel-bereydende, waerheydt-bevestigende, geloofs-bevorderende, dwalingh-stuttende, practyck-lievende, gemoet-onderrichtende* (Rotterdam: Joannes Borstius, 1671), Lord's Day VII, 158.

7. Herman Witsius, *Exercitationes Sacræ in Symbolum quod Apostolorum dicitur*, ed. sec. (Franeker: Johannes Gyselaar, 1689), exercitio III, 22-43. Note, Witsius treats the topic of faith in the *ordo salutis* (*De oeconomia foederum Dei cum hominibus*), while in the *Excercitiones Sacræ in Symbolum* the chapter on faith precedes the discussion on the doctrine of God. Other commentaries on the Apostles' Creed placing the locus of faith at the beginning of the doctrine of God are, for example, J. Pearson, *Een Uitlegging van het Geloof*, trans. M. Neef, (Utrecht: Johannes Ribbius, 1681).

8. Petrus van Mastricht, *De fide salvifica syntagma theoretico-practicum: in quo fidei salvificæ tum natura, tum praxis universa, luculenter exponitur ; cum præf. de membris Ecclesiæ visibilis seu admittendis, seu rejiciendis, oborienti scismati moderno applicanda* (Duisburg: Franc. Sas, 1671).

9. Petrus van Mastricht, *Disputationum practicarum prima de certitudine salutis ejusque natura*, Johannes Kamerling (Utrecht: Meinardus à Dreunen, 1678); idem, *Disputationum practicarum tertia de certitudine salutis, eique opposita præsumptione seu securitate carnali*, pars prima, David de Volder (Utrecht: Meinardus à Dreunen, 1679); idem, *Disputationum practicarum tertia, de certitudine salutis, eique opposita præsumptione seu securitate carnali*, pars secunda, Jacobus Hoog (Utrecht: Meinardus à Dreunen, 1680).

this, we may infer that Mastricht consciously placed the chapter *De Fide Salvifica* outside the *ordo salutis* at the beginning of the doctrine of God and at the beginning of the remainder of his system of theology. This prompts the question, therefore, of what the reason for this could be. Our examination points to two possible reasons that may have contributed to the location of the chapter on faith. The first relates to a twofold organization principle of the *TPT*. The second is connected to Mastricht's view of reason and the nature of faith.

With respect to the first organizational or methodological principle, this is obviously motivated by Mastricht's view of the division of theology.[10] He argues that the proper division of theology is faith and love.[11] He finds, like Calvin, the annotators of the *Staten-bijbel*, and Poole,[12] basis for such division in 2 Timothy 1:13. Further, he appeals to other testimonies of Scripture (Ps. 37:3; 1 Tim. 1:19, and John 13:17), to the church fathers such as Cyril of Jerusalem and Anastasias of Nicene, and to his immediate predecessors such as Polanus von Polansdorf (1561-1610) and William Ames.[13] For Mastricht, faith is discussed in the systematic theology part of the *TPT*.[14] Love, according to Mastricht, deals with the obedience of faith as discussed in his *Idea Theologiæ Moralis*. He argues that such twofold division is most accurate. Hereby, he objects to the Socinian twofold division of God and Christ and to the Arminian threefold division of faith to the divine promises, obedience to the divine commandments, and honoring the Scriptures.[15]

10. Petrus van Mastricht, *Theoretico-practica theologia: qua, per singula capita theologica, pars exegetica, dogmatica, elenchtica et practica, perpetua successione conjugantur; accedunt historia ecclesiastica, plena quidem, sed compendiosa, idea theologiæ moralis, hypotyposis theologiæ asceticæ etc. proin opus quasi novum.* (Utrecht: Thomas Appels, 1699), I.3 De Distrubutione Theologiæ, 47-49.

11. Ibid., I.3.iii, 47: "Pro ratione scopi nostri è textu impræfens nil aliud conficiemus: quod *optima sanctæ Theologiæ, seu Religionis Christianæ distributio, fiat in fidem & charitatem*." Mastricht acknowledged the use of the method in Ames's work, the *Medulla & De Casibus conscientiæ*. Cf. ibid., *præfatio*. Cf. Ames, *Marrow of Sacred Divinity*, 5. Moreover, Mastricht justifies the division that the "art of living to God" consist of two aspects. Cf. Mastricht, *Theoretico-practica Theologia*, 1102 (*Idea Theologiæ Moralis*) and I.i, 1."

12. John Calvin, *Commentary*, vol. 21, *Commentaries on the Second Epistle to Timothy*, (Grand Rapids: Baker Books, 1984), 202: "Paul has added this [the preposition ἐν] as a mark of sound doctrine, in order that we may know what it contains, and what is the summary of it, the whole of which, according to his custom, he inludes under 'faith and love.' He places both of them in Christ; as, indeed, the knowledge of Christ consist chiefly of these two parts;" *Bijbel, dat is de gansche Heilige Schrift...met nieuwe bijgevoegde verklaringen op de duistere plaatsen* (Amsterdam: Wed. G. De Groot, 1738), 102, col. 1, fn. 50: "Dit zijn de twee hoofdstukken waartoe al de artikelen of stukken van de gezonde leer gebracht kunnen worden, en waarin deze begrepen worden;" Matthew Poole, *Synopsis criticorum aliorumque S. Scripturæ interpretum*, (London: E. Flesher, 1676), 5:1107 (10): "Præpositio ἐν pendent, ...vel. 2 à verbo ἔχω ut significet, sanctum doctrinam declaratione fidei & charitatis exprimendam."

13. Mastricht, *Theoretico-practica theologia*, I.3.iii, 47. Mastricht cites respectively, *Catechism* 4, *Bibliotheca Patristica*, *Syntagma*, II.1, and *Medulla*, I.2.ii.

14. Ibid., Books I-VIII: (1) De præcognitis Theologiæ, (2) De fide in Deum triunum, (3) De operationibus Dei, (4) De hominis apstasiâ à Deo, (5) De redemptione Christi, (6) De redemptionis applicatione, (7) De Ecclesiâ & ecclesiasticalibus, and (8) De dispensatione fœderis gratiæ. One notes that Mastricht does not include the loci of eschatology.

15. Ibid., I.2.vii, 48.

However, Mastricht acknowledges that he differs with other Reformed theologians on the division but not always in the content of theology. For Mastricht, faith relates principally to that which is to be believed, both objectively (*fides quæ creditur*) and subjectively (*fides quâ creditur*).[16] Love, on the other hand, relates to obedience and should be distinguished but not separated from faith.[17] The latter, according to Mastricht, is either done by the 'theoretical' theologians, who pursue the topic of faith in detail but neglect love and the *quâ creditur*, or by the 'practical' theologians, who may know about faith and speak edifying words to others but disregard the act of faith.[18] Therefore, to synthesize *theologia theoretica* and *theologia practica*, and following in a long tradition of Reformed thought,[19] Mastricht presents theology into two parts: *Fides* and *Observantia*.[20]

The second organizational principle is less apparent but nonetheless significant in the context of covenant theology of the seventeenth century. Mastricht notes that theology ought to be taught in a certain order, because "we read in 2 Sam. 23:5 of a covenant ordered in all things and secure ברית ערוה בכל"[21] This text does not, according to Mastricht, refer only to the ordering of the covenant of grace but also contains an order for "all instruments by which theology is secured."[22] Thus, for Mastricht faith, the

16. Ibid., II.1, 50: "Primum itaque in vitâ spirituali, fides est: quâ duo concluduntur: *habitus* quo credimus, seu fides *quâ*; & obiectum *quod*, seu *in quod* cremus, & fides *quam* credimus."

17. Ibid., I.3.i, 47: "2. Distributio...Notandum, quod *fides*, respiciat credenda potissimum, & *charitas*, facienda, seu *observantiam*."

18. Ibid., I.3.viii, 49: "Vel B. fidem pariter & observantiam seu charitatem, *verbo* quidem profitentur, *re* negligunt:... *fidem* quidem urgent & *charitatem*; sed non *in fide & charitate* Jac.2:18."

19. Cf. Ames, Polanus, see Richard A. Muller, *Post-Reformation Reformed Dogmatics* (Grand Rapids: Baker Academic, 2003), 1:205, 219, 323.

20. Ibid., I.3.ix, 49. This division is presented also in the 1682 edition. The *Observantia* is divided into the *Idea Theologiæ Moralis* and the *Hypotyposis Theologiæ Asceticæ*. Mastricht states elsewhere that theology consists of faith "which we have examined in eight books." Cf.Ibid., I.3.x, 49: "*Fide,* quam octo libris, dudum exegimus." It is noteworthy to mention a twofold revision in I.3.x, *De Distrubutione Theologiæ* (1698): (1) In the 1682 edition he outlines, only, the eight books, and in the 1698 edition adds in detail the *Observantia*; (2) In the 1682 edition it is more clearly understood that the topic of faith stands at the opening of the entire theological work, as he writes "quarum *prima* fidem habeat credenda, puta *Deum triunum* libro secundo..."and observance. Cf. Mastricht, *Theoretico-practica theologia* (1682), I.3.x, 20. In respect to Mastricht's division of theology, Sprunger asserts that the Ramist conception of theology as faith and observance, which was already implicit in Calvinism and Puritanism, appeared again and again in the theological literature in England and New England. Cf. Keith L. Sprunger, *The Learned Doctor William Ames* (Chicago: University of Illinois Press, 1972), 133; idem, "Ames, Ramus, and the Method of Puritan Theology," *Harvard Theological Review*, 59 (April, 1966): 148-151. Mastricht, however, based the division on the biblical text and its exposition.

21. Petrus van Mastricht, *Theoretico-practica theologia*, I.1.iii, 2: "*Fœdus ordinatum in omnibus* בכל ערוה ברית, appellatur, non eo tantum nomine, quod ipsum gratiæ fœdus, sit...ordinatissimum;"

22. Ibid.: "sed quod ejus etiam instrumenta quibus Theologia continetur. Methodo commodissima, prostent exarata."

covenant of grace, and theology are eminently related.[23] Examining his discussion on the covenant of grace, one notes the relationship of the covenant of grace and faith. [24] The latter is the condition for one to enter into the covenant.[25]

For Mastricht, then, faith is an entry point for (1) the covenant of grace, (2) the doctrine of God, and (3) the remainder of the system of doctrine. Therefore, the art of living to God, through Christ and regulated by Scripture, gets here an additional dimension: faith. Mastricht, then, was also concerned with a living to God through faith. Other seventeenth-century Reformed theologians held, of course, to the centrality of faith, but Mastricht returned explicitly to this Protestant concept.[26] These organizational principles, then—the division of theology and the centrality of faith—may have contributed to the location of *De Fide Salvifica*.

The second reason for the location of the chapter on faith could be connected to Mastricht's view of the *principia theologiæ* and the nature of faith. With respect to the former, Mastricht recognizes Scripture as the *principium cognoscendi* received inwardly by faith at the inception of spiritual life.[27] As we have noted earlier in our discussion of reason, Mastricht rejected the rising Cartesian notion in the seventeenth century that sought to elevate reason from the ancillary, instrumental or argumentative position to a principal position. In this context, Muller argues, the question was raised as to a resident principle, in man, upon which theology might rest, or in the language of Scholasticism, a *habitus* of the soul upon which theology might be internally grounded.[28] For Mastricht

23. Faith in relation to the covenant of grace can be noted in the books V-VIII.

24. This should not lead to the assessment of Jan van Vliet, *William Ames: Marrow of the Theology and Piety of the Reformed Tradition* (Ph.D. diss., Westminster Theological Seminary, 2002), 365: "Van Mastricht's entire theological system is structured around the concept of covenant theology"; *contra* Mastricht, *Theoretico-practica theologia* I.1.iii, 2.

25. Ibid., V.1.xx, 397: "Et dictis patet, quod & quatenus fœdus gratiæ *conditionatum* agnosci debeat."; V.1.xxii, 398: "...hoc sensu *sola fides* conditionem præstat fœderis gratiæ." Mastricht explains that God is not dependent on human faith in the offering of the covenant to them.

26. The possible change in emphasis from "faith" to "regeneration" or separation of the two *loci*, in the later period of the *Nadere Reformatie* is debatable. As will be discussed below, Mastricht and his contemporaries held to a "justifying faith."

27. Ibid., I.2.i, 17: "Regulam...supra in *verbo* Dei, seu *Scriptura* posuimus. Quæ, ut *norma* est vivendi...;quo nomine Theologiæ *principium* indigitatur"; and II.1.i, 50: "*Vita* illa *Dei*, cujus *normam* præstat Scriptura...duos actus concludit: *primoum*, quo possumus operari spiritualiter, quem præstat *fides* quâ Justus vivit Rom.1:17, Gal.11:20." Here, we follow Muller's observations on the *principia theologiæ*. Cf. Richard A. Muller, *Post-Reformation Reformed Dogmatics*, 1:440-445.

28. Mastricht, *Theoretico-practica theologia*, I.1.xlvi, 14; idem, *Vindiciæ veritatis et autoritatis sacræ scripturæ in rebus Philosophicis adversus dissertationes D. Christophori Wittichii* (Utrecht, 1655). Muller, *Post-Reformation Reformed Dogmatics*, 1:445, notes, "The first hints at this principal use of reason, found in the writings of several Reformed theologians of Cartesian inclination...notably Wittich...elicited an angry response from the last generation of high orthodox theologians. These writers...raised the question of a resident principle, in human beings, upon which theology might rest, or in the language of scholasticism, of a *habitus* of the soul upon which theology might be internally grounded. The earlier development of the prolegomena...had already provided the orthodox with grounds for an answer. All that remained was for an antirationalist or anti-Cartesian, like Mastricht, to formulate it in relation to the issue of *principia*."

this disposition was the *habitus fidei* and not *habitus sciendi*. Once theological truths are received by the *habitus credendi*, then reason can use this truth as a basis for drawing conclusions. However, reason itself is never an ultimate ground of theological argument. With this theological basis, Mastricht answers the principal question by placing the chapter *De Fide salvifica* immediately between the doctrine of Scripture and the doctrine of God as a statement concerning the way in which revelation, as external to the mind and as objectively given Word, becomes effective inwardly. It is *fides*, not *ratio*, that provides the point of entry into the doctrine of God.

We can conclude, then, that the location of the chapter on faith in the *TPT* differs with the majority of other works of seventeenth-century Reformed theologians. Mastricht's understanding of Scripture (2 Tim. 1:13 and other biblical texts), patristic fathers, and immediate contemporaries shows a continuity in favor of the faith-love division of theology. In addition, Mastricht's viewpoint of faith in relationship to the covenant of grace and the rise of Cartesianism may have contributed to the location of *De Fide salvifica* at the beginning of his system of theology.

Content

The Context: Historical-Theological

Ames opens the *Marrow of Sacred Divinity*, with a definition of the nature of divinity and its distribution. He defines theology as the doctrine of living to God,[29] which is divided into faith, the beginning and first act of spiritual life, and observance.[30] Faith he defines as a "resting of the heart on God,"[31] and its object is God.[32] Ames argues that "accurately spoken" faith is "receiving (Joh.1:12)," an act of the will and assent to the promises of the gospel.[33]

In the *Synopsis purioris theologiæ*, the doctrine of God is followed by the disputations on the divine works, anthropology, Christology, and *ordo salutis*.[34] In respect to the latter, the disputation on faith and perseverance of the saints is found. Rivetus explains temporal, historic "or dogmatic," and miraculous faith.[35] He then writes, following

29. Ames, *Marrow of Sacred Divinity*, I.1, 1.

30. Ibid., II.1, 4.

31. Ibid., III.1, 5.

32. Ibid., III.7, 6.

33. Ibid., III.2, 6; III.22, 9. In the context of this chapter, we assert, however, that Ames does not reject the faculty of the intellect altogether.

34. More precisely, one could argue that the disputations on anthropology are extended in the discussion on the law of God, idolatry, oath, and Sabbath. These are followed by disputation in the gospel, Old and New Testament, and predestination, all preceding the Christology disputation.

35. Johannes Polyander *et al.*, *Synopsis purioris theologiæ* (Leiden: Elsevier, 1625, sixth edition, H. Bavinck, Leiden: D. Donner, 1881), 31.ii-iv, 301, 302.

Augustine, that saving and justifying faith are the equivalents.[36] Saving faith, Rivetus argues, includes the *intellectus* (*assensus, notitia*) and *voluntas* (*fiducia*) of the gospel promises in Christ, through the Holy Spirit planted in the heart.[37] Rivetus asserts that intellect and will aggregate in the *habitus* of faith and come to expression in the *actus* of faith. He notes in respect to the faculties of intellect and will that Durandus rejects such *potentia* and that Aquinas points to *actus* of faith having both faculties.[38] In summary, the *Synopsis purioris theologiæ* discusses the *loci* of faith after the doctrine of God. Faith then is differentiated—after the Thomistic scholastic pattern—in the *habitus* and *actus*, whereby the latter includes the faculties of intellect (*assensus, notitia*) and will (*fiducia*).

Johannes Cloppenburgh attests in his *Theologica Opera Omnia, exegetica-didactica* of a prolific and wide-ranging theological interest.[39] The disputation *De Fide Salvifica* is placed in the chapter on the calling (*De Vocatione Efficaci*), between the *loci* of regeneration and justification. In respect to the doctrine of faith, Cloppenburgh asserts that the orthodox differ over the role of the faculties of intellect and will.[40] Particularly he notes that Ames on the one hand and Beza and Perkins on the other hand differ on this matter.[41] He then meticulously reviews Ames's position[42] but concludes that faith, the character of which is found in the Heidelberg Catechism (Resp. 21), is primarily an act of the will consisting of *fiducia* in God; by grace the intellect is savingly illuminated, and the will acts.[43] In summary, Cloppenburgh's critical appreciation of Ames stresses the inclusion of the intellect and will in the *actus fidei*.

36. Polyander *et al.*, *Synopsis purioris theologiæ*, 31.v, 302: "Recte autem Augustinus (*de Fide et oper.* c. 14)."

37. Polyander *et al.*, *Synopsis purioris theologiæ*, 31.vi, 303: "Estque fides illa salvifica, ex certa revelationis divinæ notitia, firmus a Spiritu Sancto per verbum Evangelii animis nostris ingeneratus assensus...sed præsertim promissionibus salutaribus in Christo factis, quo certa fiducia in Deo acquiescens...." See also, ibid., 31.xiv, 306.

38. Ibid., 31.xv, 306, 307: "Nam præter id quod inter Scholasticos non convenit, tales esse potentias intellectum et voluntatem, id negante Durando cum suis sectatoribus, in 1 Sent. dist. 8, q. 4 qui easdem reipsa distinctas esse contendunt fatentur: actum credendi et a voluntate et ab intellectu procedere, quorum utrumque natum est per habitum perfici, et ideo oportere tam in voluntate quam in intellectu esse aliquem habitum, si debet actus fidei esse perfectus. Thom. 1.2.q.66.art.4."

39. Johannes Cloppenburgh, *Theologica Opera Omnia* (Amsterdam: Gerardus Borstius, 1684).

40. Ibid., vol.1, *Excercitationes Super Locos Communes Theologicos*, XII.2.xii, 1042: "De specialis illius assensus Subjecto absoluto constat...partim Intellectus partim Voluntas, disquiritur inter Orthodoxos."

41. Ibid., XII.2.xxviii, 1046: "Non veremur hic cum *Amesio* affirmare; *quod vera Fides, partim in intellectu, partim in voluntate collocatur... &c. Medulla, Cap. III.22*"; XII.2.xxxi, 1046 : "*A Beza & Perkinso* dissentit *Amesi* privata illa determinatio solidum illum assensum, especialem seu particularem illam Intellectus certiorationem, qua statuimus Deum esse nostrum Deum in Christo, non esse Actum primum Fidei, sed actum ex Fide emanantem § 17 & 22."

42. Ibid., XII.2, xxxii-liv, 1046-50.

43. Ibid., XII.2.lv, 1050 : "Et nobis religio est primo illo actu voluntatis quo Deum credens eligit ac suum facit...: ita nulli credimus Fiducia in Deum, credentes illum nostrum esse, per Gratiam, qua ipse prævenit, salvifica intellectus nostri illuminatione, omnem voluntatis nostræ actum quo ipsum nos diligere cœpimus aut eligere ut nostrum."; XII.2.xxvi, 1045: "Ad investigationem ergo veri characteris,

In respect to Cocceius, let us briefly examine the topic of faith from an exegetical point of view. Mastricht's foundational text for the *loci* of faith is John 1:11, 12. Here, Cocceius's exposition includes a close reading of the biblical text with the Old Testament as background. Accordingly, he asserts that Christ came to Israel, but they have not received Him; but those who believed in His name have received Him and are children of God. To receive Him, Cocceius argues, is to be united with Christ through the Holy Spirit.[44] In addition, Cocceius's work contains several places in which faith is discussed. In the context of the *ordo salutis*, he distinguishes saving faith from historic, temporal, and miraculous faith.[45] Saving faith, or justifying faith, is an assent of the total soul and includes the love and fear of God, a *fiducia* of the heart to God, and reclination to Christ.[46] Furthermore, in the context of the commentary on the Heidelberg Catechism, he follows closely question/answer twenty-one and notes that faith includes *notitia*, *assensus*, and *fiducia*. There, he mentions faith is not *notia* but requires *notitia* because "faith comes from hearing (Rom. 10:17)."[47] In summary, Cocceius appears to have Amesian notions on what faith is and is at the same time (Reformed) confessional in his exposition of faith.

In respect to the locus of faith, Burman locates this doctrine in the *ordo salutis*.[48] Philologically he notes that the Greek word πιστίς, and Hebrew אמונה has not been used by the church in the same sense as it has been used by Latin writers (perseverance, authority) but passively used as persuasion and assent.[49] Faith, according to Burman, is the first act of regeneration, the first movement of new life,[50] and is distinct from

quo utilis salvifica Fides ab inutili distinguitur, in populari quidem Catechetica Theologia, satisfacit *Responsio xxi. Catechesios Heidelbergensis. Quid est Fides? &c.*"

44. Cocceius, *Opera Omnia Theologica*, vol. 4, *Commentarius in Euangel. Johannis*, 103, § 26: "*Accipere eum* hîc notat, eum habere donatum. Et eum *habere* est in eo esse, ipsique unitum esse per Spiritum ipsius. Nam, qui spiritum ipsius habent, in ipso sunt, eumque habent cum omni jure ipsius."

45. Ibid., vol. 7, *Summa Theologiæ*, *De Fide*, cap. 46, 262, § 42-44. Cocceius places the chapter on faith after the discussion on regeneration and conversion and before (faith of the fathers), justification, and sanctification.

46. Ibid., cap. 46, 262, § 45: "Quid igitur est fides justificans, quæ, ut dictum, totam animam occupat?...Est igitur *voluntarius assensus*;" 262, § 47: "Atqui, inquies, fides à charitate Dei distinguitur Rectè. Amor Dei, ut se per testimonium offerentis, ad fœdus, distinguitur ab amore omnium attributorum Dei...;" 262, § 48: "Fides autem etiam in *timore Dei* est, quo submittimur Deo.. ;" 262, §49: "Est in fide & *fiducia*, hoc est cordis in Deum & Christum reclinatio, apprehensio arcis Dei..." Cf. Mastricht, *Theoretico-practica theologia*, II.1.iii, 51.

47. Cocceius, *Opera Omnia Theologica*, vol. 7, *Explicatio Catecheseos Heidelbergensis*, quæstio xxi, 14, § 69: "Non dicit Catechesis fidem notitiam, sed tamen ad fidem requirit notitiam."

48. Burmannus, *Synopsis theologiæ*, VI, *de Beneficiis Christi*. Book VI deals with the benefits of Christ exposited in three *loci*: the primary benefits (grace, calling, regeneration, and faith), additional benefits (justification, adoption, and Christian liberty), internal benefits (sanctification, good works, and conversion), and consummation (glorification, perseverance, assurance, and death).

49. Ibid., vol. 2, VI.4.i, 182.

50. Ibid.: "Primus regenerationis actus, primusque novi hominis motus est *fides* . . ."

historic, temporal, and miraculous faith.[51] Further, he distinguishes between faith in the Old and New Testaments, "not in its nature and essence but gradual differences."[52] Nevertheless, he asserts that to the act of faith (*actus fidei*) belongs *notitia, assensus, et fiducia*.[53] In addition, he writes that knowledge (*notitia*) is a requisite for faith but is not the act of faith itself (John 6:69; Col. 1:9; Isa. 53:11) and that assent is "the second act of faith or better, the first essential act of faith." Burman probes further and argues that even a reprobate, missing the working of the Holy Spirit, can assent to the Word of God in general, and more in particular the gospel truth—Christ, as the sufficient savior (John 3:33; 1 Tim. 1:15).[54] For Burman it is crucial that one has trust, *fiducia*, the second essential act of faith, which is owned only by the elect. It is a trust upon God and the Gospel promises, with a twofold result: *fiducia directa* and *reflexua*. This working of trust is directed to the promised matter. When the soul rests in God, then the promises are received. In that sense faith, according to Burman, is called by the Scholastics a strengthening hope.[55] From this directive arises the reflective, the assurance, joy, and peace in the conscience and charity that accompanies trust.[56] Burman notes, however, that faith and love should be distinguished.[57] He concludes that such working of faith seeks God and Christ "and does rest finally in Him after a long and laborious wandering."[58] According to Burman, faith is a leaning and resting of the soul (Isa. 10:20; Heb. 6:18), a hunger and thirst after righteousness (Matt. 5:6), a receiving (John 1:12), a union and communion with God through Christ.[59] In summary, faith is described with multiple facets, but essentially it is a trust, an act of the will, in God and His Word.

In respect to Wilhelmus à Brakel, K. Exalto has given an adequate presentation of Brakel's description of faith.[60] Brakel defines faith as a heartfelt trust in Christ—and through Him in God—in order to be justified, sanctified, and glorified, leaning upon Christ's voluntary offer of Himself and upon the promises that He will perform this to all who receive Him and rely upon Him to that end.[61] He asserts that the actual act of faith does not consist in assenting to the truths and promises of the gospel but in

---

51. Ibid., xxxii-xxxiv, 191, 192.

52. Ibid., xxxviii, 193. He argues that in the NT there is more knowledge of the mystery of faith, manner of teaching, testimony and liberty and joy. The main issue is, according to Burman, that the salvation of the OT believers was not yet merited (VT fideles, *nondum parta salute*).

53. Ibid., iv, 182.

54. Ibid., ix, 184.

55. Ibid., xii, 185.

56. Ibid., xiii, 186.

57. Ibid., xiv, 186.

58. Ibid., xi, 184.

59. Ibid., xi. 185.

60. K. Exalto, "Heilsorde" in *Theologische aspecten van de Nadere Reformatie*,182, 183.

61. Brakel, *ΛΟΓΙΚΗ ΛΑΤΡΕΙΑ, dat is Redelyke Godtsdienst*, I:32.xli, 791.

trusting in Jesus and entrusting oneself to Him.[62] In addition, Brakel provides a comprehensive description of faith of which "receiving (Joh.1:12)" is the fifth step.[63] Brakel's concern for the spiritual condition of the believer is noticeable in the chapter on *Faith* and subsequent chapter on the *Marks of Faith*. His definition of faith as a heartfelt trust may have contributed to this concern. The assurance of faith for the believer lies in the fruits of faith, the marks and experiences, though not outside Scripture.

Finally, it is the concern of Mastricht's former classmate, Theodor Undereyck, in this *magnus opus* to deal extensively with saving faith.[64] Undereyck argues that the means to enter the covenant of grace is faith in Jesus Christ.[65] Faith is described in various ways, such as refuge taking or desired (*soekende* or *verlangende*), assured (*besittende* or *genietende*) faith.[66] The main thrust of his exposition, however, is the discussion on a refuge-taking faith.[67] Nonetheless, central in faith, according to the pastor of Bremen, is a heartfelt trust upon the divine gospel promises or in God through Christ.[68] Moreover such trust is an assured trust, whereby one experiences the union and communion of God in Christ (John 1:12).[69]

We can conclude, then, that the reviewed works contribute in various ways to the topic of faith: exegetical (Cocceius) and doctrinal (Ames, *Synopsis purioris theologiæ*, Cloppenburgh, and Burman) and practical (Brakel and Untereyck), although the latter two are not presented as mutually exclusive (Burman, Brakel and Untereyck). These theologians shared in essence a similar understanding of faith as a justifying faith in which union and communion with God through Christ is experienced. This

---

62. Ibid., xxvi, 780.

63. Ibid., 784. (1) Prior to believing, through preaching of Word, conviction of misery, (2) he becomes acquainted with the offer of Christ in a general sense, (3) develops a hunger and thirst, (4) turns to Christ and takes refuge, (5) wrestles, surrenders, receives liberty to receive him by faith (John 1:12), (6) entrusts body and soul and salvation to Christ, and relies on Him. (7) This engenders, (stimulates) the assurance and the confidence that Christ is His Savior, (8) which engenders holiness. Brakel notes, however, that the above can be intertwined, not always identifiable, or in this presented sequence.

64. Theodor Undereyck, *Hallelujah, dat is, Godt in den sondaar verheerlijkt, ofte verhandelinge van het Grote Genadenwerk Godes in Christo*, trans. Wilhelm Vos (Amsterdam: Jan Bouman, 1694).

65. Ibid., XVI.1, 102: "Van het voornaamste middel van des Sondaars zaligheid . . . namelijk van het gelove in Jesum Christum . . ." The description of faith is from chapters 16 to 34. It is outside the scope of this study to examine the related chapters on faith. Therefore, we concentrate only on the definition of faith.

66. Ibid., tafel der hoofstukken, XXI.

67. Ibid., XXI-XXVII, 152-223.

68 Ibid., XXI.1, 153: "...des Saligmakenden Geloofs kan men volgens de gewoonlijke manier van spreken noemen een hertelijk vertrouwen op de Euangelische belofte Gods;" .XXI.7, 155, "Mogelijk sal dit een bekwame beschrijvinge van het saligmakende gelove, of van een Goddelijk en hertelijk Vertrouwen op Christum, en door de selven op God . . ."

69. Ibid., XXII.3, 161: "De Schrifture, en vervolgens de Catechismus, leeren ons, dat de mensch door een waarachtig geloove aller-eerst met Christo tot de gemeynschap sijner saligmakende goederen vereenigt werd (a) . . . Joh. 1:12."

understanding is also shared by Mastricht, who combines these variant expositions of faith in his fourfold approach: exegesis, doctrine, polemic, and *praxis*.

Mastricht

Mastricht begins the chapter *De Fide salfivica* with a link between his definitions of theology and faith. He notes that faith, the first act of the spiritual life, through which one lives to God, includes two aspects: the *habitus* (*fides quâ*) and the object of faith. The former is that through which one believes, and the latter is that in which one believes.[70] The *habitus* of faith is found, according to Mastricht, in John 1:11, 12, the biblical foundation of the doctrine of faith.

In order to capture the content of Mastricht's thought concerning faith, we examine the chapter *De Fide salvifica* in the following order: the exegesis of the biblical text, the doctrinal formulation, and the elenctic and practical implications.

Exegesis

Similar to Calvin and Cocceius,[71] Mastricht expounds the biblical text from the original language in two parts. The first part is about unbelief and is divided into three aspects. The second part is about faith and is divided into two sections with three aspects each.[72] This structure of the biblical text, as we will see later, is foundational for the formulation of doctrine and *praxis*. With respect to unbelief, Mastricht notes that in the

---

70. Mastricht, *Theoretico-practica theologia*, II.1.i, 50: "Primum itaque in vitâ spirituali, fides est: quâ duo concluduntur: *habitus* quo credimus seu fides *quâ*; & objectum *quod*, seu *in quod* cre[di]mus, & fides *quam* credimus." The latter is discussed in the remainder of book II, dealing with the divine existence, essence, and Trinity.

71. John Calvin, *Commentary*, vol. 17, *Commentary on the Gospel according to John* (Grand Rapids: Baker Books, 1984), 39, 40; Cocceius, *Opera Omnia Theologica*, vol. 4, *Commentarius in Euangel. Johannis*, 103, 104.

72. Mastricht, *Theoretico-practica theologia*, II.1.ii, 51. John 1:11-12 εἰς τὰ ἴδια ἦλθεν, καὶ οἱ ἴδιοι αὐτὸν οὐ παρέλαβον ὅσοι δὲ ἔλαβον αὐτόν, ἔδωκεν αὐτοῖς ἐξουσίαν τέκνα θεοῦ γενέσθαι, τοῖς πιστεύουσιν εἰς τὸ ὄνομα αὐτοῦ. Mastricht structures the biblical text as follows:

Unbelief
    Unbelievers - τὰ ἴδια
    Offer - ἦλθεν
    Unbelief - καὶ οἱ ἴδιοι αὐτὸν οὐ παρέλαβον
Faith
    Believers - ὅσοι
    Faith - ἔλαβον or παρέλαβον
    Object of faith - αὐτόν
Fruits of faith
    Source - ἔδωκεν
    Fruits of faith - ἐξουσίαν τέκνα θεοῦ γενέσθαι
    Conditions
    Act of faith - πιστεύουσιν
    Object of faith - τὸ ὄνομα αὐτου
    The relation of the act and object of faith - εἰς

context of the first chapter of John (verses 3-11), the Jewish people, who are God's own people (οἱ ἴδιοι)[73] by right of creation and government, as well as by the offered redemption and covenant, have not accepted (καὶ οἱ ἴδιοι αὐτὸν οὐ παρέλαβον) the incarnate Christ. Mastricht asserts that Christ came (ἦλθεν) to his own as their Lord and Savior in order to bring them the forgiveness of sins and salvation and to subject them to him as King (Luke 19:27). Thus, he concludes that unbelief is a rejection, a "not accepting" or receiving of Christ.[74]

According to Mastricht, the remainder of the text shows two parts: faith (ὅσοι δὲ ἔλαβον αὐτόν) and the fruits of faith (ἔδωκεν αὐτοῖς ἐξουσίαν τέκνα θεοῦ γενέσθαι, τοῖς πιστεύουσιν εἰς τὸ ὄνομα αὐτοῦ). Subsequently, based on the syntax and grammar, he divides the first part of the text into three aspects: (1) the believers (ὅσοι), (2) their act of faith (παρέλαβον), and (3) the object of faith (αὐτόν).[75] Mastricht explicates that the believer receives, which is the act of faith (*actus fidei*),[76] the only Mediator in his threefold office of prophet, priest, and king. The object of faith, then, is, according to Mastricht, not only the divine Word, the gospel promises, and the forgiveness of sin and eternal life alone, but it is also Christ. Thus, Mastricht described faith as a union and communion with Christ and His benefits (Rom. 8:32). Moreover, faith, according to Mastricht, is a receiving act (the *actus* of faith). This description, coupled with the introduction of the chapter *De Fide salfivica*, points to Mastricht's use of the scholastic terminology of *habitus-actus*, in the service of both theology and piety.

The second part of the biblical text, according to Mastricht, encompasses the source, the fruit of faith itself, and the condition of faith. Mastricht explains using a grammatical-philological approach that the word ἔδωκεν signifies that faith is divinely given for the purpose (γενέσθαι) of having the fruit of faith (ἐξουσίαν τέκνα θεοῦ γενέσθαι). The fruits of faith include, according to Mastricht, the object of faith (particularly the union and communion with Christ and his benefits) and child-adoption, whereby one receives by faith "not only Christ as Mediator but also God as

73. Mastricht notes that only the elect who have received Christ's offer are called 'His own' (ἴδιοι του Θεου, Gal.5:24). Ibid., II.1.ii, 50.

74. Ibid., II.1.i, 50, "C. Infidelitas...sui ipsum non *receperunt*." The Greek παρέλαβον is rendered by Mastricht as 'acceperunt.' Most English translations render παρέλαβον as 'receive.' Cf. *The Bible, that is the Holy Scriptures conteined in the Olde and Newe Testament* (London: Christoph. Barker, 1599), John 1:12; Poole, *Synopsis*, IV, 1152. Central in the chapter on faith is that Mastricht uses *acceperunt* as (1) to accept, (2) not to reject, (3) not to withhold obedience. The Dutch translations render this as 'aangenomen.' Cf. *Bijbel, dat is de gansche Heilige Schrift...met nieuwe bijgevoegde verklaringen op de duistere plaatsen* (Amsterdam: Wed. G. De Groot, 1738), Johannis 1:12, fol. 44. The Dutch translation of the *TPT* renders consistently *acceperunt* or its declensions as 'aangenomen, aannemen.'

75. Mastricht, *Theoretico-practica theologia*, II.1.ii, 50 and II.1.iii, 51.

76. Ibid., 50: "2. Fides, *seu actus credendi* παρέλαβον, acceperunt, *h.e* voluerunt habere, pro Mediatore unico;"

highest end."[77] Finally, the exegete notes that the receiving of the fruits of faith is conditioned upon "belief in his name." This part of the text part includes a description of faith and consists of (1) the act of faith (πιστεύουσιν; i.e. the *actus fidei*)—because "the *habitus* of faith is not sufficient, the act is required"[78]—and (2) the object of faith: "in his name." This should be understood, according to Mastricht, as "God" or "in Christ," whereby he refers to the Jewish rendering of הוא שמו ושמו הוא, which means "He is his name, and his name is He." Finally, the text τοῖς πιστεύουσιν εἰς τὸ ὄνομα αὐτου includes (3) the preposition εἰς. This preposition signifies the relationship of the act and object of faith. Faith is directed to the object in knowledge (*notitia*), but in particular it is assent in consensus with the will, whereby one wants to have "Christ as coming Bridegroom, who offers himself to his own."[79]

In summary, Mastricht distinguishes but does not separate faith and its fruits in the text. His emphasis, arising from the biblical text, in a grammatical-philological way, is that faith is the act (*actus*) of accepting or receiving[80] and is directed to God, through Christ's union and communion of his benefits. The act and object of faith are thus correlated. Moreover, keeping in mind Mastricht's introductory comments that John 1:11, 12 describe the *habitus* of faith, one notes that for Mastricht the *habitus* and *actus* of faith are integrally related.

Doctrinal

Mastricht defines faith as

"an act of the total rational soul, whereby God is received as the highest end and the union with Christ, as the only Mediator, is obtained: through him the believer has communion with all of his benefits."[81]

77. Ibid., 51, "Nobis innotecunt imprimis: quod *fides salvifica nihil aliud sit, quam actus...quo Deum accipit, quâ summum suum finem; & Christum, quâ unicum Mediatorem...*," and "Nec enim Christum, quâ Mediatorum, recipere potest, qui Deum non ante receperit, quâ *summum* suum *finem* Joh.14:6."

78. Ibid. II.1.ii, 51: "א Actus *fidei,...Neque enim* habitus *fidei* sufficit; sed actus *etiam requiritur*." This raises the question of scholastic definition and distinction of the *actus-habitus*. For example, is Mastricht referring here to the "same" *habitus* as mentioned in the preamble?

79. Ibid.: "ב Relatio,...significata in præpositione εἰς in nomen. *Qua designatur, fidem in objectum suum ferri, non notitiâ tantum; aut assensu etiam qualicunque; sed* consensu *quoque voluntatis, quâ Christum, velut sponsum venientem, seque ac sua offerentem, velis præ omnibus habere Mediatorem.*"

80. Ibid., II.1.ii, 50: "2. Fides, *seu actus credendi;* παρέλαβον, acceperunt;" II.1.ii, 51, "3. Conditio, *fructui conferendo, prærequisita....præstabat recptio jam designata*"; II.1.2.iii, 51: "Actus ejus salvificus, dicitur *recipere*," and "unà ὑιοθεσέας continentur voce, quà ex recepto Christo"; II.1.vi, 52: "Fidem istam dicimus actum;... qui consistit in *accipendo*," and "eo quod το *credere, accipere, velle*, continuus Scripturæ tenor, prærequirat ad salutem."; II.1.ix, 52: "In *voluntate*, uno verbo, fides salvifica exigit *consensum*...seriò *volumus* habere & volendo *accipimus*, Joh.1.12"; II.1.xi, 52: "Quisnam ille tandem? Textus respondet *recipere*"; II.1.xii, 52: "Consistit autem, ista Christi *receptio* in *consensu*"; II.1.xiii, 52, 53: "Hæc quidem *receptio*, diversis rationibus diversis quoque terminis, repræsentatur in Scriptura."

81. Ibid., II.1.iii, 51: "...*fides salvifica nihil aliud sit, quam actus totius animæ rationalis, quo Deum accipit, quà summum finem; & Christum, quà unicum Mediatorem, ad hoc, ut cum eo uniamur, & uniti, communionem consequamur, omnium ejus beneficiorum.*"

Thus, the doctrinal formulation arises from the biblical text and parallels the exegetical results. Subsequently, and parallel to the exegetical structure of the biblical text,[82] Mastricht exposits his definition of faith by an etymological survey of the word *faith*. He identifies, thereby, succinctly different forms of faith: a naked assent (*nudus assensus*), a historic (James 2:17-20), a miraculous (Matt. 17:20; 1 Cor. 13:2; Mark 5:34), and a temporal faith (Matt. 13:21; Heb. 6:4-6). Mastricht notes that etymologically *fides* (*fido*, I trust), πιστις (πέπεισται, he is persuaded) and אמינה (נאמן, to be firm), entail the persuasions of the soul founded upon the veracity and fidelity of the speaker (Mark 15:32; Rom. 14:2).[83] With this succinct identification of different forms of faith and their philological meaning, Mastricht continues, for the remainder of the doctrinal part, to elaborate on the act of faith. First, he argues that faith is an act of the rational soul, which consists of an *accipere* of God as the highest end and Christ as the only Mediator.[84] Though Mastricht acknowledges that there is a seminal faith granted in regeneration, for him the act of faith is essential and required for salvation. Thus, on the one hand, regeneration and faith belong, for Mastricht, distinctly together.[85] On the

82. The structure of the doctrinal part is:

Faith
  Definition (II.1.iii)
    Etymology (II.1.iv)
    Kinds of faith (II.1.v)
  The Acts of Faith (II.1.vi)
    Total rational soul (II.1.vii)
    Intellect (II.1.viii)
    Will (II.1.ix)
    Affections (II.1.x)
  Receiving (II.1.xi-xiii)
  Object of faith (II.1.xiv-xvii
Fruits of faith (II.1.xix)
  Gradations of faith (II.1.xx)
  Source of faith (II.1.xxi)

83. Mastricht, *Theoretico-practica theologia*, II.1.iv, 51: "...*firmum esse: Latinis*, quamvis notat animi, de alicujus rei veritate, persuasionem."

84. Mastricht, *Theoretico-practica theologia*, II.1.vi, 52: "Fidem istam dicimus *actum*...qui consistit in *accipiendo*."

85. Ibid.: "fides *seminalis*, infantibus etiam per regenerationem competens... est fides *habitualis*, iteratis credendi actibus...est denique fides *actualis* seu ipsum *credere*." Seminal faith, according to Mastricht, can be both present in infants and a habitual faith, the latter being characterized by the exercise of faith. In evaluating the essence of faith, one observes the similarity between Mastricht's definition of faith and regeneration, ibid., VI.3.vi, 660: "[Regeneration] is that physical operation of the Holy Spirit whereby He begets in those, who are elected, redeemed, and externally called, the first act or the principle of spiritual life, by which they are enabled to receive the offered redeemer and comply with the condition of salvation." The English translator of the chapter *Regeneration* provides an extensive footnote regarding the use of the word *physical*. He argues that Mastricht affirms Ames' and Rutherford's view by noting that God in regeneration acts after the manner of a supernatural operation, a physical cause, which is in opposition to the moral act. Cf. Peter van Mastricht, *Treatise on Regeneration, Extracted*

other hand, faith is an act of the rational soul: for "with the heart man believes" (Rom. 10:10), and this first act of spiritual life (Rom. 1:17; Gal. 2:20) encompasses the whole person. Broadening the testimony of Scripture, one notes that faith as the first act of the spiritual life is for Mastricht a justifying faith.[86] Therefore, for him regeneration, justification, and faith are united and not separate events for the believer. For Mastricht these distinctions come together in the act of faith, which unites one in communion with Christ.

Moreover, the act of faith, according to Mastricht, involves both the intellect (*intellectus*) and the will (*voluntas*).[87] The former consists of the knowledge (*notitia*) of the gospel promises of God and Christ (John 17:3; Isa. 53:11; 1 Tim. 1:12) and assent (*assensus*). This assent is not only to the entire Word of God but in particular, it is a *theoretico*-practical assent to the major proposition that "Christ is the Messiah, which is promised from ancient times, and outside him there is no hope of salvation" (John 11:25-27; 1 John 2:22; Acts 4:12). [88] The will, on the other hand, involves a consensus, whereby the Mediator offered in the gospel is accepted and affections. These affections are directed in love, desire, and joy toward God and the Mediator (Matt. 10:37; Ps. 42:1, 2; Ps. 16:5; Ps. 73:25) and result in a hate for everything that is contrary to the former (Ps. 139:22).

While Mastricht consents to the statement that knowledge, assent, consensus and trust concur in saving faith, he emphasizes that the text of John 1:11, 12 and other texts particularly states the act of faith as "receiving"[89] (Col. 2:5,6; Phil. 3:8, 9; Gal. 4:14; Matt. 26:26). The reception of Christ occurs as an unconditional consensus of the will

---

from His System of Divinity, Called Theologia theoretico-practica, trans. unknown (New Haven: Thomas and Samuel Green, in the Old Council Chamber, 1770), 18, 19.

86. The references to the texts of Rom. 1:17 and Gal. 2:20 should not be overlooked. Mastricht asserts that the appropriation of justification occurs through faith. Cf. *Theoretico-practica theologia*, VI.6.i, 700: "Appropriatio *istius justitiæ quâ justitia illa Dei*, nostra sit, per fidem Jesu Christi." He defines the justification as, "Quo modo justificatio nobis non est, nisi, Dei declaratio gratiosa quâ peccatorem, propter justitiam Christi, ei imputatam & vivâ fide ab eo apprehensam, absolvit à reatu omnium peccatorum suorum & justum eum pronunciat ad vitam æternam." (VI.6.v, 703). This definition of justification stands *contra* the central argument of E. Böhl, *Von der Rechtfertigung durch den Glauben: ein Beitrag zur Rettung des protestantischen Cardinaldogmas* (Leipzig: Gustorff; Amsterdam: Scheffer, 1890); Cf. Eduard Boehl, *The Reformed Doctrine of Jusification*, trans. C.H. Riedesel (Grand Rapids: Wm. B. Eerdmans Publ. Co., 1946), 65.

87. Mastricht, *Theoretico-practica theologia*, II.1.viii-x, 52.

88. Ibid., viii, 52: "...3. [Notitia et assensus] magnæ hujus propositionis: *Christus, est ille quondam promissus Messias, extra quem, nulla omnino salutis spes relinquitur.*"

89. Ibid., xi, 52: "Sed, cum plures, in salvifica fide, concurrant actus, notitiæ, asssensus, consensus, fiduciæ &c. observandum, esse in his unum quendam actum, qui prædominetur, quoque posito ponatur salus, & sublato, tollatur, quem *salvificum*. Quisnam ille tandem? Textus respondet *recipere*." That Mastricht actually differentiate between 'consensus' or 'fiduciæ' is open for further investigation. However, he employs the term 'consensus' or 'consensu', rather than 'fiduciæ', in his discussion of "receiving Christ." (Ibid., xii, 52; xii, 53)

assenting to the gospel offer.[90] Thus, for Mastricht, according to Muller, receiving Christ and believing the Gospel savingly are synonymous.[91] Furthermore, Mastricht notes that Scripture uses different terminology for *receptio*. In a strict sense (Col. 2:6, 7; Rev. 22:17) it means that the will of Christ is that the offer be accepted. In addition, it is a consensus, where Christ is accepted as the only Mediator but preceded by invitations and persuasions (Matt. 23:37; Ps. 81:12; John 5:40; Isa. 55:1, 2). Finally, it can mean an *electio* of Christ (Song of Sol. 5:9) or the making of a covenant, whereby the soul gives itself over in a "marriage-like" proposal (Hos. 2:20, 21; Jer. 31:33).[92]

In summary, for Mastricht the essence of faith is an assenting act of the will. Thus, he involves both the intellect and the will in the act of faith. This is the axis of his definition of faith.

Expanding his exegetical observations, Mastricht deals subsequently with the object of faith. The object of faith is essentially God as the end and Christ as Mediator.[93] Through faith, then, one receives in particular the Mediator in His threefold office, as prophet to teach the believer (Matt. 23:8, 10), as priest to acknowledge him as the only Savior for the forgiveness of sins and salvation (Isa. 10:20), and as king to acknowledge his lordship (Rom. 14:8) and be subjected to him (Ps. 2:11, 12). Mastricht remarks hereby that Christ is received through faith not only as Savior for one's righteousness but also as Lord for one's sanctification: "As ye have therefore received Christ Jesus the Lord, so walk ye in him" (Col. 2:6 KJV). Thus, both justification and sanctification flow forth from Christ.

Following the description of faith and its object, Mastricht discusses the *finis* of faith: the fruits of faith. These fruits are twofold: the union with Christ and the communion with his benefits—justification (Phil. 3:9; Acts 10:43), child-adoption (John 1:12; Gal. 3:26), sanctification (Acts 15:9), and glorification (1 Pet. 1:3-5). Mastricht distinguishes but does not separate these benefits of Christ apart from (the act of) faith.[94] Faith, he

90. Ibid., xii, 52.

91. Muller, *Post-Reformation Reformed Dogmatics*, 2:292.

92. Mastricht, *Theoretico-practica theologia*, II.1.xiii, 53: "Hæc quidem receptio, diversis rationibus diversis quoque terminis, repræsentatur in Scriptura, 1. *Receptio*...2. *Consensus* in Christum...3. *Electio* Christi...4. *Confœderatio*...ut sit in conjugio Hos. 2:20, 21, Jer. 31:33."

93. Ibid., xv, 53: "Quodnam igitur?...Deus quidem, quà *finis*, Christus quà *medium* aut Mediator."

94. Mastricht expounds from 1 Cor. 1:30 (But of him are you in Christ Jesus, who of God is made unto us wisdom, and righteousness, and sanctification, and redemption) the doctrine of the union with Christ, which is principally worked by the Holy Spirit and instrumentally by faith. Cf. ibid., VI.5.ix, 692; "Vinculâ ista quibus mediantibus, cum Christi unimur, *duo* numerantur in Scripturâ alterum *principale*, scil. Spiritus Christi Rom. 8:9...alterum *instrumentale*, scil. *fides* nostra...." The doctrine of justification is noted above. The doctrine of child-adoption is according to Mastricht, "*gratiosa Dei declaratio, quâ justificatos in familiam suam, tanquam filios admittit, eisque prærogativas filiorum Dei communicat.*" He then notes that the power of child-adoption conjugates with faith. (VI.7.v, 724). The doctrine of sanctification is formulated as "*illam Dei intelligimus operationem physicam, quâ sanctitatem suis infundit, ejusque exercitium procurat*" (VI.8.vii, 734). One notes the similarity with the definition of regeneration. The doctrine of glorification contains several affirmations from the side of God and the believer. The former is attested in the promises of the gospel, and the latter through faith. Ibid., VI.9.ix, 758: "...certitudinem

argues, can be distinguished as great faith (Matt. 15:28) and little faith (Matt. 6:30; Luke 17:6). However, in these gradual differences, faith increases (2 Cor. 10:15), is confirmed (Col. 2:7), and is brought to full assurance (Heb. 10:22). Pastorally, he notes that these differences are commonly observed from a human point of view (Matt. 8:26; 15:28; 8:10) and do not relate to more or less knowledge (*cognitio*) or assent whereby trust is more or less assured. It relates primarily to the degree of the act of faith or *receptio*.[95] Mastricht, then, closes the doctrinal part by noting that the source and origin of faith is God, who works faith in regeneration as a seed of faith, and in conversion wherein one through the act of faith obtains Christ, and in sanctification whereby faith produces fruits.[96]

We conclude, then, that doctrinal formulation and exposition in structure and content are a further elaboration of the exegesis of the biblical text. The structure of the definition and description of faith is directly correlated to the biblical text and the exegetical result. Though the exegetical section emphasizes the explication of the biblical text, the doctrinal section focuses more on the contemplative or *theoretica* aspect of theology. While the exegetical section is more restricted to the exposition of John 1:11, 12, the doctrinal section employs a widening of scriptural testimony in relationship to the topic. In terms of content, Mastricht's definition of faith consolidates the thought of how faith is related to the intellect, the will, regeneration, justification and Christ. The act of saving faith, described as faith, is central and integrally related to Christ and his benefits. Faith, then, is for Mastricht directed to God through Christ.

Elenctic

In five questions Mastricht argues subsequently about the assent of the intellect, the place of *notitia* in saving faith, the role of the divine commandments, the assurance of faith, and the question that faith could be bogus. In our examination of these questions, the structure and content will be reviewed.

The first *quæstio*, concerns whether saving faith consists only in an intellectual assent. Mastricht responds with a twofold distinction, noting that the Roman Catholics

---

glorificandis asserant, quam quæ est *fidei* divinæ 1 Joh. 4:16." Thus, we see that, for Mastricht, faith is a central link to the other *loci*. Muller notes that Mastricht discusses in detail these different *loci* later in book VI, *De Redemptione applicatione*, but here "provides a sense of purpose of the system and of the great difficulty in selecting a point of departure for discussion of doctrine." Cf. Muller, *Post-Reformation Reformed Dogmatics*, 2:292.

95. Mastricht, *Theoretico-practica theologia*, II.1.xx, 54: "Tria interim hîc observanda: *primò*, posse fidem ex una parte *robustam* esse, quando ex altera *debilis est*. ...*Secundo*, istam disparitatem, non in *diversis* modo conspici subjectis sed & in *eisdem*, diverso tempore. ...*Tertio*, nec *tantum* nec præcipuè, fidem *firmam* dici, aut infirmam, cui clarior competit ac distinctior rerum divinarum *cognitio*; vel cui *assensus* est solidior, aut confidentia immotior, aut salutis certitudo confirmatior; sed &, quin potissimum, ab appetitu, *receptione* ac submissione sui;...cum actus fidei, proprie quidem *salvificus*, non tam sit in notitiâ, aut assensu; quam in receptione."

96. Ibid., xxi, 54: "Tertio, [Operatur fidem Deus] *sanctificatione*, quâ flores etiam, & fructus fides excludit, sitque per charitatem."

understand saving faith primarily as an intellectual assent, although not denying a certain presupposition of the will towards God, in order to avoid the Protestant position that saving faith is a *fiducia* of the heart.[97] Second, he notes that most of the English practical theologians agree that saving faith consists in an assent solely of the will (*voluntas*).[98] He then states his agreement with the third position, which is, that saving faith consists of intellect and will.[99] More specifically, it consists in the intellect *radicaliter*, in the will *formaliter*, and in the remaining faculties *operative*. This middle position seems most accurate to Mastricht because "faith is the first act of spiritual life and involves the entire person." Faith, he continues based on Scripture, is not a naked intellectual assent because one believes not to God but in God and in Christ (2 Kings 17:14; Rom. 10:11; John 14:1; 3:16; 1 Pet. 2:6). Faith is πεποίθησις (trusting, 2 Cor. 3:4), θαρρέω (trusting, Matt. 9:2; 2 Cor. 5:6), παρρησία (boldness, Eph. 3:12), πληροφορία (full assurance, Rom. 4:21; Col. 2:2; Heb. 10:22), ὑπόστασις (firm foundation, Heb. 11:1), and προσαγωγὴν, (access, Rom. 5:2; Eph. 2:18). Moreover, Scripture testifies that faith is a "confidence" (Ps. 25:2), a "leaning upon" (Isa. 10:20; 50:10; 2 Chron. 16:8). Through faith one casts oneself upon God or commits oneself to God (Ps. 37:5; Prov. 22:9). Therefore, he reminds the reader that the object of saving faith is God and Christ as Mediator and that it is He who calls one to salvation through faith in the gospel. Thus, when this offer is not accepted, one rejects God and Christ.

Having stated the *quæstio* and provided an initial response, Mastricht deals subsequently with a twofold *objectio*. First, some assert that Scripture testifies in John 1:50 that faith is an assent of the intellect. Mastricht replies that such assent is not excluded but is a part of saving faith. Second, some assert that the philosophers agree unanimously that faith is an assent of the intellect, with the exception of the Cartesian philosophers, who advocate that "giving judgment" is seated in the will. Mastricht replies, "In a philosophical way, faith is an act of the rational soul, and thus includes an assent of the intellect; in a theological way, faith is more an act, namely of knowledge, assent, trust, and particular application."[100] Thus, Mastricht involves both the intellect and the will in the act of faith.

The second question discusses the role of knowledge in faith. Mastricht reminds the readers that for the Cartesian philosophers knowledge is presupposed but not a part of faith. With reference to Bellarmine's *De Justificatione*, Mastricht notes that the Roman Catholics have an implicit faith whereby knowledge is what the church believes. His

---

97. Ibid., xxii, 54.

98. Ibid., xxii, 54: "...Britannorum plerique practici, in sola voluntate ponunt fidem salvificam ... existiment, assensum nullum intellectus, sufficere ad recipiendum Christum." Note that H. Bavinck probably implies that Mastricht follows the English practical theologians. Cf. Bavinck, *Gereformeerde Dogmatiek*, 4:102.

99. Mastricht, *Theoretico-practica theologia*, II.1.xxii, 55: "Sunt, qui mediam sententiam eligunt, qua, nec in intellectu solo consistat, nec in voluntate sola: sed in universa vita hominis spirituali: in intellectu quidem, *radicaliter*; in voluntate, *formaliter*; in reliquis animae facultatibus, *operative*."

100. Ibid.: "vel *philosophice* ...vel *theologice*...."

response is that the Reformed distinguish between *scientia* and *notitia*, whereby the former is not and the latter is required for faith. This position is, according to Mastricht, argued in Scripture in Deuteronomy 4:6, Psalm 32:9, Daniel 9:22, Colossians 1:6 and 2:2, and 1 Timothy 3:7. Moreover, the Mediator cannot be received without knowledge. Three objections are dealt with, the first being that faith is the way (*via*) and means unto knowledge according Isaiah 7:9.[101] A second objection is that knowledge needs to be distinguished from faith according to 1 Corinthians 13:2. However, Mastricht argues that this text speaks about a miraculous faith, and therefore although knowledge (*notitia*) should be distinguished from faith, it is not excluded from faith. The third objection is that 2 Corinthians 10:5 seems to advocate that one's thoughts should be led by the obedience of Christ and not by reason. Mastricht replies that one should distinguish the corrupt reason (*ratio*) from knowledge (*notitia*).[102] Thus, for Mastricht knowledge (*notitia*) is a part of faith.

The third question concerns whether obedience to the commandments is part of saving faith. The Roman Catholic theologians affirm that it is because they, according to Mastricht, make faith and good works requisite for justification. The Socinians exclude the satisfaction and meritorial work of Christ and state that one is saved by the obedience of the commandments or the "works of the gospel." Objecting to the Roman Catholics and the Socinians, Mastricht argues that the Reformed, although "they do not deny that faith is a divine work and an act of obedience" (John 6:29), refute the idea that obedience to the commandments is a part of justification.

Fourth, Mastricht raises the question of whether the essence of saving faith consists of a particular application or persuasion whereby one is assured that Christ is one's Mediator.[103] He assesses the Pelagians' and Roman Catholics' denial that certitude of faith can be obtained by the means of grace in order to maintain the *liberum arbitrium*. With respect to the Protestant position, he distinguishes four trajectories.[104] First, most Protestants concur that saving faith consists of knowledge, assent, and trust (*fiducia*). Second, some of them argue that trust is a particular persuasion and application of Christ's benefits. Third, others emphasize that trust is an election of Christ and resting in Him and thus trust relates to the intellect or to the will. Fourth, there are those

who constitute trust (*fiducia*) as a marriage arrangement, whereby we, through the mediator, who offers himself to us, receive (*recipere*) to posses him upon certain laws; so that we reciprocally render ourselves to him (Song of Sol. 2:16), where after follows the particular applications and undoubtful persuasion, that Christ is our Bridegroom, that his goods, so much and great these be, are ours; thus, such persuasion or assurance is

---

101. Mastricht probably refers to אִם לֹא תַאֲמִינוּ כִּי לֹא תֵאָמֵנוּ -If you will not believe, surely you shall not be established.

102. Mastricht, *Theoretico-practica theologia*, II.1.xxiii, 55, 56.

103. Ibid., xxv, 56.

104. Ibid., 56: "Protestantes non uno modo loquuntur."

not in itself the formal saving act of faith; but a consequence of the receiving [act] (*aannemen*). [105]

This position, according to Mastricht, is the best.[106] Thus, for Mastricht, the assurance of faith is a result of the act of faith but not saving faith itself. With respect to the particular application or assurance of faith, two dangers should be avoided in his opinion. On one hand is the Roman Catholic position that excludes assurance from saving faith, which is, according to Mastricht, against Scripture (Gal. 2:20; Rom. 8:38; 2 Cor. 5:1, 2; 2 Tim 4:8; Ps. 103:1-3; 2 Sam. 12:13). On the other hand, according to Mastricht, most Protestants supplant the particular application of faith in favor of the act of faith.[107] Mastricht repudiates both dangers. First, in the assurance of faith there is no promise of justification or salvation. One does not read, according to Mastricht, in Scripture "all those which are persuaded will be saved or sins are forgiven or are justified."[108] Second, among other reasons, he stresses that a particular persuasion or assurance of faith cannot take place without saving faith. The former presupposes the latter. In other words, the believers have knowledge that Christ is their Savior and, as a result of this, that their sins are forgiven. Thus, for Mastricht, the assurance of faith belongs to the act of faith though "the particular persuasion is not always experienced" (Ps. 77:8, 9, 10; Ps. 88; Rom. 7:24).[109]

The last *quæstio* is succinctly stated and refuted and seems to Mastricht more philosophical than theological. For him there is no part in saving faith that is false, because God is the author.

We conclude our examination of these questions with the following observations regarding the structure and content. The structure of the questions in the elenctic section follows carefully the scholastic *quæstio* method. The question is stated and is *historico*-argumentatively summarized. Mastricht's *responsio* to the question is followed by the *objectio*. The latter is refuted and is followed by Mastricht's own position. In respect to the content, Mastricht's questions in this elenctical section are not immediately inferred from the biblical text. Though they seem somewhat independent, they are directly related to the formulated doctrine. However, in particular instances, for example, related

---

105. Ibid.: "Sunt etiam, qui fiduciam illam constituunt, in *receptione* quadam *coniugali*, quâ sic admittimus Mediatorem, seipsum offerentem, certis legibus possidendum; ut ei nosipsos *reciprocemus*, reddamus Cant. II. 16. quam postmodum excipit *particularis applicatio*, & indubitata *persuasio*, Christum nostrum esse *Sponsum*, eius bona, quanta quanta sunt, *nostra* esse, sic nim. ut persuasio ista, non sit ipse actus fidei formaliter salvificus; sed consequens receptionis."

106. Ibid.: "Hæc, meo quidem judicio, tutissima est sententia."

107. Ibid., 57: "De quo, ex professo videbimus, in negotio de *certitudine salutis*; in *excessu*, à plurimis Protestantibus, qui in istà *applicatione*, actum collocant fidei, *propriè* & formaliter *salvificum* quo posito, ponatur salus; & sublato, tollatur."

108. Ibid.,: "Nullibi, enim vel *verbis* dicitur, vel *re*; quicunque suerit persuasus, Christum esse *suum* Servatorem, *sibi* remissa esse peccata sua; ille justificatus est, aut justificabitur & c."

109. Ibid.,: "*Fidelis* daretur, fide salvificâ destitutus: eo quod compertum sit, nec omnibus fidelibus, adesse istam persuasionem *particularem*; nec *semper* Psal 77:8-10 & 78. per totum Rom 7:24."

to philology, the answer is a further elaboration of a linguistic discussion in the doctrinal section. On the other hand, the question on the assurance of faith, though connected to the exegetical and doctrinal section, is a concern that is more worked out in the practical section.

Practical

The foundation of the structure and the content of the practical section is the biblical text of John 1:11, 12. Mastricht parallels the structure of the practical section with the exegetical division of the text: unbelief and faith. Therefore he opens this section by following the biblical text: "his own received him not" (John 1:11).[110] Arising from this he probes the nature of, the origin of, the consequences of, and the means against unbelief.

In respect to the nature of unbelief, Mastricht asserts that the act of unbelief is "a not receiving" (John 1:11), "a not wanting" (John 5:40; Matt. 23:37), "a despising" (Matt. 13:5), and "a rejection" (John 13:48) of the object of faith, that is, God as highest end (Ps. 78:22) and Christ as Mediator (John 5:46, 47). Furthermore, he argues that ignorance is a main feature of unbelief,[111] while distinguishing gradual steps in incredulity. The highest form or step is the rejection of God and Christ, which is done by the Gentiles, Jews, and Muslims. A lesser form is heresy shown in the denial of the foundational parts of faith. The least or smallest step of incredulity is shown by those who confess faith but whose faith is not visible in their actions. Mastricht laments over the many in his time who evidence such nominal form of unbelief.[112]

Then Mastricht points to several possibilities of the origin of unbelief, including the feeling of unworthiness to receive Christ and the despising of God's grace "which is so often offered."[113] Mastricht, moreover, points out that the ultimate consequence of unbelief is a threefold death,[114] but he also offers pastorally the means of contesting

---

110. The structure of the practical section is:

> Unbelief
> > Nature
> > Origin
> > Consequences
> > Supporting means
> Faith

111. Mastricht, *Theoretico-practica theologia*, II.1.xxix, 58: "(1) Crassa *ignorantia*, Dei & Mediatoris...(2) *Incredulitas*...(3) *Non-receptio*...(4) *Diffidentia*...(5) *Contumacia*...(6) *Carnalitas*...."

112. Ibid., xxx, 58: "...qualis, in ipsis veræ fidei confessoribus, nimium proh dolor! deprehenditur frequentata."

113. Ibid., xxxi, 58: "Succidit infidelitatis *origo* (1) *Satanas*...(2) Cordis humani *perversitas*...(3) *Stupiditas*...(4) *Ignorantia* Dei, Christi, promissionum & beneficiorum...(5) *Amor* ac studium peccati...(6) *Metus* persecutionis...(7) φιλαυτία seu αὐτότη...(8) Nimia *pusillanimitas*...(9) est *contemtus gratiæ* diu multumque à Deo oblatæ...."

114. Ibid., xxxii, 59. Mastricht notes that the consequences of unbelief are manifested in hatred of God as person and his attributes, which is incapable of any work; it feeds ignorance and leads to death

incredulity. These include an acknowledgment and contemplation of the cause and consequences of unbelief (Lam. 3:40; 2 Cor. 13:5). Moreover, he urges in the conclusion that one must make use of the means of grace, "through which God commonly works faith," such as the hearing of the Word of God (John 5:25; Ezek. 37:4), prayer (Ps. 51:12), and conversation with believers.[115] Thus, for Mastricht unbelief, with its causes and characteristics, is ultimately a rejection and not receiving of Christ. The remedy, which he offers, directs one to God and his Word.

The remainder of the chapter deals with faith and is divided into seven practical reflections (*praxis*). Here also Mastricht parallels his discussion with the biblical text and its exegesis. Moreover these practical reflections, however, reveal two main themes: self-examination and exhortation, of which the latter is divided into the exercise and the life of faith. The self-examination deals with faith and the marks of faith. The former is related to the exegetical description of faith[116] and to the doctrinal description of the gradation of faith.[117] The latter is directly related[118] to the exegetical description and the division of the condition of the fruit of faith.[119] The exercise of faith is described as a prelude to the discussion of the receiving, preservation, and increase of faith. Finally, the practical section and entire chapter *De Fide salvifica* closes with a discussion on the life of faith, including the assurance of faith. The former arises from the exegesis of the biblical texts dealing with the fruits of faith and is also related to the discussion in the doctrinal part.[120] The latter, the assurance of faith, is related to the description of what faith is[121] and to the question of the assistance of faith as it was dealt with in the elenctic part.[122]

Self-examination. The self-examination of faith should be done, according to Mastricht, discriminately. In addition, such should show evidences of faith.[123] Therefore,

---

(Gen. 3), physically (2 Kings 7:2; cf. Ps. 106:26; Num. 20:8, 10-12), spiritually (Eph. 2:1, 2) and eternally (John 3:18, 36).

115. Ibid., xxxiii, 59: "Restat, infidelitatis *remedia*...in *usu* constanti & fideli *mediorum* quibus Deus solet operari fidem...."

116. Ibid., ii.I.2.i.B, 50.

117. Ibid., xx, 54.

118. The direct relationship is strengthened by the exposition in the doctrinal part on the act and object and their correlation. Cf. ibid., vi-x, 52 (act of faith), xiv-xvii, 53 (object of faith); xi, 52 (correlation).

119. Ibid., ii.I.2.ii.C, 51.

120. Ibid., xix, 53.

121. Ibid., ii.2, 50 (exegesis) and vi, 52 (doctrinal).

122. Ibid., xxv, 56.

123. Ibid., xxxv, 60, "Et, quo magis ex voto succedat, istud explorationis negotium; requiritur, ut ab *unâ parte*, in promptu nobis sint *discriminanda*, ab alterâ, discriminis *indicia*."

the examination of true faith should recognize different gradations of faith,[124] such as a great or small faith. The former is living and firm,[125] and the latter—even the smallest faith—is distinguished from unbelief, common faith, and distrust because it is still directed to God, Christ, and salvation. The smallest faith, according to Mastricht, acknowledges its weakness, complains about it (Mark 9:24), pants after a remedy (1 Pet. 2:2), but still receives God and the Mediator (Ps. 6:2-4; Ps. 77:1, 3, 4).[126]

In respect to the evidences of faith, Mastricht does not discuss the marks of faith that can be found in the believer but directs one to the parts, object, and essence of faith. He argues that saving faith consists of a sufficient knowledge to receive God and the Mediator, a firm assent to the law and gospel, and a consensus of the will.[127] In addition, one should be directed to the object of faith: Christ, the Lord and Savior as Mediator and God as highest end (John 14:1; Ps. 78:22). The modus of receiving is that all parts of saving faith are directed to God and the Mediator so that true believers are consistently directed above worldly matters (Ps. 78:25, 26; Matt. 19:27).[128] Thus, self-examination is for Mastricht primarily a habitual reflection on the gradations and evidences of faith, which are directed to God in Christ.

Exhortation—The Exercise of Faith. Mastricht underscores the inevitability of the exercise of faith.[129] He argues that these exercises accentuate the fact that faith should be acquired, conserved, and increased. With respect to the acquisition of faith, the modus is twofold: (1) to have knowledge of the nature, origin, consequences, and means against unbelief,[130] and (2) to know the way in which "God commonly works in the heart."[131]

---

124. Ibid.: "Discriminanda sunt: fides *vera* ac realis." The word *realis* is rendered in the Dutch edition as "zakelijk." Cf. Mastricht, *Beschouwende en praktikale godgeleerdheit*, II.1.xxxv, 1:148: "de dingen welke onderzocht en onderscheiden moeten worden zijn: het ware en zakelijke gelove."

125. Mastricht, *Theoretico-practica theologia*, II.1.xxxvi, 60: "Fidem verè magnæm à securitate & *præsumptione*, nervosè discernit Amesius Cas. lib. II. cap. 6. §. 16...(1) *Testimonium ejus habent in seipsis*, ...(2) *Charitatem Dei, effusam habent in suis cordibus*...(3) *Fructus illos habent & proferunt*...."

126. Ibid., xxxix, 60: "Fides *minima* itidem deficit: vel α. in *fiduciâ*...β. in *receptionis vigore*..."; ibid., xlii, 61: "Porro istæ partes, pro objecto habent: 1. non tantum *Christum* quâ Mediatorem; sed & *Deum* quâ summum *finem*."

127. Ibid., xli, 61: "...fides *salvifica* constat: (1) *Notitiâ* sufficiente Dei ac Mediatoris accipiendi...(2) *Assensu* firmo & immoto Legi & Euangelio præstito...(3) *Consensu* voluntatis..."

128. Ibid., xliii: 61. Cf. Mastricht, *De fide salvifica*, XIII.

130. Cf. ibid., xxviii-xxxiv, 57-59. Cf. Mastricht, *De fide salvifica*, XXXIV.

131. Mastricht, *Theoretico-practica theologia*, II.1.xlvi, 62: "Tum *secundò*, ut perspectos habeamus, gradus & ambages, quibus fidem actualem, Deus in corde generare consuevit...1. *Mentem convincit*...2. miseriam suam intime *sentiat* ...3. ad piam desperationem adigit...4. *cor aperit*, ei seipsum ac Filium Mediatorem, omni-sufficientissimum Redemtorem...5. *pellicit* ac permovat voluntatem, *trahit*, ut actu *veniat* Deum apprehendat ut summum finem & Christum ut unicum suum Mediatorem." Here, two comments are in order. First, Mastricht is very succinct in the description of the work of God in the conviction and misery of a sinner. Second, Mastricht also asserts that the acquisition of faith is not about

With respect to the conservation of faith, Mastricht clarifies that he speaks here about the *actus fidei*, "not the seminal faith which is granted in the regeneration, and which never can be lost" (1 John 3:9; 2 Tim 2:19; Rom. 11:29).[132] The means of conserving such faith are, then, being directed to God in prayer, exercising faith, and not grieving the Spirit. The mark of a living faith is, for Mastricht, that faith in the believer increases in the sense of Philippians 3:12, 13, 15[133] (αὐξάνω 2 Cor. 10:15; βεβαιόω Col. 2:17; ὑπεραυξάνω 2 Thess. 1:3). Mastricht's central thought is that the increase of faith occurs through the use of Word and sacrament and receiving of Christ.[134] Thus, the exercise of faith means the act of faith is continually acquired, conserved, and increased and is directed to God in Christ through Word and Sacrament.

Exhortation—The Life of Faith. Finally, to live through faith, which works through love (Gal. 5:6), involves, according to Mastricht, three elements: (1) the receiving of God and the Mediator, which is the most essential element; (2) a trusting dependency on the divine sufficiency, goodness, and veracity; and (3) an obedient submission, a walk in the strength of God and reliance upon the merits of Christ.[135] Living with these elements is, for Mastricht, a life of assured faith; it constitutes a living unto God. Without it faith is dead (James 2:16). Concerning the application of the particular persuasion or assurance of faith, Mastricht asserts that such is the apex of faith.[136] He echoes his comment from the doctrinal section that this persuasion is born out of the act of faith (Song of Sol. 2:16) but adds that the assurance of faith may also arise from the practical syllogism.[137] Here, he expands his discussion on the assurance of faith from the doctrinal section and

seminal faith, which is the *potentia* to believe that is granted immediately in the regeneration, but about the *actus* of faith; the act to receive God as highest end and Christ as the only Mediator.

132. Ibid., xlviii, 63: "*Quinta praxis, studium respicit conservandi* fidem, non utique *seminalem*, regeneratione natam, quæ amitte penitus, nunquam potest:.....sed *actualem*...."

133. "Not as though I had already attained, either were already perfect: but I follow after, if that I may apprehend that for which also I am apprehended of Christ Jesus. Brethren, I count not myself to have apprehended: but *this* one thing I do, forgetting those things which are behind, and reaching forth unto those things which are before..." (Phil. 3:12-13, KJV).

134. Mastricht, *Theoretico-practica theologia*, II.1.l, 63: " Universæ nostræ vitæ, ac perfectionis spiritualis, *incrementum* 2 Pet. 1:3-8 quatenus fide Christum recipiendo, qui vita nostra est Col. 3:4."

135. Ibid., liii, 64: "*Quod vivo, vivo per fidem Filii Dei...quam recepto Deo ac Mediatori se totum committere, ab iis, in omnibus necessariis pendere seque totum, cum omnibus suis, eisdem reciprocare; speciatim, tres actus involvit: unum essentialem,* recipere Deum & Mediatorem...*duos subsecutivos,* scil. tum *fiducialem dependentiam;* tum *obedientalem submissionem.*"

136. Ibid., lvi, 64: "Est in hac *persuasione* particulari , fidei salvificæ apex & ἀκροθινίων." Mastricht, *Beschouwende en praktikale godgeleerdheit*, II.1.lvi, 1:161: "In deze bijzondere verzekertheit bestaat het hoogste toppunt des Geloofs." Note that *persuasione* is, here, rendered in the Dutch edition as "verzekertheit," or as "overreding en verzekertheit."

137. Mastricht, *Theoretico-practica theologia*, II.1.lv, 64: "Nascitur ista persuasio è *fide*, seu fidei actu salvifico, scil. *receptione*:....Nascitur inquam virtute hujus Syllogismi practici." The syllogism runs as follows: "Quicunque, in Deum & Mediatorem *credit*; & credendo eos *recipit*; illis indubitato, Deus est & Mediator. Joh.3:16 & 1:12. ego vero credo, & credendo recipio; proinde *meus* est & c."

notes that the assurance includes three elements: faith, feeling, and reasoning.[138] However, Mastricht warns again, as in the doctrinal section, that the conclusion of having an assured faith is not saving faith itself. Nonetheless, he argues that the advantage of such particular persuasion is that one is provoked to the *pietas*, spiritual tranquility, comfort in adversity and sweetness in prosperity (Luke 21:28; Rom. 8:23). Furthermore, Mastricht points out that the means of receiving such assurance are no different than those of looking for the increase of faith.[139] He concludes the chapter *De Fide salvifica* by stating that, having understood the preceding matters, one should proceed to the well-conceived study of one's faith, its arrangements, augmentation, and appropriation.[140]

In conclusion, the structure of the practical section is directly inferred from the biblical text and its exegesis. Both unbelief and faith are discussed according to the length and content of the biblical text. In addition, the relationship between the practical and the doctrinal sections is indisputable. Thus, the explication of the biblical text guides the structure and the content of the doctrinal and the practical sections. With respect to the content of the practical section, several observations can be made. First, Mastricht directs the reader constantly to God as highest end and to Christ as Mediator. Though the spiritual condition of the believer is not ignored, Mastricht's emphasis is directive (to God and Christ) and not reflective (to the believer). This can be particularly noted in the description of the marks of faith, a practical restatement of the (doctrinal) definition of faith. Second, the practical description of faith uses biblical language. The return to the biblical text, used as the foundation for the doctrine of faith, is enhanced by other scriptural references and their exposition.

Summary and Evaluation

Our examination of Mastricht's location and content of the *locus* of faith points to several distinct threads. First, the location of the chapter on faith is not broadly shared by Mastricht's contemporaries. However, his motivation for placing this chapter at the opening of the doctrine of God is based on Scripture and an exegetical trajectory that reaches, via Ames and Calvin, back to the patristic fathers. Faith, therefore, is a very central component of Mastricht's theology. That is to say, faith as cognitive and practical *habitus*. Exegetically he shares Cocceius's reading and comments on John 1:11, 12. In respect to the doctrine, faith is for Mastricht an *actus*, an act of the intellect, the will, and the affections. It is receiving God as the *finis* and Christ as the Mediator. Although,

---

138. Ibid.: "...hanc persuasionem tria ingredi: fidem, sensum, & ratiocinationem." Mastricht notes here the following: Faith, whereby one knows Scripture and is persuaded of the veracity and divinity of the Word (2 Tim. 1:12); Feeling (Phil. 1:9), whereby one has a real sense of faith and says "I believe" (Mark 9:24); and reasoning (2 Cor. 4:13), whereby one draws conclusions from what faith has brought about.

139. Mastricht refers to ibid., II.1.l, li, lii, 63, 64.

140. Ibid., lvii, 65: "4. *Studium* hujus persuasionis, distincte impendatur, ei comparandæ, conservandæ, adaugendæ & usurpandæ." Cf. Muller, *Post-Reformation Reformed Dogmatics*, 2:293.

Mastricht's description of faith contains Amesian elements, such as the *voluntas*, he, like Cloppenburgh, broadens the definition with respect to the intellect and the affections. Mastricht's definition is the starting point of faith, while some of his contemporaries identify such as the central yet one of the steps in faith (Brakel, Untereyck) in the description of faith. Whereas others (*Synopsis purioris theologiæ*, Brakel, Untereyck) describe at length the difference between other forms of faith (miraculous, temporal, historic), it is Mastricht, who succuntly mentions these forms but concentrates predominantly on faith, that is, true or justifying faith. Furthermore, where Brakel and Untereyck are significantly concerned with the marks of faith for the believer and Untereyck exposits elborately on a refuge-taking faith and its marks, it is Mastricht who is concise in his assesment and directs the believer immediately to Christ: the benefactor and not the benefits of faith (the fruits of faith).

With these distinct threads, we identify Mastricht as a precise theologian in his description of the *locus* of faith. With respect to the utilization of different levels of scholastic method, we note three levels: the micro level (for example, the *habitus-actus* distinction), the meso level, of which the *quæstio* method is most noticeable, and the macro level (for example the integral relationship between the locus of faith and other *loci*). Actually, Mastricht's use of the scholastic method contributes to his clear and precise presentation of the *locus*. Moreover, Mastricht's fourfold approach discloses the scriptural foundation of the *locus* in its explication (exegesis), exposition (doctrine), and application (*praxis*). Finally, the exposition of faith points toward the way in which Mastricht's doctrinal and practical formulation arises from the exegesis. This is our concern in the subsequent chapter.

Part 3

A Cross-section Study of the Doctrine of God

Introduction

Thus far we have seen that Mastricht divided his theology into two parts: faith and love. In addition, each of the Reformed *loci* discussed in the *Theoretico-practica theologia* (*TPT*) consists of four parts: exegesis, doctrine, elenctic, and '*pars practica.*' This approach of the *loci communes* is unique for a seventeenth-century system of theology. This observation does not ignore the fact that other theological works in Mastricht's time are exegetical, doctrinal, polemical, and practical in nature. For example, the *Opera Omnia* of Gomarus, Cocceius, and à Marck contain a majority of volumes dealing with biblical exegesis.[1] Moreover, the Leiden *Synopsis purioris theologiæ*, characterized as the "dogmatic work of the orthodoxy of Dordt," and other systematic theology works expounded the Reformed doctrine.[2] Polemical works of P. de Witte (ca. 1621-1669) and J. Hoornbeeck[3] and practical works, such as Voetius's *TA ΑΣΚΗΤΙΚΑ* and *Disputaty van geestelicke verlatingen*,[4] illustrate the attention that was given, respectively, to the opponents of Reformed orthodoxy and to the spiritual well-being of the members of the Reformed church. However, these separate treatments related to exegesis, doctrine, elenctic, and *praxis* are integrally present in the *TPT*. Thus, in our examination of Mastricht's exposition of theology, we have to consider the scholarship of seventeenth-century Reformed orthodoxy on the topics of biblical exegesis, doctrine, polemic, and *praxis*. In addition, we have to consider Mastricht's own questions and premises with respect to the fourfold approach. Therefore, the following chapters of our study form a cross-section examination primarily of book II of the *TPT*, the doctrine of God, regarding exegesis (chapter 1), doctrine (chapter 2), elenctics (chapter 3) and *praxis* (chapter 4). Furthermore, for the exegetical section, the following questions will be considered: (1) What are the premises? (2) What exegetical method(s) did Mastricht employ? (3) Is it possible to determine in which exegetical trajectory, if any, Mastricht stood? (4) What is the trajectory of his sources? (5) Are there any doctrinal impositions on his exegesis? And (6) what is the role of the analogy of faith and Scripture in his

1. Franciscus Gomarus, *Opera theologia omnia* (Amsterdam: Johannes Jansonius, 1664); Johannes Cocceius, *Opera Omnia Theologica*, 10 vols. (Amsterdam: P&J Blaev, 1701); Johannes à Marck, *Opera Omnia*, 27 vols. (Amsterdam: Gerardus Borstius, 1699-1706).

2. Peter van Rooden, "Nut en nadeel van de biografie," in *Tijdschrift voor Sociale Geschiedenis* 15 (1989): 66-73. See for works of seventeenth-century Reformed systematic theology part I, chapter 2 footnote 55 of this study.

3. Johannes Hoornbeeck, *Summa controversiarum religionis cum infidelibus, hæreticis, schismaticis: id. Est, Gentilibus, Judæis, Muhammedanis; Papistis, Anabaptistis...ed.* secunda (Utrecht: J. à Waesberge, 1658); Petrus de Witte, *Wederlegginge der Socianiaensche Dwalingen*, 2 vols. (Amsterdam: Arent van den Heuvel en Batltes Boeckholt, 1662).

4. Gisbertus Voetius, *TA ΑΣΚΗΤΙΚΑ sive exercitia pietatis in usum juventutis academicæ nunc edita; addita est, ob materiæ affinitatem, Oratio de pietate cum scientia conjungenda, habita anno 1634* (Gorichem: Paul Vink, 1664); Gisberus Voetius and Johannes Hoornbeeck, *Disputaty van geestelicke verlatingen* (Dordrecht: Symon onder de Linde, 1667).

exegesis? For the doctrinal section, the following questions will be considered: (1) How did Mastricht formulate the doctrine? (2) What is the relationship, if any, between exegesis and doctrine? For the elenctic part, the following questions will be considered: (1) What is the relationship, if any, between elenctic and the preceding parts: exegesis and doctrine? (2) What scholastic method, if any, did Mastricht employ in the elenctic part? (3) Who are his principal opponents, and why did he oppose them? Finally, for the practical part, the following questions will be considered: (1) What is the relationship, if any, between exegesis, doctrine, and *praxis*? (2) If there is dependency on exegesis or doctrine, what is the degree of dependency? (3) In what way and to what degree does the doctrinal part dominate Mastricht's theology, and does it relate at all to the practical part? (4) Do the doctrinal and practical formulations differ or agree with the results of exegesis, and, if so, to what degree? In other words, is the assessment correct, that exegesis, doctrine, and *praxis* were not a unity?[5]

Part three of our study, then, is structured in the following manner. First, each chapter opens with an introduction and statement of the problem. Here, we will identify issues that relate to the subject at hand and that are raised in scholarly literature. Second, we will identify Mastricht's own thoughts on exegesis and doctrinal, elenctical, and practical formulations. Third, the findings regarding the latter will be used for the examination of the *TPT* chapters on the doctrine of God.

---

5. C. Graafland, "Schriftleer en Schriftverstaan in de Nadere Reformatie," in *Theologische aspecten van de Nadere Reformatie*, ed. T. Brienen et al. (Zoetermeer: Boekencentrum, 1993), 66: "Hij [Mastricht] vertegenwoordigt daarin [*Beschouwende en praktikale godgeleerdheit*] de geest van zijn tijd door het schriftmatige, dogmatische en praktische van elkaar te (onder) scheiden en niet (meer) als eenheid te behandelen."

Chapter 1
Exegesis

Introduction and Statement of the Problem

The examination of the method and practice of biblical interpretation of post-Reformation documents in the second half of the seventeenth century awaits, in general, a much needed appraisal.[1] Although this chapter does not offer an overview of the history of post-Reformation orthodox exegesis, a survey of scholarship relating to seventeenth-century post-Reformation biblical interpretation, including material on homiletic issues[2] and the exegetical labors of those portrayed in monographs,[3] indicates

---

1. This observation is underscored by a) the lack of attention given to post-Reformation biblical interpretation in studies such as Gerald Bray, *Biblical Interpretation Past & Present* (Downers Grove: Intervarsity Press, 1996); b) the deficiency of studies of exegesis in the *Nadere Reformatie*, even while one notices an increase and diversification of studies of this period (cf. F. W. Huisman, *Bibliografie van het gereformeerd Pietisme in Nederland to 1800*, [Woudenberg: Uitgeverij Op Hoope, 2001]); and c) the preliminary attention given to biblical interpretation in the era of the sixteenth- century Protestant Reformation. See, for example, Richard A. Muller and John L. Thompson, eds., *Biblical Interpretation in the Era of Reformation, Essays Presented to David C. Steinmetz in Honor of His Sixtieth Birthday* (Grand Rapids: William B. Eerdmans Publishing Company, 1996); I. D. Backus and F. M Higman, *Théorie et practique de l'exégèse: Actes du troisieme Colloqui international sur l'histoire de l'exégèse biblique au XVIe siècle* (Geneve: Droz, 1990); W. Perkins, *A Commentary on Galatians*, ed. G.T Sheppard with introductory essays by B. S. Child, G. T. Sheppard, and J. H. Augustine, Pilgrim Classic Commentaries (New York: Pilgrim, 1989), vol. 2; P. T. van Rooden, *Theology, Biblical Scholarship and Rabbinical Studies in the Seventeenth Century: Constantijn L'Empereur (1591-1648) Professor of Hebrew and theology at Leiden* (Leiden: E. J. Brill, 1989); David C. Steinmetz, "The Superiority of Pre-Critical Exegesis," in *TTs* 37 (1980): 27-38, reprinted in Donald K. McKim, ed., *A Guide to Contemporary Hermeneutics* (Grand Rapids: Wm. Eerdmans, 1986), 65-77. This obervation begins to be compensated, however, with Henry M. Knapp, *Understanding the Mind of God: John Owen and Seventeenth-Century Exegetical Methodology* (Ph.D. diss., Calvin Theological Seminary, 2002) and B. Lee, *J. Cocceius's Exegesis of the Epistle of the Hebrews* (Ph.D. diss., Calvin Theological Seminary, 2002) and marks the beginning of the appraisal of the history of post-Reformation exegesis in the (late) seventeenth century.

2. A. Nebe, *Homiletische Portretten. Eene bijdrage tot de geschiedenis der predikkunde en der evangelieprediking* (Utrecht, 1881); E. Chr. Achelis, *Die Homiletik und die Katechetik des Andreas Hyperius* (Berlin, 1901); S. Greijdanus, *Schrifbeginselen ter Schrifverklaring en Historisch overzicht over theorieën en wijzen van Schriftuitleggingen*, (Kampen: Kok, 1946); T. Hoekstra, *Gereformeerde Homiletiek* (Wageningen, 1935); C. Boer, *Hofpredikers van Prins Willem van Oranje: Jean Taffin en Pierre Loyseleur de Villiers*, (Den Haag: Historische Studie, 1951); I. Boot, *Allegorische uitlegging van het Hooglied*, (Woerden: Zuiderduijn, 1971); A. A. van Ruler, "De bevinding in de prediking," in *Theologisch Werk*, (Nijkerk: Callenbach, 1971), 3:61-81; J. v. d. Berg, "De Puriteinen en de Prediking," in *Homiletica* 17e jrg., no. 3 (1958), 27-32; T. Brienen, *De Prediking van de Nadere Reformatie*, (Amsterdam: Ton Bolland, 1981); T. Brienen, "Voetius en Hoornbeeck over de homilitiek," in *De Onbekende Voetius*, ed. J. van Oort et al. (Kampen: J. H. Kok, 1989), 48-72; W. J. van Asselt, "Hebraica Veritas: zeventiende-eeuwse motieven voor de bestudering van het Hebreeuws door predikanten," in *Kerk en Theologie* 46 (1995): 309-324.

two different lines of thought. Some assert that exegesis, doctrine, and practice are disconnected, while others argue that doctrine and *praxis* arise from the theologians' exegesis.

First, Brienen and others assert that the *explicatio* and *applicatio* are relatively independent. [4] Furthermore, Brienen argues that some of the Cocceian preachers preferred the philological exegesis[5] and the Voetian preachers were appreciative of the "scholastic analytical"[6] method of exegesis. However, in respect to the latter preachers, van den End asserts—and nuances, in our opinion, Brienen's position—that Saldenus's exposition of a biblical text is threefold: the general content of the text, the words and doctrine of the text, and the application. The application can be distinguished in *documenta* and *usus*, of which the former are axioms inferred from the text, thus doctrine inferred from the biblical text, and the latter are directed to the *praxis*. Moreover, according to van den End, Saldenus emphasized the use of the original languages, but warned against their use from the pulpit in exposition, explanation, and application of the text.[7] On the other hand, Brienen asserts, that beginning with J. Hoornbeeck, and divergent from A. Hyperius, the application, which coincides with the *usus*, is not directly inferred from the text but mediated by the *documenta*, the doctrinal explanation, which is positioned between the exegesis and *praxis*.[8] Consequently, the way was opened for dogmatic preaching, and theologically the shift was made from biblical exegesis to dogmatics.[9] According to Berkhof, this resulted in exegesis being altered from an unprejudiced explanation of Scripture to the search for dogmatic scriptural proof so that "exegesis became the handmaid of dogmatics and degenerated into a mere search of proof-texts."[10] This understanding of post-Reformation Protestant hermeneutics continues today. One reads, for example, that "the [post-reformation] Scholastics often superimposed their own sets of rationalistic guidelines upon its [the text of Holy Writ] pages, with the result that the simple message was often lost in the search for

---

3. W. J. van Asselt, *Amicitia Dei, een onderzoek naar de structure van de theology van Johannes Coccejus* (Ede: Grafische vormgeving: ADC, 1988), 50-57; T. Brienen, "Abraham Hellenbroek," in De *Nadere Reformatie en het Gereformeerd Piëtisme*, ed. T. Brienen et al ('s-Gravenhage: Boekencentrum, 1989), 181-200; G. van den End, *Guiljelmus Saldenus, een praktisch en irenisch theoloog uit de Nadere Reformatie* (Leiden: Groen en Zoon, 1991), chapter 3; F. J. Los, *Wilhelmus à Brakel*, introduced by W. van 't Spijker (Leiden: Groen en Zoon, 1991), 136, 137,

4. Brienen, *De Prediking van de Nadere Reformatie*, chapters 2 and 3; Hoekstra, De Gereformeerde Homiletiek, 120.

5. Brienen, *De Prediking van de Nadere Reformatie*, 67.

6. Ibid., 79.

7. Van den End, *Guiljelmus Saldenus*, 67, 68.

8. Brienen, *De Prediking van de Nadere Reformatie*, 173.

9. H. W. Rossouw, *Klaarheid en Interpretasie. Enkele probleemhistorische gesigtpunten in verband met die leer van die duidelikheid van die Heilige Skrif* (Amsterdam: Van Campen, 1963), 271.

10. L. Berkhof, *Principles of Biblical Interpretation* (Grand Rapids: Baker Books, 1950), 29.

methodological and doctrinal correctness."[11] In particular such exegesis, which was influenced by medieval Scholasticism, served only to proof-text dogmatic and polemic works.[12] Moreover, the development of exegesis in the period 1600-1750 was further hindered by the strong adherence to the confessions.[13] In conclusion, this line of scholarship argues that scholastic-formulated doctrine from Scripture made the exegesis and *praxis* subordinate to doctrine.

Second, D. Steinmetz, Muller, and others demonstrate that the exegesis of the early part of the seventeenth century not only as a continuation of the philological and interpretive development of the Renaissance and Reformation but also as the great era of Protestant linguistic study, whether in the biblical or in the cognate languages. The *loci* of the theological system arose directly out of meditation on specific texts. The apex of hermeneutical, philological, and text-critical work in the post-Reformation period disagrees, then, with the proof-texting characterization. The erudition of the precritical exegete was generally directed to theological and practical ends and had more in common with the medieval and patristic exegesis than with the modern higher-critical interpretation of Scripture.[14] Thus, this line of scholarship argues that doctrine and piety arises out of the exegesis of Scripture. However, it fails, in our opinion, to show the relationship, if any, between Scripture, doctrine, and piety. Related to the findings of the foregoing scholarship is the appraisal of Cocceius's work as "biblical theology." G. Schrenk asserts that Cocceius, influenced by Ramus, opposed the dominance of dogmatism and Scholasticism over exegesis, *contra* Voetius.[15] As a proficient philologist and exegete, Cocceius mined the doctrines from Scripture, whereby the unity of exegesis and doctrine directs toward the practical devotion. This practical orientation of doctrine

11. K. O'Dell Bullock, "Post-Reformation Protestant Hermeneutics," in *Biblical Hermeneutics: A Comprehensive Introduction to Interpreting Scripture*, ed. Bruce Corley, Steve Lemke, Grant Lovejoy, 2d ed. (Nashville: Broadman & Holman Publishers, 2002), 129.

12. One notes that in this line of scholarship it is often implied that the Reformation was a time of exegesis virtually without dogma, and the era of orthodoxy was a time of dogmatic system without exegesis. Cf. Richard A. Muller, "Biblical Interpretations in the 16th & 17th Centuries," in *Historical Handbook of Major Biblical Interpretations*, ed. Donald K. McKim (Downers Grove: InterVarsity Press, 1998), 135.

13. Greijdanus, *Schrifbeginselen ter Schrifverklaring*, 193.

14. Muller, "Biblical Interpretations," 123-52; Muller and Thompson, *Biblical Interpretation*; Backus and Higman, *Théorie et practique de l'exégèse*, 10; Perkins, *A Commentary on Galatians*, vol. 2, introduction.

15. On Cocceius, see G. Schrenk, *Gottesreich und Bund im Älteren Protestantismus vornehmlich bei Johannes Coccejus* (1923, reprint Darmstadt: Wissenschaftliche Buchgesellschaft, 1967), 22. On Ramus, see Rossouw, *Klaarheid en interpretasie*, 276; J. Moltmann, "Zur Bedeutung des Petrus Ramus für Philosophie und Theologie im Calvinusmus," in *Zeitschrift für Kirchengeschichte*, LXVII (1957): 296, 317; C. van der Woude, *Op de Grens van Reformatie en Scholastiek* (Kampen: Kok, 1964), 14. On Voetius, see C. Graafland, "Schriftleer en Schriftverstaan in de Nadere Reformatie," in *Theologische aspecten van de Nadere Reformatie*, ed. T. Brienen *et al.* (Zoetermeer: Boekencentrum, 1993), 35: "We krijgen niet zelden de indruk, dat de leer al lang vastaat, en dat ze alleen nog maar achteraf uit de Schrift moet worden bevestigd. Dat secundaire karakter van het Schrifbewijs is bij Voetius opvallend."

also entails an apologetic element.[16] In general, then, this line of scholarship notes that Cocceius, *contra* Voetius, advocated "biblical theology": a unity between exegesis and doctrine, whereby the *praxis* is inferior but connected to both.

In summary, the biblical interpretation of the seventeenth century Reformed theology is appraised in one of two ways: either orthodox doctrinal impositions disordered the biblical exegesis, whereby practical theology became separate from exegesis, or the exegesis of Scripture was directive and determinative for doctrinal and practical theological reflections. In addition, the secondary literature assesses the Cocceian theologians as more appreciative of biblical exegesis than the dogmatic approach of the scholastic-oriented Voetians.[17] Consequently, the question is paramount as to what exegetical method Mastricht employs, especially in light of his being characterized as a Voetian, anti-scholastic, and practical theologian. Therefore, in this chapter we examine Mastricht's view of biblical interpretation. First, we consider the sources and the context in which his views are expressed on the subject, and, second, we survey his thought on biblical exegesis in the doctrine of God of the *TPT*.

Mastricht and Biblical Interpretation

The points of departure for the examination of Mastricht's thought on biblical interpretation are primarily the *Methodus Concionandi* and the doctrine of Scripture of the *TPT*.[18] In the latter Mastricht addresses issues such as the use of Scripture and its languages, and in the former he elaborates, in the context of homiletics, on the method of biblical text analysis. In our examination, we follow Mastricht's thought as provided in the outline of the *Methodus* and, where required, interweave his thoughts as expressed in the doctrine of Scripture.[19]

16. W. J. van Asselt, *The Federal Theology of Johannes Cocceius* (Leiden-New York: Brill, 2001), 124, 125.

17. Graafland argues that Mastricht does not ignore the philological exegesis, and therefore his dogmatic work has a biblical accent (Graafland, "Schriftleer en Schriftverstaan," 61).

18. Petrus van Mastricht, *Methodus Concionandi* (Frankfurt an der Oder: M. Hübner, undated); idem, *Theoretico-practica theologia qua, per singula capita theologica, pars exegetica, dogmatica, elenchtica et practica, perpetua successione conjugantur; accedunt historia ecclesiastica, plena quidem, sed compendiosa, idea theologiæ moralis, hypotyposis theologiæ asceticæ etc. proin opus quasi novum* (Utrecht: Thomas Appels, 1699), 1225; ibid., I.2, 17-46 (In particular we consider the paragraphs xxxiii, xli, xlv, xlvi, xlvii, xlix, liii). The *Methodus* opens with the argument that a sermon consists of four parts: *inventio, dispositio, elaboratio,* and *elocutio.* The *elaboratio*, which is the major part of the *Methodus*, provides the (homiletic) context for the discussion on biblical interpretation, which, for Mastricht, includes the analysis and exegesis of the biblical text. Cf. ibid., *Methodus Concionandi*, 1226, 1227, 1228: idem, *TPT* (1682), præfatio: "primo ejus praxin analyticam & exegeticam...."

19. While this order provides a structured examination, it also avoids a coming to the document with any preconceived ideas about biblical interpretation such as are expressed in the scholarly literature.

The Sources

Prodromus. This work, which stands at the beginning of Mastricht's lifelong project of the *TPT*, contains a brief but significant section on biblical interpretation. He argues that the theological axioms, *dogmatica* or *didicatica*, *elenchtica*, and *praxis*, arise from the explication (ἀναλύω) of the scriptural text.[20] Moreover, the biblical text is foundational and underlies these axioms.[21] Thus, the formulated doctrine, elenctic, and *praxis* arise from unfolding the biblical text and are interrelated to one another.[22] Moreover, from the *Prodomus* to the final edition of the *TPT*, Mastricht adhered to the principle of connectedness of exegesis to doctrine, polemic, and practice.[23] However, the question emerges as to the way in which the biblical text is foundational and unfolded.

Methodus Concionandi. The question that emerged from the *Prodromus* is for a great part answered in the *Methodus Concionandi*.[24] First, Mastricht argues that the selected canonical text should be neither too long nor too short. The former would lead to an extensive philological exposition, and the latter prohibits a succinct perspicuous and comprehensive treatment of the text.[25] Moreover, the content of the biblical text should be sufficiently explained in its entirety and afterwards be distinguished in its parts.[26] The exposition of the text is analytical and exegetical. The former necessitates the breaking up of the whole and parts of the text.[27] In addition, the philological analysis is restricted to the literal sense of text words.[28] After the analysis, the parts need to be

---

20. Petrus van Mastricht, *Theologiæ didactico-elenchtico-practicæ prodromus tribus speciminibus* (Amsterdam: Johannes van Someren, 1666), præfatio: "In omnibus id spectavi, ut pars ejusque loci theologici dogmatica, elenchtica & practica, pari passu semper ambularent. Itaq cuique capiti illustrem quendam Scripturæ textum substerno, eumque breviter et nervose αναλύω et explico, dein axioma aut axiomata theologica, quibus ejus loci nervus continetur, ex eo produco, istorum porro confirmatione et expositione, partem didacticam; vindicationem elenchticam; applicationem practicam complector."

21. In the *Theoretico-practica theologia*, 21-23, I.2.xiv-xxi., he explains the properties of this foundation; (1) auctoritas, (2) veritas, (3) integritas, (4) sanctitas, (5) perspicuitas, (6) perfectio, (7) necessitas, and (8) efficacia.

22. Mastricht, *Prodromus*, præfatio: "Theologiæ didactico-elenchtico-practicæ specimina tria, non alio nexu inter se conjugata, quam quod singula singulæ partis ac Tomi vobis exhibent exemplum."

23. The title page read, *Theoretico-practica theologia qua, per singula capita theologica, pars exegetica, dogmatica, elenchtica & practica*, perpetuâ successione conjugantur (non-italic, AN).

24. In chapter II.2 of this study, the *Methodus Concionandi* is identified as a late 1660s work, which finds its way into *De optima concionandi methodo paraleipomena* (1681), which in turn is found in the *TPT* of 1682 and 1699.

25. Mastricht, *Methodus Concionandi*, cap. I.1 and 2, 4.

26. Ibid., cap. III.b, 10: "...contentum textus, quo nimirum totum nobis suppetat, postea in partes commode dispescendum."

27. Ibid., cap. III.c, 11: "a. ut partes immediatæ sint adæquatæ, illudque plene exhaureant... b. partes immediate substantivis nominibus contento analogis exprimantur...c. partes non sint otiosæ."

28. Ibid., cap. III.D.e.1, 18: "Cautè distinguenda explicatio verbalis ab hac reali, quod illa ulterius non enitatur, quam assequi genuinum Textus sensum literalem."

jointly paraphrased. The entire textual analysis should be done in the immediate context. On the exegetical part, he explicates that the exposition should follow the flow of content of the biblical text, taking note of demonstrative pronouns and conjunctions.[29] Furthermore, any textually obscure or controversial issue should be latent in the preaching.[30] Finally, a textual explanation is aided, after the analysis and exegesis of the text, by the *analogia fidei*, *analogia contextus*, and commentaries, including Calvin, Piscator, Poole, and others.[31] Mastricht's exegetical parts in the *TPT* specify that those others include patristic, medieval, rabbinic, and contemporary sources.[32] In 1681 Mastricht expands the categories of aid to include philology, philosophy, and history.[33] Finally, Mastricht maintains in the *Methodus Concionandi*, as stated in the *Prodromus*, that doctrine and *praxis* are consequential from exegesis.[34]

Thus, the unfolding of the biblical text is philological, analytical, grammatical, and contextual and is assisted by the analogy of faith, other discsiplines, such as philosophy and history, and a trajectory of biblical commentaries, which reaches back to the sixteenth-century Reformation and to medieval, rabbinical, and patristic exegetes. This assessment indicates the absence of doctrinal and theological considerations in Mastricht's exegesis and the necessary presence of saving faith and standing in an exegetical trajectory. The latter immediately begs the question as to what trajectory of biblical interpretation he stands in. Answering this question will assist in evaluating the allegation that Reformed doctrinal impositions played a role in Mastricht's exegesis. To ask the question another way, Is the exegesis of the biblical text as it relates to the doctrine of God formulated by Mastricht with Reformed doctrinal impositions, and does it differ from the exegetical results of non-Reformed?

Theoretico-practica theologia. Mastricht writes in the preface of the *TPT* (1699) that the biblical text is foundational for each theological chapter and is philologically explicated so that the students of theology would get familiar with the scriptural

---

29. Ibid., cap. II.4, 5.

30. Ibid., cap. III.2, 12.

31. Ibid., cap. III, 13: "*Exegeseos* adminicula repentatur, 1. Ab analogia fidei, 2. Ab analogia contextus, 3. A commentatoribus, præstantissimis cum criticis & verbalibus; tum anlyticis a realibus: Calvino, Piscatore, Pole, &c."

32. See Appendix I.2.4.

33. Mastricht, *De optima concionandi methodo paraleipomena: in usum theologiæ theoretico-practicæ*, Henricus Wagardus (Utrecht: Meinardus à Dreunen, 1681); Ibid., *Theoretico-practica theologia*, 1228: "3. Ab *extrinsecis* textui, tum philologicis, tum philosophicis, tum historicis." This category is inserted between 2 and 3 of the *Methodus*, cap. III, 13.

34. Mastricht, *Methodus Concionandi*, cap. III.D, 15: "Argumentum concionis doctrinale, ê textu consectum"; cap. III.E, 23: "Applicatio, argumenti enarrati duplex, *dogmatica*, quæ veritatem argumenti respicit; & *practica*, quæ bonitatem ejusdem."

foundation of the theology. Furthermore, he asserts that in the exposition no use has been made of logic. Rather, he has deducted the matter from the nature of the text.[35]

Beside the preface of the *TPT*, the chapter on the *Holy Scriptures* provides further insight on Mastricht's view of biblical interpretation. First, he clarifies that by the biblical text is meant the text in the original languages of Hebrew, Aramaic, and Greek.[36] Second, he argues, contrary to the Enthusiasts,[37] who insist on extracanonical revelations, and the Socinians, who adhere to the human reason as an infallible norm to explain Scripture,[38] that the things of true religion are a mystery (1 Tim. 3:16; Matt. 13:2; 1 Cor. 2:7; 4:1) and a paradox (Luke 5:26). They are spiritual (1 Cor. 2:14) and transcend human reason.[39]

The Exegete

The proper examination of Mastricht's biblical interpretation involves a review of his stated remarks on the exegete and the prerequisites for coming to the biblical text. The former includes the spiritual state and *praxis* of the exegete in respect to his inadequacy, knowledge, and spirituality (reading, prayer, and meditation). The latter, the prerequisites, includes a survey of Mastricht's thought on the analysis of the biblical text.

Inadequacy. Mastricht emphasizes that from a human perspective the infallible Scripture cannot be understood perfectly in this life but perfect understanding will be

---

35. Mastricht, *Theoretico-practica theologia*, præfatio: "Etenim in *exegeticis*, Scripturæ textus, capitibus Thelogiæ, pro fundamento substructi....In his, quantum fieri potuit, nos à terminis artis logicæ;... cohibuimus, & ex naturâ textus diduximus, ut & hîc rerum naturæ adsuescerent."

36. Ibid., I.2.x, 20, 21: "Sed quænam tandem sunt *linguæ* istæ *authenticæ? Vetus Testamentum*, Ecclesiæ Judiacæ *particulari* datum, lingua *hebræa* conditum, omnes agnoscunt nisi quod particulæ ejus quænam, in Esdra, Daniele, Esther, Jeremia, lingua prostent *Chaldæa. Novum* Ecclesiæ Christianæ *universali* scriptum, solâ lingua *græca* conscriptum agnoscitur." In the following paragraph Mastricht cites Ames's *Medulla* and argues that every translation of Scripture is human and should be in accordance with the original language. Cf. William Ames, *Marrow of Sacred Divinity, drawne out of the holy Scriptures, and the Interpreters thereof, and brought into Method* (London: Edward Griffin, 1642), 172, XXXIV.32-33; Graafland, "Schriftleer en Schriftverstaan," 65.

37. Translated in the Dutch edition as "Quakers of Geestdrijvers"; Petrus van Mastricht, *Beschouwende en Praktikale Godgeleerdheit, waarin, door alle Godgeleerde Hoofdstukken henen, het Bijbelverklarende, Leerstellige, Wederleggende, en Praktikale deel, door eenen onafgebroken schakel onderscheidendlyk samengevoegt, voorgestelt word* (Rotterdam: Hendrik van Pelt; Utrecht: Jan Jacob van Poolsum, 1749), vol.1, I.2.xxxiii, 75.

38. Mastricht, *Theoretico-practica theologia*, I.2.xxxiv, 31. Here Mastricht raises the question of whether the original text is corrupt. Mastricht argues, contrary to Moslim belief (in order to justify the Koran) and Roman Catholics (who determine the Vulgate as original language) that Scripture (Matt. 5:18; Luke 16:29) is distorted. Mastricht acknowledges the multitude of copies of text, but argues that what is transmitted in history by divine providence is that which is necessary for salvation.

39. Ibid., : "Reformati, *rationem* cogitant: vel ut *instrumentum*, vel ut *argumentum*, vel *normam* & principium:...Adeoque, si pugna videatur esse, inter Scripturam & naturam; non illi, sed huic cedendum volunt."

received in the life to come.[40] Furthermore, although the weakness of human intellect does not interfere with the clarity and the perspicuity of Scripture, there are passages in Scripture that are difficult for the human understanding.[41] Some passages seem at first sight to be contradictory or ambiguous or imperfect. Some contain difficult Hebrew phrases or figures of speech. However, Mastricht emphasized that such passages are always explained by Scripture itself.[42] Furthermore, as we have seen, Mastricht notes that for the interpretation of Scripture[43] human reason is insufficient and correct interpretation does not depend on the church.[44] Nevertheless, Mastricht urges the necessity of interpreting Scripture because Scripture is the living word of God and deals with eternal salvation (2 Tim. 3:15).

Knowledge. For Mastricht, human inadequacy does not imply a rejection of knowledge. He exhorts the learned to analyze Scripture methodically, having sufficient knowledge of Hebrew, Aramaic and Greek, and to make careful use of logic.[45] In respect to the latter, Mastricht seeks support from Ambrosius, who stated "that although the Holy writers have not written according the rules of art but in accordance to grace, which is above any art."[46]

In addition, the learned who interpret Scripture should have knowledge of rhetoric in order to explain the metaphorical and tropological matters of Scripture. The exegesis of James 1:7 illustrates Mastricht's use of metaphor. He explains that παραλλαγή can be rendered by "I change" and the root is ἀλλασσω and is rendered as "variable." Mastricht then points to the prefix παρα, indicating a succession, and explicates further that this word is metaphorically derived from astronomy, in which the sun and moon have their παραλλαγας–*kringloop*. Therefore, he concludes, the text shows that there is no (οὐκ)

40. Ibid., ii.כ.2.ב, 18: "...*& si actualem etiam velis & absolutam; tum intelligenda est, non quæ* hîc *obtinetur; sed quæ* posthac *obtinebitur.*"

41. Ibid., xviii, 22: "[*Perspicuitas*]...Est autem hoc sensu, clara ac perspicua, ut quamvis *res* Scripturæ sæpenumerò sint difficiles captu...."

42. Ibid., xlvi, 35: "Resp. Nullibi, talia in Scripturis occurrunt, circa res scitu & intellectu, ad salutem necessarias, quin alibi explicentur: ut, ad summum *non Scripturæ*; sed isthæc Scripturæ *loca* hinc dici possint obscura."

43. Ibid., xxxiv, 31: "(1) Quia *ratio; a.* est cæca...*b.* est obscura...*c.* fallax & lubrica...*d.* imperfecta...."

44. Ibid., xxxvii, 32: "Quæritur ergo primo, an divina Scripturæ auctoritas, pendeat a testimonio Ecclesiæ?...1.Auctoritas Scripturæ à *solo* suo pendet *auctore;*...2. Quia Scripturæ auctoritas est αὐτόπιστος & ἀξιόπιστος ...3. Scripturæ auctoritas, ex *infinitis* ei, divinitatis *notis*...4. Ipsa Ecclesiæ auctoritas, etiam *quoad nos* à testimonio dependet Scripturæ...5. Sequeretur, fidem nostram, non tam *fundamento Prophetarum* inniti & Apostolorum...6. *Experientia*...."

45. Ibid., lxxi, 44: "(b) prudens *Logices* usus ad methodicam Sacri textus analysin." This argument is slightly different then Mastricht's previous assessment of the use of logic. NB: double paragraph numbering lxxi on pages 43 and 44 of the *Theoretico-practica theologia* (1699).

46. Ibid.: "*Quamvis enim auctores sacri, non scripserint, secundum artem; sed secundum gratiam, quæ supra omnem artem est; attamen ii qui de arte scripserunt, in eorum scriptis, artem invenerunt.* Ait Ambros. Epistol. 8."

mutation in God and not even a shadow of mutability.[47] Thus, the (astrological) understanding of metaphor does contribute, for Mastricht, to the explication of the biblical text.

In addition to the knowledge of rhetoric, one should compare the holy and human history, as is evident in book VIII of the *TPT*, *De dispensatione foederis gratiæ*.[48]

Furthermore, in regard to the interpretation of Scripture, Mastricht stresses the need to have knowledge of the various translations and editions of Scripture. The latter is to discern the linguistic aspects and the former includes the knowledge of the Septuagint and the Syriac translation of the New Testament. An examination of the doctrine of God in the *TPT* shows the relatively greater use of the LXX than the Vulgate. Moreover, the limited use of the LXX is restricted to the exegesis of a Greek or Hebrew biblical text. For example, Mastricht explains in the context of the exegesis of Romans 11:34 ("For who hath known the mind of the Lord? or who hath been his counsellor?" KJV) that the second part of the text appeared to be taken from Isaiah 40:13, "according to the LXX."[49] Having thus noted the discriminatory use of the knowledge of linguistics, rhetoric, logic and history, he concludes that all interpretative tools are subservient to and do not rule Scripture.[50]

Pneumatology. Having shown the inadequacy of human reason but not rejecting the aforementioned knowledge to explicate Scripture, Mastricht raises the question, Who then can interpret the Scripture?[51] Here Mastricht notes that the spiritual disposition of the interpreter is of crucial importance. He emphasizes the leading of the Holy Spirit.[52] The testimony of the Holy Spirit does not, according to Mastricht, consist in an internal voice but an illumination of the intellect, whereby "the Spirit testifies with one's spirit."[53] Though this Reformed principle of exegesis is confessed since the

---

47. Ibid., II.7.ii 108: "2...*Significatur igitur, toto contextu, non tantum, nullam prorsus in Deo mutationem dari: sed ne speciem aut* umbram *mutationis etiam.*"

48. See also I.2, fn 28 of this study.

49. Mastricht, *Theoretico-practica theologia*, II.13.ii, 144: "δ...*Petita & hæc verba videntur, secundum* LXX *interp. ex* Jes. XI.13.14...." [LXX Isaiah 40:13, τίς αὐτοῦ σύμβουλος ἐγένετο Romans 11:34, τίς σύμβουλος αὐτοῦ ἐγένετο, AN] Other references to the LXX in *Theoretico-practica theologia* are found in II.4.viii, 87; II.21.ii, 219; II.26.ii, 251. Mastricht also recommends, here, a careful and prudent use of the orthodox commentaries. This will be discussed below.

50. Mastricht, *Theoretico-practica theologia*, I.2.lxxi, 44: "...[a. sufficiens *linguarum* primigeniarum, *Hebraeæ*...b. prudens *Logices* usus...c. *Rhetorices* usus...d. *Philosophiæ* adminiculum...e. *Historiæ Sacræ* cum humana collatio...f. Cum fontibus versionum tam veterum, quam modernarum, diversorum idiomatum...g. Prudens Orthodoxorum commentatorum usus...] Sic tamen (h) ut linguas omnes, artes, historias, versiones, commentarios, suo quæque loco relinquamus, nim. ut *subserviant*, non *dominentur* Scripturis"

51. Ibid., liii, 37: "*Num ergo, privato cujusvis judicio, interpretatio Scripturæ & iudicium controversiarum, sunt relinquenda?*"

52. Ibid., lxii, 40: "2. Interna Spiritus S. persuasione 1 Cor.11:12."

53. Ibid., lxii, 40: "...testimonium istud Spiritus S. non consistit in *enthusiasmo* quodam...sed in *illuminatione* & elevatione intellectus nostri..."

sixteenth-century Protestant Reformation, it is not explicitly used by Mastricht. He counsels that for the proper exegesis of Scripture, the exegete must have a life of reading, prayer, and meditation. This reminds one of the *Lectio Divina* of the late medieval time, stimulated by Bernardus. The biblical text was read (*lectio*) and followed by prayer (*oratio*). The meditation (*meditatio*) concentrated on the content of the biblical text. Thus, the *lectio divina* was a prayerful and reflective reading of Scripture. Thus, both the spiritual state and the *praxis* of the interpreter are paramount for the understanding of the biblical text.

Reading. The reading of Scripture, according to Mastricht, should be done with attention (Deut. 6:6), with understanding (Acts. 8:30), with desire (Ps. 1:2), in faith (Heb. 4:2) and with joy in respect to the promises and with trembling in respect to the judgments.[54] However, he notes that all such reading is in vain when the genuine sense of the Scripture is missed; that is, the composite literal sense.[55] Finally, Mastricht points to the necessity of interpreting Scripture. Such can take place either academically, in order to seek for the true sense, or ecclesiastically, in order to show the practical implications, or in private, in order to discern both.[56]

Prayer. The exegete also should pray for the spiritual wisdom (James 1:5) to interpret the mysteries of Scripture. Prayer is required to come to Scripture with pure eyes (Matt. 5:8), an illuminated understanding (Eph. 1:18), and with a submissive heart, because if anyone thinks that he knows anything, he knows nothing yet as he ought to know (1 Cor. 8:2).[57]

Meditation. The *meditatio* is of great importance to Mastricht. He argues that this aspect of biblical interpretation is neglected by practical writers. In respect to the meditation, Mastricht notes that the word *meditatio* can be equated biblically in a metaphoric sense with "ruminate" (Deut. 14:6; Rev. 10:9) or in a comparative sense with "desire" (Ps. 1:2), "scrutinize" (John 5:39), or "ponder"—a *soliloquium* (Luke 2:19).[58] Having asserted the biblical notion of meditation, Mastricht defines it as a matter

---

54. Mastricht, *Theoretico-practica theologia*, I.2.lxix, 42: "Studium istud, cum peculiariter sese profundat, in lectionem, auditionem, interpretationem, meditationem, collationem & praxin; de singulis horum singulatim sed breviter." idem, I.2.lxix, 43 "Fiat interim *lectio* animo: 1. attento..., 2. intelligente..., 3. avido..., 4. fideli..., 5. cum congruis *affectibus*..., 6. cum diligenti *assiduitate*..., 7. animo *puro*..."

55. Ibid., lxxi, 43: "Cum autem, citra genuinum Scripturæ *sensum* omne earundem *studium*, quod legendo, audiendo & c. impenditur, vanum plane sit: necessum omnino est, ut pro *septima* praxi." See further the paragraph below on *Sensus Scriptura*.

56. Ibid., lxxi, 43: "Scripturarum *interpretatio* succedat; seu illa, *Scholastica* sit, sensum genuinum quærens; seu *Ecclesiastica*, efficaciam potissimum practicam; seu *Privata*, utrumque suo modo ambiens."

57. Mastricht, *Theoretico-practica theologia*, I.2.lxxii, 44: "Hæc literatos potissimum concernunt: alia *quosvis* promiscue: 1. Preces...2. Gratiæ spiritu imbuti, ad Scripturarum accedamus interpretationem ...3. Scripturam continuò versemus animo *submisso*...4. Assuescamus Scripturarum lectioni ac studio, *constanti* pariter ac *methodica*...5. Instructi accedamus *analogiâ fidei*...."

58. Ibid., lxxiii, 44: "Octavus...est de *meditatione* verbi divini. Circa quam tanto erimus uberiores, quanto Ascetæ nostrates, circa eam, vel sunt rariores; vel contractiores."

contemplated in the mind and experienced in the heart.[59] The reason for meditation is, according to Mastricht, that Scripture is soul food (bread, Amos 7:2; milk, 1 Pet. 3:2; honey, Ps. 119:103) and that it illuminates the intellect, corrects the will, and excites the affections so that collectively one is directed to the eternal happiness.[60] Therefore, Mastricht states that only the regenerate can meditate (1 Cor. 2:14), purified of their sin, in a solitary place, either in the morning (Ps. 5:4), evening (Gen. 24:63), or at night (Ps. 16:7). In addition, meditation can take place at times of fasting and daily separation (Ps. 55:18) and on the Lord's Day (Rev. 1:10). Furthermore, Mastricht—as a man of order—emphasizes that meditation has a preparation, progression, and end. The preparation is required to get the mind focused, and the contemplation, interpretation, and application of Scripture characterize the progression. The end is when the true sense of Scripture is intellectually comprehended and the will and affections are strengthened.[61] One notes that, as in the *locus* of faith, the three faculties: intellect, will and affections are involved in the life of the interpreter of Scripture.

In summary, the proper interpretation of Scripture coincides with both the spiritual state and the *praxis* of the interpreter. Without a renewal and guidance by the Holy Spirit, Scripture cannot be rightly understood. At the same time, Mastricht does not ignore the various dimensions of knowledge required for such right understanding of Scripture. Both theory and (spiritual) *praxis*, including but not limited to reminders of the *lectio divina*, should characterize the life of the exegete.

Prerequisites

Having established the spiritual state and *praxis* of the biblical exegete, Mastricht discusses other prerequisites. These are of a methodological nature and include the method of analysis of the biblical text.

Translation, Hebrew, Greek, and Textual Variants. The first step in the analysis of the biblical text is a Latin translation of the original text.[62] In respect to the Hebrew text, Mastricht cites the unpointed vowel text throughout his works and makes explicit references to the Masoretes.[63] In respect to the Greek text, Mastricht includes various exegetical readings of the text. For example, the *locus* on the divine goodness is based on

---

59. Ibid. : "Ita vero nihil aliud nobis est quam *fixa quædam ac stata omnium animæ facultatum actuatio, ad hoc, ut non modo verbi divini sensum assequamur genuinum* mente: sed & vim ejus experiamur, corde."

60. Ibid., lxxv, 45: "*Quare meditandum?*"

61. Ibid., lxxvi, 46. On the authoritative text, see above.

62. We agree with Graafland that Mastricht does not favor in particular the *Staten-bijbel* but provides his own translation. C. Graafland "Schriftleer en Schriftverstaan," 65. Note, however, that the *Beschouwende en practikale godgeleertheid* uses the rendering of the biblical text as found in the *Staten-bijbel*.

63. Mastricht, *Theoretico-practica theologia*, II.8.ii, 112: "יהוה אחד...litera tertia ד in אחד majuscula est & quidem decima. Observantibus Masorethis alliisque..."

the biblical text of Matthew 19:17.[64] Mastricht refers to two possible readings. The first reading Τί με ἐρωτᾷς περὶ τοῦ ἀγαθοῦ εἷς ἐστιν ὁ ἀγαθός· ("why do you ask me for the 'good'?"), is supported by Beza, Grotius, Jerome, and the Hebrew Gospel of Matthew and is in agreement with the Vulgate as well as the *patres* such as Origenes, Chrysostomus, and Augustine. This reading, according to Matricht, means that Jesus was affirming that there is by nature no good in man. The second reading, Τί με λέγεις ἀγαθόν˙ οὐδεὶς ἀγαθὸς εἰ μὴ εἷς ὁ θεός ,why call you me good?"), leads to the intepretation that Jesus in essence responded, "You cannot call me good because you do not hold me for God, who alone is good." This reading of the text is supported, according to Mastricht, by most Greek manuscripts, the Greek commentators, such as Euthymius, Theodortus, the Syriac version, and in Mark 10:18 per Beza, Piscator, and Diodatus.[65] Therefore, he argues that the first reading would imply Christ's divinity, granting that God alone can rightly be called good. This is why, according to Mastricht, that the Jews also assert that One, אחד, is Good, "as taught by Philo."[66] The second reading, leads to the interpretation that Jesus declared his divine authority from God.[67] Mastricht then weighs both options and incorporates both readings into his following text analysis, concluding that no fallen creature is good (the first reading) but that the only and one God is good (second reading).

Other Prerequisites. After the biblical text is translated, Mastricht defines five aditional prerequisites in coming to the analysis of the text. First, he counsels that one should not seek for obscure and controversial issues in the text, unless such are present in the text. In examining this point in Mastricht's doctrine of God, one notes a somewhat strict separation between exegesis and the elenctic part. Doctrinal differences are not drawn out of the biblical text, unless variant readings give reason for doing so. Illustrative are the Socinian controversies involving, for example, the Trinity. These are not discussed in Mastricht's textual analysis, although the Socinians (*Rakov Catechism*) refer, for different reasons, to the same biblical texts.[68] Mastricht deals with such controversies primarily in the elenctic part. On the other hand, in the analysis of Psalm 2:7, 8, Mastricht refutes Grotius's reading of אתה as a vocative in order to support his

---

64. A text that, with Mark 10:18, stands in a firm exegetical tradition for the locus of the divine goodness. Cf. Richard A. Muller, *Post-Reformation Reformed Dogmatics* (Grand Rapids: Baker Academic, 2003), 2:516-518.

65. Mastricht, *Theoretico-practica theologia*, II.16.ii, 170: "Reprehensio: Quid me bonum appellas? *Duplex his occurrit lectio*: altera sic habet...*quid me rogas de bono & c.?*...altera *lectio sic habet*...quid me dicis bonum? nemo bonus est, nisi unus, Deus."

66. Ibid., 171.

67. See for J. Calvin's and S. Charnock's exegetical insights of this issue, Muller, *Post-Reformation Reformed Dogmatics*, 2:517.

68. One exception can be noted in the exegesis of Matthew 19:17 following the textual variant reading. Here Mastricht notes that Jesus does not mean that He is not good, "sicut Sociani volunt" (*Theoretico-practica theologia*, II.16, ii, 170).

anti-Trinitarian hypotheses.[69] Mastricht argues that this part of the biblcal text should be read as אתה together with בני and supplemented with a form of "to be."

The second prerequisite is that one should respect the clarity and perspicuity of the text and should not add additional explanation. This not only takes away from the time of the preacher but also makes the Scripture obscure and makes the text suspicious.[70]

Third, a sufficient explication is measured by the content of the text. This prerequiste should be understood as both quantitative and qualitative. Quantitatively, this prerequisite is determined by the length of the biblical text. The examination of the length of the exegetical parts of Mastricht's doctrine of God shows that the explication correlates with the length of the biblical text. In other words, the length of the text and grammatical-syntactical considerations determine for Mastricht the length of the biblical text analysis. Qualitatively, this prerequisite is determined by the knowledge of the exegete.

The fourth prerequisite for the analysis of the biblical text is, according to Mastricht, that the individually explicated parts should be summarized or paraphrased so that a doctrinal argument emerges.[71] Examining the chapters of Mastricht's doctrine of God, we observe that these summaries of the text analysis occur at the end of the exegtical part or at the beginning of the doctrinal part. For example, in respect to the latter, the defintion of "faith" arises from the biblical text and its exposition. We have seen that Mastricht defines saving faith as

"an act of the total rational soul, whereby God is received as the highest end and the union with Christ, as the only Mediator, is obtained; through him the believer has communion with all his benefits."[72]

However, one notes the immediate and direct correlation of the doctrinal definition and the (exposition of the) biblical text:

Structure of biblical text	Definition
Faith	
A. Believers - ὅσοι	total rational soul
B. Faith - ἔλαβον or παρέλαβον	saving faith

69. Mastricht, *Theoretico-practica theologia*, II.26.ii.2.B.1, 251: "Filiatio בני אתה Filius meus tu *supple* es אתה hîc non est pro Vocativo: O Fili mi, *ut Grotius, suis hypothesibus antitrinitariis serviens, volebat.*"

70. Ibid., 1228: "2.B. *Ut per se satis clara & perspicua, non nitatur explicare Ecclesiastes, eo, non tantum argumento tempus surrepturus; sed etiam textum declarando magis obscuraturus, quin Scripturam perpetuæ & obscuritatis damnaturus.*"

71. Ibid., "2.D. *Tandem partes explicatæ complicentur rursus, paraphrasi quâdam, ut commodius emergat argumentum doctrinale.*"

72. Ibid., II.1.iii, 51: "*...fides salvifica nihil aliud sit, quam actus totius animæ rationalis, quo Deum accipit, quà summum finem; & Christum, quà unicum Mediatorem, ad hoc, ut cum eo uniamur, & uniti, communionem consequamur, omnium ejus beneficiorum.*"

C.	Object of faith - αὐτόν	God
	Fruits of faith	
1.	Source - ἔδωκεν	God
2.	Fruits of faith - ἐξουσίαν τέκνα θεοῦ γενέσθαι	union with Christ,
3.	Conditions	communion/ benefits
a.	Act of faith - πιστεύουσιν	act
b.	Object of faith - τὸ ὄνομα αὐτου	God, Christ
c.	The relation of the act and object of faith - εἰς	received

Thus, Mastricht's summary of the biblical text analysis and exegesis is the basis for the doctrinal formulation.[73]

Finally, the fifth prerequisite in the analysis of the biblical text echoes Calvin's remark on the need for brevity in exegesis.[74] Mastricht stresses in the *Prodromus* that the biblical text should be explained *breviter* and vigorously[75] and in the *TPT* (1682, 1687) that exegesis is a concise exposition of Scripture.[76]

We conclude, then, that Mastricht carefully laid out the way in which one should approach the biblical text. The foundation of theology, the *principium cognoscendi*, has prerequisites for the exegete. These prerequisites include the spiritual state and *praxis* of the interpreter of Scripture and the method of approach to the biblical text. With these premises Mastricht moves on to discuss the method of exegesis.

Method of Exegesis

The first step in exegesis includes, according to Mastricht, a balanced articulation of the content and the individual parts of the biblical text, whereby the latter should be expressed through substantives. Mastricht usually comments briefly on the character of the biblical text, whether it is exclamation, exhortation, votum, etc. Examining Mastrichts's exegetical parts of the doctrine of God, one observes that the substantives are related to the identification of the content of the biblical text. This can be illustrated by the exegesis of Deuteronomy 6: 4 שְׁמַע יִשְׂרָאֵל יְהוָה אֱלֹהֵינוּ יְהוָה אֶחָד. This is the foundational text for Mastricht for the unity of God. Central in this text, for him, is the

73. The summaries given by Mastricht in the remainder of the doctrine of God chapters are usually more concise than the example given here.

74. J. Calvin, *Commentary*, Vol. 19, *The Epistle of Paul the Apostle to the Romans* (1844-55; reprint, Grand Rapids: Baker Books, 1989), xxvi.

75. Mastricht, *Prodromus*, Præfatio: "...Scripturæ textum substerno, eumq. breviter & nervosè ἀναλύω & explico..."

76. Mastricht, *Theoretico-practica theologia* (1682), præfatio; idem, *Theoretico-practica theologia* (1687), præfatio: "...imprimis in elenchticis & practicis: ubi brevitatis necessitate." Idem, *Theoretico-practica theologia* (1699), præfatio: "In practicis rarior accidit amplicifatio, ne in nimiam molem degeneraret Theologia nostra."

word שמע (to hear). [77] The text notes "who has to hear"—ישראל (Israel)—and "what needs to be heard"—יהוה אלהינו (the Lord our God)[78] and יהוה אחד (the Lord is One).[79] Here, one observes that the individual parts of the text can be a (biblical) phrase or individual word. Moreover, for Mastricht, the identification of the individual text parts determines the content of the biblical text. For example, the text of Romans 11:33, 34[80] is identified in its entirety as an exclamation. Mastricht divides the text further into an exclamation, an argument, and a fourfold question.[81] Thus, the structure and words of the biblical text determine the explication. Therefore, for him, the identification of the parts of the biblical text concerns the biblical words of the text and not doctrinal impositions.

The third and interrogative step in Mastricht's method should be "avoided in a sermon" but is "showed in the chapters of the *Theologia*."[82] In respect to the latter, for example, the use of interrogatives is noted in the analysis of Ephesians 3:20, 21,[83] the foundational text for the divine attribute *potestas & potentia Dei*. First, the "who" is identified in verse 20 of the text as δυναμένῳ and, in particular, Mastricht argues, the article Τῷ separates the divine one, here in the text, from any other one.[84] Second, and central to the biblical text, Mastricht identifies the "what," because the text speaks of δυναμένῳ, whereby God is the μόνος δυνάστης (1 Tim. 6:15) and has the δυναμι. Mastricht explains that the Greek word δυναμι can be rendered by power, might, potency, or strength "as is testified in 2 Thes. 2:9, and Rev. 18:3." To strengthen his argument, Mastricht notes the Hebrew form (חיל which is also rendered in Ruth 4:11 as "the mighty one." Thus, the interrogatives are used specifically in relation to the content and character of the biblical text. When the character of the text allows, however, he

77. Mastricht, *Theoretico-practica theologia* (1699), II.8.ii, 112: "*Textus, Ecclesiæ commendat auditionem...*"

78. Here Mastricht refers to the previous chapter, *De Nominibus Dei*.

79. Mastricht, *Theoretico-practica theologia*, II.8.ii, 112: "1. Auditio שמע...2. auditores, Israël...3. Audiendum, *duplex nim. Dei:...*"

80. Ὦ βάθος πλούτου καὶ σοφίας καὶ γνώσεως θεοῦ· ὡς ἀνεξεραύνητα τὰ κρίματα αὐτοῦ καὶ ἀνεξιχνίαστοι αἱ ὁδοὶ αὐτοῦ Τίς γὰρ ἔγνω νοῦν κυρίου ἢ τίς σύμβουλος αὐτοῦ ἐγένετο

81. Mastricht, *Theoretico-practica theologia*, II.13.ii, 142: "*Textus*, ἐπιφώνημα *quoddam* ἐγκωμιαστικόν...1. Exclamatio *quædam admirantis, ubi: a. Index exclamatorius, in vocula* ὡς ...b. Res, *particula admirantis, commendata...*1. Profunditas...2. Divitiarum...3. Sapientiæ & cognitionis Dei...2. Quæstio *quadruplex admirantis...*"

82. Ibid., 1227, vii.b: "*Partes immidiatæ, substantivis nominibus contento analogis exprimantur, non autem particulis interrogatoriis per quis, quid, quare, quomodo, quondo, aliisque, prout in singulis Theologiæ nostræ capitibus monstravimus.*"

83. Τῷ δὲ δυναμένῳ ὑπὲρ πάντα ποιῆσαι ὑπερεκπερισσοῦ ὧν αἰτούμεθα ἢ νοοῦμεν κατὰ τὴν δύναμιν τὴν ἐνεργουμένην ἐν ἡμῖν, αὐτῷ ἡ δόξα ἐν τῇ ἐκκλησίᾳ καὶ ἐν Χριστῷ Ἰησοῦ εἰς πάσας τὰς γενεὰς τοῦ αἰῶνος τῶν αἰώνων, ἀμήν.

84. Mastricht, *Theoretico-practica theologia*, II.20.ii, 208: "*Hic articulus* τῷ *videtur potestatem habere* διακριτικὴν *qui Deum potentem discriminet a quovis alio potente.*" God is identified as the "who" in the exegetical parts of the doctrine of God in the *Theoretico-practica theologia*, II.9.ii, 117, II.17.ii, 177, II.18.ii, 192, II.21.ii, 219 (יהוה); II.11.ii, 128 (אדני); II.15.ii, 157 (אלהים).

implicitly proceeds with the use of interrogatives through the biblical text. He does this, for example, in explicating the biblical text of Isaiah 42:8 as an edict or glorious proclamation of the divine essence and name. The glory and majesty of God are central and make this text foundational for the discussion of the divine attribute of the glory of God.[85] Finally, then, in respect to the exegesis of the biblical text, Mastricht emphazises that the text of Scripture is the foundation of the *loci communes* and is to be explicated philologically, avoiding the art of logic, which could deduct the nature of the biblical text. Mastricht's stated avoidance of the art of logic thus, here, runs contrary to the possible influence of Ramus in his exegesis.[86]

In conclusion, then, the explication of the biblical text is first and foremost, for Mastricht, a search for the grammatical, philologocal, literal, textual, and contextual understanding of a given passage.

Tools for Exegesis

The method of analysis and method of exegesis is supported by Mastricht with various exegetical tools: the analogy of faith, analogy of context, and external textual aids such as philology, philosophy and history.[87] Mastricht also recommends the use commentators such as Calvin, Piscator, Poole, and others.

Analogy of Faith and Context. Knapp's assessment of post-Reformation orthodox use of the *analogia fidei* shows that Mastricht is no exception.[88] Mastricht explains that the rule for interpretation, in the context of obscure and difficult passages of Scripture, should be the analogy of faith and the context of the biblical text. In respect to the latter, he notes further that, through parallel passages and mutual comparison of text words, Scripture explains itself.[89] One should interpret Scripture with the analogy of faith, not to allow more than one sense of Scripture but to have a united and harmonious

---

85. Ibid., II.22.ii, 225: "*Textu continetur*, edictum *quoddam, seu solemnis* promulgatio, *trium suorum quasi* Regalium...1. Essentia אני יהוה...2. nomine הוא שמי...3. Gloria וכבודי לאחר לא אתן..."

86. Ibid., præfatio: "Etenim in *exegeticis*, Scripturæ textus, capitibus Theologiæ, pro fundamento substructi...explicatius, ex philologiâ...In his, quantum fieri potuit, nos à terminis artis logicæ; ...cohibuimus & ex naturâ textus diduximus...". Cf. Keith L. Sprunger, *The Learned Doctor William Ames* (Chicago: University of Illinois Press, 1972), 140; Muller, *Post-Reformation Reformed Dogmatics*, 2:507.

87. Mastricht, *Theoretico-practica theologia*, 1228. See also part II, chapter 2 of this study for textual differences between the *Methodus Concionandi* and *Theoretico-practica theologia* (1682, 1699).

88. Knapp, *Understanding the Mind of God*, 77: "It would be difficult to overestimate the importance of the *analogy of faith* in the post-Reformation orthodox's hermeneutical strategy. Their exegetes consciously followed it, and they expressed and defended it in their theoretical writings. Yet, in practice, evidence of its use in the exegetical enterprise is only found in subtle ways. The analogy of faith did not dictate the interpretation of any particular text; what it did was limit the options which the exegete would consider as appropriate explanations of a passage. That is, the analogy of faith restricted the range of possible meanings which the exegete would consider – other potential meanings of a passage were simply not mentioned since they were excluded a priori by the *analogia fidei* assumption." Cf. Muller, *Post-Reformation Reformed Dogmatics*, 2:493.

89. Mastricht, *Theoretico-practica theologia*, I.2.xlix, 36.

understanding of Scripture. Scripture is written at different times and locations but is inspired by the same Holy Spirit who is unchangeable and the one who illuminates one's understanding. If there are conflicts, it is not because of Scripture but because of one's understanding.

The analogy of faith, based as it is on the clear and plain passages of the Bible, is basically an extension of the *analogy of Scripture*.[90] According to the *analogia Scripturæ*, the surest and truest guide for determining the meaning of a particular text is to seek its explanation within the rest of Scripture. *Sacra Scriptura sui ipsius interpres*–Scripture is its own interpreter.[91] Mastricht argues, then, that seeming contradictions in Scripture can be traced back to one of five causes. First, it may be the result of a phrase or word used at different locations in diverse senses. Second, the same word may be used in different locations in different contexts or arguments or in discussing different subjects. Third, the word may be used in relation to the same subject but does not speak of the same part of the subject. Fourth, the same subject may be considered from a different point of view. Fifth, the word may be used in a different tense.[92] Therefore, for Mastricht, one should interpret *Scripturam Scripturis*, that is, interpret Scripture with Scripture (Acts. 2:25-32). He finds support for this in Augustine, who testified to being acquainted with the practice of using the clear places of Scripture to explain the obscure places.[93] It is important to know, according to Mastricht, the economy of the Scripture—that is the order of books and the time of the author and the writing—and to memorize an outline of the book. Also one should know the scope, or the objective of the writer, and know how to become acquainted with the scope. Finally, one should know the *praxis* of Scripture because, Bernardus testifies, according to Mastricht, "that those who live the divine Scripture rightly, changes the word into deeds."[94]

In relation to exegesis, Mastricht addresses the issues of the *sensus Scripturæ*. The question is, Does Scripture admit one or more senses?[95] Mastricht answers this question from a historical perspective. The church fathers, starting with Origenes allowed for more than the *sensus literalis*, adding the *sensus allegoricus* and *mysticus*.[96] In addition, Mastricht believes that those who embrace the rule: "*verba Scriptura significant quicquid significare possunt,*" are open for multiple senses of Scripture. Finally, Mastricht states that

90. Cf. Muller, *Post-Reformation Reformed Dogmatics*, 2:493-497.

91. Knapp, *Understanding the Mind of God*, 80.

92. Mastricht, *Theoretico-practica theologia*, I.2.lxxii, 44: "Quicquid autem ἐν ἀντιοφανες ...."

93. Ibid.: "*Ubi apertius ponuntur sententiæ, ibi discendum est, quomodo in locis intelligantur obscuris.* Ait Augustin. De Doctr. Christ. Lib. 3:25."

94. Ibid.: "Is enim, *divinas Scripturas recte legit, qui verba vertit in opera.* Inquit Bernard. in Tractat. De ord. vitæ."

95. Ibid., xlvii, 35.

96. Ibid.: "E Patribus complures, in quibus chorum ducit Origenes, quod literalem Scripturæ sensum, nimium existimarent simplicem, nec talem, qui sapientiam Religionis Christianæ, posset commendare Gentilibus; a sensu Scripturae literali, ad sensus allegoricos & mysticos delabuntur: Iudæi itidem in suis Midraschim: sed comprimis Enthusiastæ omnes."

the Roman Catholics promote the quadruple sense of Scripture: literal, allegorical, tropological, and anagogical.[97] Contrary to Origen and medieval exegetes, the Reformed orthodox, according to Mastricht, allow for a single and literal sense: that which the writer intended. However, he adds, that this single sense can be composite in the tropological, typical, and mystical.[98]

Philology and Etymology. The proper exegesis of the biblical text includes, for Mastricht, philology assisted by internal and external textual aids. In respect to philology, he demonstrates the linguistic knowledge of the original languages of Scripture: Hebrew, Aramaic, and Greek.[99] Further, in the context of the analysis of the biblical text, Mastricht attests an enormous linguistic knowledge. This knowledge is utilized to come to the literal meaning of a word, phrase, or sentence of the biblical text. In our review of the doctrine of God, it can be concluded that one has to distinguish between philology and etymology. The former includes the study of literature and disciplines relevant to languages. The latter, etymology, attempts to establish the literal meaning of a word according to its origin. This involves the word or phrase analysis of its component parts, identifying its cognates and morphemes to determine whether the word is formed by composition or derivation.

Philology. Mastricht apparrently took Voetius's advice on the study of Hebrew seriously.[100] Mastricht was a professor of Hebrew for fifteen years, prior to his appointment as professor of theology at Utrecht University. Such a vocational path was

---

97. See for a comprehensive study, Henry de Lubac, *Exégèse médiévale: Les quatre sens de l'Écriture*, 4 vols. (Paris: Aubier, 1959-1964).

98. Mastricht, *Theoretico-practica theologia*, I.2.xlvii, 35: "Orthodoxi *unum* tantum; eumque *literalem*, admittunt Scripturæ sensum, illum nim. quem ipse *scriptor*, verbis suis *intendit*: interim fatentur, sensum istum, quandoque *compositum* esse, ut accidit, in phrasibus tropicis ac typicis, ubi pars sensus, propria est *verborum* significatio; pars tralatitia, *rerum*. Quin & sensus *mysticos*, ubi certo constat, à Spiritu S. eos esse intentos, *literales* appellant. Argumenta orthodoxorum sunt: 1. Quia Scripturæ sensus verus, *certus* ac firmus est 2. Pet. I. 19. quin & *purus* ac purgatissimus, hoc est, procul ab omni mixtura Psal. XII. 7. & CXIX. 140. Prov. XXX. 5. Iam vero, quod est aequivocum aut ambiguum, seu quod *plures sensus* admittit, illud non est purum, *certum* ac firmum 2. Quod non significat *unum* quid; *nihil* certò significat 3. Sensus est velut *forma verborum*: ergo, cum verba non habeant, nisi unam formam; non habent etiam, nisi *unum sensum* &c.."

99. Ibid., I.2.x, 20, 21. Besides Mastricht's extensive knowledge of the Hebrew language, he demonstrates that he is deeply acquainted with Greek, Syrian, Aramaic, Arabic, Latin, and Ethiopian, and familiar with French, English, Dutch, and Spanish. See, for example, ibid., tomus secundus, fol.637. Here Mastricht acknowledges his brother Gerard for the "*varias* Novi Testamenti *lectiones*." Ibid., II.21.ii.b, 219: "*qui ab Arabico* שרד *derivent;*" II.26.ii; ibid., II.17.ii.3, 178: "*Hinc Hispani dicunt...*"

100. Gysbertus Voetius, "Reedenvoeringe," in Isaac le Long, *Hondert-Jaarige Jubel-Gedachtenisse de Academie van Utrecht* (Utrecht: M. Visch, 1736), 51: "Betreffende verder, de Studie en Geleertheit der *Hebreeuwsche* Taale . . . dese moet men ook voor zeer nuttelyk houden. *Vooreerst*, dewyle door de *Rabbynsche* en *Thalmudische* onderzoekingen, veele Woorden en Oudtheeden, die wy in de Schrifuure vinden, soo veel te beter verklaart konnen worden."

not uncommon for the post-Reformation orthodox theologians.[101] It is therefore, then, that Mastricht demonstrates acquaintance with the lexical commentaries of Buxtorf, Reuchlin, Drusius, Aquila, Erasmus, Grotius, and rabbinic sources.[102]

Etymology. This discipline is, for Mastricht, a part of philology. Examination of the doctrine of God in the *TPT* and, in particular, the exegetical section, shows a vast etymological knowledge.

Hebrew. Mastricht's knowledge of the Hebrew words, roots, and meanings shows itself not only in an initial rendering the meaning of a Hebrew word but often by subsequent etymological analysis.[103] A few examples may illustrate our observation. He argues in the chapter on the *Divine Essence* that the phrase אשר אהיה אהיה can be rendered in four different ways: "I am who I am," "I shall be who I shall be," "I shall be who I am," and "I am who I shall be."[104] Mastricht identifies אהיה as related to יהוה and elaborates in more detail on the latter.[105] He notes that יהוה (Deut. 3:24; 9:26) is derived from the Aramaic הוה or Hebrew the היה, which both can be rendered with *esse*. Moreover, Mastricht observes that the word יהוה consists of three tenses: the future, represented by י, the present, represented by ה, and the past by וה or the ה indicating the past, the ו indicating the present, and the י indicating the future. The latter rendering is, according to Mastricht, in agreement with Revelation 1:8 and Zanchius's *De Divine Attribute* and Fuller's *Miscellanies*.[106] Mastricht continues that the LXX translates יהוה usually with κυριος, which refers more to אדני and that the French consistently and best translate יהוה with *l'Éternel*. Finally, he notes that the word יהוה even seems to have been taken over by the Gentiles in the word *Jovem*, the supreme one.[107] Furthermore, Mastricht argues that יהוה contains quiescent letters, which, "some conclude, more subtle than solid," indicate the divine rest but also that all quietness should be sought in יהוה. The alternative יאה or "beauty," is rejected by Mastricht because this is an abbreviation of

101. Muller, *Post-Reformation Reformed Dogmatics*, 2:444. In addition, two examples may illustrate our point: The *Opera Omnia* of J. Cocceius and J. à Marck consist for the greater part of Old Testament exegetical material.

102. Mastricht, *Theoretico-practica theologia*, II.21.ii.2.2, 220: "*Aquila Gen.20:5, etiam ἄπλασον h.e. non fictum;*" idem, II.4.viii, 87; II.26.ii.1, 251. See also Appendix I.2.4.

103. Ibid., II.3.ii.C, 76; II.8.ii.3, 112; II.9.ii, 117; II.10.ii.2, 122; II.11.ii, 128; II.15.ii, 157; II.17.ii, 178; II.18.ii, 192, 193; II.22.ii, 225; II.23.ii, 231.

104. Ibid., II.3.ii.c, 76: "*Nisi malis, Deum his verbis petito Mosis annuere quasi dicat: vis nomen meum, quod* Essentiam *meam repræsentet utcunque? ens est:* אהיה אהיה אשר, *sum qui sum, vel ero qui ero: vel ero qui sum: vel sum qui ero, de quo nomine Cap.seq.*" For further on the relation of אהיה and יהוה see ibid., II.4.xi, 88.

105. Ibid., II.4.vii, 86: "*Fuit nominum divinorum, Θεορία generalior; succedit specialior, juxta quam nomina Dei, vel ejus essentiam repræsentant, ut אהיה יהוה....*"

106. Ibid., viii, 87, "*Unde, in tribus ejus syllabis omnes tempororum periodos, præteritum, præsens & futurum...sic. Zanchius de divin. Attribut. Lib.1 cap.13. Fuller. Miscel. 5. Lib.ii. cap.6.*"

107. Ibid, "*Videtur ejus vocis, nonnihil defluxisse ad Gentiles quando, supremum inter Deos suos Jovem appellarunt.*"

the Tetragrammaton יהוה, caused by a fast pronunciation, with the "exception of the pronouncement אדני of the sacerdotal benediction."[108] Neither the reading with a *qametz* nor a *patach* with a *soph pasuk* excludes the meaning of the divine absolute lordship.[109] Thus, paramount for Mastricht is the analysis of the Hebrew words and their roots in order to arrive at the right (exegetical) meaning.

One other example illustrates Mastricht's own translation skills. In the analysis of the text of Psalm 139:8, in the context of verses 7-10, which serves as a foundation for the divine immensity and omnipresence, Mastricht comments on the word שאול. He asserts that the word could mean "hell," the place of the reprobate (Job. 11:8; 26:6) contrary to "heaven." However, in the context of Psalm 139:8, he argues that in "hell no one makes up his bed." Thus, he concludes that שאול better can be rendered here with "grave" (Gen. 42:6; Acts 2:27; cf. Ps. 16:80). A grave, according to Mastricht, is a bed for the dead. However, he raises the question of how one should understand this rendering in the context of the Psalm. He replies that "making a bed" denotes to hide and to live somewhere.[110] Here one observes that the right understanding of the word in the context of the biblical text illuminates the exegetical result.

Not only did the rendering of the original text have his attention; so too did even the individual letters. For example, he argues, that the ו is sometimes a connecting vowel—serving, as in Psalm 119:137, as a joint construct for the nature of justice and righteousness of judgments[111]—and sometimes it indicates a contrast with the preceding sentence part as in the context of Psalm 15:3.[112] Finally, our examination shows that Mastricht paid regular attention to the different tenses such as the hithpaël, piël, and pual. [113]

Greek. Mastricht's comments on the biblical text in the Greek language[114] are less illustrative than the Hebrew texts. Here, he could show himself as a student of Voetius. His teacher commented in de *Reedevoering* relatively briefly on the Greek New Testament language in comparison to the Hebrew.[115] We have pointed out Mastricht's critical

---

108. Ibid., xi, 88: "יאה ...abbreviatura censetur, tetragrammati, natum ex celerrimâ ejus pronunctiatione in vulgari saltem pronunciatione, natum: quamvis in sacerdotali benedictione distinctissime pronunciarint. אדני...."

109. Ibid.: "...saltem *cum Kametz*...sit pro *Patach...Dominium* Dei absolutissimum exprimit."

110. Ibid., II.10.ii.2.a, 122.

111. Ib id., II.18.ii.2, 193: "Judicia וישר משפטיך...*Copulativum* ו *justitiam* naturæ..."

112. Ibid., II.15.ii.1, 157: "*Hic præfixum conjunctionale* ו *quod ordinarie vim habet copulativem, est adversativum.*"

113. Ibid., II.22.ii.b.α, 226: "*In Pihel est laudare*"; II.11.ii.2, 128: "*vel passive, in Puhal...*"; II.21.ii.2.i, 220: "*In Hithpahel notat....*"

114. Ibid., II.1.ii, 50; II.2.ii, 66; II.6.ii, 98; II.7.ii, 112; II.13.ii, 143; II.20.ii, 208, 209; II.24.ii, 236; II.25.ii, 246; II.27.ii, 262.

115. Voetius, "Reedenvoeringe," 54.

textual reading and observed that he primarily translates the text of the New Testament taking the grammatical-syntactical context into consideration.[116]

Transliterations. Our examination of the doctrine of God shows that Mastricht provides Hebrew equivalents for Greek words in order to illuminate the rendering and meaning of the biblical text[117] but rarely provides Greek equivalents for Hebrew.[118] For example, Mastricht provides in the analysis of Romans 11:33, 34 the Hebrew equivalent for κρίματα the judgment, or חקים, that is rendered by decree and execution. Therefore, the biblical text "how deep are your judgments," should be interpreted, according to Mastricht, as the divine decrees and execution of the decrees. Thus, the doctrinal formulation arises from the biblical word study.

Commentators. *Calvin.* The overwhelming evidence of Mastricht's use of philology in exegesis is contrasted by his rare (cited) use of the "best commentators."[119] However, the limited citations of commentators in his doctrine of God should not lead immediately to the conclusion that he differs or does (not) stand in continuity with these commentators. A preliminary examination actually shows the opposite.

In respect to Calvin's biblical commentaries, we note that both Calvin and Mastricht follow overall the same line of argument in regard to the grammar and syntax of the original languages. For example, Calvin comments on "I am that I am" in Exodus 3:14,

> The verb in Hebrew is in the future tense, "I will be what I will be;" but it is of the same force as the present, except that it designates the perpetual duration of time.[120]

Moreover, Calvin argues that the text refers to the divine essence. These similar lines of exegetical argument also are found outside the chapter on the doctrine of God. For

---

116. Mastricht, *Theoretico-practica theologia*, II.1.ii, 50; II.2.ii, 66.

117. Ibid., II.1.ii.3.b, 51; II.6.ii, 98; II.13.ii.2.b, g, 143; II.20.ii.2, 208; II.25.ii, 247.

118. Ibid., II.4.iii, 86; II.13.ii.2, 143; II.21.ii, 219, 220.

119. Ibid., 1228: "*Exegeseos adminicula* repetantur...4.*Commentatoribus* præstantissimis, cum criticis & verbalibus; tum analyticis ac realibus Calvino, Piscator, Polo & c." Mastricht refers to (1) Calvin primarily in the elenctic and practical section to support his argument (cf. II.2.xxv, 73; II.4.xvi, 90; II.16.xv, 174; II.26.xix, 259), (2) Piscator in the exegetical section (cf. II.16.ii, 170), and (3) Poole is not mentioned at all.

120. J. Calvin, *Commentary*, vol. 2, *Harmony of the Four Last Books of the Pentateuch*, 73. Cf. Mastricht, *Theoretico-practica theologia*, II.3.ii.c, 76; II.3.iii, 77. Compare also on Ps. 145:3, where both formulate the same doctrine or practical result of the exegesis; Calvin, *Commentary*, vol. 6, *The Book of Psalms*, 272. Cf. Mastricht, *Theoretico-practica theologia*, II.9.ii, 117; Calvin, *Commentary*, vol.17, *Gospel according to John*, 206. Cf. Mastricht, *Theoretico-practica theologia*, II.12.iii, 135. Calvin, *The Book of Psalms*, 346. Cf. Mastricht, *Theoretico-practica theologia*, II.15.xli, 169; Calvin, *The Book of Psalms*, 18. Cf. Mastricht, *Theoretico-practica theologia*, II.18.ii, 193; Calvin, *Commentary*, vol. 8, *The Book of the Prophet Isaiah*, 296. Cf. Mastricht, *Theoretico-practica theologia*, II.22.iii, 226; Calvin, *Commentary*, vol. 20, *Epistles of Paul the Apostle to the Corinthians*, 403, 404. Cf. Mastricht, *Theoretico-practica theologia*, II.24.ii, 236.

example, it is quite clear, as we have seen, that both Calvin and Mastricht recognized the proper division of theology or "knowledge of Christ" as faith and love.[121]

Sometimes Calvin and Mastricht differ on the result or doctrinal formulation of the exegesis. For example, Calvin reads Psalm 90:2 in respect to the divine eternity and providence. Mastricht focuses exclusively on the divine eternity.[122] Finally, we note only two instances of different text interpretation. First, the exposition of John 1:12 leads to Calvin's central argument concerning the "doctrine" of adoption, while for Mastricht this text is crucial to the "doctrine" of faith, particularly the receiving or accepting of faith.[123] Second, Mastricht bases his exposition *De Immensitate et Omnipræsentia Dei* on Psalm 139:7-11. Calvin remarks on verse 7,

> David means in short that he could not change from one place to another without God seeing him....They misapply the passage who adduce it as a proof of the immensity of God's essence...this was not at present in the view of the Psalmist.[124]

Thus, both Calvin and Mastricht identify the divine omnipresence in the text, but Mastricht's exposition of the divine immensity in Psalm 139:7 is not shared by Calvin. We conclude, then, that although Mastricht rarely cites Calvin, he does not significantly differ with Calvin's exegesis and exposition of the biblical texts Mastricht used in the doctrine of God. There is continuity between Calvin and Mastricht in exegetical approach and result.

Poole. Matthew Poole finished his monumental *Synopsis* in 1676. Mastricht considers him a good commentator on the Scripture but does not cite him in his exposition of the doctrine of God. However, our examination of Poole's exposition of the biblical texts used by Mastricht in the doctrine of God is revealing. First, Poole consistently uses the Masoretic text in contrast to Mastricht who rarely uses this Hebrew text. Second, Mastricht shows more so than Poole his philological skills, especially in the Hebrew text. On the other hand, Poole provides more information on different manuscripts and references than Mastricht does. The difference in genre of the *TPT* and *Synopsis* may contribute to this difference. With this in mind, we observe that both Poole and Mastricht are similar in their grammatical, exegetical exposition.[125] Sometimes, Poole

---

121. J. Calvin, *Commentary*, vol. 21, *The Epistles to Timothy, Titus and Philemon*, 153, 154. Cf. Mastricht, *Theoretico-practica theologia*, I.1.i, 2; II.1.ix, 4; Calvin, *Commentary*, vol. 21, *The Epistles to Timothy, Titus and Philemon*, 202. Cf. Mastricht, *Theoretico-practica theologia*, I.3.ii, 47.

122. Calvin, *Commentary*, vol. 6, *The Book of Psalms*, 462. Cf. Mastricht, *Theoretico-practica theologia*, II.11.ii, 128.

123. Calvin, *Commentary*, vol. 17, *Gospel according to John*, 42. Cf. Mastricht, *Theoretico-practica theologia*, II.1.ii, 50.

124. Calvin, *Commentary*, vol. 6, *The Book of Psalms*, 211. Cf. Mastricht, *Theoretico-practica theologia*, II.10.ii, 122.

125. Matthew Poole, *Synopsis criticorum aliorumque S.Scripturæ interpretum* (London: E. Flesher, 1676), 5:1087. Cf. Mastricht, *Theoretico-practica theologia*, I.1.ii, 2; Poole, *Synopsis* 5:1106. Cf. Mastricht, *Theoretico-practica theologia*, I.3.ii, 47; Poole, *Synopsis*, 4:1147. Cf. Mastricht, *Theoretico-practica theologia*, II.6.ii, 98;

passes briefly over[126] or denotes more[127] in a biblical text, whereas Mastricht provides an exposition. At other times they differ[128] or agree[129] in rendering of the original language. Furthermore, we notice that Mastricht's exposition of Ephesians 3:20 leading to the doctrine *De Potentia Dei* is rejected by Poole.[130] Finally, both Poole and Mastricht make extensive use of Christian Hebraïsts.[131] In two instances Mastricht does not provide a reference, but thanks to Poole's work we are informed.[132] We conclude, then, that there are no major exegetical differences, in method and results, between Poole and Mastricht.

One observes a continuity of biblical exegesis and interpretation between the sixteenth-century Reformation and seventeenth-century post-Reformation orthodoxy. This continuity of biblical exegesis is actually intensified by the Protestant Scholastics such as Mastricht through the explicit attentiveness to the original languages of the biblical text. This intensification of biblical exegesis is further illustrated by Mastricht's use of non-Reformed sources.

Others: The Rabbinic Tradition or Christian Hebraism. One of the questions that arises from Mastricht's recommendation of biblical commentators in the *Methodus Concionandi* is who the "others" are. Are Calvin, Poole, and Piscator the main sources for Mastricht? Are they, although rarely used in the doctrine of God, more authoritative than any other exegetical aid? After all, these Reformed commentators could be identified as having contributed to a "central dogma or doctrinal imposition" on the exegesis of the biblical

Poole, *Synopsis*, 4:1143. Cf. Mastricht, *Theoretico-practica theologia*, II.11.ii, 128; Poole, *Synopsis*, 4:1212. Cf. Mastricht, *Theoretico-practica theologia*, II.12.ii, 134; Poole, *Synopsis*, 5:57 (emphasis is on the divine faithfulness, not veracity). Cf. Mastricht, *Theoretico-practica theologia*, II.14.ii, 152; Poole, *Synopsis*, 1:166. Cf. Mastricht, *Theoretico-practica theologia*, II.21.ii, 219.

126. Poole, *Synopsis*, 1:329. Cf. Mastricht, *Theoretico-practica theologia*, II.4.ii, 85; Poole, *Synopsis*, 2:1406. Cf. Mastricht, *Theoretico-practica theologia*, II.9.ii, 117; Poole, *Synopsis*, 2:1372-4. Cf. Mastricht, *Theoretico-practica theologia*, II.10.ii, 122; Poole, *Synopsis*, 4:1426. Cf. Mastricht, *Theoretico-practica theologia*, II.27.ii, 262.

127. Poole, *Synopsis*, 1:328. Cf. Mastricht, *Theoretico-practica theologia*, II.3.ii, 76; Poole, *Synopsis*, 2:515; Mastricht, *Theoretico-practica theologia*, II.26.ii, 251.

128. Poole, *Synopsis*, 5:1129. Cf. Mastricht, *Theoretico-practica theologia*, I.2.ii, 18. For πασα γραφη, Poole renders *omnis* and Mastricht *tota*. Cf. Mastricht, *Theoretico-practica theologia*, II.1.ii, 50. For ἔλαβον Poole renders *receperunt* and Mastricht *acceperunt*.

129. Poole, *Synopsis*, 1:498. Cf. Mastricht, *Theoretico-practica theologia*, II.17.ii.3, 178. For אֶרֶךְ אַפִּים in Exod. 34.6, both render "long nostrils." Both render more detail by noting that the Spanish people say "the nostrils of the angry are blown up." To this Poole adds, "the English: 'take pepper in the nose.'"

130. Poole, *Synopsis*, 5:784 (10): "Non loquitur de potentia Dei nuda, absoluta, & otiosa; sed de efficaci, quæ cum ejus voluntate conjuncta est *in nobis*, Pi. Be. &c."

131. See for Poole the *Catalogus Auctorum, cum Abbreviaturis quibus exprimuntur* on the back of the front page of volume I of the *Synopsis*. See for Mastricht below.

132. Poole, *Synopsis*, 1:770 (70) on Deut. 6:4: "Hinc Dei nomen est אֶחָד ...Deus...La(pide). Cf. Mastricht, *Theoretico-practica theologia*, II. 8.ii.3.2: "Hinc Dei ...Deus..."; Poole, *Synopsis*, 2:515, on Ps. 2:7: "nempe idem Rex...poeticis Gej(erus)." Cf. Mastricht, *Theoretico-practica theologia*, II.26.ii.1, 251: "*nempe idem Rex...Poëticis.*"

text. Therefore, our concern in this section is the identification of the "other" commentators Mastricht used.

The examination of Mastricht's doctrine of God shows, first, a vast evidence of the use of Christian Hebraism. Mastricht, as (former) professor of Hebrew at the universities of Frankfurt an der Oder and Duisburg, demonstrates not only his Hebrew linguistic skills but also enourmous knowledge of the rabbinical sources. Our further examination, then, concentrates on the identification of these sources and their use.

First, in respect to the sources of (Christian) Hebraism, we note Mastricht's references to rabbinical sources such as Elijah Leviata (c.1468-1549), R(abbi). Hakkadosch (1534-1572), R. Salomo (Rashi) (1040-1105), R. Jarchi, R. David Kimchi (c.1160-1235), R. Maimonides (1135-1204), R. Nacham (Rambam) (1194-c.1270), R. ben Ezra (1089-1164), R. Jonathan (first century), R. Isaac ben Abraham (?), and Manassa ben Israel (?).[133] These rabbis could be classified in the Jewish tradition of Scripture commentators as grammarians and philologists. These men were concerned with the proper meaning and interpretation of Scripture. This concern gave rise to the so-called *peshat* exegesis: the attempt to find the "plain" meaning of the biblical text, the contextual meaning, the linguistically and contextually grounded meaning. The grammatically grounded meaning became more important than the edifying relevance.[134] Second, Mastricht uses the phrase "according to the Jewish masters" multiple times in his biblical text analysis and includes references to the Targum and Mishnah. Third, he cites, in addition to the aforementioned, Hebrew grammarians and lexicons such as those of Fagius, Fuller, Alting, and Lightfoot.[135]

In respect to Mastricht's use of the rabbinic exegetical tradition, we note a primary philological use of these sources in the exegetical sections of the doctrine of God.[136] In other words, Mastricht's concern to establish the literal meaning in a grammatical context involves the reliance on (rabbinnic and other) sources that originated outside (Reformed) Christianity. Like the Jewish commentators, who employed the *peshat*

133. See Appendix I.2.4.

134. See for seventeeth-century Christian Hebraism, Aaron L. Katchen, *Christian Hebraists and Dutch Rabbis* (Cambridge, Mass: Harvard Univeristy Press, 1984); S. G. Burnett, *The Christian Hebraism of Johann Buxtorf (1564-1629)* (Ph.D. diss., University of Wisconsin, 1990); Sarah Kamin, *Rashi's Exegetical Categorization: In respect to the distinction between Peshat and Derash* (Jerusalem: Arts, 1986); Jai-Sung Shim, *Biblical Hermeneutics and Hebraism in the Early Seventeenth Century as Reflected in the Work of John Weemse* (Ph.D. diss., Calvin Theological Seminary, 1998). Peter Martyr Vermigili, *Commentary on the Lamentations,* trans. and ed. with introduction notes by Daniel Shute (Kirksville, Mo: Sixteenth-Century Essays and Studies, 2002).

135. See Appendix I.2.4.

136. It is noteworthy that both the identification and use of rabbinic sources are not restricted to the doctrine of God but are also found elsewhere in the *TPT*, as a review of the exegetical sections of books III-VIII of the *TPT*, and restricted to the biblical texts of the Old Testament, shows; Mastricht, *Theoretico-practica theologia*, III.5.ii, 312; III.6.ii, 320; II.9.ii, 365; III.11.ii, 405; III.12.ii, 415; IV.1.ii, 327; V.1.ii, 389; V.6.ii, 454; V.7.ii, 463; V.8.ii, 476; V.13.ii, 558; VI.4.ii, 675. The remainder of the book contains three *loci* derived from an Old Testament text (VII.3, VIII.2, and VIII.3), that do not have rabbinnic or Christian Hebraistic references.

method of exegesis, so Mastricht utilized their commentaries. Moreover, like these commentators, Mastricht infers from the biblical text a doctrinal *locus*.[137]

We can conclude, then, that the "other" commentators include the rabbinic sources. This underscores that Mastricht stands in a Christian Hebraist exegetical trajectory and shared the concern of these rabbinic exegetes to establish the "plain' meaning of the biblical text.[138] This finding also underscores that certain doctrines emerged, for both the rabbinic commentators and Mastricht, from the biblical text. Furthermore, we may reach a tentative conclusion in respect to the method, trajectory and character Mastricht's exegesis. The method is strongly philological-etymological, grammatical and syntactical oriented. The Word meaning and matter is determined with linguistic interpretive tools, which are utlitzed in the analysis of the biblical text. Hereby, is Mastricht accompanied by contemporary exegetes, such as Poole, and his exegetical results is shared by Reformers (Calvin) and Rabbi's. Mastricht's exegesis can be characterized as biblical and not doctrinally imposed or disorted.

137. It is important to note here that these biblical texts, foundational for the identified doctrines, are also employed by patristic fathers and by seventeenth-century Roman Catholic exegetes such as Calmet. Cf. Augustin Calmet, *Commentaire litteral sur tous Les Livre de l'ancient et du nouveau Testament*, 8 vols. (Paris: Augustins, 1724). Our examination does not answer the question of Mastricht's access to the primary sources of rabbinic material or whether he cited *via* secondary works such as one of the rabbinnic Bibles like the Bomberg Bible or Fagius's works. However, an attempt is made to answer the question of who the "other" commentators are.

138. Our findings tend to agree with the initial results of scholarship on sixteenth-century Reformers. See, for example, Rooden, *Theology, Biblical Scholarship and Rabbinical Studies*; Kalman P. Bland, "Issues ub Sixteenth-Century Jewish Exegesis," in *The Bible in the Sixteenth Century*, ed. David C. Steinmetz (Durham: Duke University Press, 1990); Stephen G. Burnett, *From Christian Hebraism to Jewish Studies Johannes Buxtorf (1564-1629) and Hebrew Learning in the Seventeenth Century* (Leiden: E. J. Brill, 1996); Jinyong Kim, *Exegetical Method and Message of Peter Martyr Vermigili's Commentary on Judges* (Louisville, Ky.: Ph.D. diss., Southern Baptist Theological Seminary, 2002).

Chapter 2
Doctrine

Introduction and Statement of the Problem

The theology of the post-Reformation Reformed orthodoxy has been appraised with different results. It has been characterized by its central dogmas,[1] and many have declared it to be a rigid dogmatism resulting in a "doctrinally correct but spiritually dead" orthodoxy.[2] In reaction to the latter, the *Nadere Reformatie* and Puritanism are perceived as movements with heartfelt piety and practical concern.[3] Thus is noted the bifurcation of *leer* and *leven*: a separation between Reformed scholastic orthodoxy with its concern for right doctrine, and "warm" practical theology, or piety, with its separation of exegesis and doctrine.[4] Recent scholarship, however, has debunked pejorative assessments of post-Reformation Reformed orthodoxy such as "dry," "dead," and "rigid,"[5] and assessed that the noted bifurcation is not tenable.[6] Nevertheless, both past

---

1. For example, A. Eekhof, *Het Gereformeerde Protestantisme* ('s-Gravenhage: Nijhoff, 1915), 15-30 (the sovereignty of God).

2. K. O'Dell Bullock, "Post-Reformation Protestant Hermeneutics," in *Biblical Hermeneutics: A Comprehensive Introduction to Interpreting Scripture*, ed. Bruce Corley, Steve Lemke, Grant Lovejoy, 2d ed. (Nashville: Broadman & Holman Publishers, 2002), 119.

3. For studies that identify the seventeenth-century Reformed orthodoxy with "dead" dogmatism and reaction to it, see, for example, A. Ypeij and I. J. Dermout, *Geschiedenis der Nederlandsche Hervormde Kerk*, 2 vols. (Breda: W. van Bergen en Co., 1819, 1822); M .F. W. Goebel, *Geschichte des christlichen Lebens in der rheinisch-westphalischen evangelishen Kirchen*, (Koblenz: Badeker, 1849); A. Tholuck, *Das akademische Leben des siebzehnten Jahrhunderts mit besondere Beziehung auf die protestantisch-theologischen Fakultäten Deutschland*, (Halle: E. Anton, 1854); H. Heppe, *Geschichte des Pietismus und der Mystik in der reformirten Kirche, namentlich der Niederlande*, (Leiden: Brill, 1879); P. Proost, *J. van Lodenstein* (Amsterdam: Brandt, 1880); F. J. Los, *Wilhelmus à Brakel*, (Leiden: G. Los, 1892); H. Visscher, *Guilielmus Ames*, (Haarlem: Stap, 1894); A. F. Krull, *Jacobus Koelman* (Sneek: Campen, 1901); C. Graafland, *De Zekerheid van het geloof* (Wageningen: Veenman, 1961); F. Ernest Stoeffler, *The rise of Evangelical Pietism* (Leiden: E. J. Brill, 1965); T. Brienen, *De Prediking van de Nadere Reformatie* (Amsterdam: Ton Bolland, 1981); C. Graafland, "Gereformeerde Scholastiek VI," *Theologia Reformata*, XXX, no. 2 (1987).

4. W. van 't Spijker, "Orthodoxie en Nadere Reformatie," in *Theologische aspecten van de Nadere Reformatie*, ed. T. Brienen *et al.* (Zoetermeer: Boekencentru, 1993), 13, 14; C. Graafland, "Schriftleer en Schrifverstaan in de Nadere Reformatie," in *Theologische aspecten van de Nadere Reformatie*, 66. In addition this and other scholarship notes an aberration in the theology of the *Nadere Reformatie* from the sixteenth-century Reformation theology.

5. On such assessment see for example, G.J. Pillay and J.W. Hofmeyr (eds.), *Perspectives on Church History. An Introduction for South African Readers* (Pretoria: De Jager-Haum Publishers, 1991), 234, "One of the after-effects of the Synod of Dort (1618) was a rigid dogmatism in ecclesiastical and theological circles. In some instances faith was reduced to an arid system of doctrine." Cf. J.W. (Hoffie) Hofmeyr and Gerald J. Pillay (eds.), *A History of Christianity in South Africa* (Pretoria: Haum, 1994) vol. 1, 12. For a most recent study *contra* the assessments of E. Bizer, W. Kickel, B. Armstrong, T. Torrance, and others see,

and recent scholarship acknowledges the importance of *doctrina* in post-Reformation Reformed orthodoxy. However, limited attention has been given to the formulation of doctrine in seventeenth-century Reformed orthodox systems of theology.[7] Therefore, in the context of our study of the *Theoretico-practica theologia* (*TPT*) in this chapter we will examine such questions as: (1) What are Mastricht's thoughts on the formulation of doctrine? (2) What is the structure of the doctrinal sections of the *TPT*? (3) What is the relationship, if any, between exegesis and doctrine? The last two questions are primarily assessed in the chapters on the doctrine of God of the *TPT*.

Mastricht and the Formulation of Doctrine

Mastricht has commented in different works on *doctrina*, or *didactica*, and on *dogmatica*, that is, "right teaching."[8] Our points of departure for the examination of Mastricht's thought on the formulation of doctrine are the *Prodromus*, the *Methodus Concionandi*, and his introductory comments in the *TPT*.

In the *Prodromus*, Mastricht states that *didactica* is confirmation and exposition that arise from the analysis of the biblical text. In other words, it is a summary of that is "ἀναλύω", thus, untied or loosed from the text.[9]

Richard A. Muller, *After Calvin. Studies in the Development of a Theological Tradition* (Oxford: Oxford University Press, 2003).

6. Jan van Vliet, *William Ames: Marrow of the Theology and Piety of the Reformed Tradition* (Philadelphia: Ph.D. diss., Westminster Theological Seminary, 2002); Henry M. Knapp, *Understanding the Mind of God: John Owen and Seventeenth-Century Exegetical Methodology* (Ph.D. diss., Calvin Theological Seminary, 2002); Gregory D. Schuringa, *Embracing Leer and Leven: The Theology of Simon Oomius in the Context of the Nadere Reformatie Orthodoxy* (Ph.D. diss., Calvin Theological Seminary, 2003).

7. Exceptions are, Richard A. Muller, *Post-Reformation Reformed Dogmatics* (Grand Rapids: Baker Academic, 2003) vol. 2, part two; Willem J. van Asselt, *Amicitia Dei, een onderzoek naar de structuur van de theologie van Johannes Coccejus (1603-1669)* (Ede: Grafische vormgeving: ADC, 1988); idem, *The Federal Theology of Johannes Cocceius* (Leiden-New York: Brill, 2001); Carl Trueman, *The Claims of Truth. John Owen's Trinitarian Theology* (Carlisle, UK: Paternoster Press, 1998).

8. Mastricht used the term "didactica" in earlier works such as Petrus van Mastricht, *Theologiæ didactico-elenchtico-practicæ, prodromus tribus* (Amsterdam: Johannes van Someren, 1666). The term "doctrina" is used in the text of works such as *Prodromus*; idem, *Methodus Concionandi* (Frankfurt an der Oder: M. Hübner, undated); idem, *Theoretico-practica theologia: qua, per capita theologica, pars dogmatica, elenchtica et practica, perpetua sumbibasei conjugantur; præcedunt in usum operis, paraleipomena, seu sceleton de optima concionandi methodo* (Amsterdam: Henricus et Vidua Theodori Boom, 1682, 1687); idem, *Theoretico-practica theologia: qua, per singula capita theologica, pars exegetica, dogmatica, elenchtica et practica, perpetua successione conjugantur; accedunt historia ecclesiastica, plena quidem, sed compendiosa, idea theologiæ moralis, hypotyposis theologiæ asceticæ etc. proin opus quasi novum* (Utrecht: Gerardus Muntendam, 1698); idem, *Theoretico-practica theologia: qua, per singula capita theologica, pars exegetica, dogmatica, elenchtica et practica, perpetua successione conjugantur; accedunt historia ecclesiastica, plena quidem, sed compendiosa, idea theologiæ moralis, hypotyposis theologiæ asceticæ etc. proin opus quasi novum* (Utrecht: Thomas Appels, 1699) and disputations. The term "dogmatica" is used as a section heading in the chapters of the *TPT* (1682 onwards).

9. Mastricht, *Prodromus, præfatio*: "...*Scripturæ textum...ex eo produco istorum porro confirmatione & expositione*, partem didacticam."

In the *Methodus,* Mastricht writes, "The doctrinal part...assembles the parts of the (biblical) text."[10] Furthermore, the investigation and proposal of doctrine are present in and arise from the biblical text,[11] and the *explicatio* can be confirmed by scriptural evidences or reason. These reasons, however, should be evident and related to the subject matter. Furthermore, such reasons are to be coherent with the immediate context of the biblical text and to be discerned from the *praxis.*[12] Mastricht concludes with the presentation of the *explicatio:* the definition of doctrine in terms of the subject and predicate of the doctrine in its entirety and in its parts. The *explicatio* discriminates, according to Mastricht, between the meaning of the words (exegesis) and the meaning of the matter (doctrine).[13] These two, he remarks, are "confused by many" in the explication of the biblical text. Finally, Mastricht notes that the main argument of the doctrinal section, which is *theoretica,* should not be digressed to the *loci communes,* except in catechetical instruction.[14]

In the 1682 edition of the *TPT,* Mastricht argues that doctrine is led out from Scripture and confirmed and illustrated by Scripture.[15] This argument however, is omitted but implied in the later edition.[16]

In conclusion for Mastricht doctrine emerges from the biblical text and is the sum of exegesis. The doctrinal section is an exposition of the biblical text, illustrated, and confirmed by Scripture. *Doctrina* (*theoretica*), thus, is distinct but directly connected to the biblical text.

Structure of Formulated Doctrine

Our examination of Mastricht's thought on the formulation of doctrine, and our examination of each doctrinal section of book II of the *TPT,* identifies the following parts in the structure: (1) a summary of the results of the interpretation of the biblical text with additional support from Scripture, (2) a provision of reasonable arguments, (3) a definition of the *locus* in general and then in its more specific nature (e.g., God), and

10. Mastricht, *Methodus Concionandi,* 15: "(D). Argumentum concionis doctrinale, e textu consectum..."

11. Ibid., (D).a: "Ejus investigatio & propositio...1. ut certo sit in textu...quo non quodvis dicat verbum Dei Ecclesiastes: sed præcisè quod est in textu suo."

12. Ibid., 16,(D).c: "Ejus confirmatio per rationes...1. Solidæ & evidentes...2. Caute discriminentur â motivis...3. Petuntur istæ rationes, vel ex natura & affectionibus subjecti...., vel ex natura & affectionibus prædicati..., vel ultiusque immediata cohærentia...."

13. Ibid., 18: "Cautè distinguenda explicatio verbalis ab hac reali...." The word *explication* is used for (the right understanding of) the literal sense of the biblical text words. The explication of the matter pertains to the nature of the word.

14. Ibid.: "Cavendum ut...non digrediamur ad locus communes..."

15. Mastricht, *Theoretico-practica theologia* (1682), præfatio: "dogmaticum, *quod capita theologica è Scripturis producit, Scripturis confirmat & illustrat.*"

16. Mastricht, *Theoretico-practica theologia* (1699), præfatio. He explains the exegetical, elenctical, and practical sections and implies that doctrine arises from the biblical text.

(4) a variable part at the end of the doctrinal section, which may include further explanation.[17] To illustrate this identified structure, let us turn to the doctrinal section of *De Beatitudine Dei.*[18]

Summary of Exegesis and Additional Testimony of Scripture

Mastricht infers the divine beatitude from Psalm 16:11: נצח בימינך נעמות את־פנך שמחות. He asserts that "beatitude" is communicated in the text by the words שׂבע שמחות.[19] Following Drusius's explanation, Mastricht notes that את identifies the divine essence in את־פנך of the biblical text.[20] Furthermore, Mastricht argues that, according to the words נעמות בימינך, this divine beatitude is communicated to creatures but in particular to the elect.[21] Finally, the word נצח points to the duration of this beatitude: eternal or everlasting. Mastricht then concludes from the grammatical-philological meaning that Psalm 16:11 refers to the (everlasting) divine beatitude. Thus, Mastricht's summary of the biblical text analysis and his exposition is the basis for his doctrinal formulation.[22]

Mastricht then begins the doctrinal section of the chapter, "from which [the exegetical section] results," by stating that the divine beatitude is *esse in se* and the source of the everlasting happiness of the elect.[23] This brief summary of the exegesis of the

---

17. Thus, one notes in Mastricht's doctrine of God, in the margin of the doctrinal sections, *Scriptura, rationibus, quid, quid Dei,* and *difficulates* or *objectiones.* The latter are distinct from the objection refuted in the elenctical sections.

18. Mastricht, *Theoretico-practica theologia,* II.23.iii, 232, 233. The margin of the doctrinal section notes, in order, (1) Deum beatum esse & omnis beatidinis fontem probatur Scripturis, (2) Et rationibus, (3) Quid beatitudo?, (4) Quid beatitudo Dei?, and (5) Difficultates adversus beatitudinem Dei tolluntur. This order parallels our identified structure (1) Scripture, (2) reason, (3) Definition (*Quid*), and (4) the variable part. We noted that Mastricht divided the divine attributes into *primitiva* and *derivativa.* The latter includes respectively the *omnisufficientia,* the *majestas & Gloria,* and the divine beatitude.

19. Mastricht notes that most commentators argue that the text refers to human and not immediately the divine beatitude. However, Mastricht asserts that only God can communicate the beatitude and the text can refer to the divine beatitude when one considers 1 Tim.1:11 and 6:15. Ibid., ii, 231: "*Nolim diffiteri, juxta plerosque interpretes, verba hæc capi posse, de beatitudine creaturarum, quâ fruuntur coram facie & ex conspectu faciei divinæ: sed tamen etiam non obstat, ob quod verba ista non capiamus, de beatudine Dei; cum procul dubio, creaturis non possit communicare, quam ipse* ἰξόχως *non habuerit cum præfertim* beatitudo, *ipsi* ῥητῶς *tribuatur* 1 Tim.1:11 *& cap.* 6:15."

20. Ibid.: "*Vocula* τα *inquit Drusius* Observat. Sac. lib.9.cap.7 *non tantum est simplex casuum nota; sed quæ simul & ipsissimam rei substantiam demonstrat.*"

21. Ibid.: "2. *Beatitudinis communicatæ* נעמות בימינך...*Hîc rursus non diffiteor, verba posse usurpari de* beatitudine *Dei: sed tamen etiam de* beatitudine *creaturarum participatâ...2.b. Significatur satietatem jucunditatum, seu beatitudinem, à fideli & gratiosa Dei potentiâ, electis communicandam esse.*"

22. See, for example, Ibid., II.18.ii, 192: "Ps. 119:137 צדיק אתה יהוה וישר משפטיך" and iii, "Est proinde, Psaltis testimonio, *Deus justus in se & justus in omnibus negotiis suis.*" The summaries given by Mastricht in other chapters of the doctrine of God and in book III to VIII are usually more concise.

23. Ibid., II.23.iii, 232: " E. quo patet, Deum non tantum *beatum* esse in se; sed etiam omnis beautitudinis *fontem* suis."

biblical text is followed by additional support from Scripture.[24] Accordingly, "beatitude" is also rendered by שׁרי (Gen. 17:1), μακαριος (1 Tim. 1:11; 6:15),[25] and "probably" ευλογητος (Rom. 9:5; 2 Cor. 11:31). Moreover, Scripture testifies that God cannot receive any good (Ps. 16:2; 50:12) and that He is the light—"which is held for the beatitude in Scripture (Ps. 112:4; Isa. 50:10)." As a result, Mastricht argues that if God cannot receive any beatitude and He is the beatitude in Himself, He therefore confers the beatitude to His people (Ps. 16:2; 27:13). Thus, Mastricht extends his concise exegetical summary with scriptural support from both the Old and the New Testaments, pays particular attention to word meaning, and links the exegetical and doctrinal expositions (Ps. 16:11 with 1 Tim 1:11; 6:15).

Reasonable arguments

Subsequently, Mastricht turns to the second aspect of the doctrinal section and furnishes reasonable arguments. He argues that the beatitude can be established by a consideration of the perfection of God, who is collectively and properly called the omni-sufficient one.[26] With a sense of rhetoric, he states, "Is the One who is the origin or source of beatitude not beatitude in Himself?" Mastricht replies in the affirmative and cites Augustine's *De Civitate Dei*: "With God only the soul can be beatified."[27] This appeal to Augustine at this location of the doctrinal section is characteristic of Mastricht.[28]

Here, a succinct excursion may help to underscore Mastricht's indebtness to Augustine. First, we have shown that the bishop of Hippo is Mastricht's most referenced author. We noted verbatim citations[29] and references to Augustine's works[30] or

24. The brief summary of the exegesis of the biblical text, followed by additional support from Scripture, is characteristic in paragraph three (iii) of each chapter throughout book II and the remainder of the *TPT*. Cf. ibid., II.4; II.6-11; II.13-15; II.17-18; and, for example, III.1-3; V.1-2; VI.6; VII.1; and VIII.4.

25. See preceding footnote. Mastricht links the biblical text of Ps. 16:2 with 1 Tim 1:1 and 6:15.

26. Mastricht, *Theoretico-practica theologia*, II.23.iv, 232: "Et sanè, qui 1. Tot tantisque *perfectionibus* gaudet, quas hactenus singulatim enarravimus, quique plures ac majores non potest, vel *habere* vel *desiderare*, nunquid *beatus* sit? Qui 2. Ex omnibus istis perfectionibus *omnisufficiens* dicitur & est (prout cap.21 demonstravimus)." Thus, Mastricht does not elaborate on the point of the divine omnisufficiency but refers to the preceding exposition.

27. Ibid.: "...aut *Deus* beatus est. Ut recte August. *De Civit. Dei* lib.ix.c.2. *Cum solo vero Deo & in solo & de eo solo anima humana, id est rationalis & intellectualis beata est.*"

28. In addition, but to a lesser extent, Mastricht cites the patristic fathers, such as Justinus, Irenæus, Hilarius, Tertullianus, and Nazianzenus. Cf. ibid., II.6.II.9.iii; II.10.iv; II.11.iii (2); II.13.iv. This observation can be extended to the remainder of the doctrinal sections of the *TPT*.

29. Mastricht, *Theoretico-practica theologia*, II.2.xxxi, 75 (practical); II.6.iii, 98 (doctrinal); II.7.iii, 108 (doctrinal); II.10.iii, 122 (doctrinal); II.10.xvi, 127 (practical); II.11.iii, 129 (doctrinal); II.11.xi, 131 (elenctical); II.12.xx, 140 (doctrinal); II.13.xii, 146 (doctrinal); II.15.xi, 160 (doctrinal); II.16.iv, 171 (doctrinal); II.16.xxii, 177 (practical); II.20.xix, 213 (elenctical); II.20.xxx, 218 (practical); II.23.iii, 232 (doctrinal).

references to his name only.[31] Second, further examination shows that Mastricht cites or refers to Augustine's work (e.g. *De Civitate Dei*, *De Trinitate*, and *Confessiones* but in particular the *Enarrationes in Psalmos*) to support positive statements of doctrine, either in the doctrinal or elenctical sections of the doctrine of God. Third, Mastricht's doctrinal formulation arising from Scripture is, furthermore, in content Augustinian in character. For example, Mastricht explains the word *eternity* in the doctrinal section of the chapter *De Æternitate Dei*. He argues that *eternal* has two basic senses. Strictly signifying what is without beginning or end, it is properly predicated of God.[32] Then, it is called "eternal" in the line of negation. Only the mode of predication is negative; deficiencies in the temporal are eliminated to yield an attribute free of imperfections. Second, the term indicates something with "a beginning but which is without end," or unending, such as the final destination of angels and humans.[33] This Augustinian formulation essentially anticipated, without necessarily influencing, Boethius's definition, cited by Mastricht: "the all-at-once whole and perfect possession of unending life."[34] Thus, Mastricht (*via* Boethius) finds agreement with Augustine in formulating a definition of eternity. Mastricht also extends this definition when he positively assesses that the "Scholastics" describe eternity as an unending, indivisible, independent duration.[35] Thus, the doctrinal formulation here is scripturally based and formulated with indebtedness to Augustine[36] and scholastic terminology. Reason does not allow carrying forward the theological formulation past the point of biblical revelation.

30. Ibid., II.7.vii, 109 (elenctical); II.8.vii, 114 (elenctical); II.8.viii, 115 (elenctical); II.16.xi, 172 (elenctical); II.17.xxxvii, 189 (elenctical); II.24.xxi, 243 (elenctical); II.24.xxi, 144 (elenctical).

31. Ibid., II.5.ii, 92 (exegetical); II.16.ii, 170 (exegetical).

32. Ibid., II.11.vi, 129: "Sonat autem *æternitas*, aliquando durationem cum principio & fine, sed longissimam & quæ finem definitum non habæt... aliquando, quæ principio pariter & fine destituitur..."; Ibid., iii, 128: "E. quo jam suâ sponte emergit: *Solum Deum æternum esse*."

33. Ibid., vi, 129: "Sic Gen. 17:13...aliquando talem quæ principium habet, sed fine caret: vel per naturam, qualis, Angelis & animabus nostris."

34. Ibid.: "Boëthio satis accurate dicitur: *interminabilis vitæ, tota simul & perfecta possessio, De Consol. Philos*.lib.v.prof. 6." Interestingly, this line of Augustinian thought is also found in Gregory of Rimini at "the beginning of the Augustinian Renaissance" leading to the establishment of the *via moderna* as the *via Gregorii* in the statutes of the University of Wittenberg in 1508. Cf. H. A. Oberman, ed., *Gregor von Rimini. Werk und Wirking bis zur Reformation* (Berlin, New York: Schuster, 1981).

35. Mastricht, *Theoretico-practica theologia*, II.11.viii, 130: "Et hæc demum illa est æternitas, quam Scholastici definiunt: *interminabilem, indivisibilem & independentem durationem*."

36. We observe also that in respect to the practical sections, Mastricht cites (limited) Augustine's comments on Ps. 36 in the context of practical pastoral counsel against hypocrisy and promoting uprightness. He notes that the divine immensity and omnipresence should exhort one to live uprightly before God, who is "total eye and sees one everywhere and is total ear, to hear everything." Cf. ibid., II.10.xvi, 127: "Quando scil. cogitamus Deum, per immensitatem...qui, *totus oculus est, ut omnia nostra videat, totus auris, ut audiat &c*. Augustin. in *Psal. 36*." Likewise in Mastricht's chapter about the *Potentia Dei*, where he concludes his exhortation that the divine potency should lead one to be submissive to God as "Augustine says." Ibid., II.20.xxx, 218: "*Quoniam, juxta Augustin. alicubi, Deus immensæ est potestatis, ideo nec locus est, in quo quis possit se abscondere; nec tempus quo possit subterfugere; nec potestas quæ ei possit*

Definition

Continuing our examination of the structure of the doctrinal section of *De Beatitudine Dei*, we note that Mastricht defines *beatitude* in general and distinguishes between the meanings of *verbalis* and *realis*.[37] With respect to the former (*verbalis*), the Hebrew word אשרי (in the plural) can be understood as the apex of every good that is the *summum bonum*, the highest good, in essence God as the source and end of all good.[38] In Greek the word μακαρισμος or μέγα χαίρων, is rendered, according to Mastricht and following Favorinus, as "blessed or very glad." With respect to the latter (*realis*), he defines *beatitude* as a total absence of evil and the possession and fruition of the *summum bonum*.[39] From this Mastricht explains that it is not sufficient to possess objective beatitude alone but that it should go together with the subjective beatitude, the fruition that consists in intellectual knowledge—that is, the *visio Dei* (John 17:3; Job 19:26), the final vision of God's glory and truth given to the blessed.[40] Thus, for Mastricht the blessedness in general consists in the perfect vision and enjoyment of God.

With this definition of beatitude in general, Mastricht moves to the definition of divine blessedness. The divine beatitude, then, consists of the absence of any evil and imperfection (1 John 1:5) and is a perfect fruition, as Mastricht mentions in regard to the text of Psalm 16:11. Such divine beatitude involves a divine knowledge (Rom. 11:34; 1 Cor. 2:11) and acquiescence, a *verzadiging van vreugde*, and joy in the communion of the divine Persons and works, recognizing that every good exists *formaliter* and *a se* in God. Thus, the divine beatitude is defined as a fullness of joy (*fruitio*) that is directly correlated with the biblical text (Ps. 16:11).[41]

Mastricht concludes the definition of divine blessedness by noting how the infinite beatitude can be communicated "to us, who are finite," even though it is written, "eye

resistere." Nonetheless, Mastricht gives Augustine a prominent place primarily in the doctrinal sections of the doctrine of God. The only *locus* where Mastricht more critically follows Augustine's position is book III.6, *De Opere Sex Dierum*.

37. Mastricht, *Methodus Concionandi*, 18.

38. Mastricht, *Theoretico-practica theologia*, II.23.v, 232: "*Beatitudo*, Hebræis אשרי in *plurali* confluxum notat omnis boni, quod sit in *summo* bono." Cf. Richard A. Muller, *Dictionary of Latin and Greek Theological Terms. Drawn Principally from Protestant Scholastic Theology* (Grand Rapids: Baker Books, 1985), 291.

39. Mastricht, *Theoretico-practica theologia*, II.23.v, 232: "...ad beatitudinem requirantur: 1.Omnis mali *absentia*.2. Omnis boni, in summo bono tum *possessio* ... ac præsentia;tum.3. *fruitio* h.e. sensus, acquiescentia ac gaudium."

40. Ibid.: "E quo perspicuum est, non sufficere ad beatitudinem, summi boni *possessionem*, ut patet in fidelibus spiritualiter desertis sed insuper possessionis istius *fruitionem*, h.e. *cognitionem*, in intellectu: *acquiescentiam* item, ac *delectationem* & gaudium, in voluntate, requiri. E quo patet, beatitudinem *objectivam* (ut loquuntur) cujus *possessione*...beatitudinem *subjectivam*, seu *actum*...esse partim *intellectum*, seu *visionem* Dei Joh.17:3, Job 19:26...partim *voluntatem*...." Cf. Muller, *Dictionary of Latin and Greek Theological Terms*, 327.

41. Mastricht, *Theoretico-practica theologia*, II.23.vi, 232: "*Dei* involvit *beatitudo*...Eâque continetur, *fruitionem*...*satietas*...*cum facie sua*." Ps.16:11 is rendered by Mastricht, "*Satietas gaudiorum est cum facie tua.*"

hath not seen, nor ear heard, neither have entered into the heart of man, the things which God hath prepared for them that love him" (1 Cor. 2:9 KJV). In other words, the divine blessedness that includes the *visio Dei* is not a vision of the eye (*visio oculi*) and is therefore impossible for the *viator*. It is accessible only to the *beati in patria*. [42] In summary, Mastricht echoes the biblical text in formulating the definition and makes use of scholastic distinctions and terms.[43]

Variable part

Finally, Mastricht closes the doctrinal section with the fourth or variable part. He notes briefly, for example, that some have difficulty with the divine beatitude as it pertains to divine repentance. However, he responds that such does not challenge the *beatitudo Dei*. [44]

We conclude, then, that the structure of the doctrinal section identified above is present in the chapter *De Beatitudine Dei* and other doctrinal sections of book II of the *TPT*. In addition, the doctrinal section is a further development or exposition of the exegetical section. This further development includes the summary of the exegetical results. In the doctrinal formulation, we also noted the influence of Augustine as well as the use of scholastic definitions and distinctions for precision and clarity. Thus, Mastricht's concern for method is extended to the structure of the doctrinal sections of the doctrine of God. His doctrinal formulations arise from Scripture, are directly correlated to the biblical text, and are biblically worded. This conclusion points to the fact that the suggested bifurcation, or separation, of exegesis and doctrine is not tenable.

---

42. Ibid. : "Sed quis tandem, *infinitam* Dei beatitudinem repræsentaverit? cum vel *nostram*, utcunque *finitam* nec *oculus viderit*; nec auris audivit; nec mens perceperit 1 Cor.2:9." Muller, *Dictionary of Latin and Greek Theological Terms*, 327.

43. This is not restricted to the reviewed chapter. For example, for the direct connection between the definition stated in the doctrinal section and the biblical text used in the exegetical section, see Mastricht, *Theoretico-practica theologia*, II.7-8; II.11; II.13; II.16; II.18.

44. The variable part differs from chapter to chapter throughout the *TPT*.

Chapter 3
Elenctic

Introduction and Statement of the Problem

Scholarship has characterized Protestant Scholasticism as polemical in nature[1] and having a important role in seventeenth-century Reformed theology.[2] Muller notes, however, that the rise of Protestant orthodoxy and, with it, the further working out of sixteenth-century Reformation ideals prompted the need for polemics in order to identify the catholicity of the Reformed church.[3] In addition, as is also true in the specific case of Mastricht, polemics was only one form of theological discourse—balanced by exegetical, homiletical, and catechetical forms, among others. This chapter, nevertheless, will not appraise studies on the polemics of the post-Reformation orthodoxy but will concentrate on the *Theoretico-practica theologia* (*TPT*) and address the following questions: (1) What is the relationship, if any, between the elenctic and preceding sections: exegesis and doctrine? (2) What (scholastic) method, if any, did Mastricht employ in the elenctic part? (3) Who are his principal opponents, and why did he oppose them? In summary, our examination focuses on the method, or structure, and content of the elenctic sections of book II of the *TPT, De Fide in Deum triunum.*

Mastricht and Elenctics

In order to appreciate Mastricht's view on elenctics, we will chronologically review his thought on the subject in his *Prodromus* (1665), *Methodus* (undated), and *TPT* (1682-1699). In the preface of the *Prodromus*, Mastricht argues that the elenctic section is primarily used for the refutation of opponents.[4] Mastricht takes this view one step further in the *Methodus*, where he speaks of three main aspects to consider in elenctics. First, Mastricht argues that one should legitimately and correctly state the controversial issue. Second, such a response should be established truthfully, with scriptural support,

---

1. K. O'Dell Bullock, "Post-Reformation Protestant Hermeneutics," in *Biblical Hermeneutics: A Comprehensive Introduction to Interpreting Scripture*, ed. Bruce Corley, Steve Lemke, Grant Lovejoy, 2d ed. (Nashville: Broadman & Holman Publishers, 2002), 129

2. J. W. Hofmeyr, *Johannes Hoornbeeck as Polemikus* (Kampen: J. H. Kok, 1975), 12, 17 fn.15, and 20. Hofmeyr restrict this note to the period of the *Nadere Reformatie*. Further, he argues that the nature of these polemics where primarily external directed (Socianism, Cartesiansm, Roman Catholicism).

3. Richard A. Muller, *After Calvin. Studies in the Development of a Theological Tradition* (Oxford: Oxford University Press, 2003), 74; idem, *Post-Reformation Reformed Dogmatics* (Grand Rapids: Baker Academic, 2003), I:217.

4. Petrus van Mastricht, *Theologiæ didactico-elenchtico-practicæ, prodromus tribus* (Amsterdam: Johannes van Someren, 1666), *præfatio: "vindicatione elenctica."*

reason, and with the consensus of the *antiquitas*. Third, the objections of opponents are refuted according to the following six rules: (1) the identification of controversies should not be sought but (2) should not be avoided either. (3) Controversies that are "dead and buried" should not be revived, and (4) the argument that seeks to repudiate should be solid and convincing. (5) One should avoid extensive elaborations because they postpone or suspend the practical application, and (6) the elenctic section leads to the strengthening of the practical section for the purpose of the manifestation of piety.[5]

These three main points are summarized in the *TPT* 1682-1687, where Mastricht states that the elenctic part deals primarily and briefly with controversies and multiple opponents and seeks to unsettle these opposing views[6] and spiritually build up in a positive way.[7] Then, in the final edition of the *TPT*, Mastricht elaborates on the content of the elenctic section. He notes that in this part all controversies and questions are brought together, including a brief description of the history of each controversy or question, so that "the reader may assert and understand the middle position of the orthodox, between the two unorthodox diverging sides."[8] In summary, Mastricht is concerned with a correct identification of the controversy that will be convincingly refuted and lead to a positive statement that will strengthen piety. [9]

---

5. Petrus van Mastricht, *Methodus Concionandi* (Frankfurt an der Oder: M. Hübner, undated), 25: "A salsitate resellendâ, nascitur usus Elenchticus seu refutatorius qui tria concludit, a. *Statum controversiæ legitimè formatum* ...b. κατασκεύασιν, quâ veritas stabiliatur (a) *Scripturis* (b) *rationibus &* (c) *consensu antiquitatis* ...c. Ἀνασκεύασιν quâ adversariorum obiectiones retundantur."

6. Petrus van Mastricht, *Theoretico-practica theologia: qua, per capita theologica, pars dogmatica, elenchtica et practica, perpetua sumbibasei conjugantur; præcedunt in usum operis, paraleipomena, seu sceleton de optima concionandi methodo*. (Amsterdam: Henricus et Vidua Theodori Boom, 1682), præfatio: "*porro elenchticum quod producta adversus quisvis hæreticorum strophas propugnat.*"

7. Ibid.: "...*proinde in elenchticis plerasque controversias, cum plerisque adversariis, breviter, constituto controversiæ statu, κατασκευασικας, ἀνασκευασικας exegi.*" Cf. Petrus van Mastricht, *Theoretico-practica theologia: qua, per capita theologica, pars dogmatica, elenchtica et practica, perpetua sumbibasei conjugantur; præcedunt in usum operis, paraleipomena, seu sceleton de optima concionandi methodo*; (Amsterdam: Henricus et Vidua Theodori Boom, 1687), præfatio **3: "... in elenchticis..ubi brevitatis necessitate, medios terminos utriusque partis adversæ..."

8. Petrus van Mastricht, *Theoretico-practica theologia: qua, per singula capita theologica, pars exegetica, dogmatica, elenchtica et practica, perpetua successione conjugantur; accedunt historia ecclesiastica, plena quidem, sed compendiosa, idea theologiæ moralis, hypotyposis theologiæ asceticæ etc. proin opus quasi novum* (Utrecht: Thomas Appels, 1699), præfatio: "In *Elenchticis*, omnes controversias, ad quæstiones redegimus, ut singularum historiam commodius tangeremus, eorum πρωτον Ψεῦδος sententiarum divortia & medium orthodoxiæ locum, inter declinantes ab utrâque parte sententias heterodoxas, facilius assequeretur lector & ab hoc utriusque exorbitantis extremitatis difficultatibus, facilius ac solidius occurreret. Existimabam enim maximum esse, in determinandis controversiis compendium, si utriusque partis exorbitationes, habeas perspectas."

9. Therefore, we opt to render "elenchticus" as elenctic and not polemic, which has in our opinion a negative connotation. The translator of the chapter on *Regeneration* renders "elenchticus" as "argumentative." Cf. Petrus van Mastricht, *A Treatise on Regeneration, Extracted from His System of Divinity, Called Theologia theoretico-practica*, trans. unknown (New-Haven: Thomas and Samuel Green, 1770).

Structure

With respect to the structure of the elenctic section of the *TPT*, we observe that Mastricht's methodology is quite similar to the medieval scholastic *quæstio* method. The medieval educational model included a *lectio-meditatio-quæstio* pattern.[10] The *quæstio* (the question or statement of the problem) was stated in order to refute a divergent opinion. The distinguishing mark of (medieval) Scholasticism was its adoption of a common method of inquiry: the method of discovering and defending philosophical or theological truth by means of Aristotelian logic or dialectic. The dialectic method involved three basic steps: the posing of a question, followed by arguments for and against answers proposed by earlier authorities, and ending in a conclusion that was logically warranted. The *quæstio* method was used to activate the student's critical thinking.

Eventually, the *quæstiones* developed as a stand-alone method, apart from the *lectio*, and functioned in the *disputatio* on certain subjects. De Rijk describes the procedure of the disputation as follows. On the day the disputation was held, other lessons were cancelled so that other professors and students could participate in the discussion. The *disputatio* was led by the *magister*, who stated the problem or question, and a baccalaureate functioned as respondent. During the discussion, objections could be raised by the participants, which usually resulted in a response from the *magister* in the afternoon or next day. In the response (the *determinatio* or *solutio*), he stated a thesis, discussed the objections, provided arguments in favor of the thesis, and refuted the objections. The published form of such disputations formed the literary genre of the *quæstio disputata*, and a collection of such disputations was called the *Summa*.[11]

This medieval educational model functioned explicitly during Mastricht's professorship. First, the *TPT*, Mastricht's "*Summa*," incorporates a significant number of disputations.[12] Second, the conducting of Mastricht's disputations was very similar to the medieval model.[13] Third, the examination of the elenctic sections of Mastricht's doctrine of God reveals a structure similar to the *quæstio* method: the margin notes (1) *Quæstio*, (2) *Argumentum* [*Reformatorum*], and (3) *Objectiones*, which is followed by a conclusion. An example, taken from the chapter *De Æternitate Dei* may suffice for our examination of Mastricht's use of the *quæstio* method. First, the question is raised as to

10. The *lectio* was a reading of an important text supplied with a commentary of the teacher, the *scholastici*. The *meditatio* was the meditation or personal digestion by the student of the material. The last phase was the *quæstio*. Cf. J. Pieper, *Scholastik Gestalten und Probleme der mittelalterlichen Philosophie* (München: Kösel, 1960); L. M. de Rijk, *Middeleeuwse wijsbegeerte, Traditie en vernieuwing* (Assen/Amsterdam: Van Gorcum, 1977), 123, 128-130; W. J. van Asselt and P. L. Rouwendal, eds., *Inleiding in de Gereformeerde Scholastiek* (Zoetermeer: Boekencentrum, 1998), 56.

11. De Rijk, *Middeleeuwse wijsbegeerte*, 129.

12. See part II, chapter 2 of this study.

13. For example the disputation of James Hog took place in the morning and afternoon. Cf. Petrus van Mastricht, *Disputationum practicarum tertia, de certitudine salutis, eique opposita præsumptione seu securitate carnali*, pars secunda, resp. Jacobus Hoog (Utrecht: Meinardus à Dreunen, 1680), title page.

whether there was eternity prior to the creation of the world.[14] Mastricht notes that Vorstius, the Arians, and Wittichius, each for their own reasons, denied or almost negated this question.[15] Mastricht then appeals to the Reformed argument for eternity being before the creation of the world.[16] He cites Psalm 90:2 and Micah 5:1, which attest to the Messiah being the eternal generation of the Father (Ps. 2:7) or מקדם, meaning "from everlasting," or, according to Mastricht "that is, from before the world." Furthermore, he asks rhetorically what the phrase "before the foundation of the world" (John 17:5; 1 Pet. 1:20) means? Mastricht supports the argument by appealing to nature, or *recta ratio*. He argues that "time" came with the creation of the world. Thus, before the world there was no time and only eternity. However, this argument is followed by an *objectio*: God can create before the world was created? Mastricht responds that according the rules of logic such a question includes a contradiction: creatures are in "time." If there is no time, there is no creature, thus creatures are in "time."[17] Mastricht consistently employs the scholastic *quæstio* method as a way of refuting his opponents and drawing out the full implications of his theology. This result is not limited to the chapters of the doctrine of God. It extends to most elenctical sections throughout *TPT*.[18]

Content

An examination of the elenctic sections of the doctrine of God demonstrates Mastricht's consistent adherence to his above-mentioned view of elenctics. We noted that, according to Mastricht, one should legitimately and correctly state the controversial issue. He does this by raising a question related to the interpretation of the biblical text and *locus*.[19] For example, the elenctic section of *De Infinitate et Magnitudine Dei* begins with the question, Is God in every mode infinite? This question is not specifically addressed in the exegetical and doctrinal section, but, according to Mastricht, it is a

14. Mastricht, *Theoretico-practica theologia*, II.11.xiv, 132: "An, quod suit ante mundum fuerit ab æterno?"

15. Ibid.: "Conradus Vorstius, in gratiam Socinianorum , aperte negat, existere ante mundum, idem esse, cum existere ab æterno....Ariani, seu *homojusiani*, quia agnoscunt Christum exstitisse *ante* hunc mundum & interim negant, ipsum ab *æterno* exstitisse...Wittichius *Theol. Pacif*. §. §. CLXXX. & CLXXXI. hic admodum lubrice loquitur de Angelis num potuerint existere ante hunc mundum...."

16. Ibid.: (*Quid Reformati? Argumenta*) "Reformati statuunt, q uicquid ante mundum fuit, id   *ab aeterno* fuisse. Sic enim, cum ipsis statuit: 1. Scriptura, cui, esse *ante mundum*, perpetua periphrasis est, *aeternitatis*, sic in textu nostro Psal. XC:2..."

17. Ibid., 133: "...imo contradictionem infert, esse creaturam, & non esse *in tempore*: creatura enim, quæ non est in tempore *nunquam* est & quod *nunquam* est: non est, prout quod *nullibi* aut nusquam est, prorsus *non* est."

18. Ibid., III.1; III.2; III.3; III.4; IV.1; IV.2; V.1; V.2; VI.2; V.3; VII.2; VIII. Sometimes the *quæstio* is present in a modified form, for example, with the absence of the *objectio*.

19. Ibid., II.1.xxii, 54; II.2.xxi, 70; II.3.vii, 77; II.5.x, 95; II.6.viii, 99; II.6.xxiii, 104; II.7.vi, 108; II.8.vi, 113; II.9.vi, 118; II.10.ix, 123; II.11.x, 130; II.13.xvii, 147; II.15.xxvii, 163; II.17.xxx, 185; II.20.xv, 211; II.22.x, 227; II.23.vii, 233; II.24.xvii, 240; II.26.xvi, 255; II.27.xvii, 265.

legitimate question for historic-theological and salvific reasons. Second, we noted that Mastricht argues that an answer should be established truthfully with scriptural support, reason, and the consensus of the *antiquitas*. Mastricht continues in the elenctic section of *De Infinitate et Magnitudine Dei* by stating that the exegesis of the biblical text of Psalm 145:3 (גדול יהוה ומהלל מאד ולגדלתו אין חקר: "great *is* the Lord, and greatly to be praised and of his greatness there is no search") is a celebration of the divine, infinite greatness. Mastricht bases this remark on the words גדול (rendered as "immense greatness") and אין חקר (rendered as "without end"; thus, "infinite"). With respect to the doctrinal section, Mastricht argues that Scripture implicitly states the infinity of God (Job 11:7-9; 36:1).[20] Therefore, he defines divine infinity as follows: "God in His essence is infinity, and He alone, so that no other is or can be infinite."[21] The relevance of the question is underscored when Mastricht places the issue in a historical perspective. First, Mastricht refers to the Anthropomorphists and Audians,[22] who taught that God is composite, thereby rejecting the doctrine of divine simplicity. Second, Vorstius denied the infinity of the divine essence in relation to Christ's dual nature (a matter related to Christology). Third, the Socinians denied the infinity of God because they did not allow the divine essence in three Persons (a matter related to the doctrine of the Trinity). Thus, the doctrine of the divine infinity, according to Mastricht, is related to the doctrine of divine simplicity, the doctrine of the Trinity, and Christology (Christ's dual nature and redemption).[23]

Third, as noted above, Mastricht argues that the objections of opponents should be refuted according to six rules. Although one finds that Mastricht in general makes limited use of these six rules, a review of each elenctic section of the chapters on the doctrine of God does reveal his use of them. Mastricht indicates in the chapters dealing with the divine attributes of life, goodness, holiness, sufficiency, and in the chapter on God the Father, that this particular *locus* is more or less not subject to controversy.[24] In addition, as we have shown in the case of Grotius's interpretation of Psalm 2:7, Mastricht does not shy away from discussing controversial issues as long as they arise out

20. Ibid., II.9.iii, 117, 118. Mastricht acknowledges that Scripture does not verbatim state the divine infinity (II.9.vi), but he insists on his exegetical result.

21. Ibid., 117: "*Deus, per essentiam, infinitus est, & solus quidem, ita etiam, ut præter eum, nec esse possit.*"

22. A sect of Christians that arose in the fourth century in Syria and extended into Scythia, sometimes called Audians, from their founder, Audius. Taking, for example, the text of Genesis 1:27, literally, Audius, like Anthropomorphists, held that God has a human form.

23. Mastricht, *Theoretico-practica theologia*, II.9.vi, 118.

24. Ibid., II.12.x, 136: "*Vita Dei, hostium telis, non ita est exposita*"; II.16.xi, 172: "*Dei bonitas cœlum & terram replens tam est nobilis ut non modo apud Christianos, Judæos, Muhammedanos; sed ne apud gentes quidem maxime barbaras, habeat, qui eam professione calumnientur, unde, quod elenchum, breves erimus*"; II.19.ix, 204: "*Quæ de sanctitate Dei diximus, tam sunt omnibus manifesta ut eis, vel ab hostibus, nulla controversia moveri possit*"; II.21.ix, 222: "*Equidem, qui omnimodam Dei perfectionem & omnisufficientiam, argumentis data opera impugnare sustineat, vix reperietur ac ne vix quidem*"; II.25.x, 248: "*Telis hostium non ita expositum est hoc caput, omnibus fatentibus Patrem esse personam esse item Deum etiam distinctum saltem à Filio.*"

of the biblical text. Rules four and five conform to Mastricht's requirement for "brevity." Only rule six seems to be an exception, unless one appraises the positively formulated Reformed position in the elenctic section as leading to the *usus* of piety.

Finally, our examination of the elenctic sections of the doctrine of God shows the following opponents: (1) Socinians (Vorstius), (2) the Roman Catholics (in particular the Jesuits), but primarily (3) the Cartesian theologians (Wittichius).[25] In the context of the latter, Mastricht refers here, and only here, to his *Gangræna Cartesiana*. Thus, Mastricht's anti-Cartesianism is most detectable in the elenctic sections of the chapters on the doctrine of God.[26] The Roman Catholic and Socinian opponents are not only refuted for doctrinal reasons in general or for reasons of the catholicity of the church but are also contested in matters of salvation. In summary, the legitimate status of the controversial issue and the rules for refuting opponents are vital to a proper understanding of Mastricht's elenctic sections: the main opponents are identified and the issues raised in the doctrine of God are related to other Reformed *loci*, but in particular Christology.

We can conclude, then, that Mastricht structures the elenctic section of the *TPT* parallel to the scholastic *quæstio* method. Returning to our main questions of concern, we can state that (1) the relationship of the elenctic section to exegesis or doctrine relates primarily to issues concerning salvation as they arise out of the biblical text and formulated doctrine; (2) in the elenctic sections, Mastricht utilizes to the full extent the scholastic *quæstio* method; and (3) his principal opponents, primarily for soteriological reasons, are the Socinians (Vorstius), the Roman Catholics, and in particular, the Cartesians (Wittichius).

The answers to our questions, coupled with the relatively concise length of the elenctical sections, do not seem to justify the characterization of these sections as central to Mastricht's theology, making such as polemic in nature. Moreover, the polemic was directed to those theological and philosophical issues raised outside the Reformed church and elenctically formulated so that *praxis pietatis* would be strengthened.

---

25. See Appendix I.2.4. Further, in respect to his opponents, Mastricht rarely discusses contemporary controversial issues in the doctrine of God chapters, with the exception of Roëll (II.26) and Bidelus (II.27).

26. This observation can be extended to the remainder of the *TPT*.

Chapter 4
Praxis

Introduction and Statement of the Problem

One of the appraisals of the theology of the post-Reformation Reformed orthodoxy is that it is characterized by a bifurcation between doctrine and *praxis*.[1] Particularly on the subject of post-Reformation Reformed piety various assessments have been made. It is described as (1) a form of mysticism, related or not to Labadism,[2] and a divergence from the *Sola fide* of the sixteenth-century Protestant Reformation;[3] (2) a reaction to the "cold, rationalistic dogmatism of the [late seventeenth century] Scholastics";[4] (3) a realization of the spiritual and ethical implications of the doctrinal foundation laid down during the Reformation, whereby orthodox doctrine and piety correlate;[5] and (4) a correlation with medieval spirituality *via* the sixteenth-century Reformation—that is, an expression of *Sola fide*: a living faith.[6] These appraisals should be evaluated in the context of our study of Mastricht's *Theoretico-practica theologia* (*TPT*). Afterall, Mastricht has been characterized as a practical theologian and pietist.[7] Therefore, the practical sections of book II of the *TPT*,

---

1. See part III. Introduction and III, chapter 2 of this study and T. Brienen, *De Prediking van de Nadere Reformatie* (Amsterdam: Ton Bolland, 1981), 182, 184; over agianst this older view, note the study of Gregory D. Schuringa, *Embracing Leer and Leven: The Theology of Simon Oomius in the Context of the Nadere Reformatie* (Ph.D. diss., Calvin Theological Seminary, 2003), who cites further instances of the problem, 7-9.

2. S. van der Linde, *Opgang en Voortgang der Reformatie* (Amsterdam: Ton Bolland, 1976), 1:171.

3. A. Ritschl, *Geschichte des Pietismus* (Bonn: Marcus, 1880), 86; S. van der Linde, "Mystiek en bevinding in het Gereformeerd Protestantisme," in *Mystiek en bevinding*, ed. G. Quispel *et al.* (Kok: Kampen, 1976), 47.

4. K. O'Dell Bullock, "Post-Reformation Protestant Hermeneutics," in *Biblical Hermeneutics: A Comprehensive Introduction to Interpreting Scripture*, ed. Bruce Corley, Steve Lemke, Grant Lovejoy, 2d ed., Nashville: Broadman & Holman Publishers, 2002), 120.

5. Richard A. Muller, *Post-Reformation Reformed Dogmatics* (Grand Rapids: Baker Academic, 2003) vol.1; Joel R. Beeke, "Gisbertus Voetius: Toward a Reformed Marriage of Knowledge and Piety," in *Protestant scholasticism: essays in reassessment*, ed. Carl R. Trueman, and R. Scott Clark (Carlisle: Paternoster, 1999); idem, *Practical Puritanism* (Grand Rapids: RHB Publishers, 2004).

6. A. de Reuver, *Verborgen omgang, Sporen van Spiritualiteit in Middeleeuwen en Nadere Reformatie* (Zoetermeer: Boekencentrum, 2002).

7. Henricus Pontanus, *Laudatio Funebris In excessum Doctissimi Et Sanctissimi Senis, Petri van Mastrigt, S. S. Theol. Doctoris & Professoris : Quam jussu amplissimi Senatus Academici D. XXIV. Februarii / postridie sepulturæ dixit Henricus Pontanus* (Rotterdam: van Veen, 1706), 20; Bernardus de Moor, *Commentarius perpetuus in Johannis Marckii Compendium Theologiæ Christianæ didactico-elencticum* (Leiden: Johannes Hasebroek, 1761), vol. 1, *præfatio*; H. Heppe, *Geschichte des Pietismus und der Mystik in der Reformirten Kirche* (Leiden: Brill, 1879), 164; J. van Genderen, *Herman Witsius, bijdrage tot de kennis der Gereformeerde theologie*

De fide in Deum triunum, deserve a separate examination. In this chapter, then, we examine the following questions: (1) What is the structure, if any, of the practical sections of the doctrine of God? (2) What is the relationship, if any, between exegesis, doctrine, and *praxis*? (3) Is the '*pars practica*' an independent, separate enterprise, or is there a dependency on exegesis or doctrine, and what is the degree of dependency, if any? The results of this examination are used to evaluate the legitimacy of the four appraisals of seventeenth-century Reformed piety in the context of the *TPT*.

Mastricht and the Formulation of Practica

The examination of the practical sections of the *TPT* immediately raises a question: What is denoted by *praxis*? Is it Pietism, a form of mysticism of Mastricht's time, which is refuted by W. à Brakel?[8] Is it a post-Reformation piety (*vroomheid*), of which Puritanism and the *Nadere Reformatie* are exponents?[9] Is it Mastricht's definition of the *praxis pietatis*?[10] In respect to the latter it should be noted that the *praktijk der godzaligheid* is discussed only in the *Idea Theologiæ Moralis* and *Theologiæ Asceticæ* of the *TPT*.[11] The *praxis pietatis* thus is placed in the context of moral and ascetic theology and is distinct, but probably not separated, from the '*pars practica*' or *praxis*.[12]   Indeed, the title of Mastricht's *magnum opus* points to *theoretico-practica theologia*, not *theologia praxeos pietatis*. The question at this point, then, remains to be answered. What does Mastricht denote with the *praxis*?

Mastricht explains his view of the practical aspect of theology in several places, including the *Prodromus, Methodus Concionandi*, and the *TPT*. In the *Prodromus* he states that the practical section is the application of the biblical text, and he voices his

---

('s-Gravenhage: Guido de Bres, 1953), 68 and 69; M. J. A. de Vrijer, *Ds. Bernardus Smytegelt en zijn "Gekrookte Riet"* (Vianen: De Banier, 1968), 10.

8. Wilhelmus à Brakel, *ΛΟΓΙΚΗ ΛΑΤΡΕΙΑ, dat is Redelijke Godtsdienst in welken de goddelijke Waerheden van het Genade-Verbondts worden verklaert* (Rotterdam: Reynier van Doesburgh, 1700), I:43, 1080-1134. Mastricht is limited in his description of Pietists such as Francken and Spener. Cf. Petrus van Mastricht, *Theoretico-practica theologia: qua, per singula capita theologica, pars exegetica, dogmatica, elenchtica et practica, perpetua successione conjugantur; accedunt historia ecclesiastica, plena quidem, sed compendiosa, idea theologiæ moralis, hypotyposis theologiæ asceticæ etc. proin opus quasi novum* (Utrecht: Thomas Appels, 1699), VIII.3.xliv, 1075. See on Pietism the overview article by Martin Brecht, "Pietismus," in *Theologische Realenzyklopädie*, ed. Gerhard Müller *et al.* (Berlin/New York: Walter de Gruyter, 1996), 26:606-31.

9. See footnote 102 of the introduction of this study.

10. Mastricht, *Theoretico-practica theologia*, *Hypotyposis Theologiæ asceticæ*, 1160, § 1: "Indolem. Est praxis pietatis, studium exercendi, quasvis virtutes Christianas." See for a discussion on *pietas* C. A. De Niet, *Gisbertus Voetius De Praktijk der Godzaligheid* (Utrecht: De Banier, 1996), 1:xxxii.

11. Ibid., Idea *Theologiæ Moralis*, 1118 and *Hypotyposis Theologiæ asceticæ*, 1160-1163 (De praxi pietatis in genere), 1164-1179 (De praxi pietatis erga Deum), 1181-1196 (De praxi pietatis versus proximum), 1200-1222 (De praxi pietatis versus semetipsum).

12. See for an historical perspective on *theologia ascetica*, see De Niet, *Gisbertus Voetius*, 1:xxvii-xxii.

appreciation of the English practical writers.[13] Mastricht advances this thought significantly in the *Methodus*. The application, he writes here, "is the soul of the sermon."[14] The homiletic purpose of the *Methodus* may have contributed to the extensive discussion of this subject. Mastricht states that the *praxis* should contain two main components: a part with a *usus* of consolation and a *usus* of admonition[15] and a part with a *usus* of self-examination and a *usus* of exhortation.[16] In respect to the *usus,* he stresses, on the one hand, the necessity to let the biblical text determine whether or not one can infer the *usus.* Furthermore, although a biblical text could allow for one or more *usus,* one should consider the circumstance of the hearers, and these aspects should be treated accordingly.[17] On the other hand, Mastricht assures the reader of the biblical origin of these "*usus.*" For example, παράκλησις (consolation) is used in Acts 4:36, νουθεσία (admonition) is used in Ephesians 6:4, πειράζω is used in Acts 5:9 in the sense of putting to the test, and παραινῶ, that is "to advise, to exhort, or urge" is used in Acts 27:22. Finally, we find a description of the *praxis* summarized in the *index analyticus* of the *TPT* (1682). He remarks here that the practical section consists of consolation, admonition of sin, the offering of a remedy, and the provision of marks, motives, and means for those in need.[18] To this, he adds in the final edition of the *TPT* that the practical section also should contain scriptural testimonies to illumine the point.[19] Thus, we conclude that, following Mastricht's outline in the *Methodus* and our examination of the chapters on doctrine of God of the *TPT,* the practical sections include specific attention to consolation, admonition, self-examination, and exhortation.

Further examination of the practical sections of the doctrine of God, however, reveals two additional and consistent themes: the glory of God and the humbling of

---

13. Petrus van Mastricht, *Theologiæ didactico-elenchtico-practicæ, prodromus tribus* (Amsterdam: Johannes van Someren, 1666), *præfatio: "Itaque cuique capiti illustrem quedem Scripturæ textum... applicatione practicam complector....Materiam huic operi, comprimis practicam quandoque suppeditabunt Authores Angli, à praxi fermè celebratissimi."*

14. Petrus van Mastricht, *Methodus Concionandi* (Frankfurt an der Oder: M. Hübner, undated), 18: "*Cavendum denique ne nimium & hic simus copiosi & applicationi quæ anima est concionis tempus præripiamus.*"

15. Ibid., 27: "*Succedit, applicatio practica, quæ vel malum respicit; cum triste cui obnititur usus* παρακλητικὸς *consolatorius; tum turpe, cui medetur usus* νουθετικὸς *reprehensorius.*" The *consolatorius* is worked out in paragrapgh xi, and the *reprehensorius* in paragraph xii of the *Methodus.*

16. Ibid., 28: "*...vel bonum, seu explorandum quo facit usus* πειραστικος *exploratorius; vel excitandum quo vergit* παραινετικὸς *adhortatorius.*" The *explorandum* is worked out in paragrapgh xiii, and the *excitandum* in paragraph xiv of the *Methodus.*

17. Mastricht, *Theoretico-practica theologia,* xv, 1235. Mastricht applies these cautions not only to the practical section but also to the exegetical, doctrinal, and elenctical sections of the *TPT.*

18. Mastricht, *Theoretico-practica theologia* (1682), 1115: "*in practicis item, casus consolationis, argumenta consolatoria, peccata reprehendenda, argumenta reprehensoria, remedia, signa, motiva, media &c. passim occurrere, quæ in hoc indice, frustra quæres.*"

19. Mastricht, *Theoretico-practica theologia* (1699), *præfatio: "...cum præsertim lector attentus amplificationes, ex congestis Scripturæ testimoniis...sed nonnulla illustrationi tantum fuisse adjecta."*

man. These two themes are succinctly present, and in the identified order, in almost every chapter of *De fide in Deum triunum* at the opening of each practical section. Frequently, Mastricht first directs one to the glorification of God[20] and thus prior to the four identified aspects of the practical section: consolation, admonition, self-examination, and exhortation. Second, such directive correlates to the other theme: the humbling of man.[21] This observation may answer partly the question of what Matricht means by *praxis* or *'pars practica.'* The Scholastics denoted *theologia practica* as leading or tending toward a goal.[22] If Mastricht, then, directs in the practical sections to God, his theology is goal- and God-oriented.

Structure of Formulated of the Practical sections

The examination of Mastricht's thought on the formulation of *praxis*, and further examination of the practical sections of book II of the *TPT*, identified the following parts: (1) the glory of God and the humbling of man, (2) consolation, (3) admonition, (4) self-examination, and (5) exhortation. To illustrate these parts of the structure of the practical sections, we examine their content in the chapters of the doctrine of God of the *TPT*. This examination may assist in answering our introductory questions and the quest for the meaning of the *praxis* for Mastricht.

The Glory of God and the Humbling of Man

We observe that both these themes, while consistently present in the practical sections of the doctrine of God, are also rather consistent in their content. Mastricht refers to the *locus* under consideration, e.g., the divine goodness, and argues that this doctrine should lift one up to the goodness of God, should lead one to expect all good from Him, yet one misses this by nature (humbling). He subsequently directs one to God, who is the *summum bonum*.[23] Thus, both these themes—the glory of God and the humbling of man—are related in the *praxis*. *Vroomheid* is, for Mastricht then, directed to God, and thus the godly living (*[het] godzalig(e) leven*) contains both aspects. This reminds

---

20. Ibid., II.5.xii, 97; II.7.ix, 110; II.9.xi, 120; II.11.xv, 133; II.12.xiv, 139; II.12xxiii, 141; II.13.xxiv, 150; II.18.xvii, 199; II.22.xvi, 229; II.23.xi, 233; II.24.xxiii, 244; II.26.xx, 259. Not prior to but at the beginning, middle, or end of the practical section; ibid., II.3.xxvi, 84; II.4.xviii, 91; II.16.xxii, 177; II.17.xlii, 191; II.19.xix, 208; II.20.xxxiii, 218; II.21.xiv, 223. This observation can be extended to the remainder of the *Theoretico-practica theologia*.

21. The humbling of man can often be found immediately following or in the paragraph on the glory of God (see preceding footnote).

22. See this study II.1 for the discussion on *theologia theoretica* and *theologia practica*

23. Mastricht, *Theoretico-practica theologia*, II.5.xii, 97; II.7.ix, 110; II.9.xi, 120; II.11.xv, 133; II.12.xiv, 139; II.12xxiii, 141; II.13.xxiv, 150; II.18.xvii, 199; II.22.xvi, 229; II.23.xi, 233; II.24.xxiii, 244; II.26.xx, 259 and II.3.xxvi, 84; II.4.xviii, 91; II.16.xxii, 177; II.17.xlii, 191; II.19.xix, 208; II.20.xxxiii, 218; II.21.xiv, 223.

one of the opening of Calvin's *Institutes*: the knowledge of God and the knowledge of self.[24]

Consolation

The consolatory aspect consists of identifying sin, providing comfort, and taking away objections.[25] Furthermore, Mastricht recommends the following rules for the consolatory aspect. First, consolation should be given the first place in the practical application, not so much for the benefit of the spiritually afflicted pious person but, he argues, because it weakens rhetorically the practical application when such is moved to the end.[26] Second, in all other parts of the practical application, the consolation should be rarely presented, because "the spiritually afflicted (*de geestelijk verdrukten en aangevochtenen*) are rare in a congregation."[27] Third, the consolation should be discriminatively presented and not in general so that the "worldly ones" will not wrongly apply and misuse the provided comfort.[28]

The examination of the doctrine of God of the *TPT* affirms that Mastricht takes the consolatory aspect of the practical application seriously.[29] We observe two particularities: location and structure. With respect to the location in the practical section, one notes a difference with his suggested homiletic advice. In the practical sections of the doctrine of God, Mastricht does not usually begin with comfort[30] but, as we have seen, with the glory of God. With respect to the structure of the consolatory part, a similar structure is seen, with parts we can identify as (1) thesis or argument, (2) consideration, (3) question,

---

24. John Calvin, *The Institutes of Christian Religion*, ed. John T. McNeil, trans. Ford L. Battles (Philadelphia: The Westminster Press, 1960), 35.

25. Mastricht, *Methodus Concionandi*, 28: "Hunc usum tria possint ingredi: 1. Mala recensenda...spiritualia, corporalia...2. Argumenta consolatoria...3. Objectiones...præoccupandæ & tollendæ."

26. Ibid.: "a) *Consolationi* in praxi primum arbitror esse dandum locum, non tam quod piorum affictorum, prima nobis & præcipua debeat esse cura; quam ne ultimo loco posita, præcendentis praxeos acumen & efficaciam obtundat."

27. Ibid., 29: "b) *Rarior* reliquis usibus practicis, sit consolatio, quod spiritualiter afflicti, rariores in quavis Ecclesiâ existant & his qui sunt argumenta consolatoria, privatim comodius applicari queant." The question can be raised, that Mastricht saw the spiritual condition of the congregation different than his teachers, who saw enough reason to provide help for the spiritual afflicted. Cf. Gisbertus Voetius and Johannes Hoornbeeck, *Disputaty van geestelicke verlatingen* (Dordrecht: Symon onder de Linde, 1667), A 2.

28. Ibid.: "c) *Argumenta* consolatoria non promiscuè profunduntur; ne ab impiis arrepta, perperam usurpentur, in sui indurationem ac perniciem Matth. 7:6 sed cautè discriminentur ab aliis quibus consolatio dicitur."

29. Mastricht, *Theoretico-practica theologia*, II.3.xxiv, 83; II.10.xiv, 126; II.11.xvii, 133; II.12.xvii, 139; II.12.xxv, 141; II.13.xxix, 151; II.14.xiv, 156; II.15.xli, 169; II.18.xxiii, 201; II.19.xviii, 207; II.21.xii, 222; II.22.xix, 230; II.23.xv, 234; II.25.xix, 250.

30. Located at the opening of the practical section: II.3.xxiv; II.10.xiv; II.21.xii; at the middle of the practical section: II.11.xvii; II.12.xvii; II.12.xxv; II.13.xxix; II.14.xiv; II.25.xix; at the end of the practical section: II.15.xli; II.18.xxiii; II.19.xviii; II.22.xix; II.23.xv.

and (4) response. To illustrate, consider the consolation part of the practical section of the *locus de Essentia Dei*. Mastricht argues that the first *usus* of the divine essence is consolation in adversity.[31] This remark is echoed throughout the consolation sections of the doctrine of God—a divine attribute or subject such as God the Father provides "comfort in adversity."[32]

He then states his thesis: sorrow and hardship arise most times from what one does not have or from what one desires to have. However, he consoles, one should consider the divine essence, which gives comfort for those who have lost goods or happiness such as friends (Job, Job 1:19; Rachel, Matt. 2:18; Naomi, Ruth 1:3), or honor (1 Cor. 4:13). Consider, Mastricht counsels, those who have lost health (Isa. 1:6, 53:3; Ps. 73:26)[33] or rest and are troubled in their souls because of missing faith, hope, or love or because of spiritual desertion. Then Mastricht raises the following question, present in almost every part of the consolation section: What can strengthen one?[34] Mastricht replies, in the context of the chapter on the divine essence, that the text reveals that "God is through His essence, the divine foundation to strengthen the Israelites." Here one may raise the question as to how Mastricht makes this objective truth a subjective personal matter or, as he words it, how "from these grounds of consolation flows our consolation." The way of appropriation (*toeëigening*) is, according to Mastricht, that one "in all his misery" must do one thing: make a covenant with God, through which He becomes "our God" (Jer. 31:33), "so that Moses announces also to us as he did to the Israelites in the text that the God of your fathers . . . is your God."[35]

Thus, Mastricht reaches back from the practical section to the biblical text for the foundation for the divine essence (Exod. 3:13,14), and there finds that appropriation takes place *via* the covenant. Further examination shows that for Mastricht the objective truth becomes personally subjective through the covenant and through faith, or as he states, "through faith as covenanting with God" (Gen. 17:1).

To provide one more illustration from the section on consolation, let us turn to the chapter *De Vita Dei*. The attribute of divine life, according to Mastricht, is a resting

31. Ibid., II.3.xxiv (note the 1699 has a print error, xxv), 83: "Jam, usus observationis de essentiâ Dei esse possit: *primo consolationis* in quibusvis adversis."

32. Ibid., II.10.xiv, 126 (divine omnipresence); II.11.xvii, 133 (divine eternity); II.13.xxix, 151 (divine omniscience); II.14.xiv, 156 (divine veracity and faithfulness); II.15.xli, 169 (divine will); II.18.xxiii, 201 (divine justice); II.19.xviii, 207 (divine holiness); II.21.xii, 222 (divine omnisufficency); II.22.xix, 230 (divine majesty and glory); II.23.xv, 234 (divine beatitude); II.25.xix, 250 (God the Father). This notion is not restricted to book II but is also found throughout the remainder of the TPT. A sampling of references may illustrate our point: III.1.xi, 274 (divine action); III.3.xxvi, 300 (divine election); III.10.xliii, 403 (divine providence); absent in book iv; V.1.xlvi, 408 (covenant of grace); V.2.xxx, 419 (mediator of covenant of grace); V.12.xxxiv, 551 (death of the mediator); VI.6.xxxvi, 722 (justification); VI.9.xxiii, 762 (glorification); VIII.3.lii, 1090 (dispensation under Christ); VIII.4.xxii, 1100, (dispensation in eternity).

33. Note Mastricht takes these texts literally.

34. Mastricht, *Theoretico-practica theologia*, II.3.xxv, 83: "...quid efficacius erigere possit?

35. Ibid., 84: "Ut & nobis Moses possit denunciare, quod Israëlitis in textu denunciat: *Deus patrum vestrorum &c.* imo & *vester.*"

ground for all kinds of difficulties in one's life. First, he considers difficulties in natural life. These difficulties include sickness, which can lead to the consideration of ending one's life, or poverty and the lack of life's necessities, or enemies who seek after one's life. Mastricht asks, "What shall lift one up?" He answers by pointing to the divine life. It is God Himself who gives, restores, sustains, and protects one's life. He lives, according to John 5:26, which is the foundational text for the chapter on *De vita Dei*, and makes alive by the Spirit of life (Rom. 8:3). Second, in spiritual life, when one feels dead in sin or unfit for any spiritual work, Mastricht asks, "What shall lift one up?" He answers that one should contemplate the fact that God has life in Himself (John 5:26), that he has given his Son, who in turn has given Himself so that one may live (1 John 4:9). Indeed, Christ is our life (Col. 3:4) and is the way, the truth, and the life (John 14:6). Third, when there are struggles for eternal life, when there is fear of death (Heb. 2:15) and when one sighs, "Who shall deliver me?" (Rom. 7:24), Mastricht asks, again, "What shall lift one up?" He replies that nothing else will do but to acknowledge that God is a living God (Ps. 42:3) and lives; that "our Redeemer" lives and that He is one's life; and that the Holy Spirit is a Spirit of life (John 5:63).

With this Trinitarian approach, Mastricht concludes the consolation part by stating that one should live unto God, *Deo vivere*, (Rom. 6:2).[36] One observes that the *consolatio* relates immediately to the biblical text, which is foundational for the discussed *locus*. Moreover, the consolation is biblically formulated and practically appropriated through faith and covenant.

Admonition

In contrast to the significant presence of the consolation part, the part on admonition in the practical sections is much more concise. Admonition is to be used, according to Mastricht, as medicine and is sometimes called a dissuasion.[37] The examination of the practical sections of the doctrine of God shows that discussion of admonition is limited.[38] Admonition is mostly directed to those who deny God[39] or

---

36. Ibid., II.12.xiv, 139: "In praxi, suppetit nobis à *vitâ* Dei...;" ibid., xvii, !39, 140: "Suppetit, *quartò*, fundamentum solatii, in quibusvis difficultatibus, omnis *vitæ* nostræ Psal.27:1. Nominatim in difficultatibus: 1. *Vitæ naturalis*...2. *Vitæ spiritualis*...3. *Vitæ æternæ*...."

37. Mastricht, *Methodus Concionandi*, 32: "*Succedit*, malo tristi, malum turpe, cui reprehensio medetur, aliis nominibus, pro diverso tractandi modo, jam admonitio, jam dehortatio, jam quærela designata."

38. Mastricht, *Theoretico-practica theologia*, II.1.xxviii-xxxiii, 57-59; II.2.xxiii-xxviii, 72-74; II.3.xxv, 84; II.12.xvi, 139; II.21.xiii, 223; II.23.xiii, 234. Note 1. The paragraphs II.1.xxviii-xxxiii, 57-59, could be considered as a reprehension but is a practical formulation derived from the biblical text of John 1:11 and lays out unbelief, its nature, causes, and remedy (xxxiii: "Restat, infidelitatis *remedia* subjungamus; à Medico spirituali applicanda..."). Note 2. The paragraphs II.2.xxiii-xxvii, 72-74, deal with atheism (in a seventeenth-century context).

39. Ibid., II.3.xxv, 84: "*Secundus* usus, esse possit *reprehensorius*, eorum omnium, qui: 1. apertè *essentiam* & existentiam Deo abrogatam vellent Psal. 14:1, 10:4. Qui 2. saltem *interpretativè*, ita dicam, essentiæ divinæ aseitatem & independentiam, infringunt: quando gratiam Dei, in negotio

who, "not so much in words but in deeds," testify that God does not live[40] and seek their own beatitude.[41] Further, Mastricht admonishes those who show that God is not sufficient for their needs, not only the ungodly but also the regenerate.[42] In summary, Mastricht is limited in his admonitions, which are primarily directed to the ungodly.

Self-examination

According to Mastricht, self-examination consists of motives, marks, and an end. The motivation for self-examination is for one to receive spiritual tranquility and joy.[43] The marks of self-examination are meant to discern whether one is in a natural state or in the state of grace. One should proceed with great caution, however, (1) because the "pious" should be brought neither into doubt nor into anguish (when such doubt happens, Mastricht argues, it is difficult for one to be led out of it) and (2) because hypocrites should not be strengthened and hardened in their carnal rest. The end (*finis*) of self-examination is, according to Mastricht, that the pious are confirmed in the state of grace and desirous of heaven.[44] With this as background, the examination of the practical sections of the doctrine of God shows three features. First, Mastricht makes limited use of self-examination, much as he does with admonition.[45] Second, the limited use of self-examination is restricted to faith. Third, his suggested structure—motives, marks and end—is consistently employed throughout the practical sections of the doctrine of God of the *TPT*.

A further examination of this structure of the chapters of the doctrine of God show that in respect to the motives they are rarely present but always indicate the relationship

prædestinationis, suspendunt à libero hominis arbitrio, à fide & infidelitate, aut etiam a bonis prævisis, eoque, ab una parte, Deum omnimoda sua independentiâ exuunt; ab alterâ parte homini, eiusque arbitrio, independentiam commodant, coelum terræ permiscentes. Quin 3. qui *practicè* saltem, independentiam Dei vellicant, quando eius auxilium, a mediis suspendunt: seu per totalem *desperationem* 2. Reg. 7:2. seu per qualemcunque *diffidentiam*. Num. 11:21, 23. Joh. 11:21 & 4:49."

40. Ibid., II.12.xvi, 139: "Suppetit, *tertiò* argumentum *reprehensionis*, eorum omnium, qui: 1. non tam *voce*, quam *facto* cum Deo agunt ac si ἄζωον haberent & ἀναισθητον qui nec videat, nec audiat, nec observet...."

41. Ibid., II.23.xiii, 234: "*Tertiò*, reprehendit quoque eorum *stultitiam* qui præteritâ verâ omnis beatitudinis *venâ*, beatitudinem suam in *quibusvis*....secluantur."

42. Ibid., II.21.xiii, 223: "*Tertiò, reprehendunt* eos omnes, qui non tam *verbis*, istam Dei negant omnisufficientiam...quam *factis*. Quod sit (1) Ab *apertè impiis*, quando *derelicto* Deo, sibi suisque *mundanis...,sufficientiam* perspiciunt. (2) A *clam hypocritis*, qui *aliqualem* in Deo sufficientiam deprehendunt...(3) Ab ipsis etiam verè *regenitis*, prout videre est in tergiversatione Mosis Exod.3:11,12 in mendacio Abrahami Gen.20:2...."

43. Mastricht, *Methodus Concionandi*, 39.

44. Ibid.: "[3] Finis exploratorius ut facta investigatione confirmentur virtute salutari prædeti & in statu gratiæ eo ipso deprehensi: Contra qui vitiis laborant, exitialibus potissimum ad solicitudinem, metum & curam emendationis pertrahantur."

45. Mastricht, *Theoretico-practica theologia*, II.1.xxxiv,xxxv, 59, 60; II.2.xxx, 74; II.6.xv, 102; II.17.xl, 190; II.27.xxiv, 270.

with the *locus*. For example, Mastricht states in the chapter *De Existentia & Cognitioni Dei* that one should examine the possession of true knowledge of God,[46] or examine in spirit and in truth (*De Spiritualitate et Simplicitate Dei*),[47] or search whether one has received the Spirit (*De Deo Spiritu Sancto*).[48] With respect to the marks, an examination shows also a rare use of the marks but one that is always directly connected to the biblical text. For example, Mastricht discusses the marks of one's possession of the true knowledge of God in the practical section of *De Existentia et Cognitione Dei*. The biblical text for this chapter is Hebrews 11:6.[49] Mastricht then raises the question as to whether one possesses some knowledge of God and "in such a way that the [biblical] text provides criteria."[50] He responds that one has this knowledge of God when there is (1) faith generated by the "rewarder"; (2) a desire to know God as to ἐκζητεῖν, to "seek Him"; (3) a coming to God, εἰς προσέρχεσθαι, "to come to and receive Him"; and (4) an excitement that causes one to do everything "to please Him."[51] This example corroborate a direct relationship between the biblical text and identified marks but also that these marks (of grace) are Scriptural expressed.

At other times such a direct relationship is less present, and the marks are established from the biblical text *via* the exposition and doctrinal formulation. The marks present in the chapter on the *Holy Spirit* illustrates this point. In the text analysis of John 14:26, Mastricht identifies the proper name of the Holy Spirit.[52] He then explores further in the doctrinal section that Scripture uses several names to identify the Holy Spirit, such as the *goede Geest* (Ps. 143:10), the Spirit of grace (Heb. 10:29), the Spirit of life (Rom. 8:2), and the Spirit of glory (1 Pet. 4:4).[53] Then in the practical section he refers to the question of Acts 19:2, "Have you received the Holy Spirit?" Mastricht replies, that one should discern personally (1) the Spirit of life who makes alive, (2) the Spirit of sanctification who brings a desire for holiness in life, and (3) the Spirit of light who enlightens the mind. In addition, one should discern and seek to have (4) the Spirit of ignition, so that one is not cold and lazy but "*vurig en yverig*," and,

46. Ibid., II.2.xxx, 74: "*Tertia praxis, circa scrutinium distinetur veræ cognitionis Dei.*"

47. Ibid., II.6.xv, 102: "*Proinde tertiò suadet, cultum nostrum solicitè examinemus sitne convenienter naturæ divinæ, in spiritu & veritate.*"

48. Ibid., II.27.xxiv, 270: "*Est quartò, quod Spiritum exploremus num ex Deo sit?* 1 Joh. 4:1, 1 Thess.5:21. Exploremus: A. num Spiritum Sanctum *simus consecuti* Act 19:2 *Num Spiritum S. accepistis?.*"

49. πιστεῦσαι γὰρ δεῖ τὸν προσερχόμενον τῷ θεῷ ὅτι ἔστιν καὶ τοῖς ἐκζητοῦσιν αὐτὸν μισθαποδότης γίνεται. "For he that cometh to God must believe that he is, and *that* he is a rewarder of them that diligently seek him" (King James Version).

50. Mastricht, *Theoretico-practica theologia*, II.2.xxx, 74: "...exploratione opus est, ut sciamus, num *ullâ* simus præditi cognitione Dei? & num tali? Cujus hæc suppeditat κριτήρια textus."

51. Ibid.: "Si (1) fidem generet...(2) appetitum erigat ad *quærendum* agnitum...(3) *perducat* ad Deum...*ad accedendum*, h.e. ut inventum *recipiamus*...(4) studium excitet, in omnibus...."

52. Ibid., II.27.ii, 262.

53. Ibid., iv, 263.

finally, (5) the Spirit of Christ, through whom Christ lives in one and glorifies Christ.[54] Here one observes the intrinsic correlation between the biblical texts and the practical formulation.

Although Mastricht infers the marks, where allowed, from the biblical text, the question could be raised as to what their function is. He appears to point in the direction of the use the marks in a practical syllogism. For example, he argues that if one provides the mark of the Spirit of sanctification, whereby one has a desire to live holy before God, one can "assuredly conclude, from this that we have received the Holy Spirit,"[55] and "since we have asserted these things in us we may be completely convinced and trust that we have received the Spirit of Christ,"[56] which is, according to Mastricht, revealed by the fruits of the Spirit. Thus, having the fruits of the Spirit, one can draw assurance of possessing the Spirit.[57] However, Mastricht also argues that such (practical) knowledge rests alone upon "the foundation of the Prophets and Apostles, is rooted in the 'inward parts of the heart' (Col.2:6:7), and is received from heaven (Jam.3:17)."[58] Thus, practical knowledge is founded not so much on practical syllogism as on the Word applied through the Holy Spirit. Therefore, the function of the marks in the part on self-examination is limited although directive to the Word and the working of God's Spirit.

Finally, the goal of self-examination is to move the affections to fear deception, to produce the love and desire of confirming one's spiritual state, and to promote assurance of faith.[59] Thus, though Mastricht's use of self-examination is restrained, when it is used, it is primarily directed toward God, resting upon the Word and the work of the Spirit.

---

54. Ibid., xxiv, 270: "...eosque conferamus cum cordibus nostris. Est (1) Spiritus, *vitæ*...(2) Spiritus S πνεῦμα ἀγιωσύνης...(3) Spiritus *lucis*...(4) Spiritus *igneus*...(5) Spiritus *Christi*...."

55. Ibid.: "(2) Spiritus S. πνεῦμα ἀγιωσύνης Rom.1:4. Quod si igitur, *studium* serium in nobis observemus *sanctitatis* ac *detestationem* omnis impuritatis; poterimus inde tutò conficere, nos Spiritum Sanctum adeptos esse."

56. Ibid.: "Est [5] Spiritus *Christi*...Ista igitur si penes nos deprehenderimus; certo certius simus persuasi, nos *spiritum Chrsiti* infallibiliter consecutos esse."

57. Ibid., II.17.xl, 190: "Sed quibus tandem indiciis propensionem illam electis *peculiarem*...certò agnoscemus ac discriminabimus? Resp. 1. Discrimen non quæremus, in ipso Dei *affectu*...sed in *effectis*...illis quæ peculiariter χαρίσματα, *fructus Spiritus S.* "

58. Ibid., II.2.xxx, 74. Mastricht comments here on the knowledge of God and its marks, and writes, "(c) ut sit *profunda* nitens *fundamento Prophetarum & Apostolorum* Eph.2:20 radicata in imo pectoris Col.2:6,7 è cœlis accepta...."

59. Mastricht, *Methodus Concionandi*, 39, 40: "Affectus in exploratione movendi, sunt primo: metus fallaciæ ac deceptionis...secundò, amor & desiderium certiorandi εὐεξίαν status nostri spiritualis...tertio, audacia & conatus applicandi quævis studia & labores, quo assequamur certitudinem boni status nostri."

Exhortation

As a further exposition of the doctrinal argument, the exhortation, according to Mastricht, is used to encourage good works.[60] Exhortations are to act by means of the working of the Holy Spirit to the *exercitia pietatis*, encouraging the reading and hearing of Scripture, the communion of the saints, and prayer. Together, these should lead to a heavenly walk (Col. 3:1, 2).[61] An examination of the exhortation part in the practical sections of the doctrine of God reveals several features. First, Mastricht uses different words in these sections, such as "meditation,"[62] "invitation,"[63] (positive) "arguments,"[64] and "imitation."[65] For Mastricht the exhortation is meditative in character and invites the believer to the *navolging* of Christ. Second, these exhortations aim to direct the believer to God. For example, Mastricht comments in the chapter *De Potestate et Potentia Dei* that the divine power should lead one to trust in God and being His possession by creation and redemption. Therefore, one is exhorted that His power will overcome one's enemies because He is the Lord Sabaoth.[66]

Further examination of this part of the practical section demonstrates Mastricht's expressed view of the exhortation as a further exposition of the doctrinal argument that is used to encourage good works. For example, in the chapter *De Immutabilitate Dei*, he first identifies the close connection between the biblical text, its exposition, and doctrinal and practical formulation.[67] Second, the practical section works out in more detail Mastricht's doctrinal formulation of God's unchangeableness. Such knowledge in itself is not sufficient, however; it should exhort one to live a consistent life unto God. In conclusion, Mastricht does not structure the exhortation part as precisely as the other parts of the practical section. Moreover, exhortation is expressed with different words, but collectively they aim to exhort one unto God.

Our examination of the practical sections, then, reveals that Mastricht employed a distinct structure, the content of which, distinguished in five aspects, collectively aimed to direct one to God. In addition to the structure of (a) the *TPT*, (b) the doctrine of God, and (c) the individual *locus*, we identify, here, another structure, that of the practical section. The content of the practical sections are biblically expressed and correlated to

---

60. Ibid., 42, 43: "Succedit usus adhortatorius, quo argumentum doctrinale accuratur ad excitandum studium virtutis aut boni alicujus operis."

61. Ibid., 43, 1-4.

62. Mastricht, *Theoretico-practica theologia*, II.4.xx, 91; II.15.xxxix, 168; II.20.xxxi, 218; II.20.xxxii, 218.

63. Ibid., II.7.xiv, 111; II.11.xix, 133; II.12.xxvi, 142; II.13.xxx, 151; II.15.xl, 168; II.21.xv, 224; II.24.xxv, 245; II.24.xxviii, 245; II.25.xx, 250; II.26.xxiii, 260.

64. Ibid., II.12.xviii, 140; II.13.xxvi, 150; II.13.xxviii, 151; II.24.xxv, 245; II.26.xxv, 261.

65. Ibid., II.17.xlii, 191; II.21.xvii, 224; II.27.xxiii, 269.

66. Ibid., II.20.xxxii, 218: "Struit *septimò, potestatis & potentiæ* divinæ devota cogitatio, solidam *fiduciam*...Quod 1.per ejus potestatem ac dominium ejus simus *peculium*, qui nos sibi comparaverit *creatione &* redemptione..."

67. See Appendix III.4. The Structure of *De Immutabilitate Dei*.

the biblical text foundational to the *locus*. Thus, on the one hand, the biblical text and exegesis is at work throughout the practical formulation of the *loci*. On the other hand, the *praxis* is bound to Scripture. Finally, the collective content of the practical sections points to Mastricht's understanding of the *theologia practica* as theology directed to God, dependent and formulated upon the divine Word, and worked by the Holy Spirit, resulting together in a oneness of *leer* and *leven*.[68]

68. Gregory D. Schuringa, *Embracing* Leer *and* Leven: *The Theology of Simon Oomius in the Context of the* Nadere Reformatie *Orthodoxy*, 314-322.

Part 4

An In-depth Study of the Doctrine of God

Introduction

Introduction and Statement of the Problem

Thus far we have seen that theology for Mastricht means a reflection upon the *principium cognoscendi*: Scripture. It is a reflection on the biblical text in a grammatical-philological exegetical way that leads to the formulation of doctrine and *praxis*. This reflection is goal-oriented and through faith[1] directed to the *principium essendi*: God. Although the foregoing chapters demonstrate a most probable interrelation between Mastricht's biblical interpretation, doctrine, and *praxis*, it leaves two main questions unanswered. First, how does the probable interrelated approach of Mastricht to theology unfold in a specific *locus*? Second, does Mastricht's doctrine of God in the *Theoretico-practica theologia* (*TPT*) confirm the critique of the doctrine of God of the seventeenth-century post-Reformation Reformed orthodoxy? This doctrine has been appraised in whole or in part in various ways. These include the assessment that this doctrine is (1) controlled by a "static" thinking of eternity so that one encounters and describes only a transcendent God[2] and (2) that it is a return to medieval metaphysics[3] and philosophical construction of God.[4] From this arises the central question of whether the God of Mastricht is the God of the covenant or is a "metaphysical idol."[5]

Therefore, in the following chapters, we examine the presentation of the *loci* of the doctrine of God of the *TPT* and whether the critique of this doctrine is justifiable. These two lines of investigation may answer the central question about the God of Mastricht.

---

1. Petrus van Mastricht, *Theoretico-practica theologia qua, per singula capita theologica, pars exegetica, dogmatica, elenchtica et practica, perpetua successione conjugantur; accedunt historia ecclesiastica, plena quidem, sed compendiosa, idea theologiæ moralis, hypotyposis theologiæ asceticæ etc. proin opus quasi novum* (Utrecht: Thomas Appels, 1699), II.1.iii, 51. Mastricht defined faith as, "an act of the total rational soul, whereby God is received as the highest end and union with Christ, as the only Mediator, is obtained and through him communion with all his benefits."

2. See for example, S. van der Linde, *Opgang en Voortgang der Reformatie*, (Amsterdam: Ton Bolland, 1976), 165; B. Loonstra, "De leer van God en Christus in de Nadere Reformatie," in *Theologische Aspecten van de Nadere Reformatie*, ed. T. Brienen *et al.* (Zoetermeer: Boekencentrum, 1993), 99-150.

3. H. Cremer, "Die christliche Lehrer von den Eigenschaften Gottes," in *Beiträge zur Förderung christlicher Theologie* ed. H. Cremer (Gütersloh Verlagshaus G. Mohn, 1897); Brian G. Armstrong, *Calvinism and the Amyraut Heresy* (Madison: The University of Wisconsin Press, 1969), 122; John S. Bray, *Theodor Beza's Doctrine of Predestination* (Nieuwkoop: B. De Graaf, 1975), 12-15; John M. Frame, *The Doctrine of God* (Phillipsburg: P&R Publishing, 2002), 230. See for additional literature on this subject, Richard A. Muller, *Post-Reformation Reformed Dogmatics*, (Baker Academic, 2003), 3:154-56.

4. K. H. Miskotte, *De praktische zin van de eenvoud Gods* (Amsterdam: Uitgeversmaatschappij Holland, 1945); Emil Brunner, *Dogmatics* (London: Lutterworth Press, 1949), I:241-47; Wolfhart Pannenberg, "The Appropriation of the Philosophical Concept of God as a Dogmatic Problem of Early Christian Theology," in *Basic Questions in Theology: Collected Essays*, trans. George H. Kehm (Philadelphia: Fortress Press, 1971), II:119-83.

5. F. G. Immink, *Divine Simplicity* (Kampen: J. H. Kok, 1987), 182.

Our examination in the first chapter provides a general historical-theological context for Mastricht's discussion of the doctrine of God and in particular of the doctrine of the divine spirituality and simplicity and the doctrine of the Holy Trinity. The second and third chapters deal respectively with the doctrines of the *Divine Simplicity* and the *Holy Trinity* as expounded by Mastricht. One might wonder why a full description of the divine attributes is not undertaken, given the relatively large number of pages in the *TPT* on this subject.[6] Three reasons seem to favor giving attention to the doctrines of divine simplicity and the Holy Trinity. First, Mastricht, as we will see, relates many divine attributes to the divine simplicity, which he also links to the doctrine of divine spirituality. Second, in regard to the doctrine of the divine attributes, Muller has addressed two misapprehensions concerning Scholasticism by noting that a greater allotted space to the doctrine of the divine attributes is not necessarily a sign of greater importance and that the location of the doctrine of the Trinity following the discussion of the divine attributes does not indicate "a subordination of the doctrines concerning the personal God of the Bible to metaphysical concerns."[7] Third, the chosen doctrines address the tri-unity of God. These three reasons, then, permit the focus on Mastricht's expositions of the doctrines of divine simplicity and Holy Trinity. Our examination of these doctrines primarily gives attention to Mastricht's formulation but will include reflections of his contemporaries on the subjects. In addition, the examination will conclude with an analysis of Mastricht's presentation of these doctrines and their relationship, if any, and attempt to answer the questions of the interrelationship of exegesis, doctrine, elenctic, and *praxis*, the plausibility of the noted critique, and the quest of Mastricht's God.

6. Mastricht, *Theoretico-practica theologia*, II.5-23, 92-234.

7. Muller, *Post-Reformation Reformed Dogmatics*, 4:145, 146.

Chapter 1
The Structure of the Doctrine of God

Mastricht begins *De fide in Deum triunum*, book II of the *Theoretico-practica theologia* (*TPT*), as we have seen, with a discussion of the *locus* of faith. Subsequently, he argues that one who, through faith, seeks and receives God as highest end should be persuaded and assured that God is (Heb. 11:6) and that He communicates His all-sufficiency.[1] With this point of departure, one enters the further discussion of the doctrine of God: (1) *De Existentia & cognitione Dei*: chapter 2, (2) *De Essentia Dei*: chapters 3 to 23, and (3) *De Subsistentia Dei*: Trinity, chapters 24 to 27. This outline of the doctrine of God, which moves from the divine existence to the divine essence, subdivided into the divine names and attributes, to the discussion on the Trinity, is shared by other seventeenth-century Reformed theologians. A brief excursus on the doctrine of God in the writings of several of these theologians will contribute to the understanding of Mastricht's exposition of the doctrine of God.

The Reformed Orthodox Doctrine of God

In contrast to limited attention in the secondary literature to the doctrine of God of the seventeenth-century Reformed orthodoxy,[2] these sources attest to a diverse explication of theology proper. The teaching of the doctrine of God was expressed, for example, in works of exegesis (Scripture commentaries[3] and homily[4]), doctrine (systematic theology[5] and catechetical instructions[6]), polemic (exegetical-elenctic,[7]

---

1. Petrus van Mastricht, *Theoretico-practica theologia qua, per singula capita theologica, pars exegetica, dogmatica, elenchtica et practica, perpetua successione conjugantur; accedunt historia ecclesiastica, plena quidem, sed compendiosa, idea theologiæ moralis, hypotyposis theologiæ asceticæ etc. proin opus quasi novum* (Utrecht: Thomas Appels, 1699), II.2.i, 65: "'Fide salvifica, quò Deum appetamus, recipiamusque, velut *summum* nostrum *finem*: necessum omninò est, persuasi simus...Qui 3. Istam suam *sufficientiam*, nobis *communicare* possit & velit, per suam *efficientiam*, seu operationes."

2. An exception is the study of Richard A. Muller, *Post-Reformation Reformed Dogmatics*, (Grand Rapids: Baker Academic, 2003), vol.3, *The Divine Essence and Attributes*.

3. Franciscus Gomarus, *Opera Theologica Omnia* (Amsterdam: Joh. Janssonius, 1664); Johannes Cocceius, *Opera Omnia Theologica* (Amsterdam: P&J Blaev, 1701); Herman Witsius, *Miscellaneorum sacrorum* (Utrecht: Franciscus Halma, 1692).

4. Petrus van der Hagen, *Verborgenheyt der Godsaligheit*, (Amsterdam: Johannes van Someren, 1677).

5. William Ames, *Marrow of Sacred Divinity, drawne out of the holy Scriptures, and the Interpreters thereof, and brought into Method* (London: Edward Griffin, 1642); Samuel Maresius, *Collegium Theologicum sive Systema Breve Universæ Theologiæ*, (Groningen: Franciscus Brochorstius, 1656); Simon Oomius, *Institutiones Theologiæ Practicæ* (Bolsward: Samuel Haringhouk, 1676); Theodor Undereyck, *Hallelujah, dat is, Godt in den sondaar verheerlijkt, ofte verhandelinge van het Grote Genadenwerk Godes in Christo*, trans. Wilhelm Vos, (Amsterdam: Jan Bouman, 1694); Franciscus Burmannus, *Synopsis Theologiæ & speciatim*

doctrinal-elenctic[8]) and *praxis* (systematic theology[9]). Thus, the doctrine of God of the Reformed Orthodox in the seventeenth-century was articulated in different settings, such as the academy and the congregation.[10] Therefore, before we examine the doctrine of God of the *TPT* in more detail, we provide here a succinct overview of some of Mastricht's contemporaries. Two remarks are in order to justify the selected authors and works. First, our examination focuses primarily on the structure of and summarized content of their doctrine of God. Second, the choice of these theologians is prompted by the life and work of Mastricht. The *Synopsis purioris theologiæ* (1625) was one of Mastricht's textbooks during his study at the University of Utrecht. The University of Franeker, as we have pointed out, was aware of Mastricht's qualities and was previously served by William Ames (1576-1633) and Johannes Cloppenburgh (1592-1652). Furthermore, Mastricht's reference to Ames[11] necessitates the review, in particular, of Ames's *Marrow*. In addition, the theological thought of Cloppenburgh, which awaits a much needed appraisal,[12] although sparingly cited by Mastricht,[13] belongs to the texture

Oeconomiæ Foederum Dei (Utrecht: C. J. Noenardus, 1671); Herman Witsius, *Excercitationes Sacræ in Symbolum quod Apostolorum dicitur* (Franeker: Johannes Gyselaar, 1689). A work with a somewhat similar order but more comprised is J. Polyander, A. Rivetus, A. Walaeus, A. Thysius, *Synopsis purioris theologiæ* (Leiden: Elsevier, 1625, sixth edition, H. Bavinck, Leiden: D. Donner, 1881). Other works with similar structure of the doctrine of God are, Andreas Essenius, *Compendium theologiæ dogmaticum: ubi præter explicationes theticas, & assertiones scripturarias, in controversiis vera sententia passim confirmatur argumentis, ad certas & paucas classes revocatis: præcipuæ adversariorum exceptiones atque objectiones clare proponuntur, & solvuntur: usus autem practici suis locis etiam adscribuntur* (Utrecht: Meinardus à Dreunen, 1669); Abraham Heidanus, *Corpus Theologiæ Christianæ in Quindecim Locos*, 2 vols. (Leiden: Johannes de Vivie & Jordanus Luchtmans, 1686); Franciscus Turrettinus, *Institutio theologiæ elencticæ* (Geneva: Samuel de Tournes 1688-1689); Johannes Braunius, *Leere der Verbonden*, 3rd ed. (Amsterdam: Isaac Stokmans, 1723).

6. Franciscus Ridderus, *Sevenvoudige Oeffeningen over de Catechismus zijnde, ziel-bereydende, wærheydt-bevestigende, geloofs-bevorderende, dwalingh-stuttende, practyck-lievende, gemoet-onderrichtende,* (Rotterdam: Joannes Borstius, 1671).

7. Friedrich Spanheim, *Opera*, vol. III, *Qui complectitur theologica scripta omnia, exegetico-didactico-elenctica* (Leiden: Johannes du Vivie, Isaaco Severino, 1701-1703).

8. Essenius, *Compendium*.

9. Wilhelmus à Brakel, *ΛΟΓΙΚΗ ΛΑΤΡΕΙΑ, dat is Redelijke Godtsdienst in welken de goddelijke Waerheden van het Genade-Verbondts worden verklaert* (Rotterdam: Reynier van Doesburgh, 1700).

10. We do not suggest here a dichotomy. The "academy" was involved in the congregations by preaching and participating as elder, minister in the consistory, classis, and synodical meetings.

11. Petrus van Mastricht, *Theologiæ didactico-elenchtico-practicæ prodromus tribus speciminibus* (Amsterdam: Johannes van Someren, 1666), præfatio: "...(teste Amesio in paraenesi ad Studiosos suffixâ ejus Casibus conscientiæ," idem, *Theoretico-practica theologia* (1699), præfatio: "Methodum sectatus sum, Cl. Amesii, in *Medullâ & Casibus conscientiæ*, quæ mihi visa est, adeò commoda, ut aliam ei substituere, nec voluerim, nec debuerim."

12. David N. J. Poole, *The History of the Covenant Concept from the Bible to Johannes Cloppenburgh: De foedere Dei* (San Francisco: Mellen Research University Press, 1992).

13. Mastricht, *Theoretico-practica theologia*, II.27.xviii, 266, 267: "(267) Ex professo & accuratè, hoc argumentum tractavit Cl. Cloppenburghius in suis *Vindiciis, pro deitate Spiritus S. adversus Bidellum.*"

of the seventeenth-century Reformed theology. The *Opera Omnia* of Johannes Cocceius (1603-1669) is included partly because of the noted influence of the University of Leiden on the Reformed churches of the Lower Rhineland region. Furthermore, during Cocceius's tenure, Mastricht probably studied briefly at the University of Leiden. Finally, Mastricht's acquaintance with Theodor Undereyck (1635-1693) and Wilhelmus à Brakel (1635-1711), and Simon Oomius's (1630-1706) recollection of Mastricht's *Prodromus*, as well as Mastricht's familiarity with Franz Burman (1628-1679), his colleague at the University of Utrecht, provide sufficient reasons to include these theologians in our review.

William Ames wrote at the opening of the *Medulla*, or *Marrow of Sacred Divinity*,[14] that God may be known by the two pillars of faith: the divine sufficiency—the divine essence and subsistence—and divine efficiency.[15] Limiting ourselves to the former, we note that Ames first argued that the divine essence is affirmed in the divine name and attributes.[16] The divine perfections, "abstract and concrete," then, are attributed to God and are to be distinguished among themselves and from the divine essence. They belong to the divine essence, being distinct "virtually" or "emmently," whether incommunicable, such as omnipotence, immensity, and eternity, or communicable.[17] Accordingly, God's attributes set forth what and who God is.[18] The former comprises the divine spirituality and life.[19] The latter includes the divines oneness and infinity, and thus He is immeasurable, incomprehensible, and eternal.[20] Moreover, as part of the "who God is," Ames then states, "the greatness of God" also includes the divine simplicity, immutability, eternity, and immensity.[21] Ames distinguishes the divine understanding and will. Both God's intellect and His will are without composition, unchangeable, eternal, and infinite.[22]

Ames then proceeds to the discussion on the Holy Trinity: the subsistence of God. Here, following the classical creedal description of the Trinity,[23] Ames concludes that

---

14. Ames, *Marrow of Sacred Divinity*, I.4.xxvi, 13. See for a discussion on the terminological distinctions in the doctrine of the "attributes," Muller, *Post-Reformation Reformed Dogmatics*, III:215. Note, the translation by Eusden, William Ames, *The Marrow of Theology*, ed. John D. Eusden (Grand Rapids: Baker Books, 1997), 85, fn. 10, is incorrect.

15. Ames, *Marrow of Sacred Divinity*, I.4.xiii-ix, 11.

16. Ibid., xiv-lxvi, 11-16.

17. Ibid., xx-xxi, 12, 13.

18. Ibid., xxxi, 13.

19. Ibid., xxxiii-xxxv, 13, 14.

20. Ibid., xli-xlviii, 14, 15.

21. Ibid., l, 15.

22. Ibid., lii-lxi, 15, 16.

23. Ibid, I.5.ii, 17. Eusden writes in William Ames, *The Marrow of Theology*, ed. John D. Eusden, 22: "The Savior-Son is begotten in spiritual generation from the Creator-Father, the Sanctifier-Holy Spirit, proceeds from both Father and Son. Spiritual generation is not the same as physical or temporal

such a Triune God, the object of faith, provides everything for living well.[24] Thus, in respect to the structure, Ames writes of three modes of divine being using a scholastic pattern. God is known is His essence (*essentia*), His subsistence (*subsistentia*), and His efficiency or working power (*efficientia*). The divine essence, then, consists of the divine name and attributes, whereby the latter are distinguished as incommunicable and communicable attributes, which collectively describe the *Quid* (spirituality and life), *Quantus* (unity and infinity), and *Qualis* (will and intellect) *sit Deus*. In respect to content, the doctrine of the Trinity points ultimately to Ames's goal: a doctrine of living to God.

The *Synopsis purioris theologiæ* discusses the doctrine of God after setting forth the prolegomena of theology and the doctrine of Scripture.[25] The former is defined by Polyander as a *scientia* and *sapientia* of divine things.[26] God is the object of theology: the doctrine of God and divine benefits and creation.[27] He then states that theology should be studied theoretically and practically.[28] Its ultimate aim, however, is the glorification of God.[29] With these preceding *loci* and premises of theology, the doctrine of God is discussed beginning with the divine nature and attributes, with subsequent reflection on the Trinity. In respect to the former, the chapter is structured as follows: existence, name, essence, and attributes of God. Examining the chapters on the divine attributes, Thysius argues that God's essence, ascribed with properties, is spiritual. These properties, the incommunicable and communicable attributes,[30] vary among themselves, not *realiter* but comparatively as far as they can be humanly perceived.[31] To the incommunicable

generation. Father, Son and Holy Spirit are of God eternally and equally; there was not a time when one existed without the others. They consist of each in his own way, the divine subsistence known to man in creation, salvation and spiritual maintenance."

24. Ames, *Marrow of Sacred Divinity*, I.5.xxiv, 21.

25. In respect to the doctrine of Scripture, Walaeus states regarding its interpretation that the grammatical-historical sense is prevalent. However, Scripture can be explained anagogically, tropologically and analogically but not allegorically except where Scripture permits. See Polyander *et al.*, *Synopsis purioris theologiæ*, 5. corollarium.i, 48: "Etsi S. Scriptura per Anagogen, Tropologiam, Analogiam, similesque explicandi modos, ad Ecclesiæ usus, in multis locis applicari possit, unicus tamen immediatus et certus ejus sensus est, sensus grammaticus seu historicus."

26. Ibid., 1.ix, 2: "Theologiam definimus, scientiam vel sapientiam rerum divinarum."

27. Ibid., xii, 3: "Objectum Theologiæ cum res divinas esse asserimus, sub hac applicatione complectimur: 1. Deum ipsum. 2. Dogmata et beneficia divina ad salutarem Dei cognitionem, communionem et fruitionem necessaria. 3. quæcunque sunt in rerum natura a Deo creata et ordinata, quatenus ad Deum tamquam ad suum principium et finem sunt referenda."

28. Ibid., xxii, 5. On the question of whether theology is theoretical or practical, Polyander answers that some state that it is either theoretical or practical, and some affirm both. Of the latter Polyander notes, "Nos postremorum responsioni sic astipulamur, ut censeamus eam et theoreticam et practicam esse nuncupandam."

29. Ibid., xxi, 5: "Ultimus Theologiæ finis est Deo gloria."

30. These are also identified respectively as *attributa primi generis* and *attributa secundi generis* (Ibid., 6.xxiv and xxx, 54, 56)

31. Ibid., xxi, 53.

attributes belong the divine *simplicitas, immutabilitas, infinitas, æternitas,* and *immensitas.* The communicable perfections are divided into the immanent—divine life, intellect and will—and the emanant attributes—divine power, dominion, affection, and virtues.[32] The chapter is closed with a polemic section refuting the atheists, Manicheans, Anthropomorphists, and idolatry.

Examining the chapters on the Trinity, one notes that a general discussion is followed by two separate chapters, one on the Father and Son and one on the Holy Spirit. In respect to the disputations on the Trinity, the general chapter examines the meaning of the words *trinity,* and *person,* and discusses the relationship and unity of the divine essence and Persons. Polyander points to a certain danger in defining "this mystery through human reason," which should be "adored through a humble faith."[33] With additional testimony of Scripture, including an appeal to the divine name Elohim,[34] the chapter concludes polemically by refuting the antitrinitarians and Socinians.

Walæus deals in the subsequent chapter with the Person of the Father and the Son. The latter, generated by the Father (Ps. 2:7), is equal with the first Person of the Trinity, and the divine names and attributes apply to both. Polemically, the Leiden professor rebuts the Samosatians, Arians and the Socinians. The final chapter on the Trinity defines the Holy Spirit as Person, ascribed with the same divine attributes in relation to the Father and the Son and in His work.[35] Thysius concludes this chapter by contesting the heresies of the Macedonians, antitrinitarians, libertines, and Campanus. The content of the doctrine of the Holy Trinity here, as in Ames's *Medulla,* follows the classic western creedal formulation. The Person and His work always reflect the divine attributes and essence. Moreover, the Leiden professors formulated the doctrine of the Trinity based on Scripture and clarified their position by rebutting divergent views.

Johannes Cloppenburgh attests in his *Theologica Opera Omnia,* a prolific and wide-ranging theological interest.[36] In the context of our study, we are interested in the

---

32. Ibid., xxxi, and xxxvi, 56, 57.

33. Ibid., 7.xiv, 62, "Modus ergo hujus mysterii, ut rationi humanæ inexplicabilis, humili potius fide adorandus, quam periculosis locutionibus definiendus est."

34. Ibid., xli, 66. Polyander refers to the following Old Testament texts: Ps. 45:7; Gen. 1:26; Num. 6:23; Isa. 6:3; Gen. 48:16; Exod. 14:19. New Testament testimonies include Matt. 3:16; John 14:16; 2 Cor. 13:13; 1 John 5:7; Rev. 1;4, 5.

35. Ibid., 9.iv, 77: "Est autem Spiritus Dei sive Sanctus, tertia Deitatis seu Sacro-Sanctæ individuæ Trinitatis hypostasis, id est, persona, a Deo Patre Filioque ineffabili spiratione, sine ulla perpessione ab æterno procedens: adeoque ab utriusque persona singulari distincta, et essentiæ unione et communione conjuncta."

36. Johannes Cloppenburgh, *Theologica Opera Omnia* (Amsterdam: Gerardus Borstius, 1684). Volume 1 is exegetical-didactical oriented and includes disputations and chapters on, (1) *Sacrificiorum Patriarchalium Schola Sacra,* (2) *Epistola ad Clariss. Virum Ludovicum de Dieu,* (3) *Exercitationes Juveniles,* (4) *De Foenore et Usuris,* (5) *Syntagma Exercitationum Selectarum* (including disputations on *de Foedere Dei et Testamento V & N*), and (6) *Excercitationes Super Locos Communes Theologicos.* Volume 2 is more elenctically oriented and includes (1) *Disputationes xv De Canone theologiæ et Judicio Controversiarum,* (2) *Gangræna Theologiæ Anabaptisticæ,* (3) *Disputationes vii ad quinque articulos Remonstrantium,* (4) *Compendiolum*

Excercitationes Super Locos Communes Theologicos, which addresses the doctrine of God. He opens this section of the *Opera* by defining theology as a *doctrina* Θεοδιδακτώ or a Christian religion *sapientia spiritualis*, whereby one has knowledge of the reconciling and redemptive work of Christ unto eternal life and gratitude is shown in the *observantia Deo*.[37] The chapter on *Theology* is followed by several disputations on *Scripture*.[38] Subsequently, Cloppenburgh deals with the doctrine of God respectively on the divine existence, names, and attributes.[39] Then, he discusses the doctrine of predestination, which is followed by the disputation *De Essentiæ Dei Unitate in Trinitate Personarum* and ensuing chapters on *God the Father*, *God the Son*, and *God the Holy Spirit*. In respect to the divine attributes, Cloppenburgh argues very succinctly, for example, that the divine simplicity belongs with infinity to the *negativa Dei attributa*, and immutability (James 1:17; Ps. 102:27, 28; Heb. 1:11, 12) is an *essentia Dei modus singularis*,[40] along with divine incorruptibility and immortality.

In respect to the doctrine of the Trinity, Cloppenburgh develops the *locus* in conjunction with the doctrine of the divine unity. The latter, is, according to the Franeker professor, inferred from Deuteronomy 6:4: יהוה אלהינו יהוה אחד. The former, the doctrine of the Trinity, which is "a mystery," is argued by Cloppenburgh with the testimonies of Tertullianus, Augustine, Boetius, and ecumenical creeds that God is *una essentia et tres substantiæ*. Cloppenburgh discusses the ontological Trinity, including the generation of the Son from the Father and the procession of the Holy Spirit from the First and Second Persons of the Godhead and their works.[41] We conclude, then, that Cloppenburgh's structure of the doctrine of God has its peculiarities, especially the exposition on *Predestination* between the discussion on the *Divine attributes* and *Trinity*. Furthermore, the divine attributes are structured like the Leiden *Synopsis purioris theologiæ* and Ames's *Marrow* but differ in that some divine properties are discussed in one disputation. Finally, as the title of his work indicates, each *locus* includes an exposition of the biblical text and develops from it the related doctrine.

Socinianismi Confutatum, (5) *Vindiciæ pro Deitate Spiritus Sancti*, (6) *Anti-Smalcius*, (7) *Res Judicata*, and (8) *Tractatus Brevis de Sabbatho Christiano*.

37. Ibid., vol. 1, *Excercitationes Super Locos Communes Theologicos*, I.1.iii, 696; I.1.xxi, 699: "Theologia seu Religio Christiana est Sapientia spiritualis, per notitiam Dei Redemptoris jam per Christum exhibitum reconciliati, ac nobis obsignantis firmam spem vitæ æternæ jam quæsitæ, conscientiam stimulans, ad gratitudinis demonstrationem, in cultu & observantia Deo debita."

38. Ibid., 700-723. Cloppenburgh deals in five disputations *De Canone Theologiæ Christianæ*, *De Methodo Fidei qua Scripturis creditur*, *De Ecclesiæ officio circa Scripturam Sacram*, *De Censura librorum Apocryphorum Generalis*, *De Censura librorum Apocryphorum Specialis*, and *De Codicis Bibliorum & Contextus Authentici Integritate*.

39. Ibid., 731-752. The attributes are structured as follows: *Dei Immutabilitate & Immensitate*, 731-35; *Simplicitate Essentiæ Dei absoluta*, 735-38; *Dei Scientia*, 739-40; *Dei Præscientia*, 741-42; *Dei Sanctitate & Justitia*, 743-46; *Dei Potentia, Potestate & Adorabilitate*, 747-50; *Voluntatis Dei Consilio & Decreto*, 750-52.

40. Ibid., II.2.iv-vii, 732.

41. Ibid., I.3.i, 756.

Johannes Cocceius's work is intriguing in the context of our study, because he not only defined theology as *doctrina est secundum pietatem*,[42] as Mastricht did, but Cocceius's *Opera* also attests to vast exegetical labors. At the same time, with the exception of the *loci* of faith, the doctrine of God has been adequately examined in the context of his *Summa Theologiæ*.[43] Our examination of Cocceius's work, then, concentrates briefly on the exegesis of the biblical texts foundational to Mastricht's *loci* of the divine attributes (*Quid sit Deus*)[44] and doctrine of the Holy Trinity (2 Cor. 13:13, v. 14 in English versions)—God the Father (Eph. 3:14-15), God the Son (Ps. 2:7-8), and God the Holy Spirit (John 14:26). Commenting on 2 Corinthians 13:13, Cocceius parallels this text[45] with other Pauline texts.[46] He argues that the text of 2 Corinthians 13:13 attests to a prayer to the Trinity.[47] In addition, he notes that love χάρις ("distinct from ἀγάπη") is attributed to Christ, which should result in the understanding that "to live a life of love, just as Christ loved us and gave himself up for us as a fragrant offering and sacrifice to God (Eph. 5:2)." The final part of the text ἡ κοινωνία τοῦ ἁγίου πνεύματος μετὰ πάντων ὑμῶν , then, attests to the fellowship that is dependent only on God.[48] In respect to Ephesians 3:14-15 (God the Father), Cocceius divides the text into four parts: (1) Τούτου χάριν (2) κάμπτω τὰ γόνατά μου (3) πρὸς τὸν πατέρα τα Κυρια Ιησου Χριστου, (4) ἐξ οὗ πᾶσα πατριὰ ἐν οὐρανοῖς καὶ ἐπὶ γῆς ὀνομάζεται. In the second part, he identifies God the Father as Lord and Judge.[49] In respect to Psalm 2:7-8 (God the Son), one notes that Cocceius's commentary contains a layout parallel to the syntactical-grammatical structure of the Psalm. He argues that the second psalm speaks of Christ's enthronement, describes the hostility of the nations, and asserts the honor of God and Christ, God the Son, and the

---

42. Cocceius, *Opera Omnia Theologica*, vol. 7, 17, § 1: "Theologia vel significat doctrinam, quæ est secundum pietatem...Receptio hujus doctrinæ *fides* dicitur, quatenus causa recipiendi est testimonium Dei;" § 2: " Igitur Theologia est practica." Cf. Mastricht, *Theoretico-practica theologia*, I.1.ix, 4.

43. W. J. van Asselt, *The Federal Theology of Johannes Cocceius* (Leiden-New York: Brill, 2001), part two, 139-192. According to Van Asselt, Cocceius views faith, bestowed by the Holy Spirit, as the instrument to enter into the covenant of grace (42, 43). For an overview of Cocceius's structure of the divine attributes see *The Federal Theology of Johannes Cocceius*, 160.

44. This will be discussed in part IV, chapter 3 of this study.

45. Η χάρις τοῦ κυρίου Ἰησοῦ Χριστοῦ καὶ ἡ ἀγάπη τοῦ θεοῦ καὶ ἡ κοινωνία τοῦ ἁγίου πνεύματος μετὰ πάντων ὑμῶν

46. 1 Cor 16:23; Rom. 16:24; Gal. 6:18; Eph. 6:24; Phil. 4:23; 1 Thess. 5:28; 2 Thess. 3:18; Philem. 25.

47. Cocceius, *Opera Omnia Theologica*, vol. 5, *Epist. Ad Corinthios II*, cap. xiii, 455, § 55: "Vers 13...Est in distinctis hisce comprecationibus typus & unitatis & trinitatis. Invocatur hic Trinitas ut & Apocal. 1:4, 5."

48. Ibid., § 60, "Μετὰ πάντων ὑμῶν neque enim est in cœtu discrimen inter fidelis quoad hoc. Et ita à solo Deo in omnibus dependent & consummantur."

49. Ibid., vol. 5, *Commentarius in Epistol. Ad Ephesios*, cap. iii, 176, § 87: "Deus igitur ab homine, quem ad imaginem suam condiderat, debebat adiri, ut *dominus & judex*...." The text division (1)-(4) takes place respectively in § 82-83, 84, 85, and 91-94.

dedication of Christ.[50] On verse 7, he comments that the text points to the eternal *pactum*, which legally is immutable, "as indicated by אל (Isa. 38:19)."[51] Central for Cocceius is the christological interpretation of this psalm, though he does not dismiss the idea present in the text of the relationship of God the Father and the Son. In respect to John 14:26 (God the Holy Spirit), he comments that the Holy Spirit proceeds from the Father and the Son. The Spirit, who, according to Cocceius, is a Person ("ἐκεῖνο *ille*. Antecedit πνευμα. Indicat, esse personam..."), the *paracletus*, the comforter, and the "doctor or teacher."[52] We thus note Cocceius's careful attention to philological and grammatical issues in the biblical text. Further, he rarely mentions doctrinal issues with the exception of the exegesis of Psalm 2, where he recognized the (eternal) covenant. Exegesis is, for Cocceius, a biblical search for the literal meaning of the text, resorting to the original biblical languages and other scriptural testimonies in order to interpret the text rightly.

Franz Burman opens his *Synopsis Theologiæ* by noting the centrality of the covenant in the exposition of theology.[53] Theology is described by Burman as the doctrine of the true religion, divinely revealed, directed to His honor and our salvation,[54] and divided into faith and love (2 Tim. 1:13).[55] Subsequently, Burman deals with the doctrine of Scripture followed by the doctrine of God.[56] The attributes of the divine spirituality and the *locus* of the divine simplicity and immutability are located, respectively, almost at the beginning and end of the *locus*. He argues that the distribution of the divine attributes

50. Ibid., *Opera Anekdota Theologica et Philologica*, vol. 1, *Analysis Psalmorum*, Ps. II, 382: "A. Descriptio & exsibilatio hostilium motuum & conatuum per I. Interrogationem causæ motus gentium...II. Narrationem studii Judæorum...B. Assertio honoris Dei & Christi...C. Prædicatio Christi...."

51. Ibid., (C.I): "Præfatio vers 7. Narrabo *juxta statutum*, quemadmodum audivi & vidi apud Patrem meum, utque is mecum ab æterno pactus est lege immutabili, ita exponam hominibus אל, *ad* conventiæ. Sic. Isa.38:19."

52. Ibid., *Opera Omnia Theologica*, vol. 4, *Commentarius in Euangel. Johannis*, cap.xiv, 219, § 67: "Unde apparet, verè videri Patrem & Filium ab eo, qui accipit Spiritum Sanctum." See also § 68-69 for *paracletus*, doctor.

53. Burmannus, *Synopsis Theologiæ*, title page and I, 1 (chapter heading).

54. Ibid., I.2.xxx, 9: "Doctrina, quæ hanc veram religionem tradit, *Theologia* vocatur; veteribus *Theologice* dicta. Quæ inde describitur: doctrina veræ religionis à Deo nobis patefactæ, eam dirigens ad ipsius gloriam & nostram salutem."

55. Ibid., lxxi, 17: "Cum autem religio, quam tradit Theologia, constet ex vero de Deo sensu, & recto ejus cultu, inde commodè distribui potest Theologia in duas partes, quæ vitam spiritualem constituunt, nimirum in notiam seu fidem, & obedientiam seu charitatem... 2 Tim.1:13."

56. Ibid. The second *locus De Deo* is divided into the divine existence (I.14), aseity and unity (I.15), names (I.16), spirituality & invisibility (I.17), infinity and perfection (I.18), the attributes in general (I.19), divine life (I.20), intellect and knowledge (I.21), will (I.22), the attributes belonging to: the affections (I.23), the virtues (I.24), the divine omnipotence (I.25), omnipresence (I.26), eternity (I.27), simplicity and immutability (I.28), glory and beatitude (I.29). The third *locus S.S. Trinitate* I.31-36, deals in four lengthy chapters on the Trinity, Persons, and the economy of the three Persons.

varies: (1) proper and metaphoric, (2) positive and negative, (3) absolute and relative, and (4) incommunicable and communicable.[57] This differentiation of the divine attributes, Burman argues, is *modalis & rationis* but *realiter* not distinct in God.[58] Notably in his discussion on the divine spirituality and simplicity, he does not seek scriptural support in John 4:24 but combines the attributes of simplicity and immutability because, he argues, God is simple and therefore immutable.[59]

In respect to the Trinity, Burman first gives a general description of the doctrine of the Trinity, modeled after the language of the classic western creeds.[60] However, in addition, he discusses the economic Trinity in a distinct chapter. He argues that the Trinity can be distinguished in the *modus operandi*; the Father and the creation, the Son and the redemption, and the Holy Spirit and the consummation.[61] In his further exposition, Burman gives slightly more attention to the work of the Holy Spirit. In particular he emphasizes the practical implication that the third Person of the Trinity should not be grieved as the Comforter and Teacher of the believer.[62] Burman's structure of the doctrine of God, then, resembles the preceding examined works but differs in the organization of the divine attributes.

Wilhelmus à Brakel defined theology as a reasonable service.[63] Following the opening chapters on theology and Scripture, Brakel proceeds with the doctrine of God. The divine essence, expressed in Exodus 3:14 is revealed in His names and attributes.[64] The latter are divided into communicable and incommunicable.[65] Moreover, the

57. Ibid., I.19.xvi, 111.

58. Ibid., viii, 110: "Cum autem omnis rerum distinctio triplex sit, maxima, media, & minima, *realis* nimirum, *modalis & rationis*, attributa Dei *realiter* à Deo non differunt, neque ab essentia ejus quid diversum sunt."

59. Ibid., I.28.i, 156 (*De Simplicitate & Immutabilitate Dei*): "Ultimum Dei attributum, ex omnium unione fluens, est simplicitas ejus; quæ omnium attributorum Dei arctissimum nexum, & individuam unitatem & identitatem dicit; unde illa nec seperationem nec mutationem ullam pati possunt Exod. 3:14."

60. Ibid., I.30.ii, 161: "Ubi nobis occurrit augustum illud S.S. Trinitatis mysterium. Cujus summa est, unicam esse divinam naturam & essentiam, tribus personis communem, quæ per incommunicabiles proprietates sunt à sese invicem distrinctæ."

61. Ibid., I.36.x, 230: "*Patri*, ut primæ personæ, primum tribuitur opus, nempe *Creationis...*;" ibid., xi, 230: "*Filio* in œconomiâ operum speciatim attribuitur operis redemtionis peractio;" ibid.,xiii, 231: "Similiter *Spiritui S.* quo ad ordinem agendi tribuitur rerum consummatio."

62. Ibid., I.36.xvi, 233: "Est ergo ille perpetuus Ecclesiæ custos & rector...estque individuus ejus in terris hisce comes ac dux & Paracletus ac advocatus, cum apud Deum, religiosos motus atque affectus in fidelibus ciendo, & tenerum balbumque ipsorum os figurando, precesque ipsis veluti præformando Rom. 8:26, 27. See also ibid., xvii-xviii, 233, 234.

63. Brakel, *ΛΟΓΙΚΗ ΛΑΤΡΕΙΑ, dat is Redelyke Godtsdienst*, I:1, 1.

64. Ibid., 3.v, 68.

65. Ibid., 69-107. The incommunicable attributes include, for Brakel, the divine perfection (III.viii), eternity (III.ix), infinity and omnipresence (III.x), simplicity and unity (III.xiii), and immutability (III.xiv). The communicable attributes are the divine science (III.xvi), will (III.xxiv), holiness (III.xxxi), goodness

exposition of Brakel's doctrine of the divine attributes and Trinity is in agreement with other Reformed orthodox explications. Where Brakel differs in his system of theology is the practical dimension to the exegetical and doctrinal reflection of the *loci*. Here, he directs and counsels the reader toward God in Christ. For example, he concludes the chapter on the Trinity with the question,

> "Siet dær, is 'er nu geene nuttigheyt in het geloove van de Heylige Drie-Eenigheyt? Is het niet alleen de grondt van een waerlyk Godsalig leven, ende fonteyne van alle vertroostinge?[66]

We conclude, then, that Brakel provides a more practical dimension to the exposition of the doctrines and in particular points to the comfort for the believer.

Theodor Undereyck's central concern of the *Hallelujah* is—in question-and- answer format—about how God will be glorified in the sinner and about the great work of God's grace through Christ. Moreover it is about the covenant of grace, which "after the eternal *pactum* between the Father and the Son" pertains to the sinner in the Old and New Testament dispensation. Undereyck opens his work with the question, "What do all people desire?" and answers, "Everything necessary for one's comfort and salvation."[67] This comfort, he argues, is found in Scripture, where God reveals His perfections: as a living Spirit (John 4:24), one who is self-existent, incomprehensible, eternal, omnipresent, and immutable (Mal. 3:6, James 1:17). He possesses intellect and will and is holy and righteous, loving, merciful, and gracious. Moreover, God is a simple being (John 17:3), one in Three Persons (1 John 5:7).[68] Thus, Undereyck's distribution of the divine attributes resembles the scholastic division of *Quid sit Deus* (spirituality, aseity), *Quantus sit Deus* (incomprehensibility, eternality, omnipresence, and immutability) and *Qualis sit Deus* (intellect, will, holy and righteous, loving, merciful and gracious).[69]

Following the discussion on the divine attributes, Undereyck moves to questions regarding the Trinity. First he discusses the ontological Trinity and notes that the Three Persons are one in essence, whereby the Son is generated from the Father (Ps. 2:7) and the Holy Spirit proceeds from the Father and the Son.[70] However, he raises the question

(III.xxxii), love (III.xxxiii), grace (III.xxxiv), mercy (III.xxxv), patience (III.xxxiv), justice (III.xxxviii), and power (potentia) (III.xli).

66. Ibid., 4.i, 153.

67. Undereyck, *Hallelujah*, I.1, 1: "Wat begeren, en waar na trachten alle mensen? Naar alles, 't geen een yder oordeeld tot syn hoogste vergenoeginge, troost, and zaligheyt nut en goet te zyn." NB. Each answer, through the entire work, is supported by scriptural references.

68. Ibid., II.1, 4: "Spreekt de H. Schrift, behalven 't geen van Godts opperste volmaaktheyt, tot des sondaars hooghste vergenoeging en troost? Ja gewisselyk...soo God is een levendige Geest...en evenwel Vader, Soon, en H. Geest."

69. Ibid.: "God is...syne grootheid...syn verstand en wil..." We infer from this division, God is (*Quid sit*)...syne grootheid (*Quantus sit*)...syn verstand en wil (*Qualis sit*).

70. Ibid., III.1, 10,11: "de Soon is van de Vader gegenereert geworden, en doet met den selven den H. Geest uytgaan."

of why, if the Father and Son are equal, Scripture indicates that the Father and Son are, respectively, Lord and Servant. The reason is, according to the pastor of Bremen, "the great work of redemption."[71] God the Father is infuriated as Lord and Judge by the sinner, and the Son, in the council of peace, took the form of Servant and through His work on earth glorified the Father.[72] In summary, Undereyck describes the Trinity ontologically in a classic western formulation but pays special attention to the economic Trinity in relation to the work of redemption, proceeding from the council of peace to the covenant of grace.

Simon Oomius's work on the doctrine of God in his *Institutiones Theologiæ Practicæ* has recently been examined in detail.[73] However, it is noteworthy, in the context of our study, to point out that Oomius's lengthy expositions of the doctrines focus on the practical aspects of theology, particular in his discussion on the Holy Trinity. [74]

We conclude, then, that our examination demonstrates the attention of the Reformed orthodox of the seventeenth century to the doctrine of God—exegetically (Cocceius), doctrinally (Ames, *Synopsis purioris theologiæ*, Cloppenburgh, Burman), elenctically (*Synopsis purioris theologiæ*), and practically (Brakel, Undereyck, Oomius). Moreover, the doctrine of God resembles a similar structure of moving from the doctrine of the divine existence and essence to the doctrine of the Trinity. However, the doctrine of the divine attributes reveals a variety of ordering of the divine perfections, with the scholastic division of *Quid, Qualis, Quantus* sometimes present. Further, in respect to the doctrine of the Trinity, which is stable in its expression of western creedal formulation, attention is given to the discussion of the ontological Trinity, whereby federal theologians such as Cocceius, Burman, and Undereyck give particular attention to the economic Trinity. The Reformed orthodox doctrine of God thus is consistent in its articulation but varies in its approaches. Mastricht's approach, as we will see, combines the different approaches of his contemporaries.

71. Ibid., III.3, 12.

72. Ibid.: "By aldien de Sone den Vader gelijk is, waarom schijnt dan de H. Schrift vanden Vader meestendeel te spreken, als van een grotere dan de Soon, so datse beyde genoegsaam, als Heer en Knecht van malkander onderscheyden werden? Het groote werk der Verlossing is daar van de oorzaak. . ."

73. Gregory D. Schuringa, *Embracing Leer and Leven: The Theology of Simon Oomius in the context of the Nadere Reformatie Orthodoxy* (Grand Rapids: Ph.D. diss., Calvin Theological Seminary, 2003).

74. Simon Oomius, *Institutiones Theologiæ Practicæ* (Schiedam: Laurens van der Wiel, 1680), cap. v-viii, 166-260.

Chapter 2
The *Quid Sit Deus*

The *Quid sit Deus* consists, for Mastricht, in the divine spirituality, simplicity, and immutability.[1] In this chapter we examine Mastricht's exposition of the divine spirituality and simplicity. This examination is concerned with the structure and content of Mastricht's description of these divine "essential" attributes.[2] In addition—and, in particular, in light of a rather negative assessment of the scholastic metaphysically constructed doctrine of divine simplicity[3]—an attempt is made to answer the question of how and why Mastricht exposited these two divine attributes together. The chapter, therefore, offers a descriptive analysis of Mastricht's understanding of the divine spirituality and simplicity as found in the *Theoretico-practica theologia* (*TPT*).

Mastricht explicates the divine spirituality and simplicity by beginning with an exegesis of the Johannine text, πνεῦμα ὁ θεός, καὶ τοὺς προσκυνοῦντας αὐτὸν ἐν πνεύματι καὶ ἀληθείᾳ δεῖ προσκυνεῖν.[4] In order to evaluate Mastricht's approach to these divine attributes, exegetically, doctrinally, elenctically, and practically, we will succinctly review the biblical interpretation of this text by Reformed orthodox theologians or works between 1625 and 1700, namely, the *Synopsis purioris theologiæ* (1625), the *Staten-bijbel* (1637), Johannes Cloppenburgh (1592-1652), Johannes Cocceius (1603-1669), Franciscus Ridderus (1620-1683) , Simon Oomius (1630-1706), Wilhelmus à Brakel (1635-1711), Theodor Undereyck (1635-1693), and Herman Witsius (1636-1708). These theologians, so-called Voetian or Cocceian, offer a context for Mastricht's work. Moreover, in order to preserve the trajectory of the biblical interpretation of John 4:24, the material will be examined in the order of the first publication date.

---

1. Petrus van Mastricht, *Theoretico-practica theologia qua, per singula capita theologica, pars exegetica, dogmatica, elenchtica et practica, perpetua successione conjugantur; accedunt historia ecclesiastica, plena quidem, sed compendiosa, idea theologiæ moralis, hypotyposis theologiæ asceticæ etc. proin opus quasi novum* (Utrecht: Thomas Appels, 1699), II.6 (*De Spiritualitate & Simplicitate Dei*), 98-107, and II.7 (*De Immutabilitate Dei*), 107-111. He concludes his doctrinal part on divine spirituality by stating that the divine simplicity and immutability flows forth from the spiritual nature of God. Cf. ibid., II.vi.7, 99. See also Adriaan C. Neele, *A Study of Divine Spirituality, Simplicity, and Immutability in Petrus van Mastricht's Doctrine of God* (Th.M. thesis, Calvin Theological Seminary, 2002).

2. See for a discussion of the treatment of the essential attributes in post-Reformation Reformed orthodox theology, Richard A. Muller, *Post-Reformation Reformed Dogmatics*, (Grand Rapids: Baker Academic, 2003), 3:271-72.

3. Alvin Plantinga, *Does God Have a Nature?* (Milwaukee: Marquette University Press, 1980), 144; John M. Frame, *The Doctrine of God. A Theology of Lordship* (Phillipsburg: P&R Publishing, 2002), 220-30; Brian Davies, "Classical Theism and the Doctrine of Divine Simplicity," in *Language, Meaning and God: Essays in Honor of Herbert McCabe, OP*, ed. Brian Davies (London: Cassell, 1987), 59; Gerrit Immink, "The One and Only: The Simplicity of God," in *Understanding the Attributes of God*, ed. Gijsbert van den Brink, Marcel Sarot (Frankfurt an Main: Peter Lang, 1999), 117 (Aquinas).

4. John 4:24, "God is Spirit and those who worship him must worship [him] in spirit and in truth."

The Context

The Leiden *Synopsis purioris theologiæ* refers to John 4:24 as a scriptural foundation for divine simplicity, linking it to spirituality as the attribute of God's essence.[5] Many after 1625 echoed this scriptural testimony for the doctrine of divine simplicity and spirituality. The *Staten-bijbel* annotates on the text:

> Dat is [God is een Geest] een geestelijk, onzienlijk wezen, en wil daarom gediend worden met een dienst, die met zijne natuur overeenkomt, dat is, die inwendig en geestelijk is, voortkomende uit een oprecht en gelovig hart; Rom. 12:1,2.[6]

Thus, the annotators infer divine spirituality and invisibility from the text, arguing that this should lead one to serve God in accordance with His essence: spiritually and uprightly.

Cocceius comments in his commentary on the Gospel of John that the words *Deus est Spiritus* in John 4:24 point to who God is: eternal, immutable, omniscient, holy, mighty and good.[7] He also notes that the words in the remainder of the text reveal how one should glorify God. Cocceius takes a philological view of the text, and his primary emphasis centers on a discussion of the divine attributes by which one comes to know who God is. Specifically, in his *Summa theologiæ*, John 4:24 is used as the biblical foundation for his discussion of the spirituality of God as an incommunicable attribute.[8] Thus, according to Cocceius, the philological exegesis of John 4:24 leads primarily to doctrine but also should lead one to worship God.

Ridderus discusses John 4:24 in the context of the divine attributes in the *Sevenvoudige oefeningen over de Catechismus*[9] in the chapter on Lord's Day eight on the opening of the Apostles' Creed. In a sevenfold approach, the pastor of Rotterdam discusses the essence and attributes of God. The various "*oefeningen*" include soul-preparing, truth-confirming, historic-beneficial, faith-stimulating, heresy-stopping, practical loving, and conscience-relieving (*gemoed-ontlastende*), which contribute to his explanation of the attributes. On the simplicity or spirituality of God, Ridderus notes that it points to God's perfectness, that He is of no composition.[10] It is Ignatius, according to Ridderus, who said in several places, "God is eternal, God is invisible: God

---

5. J. Polyander, A. Rivetus, A. Walaeus, A. Thysius, *Synopsis purioris theologiæ* (Leiden: Elsevier, 1625).

6. *Biblia, dat is de gantsche H. Schrifture, vervattende alle de canonijcke boeken des Ouden en des Nieuwen Testaments* (Leyden: Paulus Ærtsz. van Ravensteyn, 1637).

7. Johannes Cocceius, *Opera Omnia Theologica* (Amsterdam: P&J Blaev, 1701), vol. 4, *Commentarius in Euangel. Johannis*, (Amsterdam: P&J Blaev, 1701), 131, § 13-16.

8. Ibid., vol. 7, *Summa Theologiæ*, 169, § 35.

9. Franciscus Ridderus, *Sevenvoudige Oeffeningen over de Catechismus zijnde, ziel-bereydende, wærheydt-bevestigende, geloofs-bevorderende, dwalingh-stuttende, practyck-lievende, gemoet-onderrichtende*, (Rotterdam: Joannes Borstius, 1671), 186-213.

10. Ibid., 191.

is a Spirit."[11] The majority of the discussion on Lord's Day eight, however, is on heresy-stopping and the faith-stimulating points. In the latter, Ridderus focuses on the practical aspects of the essence and attributes of God. The divine simplicity should lead one to go his way in simplicity and uprightness (2 Cor. 1:12). Furthermore, John 4:24 teaches one to worship God in spirit and in truth and to glorify Him in one's spirit.[12] In summary, Ridderus finds support in this biblical text to discuss divine simplicity from a doctrinal, argumentative, and practical perspective in the context of catechetical teaching.

Undereyck discusses the divine attributes, "exposited and described of the Holy Scriptures," in the second chapter of his *Hallelujah*.[13] Following the introduction question, in which he outlines the structure of the divine attributes, he argues the question, "Why do you call God a living Spirit?" Undereyck responds that God is invisible. Though He sometimes reveals Himself to us in an anthropomorphic way, His spiritual essence is the almighty and ever present power of God by which He upholds all creatures (Acts 17:25-28; cf. John 4:24).[14] Undereyck continues his exposition of other divine attributes and closes the chapter with an explication on the divine simplicity. He asks, "Why do you ascribe the simplicity to such a great God?" He replies that the ultimate perfection of God is not a result of the combined divine attributes. No, he asserts, the divine simplicity is like a "stone with multiple perfections, but has only one brilliance, or the sun, with its seemingly one brightness consisting of many colors."[15] He rejects the notion that the divine simplicity is a hindrance for the doctrine of the Trinity because "God reveals Himself in His Word as a simple one in Three Persons."[16] It is noteworthy that Undereyck's answer to the question of the divine simplicity does not refer to a biblical text. In summary, then, he describes as first divine attribute the spirituality of God and as last the simplicity of God.

In his *Institutiones* Oomius deals in one chapter with the divine simplicity and, flowing from this, God's unity, spirituality, invisibility, intangibility, and indepictability.[17] According to Oomius, the teaching of the divine simplicity serves to refute divergent thoughts on the subject, such as those held by heathens, the Manicheans, Audians, Remonstrants, and the papists, all of whom deny the simplicity of God.[18] This attribute

---

11. Ibid., 193. Of particular interest is the *oefening* on the immutability of God, where the author addresses other divine attributes but does not explain their relationship. He notes, here, that the simplicity of God emphasizes that He is the first Being. Cf. ibid., 194.

12. Ibid., 208.

13. Theodor Undereyck, *Hallelujah, dat is, Godt in den sondaar verheerlijkt, ofte verhandelinge van het Grote Genadenwerk Godes in Christo*, trans. Wilhelm Vos, (Amsterdam: Jan Bouman, 1684), I.2, 4.

14. Ibid., I.2, question 2, 5.

15. Ibid., question 21, 10.

16. Ibid., I.3, question 1, 10.

17. Simon Oomius, *Institutiones Theologiæ Practicæ* (Bolsward: Samuel van Haringhouk, 1676), II.2.iii.2.i.2, 177, 178: "Uyt dese Eenvoudigheyt Godts . . . brengen wij af . . . 1. Sijne Eenheit . . . 2. Sijne Geestelickheyt . . . (Joh.4:24)."

18. Ibid., 181-93.

also serves as a warning against thinking of God corporeally, and it encourages the believer to practice true simplicity and uprightness before God and to worship God in spirit and in truth.[19] Here, then, Oomius connects the divine simplicity with the divine spirituality.

Cloppenburgh refers to John 4:24 when he briefly discusses the simplicity of God in his *Loci Communes*. According to him the divine simplicity belongs with divine infinity to the *negativa Dei attributa*. He understands the simplicity, with the other divine attributes, to be identical with and inseperable from the *essentia Dei*.[20] Moreover, he refutes heretical teachings such as those of the Anthropmorpists and Vorstius, and finds scriptural support in "Christ's affirmation, *Deus est Spiritus*, John 4:24."[21] Thus, Cloppenburgh's *disputatio* on divine simplicity is scripturally based on John 4:24 and formulated doctrinally and polemically.

Witsius discusses the article on the Holy Spirit of the Apostlic Creed that one should distinguish between the spirit referring to the essence of God, "like in John 4:24"[22] and the third Person of the Trinity. It is noteworthy that Witsius does not refer to the text of John 4:24 as biblical support when he discusses the first article of the Creed in the chapter that deals with the essence of God as being the object of faith.[23]

Brakel does not rely on John 4:24 in his discussion on the divine essence and the attributes in particular. In this context he argues, although distinguishing between several kinds of composition such as logical, physical, and metaphysical, that in God there is no composition. Regarding the logical composition, Brakel writes:

En als Godt een Geest genoemt wordt, dan wordt het woordt Geest, Gode ende Engelen niet toegeschreven, als een gemeene nature, waer aen Godt en Engelen even gelyk deel hadden; maer de naem is alleenlyk gelyk, en Godt wordt een Geest genaemt, op dat wy daerdoor Godts onsienlykheyt souden verstaen.[24]

Thus, Brakel links divine spirituality to God's invisibility. However, he refers to John 4:24 in his trinitarian discussion specifically on the Holy Spirit and writes:

19. Ibid., 177.

20. Johannes Cloppenburgh, *Theologica Opera Omnia*, (Amsterdam: Gerardus Borstius, 1684), I:735. Cf. Richard A. Muller, *Dictionary of Latin and Greek Theological Terms, Drawn Principally from Protestant Scholastic Theology* (Grand Rapids: Baker Books, 1985), "simplicitas," 283.

21. Ibid., 736.

22. Herman Witsius, *Oefenningen over de Grondstukken van het Algemeyne Christelyke Geloove*, 3d ed. (Rotterdam: Jan Daniel Beman, 1743), 423.

23. Ibid., 44-60.

24. Wilhelmus à Brakel, *ΛΟΓΙΚΗ ΛΑΤΡΕΙΑ, dat is Redelijke Godtsdienst in welken de goddelijke Waerheden van het Genade-Verbondts worden verklaert* (Rotterdam: Reynier van Doesburgh, 1700), I: 3.xiii:75.

En om de geestelyke nature Godts uyt te drukken, soo is er geen gepaster woordt voor ons als het woordt Geest. Somtydts wordt dit woordt wesenlyk genomen, en beteekent de Godtheyt, het Goddelyke Wesen, bestaende in drie Personen, Joh. IV:24.[25]

Thus for Brakel John 4:24 points to the divine essence, whereby His spirituality is related to His divine invisibility. Here, Brakel does not argue with his opponents, as he does in his discussion of the other divine attributes, but gives practical instruction that the doctrinal presentation of the divine essence and attributes:

Deze [Godt] is het voorwerp van onsen Godtsdienst. Daerom is het de plicht van alle Godtsdienstigen, Godt als soodanigh sich gedurigh voor te stellen, in de beschouwinge van hem te leven ende voor syn aengesicht te wandelen.[26]

For Brakel the text of John 4:24 is foundational for his discussion of the divine essence. His doctrinal discussion leads to the practical consequence that God is the object of "our religion," and thus, he asserts, it is our duty to live and walk before God.

With the foregoing overview we are in a position to summarize our findings on Joh. 4:24 as follows:

Year	Source	Material	Inferred from text
1625	Leiden *Synopsis*	Doctrinal	doctrine of divine simplicity and spirituality
1637	*Staten-bijbel*	Annotation	doctrine of divine spirituality
1662	Cocceius	Doctrinal	doctrine of divine attributes
		Exegetical	particularly spirituality
1671	Ridderus	Doctrinal	doctrine of divine spirituality
		Practical	worship of God in "spirit and truth"
		Polemic	
1676	Oomius	Doctrinal	doctrine of divine spirituality
		Practical	living to God
1678	Undereyck	Doctrinal	doctrine of divine spirituality
1684	Cloppenburgh	Doctrinal	doctrine of divine simplicity
		Polemic	
1681	Witsius	Doctrinal	doctrine of divine essence
1700	Brakel	Doctrinal	doctrine of Holy Spirit
		Practical	living to God

25. Ibid., 4.xxvi, 132.

26. Ibid., 3.xliv, 104.

Thus, one observes that the text of John 4:24 is primarily used as scriptural basis for both the doctrine of divine simplicity and the doctrine of spirituality. Cocceius explicates the text philologically before he formulates the doctrine. The Leiden *Synopsis purioris theologiæ* and Untereyck infer from the text principally the doctrinal aspect. Ridderus and Brakel infer from the text, like the annotators of the *Staten-bijbel*, the practical consequence: to live to God in spirit and in truth. It is noteworthy that this practical consequence is stated in different genres, namely, catechetical (Ridderus) and doctrinal-practical (Brakel). Ridderus and Cloppenburgh are polemical or argumentative in the context of their discussion on divine simplicity. They argue against the Anthropomorphists, and whereby Ridderus seeks support from the early church fathers. Thus, our preliminary conclusion is that the biblical interpretation of John 4:24 by these theologians contains in variable degrees aspects of exegesis, doctrine, polemic, and practice. However, it is Mastricht who, at the close of the seventeenth century, codifies and combines the biblical interpretation of John 4:24 of the preceding era in a fourfold approach: exegesis, doctrine, elenctic, and practice.

De Spiritualitate Dei

Mastricht begins the chapter by noting that the attributes or perfections of spirituality and aseity correspond respectively with the divine simplicity and immutability of God. He argues that divine spirituality and simplicity have been merged in this chapter for the reason that "God is a Spirit of Himself."[27]

Exegesis

Mastricht argues that John 4:24 speaks about the nature of God and its consequence: the *praxis pietatis*.[28] The former is distinguished in the descriptor and description. The descriptor is identified in the subject of the sentence ὁ θεός ("note the definite article") and the description of the subject is, πνευμᾶ[29] Mastricht explains that πνευμα is understood in an improper sense when it is rendered in Hebrew and Latin by the linguists as blowing but is understood in a proper sense as signifying the immaterial and simple. The practical consequence is discussed in three parts: the worship of servants—civil (Gen. 23:7; Matt. 18:26) and religious (John 4:23; Ps. 96:9; Matt. 4:10)—the worship in spirit (Ps. 51:8; Matt. 22:37; Rom. 1:9) and truth (1 Cor. 5:8; John 1:17), and the obligation or necessity to worship. He asserts that this part of the text expresses matters for the worshipers, the subject of worship, and its necessity. In other words, the προσκυνοῦντας, which like the Hebrew הׁמתחוה, is rendered as the ones who

27. Mastricht, *Theoretico-practica theologia*, II.6.i, 98. He notes that God's aseity and independence are discussed in the preceding chapters (which is II.2 and II.3, AN).

28. Ibid., ii, 98: "*Cujus verbis, responsum continetur, de naturâ Dei, ejusque, ad praxin pietatis* ἐνεργείᾳ."

29. Ibid.

bow down and worship God, should worship in spirit and in truth. Moreover, Mastricht directs the reader, as pointed out by the word δει, to the practical necessity of the text. This necessity is because, on the one hand, God is a Spirit and therefore is delighted with spiritual matters, as is demanded in the New Testament, and, on the other hand, He rejects the ceremonial worship. In summary, Mastricht grammatically expounds succinctly the text of John 4:24 and infers from it the divine spiritual essence—immaterial and simple—and the consequence for one's worship.

Doctrine

Following the further testimony of Scripture (Num. 24:2, Judg. 3:10, Ezech. 11:24, 2 Cor. 3:17, Acts 3:10) and church fathers (Origene, Augustine) for the doctrine of divine spirituality, Mastricht argues that God is a spirit because, He is the first absolute being, independent (Rom. 9:36), simple ("which we will explain in more detail,") infinite, immutable, and perfect (Matt. 5:48).[30] This description can be noted as an echo of Aquinas's discussion on the divine simplicity, in which he states that God is the first being, infinite and perfect.[31] Mastricht, then, continues to describe in what sense God is a spirit. He is, according to Mastricht, not a spirit in a *sensus tropicus* and *sensus analogicus*, although both the former, such as the wind, animals, and chemicals, and the latter, such as the angels and human souls, are called spirits. However, understood in a proper sense, the divine spirituality is a singular personal divine essence without composition.[32] This singularity of the divine essence is, for Mastricht, not in contradiction to the Trinity. The third Person of the Trinity, he notes, proceeds "with ineffable blowing" from the Father and the Son, yet all Three Persons are an immaterial essence.[33] Mastricht states that the spiritual essence of "anyone but in particular of an uncreated Spirit" consists of *substantia* and not accidents, is immaterial and incorporeal (Luke 24:39), is a quickening power (Rom. 8:2), has intellect (1 Cor. 2:2) and will (*voluntas*). Moreover, he argues that a spirit is invisible, untouchable, and unimaginable and, therefore, that God cannot be captured in images (Deut. 4:14; Acts 17:29).[34] In summary, Mastricht defines in the doctrinal section, along the same division as the exegetical section, in what sense there is a divine spirituality that cannot be represented by images, a notion related to worship.

---

30. Ibid., iv, 99.

31. Thomas Aquinas, *Summa Theologica*, trans. by the Fathers of the English Dominican Province (Benziger Bros. edition, 1947), part I, question 3. For the Latin edition, we have made use of http://www.thelatinlibrary.com/quinas- *Summa Theologica*, prima pars.

32. Mastricht, *Theoretico-practica theologia*, II.6.v, 99: "Spiritus autem Deus est, non sensu *tropico*...nec *analogico*: sed, vel maximè *proprio & univoco*: cum ipse remotissimus sit, ab omni compositione."

33. Ibid.: "Sic autem *spiritus* dicitur, non tantum tertia Persona ὑπόστατικως per appropriationem, quod subsistat, per ineffabilem quandam Patris & Filii spirationem; sed singulæ personæ οὐσιωδως, quod omnes eandem habeant essentiam immaterialem."

34. Ibid., vi and vii, 99.

Elenctic

An examination of the structure of the elenctic section of the divine spirituality shows that Mastricht argues five questions that relate to the twofold division he established in the exegetical section and continued in the doctrinal section: the divine spirituality and worship. The main concern in the first three questions relates to the issues raised in the doctrinal part as to the sense in which God is a spirit and then, in particular, "whether God is a body." This central concern of Mastricht, here, whether God is a body is actually Aquinas's opening question of his discussion of the divine simplicity. Here the question is followed by five objections that are refuted "On the contrary, It is written in the Gospel of St. John (John 4:24): 'God is a Spirit.'"[35] The main concern of Mastricht's last two questions deals with worship and specifically whether God can be represented by images. With the identified structure of the elenctic section, we proceed to examine the structure and content of each of these questions.

The first *quæstio* reads: Is God a Spirit? Mastricht notes that the Anthropomorphist, in order to explain the creation of humanity, argues that God is not a spirit but that He has a thick body.[36] Contrary to this argument, Tertullian seemed to argue in *Adversus Praxean* that God has a thin body. However, according to Mastricht, others understand by this that Tertullian meant *"quod Deus sit, non accidens; sed substantia."*[37] More problematic for Mastricht were the views of Vorstius, the Socinians, and the Cartesian theologians. The latter argue that the word *Spiritus* is not "cartesianized" enough. Mastricht notes that the ideas of Wittichius and other Cartesians run contrary to Scripture as "they would rather have a word that indicates that God is a thinking Essence."[38] Vorstius and the Socinians attribute to God a physical body with a Spirit. Mastricht responds that the Reformed acknowledge the linguistic distinctions related to the word *Spiritus* or *spirare*, as well as πνευμα and רוח, which is to blow, to breathe as pertaining to creatures. He insists, however, that the meaning of spirit points to an immaterial, simple independence. In summary, Mastricht follows structurally the medieval *quæstio* method by raising the question and objections followed by a response. Further, one notes a *historico*-elenctic approach in answering the question. Finally, Mastricht restates his doctrinal position of the divine spirituality: God's aseity and simplicity.

The second question continues the theme of the corporeality of God. Again Mastricht replies from an historic perspective by noting the position of the Anthropomorphist and Tertullian that God has bodily members. Mastricht argues that although the Reformed acknowledge that Scripture uses anthropomorphic language for God, they state that He is "invisible, neither has flesh (Luke 24:39) nor is incorruptible

---

35. Aquinas, *Summa Theologica*, part I, question 3, article 1.

36. Mastricht, *Theoretico-practica theologia*, II.6.viii, 99: "An Deus, proprie & accurate, sit spiritus?"

37. Ibid.

38. Ibid., viii, 100. Mastricht writes here, "Plura huius generis, si aveat lector, conferre poterit *Gangrænam* nostram, Sect. II. cap. VII."

(Rom. 1:23)."[39] Therefore, the notion of the corporeality of God must be rejected based on the right understanding of Scripture. In addition, he argues in the third question, that "even not a thin body can be ascribed to God."[40] In particular this notion is to be rejected, according to Mastricht, because Vorstius probably denies the personal union of the two natures of Christ because he insists that God has a bodily essence in heaven but His power is omnipresent. Therefore, Christ on earth was not united with his divine nature. In summary, the issue of the corporeality of God has, for Mastricht, a soteriological dimension. Thus, Mastricht's three questions related to the essence of the divine spirituality do not concern only the matter of preserving the careful doctrinal formulation arising from Scripture and defined with scholastic method and distinctions. Ultimately they have salvific implications.

Question four states, Can God, who is a spirit, be showed or represented by images? Mastricht articulates the affirmative views of the heathens, Roman Catholics, and Lutherans. The heathens held the idea of the corporeality of gods. Both the Catholics and Lutherans acknowledge the spirituality of God but "have a love for images,"[41] although the Lutherans do not agree with the Λατρεια. In refuting them, Mastricht argues that the Reformed theologians negate the question based on the immateriality of God and therefore God cannot be depicted (Isa. 40:18; Deut. 4:15). In addition, making images of God transgresses the second commandment (Acts 17:29), changes the incorruptible glory of God (Rom. 1:23), and initiates improper thoughts, "which is noted by the heathen philosophers who have vain deliberations."[42] Then the *objectio* is raised that the Roman Catholics and Lutherans refer to the Old Testament, in which God even appeared in human form. Mastricht rejects this objection by stating that the second commandment forbids the depicting of God.

The last question addresses whether it is licit to depict God as an old man in prayer during worship. The Lutherans, according to Mastricht (referring to *Casus Conscientia*, *cap. 2 casus 1* of Franciscus Balduinus), allow images in public worship and do not see this type of depiction as sin. The Reformed on the contrary, although they allow for a concept of God, "if we do not want to be an atheist,"[43] reject this type of representation of God. The main reason for the Reformed position is, according to Mastricht, based on John 4:24. All other conceptions of God are false and vain deliberations that are caused by a darkened understanding. Therefore, Balduinus's first objection, that one has a better concept of God through an image, is not valid for Mastricht because it presupposes that a conception and the understanding of an image are the same. The second objection of Balduinus, that God appeared in the Old Testament in human form, is rejected by Mastricht by referring to Genesis 18: 2, Joshua 5:3, Daniel 7:9, and

39. Ibid., ix, 100.

40. Ibid., x, 100: "An Deo, si non membra corporea, corpus, saltem *subtile*, competat?"

41. Ibid., xi, 101.

42. Ibid.

43. Ibid., xii, 101.

Isaiah 6:1, where the "spectators" understood His extraordinary presence, which directed them to Him but in no way depicted God inwardly or outwardly. Thus, one notes that these questions are answered by Mastricht by articulating the issue at stake (*thesis*), indicating the Reformed theological position (*argumentum Reformatum*), raising *objectiones*, and formulating a *determinatio* or *solutio*. Again, the use of the medieval *quæstio* technique as an important scholastic education method cannot be overlooked. However, as we have seen before, for Mastricht, the proper understanding of Scripture, here, leads one to the right manner of worship.

In summary, the structure and content of the elenctic section shows a continuation of Mastricht's exegetical work on John 4:24 and his doctrinal formulation.[44]

Practical section

In the final section, Mastricht discusses the practical consequence of the text: those who worship Him must worship [*Him*] in spirit and in truth.[45] Therefore, for Mastricht the first application or *conscientiæ casus* of worship implies prayer, particularly one's understanding, comprehension, and impression of how to think about God in prayer.[46] He argues that one should think about God as one's own soul or as an omniscient, incomprehensible, spiritual, invisible, almighty Being without flesh and bones (Luke 24:39). Moreover, one should direct one's self to God's glorious attributes as He manifests Himself "to us in the words of Exodus 34:6."[47] Thus, Mastricht directs one in the first place to the glory of God.

Mastricht then briefly warns the hypocrites who pray to Him with their lips and minds alone and not spiritually with their hearts.[48] He urges examination of one's worship to be sure it is truly in spirit and truth.[49] The criteria for such self-examination are provided by Mastricht: in the external worship, the spirit and body together glorify God.[50]

---

44. See further Appendix IV.2.1 on the structure of the chapter the *Spiritualitate Dei*.

45. Mastricht, *Theoretico-practica theologia*, II.6.ii, 98: "*Deus est Spiritus, & qui adorant eum, in spiritu & veritate oportet adorent.*" The *Beschouwende en praktikale godgeleerdheit* follows the *Staten-bijbel*: "Ende die Hem aanbidden moeten Hem aanbidden in geest en waarheit."

46. The link in Dutch language is notable. The dutch verb "bidden" is in english "to pray," and "aanbidden" can be rendered with "pray to." Thus, a literal rendering of Joh. 4:24 (*Staten-bijbel*) is "those who pray to Him must pray to Him in Spirit and in truth."

47. "Jehovah passed by before him, and proclaimed, Jehovah, Jehovah, a God merciful and gracious, slow to anger, and abundant in loving-kindness and truth."

48. Mastricht, *Theoretico-practica theologia*, II.6.xiv, 102.

49. Ibid., xv, 102: "Proinde *tertiò* suadet, cultum nostrum solicitè *examinemus* sitne, convenienter naturæ divinæ *in spiritu & veritate.*"

50. Ibid.: "Quod his assequemur criteriis: 1. si in cultu nostro externo, spiritus semper coëat cum corpore, ut *spiritu & corpore* Deum glorificemus...2. si spiritus, qui, in cultu externo, coit cum corpore, sit *spiritualis*, non carnalis...3. si finis, cultus nostri externi, non sit *carnalis* conservatio aut incrementum famæ...si 4. in cultu, omnes animæ facultates sese exserant: *intellectus...voluntas* amor...si 5. non in propatulo tantum simus Christiani...*in spiritu, non in literâ*...si 6. in *simplicitate cordis*...si denique 7.

Subsequently, Mastricht admonishes to subject "our spirit to God's Spirit."[51] In what manner could one perform such devotion? he asks.[52] He replies that one should deny one's self and entrust himself to God's glory. By faith one should cleanse his unclean spirit by the rule of Scripture and prayer, commending his spirit to Him who takes it to Himself in the hour of death.[53]

Finally, Mastricht exhorts that one needs to be purified from all evil desires, to be cleansed by the blood of Christ, and to "pray and implore God that according to the promises of the covenant of grace He gives one heart (Ezech. 11:19) and creates a clean Heart (Ps. 51:10)."[54] One needs, "like our text demands," to exercise prayer in spirit and in truth, that is, from the heart, with mind and attention in faith, hope, and love "expectantly waiting upon what is desired" and not using form prayers.[55]

In summary, the *praxis* of the divine spirituality arises from the biblical text (John 4:24). The structure of the practical section reflects on one hand the exegetical division and on the other hand contains characteristic aspects such as the glory of God, admonition, self-examination, and exhortation.

We conclude, then, with the following remarks on the structure and content of Mastricht's exposition of the divine spirituality. In respect to the structure, this exposition is fourfold: exegesis, doctrine, elenctic, and practice. The biblical text of John 4:24 is divided (grammatically) into two main parts: one related to God and one related to the worshiper. This twofold division is consistently maintained by Mastricht throughout the remainder of the chapter in the doctrinal, elenctical, and practical sections. Moreover, the structural notions of each section, which have been identified in part III of this study, are present in the exposition of the divine spirituality. The exegesis contains philological and grammatical-syntactical study and is foundational for further discussion, whether doctrinal or practical. Further, the doctrinal formulation arises from the biblical text and is broadened by other testimonies of Scripture and stands in a trajectory reaching back to the patristic fathers. The elenctic section follows the scholastic *quæstio* method, in which Mastricht's main opponents, the Cartesian theologians and Socinians, are refuted. Finally, the '*pars practica*' includes words of admonition and exhortation and emphasizes the glory of God. In summary, exegesis, doctrine, elenctic, and practice are integrally related, arising from the biblical text.

In respect to the content, the centrality of the biblical text of John 4:24 for the exegesis and practice of the doctrine of the divine spirituality reflect Mastricht's

---

exercitiis spiritualibus, abnegationi nostri, mortificationi cupiditatum, imitationi Christi, fidei, spei, charitati."

51. Ibid., xvi, 102: "Quartò, quod Deus *spiritus* sit, nos monet spiritum nostrum Deo addicamus quippe qui: 1. Spiritu gaudet ac delectatur Joh.4:23..."

52. Ibid.

53. Ibid., xvii, 102.

54. Ibid., xxvii, 106.

55. Ibid., xix, 103: "...disertè exigente textu...non affuetis precandi formulis adstricti, precemur."

definition of theology. The exegetical result with both the spiritual essence of God and the practical implication for those who worship Him are the *basso continuo* for the doctrinal and practical formulation. God is a spirit: a simple, noncorporeal being, who deserves to be worshiped in spirit and truth, and thus without images.

De Simplicitate Dei

Mastricht treats the doctrine of the divine simplicity in three parts: doctrine, elenctic, and practice. This structure should not be seen as a deviation from Mastricht's characteristic fourfold approach to a *locus*. Rather, the discussion on both divine spirituality and simplicity arises out of the same biblical text. Structurally, therefore, both doctrines are discussed in a single chapter, which is opened by an exegetical section on John 4:24. Consequently, what follows is a descriptive-analytical explanation of the three parts, doctrine, elenctic, and practice, of the divine simplicity.

Doctrine

Mastricht begins the doctrinal section of the divine simplicity by restating his final sentence of the doctrinal section of the divine spirituality—that the simplicity is a consequence of the spirituality of God.[56] The simplicity is, accordingly, not a communicable perfection for God is a Spirit *à se & univocè*. The divine simplicity, furthermore, is not "participative and restrictive," as in the case of created spirits, but "original and omnimodal."[57] The latter term "omnimodus simplicitas," is employed to designate a ruling out of all manner of composition and, as Muller argues, has a long history, tracing back to Alexander of Hales.[58] That God is of Himself and simple is, according to Mastricht, taught in Scripture, where God is represented not only *in concreto* but also *in abstracto* and is called love (1 John 4:8, 16), life (1 John 5:20) and a light in which there is no darkness (1 John 1:5).[59] Mastricht summarizes that God, therefore, is not heterogeneity but a *pura deitas*. This initial definition of the divine simplicity is supported by Mastricht with seven reasons. Accordingly, God is the absolute first Being, independent, immutable, infinite, eternal, perfect. Moreover, if there is composition in God, then He is not a *pura deitas*.[60] Mastricht argues that the patristic Justinus explicated the subject well in *Quest. & Resp. ad Orthodox*, question 144, stating that in God there is

---

56. Ibid., xx, 103: "Spiritualitati consectaria est *simplicitas*"; Ibid., vii, 99: "Consequitur 2. naturam Dei spiritualem, ejus omnimoda *simplicitas*. Consequitur 3. *immutabilitas*, de quibus, totidem theorematis ex prosesso."

57. Ibid., xx, 103: "sed *originalis & omnimoda* propterea, quod Deus sìt spiritus *à se & univocè*."

58. Muller, *Post-Reformation Reformed Dogmatics*, 3:280.

59. Mastricht, *Theoretico-practica theologia*, II.6.xx, 103: "Docet istam Scriptura, quoties terminis Deum repræsentat, non compositis tantum & *concretis*; sed simplicibus etiam & *abstractis*..."

60. Ibid., xxi, 103, 104, (confirmat ratio) "1. ens *absolutè primum*...2. *independens*...3. *immutabilis*...4. *infinitus*...5. *æternus*...6. *perfectissimus*...7. si in Deo est compositio; tum non est *lux, in quâ non sunt tenebræ*, non pura deitas: partes enim, proculdubio diversæ, eandem puram deitatem non constituerent."

no composition and as such it should be understood that He is and that He has.[61] Mastricht continues to explain in the remainder of the doctrinal part that God is without composition. Here, Mastricht parallels, though with discernment, Aquinas reflection on the divine simplicity.

Aquinas argued concerning the divine simplicity that there are eight points of inquiry.[62] Mastricht follows a similar structure and summarizes the content of Aquinas's first five questions. First, there is no corporeal composition in God because He is a Spirit. Second, His essence is not composed of matter and form. The second point is the most succinct of Mastricht's five reasons and thereby differs with Aquinas, who gives considerable attention to the Aristotelian form-matter distinction. Third, Mastricht deals with the *substantia* and *accidentia*, thereby concentrating, as does Aquinas in point six *Utrum in Deo sint aliqua accidentia*, on the argument that an accident is subject to mutation and therefore cannot belong to the divine simplicity.[63] Fourth, Mastricht argues that God is His own existence and not merely His own essence, because the divine existence is not an act of the divine essence, which would imply compositeness.[64] Finally, for Mastricht, the divine simplicity is without composition because God cannot be a species of any genus because a species is constituted of genus and difference. Mastricht does not explain this further but could have in mind what Aquinas wrote before: "Now that from which the difference constituting the species is derived, is always related to that from which the genus is derived, as actuality is related to potentiality."[65]

---

61. Ibid., 104: "*Quæst. & Resp. ad Orthodox.* quæst 144. *Non ad instar creaturæ Deus est, ut id quod sit & habeat, pro compositionem intelligatur, sicut natura creata; verum pro eo, atque naturam obtinet, ita etiam intelligendus est, id quod sit & quod habeat, obtinere supra compositionem.*" Mastricht refers to Pseudo-Justinus, Theodoretus of Cyrus, *Quæstiones & Responsiones ad Orthodoxos*. Dr. C. A . de Niet is acknowledged.

62. Aquinas, *Summa Theologica*, prima pars, quæstio 3, De Simplicitate Dei: "*Circa primum quæruntur octo: Primo: utrum Deus sit corpus; Secundo: utrum sit in eo compositio formæ et materiæ; Tertio: utrum sit in eo compositio quidditatis, sive essentiæ, vel naturæ, et subiecti; Quarto: utrum sit in eo compositio quæ est ex essentia et esse; Quinto: utrum sit in eo compositio generis et differentiæ; Sexto: utrum sit in eo compositio subiecti et accidentis; Septimo: utrum sit quocumque modo compositus, vel totaliter simplex; Octavo: utrum veniat in compositionem cum aliis.*" Cf. Mastricht, *Theoretico-practica theologia*, II.6.xxii, 104: "Nominatim compositionis: 1. ex *partibus* corporeis quantitativis; est enim spiritus...2. ex partibus *essentialibus*, materiâ & forma...3. ex *substantia* & accidente...4. ex essentiâ & existentiâ...5. ex *genere* & differentia..."

63. Mastricht, thus, changed the order of Aquinas's questions. Mastricht's third reason to explain the non-compositionality of God parallels Aquinas's sixth question.

64. Cf. Aquinas *Summa Theologica*, prima pars, quest. 3, art. 2: "Secundo, quia omne compositum ex materia et forma est perfectum et bonum per suam formam: unde oportet quod sit bonum per participationem, secundum quod materia participat formam. Primum autem quod est bonum et optimum, quod Deus est, non est bonum per participationem: quia bonum per essentiam, prius est bono per participationem. Unde impossibile est quod Deus sit compositus ex materia et forma."

65. Aquinas, *Summa Theologica*, prima pars, quæstio 3, article 5.

In summary, the central concern and definition of the divine simplicity for Mastricht is that God is without *omnis omnino compositio*.[66] Further, in respect to the structure of the doctrinal part, Mastricht begins to link the divine spirituality and simplicity, whereby the latter is inferred from the former, which results from John 4:24. Subsequently, he broadens the explication with other testimonies of Scripture and support from patristic sources and provides a description that reflects Aquinas's treatise on the doctrine of the divine simplicity, whereby any composition is denied in God or "How God is not" (*Deus quomodo non sit*).

Elenctic

Mastricht deals with two questions in the elenctic section. The structure of each question is similar to the medieval *quæstio* method.[67] The content of both questions relate immediately to the doctrine section. First, he asks, Is God a simple being?[68] This first question actually reflects Aquinas's seventh question of his treatise on the divine simplicity, which states, "Deus sit omnino simplex."[69] In the second question, Mastricht addresses the intriguing issue of whether the doctrine of the divine simplicity is taught in Scripture.

Mastricht's response to the first question resembles the answer to the first elenctic question on the divine spirituality.[70] Mastricht asserts that both the Anthropomorphists and the Socinians deny a scriptural foundation for the simplicity of God and "omit this divine attribute."[71] However, they differ in this respect: the Anthropomorphists taught that humanity is created in the image of divine physical parts, and the Socinians want to have a finite God who in is heaven and who cannot be united with Christ's human nature on earth. Thus, Mastricht shows that the question was debated in early church history as well as in his own time. It was addressed by, among others, Aquinas, who raised the objection of the Anthropomorphists to the question of "whether God is

---

66. Mastricht, *Theoretico-practica theologia*, II.6.xxii, 104: "Per simplicitatem, Deus expers est *omnis omnino compositionis*, in quâ res & res coëunt."

67. Although we follow Mastricht's structure of each question, no further comment will be made on the structure itself.

68. This is also confirmed in Mastricht's answer to question one of the elenctic section, where he writes, "Sociniani...negant Deum esse ens simplicissimum. Reformati, ex adverso, Deum, omnibus modis, simplicissimum esse, docent, Scripturis & rationibus, quas designavimus § 20 & 21" (Mastricht, *Theoretico-practica theologia*, II.6.xxiii, 104).

69. Aquinas, *Summa Theologica*, prima pars, quæstio 3, article 7: "Utrum Deus sit omnino simplex." Cf. Mastricht, *Theoretico-practica theologia*, II.6.xxiii, 104: "An Deus sit ens simplicissimum?"

70. Mastricht, *Theoretico-practica theologia*, II.6.viii, 99 : "An Deus proprie sit Spiritus?"

71. Ibid., xxiv, 104. See for the Anthropomorphists and Audians, Vorstius's *Tractat. De Deo,& notis ad Disputat.3 de Nat. Dei* and Socinius's *Defense Animadversionum in assert. Posnanienses & Catechesis Racov.* Cap. 5.

altogether simple."[72] However, the remainder of Mastricht's response differs from Aquinas. First, Mastricht's concern about the Socinian position is also articulated at the close of question one. Namely, the objection is raised that where two natures are united in one person, there is composition. Mastricht refutes this by arguing that such unity of two natures does not constitute a composition in God but an extraordinary θεανθρωπος—a God-Man.[73] Again, as previously noted, this issue has soteriological implications. Second, Mastricht raises and succinctly refutes six objections.[74] These objections, with the exception of the first one, which refutes any ascription of corporeality to God, concern the difference between *distinctio realis* and *distinctio formalis*. Mastricht argues, for example, that the Three Persons and divine essence are different in our conception but are not different in and of themselves: "The personality is nothing else than the *subsistantia* of the essence."[75] The Persons are not distinct in essence, but they are distinct in number, which excludes composition.[76] In summary, God's simplicity is affirmed by Mastricht's description of the divine simplicity as an absence of composition. The *unitas Dei* is not a matter of metaphysical speculation but of salvific significance: it is related to the doctrine of the Trinity and Christology.

Mastricht then states the second question: Is the simplicity of God taught in Scripture?[77] Mastricht notes, as before, that the Anthropomorphists, Vorstius, and the Socinians omit divine simplicity from the divine attributes.[78] In addition, the apologetic Remonstrants, "although not denying the divine simplicity otherwise they must be banished from society," teach (1) that God's simplicity is not found anywhere in Scripture, (2) the entire doctrine is metaphysical, and (3) it is not necessary to believe in

---

72. Aquinas, *Summa Theologica*, prima pars, quæstio 3, article 7: "1. Ea enim quæ sunt a Deo, imitantur ipsum... Sed in rebus quæ sunt a Deo, nihil est omnino simplex. Ergo Deus non est omnino simplex."

73. Mastricht, *Theoretico-practica theologia*, II.6.xxiii, 104: "Quod 6. *duæ naturæ* uniantur in unam personam. Resp. Hinc nulla emergit compositio in *Deo* quamvis emergat, quam diximus, extraordinaria in θεανθρώπω."

74. Ibid.: "Præcipua quæ oggerunt adversarii, sunt: 1. Quod *membra* humana, Deo tribuantur...2. Quod actiones *externæ* differant ab ipso agente...3. Quod actiones, etiam *internæ*, v.g. decreta, procul dubio, diversæ sint ab agente à decernente...4. [Quod] *attributa* differant ab essentiâ v.g. misericordia à justitia vindicante...5. Quod *personæ* tres obtineant, in unâ essentiâ...6. [Quod] *duæ naturæ* uniantur in unam personam."

75. Ibid.: "Resp. Nec 1. essentia differt à personalitate...personalitas enim, non est nisi *subsistentia* essentiæ, nec subsistentia, nisi *existentia* substantiæ actualis, quæ, procul dubio, non differt ab ipso existente Deo."

76. Ibid.: "Et 2. Personæ in abstracto, differunt inter se, non ut tres subsistentiæ; sed ut unius subsistentiæ, tres *modi*, qui cum non sint entia, non *componunt*; sed *distinguunt* & modificant tantum."

77. Ibid., xxiv, 104: "An omnimodam Dei simplicitas doceatur in Scriptura?"

78. Ibid.: "Anthropomorphitæ, seu Audiani, Vorstius in *Tractat. De Deo,& notis ad Disputat.3 de Nat Dei*. Socinus in *Defens. Animadversionum* in assert. Posnanienses & *Catechesis Racov.* Cap.1."

the simplicity of God.[79] Contrary to them, Mastricht argues that until the coming of Socinius the Reformed theologians always were in agreement about the simplicity of God, based on Scripture, "although not literally stated."[80]

Mastricht contends that the doctrine of the divine simplicity is not merely a philosophical question but a matter of faith. Thus, he argues[81] that Scripture attests that (1) God is a spirit (John 4:24), who is an immaterial and simple being who differs from angel and human spirits; (2) God is the first absolute being (Rev. 1:8; Jer. 41:4; 44:6; Rom. 11:35, 36) and (3) is immutable (Mal. 3:6; James 1:17; Ps. 102:27, 28; Heb. 1:11, 12). Moreover, God is (4) incorruptible (Rom. 1:23; 1 Tim. 1:17), for that which is without composition is unchangeable and cannot be corrupted. Finally, (5) God is infinite (Jer. 23:23, 24; Job 11:8; 1 Kings 8:27) and perfect (Job 11:8; Matt. 5:48), for that which is finite and imperfect is composite. In summary, Mastricht demonstrates from Scripture with other divine attributes that the divine simplicity is grounded in God's Word.

Those who still have objections, contrary to this testimony of Scripture, according to Mastricht, should be refuted. First, even though the word *simplicity* is not found in Scripture, this does not mean it is not scripturally based, since the words *trinity, personal union, satisfaction* and "other mysteries" are also not found in Scripture but are biblical.[82] Second, it is a heresy to deny simplicity because to do so is to interfere with the divine free action and will. Mastricht asserts that the divine will is not affected by God's simplicity and that He wills what He has decreed.[83] The third and fourth objections deal with the distinctions of the divine essence, attributes, three Persons, and Trinity. Both objections are refuted with arguments similar to those stated in the preceding question.[84] In summary, the question and response is concerned with the preservation of the scriptural foundation of the doctrine of divine simplicity.

---

79. Ibid., xxiv, 105: "Remonstrantes Apologetæ, in sua *Apologia* non negant quidem simplicitatem Dei; sic enim in Socinianorum castra transirent, qui à nostris oris, legibus civilibus, proscripti sunt: ne à communione sua proscribere cogerentur Socinianos, rem de simplicitate Dei, his tribus axiomatis complectuntur: 1. *Quod de simplicitate Dei, ne iota quidem habeatur in Scriptura. 2. Quod tota ejus doctrina, sit metaphysica sive terminum; sive rem spectes. 3. Quod simplicitas Dei, non sit creditu necessaria.*"

80. Ibid. (objectiones): "β. Non exstet ρητῶς exstat tamen virtute & διανοία."

81. The *Beschouwende en praktikale godgeleerdheit* (vol. 1, II.6.xxiv, 258) states "Iets 't welke de Rechtzinnigen met deze bewysreden trachten te verwerven." Cf. Mastricht, *Theoretico-practica theologia*, II.6.xxiv, 105: "Id quod his argumentis conantur obtinere."

82. Mastricht, *Theoretico-practica theologia*, II.6.xxiv, 105: "Sic enim 3. nec Trinitas nec unio personalis, nec satisfactio, aliaque mysteria docerentur in Scripturis, quatenus totidem syllabis, forte non exstant."

83. Ibid.: "2. Quod omnimoda simplicitas, neget actiones & volitiones Dei liberas, vere distinctas esse, ab ejus essentia id quod cum Scriptura non consistit...Resp.... Libertas volitionum divinarum, nihilominus farta tecta subsistit, quod, non obstante simplicitate agat ex consilio...in quo libertas consistit."

84. Ibid., xxiii, 104 and xxiv, 105.

Practical section

This section is structured in five *praxeis* (*usus*) that deal with the practical application of the divine simplicity. This structure resembles the previously identified outline: (1) the glory of God and the humbling of man, (2) consolation, (3) admonition, (4) self-examination, and (5) exhortation. Mastricht notes that some of the practical *usus* of the divine spirituality can be used *mutatis mutandis* for the divine simplicity.[85] The divine simplicity is, according to Mastricht, foundational for the teaching of the imperfectness of creatures and the perfectness of God. His simplicity is the foundation of His perfection, and it reveals our imperfection. Nevertheless, the divine simplicity (*Simplicitas Dei*) commends us to an upright association with people, as well as reminds us of the need to be satisfied with our lot, even when this is of a humble condition. Moreover, the divine perfectness also is explicated in Scripture by the fact that God is a light in whom there is no darkness (1 John 1:5), which, according to Mastricht, points to the divine majesty and glory.[86] The divine simplicity should direct one to the glorification of God, as the simple goodness, through faith and covenant making, because "Blessed *is* the nation whose God *is* the Lord! Ps. 33:12."[87]

Second, Mastricht consoles and instructs by pointing out that because of the divine simplicity, one should, with simplicity of heart, rest in uprightness and integrity ("which coincide with the simplicity") in God alone. Entrusting upon divine simplicity is based on the pure, infinite and general goodness of God so that one may say in agreement with the psalmists,

The Lord *is* the portion of mine inheritance (Ps. 16:5); and, Whom have I in heaven *but You?* And *there is* none upon earth *that* I desire besides You. My flesh and my heart fail; *But* God *is* the strength of my heart and my portion forever (Ps. 73:25-26).[88]

Third, Mastricht continues with an admonition to serve God with simplicity of heart (Matt. 10:16). One should in all work follow the apostle Paul's counsel in Ephesians 6:5 "that the servants obey their masters in simplicity of heart" and in 2 Corinthians 1:12 that one should "live in simplicity and righteousness of heart."[89] This simplicity of heart, Mastricht notes, is to be directed toward God in all things, which is

---

85. Ibid., xxv, 105: "...manet, usus nonnullos practicos, quos spiritualitati divinæ, jamjam subjecimus, mutatis mutandis, apud simplicitatem usurpari posse . . ."

86. Ibid., xxv, 106: "1. Deum ex ea, velut radice omnis perfectionis glorificemus. Notum est Scripturis, majestatem & gloriam Dei designari *Luce*...." Here Mastricht reaches back to the doctrinal section, where he attested of the divine simplicity from Scripture and referred to God as light.

87. Ibid.: "3. ex istis omnibus, Deum, ut simplicissimam *bonitatem*, a qua *solus bonus* dicitur Matth. 19:17, fide, resipiscentia, studio complacendi ei & imprimis confœderatione cum eo: *quam* enim *beata gens*, cujus Deus est Jehova! Ps.33:12."

88. Ibid., xxvi, 106: "Ut non sit, quamobrem non dicamus cum Davide: *ipse portio mea* Psal. 16:5. cum Assapho: *Quis mihi in cælis?*..."

89. Ibid., xxvii, 106.

distinguished in three aspects: (1) one's heart should be pure and be delivered from any form of corruption (Ps. 12:3, 4), so that with a pure and simple heart one object needs to be kept in mind: the glory of God (Phil. 1:20, 21); (2) one should seek the benefit of one's soul and that of one's neighbor; and (3) the simplicity of heart should cause one to stand firm in all things, as one is often inclined to be inconsistent in one's ways.[90] Fourth, Mastricht admonishes and infers from the divine simplicity that one should serve in public in simplicity of heart. He argues that one's behavior in society is inferred from this attribute. The reason for this application, according to Mastricht, is that in one's simplicity lies one's assurance, security (Ps. 25:21), rest, and honor. Contrary to this a deceitful communion with God is a curse (Ps. 5:7; Prov. 11:20).

Finally, the practical section and chapter ends with the exhortation for one to live in simplicity. Mastricht urges one to be satisfied with one's lot since a plain life provides consistency, contrary to a composite life that is more changeable. He argues, with a link to the divine immutability, "God is immutable because He is simple."[91] He continues, that the more one possesses in treasures, honorary offices, and friends, the more one is changeable and less endurable, because "the more involved you are with these belongings the more you are subdued to all kind of concerns and trial and the more you have the more can be taken away, Luke 10:41."[92] Therefore, he concludes that it is important to be acquainted with, by a God-fearing conscience, simplicity instead of changeable matters. One should rest in the simplicity that God is sufficient for all things, just as the apostle Paul exemplifies that godliness with contentment is great gain (1 Tim. 6:6). In summary, the practical section parallels the identified structure of the 'pars practica' except that, here, the self-examination is omitted. Further, in respect to the content, Mastricht concentrates primarily on the practical application of the divine simplicity, and thus is the application is integrally related to the doctrinal and elenctical sections. The divine simplicity is, for Mastricht, based on Scripture and the absence of composition and should lead in private and public to a Christian piety that is simple, uncompounded, and directed to God's glory and the welfare of one's neighbor.

We can conclude this chapter of Mastricht's discussion *De Spiritualitate et Simplicitate Dei* with several remarks in respect to structure and content. In respect to the structure, Mastricht presented the *loci* with his fourfold division, although in this case he infers from a single biblical text (John 4:24) and its exegesis two distinct but related divine attributes: the divine spirituality and simplicity. Here Mastricht differs with most of his contemporaries, who begin with the treatment of the doctrine of the divine simplicity rather than with the exegesis and divine spirituality, as Mastricht does. In addition, we

90. Ibid.: "Quo quidem, tria distinctè concluduntur: 1. Ut cor intus sit *purum*...2. Ut corde puro ac simplici, in *unum scopum* collimet...3. Ut cor purum ac *simplex*, in *simplicem* suum scopum contendat constanti..."

91. Ibid., xxix, 107: "Unde Deus, maximè immutabilis est quia maximè *simplex*."

92. Ibid.: "Prorsus ita *sors*, quo simplicior, eo solidior; & quo magis variegata, ex compositione, opibus, honoribus, amicis, eo mutabilior: & quo magis distraheris, in tot obiecta, eo pluribus curis & angoribus es obnoxius Luc. X. 41."

have seen that each section confirms the previous findings on structure, namely, that the doctrinal section moves from a broadening of scriptural testimonies to references of church fathers to definition of the doctrine, thereby employing medieval scholastic distinction and definitions, just as the elenctic section parallels the *quæstio* method in defending, for soteriological reasons, the Reformed orthodox position, primarily against the Socinians. The practical section corresponds, as we have seen, with the five aspects, of which the glory of God and Mastricht's directive of the believer toward God should not be overlooked.

In respect to the content, Mastricht stands in an exegetical, doctrinal, and practical trajectory with the scriptural foundation for these doctrines, reaching back with contemporaries such as Cocceius, Oomius, and Brakel and the annotators of the *Staten-bijbel* and the writers of the Leiden *Synopsis purioris theologiæ*, via Aquinas and early church fathers to the Scriptures. However, where Mastricht's contemporaries refer to John 4:24 in their explication of the doctrine and practice of the divine simplicity or spirituality, it is Mastricht who consolidates the diverse explications—exegesis, doctrine, elenctic, and practice—into a single chapter. The study of this chapter demonstrates that, for Mastricht, doctrine, elenctic, and practice arise from Scripture. That a solid exegesis is demanded for such a consolidated approach is not surprising, but it is often absent from the works of Mastricht's contemporaries. In addition, Mastricht presents and argues the divine spirituality prior to the divine simplicity. In this he differs in order but not in content with other seventeenth-century Reformed theologians, for all of whom the *unitas simplicitatis* is central. Mastricht also relies in a sophisticated way on Aquinas's exposition of the divine simplicity. On the one hand, Mastricht follows selectively Aquinas's stated objections, arguments, and refutations, but on the other hand, he limits Acquinas's reliance on Aristotelian distinctions such as actuality-potentiality and form-matter. Nevertheless, Mastricht's basic definition of the divine simplicity does not differ with his contemporaries and Aquinas, whereby the latter refutes the objections to the doctrine of divine simplicity with one biblical text: John 4:24, the foundation for Mastricht's doctrine of divine spirituality and simplicity.

Mastricht's definition of the divine simplicity flows forth, according to him, from the divine spirituality. This could arguably point to Mastricht's rejection of a metaphysical description of God. This point is supported by the fact that Mastricht relates many divine attributes to the divine simplicity, such as the immutability, invisibility, and other "essential" attributes, which together he links via the divine simplicity to the divine spirituality. Another argument could be that, for Mastricht, a metaphysical-philosophical description of the divine spirituality and simplicity prohibits the soteriological implications of these doctrines. He demonstrates this concern in his refutation of the Socinian, Cartesian, and apologetic Remonstrant opponents. There, where the *unitas simplicitatis* is denied, the Christology, according Mastricht, is under assault. Thus, Mastricht's doctrinal and elenctical explications of both *loci* are related to the doctrine of Christ and salvation. Moreover, as we have seen, these doctrines are also related to the doctrine of the Trinity: the *simplicitas* is not transverse to *trinitas* but is converse to composition.

Finally, the practical dimension of the divine spirituality and simplicity contains, for Mastricht, both a vertical and a horizontal dimension. On the one hand, he directs the believer to God and His glory, while at the same time the believer is guided to live spiritually and in simplicity. In summary, for Mastricht the exegetical method, the formulation of doctrine, and practice are integrally related and provide a scriptural explication, and not a metaphysical construct, of the divine spirituality and simplicity. Furthermore, his reliance on the medieval *quæstio* method in the elenctic sections and discriminative use of Aquinas's *Summa Theologica* contribute to a clear definition and defense of the doctrines of divine spirituality and, in particular, the divine simplicity. Therefore, for Mastricht, a living to God with the *theoretico-practica* knowledge of these divine attributes involves anthropology, Christology, soteriology, and the doctrine of the Trinity. The next chapter deals with Mastricht's treatment of the latter.

Chapter 3
The Holy Trinity

Introduction and Statement of the Problem

Studies on the doctrine of the Holy Trinity of the post-Reformation era are limited.[1] Despite the fact that this doctrine is surveyed in major Reformed dogmatics[2] and history of doctrine,[3] only a few monographs examine this doctrine.[4] Nevertheless, seventeenth-century post-Reformation systems of theology attest to the importance of the doctrine of the Holy Trinity.[5] Furthermore, these systems attest that this doctrine is based on

1. F. W. Huisman, *Bibliografie van het gereformeerde Pietisme in Nederland to 1800* (Woudenberg: Uitgeverij Op Hoope, 2001). This bibliography (1,000+ publications) does not list one publication devoted to a study of the Holy Trinity. An exception is B. Loonstra, "De Leer van God en Christus in de Nadere Reformatie," in *Theologische Aspecten van de Nadere Reformatie*, ed. T. Brienen et al. (Zoetermeer: Boekencentrum, 1993), 107-10.

2. Eduard Böhl, *Dogmatik, Darstellung der Christlichen Glaubenslehre auf Reformirt-Kirchlicher Grundlage* (Amsterdam: Von Scheffer & Co., 1887); E. C. Gravemeijer, *Leesboek over de Gereformeerde Geloofsleer* (Utrecht: H. Ten Hove, 1896); Herman Bavinck, *Gereformeerde Dogmatiek* (Kampen: Kok, 1921); Louis Berkhof, *Systematic Theology*, with a new preface by Richard A. Muller (Grand Rapids: Eerdmans, 1996); J. T. Mueller, *La Doctrine Chrétienne* (La Petite Pierre: Éditions "Le Luthérien" Église Évangélique Luthérienne, 1956); Herman Hoeksema, *Reformed Dogmatics* (Grand Rapids: Reformed Free Publishing Association, 1966); Karl Barth, *Die Kirchliche Dogmatik* (Zürich: EVZ-Verlag, 1970).

3. Reinhold Seeberg, *Lehrbuch der Dogmengeschichte* (Leipzig: Erlangen, 1923); Heinrich Heppe, *Reformed Dogmatics*, trans. G. T. Thomson (London: Allen & Unwin, 1950); Bernard Sesboüé and Joseph Wolinski, *Histoire des Dogmes: Le Dieu du Salut* (Paris: Desclée, 1994). See for additional literature Robert D. Preus, *The Theology of Post-Reformation Lutheranism* (St. Louis: CPH, 1972), 2:113; Richard A. Muller, *Post-Reformation Reformed Dogmatics* (Grand Rapids: Baker Academic, 2003), 4:22, 23

4. W. J. van Asselt, *Amicitia Dei: een onderzoek naar de structuur van de theologie van Johannes Coccejus (1603-1669)* (Ede: Grafische vormgeving: ADC, 1988): idem, *The Federal Theology of Johannes Coccejus* (Leiden-New York: Brill, 2001), 175-93; Carl Trueman, *The Claims of Truth: John Owen's Trinitarian Theology* (Carlisle: Paternoster Press, 1998), 129-33; Gregory D. Schuringa, *Embracing Leer and Leven: The Theology of Simon Oomius in the Context of the* Nadere Reformatie *Orthodoxy* (Ph.D. diss., Calvin Theological Seminary, 2003). See also studies on Jonathan Edwards's doctrine of the Trinity, rooted in the seventeenth-century Reformed theology, Bruce M. Stephens, *God's Last metaphor: The Doctrine of the Trinity in New England Theology* (Chico: Scholars Press, 1981); Amy Plantinga Pauw, *The Supreme Harmony of All. The Trinitarian Theology of Jonathan Edwards* (Grand Rapids: William B. Eerdmans Publ. Co., 2002); Muller, *Post-Reformation Reformed Dogmatics*, vol. 4.

5. J. Polyander, A. Rivetus, A. Walaeus, A. Thysius, *Synopsis purioris theologiæ* (Leiden: Elsevier, 1625); William Ames, *Marrow of Sacred Divinity, drawne out of the holy Scriptures, and the Interpreters thereof, and brought into Method* (London: Edward Griffin, 1642); Samuel Maresius, *Collegium Theologicum sive Systema Breve Universæ Theologiæ* (Groningen: Franciscus Bronchorstius, 1656); Simon Oomius, *Institutiones Theologiæ Practicæ* (Bolsward: Samuel van Haringhouk, 1676); Theodor Undereyck, *Halleluja, das ist, Gott in dem Sünder verkläret oder Des sünders Wanderstab zur Erkäntnüs, Geniessung und Verklärung Gottes, alß des höchsten Gutes* (Bremen: 1678); Johannes Hoornbeeck, *Theologiæ practicæ* (Frankfurt: Ernst Claudium

Scripture and has polemical and practical implications. The former was forced by the rise of Socinianism,[6] and the latter as a result of the fundamental character of the doctrine of the Holy Trinity for the life of faith and obedience.[7] In summary, the Reformed theology of the seventeenth century paid attention to the teachings of the Trinity in several ways, namely, exegetical, doctrinal, polemical, and practical. Mastricht offers a combined treatment of the doctrine in the *Theoretico-practica theologia* (*TPT*) in his characteristic fourfold manner.

The aim of this chapter is, in response to the limited attention to the post-Reformation Reformed doctrine of the Holy Trinity, to illumine Mastricht's thoughts on this doctrine in structure and content and, second, to pursue the main quest of our study: the relationship, if any, of exegesis, doctrine, elenctic, and *praxis*. The following questions will be considered: (1) To what degree is the formulation of doctrine and *praxis* the result of the exegesis of the biblical text? (2) Do the doctrinal and practical formulations differ or agree with the results of exegesis? (3) Is the constructed doctrine of the Trinity related to other parts of Mastricht's theology? Our examination of Mastricht's doctrine of the Trinity, however, demands a different approach than the preceding assessments of the *loci* of faith and divine spirituality and simplicity. A close reading of the four chapters on the Holy Trinity shows a high degree of structural and content interrelationship. In addition, there are modifications from the 1682 to the final edition of the *TPT*. Therefore, we approach our examination, in dialogue with Mastricht's contemporaries, with (1) general observations, (2) a review of structure, and (3) a descriptive analysis of Mastricht's explication of the Holy Trinity. This descriptive-analytical part commences with the first and general chapter of the Holy Trinity, in which Mastricht identifies the Three Persons and proceeds with an individual exposition of the Persons of the Holy Trinity.

Bailliar, 1680); Johannes Cloppenburgh, *Theologica Opera Omnia* (Amsterdam: Gerardus Borstius, 1684); Abraham Heidanus, *Corpus theologiæ christianæ in quindecim locos* (Leiden: Johannes de Vivie & Jordanus Luchtmans, 1686); Franciscus Burmannus, *Synopsis Theologiæ & speciatim Oeconomiæ Foederum Dei* (Utrecht: C. J. Noenardus, 1671); idem, *Synopsis, dat is Kort Begrip der Heilige God-geleerdheit, en insonderheit van de Huishouding der Verbonden Gods*, trans. Dirk Smout, (Utrecht: Franscois Halma, 1688); Herman Witsius, *De oeconomia Foederum Dei cum hominibus* (Herborne, Nassau: Johannes N. Andreas, 1712); idem, *Oefeningen over de Grondstukken van het Algemeyne Christelyke Geloove en het Gebed des Heeren* (Rotterdam: Daniel Beman, 1699);Wilhelmus à Brakel, *ΛΟΓΙΚΗ ΛΑΤΡΕΙΑ, dat is Redelyke Godtsdienst, in welken de Goddelijke Waerheden des Genade-Verbondts worden verklaert, tegen partyen beschermt, en tot de practyke aengedrongen* (Rotterdam: Reynier van Doesburgh, 1700); Johann Heinrich Heidegger, *Corpus theologiæ christianæ* (Zürich: David Gessner, 1700).

6. John Owen, *The Works of John Owen* (London: Johnstone and Hunter, 1850-1855), vol. 12; Johannes Hoornbeeck, *Summa controversiarum religionis cum infidelibus, hæreticis, schismaticis: id. Est, Gentilibus, Judæis, Muhammedanis; Papistis, Anabaptistis...*ed. secunda (Utrecht: J. à Waesberge, 1658).

7. Cf. Muller, *Post-Reformation Reformed Dogmatics*, 4:154-56.

General Observations

Psychological and Social Analogy

The examination of the doctrine of the Holy Trinity reveals that Mastricht gives considerably more attention to the social analogy than to the psychological model. The latter depicts the Son and Spirit as the Wisdom and Love of the one God, thus accentuating divine unity. This analogy has a long tradition of inquiry established by Augustine in *The Trinity*, where he wrote:

> But in these three, when the mind knows itself and loves itself, a Trinity remains: the mind, love, and knowledge; and there is no confusion through any commingling, although each is a substance in itself, and all are found mutually in all...These three, therefore, are in a marvelous manner inseparable from one another; and yet each of them is a substance, and all together are one substance or essence, while the terms themselves express a mutual relationship.[8]

In comparing the Trinity to a human mind and its interior operation of knowledge and love, Augustine portrayed the Son as the Idea or Image of God and the Spirit as divine Love or Joy. Mastricht employs this analogy in a limited way.[9] The social analogy, on the other hand, depicts the Godhead as a society or family of persons. The immediate implication of this analogy is the "economy of the Trinity." The word *economy* has its roots in the Greek word *oikonomia*, which can be rendered as "dispensation," "administration," or "order of acting," and originally applied to the management of a household. Mastricht, then, employs terms such as *familia, pater familias, filius familias,* and *œconomia*.[10] Where the "economic" Trinity usually refers to the manifestation of the divine activity *ad extra*, Mastricht includes in his understanding of the term 'economy'

8. Augustine, "The Trinity," in *Fathers of the Church*, vol. 45, trans. Stephen McKenna (Washington, D. C: Catholic University Press, 1963), IX.v.8, 277-78. Cf. Willam J. Danaher, *The Trinitarian Ethics of Jonathan Edwards* (Ph. D. diss., Yale University, 2002), 23; Plantinga Pauw, *The Supreme Harmony of All*, 12.

9. Petrus van Mastricht, *Theoretico-practica theologia qua, per singula capita theologica, pars exegetica, dogmatica, elenchtica et practica, perpetua successione conjugantur ; accedunt historia ecclesiastica, plena quidem, sed compendiosa, idea theologiæ moralis, hypotyposis theologiæ asceticæ etc. proin opus quasi novum* (Utrecht: Thomas Appels, 1699), II.26.v, 253: "Ista omnia, aliaque, pro divina Filii personalitas . . . item *imago Dei invisibilis* scil. Patris, Col. 1:15." See for the use and limitations of the Augustian metaphors, Muller, *Post-Reformation Reformed Dogmatics*, 4:157-159, 266.

10. Ibid., 25.ii, 246: "2. Invocatum...A. Pater familias, ad Patrem...B. Filius familias, Domini...C. Familia...*universa* œconomia"; 24.iii, 236: "...hoc voto contineatur adoratio (Deo propria Matth. 4:10) adoratio *unius Dei* & adoratio *trium*, trium *uniformis* & pro triplici beneficio *œconomico*"; 24.vii, 237: "*Rem* eis designatam, tum percipiemus ubi, velut per partes, explicuerimus: 1. Trium istorum *convenientiam*, seu communionem...3. *Officium œconomicum*"; 24.xi, 238: "Atque adeo, huic *communioni* trinum distinctarum personarum, innituntur: œconomia quædam..."; 24.xiii, 239 (Gubernandi vices personis œconomicæ); 24.xiv, 239: "Oeconomicæ huic gubernationi œconomica porro respondent *attributa...*"; 25.xiii, 249: "Praxis hujus capitis, consistit in cultus œconomici officiis, Patri peculiaribus. In quibus *primò* Patri...Capiti-familiâs." See also, 26.iii, 252; 26.xiii, 255; 26.xx, 259; 27.i, 261; 27.iii, 263; 27.xi, 264.

the interaction, deliberation, and organization of the Persons of the Trinity prior to the work of redemption.

Ontological and Economical Trinity

In relation to the preceding paragraph, one notes furthermore that Mastricht concentrates more on the economical than the ontological Trinity. That is to say, Mastricht discusses the latter in respect to the essence, nature, or attributes of the Trinity[11] but gives more attention to what each of the Three Persons do (economic Trinity).[12] The economic Trinity reveals, for Mastricht, the ontological Trinity. However, he argues, that the Persons of the Trinity are equal ontologically but not economically.[13] A similar approach is noted in Undereyck, who describes the Trinity ontologically in a classic Western creedal formulation but notes the economical Trinity especially in relation to the work of redemption, proceeding from the council of peace to the covenant of grace.[14]

Greek and Western Theology of the Trinity

In reading the chapters on the Holy Trinity and the Three Persons, one notes that Mastricht consistently uses words from the Latin or Western Trinitarian theology, such as *substantia* (instead of οὐσία), *essentia, subsistentia,* and *persona.* That, however, does not mean that Mastricht always uses the same Augustinian formulated definitions. For example, it was Boethius who defined a "person" as "an individual substance of a rational nature" (*persona est individua substantia rationalis naturæ*), while Richard of St. Victor defined the divine person as "an incommunicable existence of a divine nature" (*persona divina est divinæ naturæ incommunicabilis existentia*).[15] The Boethian definition prevailed in most works of the seventeenth-century Reformed theologians.[16] However,

---

11. Mastricht, *Theoretico-practica theologia,* II.24.v, 237: "Demonstrationes *naturæ,* hîc frustra expectabis, quod *mysterium* excedat naturam..." See also Appendix IV.2.b for the paragraphs on the trinitarian attributes.

12. Ibid., 24.xii, 238; 25.ix, 248; 26.xiii, 255; 26.xv, 255; 27.xi, xiii, xiv, 264.

13. Ibid., 24.iii, 236: "...fieri non potest, quin in *uno* Deo *tres* sint distinctæ *personæ* etiam *munere & beneficiis* œconomicis diversæ."

14. Theodor Undereyck, *Hallelujah, dat is, Godt in den sondaar verheerlijkt, ofte verhandelinge van het Grote Genadenwerk Godes in Christo,* trans. Wilhelm Vos, (Amsterdam: Jan Bouman, 1694).

15. Cf. Muller, *Post-Reformation Reformed Dogmatics,* 4:34.

16. Polyander *et al., Synopsis purioris theologiæ,* 7.iii, 61: "Vox personæ apud Latinos, ut τοῦ προσώπου apud Græcos, est aequivoca. Interdum enim larvam et qualitatem hominis, seu conditionem externam denotat, ut Act. 10:34 interdum subsistentiam ratione præditam, ut 2 Cor. 1:11. Nos hanc vocem analogice ad personas Trinitatis accommodantes, eam posteriori significatu usurpamus."; Franciscis Gomarus, *Opera Theologica Omnia* (Amsterdam: Joannis Janssonius, 1664), Disputationes Theologicæ, 6.xl, 18: "*Substantiam* autem vocat: quia est ens, per se subsistens, completum; non verò accidens, neque pars substantiæ: *rationalis naturæ,* hoc est (per *synecdochen speciei,* pro genere) intellectualis;" Gomarus cites here Aquinas, Bonaventura, and Boethius. Undereyck, *Halleluja* (1678), III.1, 10: "'t is wel sulx dat yeder Persoon het selvige wesen heeft"; Cloppenburgh, *Theologica Opera Omnia,* vol. 1, Exerc. Theol. Locus III

Mastricht defines a "person" as "an incommunicable rational substance" (*substantia rationalis incommunicabilis*), thereby combining the Boethian and Victorian formulations.[17]

Although, these observations point to Mastricht's appreciation of the Western theology of the Trinity, we note his discernment on the issue of the *filioque*. He raises, like *Synopsis purioris theologiæ*, Cocceius, Burman, and Brakel,[18] the issue of whether the Holy Spirit proceeds from the Father or from the Father and the Son.[19] Mastricht first provides a historical account of the *filioque* and mentions that both the Latin and Greek Church have "sinned."[20] Second, he sympathizes with the later Greek fathers who argued that the Holy Spirit proceeds from the Father through the Son.[21] He recognizes that the Reformed theologians agreed with the Latin Church in defining the double procession of the Holy Spirit. Mastricht does not want to deviate from this consensus and agrees that John 15:26 cannot be used by the Greeks against the *filioque*.[22] However, he argues that if the Greek fathers did mean with ἐκ, δια, and εἰς "through or from," meaning that the Holy Spirit in the Johannine text proceeds from the Father through

disp. 1.xiii, 758: "Illa veteri notione Substantiæ, Substantia ingreditur Personæ definitionem. Definitur enim, & *Boëthio* olim, *Rationalis naturæ Substantia individua*"; Brakel, *ΛΟΓΙΚΗ ΛΑΤΡΕΙΑ, dat is Redelyke Godtsdienst*, I:4.iv, 111: "Als het woordt ὑπόστασις *Hypostasis* van eene verstandige selfstandigheyt gesegt wordt, dan beteekent het een Persoon, daer door verstaen wij een levendige, verstandige, onmededeelbare...op zich zelf bestaende selfstandigheyt." Burman describes a "person" following Tertulianus. Cf. Burmannus, *Synopsis Theologiæ*, I.30.x-xiv, 162. Oomius notes several definitions including Boethius, Richard of St. Victor. Cf. Oomius, *Institutiones Theologiæ Practicæ*, III.2.i, 6. See also on the prevailing (modified) definition of Boethius in post-Reformation Reformed theology, Muller, *Post-Reformation Reformed Dogmatics*, 4:178-79.

17. Mastricht, *Theoretico-practica theologia*, II.24.vi, 237: "Ut ab hac, *persona* nihil aliud sit, quam *substantia rationalis, incommunicabilis*."

18. Polyander et al., *Synopsis purioris theologiæ*, 9.xix, 80; Brakel, *ΛΟΓΙΚΗ ΛΑΤΡΕΙΑ, dat is Redelyke Godtsdienst*, I:4.xxxii, 138; Burmannus, *Synopsis Theologiæ*, I.31.xxxvi, 177; Cocceius, *Opera Omnia Theologica*, vol. 7, *Summa Theologia*, cap.xii, 180-82, § 3-18. Cf. Van Asselt, *The Federal Theology of Johannes Cocceius*, 180-83; The following theologians do not discuss the *filioque* in the discussion on the Holy Spirit, Ames, *Marrow of Sacred Divinity*; Oomius, *Institutiones Theologiæ Practicæ*, III.2.iii; Undereyck, *Halleluja* (1678), IV; Cloppenburgh, *Theologica Opera Omnia*, vol. 1, Exerc. Theol. Locus III Disp. II prima, secunda; Witsius, *Oefeningen*, XXIII. See also for a discussion of the *filioque* in the context of post-Reformation Reformed theology, Muller, *Post-Reformation Reformed Dogmatics*, 4:373-75.

19. Mastricht, *Theoretico-practica theologia*, II.27.xx, 267: "An Spiritus S. procedat à solo Patre, an vero à Patre & Filio?"

20. Ibid.: "Peccatum hîc utrinque: à Latinis, quod symbolo Constantinopolitano, aliquid addiderint, eoque Papæ auctoritatem Græcis, ex obliquo obtenderent; à Græcis autem, quod dogma Scripturis consentaneum & à vetustioribus Ecclesiæ Patribus agnitum, sola nominis Latini invidia, temere recusarint."

21. Ibid.: "Non desunt tamen, qui existiment...& imprimis recentiores Græcos, sibi nihil aliud velle, quam Spiritum S. à Patre solo per Filium, procedere."

22. Ibid., 268 (objectiones): "Sed 3. Nihilominus satis accurate obtinebit *ordo subsistendi* si statuatur Spiritum S. procedere à Patre & à Filio...."

the Son, there are no objections.[23] In summary, Mastricht has empathy for the position of the Eastern Church but favors the Latin dominance of the *filioque* issue. Finally, Mastricht's citations and references to both Eastern theological sources, such as the Cappadocian Fathers—John Chrysostom, Basil the Great, and Gregory Nazianzus—and the Western theological sources attest to a dual indebtness.[24]

The Doctrine of the Trinity Expounded and Used in the *TPT*

Knowing that the *TPT* was written for students of theology and in particular was meant for homiletic use, it is noteworthy that the subsequent chapters on the Trinity parallel a (Reformed) liturgy. The particular biblical texts foundational for the exposition of the doctrine are, respectively, a *votum* (*Holy Trinity*), an invocation (*God the Father*), a proclamation (*God the Son*) and a promise (*God the Holy Spirit*).[25] The proclamation is exemplified in Mastricht's *Methodus Concionandi*, in which he outlines a sermon on Colossians 3:1—living to God through Christ, whereby the work of the Holy Spirit is indispensable for exercises of faith.[26] Maybe this was the liturgical essence for Mastricht.

Finally, the chapters on the doctrine of the Trinity are referenced throughout the *TPT*[27] but in particular in the chapter on the *Covenant of Grace*.[28] Thus, the inference can be made that the doctrine of the Trinity, in particular, is foundational for Mastricht's theology. In summary, Mastricht's discussion of the Holy Trinity overall parallels that of his contemporaries. The tri-unity is underscored by Mastricht to define the Trinity as the incommunicability of each of the divine Persons together with the communal analogy. With this description he stands in the trajectory of the Western formulated doctrine of the Trinity.

Structure

Mastricht's exposition on the Holy Trinity is at the close of the book *De Fide in Deum Triunum*. In this he does not differ from his contemporaries, who also closed the discussion of the doctrine of God with a treatment on the Trinity. However, Mastricht

---

23. Ibid.: "2. Si non aliud intendant, quam ipsum procedere à solo Patre, sed *per* Filium; non suppetit mihi, quod multum opponam. Interim 3. locus loqui videtur, non tam de *hypostaticâ* eius processione, quam de *oeconomica*, quæ fit in tempore. β Quod Scriptura nihil habeat de processione Spiritus S. à Filio. .... usurpari videantur, prout Basilius, Theophylactus, Damascenus, aliique teste Bessarione in Concilio Florentino. . .resp. 1. me nonmagnopere obtini."

24. See appendix I.2.4.

25. The biblical texts are, respectively, 2 Cor. 13:13 (Holy Trinity); Eph. 3:14, 15 (God the Father); Ps. 2:7, 8 (God the Son); and John 14:26 (God the Holy Spirit).

26. Petrus van Mastricht, *Methodus Concionandi* (Frankfurt an der Oder: M. Hübner, undated).

27. Mastricht, *Theoretico-practica theologia*, II.2.i, 65, *De Existentia et Cognitione Dei*; III.5.i, 311, *De Creatione in genere*; III.9.i, 365, III.9.iv, 368, *De Homine et Imagine Dei*; IV.3.xvi, 362, *De Peccato Actuali.*; V.2, 409-22, *De Mediatore Fœderis Gratiæ*; V.3, 422-35, *De Nominibus Mediatoris*; VII.1.vi, 768, *De Naturâ Ecclesiæ*.

28. Ibid., V.1.iv, 372; V.1.vi, 373; V.1.viii, 375, cf. II.24.xii-xvii; V.1.ix, xv, 394, 395.

differs insofar as he commences with an introductory chapter followed by individual discussion on Father, Son and Holy Spirit.[29] These chapters were present in the 1682 edition. However, a comparison with the 1698 edition reveals several modifications, such as an expanded[30] or added paragraph.[31] The expanded paragraphs are primarily found in the exegetical or elenctic parts and the added paragraphs in the doctrinal and elenctic parts of the 1698 edition. The modifications in the 1698 edition indicate Mastricht's continuing dialogue with his time. He writes extensively about a "certain Dutch theologian" who challenges the classic doctrinal understanding of the generation of the Son. Mastricht's approval of Campegius Vitringa and in particular the expansion on the generation of the Son in the exegetical section of the chapter on *God the Son* points to the H. A. Roël controversy.[32]

Returning to the differences of Mastricht's work from his contemporaries, one notes that where the *Synopsis purioris theologiæ*, Ames, Cloppenburgh, Burman, and Undereyck primarily exposited the doctrine and Brakel and Oomius concentrated, beside the doctrine, on the *praxis* of the doctrine of the Trinity and Hoornbeeck explained this doctrine polemically and practically,[33] it is Mastricht who presents the entire doctrine in his characteristic fourfold approach: exegesis, doctrine, elenctic, and practice. Furthermore, this fourfold approach is extended across the individual chapters.[34] The

29. Ibid., II.24 (De SS. Trinitate), II.25 (De Deo Patre), II.26 (De Deo Filio) and II.27 (De Deo Spiritu S.); Polyander *et al.*, *Synopsis purioris theologiæ*, 7 (De SS Trinitate), 8 (De Persona Patris et Filii), 9 (De Persona Spiritus Sancti); Ames, *Marrow of Sacred Divinity*, V (Of the Subsistence God); Oomius, *Institutiones Theologiæ Practicæ*, I.2.iii cap. I (H. Drie-eenigheyt), cap.II (God den Vader), cap.III (God den Soone), cap.IV (God den H.Geest), cap.V (Bedroeven des H. Geestes), cap.VI (Uytblusschen des Geestes), cap.VII (Tempelen des H. Geestes), cap.VIII (laeten Leyden door den H. Geest); Undereyck, *Halleluja*, III (H.Triniteit); Cloppenburgh, *Theologica Opera Omnia*, vol. 1, Excerc. Theol., locus III. Disp. I prima (De Mysterio SS. Trinitatis: Essentiæ Dei Unitate in Trinitate Personarum), secunda (De Persona Patris & Filii), Disp. II prima (De Persona Patris & Filii), secunda (De Persona Filii & Spiritus S.), Disp. III prima (De Filii Dei vera Divinitate), secunda (De Spiritus Sancti vera Divinitate); Burmannus, *Synopsis Theologiæ*, III De SS. Trinitate: III.30 (De SS. Trinitate & Personarum distinctione), III.31 (De Personis divinis in specie), III.32 (De SS. Trinitate demonstrandæ), III.33 (De Deitate Filii), III.34 (De Deitate Spiritus Sancti), III.35 (De Hæreticorum circa SS. Trinitatem erroribus), III.36 (De Oeconomia trium Personarum); Brakel, *ΛΟΓΙΚΗ ΛΑΤΡΕΙΑ, dat is Redelyke Godtsdienst*, I:4 (Van de Goddelyke Personen). For Johannes Cocceius see Van Asselt, *The Federal Theology of Johannes Cocceius*, 175-93.

30. Mastricht, *Theoretico-practica theologia*, II.24.xix, II.24.xxi (*De SS Trinitate, pars elenchtica*); II.25.xii (*De Deo Patre, pars elenchtica*); II.26.ii (*De Deo Filio, pars exegetica*); II.27.ii (*De Deo Spiritus Sancto, pars exegetica*); II.27.iii, iv (*De Deo Spiritus Sancto, pars dogmatica*).

31. Ibid., II.24.xvii (*De SS Trinitate, pars elenchtica*); II.26.iii-vii (*De Deo Filio, pars dogmatica*).

32. In 1689 Roëll held a disputation on the generation of the Son at Franeker. Mastricht added in the chapter on *God the Son* the paragraph in the elenctic part about the generation of the Son, opposing a certain Dutch theologian and citing favorably C. Vitringa. See for H. A. Roëll, J. van Sluis, *Herman Alexander Roëll* (Leeuwarden, 1988); idem, "De Cartesiaanse Theologie van Herman Alexander Roëll," in *Vier Eeuwen Theologie in Utrecht*, ed. A. De Groot and O. J. De Jong (Zoetermeer: Meinema, 2001), 145.

33. Hoornbeeck, *Theologia practica*, II.1 (*De Deo*); idem, *Summa Controversiarum*, VII (*De Socianismo*). See for the other authors the above mentioned works.

34. See Appendix IV.2.a for the structure of chapters 24 to 27 of the *Theoretico-practica theologia*.

first chapter (on the *Holy Trinity*) can, therefore, be understood as an introduction to and foundation for the subsequent chapters. As the structure of the chapters show, the four chapters are integrally linked and contain shared themes: God the Son as Mediator, God the Father as Creator (Lawgiver) and God the Holy Spirit as Applicator (Teacher). Contrary to Cocceius, Brakel, and Oomius, who give most attention to the discussion of God the Holy Spirit, Mastricht gives an equal amount of space to the exposition of God the Son and God the Holy Spirit.[35] Further examination of the chapters on the *Holy Trinity* (24), *God the Father* (25), *God the Son* (26) and *God the Holy Spirit* (27) shows a comparable doctrinal section. The communion and economy of the Three Persons thus draws one's attention throughout the chapters.[36] In summary, then, though Mastricht, like other Reformed theologians of his time, discusses the doctrine of the Holy Trinity as part of the doctrine of God, he varies with them in the order of presentation of the Trinity and Three Persons, whereby a christological and pneumatological importance is noted.

Content: a Descriptive Analysis

With the preliminary remarks and identified structure of Mastricht's doctrine of the Holy Trinity, we proceed to the descriptive-analytical part of the examination of the doctrine. Our starting point is the exegetical section of chapter 24 (*Holy Trinity*). Here, Mastricht identifies in the text of 2 Corinthians 13:13 (verse 14 in English versions) the Three Persons: the Son, the Father and the Holy Spirit. This order, then, will be followed in our ensuing examination of God the Son (exegetical, doctrinal, and practical sections of chapters 24 and 26), God the Father (exegetical, doctrinal, and practical sections of chapters 24 and 25), and God the Holy Spirit (exegetical, doctrinal, and practical sections of chapters 24 and 27). The elenctic sections of these chapters will not be discussed. The exclusion of these sections in our examination is based on (1) Mastricht's historical treatment of trinitarian controversy in the chapter on the *Holy Trinity*,[37] which is not the focus of our study, (2) his remark that the doctrine of God the Father is less contested,[38] and (3) the size and scope of the H. A. Roëll controversy in the chapter on *God the Son*,[39] which should be treated separately and falls outside the aim of

---

35. The number of pages in the chapter on the *Holy Trinity*: 11; on *God the Father*: 4; on *God the Son*: 11; on *God the Holy Spirit*: 10. All exegetical sections are approximately equal in length, and the doctrinal and practical sections of the chapters on God the Son and God the Holy Spirit are equal in length. The elenctic section of the chapter on *God the Son* is most extensive, and the overall treatment of *God the Father* is most succinct. For Cocceius, Brakel, and Oomius see footnote 29 of this chapter.

36. See Appendix IV.2.b for the structure of the doctrinal sections of chapters 24 to 27 of the *Theoretico-practica theologia*.

37. Mastricht, *Theoretico-practica theologia*, II.24.xvii-xviii, 240, 241.

38. Ibid., 25.x, 248: "Telis hostium, non ita expositum est hoc caput, omnibus fatentibus, Patrem esse *personam* esse item *Deum* etiam *distinctum*, saltem à Filio."

39. Ibid., 26.xvi-xviii, 255-59.

our study. In addition, (4) the structure of each elenctic section parallels the *quæstio* method, which is identified and described in preceding chapters of our study.

The Holy Trinity

Mastricht reminds the reader at the opening of the chapter on the *Holy Trinity* that faith rests upon two foundations: the divine sufficiency and efficiency, whereby one obtains eternal life and happiness. Moreover, the sufficiency is to be distinguished in *essentia* and *subsistentia*. The latter includes the economy of the divine Persons in which each has His own task in the work of one's salvation "as taught by the apostle in 2 Cor. 13:13."[40] This text is, according Mastricht and Cocceius,[41] a *votum* wherewith the apostle imparts a trinitarian blessing for the Corinthians. This wish involves the Son, "the grace of the Lord Jesus Christ," the Father, when "the apostle speaks of the love of God," and the Holy Spirit, namely the "communion of the Holy Spirit."[42] The biblical text, then, contains parts on God the Son, God the Father, and God the Holy Spirit, as also is attested in the *Staten-bijbel*.[43] Mastricht identifies each part as containing a benefit and benefactor.[44]

God the Son: Exegesis

Mastricht argues that in the text the apostle Paul let the Father be preceded by the Son. This should not be understood as an order of *subsistentia* between the divine Persons, as the *Staten-bijbel* also attests,[45] but as an order in conferring the saving benefits, insofar as this relates to the execution: the first benefit is the redemption of the Son.[46]

---

40. Ibid., 24.i, 235: "*Fidem* quâ in Deo quiescimus, ad vitam & beatitudinem æternam, duobus niti fundamentis, supra monuimus: quod Deus *sufficiat*; & quod *efficiat*. *Sufficit* autem, partim per *essentiam* & attributa essentialia, quibus existit אשר שדי: partim per *subsistentiam*, qua tres Deitatis personæ...docente Apostolo 2 Cor. 13:13."

41. Cocceius, *Opera Omnia Theologica*, vol. 5, *Epist. Ad Corinthios II*, cap. xiii, 455, § 55: "Est in distinctis hisce comprecationibus typus & unitatis & trinitatis. Invocatur hic Trinitas."

42. 2 Corinthians 13:13, Ἡ χάρις τοῦ κυρίου Ἰησοῦ Χριστοῦ καὶ ἡ ἀγάπη τοῦ θεοῦ καὶ ἡ κοινωνία τοῦ ἁγίου πνεύματος μετὰ πάντων ὑμῶν. Cf. Mastricht, *Theoretico-practica theologia*, II.24, 235: "*Gratia Domini Jesu Christi & charitas Dei, & communicatio Spiritus Sancti, sit cum omnibus vobis, Amen.*"

43. *Bijbel, dat is de gansche Heilige Schrift...met niewe bijgevoegde verklaringen op de duistere plaatsen* (Amsterdam: Wed. G. De Groot, 1738), 2 Cor. 13:13 fn. 36, fol. 105: "Alzoo dat hier een klaar getuigenis is van de Heilge Drievuldigheid."

44. Mastricht, *Theoretico-practica theologia*, II.24.ii, 235, 236: "1. Filium, gratia Domini Jesu Christi...A. Beneficium, *quod oratur*, gratia: B. Benefactor, *repræsentatus*: 2. Patrem, amor Dei. A. Beneficium, amor ἀγάπη. B. Benefactor, Deus. Scil. Pater. 3. Spiritum Sanctum, communicatio Spiritus S. A. Beneficium, κοινωνία, communicatio. B. Benefactor, qui appellatur 1. Spiritus...2. Sanctus....."

45. *Bijbel, dat is de gansche Heilige Schrift*, 2 Cor. 13:13 fn.36, fol. 105: "hoewel de orde der personen hier niet gesteld wordt gelijk Matth. 28:19."

46. Mastricht, *Theoretico-practica theologia*, II.24.ii, 235: "*Præmittendo Patri Filium, non tam respicit ordinem* subsistendi *in personis*"; and II.24.ii, 236: "*Patrem*...(B) Est autem Deus...sed etiam, *ut* Filii, *ratione* ordinis *subsistendi*...."

Mastricht then identifies in the text a prayer for a benefit: grace. The text, he explains, does not refer to the grace *naturalis* belonging to the entire Trinity.[47] It refers to the grace *personalis*, which belongs in the household of the Trinity to the Son,[48] "who has acquired redemption for miserable people."[49] One notes the redemptive or salvific character of this part of the biblical interpretation. Here Mastricht echoes the explication of Calvin[50] and Poole.[51] Calvin's reading of the text is also noticeable in Mastricht's threefold division of the prayer and benefactor: Lord, Jesus, and Christ.[52] These three names are distinctive but point to a single interpretation: the Son as mediator.[53]

This central notion of God the Son as Mediator is further explicated in the exegetical section of *God the Son*, an exposition of Psalm 2:7, 8.[54] This text, according to Mastricht, proclaims (1) the household pact (*œconomicum officium*), (2) the Second Person of the Trinity, and (3) His office.[55] Also, the analysis of the biblical text includes, for Mastricht, the covenant of the divine economy, אספרה אל חק, and the Son as 'economicus' (Persona *Filii ceu oeconomi*). The Second Person of the Trinity is treated

47. Ibid., II.24.ii, 235: "Beneficium *quod oratur, gratia: non naturalis illa, toti Trinitati communis, de qua supra*; sed personalis...." Mastricht refers here indirectly to II.17.xiv, 180, "Quid gratia, re tenus? ...Quod *naturalia, cum ex benevolâ Dei constitutione, creaturæ cuivis, si non individuo saltem specie tenus*, q. debeantur."

48. The word *oikonomia* (II.24.ii), or household, is a recurring word throughout the chapters on the Trinity.

49. Mastricht, *Theoretico-practica theologia*, II.24.ii, 235: "*sed personalis, quæ consistit* in redemptione *miseri*."

50. John Calvin, *Commentary*, vol. 20, *The Second Epistle to the Corinthians* (1844-55; reprint, Grand Rapids: Baker Books, 1989), 403: "*The grace of the Lord Jesus.* He [Paul] closes the Epistle with a prayer...in which the sum of our salvation consist...The term *grace* does not here mean unmerited favour, but is taken by metonymy, to denote the whole benefit of redemption."

51. Matthew Poole, *Synopsis criticorum aliorumque S.Scripturæ interpretum* (London: E. Flesher, 1676), 5:663: "[vers.]13. *Gratia Domini* &c. Sic vocat totum redemptionis beneficium, vel gratuitam beneficentiam Christi Redemptoris nostri, gratiam quæ datur, vel à Christo ut authore, secundum Divinam naturam."

52. Calvin, *Commentary*, vol. 20, *Second Epistle to the Corinthians*, 403: "...the prayer, which contains three clauses..."

53. Mastricht, *Theoretico-practica theologia*, II.24.ii.1.B, 236: "Benefactor; *1. Ab auctoritate*, Domini. Est triplex *Dominium in Sripturis obvium. 1. Dominium naturæ divinæ...2. Dominium personæ...3 Dominium mediatorium...Istud hoc loco Apostolus, Filio peculiariter tribuit. 2. A nomine proprio*, Jesu. *Quo redemptor ex officio designatur...3. A nomine appellativo*, Christo, *quo unctus & vocatus ad* officium *mediatorium designatur*." See for additional explanations of the names Mediator, Jesus, and Christ, Mastricht, *Theoretico-practica theologia*, V.3.x and V.3.xi, 425.

54. Psalm 2:7-8, "I will declare the decree: the LORD hath said unto me, You are my Son; this day have I begotten You. Ask of me, and I shall give You the heathen *for* Your inheritance, and the uttermost parts of the earth *for* Your possession." Cf. Mastricht, *Theoretico-practica theologia*, II.26, 250: "*Narrabo ipsum decretum: Filius meus tu es, ego hodie genui te, postula à me & dabo Gentes hæreditatem tuam.*"

55. Mastricht, *Theoretico practica theologia*, II.26.ii, 250: "Proinde...*Filium* contemplabimur qui sui προσωπογραφίαν, & officium œconomicum, ex *pacto* œconomico refert, verbis præfix, ex Psalmo 2:7,8."

from the perspective of the speaker, יהוה, and the saying, אמר. The latter includes, then, a discussion on the Sonship, בני אתה, the generation, אני היום ילדתיך, and the heritage, גוים נחלתך ואחזתך. In addition, the generation of the Son is worked out in meticulous detail, discussing who generates, אני, the time of generation, היום, the act of generation, ילדתי, and the generated one, David, a type of Christ.[56] Thus Mastricht, like Cocceius and Poole,[57] takes the entire text and breaks it down into individual (identifiable) parts. He then expounds each part individually and brings it all together in closing. To show the depth of his argument, we will examine Mastricht's first part of the biblical text: the Son and covenant.[58]

The text (Ps. 2:7) begins with the covenant between the Father and the Son. The Son is introduced in a speaking manner, "such as one finds in verse 6 and Song of Solomon and other poetry."[59] These words, accordingly, can be understood as a *typus*, the confirmation of the kingdom to David, and *antitypus*, the proclamation of the eternal covenant to Christ. Mastricht assures the reader that the biblical text really speaks of a covenant. He argues that the word חק constitutes a *concilium pacis*, or council of peace.[60] That it is a divine covenant is based on the word אל, which is used instead of את (Judg. 7:25; Isa. 38:19; Jer. 4:23; 10:2). Mastricht notes that some read אל (El) as the Arabic word אל (Al), which points to an accusative. Others render אל (El) as "till," which results in the reading of coming to a *decrectum* or coming to a law. Others, he continues, render the word as "of": "I will declare *of* the degree" (Job 42:7; Ps. 79:27; Jer. 27:19; Ezek. 21:28). In addition, he notes the rendering "according to" (indicating a proclamation of what has been decided, and thus synthesizing the preceding text words) or emphatically or the genitive reading of אל (LXX translators, the Targum, Arabic, Ethiopian, and Vulgate translations, following the Masoretes). Whatever reading one follows, Mastricht writes, the text indicates the covenant between the Father and the Son (Isa. 53:10 or Zech. 6:10, the council of peace—*concilium pacis*) by which the Father says, "You are my Son." The christological and covenantal interpretation is obvious. Calvin attests the former, though he renders a stronger Davidic interpretation than Mastricht.[61]

56. Ibid., 251, 252: "*1. Fœdus œconomicum, inter se & Patrem*: Narrabo ipsum decretum...2. Persona *Filii, ceu œconomi*: Filius meus tu...a. dicens *Jehova*...B. Dictum: Filius meus tu es...1. Filiatio בני אתה ...2. Generatio *æterno*...α. generans אני...β. generandi tempus, היום...γ. generandi actus ילדתי...δ. genitus, te...3. Hæreditas...a. Stipulatio *Patris œconomica*...b. Promissio *reciproca*..."

57. Cocceius, *Opera Anekdota Theologica et Philologica*, vol. 1, *Analysis Psalmorum*, Ps. II, 382; Poole, *Synopsis*, vol. 2, Psalmorum, Ps. II, 509-25.

58. Mastricht, *Theoretico-practica theologia*, II.26.ii, 251, 252. The remainder of the biblical text is also expounded by Mastricht in depth, but we will summarize his exegetical results.

59. Ibid., 251: "*1. Fœdus œconomicum...Ex abrupto introducitur persona secunda loquens, nempe idem Rex, de quo vers.6 quales sermonum alternationes, non raræ sunt, in Cantico, aliisque scriptis Poëticis.*" This sentence is *verbatim* present in Poole's commentary, with the reference "Gej[erus]." Cf. Poole, *Synopsis* 2:509.

60. Mastricht, *Theoretico-practica theologia*, II.26.ii, 251: "הק, *statutum notat, quod constitutum sit, in æterno consilio Pacis, inter Patrem & se.*"

61. Calvin, *Commentary*, vol. 4, *The Psalms*, 16-18.

In addition, the messianic reading of this psalm was, according to Poole and Cocceius, also argued by the rabbis.[62] The covenantal interpretation is shared by Poole, who, like Cocceius, Witsius, and the annotated *Staten-bijbel*, defends the interpretation of the eternal decree, or *pactum*, between God Father and the Son.[63] In summary, Mastricht's identification and interpretation of the covenant, or *pactum*, and Messiah in Psalm 2 is shared by other Reformed as well as Jewish commentators. In respect to the Reformed exegetes, the christological importance is particular further noted in Mastricht's remaining text analysis.[64]

The speaker in the text is יהוה and should be taken here, according to Mastricht, as a personal and household name of the Father as "is confirmed in the text."[65] The question then arises, "When, did He say?" Some, according to Mastricht, answer by pointing to the baptism (Matt. 3:17) or to the time of the transfiguration (Matt. 17:5). However, Mastricht argues that the biblical text word points to an eternal stability. Thus, from eternity to eternity is the divine "now," היום.[66] The saying אתה, Mastricht notes, speaks of the Second Person, as אתה relates grammatically to the Sonship, בני. Accordingly, one should not follow the vocative reading of Grotius's antitrinitarian hypothesis, "O! my son."[67] No, Mastricht argues it should be read emphatically, "My son you are! . . . not by creation, as Adam (Luke 3:38) or angels (Job 38:7), and not by adoption, which belongs to the believers (John 1:12; 1 John 3:1), but by nature and generation." Thus, the Second Person, generated by the Father, is divine. Mastricht also counters the Socinians by stating that the one generated, "You," is not ultimately David. He notes that others interpret this (You) as David—an example of Christ—or as Solomon (2 Sam. 7:14). However, he comments that most interpret the text as speaking about the

62. Cocceius, *Opera Anekdota Theologica et Philologica*, vol. 1, *Analysis Psalmorum*, Ps. II, 382: "Christi ἐνθρονισμὸς inthronisatio & communiter Status regni ejus inter hostes hoc Psalmo depingitur. Veteres Hebræi cum Chaldæo absque omni dubitatione de Christo accipiunt"; Poole, *Synopsis criticorum aliorumque S.Scripturæ interpretum*, 2:509 (20): "De Messia, de quo veteres *Rabbini intellexerunt*, ait K[imchi] in sine hujus Psalmi. Hic *Psalmus aut de Davide agit, aut de Messia*...R. Obadiah Haggaon...R. Johanan in Midras Tillim...& Maimon[ide]...R.S. Jarchi in commentariis ad hunc Psalmum hæc habet; *Doctores nostri exposuerunt* [hujus Psalmi] *significatum de Rege* Messiah."

63. *Bijbel, dat is de gansche Heilige Schrift*, Ps. II.7 fn.17, fol. 262: "Of, *inzetting, ordinantie*, die de Vader gemaakt heeft over mij, als zijn eenigen eeuwigen Zoon...als een fondament, waarop God Hem tot een Hoofd en Heere over zijne kerk gesteld heeft"; Cocceius, *Opera Anekdota Theologica et Philologica*, vol. 1, *Analysis Psalmorum*, Ps. II, 382: "*Narrabo juxta statutum*, quemadmodum audivi & vidi apud Patrem meum, utque is mecum ab æterno pactus est lege immutabili, ita exponam hominibus"; Poole, *Synopsis*, 2:516 (20): "decretum"; Witsius, *De oeconomia Foederum Dei*, II.2.vii, 133: "Denique huc referri potest, quod Zach. 6:13 exstat; *Consilium Pacis est inter Utrumque*."

64. Mastricht, *Theoretico-practica theologia*, II.26.ii, 251, 252: "a. Dicens...b. Dictum...1. Filiatio...2. Generatio...α. generans...β. Generandi tempus...γ. Generandi actus...δ. Genitus...."

65. Ibid., 251: "a. Dicens *Jehova*...hic personaliter & *oeconomice capitur, pro* Patre, *sicut passim* Ps. 33:6."

66. Ibid.: "Dixit, *quando?* ...*cum ratione* decreti, *ante omne tempus; ratione* exsecutionis *in tempore, dixerit, dictat & dicturus sit*."

67. See further part III, chapter 1 of this study.

Messiah, as is testified in the New Testament (Acts 13:33; Heb. 1:5), and that the Son is not spoken of as adopted but as His own (*proprio*) Son (Rom. 8:32, John 1:4; 3:16). Mastricht concludes, then, by affirming the divinity of the Son and the personal distinction between the Father and the Son.[68]

In the second part of the text, Mastricht concentrates on the heritage of "the nations." According to him, the text speaks here of a promise, in which is made known the lordship of the Mediator, resulting from His redemptive work.[69]

In summary, the exposition of 2 Corinthians 13:13, whereby God the Son as Mediator is explicated as central to the redemptive work, is deepened by Mastricht with the exegesis of Psalm 2:7, 8. Like other exegetes such as Cocceius, Poole, and rabbinic commentators, he identifies in this psalm the covenant relationship between God the Father and the Son, the Mediator. In respect to method, Mastricht utilizes his Hebrew language skills extensively in order to determine the literal meaning of the biblical text words. Thus, for Mastricht, the Second Person of the Holy Trinity and God the Father are in eternal *pactum*, in which God the Son is identified as the Mediator.

God the Son: Doctrine

Following the exposition of 2 Corinthians 13:13, Mastricht argues at the opening of the doctrinal part (on the *Holy Trinity*) that this wish (*votum*) is an adoration of the divine one-ness and three-ness and of a threefold benefit of the household, "so it cannot be otherwise that there is one God in three distinct Persons, and also distinct to their offices and benefits in the diverse economy."[70] This multiplicity of persons and unity of God is, according to Mastricht, attested in Scripture in several places. First, there are places where God speaks as the plural one (Elohim, Gen. 1:26; 3:22; 11:7). This argument is present, for example, in *Synopsis purioris theologiæ*, Cloppenburgh, Oomius, and Brakel[71] but not by Cocceius.[72] Mastricht moderates this proof as he considers that (1) the same grammatical structure is used for idols (Judg. 16:23, 24) and humans (Exod. 4:16) and one person of the Godhead (Ps. 45:8) and that syntactically one could construct three essences as well as three persons. For these reasons and his reminder of

---

68. Mastricht, *Theoretico-practica theologia*, II.26.ii, 251: "*Ex quo patet, tum Filii* deitas; *tum* distinctio *personalis inter Patrem & Filium.*"

69. Ibid., 252: "(3.b) *Denotatur* dominium Mediatorium, *ei, ex redemptione....*"

70. Ibid., 24.iii, 236: "Cum igitur ὁμολογουμένως, hoc voto contineatur adoratio (Deo propria Matth.4:10) adoratio *unius* Dei & adoratio *trium*, trium *uniformis*, & pro triplici beneficio *œconomico.*"

71. Polyander *et al.*, *Synopsis purioris theologiæ*, 7.xl, 65: "Prima classis est eorum locorum, in quibus Elohim"; Cloppenburgh, *Theologica Opera Omnia*, vol. 1, Exerc. Theol. Locus III Disp. I secunda, 759: "Plures unâ Deitatis Personas *indefinite* indicant loca illa. *Faciamus hominem ad imaginem & similitudinem nostram* Gen. 1:26"; Oomius, *Institutiones Theologiæ Practicæ*, III.2.i, 21: "Wie soude een klaerder bewys begeeren? Want wy sien de persoonen in het getal van velen, *Laet ons, na onse gelijckenisse*"; Brakel, ΛΟΓΙΚΗ ΛΑΤΡΕΙΑ, *dat is Redelyke Godtsdienst*, I:4.v, 111. The marginal note is explained in paragraph 5: "In het Goddelyke Wesen zyn DRIE Personen, 't Welk blykt: 1. Uyt de benaming ELOHIM."

72. Cocceius, *Opera Anekdota Theologica et Philologica*, vol. 1, *Curæ priores in Genesin*, caput I, 1, § 4. Cf. ibid., *Opera Omnia Theologica*, vol. 7, *Summa Doctrinæ*, cap. xi, § 177, § 46.

Calvin's "response to the antitrinitarians," Mastricht sets aside this option. Other options to consider, according Mastricht are (2) those places where Jehovah is distinct from Adonai (3) and those places where God's name is repeated differently in the text. Nevertheless, he affirms with the ecumenical creeds and other Reformed theologians of his time that one God is three in Persons.

From the foregoing exegesis, we have seen that Mastricht described God the Son primarily as Mediator.[73] In the doctrinal sections, a fuller explanation is given of the Mediator. God the Son is generated from eternity by the Father (Mic. 5:1)[74] and is distinct from the Father and the Holy Spirit as the second *Person* of the Trinity.[75] He is divine, has names (Jehovah, Hos. 1:7; Lord [of glory]; 1 Cor. 2:8) and attributes (for example, spiritual, independent, eternal), and should be honored.[76] With these descriptions Mastricht emphasizes the unity of the Godhead. However, in the context of the offices of the divine household, Mastricht argues that based on the text (Ps. 2:7), God the Son is the *expromissor* (one relieving another of debt by taking it upon himself, Heb. 7:22), Goël (Job 19:25; 17:3; Isa. 38:14), and Redeemer.[77] The Son, he continues, is the dispenser of the covenant and the *expromissor* (Heb. 7:22, ἔγγυος, "By so much was Jesus made a surety of a better testament"), the Envoy of the Father, the Logos to explain the Word, the Head of the church, and Judge of the living and dead (Rom 11:16).[78] Thus, Mastricht posits Christ in the Trinity as Mediator from eternity: *expromissor*, not *fideiussior*. Hereby, he differs from Cocceius,[79] although Mastricht emphasizes in the chapter the *Covenant of Grace* that one should not strictly demand the *expromissor* position.[80]

---

73. Mastricht, *Theoretico-practica theologia*, II.24.ii, 236: " (b.1) *Dominium* mediatorum... *Istud hoc loco Apostolus, Filio peculiariter tribuit.*"

74. Ibid., 26.iv, 253: "Est igitur nobis, *Filius* secunda Trinitatis persona, ab æterno à Patre genita Mich.v.1.... See also II.26.vii, 253. For a representative description of Mastricht's argument of the eternal generation of the Son, see Heppe, *Reformed Dogmatics*, 125.

75. Mastricht, *Theoretico-practica theologia*, II.26.vi, 253: "*Secundo,* discrimen ejus à Patre & Spiritu S. distingui agnoscunt...sed 1. ut *persona* divina...2. ut *secunda* è tribus personis. Differt 3. per suas *proprietates* personales..."

76. Ibid., viii-xii, 254.

77. Ibid., 24.xii, 238, 239: "*Gubernium* hujus familiæ, personæ susceperunt...Rursus *secunda* persona, ut media, *Mediatoris* pensum suscepit....Ibid. *Expromissoris...Goëlis...Redemptoris*"; 26.ii, 251: "*Quibus continetur* promulgatio *fœderis æterni, quod coiit inter Patrem & Filium, super officio Filii Mediatorio, penes quod repræsentatur:...ita Filius, expromissoris, dispensatoris, redemptoris*"; 26.xiii, 255: "Tandem *quarto, officium œconomicum* quod Filius...ex statuto œconomico, narrat in textu, & ex *consilio pacis* inter personas, suscepit....Secundo, sponsor seu *expromissor...*Tertio, Mediator...*Quarto, Redemptor.*"

78. Ibid., 26.xiii, 255.

79. Cocceius, *Opera Omnia Theologica*, vol. 7, *Summa Doctrinæ*, cap v, 61-66, §§ 91-117. See also Asselt, *Amicitia Dei*, 100-102.

80. Mastricht, *Theoretico-practica theologia*, V.1.xxxiv, 402: "An sponsio Filii in fœdere gratiæ æterno habuerit rationem *fidejussionis*, an *expromissionis*?. . .Reformati reliqui existimant Filium æternâ illâ sponsione, solutionem seu satisfactionem *absolutè* spopondisse...quamvis interim adjiciant, divinam hanc

In summary, Mastricht provides an extensive discussion of the Second Person of the Trinity in relation to the work of redemption grounded in the eternal *pactum*.[81] Where, for example, Ames and Brakel do not deal with this aspect in their discussions of the divine Persons but give attention to the eternal generation of the Son,[82] Mastricht is accompanied on this issue by federal theologians such as Burman and Undereyck.[83] For Mastricht, the exegesis of 2 Corinthians 13:13 gives the primacy to God the Son as Mediator in the explication of the biblical text. The exposition of Psalm 2:7 gives Mastricht reason not only to identify God the Son as Mediator but also to recognize the eternal *pactum* between the Father and the Second Person. In the doctrinal section, Mastricht expounds his exegesis with additional testimony of Scripture and describes the Mediator as the *expromissor* of the *pactum*. In other words, the work of redemption takes center stage in the discussion of the Second Person of the Godhead in the context of the doctrine of the Holy Trinity. The *basso continuo*, here, is for Mastricht the redemptive mediatorial character of God the Son.

God the Son: Practical

The teaching of the Holy Trinity should lead to the glory of God[84] and a seeking of the communion of the Three Persons.[85] This is a thought shared, for example, by Oomius.[86] This communion, Mastricht argues, is reflected in the covenant and communion of the saints.[87] In respect to God the Son, the Mediator, Mastricht states that one should desire to know more and more the Son, for it is He who is proclaimed, according to the decree, by the Father to us.[88] Therefore, Mastricht urges that the Son should be known as dispenser, like Joseph (Gen. 39:4, 8, 9), so that one bows the heart before Him (Phil. 2:10, 11). To know Him as *expromissor* is to deny one's own

expromissionem, ad leges civilis cujusvis expromissionis, non ita rigidè & per omnia, esse exigendam." See also, W. J. van Asselt, "Christus Sponsor. Een bijdrage tot de geschiedenis van het coccejanisme," in *Kerk en Theologie*, 53 (2002), 108-124.

81. This is further explicated by Mastricht in his discussion of the covenant of grace (Ibid., V.1.vii, 375).

82. Ames, *Marrow of Sacred Divinity*, V.12-13, 17, 18; Brakel, *ΛΟΓΙΚΗ ΛΑΤΡΕΙΑ, dat is Redelyke Godtsdienst*, I:4.ix-xxv, 116-31.

83. Burmannus, *Synopsis Theologiae*, I.36.xi, 230; Undereyck, *Halleluja* (1678), III.5, 13.

84. Mastricht, *Theoretico-practica theologia*, II.24.xxiii, 244: "*Secundò*, argumentum nobis suppeditat S. Trinitas *glorificationis*..." Mastricht diverges, here, reversing his usual order in the practical section: (1) the glory of God and the humbling of man, and (2) admonition or warning. The first paragraph of the practical section of chapter 24 deals with a warning against atheism.

85. Ibid., xxv, 245: "*Quartò*, allicit communionem SS. Trinitatis omni *conatu ambiamus*..."

86. Oomius, *Institutiones Theologiae Practicae*, III.2.i, 49.

87. Mastricht, *Theoretico-practica theologia*, II.24.xxvi and xxxvii, 245.

88. Ibid., 26.xxi, 259: "*Secundò*, accendit *desiderium*, Filium istum, qui ex statuto Patris, seipsum nobis narrat..."

righteousness and seek Him for all one's needs (Phil. 3:9, 10), thus resting in one's salvation.[89] Thus, Mastricht carries the redemptive theme, arising from the biblical text and formulated doctrine, to the practical section. The believer is directed to the Second Person: He is the all-sufficient one because He is divine. His sufficiency originates and flows forth from the council of peace (Ps. 2:7).[90] This doctrine, he argues, excites our hope and trust of eternal life in the Son (Ps. 2:12).[91] In summary, the *praxis* of the *locus God the Son* has a soteriological and an eschatological dimension. These practical dimensions arise, according to Mastricht, from the formulated doctrine, which in turn is developed from the exegesis of the immediate text, connected with and derived from the initial exegesis of 2 Corinthians 13:13 and following the exegesis of Psalm 2:7. In respect to the structure, we note the fourfold approach in an extended manner, and a parallel with the identified individual section structure.[92] In respect to the content of these sections, we note that the doctrine of the *pactum*, in which the Son has a prominent role, is a central throught in Mastricht's development of the doctrine of the Holy Trinity.

We conclude, then, that Mastricht's exposition, exegetical and doctrinal, of the Second Person of the Trinity emphasizes the eternal *pactum* and the position of God the Son in it as Mediator and *expromissor*. The soteriological implications are notable in the practical section, where Mastricht points the believer to Christ.

God the Father: Exegesis

In respect to the Father, the text of 2 Corinthians 13:13 speaks of a benefit: the "love of God." Mastricht argues that ἀγάπη should be understood as (1) an electing love, "which the apostle derives from προγινώσκω (Rom. 8:29), namely the foreknowledge and gift of the Son (John 3:16)"; (2) benevolent love, which signifies that the Father has given the Son for redemption and precedes the redemption and faith in the Redeemer; and (3) a well-pleasing love, which follows upon faith (Heb. 11:3) and whereby the Father is reconciled in Christ with the redeemed.[93] The first interpretation of Mastricht concurs with Calvin, who comments,

---

89. Ibid., xxi, 260: "Tum 2. ut *Expromissor* ut abnegatâ penitus omni *propria* justitia....Porro 3. ut *Mediator*....Etiam 4. ut *Redemptor*..."

90. Ibid., xxii, 260: "Hinc *tertiò*, nobis commendat *sufficientiam* & perfectionem Mediatoris nostri...Quæ quidem *sufficientia*, oriunda est: 1. A *personæ* dignitate & præstantia...sed *Filius* Dei...2. oriunda hæc est sufficientia, ex *statuto* Patris quod Filius nobis narrat Ps. 2:7 ex *consilio Pacis* Zach. 6:13..."

91. Ibid., xxvi, 261: "Ad hæc *septimò*, nos excitat *spem* & fiduciam vitæ eternæ, in Filio collocemus Ps. 2:12...."

92. See III.1, III.2, III.3, and III.4 of this study. The only exception is that the practical part of *God the Son* contains more exhortations than identified in III.4.

93. Mastricht, *Theoretico-practica theologia*, II.24.ii, 236: "*Beneficium*, amor ἀγάπη. *Intelligitur* amor electionis... *Proinde non tantum* amor iste benevolentiæ, *qui præcedit ordine naturæ redemptionem, & fidem in Redemptorem; sed etiam* complacentiæ, *qui sequitur* fidem Heb. XI. 3. *quo iam reconciliatus eos complectitur, propter gratiam Filii:*"

The order [grace and love] however, may appear to be here inverted, because the *love of God* is placed *second*, while it is the source of that grace and hence it is *first* in order,[94]

and Poole, who refers to John 3:16.[95] Mastricht, then, identifies further in 2 Corinthians 13:13 the benefactor: God the Father is appropriated in the economy as Lord, Creator, Lawgiver, and *Pater familias*.[96] Consequently, God is Father in respect to humanity and to the Second Person of the Trinity, particularly as Mediator. The latter is the case because, Mastricht concludes, the Son became in the council of peace a debtor for the debt of the elect, and thus the Son is subjected to the Father.[97] Here one notes the link with the preceding exegesis and doctrinal formulation on God the Son and the eternal *pactum* of which God the Father is the *pater familias*.

The language of Father of the divine household is repeated in the exegesis of the chapter on *God the Father*. Here Mastricht expounds the text of Ephesians 3:14, 15, Τούτου χάριν κάμπτω τὰ γόνατά μου πρὸς τὸν πατέρα, ἐξ οὗ πᾶσα πατριὰ ἐν οὐρανοῖς καὶ ἐπὶ γῆς ὀνομάζεται.[98] The text, he argues, as does his student Petrus Dinant,[99] is a part of an invocation, a prayer of the apostle Paul for the Ephesians. Mastricht distinguishes two major parts of the text: the prayer and the one prayed to.[100] The former is κάμπτω, a prayer to God the Father, a "submission to the Father as head of the household."[101] The second part of the text refers, according to Mastricht, to the Father of the divine household, as Gubernator, Legislator, Judge, and Vindicator but above all as the benevolent Curator of the family. The judicial aspect of God the Father

---

94. Calvin, *Commentary*, vol. 20, *Second Epistle to the Corinthians*, 403.

95. Poole, *Synopsis*, 5:664 (10): "*Patri tribuit charitatem, qui sic dilexit mundum* &c Joh. 3:16."

96. Mastricht, *Theoretico-practica theologia*, II.24.ii, 236: "*Pater, qui Deus est...In œconomia enim, quâ Dominus, Creator, Legislator, Pater familias.*" Œconomia is rendered as "huishouding der Genade" in Mastricht's *Beschouwende en Praktikale Godgeleerdheit, waarin, door alle Godgeleerde Hoofdstukken henen, het Bijbelverklarende, Leerstellige, Wederleggende, en Praktikale deel, door eenen onafgebroken schakel onderscheidendlyk samengevoegt, voorgestelt word* (Rotterdam: Hendrik van Pelt; Utrecht: Jan Jacob van Poolsum, 1749), 1:II.24.ii, 578.

97. Mastricht, *Theoretico-practica theologia*, II.24.ii, 236: "*Est autem Deus...nec tantum respectu Christi...aut ut Mediatoris...& potissimûm respectu provinciæ redemptoriæ, quâ in consilio pacis, pro reatu electorum, Patris debitor factus est adeoque subjectus velut Deo.*"

98. Ephesians 3:14-15, "For this cause I bow my knees unto the Father of our Lord Jesus Christ, Of whom the whole family in heaven and earth is named" (King James Version).

99. Petrus Dinant, *De Brief van de H. Apostel Paulus aan die van Efeze, verklaart en toegepast*, 2ᵈᵉ druk (Rotterdam: Jan Daniel Beman, 1726), 2:200: "...namelijk een aanspraak...die de Apostel doet...tot wie hij zijne bede richt, te vinden in het viertiende en vijftiende vers...."

100. Mastricht, *Theoretico-practica theologia*, II.25.ii, 246: "*Quibus pars continetur voti illius, seu invocationis illius...*1. Invocationem...2. Invocatum."

101. Ibid.: "*...arguit invocatum Patrem, esse Deum: & subjectionem quæ Patri.... œconomicè peculiaris est.*"

is also noted by Dinant, but he does not speak of the divine economy.[102] Mastricht also notes that the biblical text speaks of the Son of the household, "our Lord Jesus Christ, particularly as Mediator."[103] This household includes the family (πᾶσα πατριά, celestial (οὐρανοῖς) and terrestrial (ἐπὶ γῆς): the universal church militant.[104] This explication is not shared in its entirety by Calvin, Poole, and Dinant, who nevertheless identify this text part as a prayer.[105] The difference is that these exegetes do not explicate the text in reference to either God the Father or the economic Trinity or divine family. Cocceius, on the other hand, explicates this text part at length and notes the divine familial element but not to the extent of Mastricht's exposition.[106] Thus, Mastricht is arguably different from his exegetical contemporaries on the exposition of Ephesians 3:13, 14. The importance of the economic Trinity cannot be overlooked, whereby God the Father as Lawgiver is placed over against God the Son as representative of the elect in the eternal *pactum*.

God the Father: Doctrine

The description of God the Father defined in the exegetical section is further expounded by Mastricht in the doctrinal part in the context of the offices of the divine economy. He argues that the First Person as Father of the family conducts Himself as Lord in predestination in order to prepare the future family (Eph. 1:2; Acts 4:28)[107] and, "as is seen in the exegetical part,"[108] as Creator (Gen. 1:1; Ps. 33:6) and Legislator and Judge (Gen. 18:25). Here one notes that the exegesis of Ephesians 3:14 is succinctly expanded with other scriptural references and contextualized in the covenant of the divine economy. God the Father, according to Mastricht is (1) Lord (Matt. 11:25; Eph. 4:5): the one who prepared to build the household (Heb. 3:4); and (2) Creator (Exod. 20:11): the one who built the house and is its owner. Therefore, (3) He is the Legislator (James 4:12): the one who gives created humanity the law of nature (Gen. 2:17),

---

102. Dinant, *De Brief van de H. Apostel Paulus aan die van Efeze*, 2:204, 205: "Dit [De Vader] ziet op den eerste Persoon in het Goddelijke Wezen...die zich gedraagt als Rechter in het werk der verlossing . . ."

103. Mastricht, *Theoretico-practica theologia*, II.25.ii, 246.

104. Ibid., 246, 247: "2. Invocatum, *quem repræsentat sub* σχέσει ...c. Familia...1. Cœlestis...2. Terrestris...3. *Utriusque* origo...."

105. Calvin, *Commentary*, vol. , *Epistle of Paul to the Ephesians*, 259: "His prayers"; Poole, *Synopsis*, 5:781; Dinant, *De Brief van de H. Apostel Paulus aan die van Efeze*, 2:202. Dinant identifies three parts in the text: (1) His [Paul] reverend prayer; (2) the object of prayer: God and Father of our Lord Jesus Christ; and (3) the assurance of this prayer: the whole family in heaven and earth is named.

106. Cocceius, *Opera Omnia Theologica*, vol. 5, *Commentarius in Epistol. ad Ephesios*, 176, § 85: "Domus pro familia...": § 86: " & indicando rationem Dei appellandi *Patris*."

107. Mastricht, *Theoretico-practica theologia*, II.25.vii, 247: "...Pater est: 1. *Dominus*...æterna prædestinatione, futuræ *familiæ*..."

108. Ibid., 24.xii, 238: "...proinde *Deum*, non tantum θεολογικως; sed & οικονομικως h.e.non tantum per *naturum* & *essentiam*, (quod omnibus personis est commune) sed etiam q. per officium œconomicum...ut vidimus in exegeticis 2 Cor. 13:13."

confirming this in a covenant with humanity.[109] Moreover, He is (4) Vindicator of the violated law and (5) the merciful Father (Ps. 103:13) who "provides in the council of peace a Mediator for redemption."[110] In summary, the doctrinal part restates Mastricht's exegetical observations and expands these with additional Scripture testimonies. Doctrinally, the position of the Father is primarily that of Lawgiver in the eternal *pactum*, though He also provided a Mediator.

God the Father: Practical

Mastricht's exegetical observations are continued in the practical section of the chapter on *God the Father*. First, he argues that the lordship of God the Father as head of the family demands honor and glory. Here Mastricht refers to the chapter *De Gloria Dei*, where he notes in the doctrinal part that the glory of God is propagated, among other things, by humanity when people publicly acknowledge the divine glory;[111] and in the practical part, he asserts that the glory and majesty of God provokes one to glorify His name (1 Cor. 6:20), with the heart and mouth. Indeed, the entire book of Psalms gives reasons to proclaim His glory.[112] Furthermore, His lordship stimulates one to patiently (1 Sam. 3:18) and with thanksgiving (Job 1:21) bear divine chastening, "like it is not unusual for a natural father to chastise."[113] Here, one notes the typical structure of the practical part: the glory of God and the humbling of man.

Mastricht also refers to the practical part of the chapter *De Potestate & Potentia Dei*. He notes here that "His people" should acknowledge more the omnipotent one and promptly confess to be owned by Him, whatever is brought upon their way, so that they are more ready to be thankful in prosperity, patient in adversity, and to trust in him for the future.[114] The lordship of God the Father instructs one to live in submission and obedience to His glory. In addition, Mastricht points to the practical aspect of God as Creator. He argues that "Eph.3:14 πρὸς τὸν πατέρα" should lead one to submissive thankfulness for the giving of natural life (Acts 17:25, 28) and spiritual life (Eph. 2:1) and eternal life, which will be granted in the time to come (1 John 1:2). In addition, it should lead one to total dedication to God for everything that is received,[115] as well as fidelity in

---

109. Ibid., 25.vii, 247: "Pater est:...3. Legislator...*instruxit* lege *naturæ*...& lege *positiva* Gen. 2:17, illamque *sancivit* communicatione & promissione, inito quodam cum homine *fœdere.*"

110. Ibid.: "Pater est:...5.misericors *Pater* Psal. 103:13 qui, juxta æternum *pacis consilium*, peccatoribus *Mediatorem* elegit..."

111. Ibid., 22.viii, 227: "[Quartum, ejusdem celebratio seu manifestatio]...concurrit ad gloriam agnitæ per fulgorem eminentiæ...(3) Ab Angelis & hominibus, quando agnitionem, sensum & æstimationem gloriæ Divinæ, manifestam faciunt..."

112. Ibid., xvi, 229: "...quibus argumentum præstabit universum Psalterium quod hinc תהלים dicitur..."

113. Ibid., 25.xv, 249: "*Tertiò* eidem quâ Creatori...competit: (1) submissa *gratitudo*, quam lex, cuivis Parenti requirit..."

114. Ibid., 20.xxvi, 216.

115. Ibid., 25.xiii, 249; cf. 20.xxix, 217.

the use of the received goods, which is to the advantage of God's honor and glory and the well-being of the household.[116] Furthermore, in respect to God the Father as Legislator, Judge, and Vindicator, one should be prompted to a general and complete obedience and honor, which one shows, according to the divine will, to earthly parents.[117] Thus one notes the direct interrelationship and extended exposition between the exegesis, doctrine, and *praxis* throughout the chapter(s) on the *Holy Trinity* and *God the Father.*

This extended exposition is finally observed between the chapters on the *Holy Trinity* and *God the Father* in the exposition of the benefit: love. In the exegesis of 2 Corinthians 13:13, Mastricht argues that the benefit, love, is threefold: electing love, benevolent love (redemption), and a well-pleasing love (gratitude following faith). In the practical part of the chapter on *God the Father* Mastricht returns to this benefit. Here he states that God's love "toward us" is exceeding great "as He is occupied with us, 2 Cor. 13:13." This is a mutual and reciprocal love, whereby one's communion with Him is eternal, the same, and immutable (Hos. 2:18; Rom. 11:29; Isa. 54:9, 10), and therefore one's love to God should be eternal, not *ante* but *post*,[118] consistent, and immutable (Rev. 2:10). Finally, God's love is distinct: He loves His creation as the work of His hands, but this differs from His love for His creatures (Rom. 9:13). Therefore, one's love for God's word should be distinct from one's love for His will (Ps. 78:25).[119]

In summary, regarding the structure of the practical sections of the chapters on the *Holy Trinity* and *God the Father*, in respect to the first Person of the Trinity, both chapters conform to an identified structure: glorification, consolation, reprehension, and exhortation. Also, a strong connection between exegesis, doctrine, and *praxis* is noted, whereby the biblical text is foundational to the doctrinal and practical formulation. This is particularly observed with the exegesis of 2 Corinthians 13:13 (*Holy Trinity*) on threefold love, a theme that returns in the practical section of *God the Father*. In respect to the content, the position of the Father is contextualized in the divine economy or *pactum*, primarily as upholder of the law and provider of redemption.

God the Holy Spirit: Exegesis

In respect to the Third Person of the Trinity, Mastricht exegetes the last part of the text of 2 Corinthians 13:13, "the communion of the Holy Spirit," and affirms the benefit: the κοινωνία that communicates sanctification and comfort through the grace of Christ and the love of the Father. This communication is, then, the designated work

---

116. Ibid., 25.xiii, 249: "In quibus *primò* Patri, ut *Domino*, Hero...competit *honor.* "

117. Ibid., xvi, 249: " obedientia, quem & terrenis Parentibus, ex præscripto divino debemus Exod. 20:12."

118. Ibid., xvii, 250: "sit et noster [amor] *æternus* ...versus ipsum, si non à parte *ante* (ut loquuntur) saltem à parte *post*."

119. Ibid., 249: "*Quintò*, velut Patri ac *benefactori*, ipsi competit: 1. *Amor*...2 Cor. 13:13..."

of the Holy Spirit in the economic Trinity.[120] The work of the Third Person of the Trinity as distributor of Christ's benefits is also identified in the exegesis of Calvin and Poole[121] but not in the *Staten-bijbel*, which points to the Spirit's work in the doctrine of adoption.[122] Mastricht's exegesis identifies the benefactor. He is called (1) Spirit, not in respect to the *essentia* because the Son and Father are also spirit but in respect to the *subsistentia*, and (2) Holy, in respect to His office, by which He is called the πνεῦμα ἁγιωσύνης, Spirit of holiness (Rom. 1:4). This differentiation in the text of Spirit and Holy is, so far as studied, not shared by other contemporary exegetes. Mastricht then marks three aspects in this part of the exegesis of 2 Corinthians 13:13: the Third Person, who is (1) Spirit and (2) Holy and is the (3) applicator of the redemptive work. These three aspects are expanded in Mastricht's explication of John 14:26, the foundational text for the exposition of *God the Holy Spirit*.

Mastricht exposits this text meticulously in a grammatical and philological way.[123] In respect to the structure, one notes a parallel with the exegesis of Psalm 2:7 (God the Son)

---

120. Ibid., 24.i, 236: "A. *Beneficium* κοινωνία, communicatio...*Spiritus* S. officium & *beneficium* œconomicum *designat*..."

121. Calvin, *Second Epistle to the Corinthians*, 404: "The fellowship of the Holy Spirit is added, because it is only under his guidance, that we come to posses Christ, and all his benefits....and...distributes to each according to the measure of grace..."; Poole, *Synopsis*, 5:664: "gratiam Filio qui nos nihil promeritos redemit communionem Spiritui per quem Dononrum distributio sacta est."

122. *Bijbel, dat is de gansche Heilige Schrift*, 2 Cor. 13:13 fn. 36, 105: "Namelijk waardoor wij in deze genade meer en liefde meer en meer gesterkt, en daarvan verzekerd worden, Rom. 8:15." In Rom. 8:15 the annotators of the *Staten-bijbel* comment, "Hierdoor wordt verstaan de genadige werking des Heiligen Geestes door de predikatie des heiligen Evangelies, die de harten der geloovigen verkwikt en van hunne aanneming tot kinderen verzekert."

123. τὸ πνεῦμα τὸ ἅγιον, ὃ πέμψει ὁ πατὴρ ἐν τῷ ὀνόματί μου, ἐκεῖνος ὑμᾶς διδάξει πάντα καὶ ὑπομνήσει ὑμᾶς πάντα ἃ 'εἶπον ὑμῖν "But the Comforter, *which is* the Holy Ghost, whom the Father will send in my name, he shall teach you all things, and bring all things to your remembrance, whatsoever I have said unto you" (King James Version).

1. The Benefactor: Person of the Holy Spirit
   1. ὁ παράκλητος   his office of the economy
   2. τὸ πνεῦμα τὸ ἅγιον   his proper name
      a. πνεῦμα   essentia immateriali
      b. ἅγιον   sanctification

2. The Mission of the Holy Spirit per *pactum œconomicum*
   ὃ πέμψει ὁ πατὴρ ἐν τῷ ὀνόματί μου
      1. ὁ πατὴρ   the Sender
      2. ὃ πέμψει   the Mission
      3. ἐν τῷ ὀνόματί μου   the Mode of sending

3. The Benefits
      1. ἐκεῖνος ὑμᾶς διδάξει πάντα   his teaching (*doctrinam*)
         a. ἐκεῖνος   the teacher (*doctor*)
         b. ὑμᾶς   the student (*docendi*)

and Ephesians 3:14 (God the Father) with the delineation of the benefactor and the benefits. However, Mastricht inserts in the exposition of John 14:26 the mission. This extensiveness of exegesis is not found, for example, in the commentaries of Calvin, Cocceius, or Poole on the text of John 14:26. We noted before, from a structural point of view, that Mastricht gives equal attention to God the Son and God the Holy Spirit in his treatment of the Holy Trinity. This factor and the elaborated exegesis of John 14:26 gives rise to the question of the importance of the Holy Spirit in Mastricht's trinitarian discussion. Also, we noted the centrality and the respective roles of the Father and the Son in the trinitarian pact. Thus, the additional question rises as to what the allotted role of the Holy Spirit is in the *pactum consilium*. These questions, then, will be considered in our examination of the exegesis, doctrine, and practice of Mastricht's discussion of God the Holy Spirit.

The first part of the biblical text analysis comprises the two names designated to the Holy Spirit: the official and the proper name.[124] The former, can be identified, according to Mastricht, with the emphatic article ὁ, which indicates the excellence of the Comforter, who is in the Trinity the only *ex officio* Paraclete.[125] To underline his assessment of the παράκλητος, Mastricht probes further the meaning. The original word παράκλητος, he argues, is commonly rendered by the Jews in the Aramaic translation and by the Talmudists, not in the sense of one who consoles or comforts, but as one who represents an accused one.[126] This understanding of παράκλητος is shared by Poole, who comments, not on John 14:26 but on John 16:7, that the Paraclete is an advocate, one who represents an accused one.[127] Moreover, Mastricht, like Poole, comments that the word παράκαλεω originates from "to advocate." Thus, he concludes, that the Holy Spirit is an advocate in court who represents all kinds of cases. In other words, one may conclude that παράκλητος can be rendered as "advocate of a case," "a teacher," "a comforter," "admonisher," and "intercessor."[128] In summary, Mastricht designates to the Third Person of the Trinity primarily the role of advocate.

c. διδάξει	the study (*doctrina*)	
d. πάντα	the requirement (*docendum*)	
2. ἃ᾽εἶπον ὑμῖν	the reminder	
a. the reminding act (*rememoratio*)		
b. πάντα ἃ᾽εἶπον ὑμῖν	the remembrance (*rememoranda*)	

124. Mastricht, *Theoretico-practica theologia*, II.27.ii, 262: "1. Personam, *ceu benefactorem, cujus designatur duplex* nomen: A. Appellativum, *ab* officio, *ejus œconomico:* ὁ παράκλητος...B. Proprium τὸ πνεῦμα τὸ ἅγιον."

125. Ibid.: "(1.A)...*qui per excellentiam est Paracletus, imo & qui in Trinitate, solus* ex officio *est Paracletus.*"

126. Ibid.: "Παράκλητος *vox frequens est apud Judæos in versione Chaldaica & apud Thalmudicos, non pro consolatore; sed pro eo qui causam agit alterius, & quadum* rei."

127. Poole, *Synopsis*, 4:1338: "Paracletus. Ex hoc loco constat vocem παράκαλεω sumi in notione *advocati, sive actioris, cujus hoc est officium convincere accusatorem.*"

128. Mastricht, *Theoretico-practica theologia*, II.27.ii, 262: "(1.A)...*ut sonet advocatum, ad hoc, ut alicui patrocinetur in* judicio; *aut consilio succerat*...παράκλητος...Doctorem, consolatorem, adhortatorem, intercessorem."

The exegesis continues with the discussion of the proper names: Spirit and Holy. According to Mastricht, these two names represent a composite single name.[129] The question this raises is why there are two articles: τὸ πνεῦμα τὸ ἅγιον . Mastricht explains that this distinguishes the Third Person of the Trinity from any other unclean or created spirit.[130] With this in mind, Mastricht expounds the names Spirit and Holy. The former, he notes, refers neither to the immaterial divine essence, which belongs to all the Persons of the Godhead, nor to the divine operation that makes one spiritual but refers to the *modus subsistendi*, "which will be expounded in the doctrinal part."[131] In respect to the proper name ἅγιον, Mastricht argues that this refers not so much to the divine holiness, which is an essential attribute of all divine Persons, but to the operation of sanctification insofar as this belongs to the office of the economy, "of which will come more in the doctrinal and practical part."[132] In summary, Mastricht designates to the Third Person of the Trinity in this part of the exegesis the *modus subsistendi* and the redemptive operation. Furthermore, he establishes the link between the exegetical part and the doctrinal and practical sections.

Mastricht, then, explicates the mission of the Holy Spirit per *pactum œconomicum*.[133] It is, accordingly, the Father (ὁ πατὴρ) who sent *simpliciter a se*.[134] Moreover, the mission (ὁ πέμψει) is a twofold procession of the Holy Spirit: the one is eternal or personal proceeding from the Father and the Son (Matt. 10:20, the Spirit of the Father; 2 Cor. 3:3, the Spirit of God; Gal.4:4, the Spirit of Christ), and the other is temporal and economic: "according to His office of the [divine] economy He is the Paraclete."[135] Finally, the mission occurs "in my name," which means "of Me" and "because of Me." It is, according to Mastricht, that the Spirit is sent of and because of Christ. The latter means that Christ merited the Spirit for His people.[136] In summary, Mastricht designates to the Third Person of the Trinity His mission as a result of the *pactum* and for the work of redemption.

129. Ibid.: "(1.B) Proprium...*Voces duæ*, Spiritus Sanctus, unum *tantum efformant, tertiæ personæ* nomen: *sed* compositum *non duplex, proprium & appellativum*."

130. Ibid.: "*Interim articulus* τὸ *utrique ejus parti, distincte præfigitur, ad hoc, ut prius* τὸ *discriminet in Trinitate, personam tertiam...ut Spiritum S. discernat à Spiritu quovis alio, impuro, creato...*"

131. Ibid.: "*...prout in dogmaticis uberius dicemus.*"

132. Ibid.: "*De quo itidem plura venient in dogmaticis & practicis.*"

133. Ibid.: "2. Missionem *per pactum œconomicum.*"

134. Ibid.: "*Mittens,....Spiritum S. principium, nec procedens, nec missum ab alio; sed* simpliciter *à se.*"

135. Ibid.: "*Missio...Significatur Spiritus S. processio...Est autem duplex: altera æterna seu personalis, quâ* procedit *à Patre..& à Filio...altera* temporalis *& œconomica, juxta* officium *ejus œconomicum, per quod Paracletus est.*"

136. Ibid.: "*Modus mittendi...in nomine meo. Hoc est, partim à me...partim propter me Gal. 4:4. Utpote qui merito & intercessione mea, Spiritum illum meis impetravi.*"

Mastricht concludes his exegesis of John 14:26 with the exposition of a double benefit: intellect and memory.[137] The former is enriched through the teaching of he Holy Spirit (ἐκεῖνος ὑμᾶς διδάξει πάντα). He is the Teacher, a Person (ἐκεῖνος) and not an accidental power of God, who makes known all divine things.[138] He instructed (ὑμᾶς) the patriarchs, prophets, and apostles and teaches, in different degrees but sufficient for salvation, the elect.[139] He will teach (διδάξει) outwardly and inwardly, by comforting, admonishing, and leading, all that is necessary for eternal life.[140] Here Mastricht echoes Calvin on the exegesis of this text part, who wrote,

> The two ways of teaching are that he [Christ] sounds in our ears by the mouth of men and he addresses us inwardly by his Spirit.[141]

In respect to the work of the Holy Spirit in bringing to remembrance all the divine teachings, Mastricht argues that this refers to the memory. This takes place when matters are recalled or are brought back into remembrance. He is aware that Beza follows Erasmus and the Vulgate in using here the word *suggeret* (to furnish, to suggest) instead of ὑπομνήσει. Mastricht is doubtful that their rendering is correct, because it could mean that the Holy Spirit will teach things that are not known, rather than bringing to remembrance previously known things, namely, the teachings of Christ.[142] In summary, Mastricht designates to the Third Person of the Trinity the task of teaching those things necessary for salvation and, in particular for the elect, bringing to remembrance Christ's work.

We conclude, then, that Mastricht in his rather extensive exposition of John 14:26 is not accompanied by many of his contemporaries. Nevertheless, he shares with them the understanding that the Holy Spirit, the Paraclete, is the Third Person of the Trinity. On the other hand, the length and depth of Mastricht's exposition demonstrates the importance of God the Holy Spirit in the divine economy, next to God the Son. This importance is further underscored with the centrality of the *pactum* in Mastricht's

---

137. Ibid.: "Beneficium *œconomicum duplex...*1. Doctrinam, *quæ respicit* mentem *seu intellectum...*a.doctor...b. docendi...c. doctrina...d. docendum...2. Rememorationem, *quæ respicit memoriam...*a. rememoratio...b. rememoranda...." The question could arise as to why these benefits differ from the benefit Mastricht identified in the exegesis of 2 Cor. 13:13: communion. These benefits are not contrary to one another, however, but complementary and arise from the biblical interpretation.

138. Ibid.: "A. Doctor...*non virtutem Dei* accidentalem; *sed personam.*"

139. Ibid.: "B. Docendi.... ὑμᾶς... Apostolos...*verùm quovis* electos... *quamvis dispari gradu & modo...quantum quidem illis sufficit ad salutem.*"

140. Ibid.: "C. Doctrina *seu docendi actus...qui requiruntur ad procurandam vitam æternam...*D. Docendem, πάντα *omnia...quæ sunt ad salutem* necessaria...."

141. Calvin, *Commentary*, vol. 17, *Commentary upon the Gospel according to John*, 101.

142. Mastricht, *Theoretico-practica theologia*, II.27.ii, 263: "Rememorationem, *quæ respicit* memoriam...*Vulg. Eras. aliique est* suggeret. *Non male quidem, inquit* Beza...*Hîc verò, de auditis intelligendis & in memoriam revocandis agitur,*" and "Rememoranda...*Christi doctrinam illustravit....*"

exegesis of 2 Corinthians 13:13, Psalm 2:7, Ephesians 3:14, and John 14:26. Consistent throughout, the Father is the Lawgiver, Judge, and merciful Provider of redemption, the Son is Mediator and *expromissor*, and the Holy Spirit is the Paraclete—Advocate, Comforter, and Teacher. The First and Second Persons stand in a legal relationship (inter-*pactum*), and the Third Person stands in relation to the history of redemption (extra-*pactum*).

God the Holy Spirit: Doctrine

Doctrinally Mastricht affirms, although critically as we have seen, the formulation of the Latin or Western Church that the Holy Spirit proceeds from the Father and the Son.[143] Further, he writes that the operations of the Three Persons in the divine economy are distinct: the Father in relation to the creation, the Son in relation to the dispensation and redemption, and the Holy Spirit in relation to the consummation and sanctification. The Spirit's office designates Him as the Emissary, Teacher, and Comforter of the divine economy.[144] Moreover, Mastricht argues that the Holy Spirit is a Person, which "is indicated by ἐκεῖνος," distinct from but "sent from the Father in My name" (ὃ πέμψει ὁ πατὴρ ἐν τῷ ὀνόματί μου).[145] Here, Mastricht further explicates the *modus subsistendi* of the Holy Spirit: a Person of the divine essence, distinct from yet consubstantial with the Father and the Son; having divine names (Jehovah, Isa. 6:9; cf. Acts 28:26; Θεος, Acts 5:3; 1 Cor. 3:16; κυριος, 2 Cor. 3:17), divine attributes (eternal, Heb. 9:14; infinite, Ps. 139:7; omniscient, 1Cor. 2:10; omnipotent, 1 Cor. 12:4, 6, 11), and divine operations (creation, Gen. 1:2; miracles, Matt. 12:28; healing, 1 Cor. 12:9, 10; unction of Christ, Isa. 61:1; cf. Luke 4:18; regeneration, conversion, sanctification, and strengthening the believers).[146]

One notes here that Mastricht continues and extends the discussion of the *modus subsistentiæ*, which he commenced in the exegetical section. Such expanded discussion also can be noted when he treats the official operation of the Holy Spirit. For Mastricht, the Third Person is the Applicator of the redemptive work promoting the salvation of

143. Ibid., 24.xi, 238: "Pater...Filius...est qui à duobus *procedit, Spiritus S.*"

144. Ibid. x, 238: "A quo etiam *primæ* Personæ *primum* opus, *creatio; secundæ, secundum: dispensatio &* redemptio; *tertiæ* ac postremæ, *postremum, consummatio &* sanctificatio appropriatur." See also xii, 238 : "per quod *prima* persona... *Creatorum... Judicem*"; 239; "*secunda* persona... *Mediatoris... Expromissoris... Redemptoris... tertia* persona... *Emissarii... Doctorem... Consolatorem*"; and xiv, 239: "3. *Spiritui Sancto* ut *consummatori, potentia* Luc. 1:35 ut *communicatori,* sanctificatori, Doctori, ductori, consolatori, *bonitas* communicativa Ps.143:10."

145. Ibid., 27.iii, 263: "...ipsum *personam* esse, innuit ἐκεῖνος, *ipse,* item ejus missio & operationes personales *docebit &* in *memoriam revocabit*; ejus distinctionem à Patre & Filio tradunt verbâ"; v, 263: "Ipsum *personam* esse ... Quod 3. πνεῦμα *neutrius* generis, construatur cum pronomine *masculini* generis ἐκεῖνος ille. Here, Mastricht reaches back to the exegetical section of the chapter.

146. Ibid., vi, 263: "Esse quoque *distinctam,* à Patre & Filio personam..."; 264: "B. Ordo peculiaris in *subsistendo,* quo à Patre & Filio, quippe ab ipsis procedens, *subsistit...*"; vii, 264: "Esse etiam personam, non *creatam* sed *divinam,* Patri ac Filio *coæternam...primò nomina* divina..."; viii, 264: "*Secundò, attributa* divina..."; ix, 264: "*Tertiò, operationes* divinæ...."

humanity according to the council of peace (*concilium pacis æternum*).[147] He is the Paraclete (παράκλητος) of the Trinity who completes the salvation, which originates with the Father and is merited by the Son.[148] The Holy Spirit is the (1) Teacher, who "sent, provides gifts and leads the teachers in all truth," (2) the Sanctificator, and (3) Consolator.[149] The parallel here with the exegetical section is noted particularly when Mastricht expands his discussion on sanctification insofar as this belongs to the office of the Third Person of the economy: faith, through the regeneration (the first act of spiritual life), conversion (the act of faith), sanctification (the fruits of faith), strengthening (the exercise of faith), and excitation (the initiation of that which is good).[150] Here one notes that the application of redemption is extended to the doctrine of faith. This work of the Holy Spirit, concludes Mastricht, will continue in leading God's church until the Son hands over the kingdom to the Father.[151] In summary, the content of the doctrinal section of *God the Holy Spirit* is an expansion of Mastricht's discussion that he commenced in the exegetical section: the Third Person of the Trinity is the Paraclete, the Advocate, Comforter and Teacher. Mastricht pays attention to the *modus subsitentiæ* and the representation of the eternal *pactum* by the Holy Spirit: the application of salvation. In the context of Mastricht's contemporaries, one notes that the former is predominantly present in the chapters on the Trinity or God the Holy Spirit in the works of the *Synopsis purioris theologiæ*, Ames, Maresius, Undereyck, Cloppenburgh, Burman, and Brakel.[152] The alloted position of the Holy Spirit as Paraclete in the

147. Ibid., iii, 263: " Spiritus S. ...hoc in *divinis* obtinere, totus contextus arguit...ac de divino utriusque Emissario loquitur...exigere videtur, salutis humanæ procurandæ ratio, juxta consilium pacis æternum."

148. Ibid., xi, 264: "Quantum ad *officium* œconomicum, Spiritus S. est quasi *Emissarius* Trinitatis...Ibid. Est παράκλητος *advocatus* Trinitatis, *ad causam* perficienda salutis humanæ, quam Pater designarit, Filius impetratit."

149. Ibid., xii, 264: "Id quod Spiritus S. triplici potissimum peragit operatione:...primò, *docendo* Joh. 14:26 quod agitur, doctores *emittendo*...missos *exornando &* instruendo donis necessariis... A. quibus omnibus *Spiritus veritatis* appellatur Joh. 14:17."; xiii, 264: "Secundò, *sanctificando, à quo Spiritu S.* dicitur."; and xiv, 265: "Tertio *consolando* (à quo παράκλητος peculiariter dicitur) quod sit."

150. Ibid., xiii, 264: "Secundò,...Id quod laxiori significatione concludit (1) *regenerationem*... actus primus vitæ spiritualis animæ... (2) *conversionem* quâ vivificatus ad actum fidei perducitur...(3) *sanctificationem* 1 Cor. 6:11 per quam fidei *fructus* excluduntur... (4) *corroborationem* in veritate & praxi...(5) *excitationem* & incitationem, ad bonum quodvis...."

151. Ibid., xvi, "265: "Sunt etiam *officia* œconomica, quæ Spiritui S competunt... *ducens* Ecclesiam Dei... *quod nim. Filius regnum Patri tradet* . . ."

152. Polyander *et al.*, *Synopsis purioris theologiæ*, 9, 76-82; Ames, *Marrow of Sacred Divinity*, V.14, 18; Maresius, *Collegium Theologicum*, locus tertius, 43-64; Undereyck, *Halleluja* (1678), III.4, 12; Cloppenburgh, *Theologica Opera Omnia*, vol. 1, Exerc. Theol. Locus III Disp. III.2, 770-72; Burmannus, *Synopsis Theologiæ*, I.34, 212-16; Brakel, *ΛΟΓΙΚΗ ΛΑΤΡΕΙΑ, dat is Redelyke Godtsdienst* I:4.xxvi-xxxiv, 131-40.

pactum is more or less present in works of Cocceius, Oomius, and Witsius.[153] Mastricht combines both elements in one chapter, *God the Holy Spirit*. In respect to the structure, the parallel between both sections is prominent.[154] Thus, for Mastricht, the doctrine of the Holy Spirit arises from the biblical text and is scripturally formulated.

God the Holy Spirit: Practical

Mastricht commences the practical section of the chapter *God the Holy Spirit* with a return to the stated benefit in the exegesis of 2 Corinthians 13:13 (the chapter *Holy Trinity*): communion. He argues that in respect to the *praxis* one should aim foremost for the κοινωνία of the Holy Spirit (2 Cor. 13:13) in order to be partaker and receiver of Him.[155] This communion is granted from God's side for free. The Holy Spirit is sent "to us" from the Father and poured out (Joel 2:28). On the other hand, this communion is received "from our side," through faith. One apprehends the Holy Spirit as the Spirit of promise (Eph. 1:13) by prayer (Zech. 12:10, the Spirit of prayer) and received by the hearing of the Word (Acts. 10:34). He concludes, then, that one should aim for this communion because of the excellency of the Holy Spirit, who is one in essence with the Father and the Son, and communicates the "grace of our Lord Jesus Christ and the love of the Father, 2 Cor. 13:13."[156] The importance of this communion is unambiguous: without the Third Person of the Trinity, there would be no communion with Christ (Rom. 8:9).[157] Thus, reaching back to the text of 2 Corinthians 13:13, Mastricht works out the *praxis* of the communion with the Holy Spirit in the chapter *God the Holy Spirit*. Therefore, and because of the importance of the communion with the Holy Spirit, he

---

153. Oomius, *Institutiones Theologiæ Practicæ*, III.4, 115-65; Cocceius, *Opera Omnia Theologica*, vol. 7, *Summa Doctrinæ*, 61, § 89. Cf. Van Asselt, *The Federal Theology of Johannes Cocceius*, 233, 234; Herman Witsius, *Exercitationes Sacræ in Symbolum quod Apostolorum dicitur*, XXII.9, 424.

154.

Exegetical section	Doctrinal section	§
1. The Person of the Holy Spirit,	as benefactor	
1. ὁ παράκλητος	his office of the economy	III
2. τὸ πνεῦμα τὸ ἅγιον	his proper name	IV, VII
a. πνεῦμα	*essentia immateriali*	V, VIII
b. ἅγιον	sanctification	XIII
2. The Mission of the Holy Spirit	per *pactum œconomicum*	VI
3. The double economical benefit		IX
1. ἐκεῖνος ὑμᾶς διδάξει πάντα	his teaching (*doctrinam*)	XII
2. ἃ' εἶπον ὑμῖν	the reminder	

155. Mastricht, *Theoretico-practica theologia*, II.27.xxi, 268: "Est igitur hîc (quantum ad *praxin*) ob quod, *primò* omni conatu enitamur in κοινωνίαν Spiritus S."

156. Ibid., 269: "2. *Officii* oeconomici *scopus*, scil. consummare negotium salutis humanæ. H. e *gratiam* Domini nostri Jesu Christ, *charitatem* Patris & quicquid illæ possunt nobis communicare 2 Cor.13:13."

157. Ibid., xxi, 269: "4. Absoluta ejus *necessitas* utpote absque quo, ne *Christum* quidem *Dominum* possumus salutare 1 Cor. 12:3, neque ulla nobis cum Christo *communio* esse potest Rom. 8:9."

argues extensively to hold fast to Him, because quenching the Holy Spirit (1 Thess. 5:19) may result in a declension of the fruits of salvation, faith, hope and love.[158] Therefore, in order to experience the presence of the Third Person of the Trinity, one should in obedience use the gifts of the Spirit (Gal. 5:25),[159] discern the leading of the Holy Spirit in one's life, and not to grieve the Spirit (Eph. 4:30).[160]

Mastricht returns throughout the practical section to the two aspects identified in the text of John 14:26: Holy and Spirit. The former is noted primarily in respect to sanctification, and the latter coincides with his discussion of the Person of the Holy Spirit.[161] The focus is clear that one should avoid all hindrances so that the communion with the Holy Spirit is not stalled. In summary, the central concern here is the practical working out of what it means to have the communion of the Holy Spirit. This spiritual union connects to a Triune God in the redemptive work. Mastricht's practical working out is succinct and directly related to the exegesis of the biblical text and the doctrinal formulation. The integral exposition of 2 Corinthians 13:13 (*Holy Trinity*) and John 14:26 (*God the Holy Spirit*), exegetically, doctrinally, and practically, sets Mastricht apart from his contemporaries. In addition, he also differs with some of them, such as Brakel and Oomius, in the succint practical explanation.[162]

We conclude, then, that this investigation has attempted to render a contribution to the limited number of studies concerning the post-Reformation Reformed doctrine of the Holy Trinity. Second, this examination contributes to our quest for the relationship between exegesis, doctrine, and practice.

In response to the questions raised in the introduction of this chapter, we can provide the following probable answers. First, the exegesis of the biblical texts (2 Cor. 13:13; Ps. 2:7, 8; Eph. 3:14; John 14:26) can be characterized as robustly grammatical-philological. We noted diverse exegetical trajectories, including contemporaries, sixteenth-century Reformed, and medieval rabbinic exposition. The latter underscores that Mastricht's exegesis is shielded from doctrinal eisegesis. In addition, both the grammatical-syntactical structure of the biblical text and the content of Mastricht's exegesis lead to and guard the doctrinal and practical formulation. Arising from the examined biblical texts, Mastricht carefully exposited and formulated the divine economy of the Holy Trinity, with a strong christological and pneumatological dimension, as the eternal *pactum* with the allotted positions of the Father as Originator,

---

158. Ibid., xxii, 269: "...potest eatenus *exstingui* 1 Thess. 5:19...potest quantum ad *fructus* salvificos, fidem, spem, charitatem...."

159. Ibid.: "[1] *Cura* circa *motus* Spiritus Sancti, in cordibus nostris...[2] *usus charismatum*....Gal. 5:25."

160. Ibid., xxv, xxvi, 270, 271.

161. Ibid., xxiii, 269: "(2) *Sanctificationem*...Spiritus *Sanctus & sanctificationis*...Sanctificatos *roborare* in studio boni..."; xxiv, 270: "Quod si igitur, *studium* serium in nobis observemus sanctitatis...."

162. Oomius, *Institutiones Theologiæ Practicæ*, III.5, III.5, III.7, III.8, 166-260; Brakel, ΛΟΓΙΚΗ ΛΑΤΡΕΙΑ, *dat is Redelyke Godtsdienst*, I:4.xxxiv-l, 140-153.

Lawgiver, and merciful Provider of redemption, the Son as Mediator and *expromissor*, and the Holy Spirit as Paraclete and Applicator in the work of salvation. The identification and centrality of the eternal *pactum*, or council or peace, in Mastricht's discussion of the doctrine of the Holy Trinity is distinctive in relation to other seventeenth-century Reformed theologians. Although the covenant and its various aspects have a place in this part of the *TPT*, and arises, here, from Mastricht's exegetical understanding of the biblical texts related to the doctrine of the Holy Trinity, it ought not to be explained as a result of a federal theological motif employed by Mastricht. Rather it is a result of his meticulous exegesis of Scripture. Additionally, we noted the importance of the doctrine of the Trinity throughout the *TPT*, especially in relation to the covenant of grace. The centrality of the *pactum* addresses two concerns: the tri-unity of God and the covenantal aspect of God. The former is complementary to his doctrine of divine spirituality and simplicity. The latter establishes that the God of Mastricht is not a metaphysical construct but a Triune God of Abraham, Isaac, Jacob, and of all His people throughout the ages: the God of the covenant.

Conclusion and Prospect

This study has addressed the post-Reformation Reformed concern for right doctrine and piety. In particular, this study has concentrated on the method and piety in the *Theoretico-practica theologia* (*TPT*) of Petrus van Mastricht. At the close of this study, it seems appropiate to draw several finalizing thoughts. The order of our conclusion follows the order of the four parts of our study.

Part 1 presents a more detailed account of the life and work of Mastricht than has previously been identified. The previous characterizations of the man and his work by Heppe, Goeters, Reuter and Roessingh[1] do not resemble our findings, namely that the three main and consistent threads throughout his life and work were that of theologian, Hebraist, and anti-Cartesian. Mastricht, the theologian, worked on a lifelong project: the *TPT*. Placed in the context of his time and in dialogue with other seventeenth-century theological works of the same genre, we have demonstrated that this work is a consolidation and mediating codification of post-Reformation Reformed theology: exegesis, doctrine, elenctic, and *praxis*. Throughout his life as a Reformed pastor and professor of theology, all of his theological writings, in the form of disputations or books, have contributed to the immense work of the *TPT*. His other writings, therefore, show Mastricht, the Hebraist, not immediately as a scholar in the field of Hebrew literature, but as one whose Hebrew and Oriental language expertise served him as an able Old Testament exegete. Moreover, this expertise was in the service of his lifelong passion of Reformed theology, as far is exemplified in his Old Testament texts analysis in the *TPT*. In the opinion of the present author, the finding of Mastricht as Hebraist should be maintained, primarily for the following reason. Old Testament exegesis was for Mastricht not only a philological and etymological quest but also a careful listening to and standing in a rabbinnic exegetical trajectory before arriving at the results of biblical exegesis as foundation for doctrine and practice. The third part of the portrait of Mastricht, the anti-Cartesian, emerges from his (philosophical) publications and in the context of the *TPT*, as shown in his critique of this philosophy and primarly in connection to soteriological concerns. It is therefore, that Mastricht understood early on, as none other of his time, the significance of Cartesianism and its detremental impact on Reformed theology.

Part 2 demonstrates that for Mastricht theology is a matter of faith. This make the assessment of Tholuck, Althaus, and Weber on the nature of post-Reformation Reformed theology,[2] at least in the case of Mastricht, no longer tenable. Moreover, the prolegomena, in which Mastricht lays out the premises of his theological enterprise, parallels the work of the sixteenth- and early seventeenth-century Reformed theologians.

1. See the discussion in this study pages 16-18.

2. Ibid., 83.

This is seen in his division of theology into faith and obedience, which was already identified by the patristics and Calvin, his definition of theology, which resembles descriptions of Ames (*doctrina est Deo vivendi*) and Cocceius (*doctrina est pietas*), and his description of theological topics, which echoes at times the Leiden *Synopsis purioris theologiæ*. This obervation leads us to conclude that Mastricht's theology, at the close of the seventeenth-century, resembles more the earlier Reformed theology than of his own time. This conclusion is further underscored by the location and content of the *locus* of faith. It also repudiates the critique of Bavinck, Brienen, Exalto and Graafland[3] of the discontinuity of the sixteenth- and seventeenth-century Reformed theologians on the nature of faith.

The centrality of faith for Mastricht cannot be overlooked when the location of the chapter of faith is considered. First, he differs in this with most of his contemporaries, who located the discussion of faith in the context of the *ordo salutis*. Second, his view of reason and the covenant of grace may have contributed to the unique location of *De Fide salvifica*, which preceeds another 1,200 pages of his theological system. The centrality of faith for Mastricht is moreover confirmed by its precise and long-standing definition. In respect to the latter, he had provided the same definition twenty years before his publication of the *TPT*. The same definition is worked out in an extensive treatise, *De fide salvifica syntagma theoretico-practicum* (1671), of which the chapter on faith in the *TPT* is a synopsis. In respect to the preciseness of his description of faith, this is reflected in several ways. First, the definition of faith arises from a careful exegesis of Scripture. The direct correlation between the text and text parts and the definition of faith cannot be disregarded. Second, the definition is supported by the context of the text (John 1:11, 12) and other testimonies of Scriptures, which provide, for Mastricht, the essence of faith: the union and communion with Christ, thereby receiving God as highest end. Further such habitual faith is, for Mastricht, directed to God. His lesser attention to the marks of faith and the inward concerns of the believer set him apart from his contemporaries and points also to an adherence to the understanding of faith as found in earlier Reformed (confessional) expressions, such as the Heidelberg Catechism. Part 2 of this study, then, addresses one part of the title of this book. Living to God is, for Mastricht, a living by faith through Christ.

Part 3 shows that method and piety are, in the doctrine of God in the *TPT*, not bifurcations but integrally related in Mastricht's theology. In respect to method, then, we may conclude that Mastricht employed three main approaches in respect to the structure of theology. First, based on Scripture (1Tim. 6:2), he employed a twofold structure in his theology: faith and obedience or love. The latter refers, for Mastricht, primarily to the *praxis pietatis* or moral theology. The former, faith, comprises for him the Reformed theological *loci* such as theology proper, anthropology, Christology, soteriology and ecclesiology. Each of these loci contains individual topics, which are divided in Mastricht's characteristic structure, our second identified approach: exegesis, doctrine, elenctic and *praxis*. This approach was employed early on in Mastricht's theological

---

3. Ibid., 103.

writings and is unique for any of the seventeenth-century Reformed systematic theological works. That is to say, Mastricht presents this fourfold approach to describe a single *locus* of theology. Exegesis, doctrine, polemic, and *praxis* are present in other works of seventeenth-century Reformed theology but in their mutual interplay and the forcefulness of their presentation as lucidly deliniated are typical only of Mastricht himself.

In addition, we can conclude that on each separate aspect Mastricht employed a third approach. This approach relates to the individual *loci* sections: exegesis, doctrine, elenctic and *praxis*. In respect to exegesis, Mastricht employed primarily a historical-grammatical method of exegesis, with an emphasis on philology and etymology. This emphasis stands in a trajectory of the rabbinic *peshat* interpretation of Scripture. Furthermore, he employed a biblical exegesis that stands in an exegetical trajectory of sixteenth-century Reformed interpretation, reaching back to the patristic interpretation of Scripture and ultimately Scripture itself. That is to say, in his exegesis, Mastricht rarely comments on doctrinal issues, except when the biblical text gives way to this, as we have seen in the exegesis of Psalm 2:7 in relationship to the covenant. These findings combined, as it relates to Mastricht's exegesis examined in the doctrine of God in the *TPT*, makes the so-called proof-text theory not longer tenable[4] and the suggested distinction of Voetian and Cocceian exegesis less probable.[5]

In respect to doctrine, Mastricht employed in structure and content a distinct approach. We have demonstrated that the doctrinal formulation emerges from Scripture and Mastricht's exegesis. The results of exegesis are, for Mastricht, the foundation and building blocks of the doctrinal formulation. This formulation is surrounded by other testimonies of Scriptures, is Augustinian in character and expressed in a biblical and early Reformed theological manner. Here Mastricht's use of scholastic distinctions and definitions has, in our opinion, contributed to the precision of his doctrinal formulation.

The employment of scholastic method is furthermore distinctly present in the elenctic sections of the *TPT*. In respect to elenctic, Mastricht adhered closely to the medieval scholastic *quæstio* method, whereby he, in several instances, as we have observed, made discriminating use of Aquinas's *Summa*. It is important to note here that in our opinion Mastricht's use of the scholastic method, distinctions, and definitions is safeguarded by Mastricht's exegesis and by Scripture itself. The authority of Scripture and the influence of the exegetical results are for Mastricht the parameters and boundaries for the employment of rhetoric (Renaissance humanism) and medieval scholastic devices. Ultimately, the elenctic sections were, for Mastricht, not only a refutation of diverse thought, primarily Roman Catholicism, Socinianism and Cartesianism, but predominently related to the concern of the work of redemption.

In respect to the *praxis*, Mastricht consistenly employed a similar structure, which in content directs the believer to God in Christ. The content, like in the doctrinal sections,

---

4. Ibid., 134, 135. Our conclusion is *contra* the findings of Berkhof and O'Dell Bullock.

5. Ibid., 134. Our conclusion differs from Brienen's view of Voetian and Cocceian preachers.

moreover arises from Scripture and is biblically expressed but reflects, here, the character of the theology of Bernardus. The *praxis* was, for Mastricht, not a form of mysticism or divergence of sixteenth-century Reformed piety as is suggested by Ritschl and others[6] but an expression of living faith.

The *basso continuo* of the foregoing and third identified approach is that, for Mastricht, doctrine and *praxis* arise from Scripture. Exegesis, doctrine, elenctic, and *praxis* are distinct but integrally related: *contra* the assessment of Brienen regarding the independency of *explicatio* and *applicatio*.[7] These three approaches, then, are cumulated, for Mastricht, in the exegete. Only the exegete who possesses faith can, under the guidance of the Holy Spirit, faithfully expound the Scriptures and formulate exegetical results, doctrine, and *praxis* in a *theoretico*-practical manner. That is to say, the method (*theoretica*) employed by the exegete is interrelated to the *praxis* and vice versa. Here, we can conclude that Mastricht's concern for *theoretico-practica* theology parallels the medieval concern of scholastic system and piety. However, in respect to piety, it would be tenable to say that Mastricht works out a combination of the medieval concern and the Amesian defintion of theology. Nevertheless, although Mastricht's theology, as far as noted in the doctrine of God, aims to direct one to God (*theologia practica*), the unity of *theologia theoretica* and *theologia practica* cannot be ignored—every speculative truth in theology has a practical implication. This may point us to Mastricht's ultimate understanding of theology as *habitus*. In addition, this may point to a mediating position of Mastricht in post-Reformation Reformed theology, characteristic for one who wrote, as we have seen in various occasions in this study, that the "middle" way was preferable. Part 3 of this study, then, addresses another part of the title of this book. The art is, for Mastricht, an employment of an exegetical and a scholastic yet a Scriptural guarded method.

Part 4 illumines that the overall approach of Mastricht to theology, and primarily restricted in this study to the doctrine of God, lead to some distinctive results. First, theologically, the unity of God is exposited by Mastricht through the doctrine of the divine spirituality and simplicity (and in that order). In the context of his time, we have seen a variety of structure and order of the divine attributes. Mastricht's threefold division of *Quid sit Deus, Quantus sit Deus,* and *Qualis sit Deus* is not quite shared with his contemporaries. Moreover, for Mastricht, the doctrine of the divine simplicity is grounded in Scripture via the formulated doctrine of the divine spirituality. In addition, Mastricht's scriptural foundation for the doctrine of the divine simplicity (John 4:24) was shared by his contemporaries, sixteenth-century Reformed commentators, and Aquinas. This point, that the the doctrine of the divine simplicity is not a metaphysical construct *per se* but should be understood in relation to the doctrine of the divine spirituality, is grounded upon the Word of Christ, so that, for Mastricht, the unity of God is preserved. This preservation of the unity of God, as this study shows, has redemptive significance (Christology). Furthermore, Mastricht's connection of these two

6. Ibid., 173.

7. Ibid., 134.

doctrines is also shared with the Leiden *Synopsis purioris theologiæ*. Again, this may point to the fact that Mastricht's theological orientation was more directed to the sixteenth-century and early seventeenth-century Reformed theology.

Second, the Three-ness of God is expounded in the chapters on the *Holy Trinity*. We conclude, from this study, that, for Mastricht, the economic Trinity is central to his exposition and also has a redemptive significance (*pactum salutis*). Here, in the context of his time, Mastricht is rather unique. His treatment of the *pactum* in the context of his discussion on the Holy Trinity is not shared by most of his contemporaries. However, the strong notion of the covenant, present in these chapters on the Three Persons, may lead us to identify Mastricht as a federal theologian. He concurs with his exposition of the Holy Trinity with covenant theologians such as Cocceius, Burman, and Untereyck. Mastricht shared their exegesis and doctrinal formulation of, for example, God the Son. The argument should, of course be balanced in that Mastricht differs with Cocceius on the position of the Mediator in the *pactum*. But combined, this could point again to a mediating position of Mastricht, and in this case, on the covenant.

Third, then, our study shows that the foundational character of the doctrine of God for the theology of Mastricht, in *leer* and *leven*, underscores that the assessment of this doctrine by Loonstra and Graafland[8] is not justifiable. The catholicity of Mastricht's formulation of the doctrine of God is rooted in the thought of the patristic fathers and medieval doctors, notably Aquinas, and concurs with the work of the sixteenth-century Reformers, especially Calvin. The One and Triune God who emerges from the writing of Mastricht is not merely an abstract doctrinal exposition but the God of Salvation.

We end this study by outlining three main finalizing thoughts in respect to the life and work of Petrus van Mastricht in general and in respect to his doctrine of God in particular. First, the emerging portrait of Mastricht as a seventeenth-century post-Reformation Reformed theologian, Hebraist, and philosopher differs from previous assessments of his life and work as presented in the introduction of this study. Second, the *TPT* can be seen as a synthesizing codification of seventeenth-century Reformed orthodox theology, with some distinctive characteristics. The fourfold approach to theology combined the elements, which are individually or two- or threefold present in Reformed theology of the post-Reformation: exegesis, doctrine, polemic or elenctic, and practice. Further, the sources of the *TPT* attest to exegetical trajectories that are beyond the sixteenth-century Reformation and include rabbinic and patristic explications. Third, this study finds that, for Mastricht, method (*ars*) and piety (*theologia practica* and *praxis pietatis*) are related. Thereby, we return to our proposition that the doctrinal and practical formulation of theology and the scholastic method employed by Mastricht are guarded by Scripture and exegesis. This result that theology, then, is for Mastricht trinitarian and redemptive in nature: the art of living to God. Mastricht's existential

---

8. Ibid., 28.

nature of his teaching is grounded in Scripture. He brings, as once was argued for Bernardus, "us back to the sources and to the Source of all Christian spirituality."[9]

Several times during this study, the question was asked what the (theological) influence or contribution was of Mastricht to Reformed theology. Although the question is of historical-theological interest and falls outside the scope of this study, the following points, arising from this study, may give some direction.

First, the life and work of Mastricht was interweaved with church (the Cocceian oriented classis of the Lower Rhine area, the Voetian oriented classes of Utecht), politics (the Brandenburg expansion), and academics (Frankfurt an der Oder, Duisburg, and Utecht). Moreover, we note a continuing dialogue with current issues of his time (Labadism, Cartesianism, and Bekker). These aspects combined invite further study of Mastricht's life and work, so that a fuller portrait may emerge and more completeness may be achieved in respect to the content of his publications. In particular, a more complete understanding of his doctrine of God would be obtained when the scope of study goes beyond the *TPT* and includes, at least, his philosophical work the *Novitatum Cartesianarum Gangræna*.

Second, our study points to the foundational character of the doctrine of God in the *TPT* as a whole. In particular, our study invites a specific study on the doctrine of the covenant of Mastricht. Such study, should take into consideration his doctrine of the Trinity and the disputation *Diatribe theologica de æterna Christi sponsione*. Furthermore, such study may contribute to three additional issues. One study should consider Jonathan Edwards's indebtedness to Mastricht regarding covenant theology. If the thesis of the trinitarian theology of Edwards is attainable, it should not come as a surprise that probably most of the underpinnings are of Mastricht. Another study should consider Mastricht's indebtedness to Cocceius, not only as exegete but also as covenant theologian. Finally, a study should explore the indebtedness of the theology of the Scottish Marrow-men to Mastricht.

Third, the absence of the *loci* of eschatology, while embedded in book VIII of the *TPT*, *De dispensatione foederis gratia*, invites exploration of Mastricht's view of the covenant of grace and eschatology.

Last, but not least, the findings of this study in regard to Mastricht's Old Testament exegesis and the rabbinic exegetical trajectory underscores the eminent need to gain more insight into the continuity of exegetical trajectories beyond the sixteenth—and seventeenth—century exegesis of Reformed theologians and commentators.

9. Bernard of Clairvaux, *Selected Works*, trans. G.R. Evans and introd. Jean Leclercq, O.S.B (New York: Paulist Press, 1987), 57.

Samenvatting

Deze studie richt zich op de verhouding van de gereformeerde leer en vroomheid zoals die is weergegeven door Petrus van Mastricht (1630–1706) in zijn belangrijkste theologische werk de *Theoretico-practica theologia* (hierna vermeld als *TPT*). In de inleiding van de studie wordt duidelijk dat de theologische gedachte van Mastricht nauwelijks is onderzocht. De beeldvorming van deze hoogleraar aan de universiteit van Frankfurt an der Oder, Duisburg en Utrecht is tweeledig. In het Europese onderzoek betreffende de Nadere Reformatie wordt hij beschouwd als Voetiaan, anti-Coccejaan, anti-Cartesiaan, anti-chiliast, dogmatische-scholasticus, verbonds- en praktikaal theoloog. Het Amerikaanse onderzoek ziet in Mastricht een evenwichtig bemiddelend vertegenwoordiger van de gereformeerde scholastiek. Vanuit dit tweeledig beeld rijst de vraag: Klopt dit beeld? Op deze vraag wordt in het eerste hoofdstuk van deel I een voorlopig antwoord geformuleerd, dat meer genuanceerd en gedetailleerd is dan de antwoorden van voorheen.

In hoofdstuk twee wordt onderzocht hoe de *TPT* tot stand is gekomen, welke bronnen Mastricht heeft gebruikt, hoe het gehele werk is gestructureerd en wat de globale inhoud van het werk is.

Met de voorgaande gegevens worden de premissen van Mastrichts theologie nagegaan. Het blijkt dat hij theologie verdeelt in geloof en gehoorzaamheid: een twee-deling die ook bij de patres en bij Calvijn is waar te nemen. Verder sluit Mastrichts definitie van theologie aan bij de formuleringen van Amesius (*doctrina est Deo vivendi*) en Coccejus (*doctrina est pietas*). Voorts, de beschrijving van de theologische onderwerpen (loci) door Mastricht herinnert op sommige momenten aan de vroeg zeventiende-eeuwse *Synopsis purioris theologiæ*. Al met al kan dit er op wijzen dat Mastricht zich meer verbonden weet met de theologie van de vroege zeventiende eeuw dan met die van zijn eigen tijd. Dit wordt in het bijzonder onderstreept door de relatief unieke plaats die het hoofdstuk over het geloof inneemt: tussen de beschrijving van de prolegomena en de overige *loci* van gereformeerde theologie. Daarom is de plaats en inhoud van het hoofdstuk betreffende het geloof verder onderzocht in hoofdstuk twee van deel II van deze studie.

Het blijkt dat de centrale positie van het geloof voor Mastricht onmisbaar is voor het verstaan van zijn theologische ontwerp. Allereerst, het hoofdstuk staat niet in de zogenaamde *ordo salutis*-behandeling, maar vooraan in de *TPT*. Hierin verschilt Mastricht met velen van zijn tijd. Verder blijkt dat Mastricht elders al eerder een omschrijving van het geloof heeft geboden, namelijk in een publicatie uit 1671, die specifiek en uitsluitend dit thema regardeert. Ook daarin is Mastricht uniek in zijn tijd. De vorm en inhoud van het hoofdstuk over het geloof in de *TPT* komt overeen met die van de publikatie uit 1671. Mastrichts definitie van het geloof is identiek. Deze definitie komt tot stand door een zorgvuldige exegese van de bijbeltekst Johannes 1: 11, 12. De exegese van de tekst vormt de basis niet alleen voor de definitie maar ook voor de verdere uitwerking van wat het geloof is. Dit geloof is voor Mastricht: de vereniging en gemeenschap met Christus, waarbij God wordt ontvangen als het hoogste einddoel. Aan de kenmerken van het geloof schenkt hij slechts beperkt aandacht. Hierin verschilt hij met bijvoorbeeld zijn tijdgenoten Wilhelmus à Brakel en Herman Witsius. Het leven voor God is voor Mastricht het leven door het geloof in Christus.

Deel drie van deze studie laat zien dat theologische methode en vroomheid in Mastrichts theologie geen tweespalt vormen, maar geïntegreerd zijn. Zoals gezegd wordt theologie door Mastricht gestructureerd in geloof en gehoorzaamheid. Hieronder moet worden verstaan dat het geloof de Godsleer, antropologie, Christologie, soteriologie en ekklesiologie omvat. De *locus* over de eschatologie heeft een eigen karakter in Mastrichts theologie: een beschrijving van het genadeverbond van de tijd van Adam tot Mastrichts eigen tijd en de toekomende tijd. Gehoorzaamheid wordt door Mastricht geschetst als ascetische theologie.

Als we ons beperken tot de *loci*, dan valt op dat ieder hoofdstuk bestaat uit vier aspecten: exegese, leer, elenctiek en *praxis*. Mastricht heeft deze viervoudige benadering van een theologisch onderwerp vanaf het begin van zijn loopbaan in de theologie gebruikt: de *Prodomus* van 1666 en vele disputaties getuigen ervan. Ook daarin is Mastricht zijn eigen weg gegaan, vergeleken met andere zeventiende-eeuwse theologische werken. Het eigene is niet zozeer gelegen in het feit dat er geen exegese, leeromschrijving, polemiek en *praxis* werd beoefend, maar dat Mastricht deze vier onderdelen samenbrengt in elk theologisch onderwerp.

Vervolgens, naast de tweedeling van theologie en de viervoudige benadering van de theologische onderwerpen valt het volgende op. Mastrichts exegese is vooral historisch-grammaticaal getint, met grote nadruk op filologie en etymologie. Verder toont hij welbewust te willen staan in de lijn van de rabbijnse peshat-methode en van Schriftinterpretatie zoals die wordt gevonden in de patristiek. Deze observatie wordt ondersteund door het nagaan van de exegese van Psalm 2:7 in verband met de triniteits- en verbondsleer. Het blijkt daarbij dat de "bewijs-teksten theorie" en het in de wetenschappelijke literatuur gesuggereerde onderscheid tussen voetiaanse en coccejaanse exegese niet houdbaar is. Mastrichts leeromschrijving is, zoals wordt aangetoond, het resultaat van zorgvuldige uitleg van de Schrift. De inhoud van de leer blijkt Schriftuurlijk te worden geformuleerd, waarbij de omschrijving doet denken aan de theologie van Augustinus.

Verder, het gebruik van scholastieke onderscheidingen en definities draagt, in onze opinie, er toe bij dat Mastricht helder en precies te werk gaat. Het gebruik van de scholastieke *quæstio*-methode komt vooral tot uiting in het elenctische gedeelte. Echter, het is belangrijk om op te merken dat Mastrichts gebruik van scholastieke methode, onderscheidingen en omschrijvingen wordt begrensd door zijn exegese en door de Schrift zelf. Voor wat betreft de *praxis*-gedeelten kan worden opgemerkt dat zij eenduidig zijn in structuur en dat zij qua inhoud de gelovige richt op God in Christus. De inhoud komt, zoals in de doctrinaire partijen, op uit de Schrift en wordt bijbels uitgedrukt, waarbij zij parallellen vertoont met de theologie van Bernardus van Clairvaux. De *praxis* is voor Mastricht niet een vorm van mysticisme of een ontsporing van de zestiende-eeuwse vroomheid, zoals wordt beweerd door Ritschl en anderen, maar is een uitdrukking van levend geloof.

De *basso continuo* van het voorafgaande is, dat voor Mastricht leer en leven (*praxis*) opkomen vanuit de Schrift. Exegese, leer en *praxis* zijn te onderscheiden, maar niet te scheiden. De opvatting van Brienen, die een diepe kloof meent te bespeuren tussen de *explicatio* en de *applicatio*, is af te wijzen.

De viervoudige benadering van de theologische onderwerpen door Mastricht hebben, voor hem, alles te maken met de exegeet. Alleen de exegeet die gelovig is en zich onder de leiding van de Heilige Geest stelt, is in staat getrouw de Schrift uit te leggen en formuleert het exegetisch resultaat in leer en *praxis* op een *theoretico*-praktische wijze. Dat wil zeggen dat de methode (*theoretica*) die door de exegeet wordt gebruikt is verbonden met de *praxis*, en andersom. Hier kunnen we concluderen dat Mastrichts *theoretico-practica*-ideaal parallel loopt met die van de middeleeuwse scholastieke methode en vroomheid, zij het dat deze laatste voor Mastricht samengaan met een gemodificeerde Amesiaanse omschrijving van theologie.

Deel IV richt zich op de Godsleer van Mastricht, die met in achtneming van het voorgaande leidt tot onderscheiden resultaten. Ten eerste, theologisch laat Mastricht zien dat de eenheid van God is gewaarborgd in de geestelijkheid en eenvoudigheid van God. Mastrichts benadering van de eigenschappenleer, door middel van de driedeling *Quid sit Deus*, *Quantus sit Deus* en *Qualis sit Deus* wordt niet of nauwelijks gedeeld door zijn tijdgenoten. De leer van de eenvoudigheid van God is geworteld in de Schrift en wordt geformuleerd via de leer van de geestelijkheid van God (hetgeen zijn Schriftuurlijke grond heeft in Johannes 4:24). Dit stemt overeen met zijn tijdgenoten, alsook met zestiende-eeuwse commentaren en Aquino. Dit betekent ons inziens dat de leer van de eenvoudigheid van God voor Mastricht niet een metafysische constructie is, maar gegrond is op het Woord van Christus en niet los gezien kan worden van de geestelijkheid van God. Het accent op de eenheid van God is voor Mastricht van soteriologisch belang.

Ten tweede wordt Mastrichts omschrijving van de Drie-eenheid onderzocht. Geconcludeerd kan worden dat voor hem de oeconomische Drie-eenheid centraal staat in zijn uitleg, welke een redemptieve betekenis (*pactum salutis*) heeft. Hier is Mastricht in het raam van zijn tijd uniek. Dat het *pactum* in de context van de omschrijving van de Drie-eenheid wordt behandeld, treft men bij zijn tijdgenoten niet aan. De geprononceerde aandacht die hij aan het verbond besteedt, geeft ons reden om Mastricht te identificeren als een verbondstheoloog. Mastricht deelt daarin de opvattingen met verbondstheologen zoals Coccejus, Burman en Untereyck. Deze conclusie wordt genuanceerd door op te merken dat Mastricht verschilt van Coccejus ten aanzien van de positie van de Middelaar in het *pactum*. Dit leidt ons tot de stelling dat Mastricht een middenpositie inneemt wat betreft de verbondsleer.

Ten derde, onze studie laat zien dat de Godsleer voor Mastricht van fundamenteel belang is voor zijn theologie, in leer en leven. Van Mastrichts formulering van de leer van God wordt gedeeld door de vroege kerkvaders, middeleeuwse doctors, in het bijzonder Aquino, en komt overeen met de uitleg van de zestiende-eeuwse reformatoren, in het bijzonder Calvijn. De Drie-enige God, zoals die door Mastricht wordt beschreven, is niet een abstract, doctrinair idee, maar de God van zaligheid.

Wij sluiten deze studie af met drie opmerkingen over het leven en werk van Petrus van Mastricht. Ten eerste, het beeld van Mastricht als zeventiende-eeuws gereformeerd theoloog, filosoof en hebraïcus verschilt van de karakterisering die voorheen wel is gegeven, zoals in de inleiding van deze studie is geschetst. Ten tweede, de *Theoretico-practica theologia* moet worden gezien als een synthese en codificatie van zeventiende-eeuwse gereformeerde theologie, zij het met onderscheiden karakteristieken: exegese, leer, elenctiek en *praxis*. Verder, de gebruikte bronnen in de *TPT* getuigen van exegetische trajecten die verder gaan dan de zestiende-eeuwse Reformatie: zij sluiten de rabbijnse en patristisch uitleg van de Schrift in. Ten derde zijn voor Mastricht de theologische methode (*ars*) en de vroomheid (*theologia practica* en *praxis pietatis*) onlosmakelijke met elkaar verbonden. Hierbij keren wij terug tot onze stelling dat voor Mastricht de leerstellige en pralicale formulering van theologie en het gebruik van de scholastieke methode worden begrensd door Schrift en exegese. Dit betekent dat theologie voor Mastricht trinitarisch en redemptief is van karakter: the art of living to God. Het existentiële karakter van zijn theologie is gegrond op en geworteld in de Schrift. Hij brengt ons, zoals ooit gezegd is van Bernardus "terug naar de bronnen en tot de Bron van alle christelijke spiritualiteit."

Appendix I.1.1 Works of Petrus van Mastricht[1]

1. *Vindicæ veritatis et autoritatis sacræ scripturæ in rebus Philosophicis adversus dissertationes D. Christophori Wittichii.* Utrecht: J. à Waesberge, 1655. (*)

2. *Theologiæ didactico-elenchtico-practicæ prodromus tribus speciminibus.* Amsterdam: Johannes van Someren, 1666.

3. *Perpetua praxeos cum theoria in theologicis pariter et theologis Συμβιβασις, oratione inaugurali lectionibus Hebræo-theologicis præmissa ... accedit ... programma invitatorium.* Frankfurt an der Oder: M. Hübner, 1668. (*)

4. *Methodus Concionandi.* Frankfurt an der Oder: M Hübner, undated.

5. *De fide salvifica syntagma theoretico-practicum: in quo fidei salvificæ tum natura, tum praxis universa, luculenter exponitur; cum præf. de membris Ecclesiæ visibilis seu admittendis, seu rejiciendis, oborienti scismati moderno applicanda.* Duisburg: Franc. Sas, 1671.

6. *Diatribe Theologica ... De Casu Conscientiæ: An Viduus Uxoris Novercam, Salva Conscientia, Ducere possit?: An saltem non sit dispensabile, tale Matrimonium? Immo &, si partibus de eo convenerit, per Magistratum dispensandum?* Pars 1 et 2, resp. Johannes Adolphus Eylerdt. Duisburg: Franc. Sas, 1676.

7. *Vita viatoris quasi transitus, omnia finem ... In: Lachrymæ Academiæ Duisburgensis In Obitum Admodum Reverendi, Clarissimi, Acutissimi Viri, D. Johan. Hermanni Hugenpoth, S.S. Theologiæ & purioris Philosophiæ Doctoris, earundemque Facultatum in alma Electorali, quæ est Duisburg, Professoris Celeberrimi, V.D. in eadem perantiqua Germanorum sede Præconis Facundissimi.* Duisburg: Franc. Sas 1676. (*)

8. *Theologiæ Theoretico-Practicæ Disputatio Quinta, De Existentia Et Cognitione Dei,* resp. Wilhelmus Mercamp. Duisburg: Franc. Sas, 1677.

9. *Novitatum Cartesianarum Gangræna, Nobiliores plerasque Corporis Theologici Partes arrodens et exedens, Seu Theologia Cartesiana detecta.* Amsterdam: Jansson, 1677.

---

1. Works marked with an asterisk (*) have not been reviewed. All other works have been consulted.

10. *Academiæ ultrajectinæ votum symbolicum: Sol justitiæ, illustra nos : pro themate inaugurali dictum a Petro Van [_sic_] Mastricht... die 6 septembris anno 1677.* (*)

11. *Theologiæ theoretico-practicæ disputatio septima de essentia, nominibus et atrributis Dei in genere*, pars 2, resp. Balduinus Drywegen. Utrecht: Meinardus à Dreunen, 1677.

12. *Theologiæ theoretico-practicæ disputatio septima de essentia, nominibus et attributis Dei in genere*, pars 3, resp. Jacobus de Clyver. Utrecht: Meinardus à Dreunen, 1677.

13. *De omnisufficientia Dei*, pars prior Theologiæ theoretico-practicæ disputatio sexta, resp. Theodorus Groen. Utrecht: Meinardus à Dreunen, 1677.

14. *De omnisufficientia Dei*, pars posterior, Theologiæ theoretico-practicæ disputatio sexta, resp. Theodorus Groen. Utrecht: Meinardus à Dreunen, 1677.

15. *Diatribes theologicæ determinantis casum conscientiæ: an Socinianus, a Socinianis, more sociniano baptizatus, ad catholicos transiturus, sit baptizandus ante?* pars posterior, resp. Theodorus Groen. Utrecht: Meinardus à Dreunen, 1677.

16. *Disputationum practicarum prima de certitudine salutis ejusque natura*, resp. Johannes Kamerling. Utrecht: Meinardus à Dreunen, 1678.

17. *Theologiæ theoretico-practicæ disputatio septima de essentia, nominibus et attributis Dei in genere*, pars 4, resp. Isaacus Ravensbergius. Utrecht: Meinardus à Dreunen, 1678.

18. *Disputatio historico-theologica peri tês moschopoiias. Act. vii.41. Exodi xxxii*, pars prior, resp. Jacobus Broedelet. Utrecht: Meinardus à Dreunen, 1679.

19. *Disputationum practicarum tertia de certitudine salutis, eique opposita præsumptione seu securitate carnali*, pars prima, resp. David de Volder. Utrecht: Meinardus à Dreunen, 1679.

20. *Exercitatio theologica de præcepto decalogi quarto*, resp. Nanningius Berckhout. Utrecht: Meinardus à Dreunen, 1679.

21. *Theologiæ theoretico-practicæ, sub relo sudantis, specimen de natura theologiæ*, primum, resp. Petrus Dix. Utrecht: Meinardus à Dreunen, 1680.

22. *Theologiæ theoretico-practicæ specimen, de natura theologiæ*, secundum, resp. Hugo Fittz. Utrecht: Meinardus à Dreunen, 1680.

23. *Theologiæ theoretico-practicæ specimen de natura theologiæ*, tertium, resp. Johannes Best. Utrecht: Meinardus à Dreunen, 1680.

24. *Theologiæ theoretico-practicæ specimen de natura theologiæ*, quartum, resp. Johannes Kelfkens. Utrecht: Meinardus à Dreunen, 1680.

25. *Disputationum practicarum tertia, de certitudine salutis, eique opposita præsumptione seu securitate carnali*, pars secunda, resp. Jacobus Hoog. Utrecht: Meinardus à Dreunen, 1680.

26. *Ad illust. episcopi Condomensis expositionem doctrinæ, quam vocat, Catholicæ, diatribe prima de consilio*, resp. Rutgerus van Bemmel. Utrecht: Meinardus à Dreunen, 1680.

27. *Ad illust. episcopi Condomensis expositionem doctrinæ quam vocat Catholicæ, diatribe tertia de adoratione creaturarum*, resp. Petrus Westwoude. Utrecht: Meinardus à Dreunen, 1680.

28. *Ad illustr. episcopi Condomensis expositionem doctrinæ quam vocat Catholicæ, diatribe quinta de invocatione sanctorum*, secunda, resp. Petrus Lastdrager. Utrecht: Meinardus à Dreunen, 1680.

29. *Ad illustr. episcopi Condomensis expositionem doctrinæ quam vocat Catholicæ, diatribe septima de cultu imaginum et reliquiarum*, secunda, resp. Johannes Rodenborgh. Utrecht: Meinardus à Dreunen, 1680.

30. *Disputationum practicarum de desertione spirituali prima*, resp. Henricus Nahuys. Utrecht: Meinardus à Dreunen, 1680.

31. *Disputationum practicarum de desertione spirituali secunda*, resp. Daniel Bongart. Utrecht: Meinardus à Dreunen, 1680.

32. Cephas Scheunenus. *Cartesianismi Gangræna insanabilis. Duodecim erotematum illustrium decadibus, frustra curata per P. Allingham, pastorem . . . enneade erotematum vulgarium*, demonstrata à C. Scheuneno. Utrecht: Meinardus à Dreunen, 1680. (*)

33. *De optima concionandi methodo paraleipomena: in usum theologiæ theoretico-practicæ, quæ, duabus disputationibus*, resp. Henricus Wagardus. Utrecht: Meinardus à Dreunen, 1681.

34. *De Foedere Gratiæ*, pars prima, ex theologiæ theoretico-practicæ, libro quinto, caput primum, resp. Hemmo Hovius. Utrecht: Meinardus à Dreunen, 1682.

35. *De mediatore foederis gratiæ*, pars tertia, ex theologiæ theoretico-practicæ, libro quinto, caput secundum, resp. Theodorus van Breen. Utrecht: Meinardus à Dreunen, 1682.

36. *Theoretico-practica theologia: qua, per capita theologica, pars dogmatica, elenchtica et practica, perpetua sumbibasei conjugantur; præcedunt in usum operis, paraleipomena, seu sceleton de optima concionandi methodo.* Vol. I. Amsterdam: Henricus et Vidua Theodori Boom, 1682.

37. *Disputationum practicarum de desertione spirituali*, pars tertia, resp. Daniel le Roy. Utrecht: Meinardus à Dreunen, 1683.

38. *Disputationum practicarum de desertione spirituali* pars quarta, resp. Samuel Kaposi. Utrecht: Meinardus à Dreunen, 1683.

39. *Disputationum practicarum de desertione spirituali*, pars quinta, resp. Johannes Chasse. Utrecht: Franciscus Halma, 1684.

40. *De dispensatione foederis gratiæ sub Patriarchis, ex Theologiæ Theoretico-Practicæ propediem ex ituræ libro octavo caput primum*, resp. Nicolaus de Goyer. Meinardus à Dreunen, 1686.

41. *De dispensatione foederis gratiæ, sub æternitate, ex Theologiæ theoretico-practicæ, parte posteriore, jam exituræ, caput postremum*, resp. Johannes Georgius Barovius. Meinardus à Dreunen,1686.

42. *De miraculis circa mortem Christi, disputationis philosophico-theologica*, resp. Mauritius Seelig. Meinardus à Dreunen, 1687.

43. *Theoretico-practica theologia: qua, per capita theologica, pars dogmatica, elenchtica et practica, perpetua sumbibasei conjugantur; præcedunt in usum operis, paraleipomena, seu sceleton de optima concionandi methodo*; auctore Petro van Mastricht. Vol. II. Amsterdam: Henricus et Vidua Theodori Boom, 1687

44. *De transubstantiatione*, resp. Joannes Wilhelmus Walschardt. Utrecht: Franciscus Halma, 1688.

45. *Diatribe theologica de æterna Christi sponsione*, resp. Arnoldus de Blankendæl. Utrecht: Franciscus Halma, 1690.

46. *Diatribes Theologicæ, De Usuris*, pars prior, resp. Jacobus Schuarz. Utrecht: Franciscus Halma, 1690.

47. *Diatribes Theologicæ, De Usuris*, pars posterior, resp. Jacobus Schuarz. Utrecht: Franciscus Halma, 1690.

48. *Disputatio theologica, De Electione ad salutem*, resp. Joannes von Ham. Utrecht: Franciscus Halma 1691.

49. *Disputatio theologica de obedientia fidei*, par. 1, 2, J. Witzonius. Utrecht: Franciscus Halma, 1691.

50. *Disputatio theologica De obedientia fidei*, par. 3, J. A. Breen. Utrecht: Franciscus Halma, 1691.

51. *Ad virum clariss. Balthasarem Beckerum epanorthosis gratulatoria occasione articulorum*, quos venerandæ Classi Amstelodamensi exhibuit, die 22 Janu. 1692, Exarata à Petro van Mastricht. Utrecht: Anthonium Schouten, 1692.

52. *Exercitationum analyticarum exegeticarumque, in caput Jesaiæ quinquagesimum-tertium*, prima [pars], resp. Henricus Revius. Utrecht: Franciscus Halma, 1693.

53. *Exercitationum analyticarum exegeticarumque, in caput Jesaiæ quinquagesimum-tertium*, secunda & tertia [pars], resp. Lambertus Wagardus. Utrecht: Franciscus Halma, 1693. (*)

54. *Exercitationum analyticarum exegeticarumque, in caput Jesaiæ quinquagesimum-tertium*, quarta & quinta [pars], resp. Theodorus Hagendyck. Utrecht: Franciscus Halma, 1694. (*)

55. *Exercitationum analyticarum exegeticarumque, in caput Jesaiæ quinquagesimum-tertium*, sexta & septima [pars], resp. Laurentius Le Brun. Utrecht: Franciscus Halma, 1694. (*)

56. *Theoretico-practica theologia: qua, per singula capita theologica, pars exegetica, dogmatica, elenchtica et practica, perpetua successione conjugantur; accedunt historia ecclesiastica, plena quidem, sed compendiosa, idea theologiæ moralis, hypotyposis theologiæ asceticæ etc.* 2 vols. Utrecht: Gerardus Muntendam, 1698.

57. *Dissertationis historico-philologico-theologicæ, tremendum vindictæ divinæ monumentum, in perennem memoriam, Ananiæ et Sapphiræ Actor. Cap. v vs. 1.-12. miraculose erectum exhibentis, pars prior*, resp. Johannes Pelsöczi. Utrecht: Franciscus Halma, 1699.

58. *Theoretico-practica theologia: qua, per singula capita theologica, pars exegetica, dogmatica, elenchtica et practica, perpetua successione conjugantur; accedunt historia ecclesiastica, plena quidem, sed compendiosa, idea theologiæ moralis, hypotyposis theologiæ asceticæ etc.*

proin opus quasi novum. Ed. nova, priori multo emendatior et plus quam tertia parte auctior. Utrecht: Thomas Appels, 1699.

59. *Historia ecclesiastica plena quidem compendiosa: Idea theologiæ Moraliæ hypotyposis theologiæ asceticæ. Theoretico-practica theologia, qua, per singula capita theologica, pars exegetica, dogmatica, elenchtica et practica, perpetuâ successione conjugantur: accedunt historia ecclesiastica, plena quidem; sed compendiosa.* Utrecht: Thomas Appels, 1699.

Reprints and Translations

60. *Theoretico-practica theologica: qua per singula capita theologica, pars exegetica, dogmatica, elenchtica et practica, perpetua successione conjugantur; auctore Petro van Mastricht. Editie Ed. nova, priori multo emendatior, et tertia saltem parte auctior / accedunt Historia ecclesiastica plena ferè, quanquam compendiosa, idea theologiæ moralis, hypotyposis theologiæ asceticæ etc.. . . ; huic novæ editione adjecta est auctoris vita a Pontano descripta.* Utrecht: sumptibus Societatis, 1715.

61. *Theologia Cartesiana detecta, seu gangræna Cartesiana: nobiliores plerasque corporis theologici partes arrodens et exedens Editio Ed. 2a.* Deventer: Daniel Schutten, 1716. (*)

62. *Theoretico-practica theologia: qua, per singula capita theologica, pars exegetica, dogmatica, elenchtica et practica, perpetua successione conjugantur; auctore Petro van Mastricht accedunt Historia ecclesiastica plena fere, quanquam compendiosa, idea theologiæ moralis, hypotyposis theologiæ asceticæ etc. Ed. nova / accedunt Historia ecclesiastica plena fere, quanquam compendiosa, idea theologiæ moralis, hypotyposis theologiæ asceticæ etc.* Utrecht: W. van de Water, J. v. Poolsum, J. Wagens, G. v. Paddenburg. 1724.

63. *Beschouwende en Praktikale Godgeleerdheit: waarin, door alle de Godgeleerde hoofdstukken henen, het Bybelverklarende, Leerstellige, Wederleggende,, en Praktikale deel door eenen onafgebroken schakel, onderscheidenlyk samengevoegt, voorgestelt word. Hierby komt een volledig Kort-begrip der Kerklyke Geschiedenisse, een vertoog der zedelyke, en een schets der plichtvermenende godgeleerdheit, enz. In het Latyn beschreven. Naar den laatstendruk in het Nederduitsch vertaalt, benevens de lykrede van den vermaarden hoogleeraar Henricus Pontanus, over het afsterven van den hoogwaardigen autheur; met eene voorrede van den heer Cornelius van der Kemp,* 4 vols. Rotterdam: Hendrik van Pelt, de Wed. P. Van Gilst, Jacobus Bosch, en Adrianus Douci; Utrecht: Jan Jacob van Poolsum, 1749-1753.

64. *A Treatise on Regeneration. By Peter Van Mastricht, D.D. Professor of Divinity in the Universities of Francfort, Duisburgh, and Utrecht.; Extracted from His System of Divinity, Called Theologia theoretico-practica; and Faithfully Translated into English; with an*

Appendix, Containing Extracts from Many Celebrated Divines of the Reformed Church, upon the Same Subject. New-Haven: Printed and sold by Thomas and Samuel Green in the Old-Council-Chamber, 1770.

65. Petrus van Mastricht, *A Treatise on Regeneration.* Reprint, ed. Brandon Withrow (Morgan: Soli Deo Gloria Publications, 2002).

66. *Beschouwende en Praktikale Godgeleerdheit: waarin, door alle de Godgeleerde hoofdstukken henen, het Bybelverklarende, Leerstellige, Wederleggende, en Praktikale deel door eenen onafgebroken schakel, onderscheidenlyk samengevoegt, voorgestelt word. Hierby komt een volledig Kort-begrip der Kerklyke Geschiedenisse, een vertoog der zedelyke, en een schets der plichtvermenende godgeleerdheit, enz. In het Latyn beschreven. Naar den laatsten druk in het Nederduitsch vertaalt, benevens de lykrede van den vermaarden hoogleeraar Henricus Pontanus, over het afsterven van den hoogwaardigen autheur, met eene voorrede van den heer Cornelius van der Kemp,* 4 vols. 1749-1753. Reprint. Ermelo: F. N. Snoek, 2003.

Disputations presided by Petrus van Mastricht as *rector-magnificus* 1682-1683.

67. *Disputatio medica inauguralis De Martialium operandi modo [et] usu.... pro gradu Doctoratus summisque in medicina honoribus [et] privilegiis rite ac legitime consequendis, publico examini,* resp. Johannes Fridericus Jani. Utrecht: Appellarianis, 1682. (*)

68. *Disputatio medica inauguralis De natura contagii ejusque effectibus,* resp. Zacharias Moeser. Utrecht: Appellarianis, 1682. (*)

69. *Dissertatio medica inauguralis De febribus continuis acutis,* resp. Abrahamus Gruber. Utrecht: Appelarianis, 1682. (*)

70. *Dissertatio medica inauguralis Quædam positiones medico-chymicæ,* resp. unknown. Utrecht: Appellarianis, 1682.

71. *Disputatio juridica inauguralis De tributis & vectigalibus, eruditorumexamini,* resp. Gerardus Brejerus. Utrecht: Strick, 1683.

72. *Dissertatio medica inauguralis De pleuritide vera,* resp. ? Utrecht: Appellarianis 1683. (*)

About Petrus van Mastricht

73. Pontanus, Henricus. *Laudatio Funebris In excessum Doctissimi Et Sanctissimi Senis, Petri van Mastrigt, S. S. Theol. Doctoris & Professoris : Quam jussu amplissimi Senatus Academici D. XXIV. Februarii / postridie sepulturæ dixit Henricus Pontanus.* Rotterdam: Petrus van Veen, 1706.

74. Pontanus, Henricus. *Liick En Lof-Reden Op het Afsterven van den Hooghgeleerden en seer Godsaligen Ouden Man, Petrus van Maastricht, Doctor en Hoogleermeester der H. Godtsgeleertheyt. Welke uyt last van de Hooghænsienlijke Raad der Academie op den 24. van Sprockelmaand des Jaars 1706. 's anderen daags na de Begræffenis, gedæn heeft Henricus Pontanus, ... Vertaalt door C.T.V.D.M.*

Handwriting of Mastricht[2]

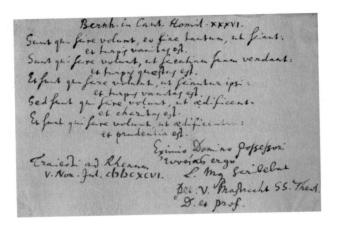

BERNH[ARD] IN CANT[ICUM] HOMIL[IAM] XXXVI
SUNT QUI SCIRE VOLUNT, EO FINE TANTUM, UT SCIANT:
    ET TURPIS VANITAS EST.
SUNT QUI SCIRE VOLUNT, UT SCIENTIAM SUAM VENDANT:
    ET TURPIS QUAESTUS EST.
ET SUNT QUI SCIRE VOLUNT, UT SCIANTUR IPSI:
    ET TURPIS VANITAS EST.
SED SUNT QUI SCIRE VOLUNT, UT AEDIFICENT:
    ET CHARITAS EST.
ET SUNT QUI SCIRE VOLUNT, UT AEDIFICENTUR:
    ET PRUDENTIA EST.

                Eximo Domino Possessor

Traject[um] ad Rhenum   εὐνοίας ergo
V. Non. Jul. MDCXCVI.   L. Mg. Scribebat Pet[rus] v[an] Mastricht SS Theol[ogiae]
                D[octor] et Prof[essor]

2. A. E. van Tellingen, *Het leven en enige aspecten uit de theologie van Petrus van Mastricht (1630-1706)* (Utrecht: Master thesis Faculty of Theology University of Utrecht, 2003), 50. Prof. Dr. Christoph Eggenberger of the Zentralbibliothek Zürich, Switzerland is acknowledged for his helpful assistance and copy of Mastricht's handwriting—probably written in an *album amicorum*—during my visit of August 23, 2005 at the department of handwritings.

Appendix I.2.1 Comparative Overview of the *Theoretico-practica theologia* 1682-1687 and 1699 edition

1699   1682-1687[1]

Liber Primus, de præcognitis Theologiæ.

1699	1682-1687
1. *De Theologiâ*	*De natura Theologiæ, tribus theorematis De Methodo Thelogiæ. De Definitio seu Theologia Christiana. De Definitione Theologiæ*
2. *De Scriptura*	*De Sacra Scriptura*
3. *De distributione Theologiæ*	

Liber Secundus, de fide in Deum triunum.

1699	
1. *De fide salvifica*	
2. *De existentia & cognitione Dei*	
3. *De essentia & independentiâ*	
4. *De nominibus Dei*	
5. *De attributis Dei in genere*	
6. *De spiritualitate & simplicitate Dei*	
7. *De immutabilitate Dei*	
8. *De unitate Dei*	
9. *De infinitate & magnitudine Dei*	
10. *De immensitate & omnipræsentiâ Dei*	
11. *De æternitate Dei*	
12. *De vita & immortalitate Dei*	
13. *De intellectu, scientia & sapientia Dei*	
14. *De veracitate & fide Dei*	
15. *De voluntate & affectibus Dei*	
16. *De bonitate Dei*	
17. *De amore, gratiâ, misericordiâ, longanimitate & clementiâ Dei*	
18. *De justitiâ Dei*	
19. *De sanctitate Dei*	
20. *De potestate & potentiâ Dei*	
21. *De omnisufficientia & perfectione Dei*	

[1] Book I – IV 1682, Book V – VIII 1687

22. *De majestate & gloriâ Dei*	
23. *De beatitudine Dei*	
24. *De SS. Trinitate*	
25. *De Deo Patre*	
26. *De Deo Filio*	
27. *De Deo Spiritu S.*	

Liber Tertius, de operationibus Dei.

1. *De actionibus & decretis Dei*	
2. *De prædestinatione*	
3. *De electione*	
4. *De reprobatione*	
5. *De creatione in genere*	
6. *De mundo & opere sex dierum*	
7. *De Angelis bonis*	
8. *De malis Angelis*	
9. *De homine & imagine Dei*	
10. *De providentiâ Dei generali*	
11. *De providentiâ speciali*	
12. *De fœdere naturæ*	

Liber Quartus, de hominis apostasiâ à Deo.

1. *De violatione fœderis naturæ*	
2. *De peccato originali*	
3. *De peccato actuali*	
4. *De pœna & statu peccati*	

Liber Quintus, de redemptione Christi.

1. *De fœdere gratiæ*	
2. *De Mediatore fœderis gratiæ*	
3. *De nominibus Mediatoris*	
4. *De persona Mediatoris*	
5. *De Trinitate officii Mediatorii*	
6. *De Mediatore Propheta*	
7. *De Mediatore Pontifice*	*De Mediatore Sacerdote*
8. *De Mediatore Rege*	
9. *De Mediatoris humiliatione*	
10. *De Mediatoris incarnatione*	
11. *De Mediatoris vitâ*	
12. *De Mediatoris morte*	
13. *De Mediatoris descensu*	
14. *De Mediatoris exaltatione in genere*	*De Mediatoris exaltatione*
15. *De Mediatoris resurrectione*	
16. *De Mediatoris ascensione*	
17. *De Mediatoris sessione ad dextram*	
18. *De ipsa Mediatoris redemptione*	

Liber Sextus, de redemptionis applicatione.

1. *De naturâ applicationis*	
2. *De redimendorum vocatione*	
3. *De redimendorum regeneratione*	
4. *De redimendorum conversione*	
5. *De redimendorum unione cum Christo*	
6. *De redimendorum justificatione*	
7. *De redimendorum adoptione*	
8. *De redimendorum sanctificatione*	
9. *De redimendorum glorificatione*	

Liber Septimus, de Ecclesiâ & ecclesiasticalibus.

1. *De naturâ Ecclesiæ*	
2. *De Ecclesiæ Ministris*	
3. *De Ecclesiæ Sacramentis in genere*	
4. *De Sacramentis regenerationis*	
5. *De Sacramentis nutritionis*	
6. *De Ecclesiæ disciplinâ*	
7. *De Ecclesiæ gubernatione*	

Liber Octavus, de dispensatione fœderis gratiæ.

1. *De dispensatione sub Patriarchis*	
2. *De dispensatione sub Mose*	
3. *De dispensatione sub Christo*	
4. *De dispensatione sub æternitate*	

Included in the 1699 edition and missing in the 1682-87 edition are the *Idea Theologiæ Moralis* and *Hypotyposis Theologiæ Asceticæ*.

Appendix I.2.2 Contributive Publications of Mastricht to His *Theoretico-practica theologia*

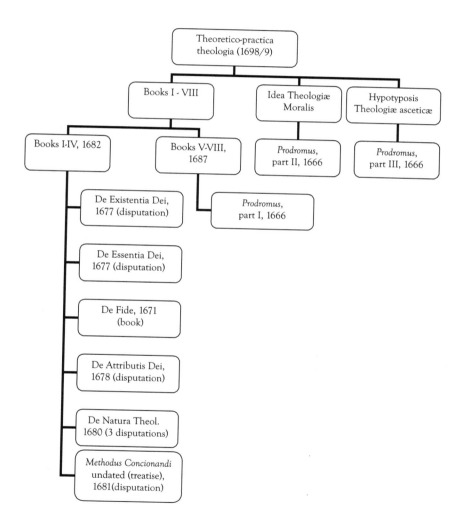

Appendix I.2.3 Structure of *De Fide in Deum triunum*

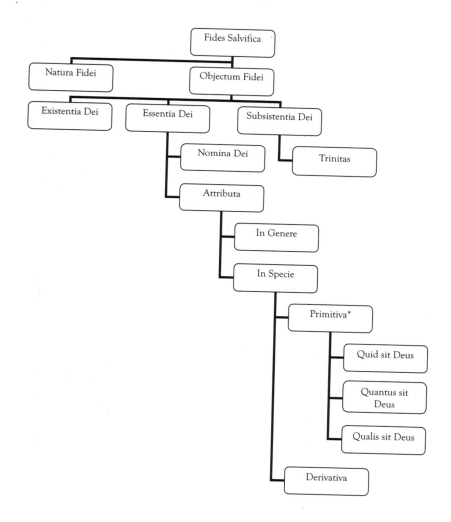

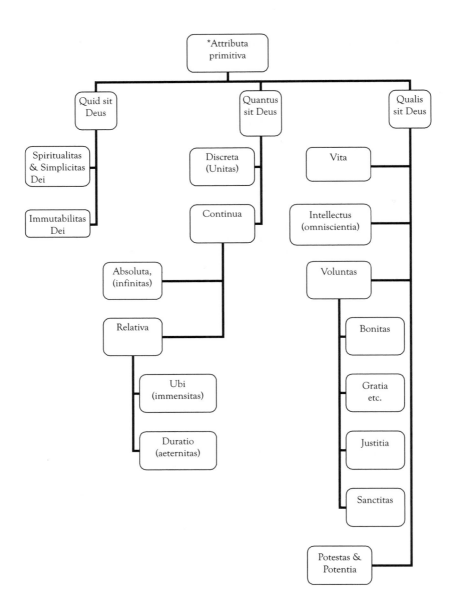

Appendix I.2.4 Sources of Book II, *De Fide Deus Triunum*

Citations with Reference

Ambrosius[1]
Amesius[2]
Anselmus[3]
Athanasius[4]
Augustinus[5]
Bernardus (of Clairvaux)[6]
Boethius[7]
Burtorius[8] but cites from Reuchlinus De Arte
Cabbal/ Lexico Talmud
Burmannus[9]
Canus, Melchior[10]
Calvinus[11]
Cyprianus[12]
Cyrillus[13]
Descartes[14]
Drusius[15]
Fulgentius[16]
Gerhardus, Joh.[17]
Gregorius (the Great)[18]
Haccados (rabbi)[19]
Hilarius (of Poitiers)[20]
Homerus[21]

Horatius[22]
Ireneus[23]
Justinus[24]
Juvenalis[25]
Lactantius[26]
Leo X[27]
Lirinensis, Vincentius[28]
Nazianzenus[29]
Origenes[30]
Orpheus[31]
Philo[32]
Plato[33]
Polydor, Virgil.[34]
Prudentius[35]
Proclus[36]
Richardus (of St. Victor)[37]
Seneca[38]
Smalcius[39]
Sophocles[40]
Statius[41]
Tertullianus[42]
Wittichius[43]
Wolzogius[44]

1. II.9.
2. II.3; II.13.
3. II.17.
4. II.8.
5. II.2; II.6; II.7; II.10; II.11; II.12; II.13; II.15; II.16; II.20, II.23.
6. II.4; II.10; II.11; II.12; II.16
7. II.11.
8. II.5.
9. II.14.
10. II.19.
11. II.2.
12. II.14.
13. II.8.
14. II.2.
15. II.23.
16. II.14.
17. II.20.
18. II.21.
19. II.26.
20. II.7; II.10; II.11.
21. II.8.

22. II.2.
23. II.11.
24. II.6; II.7.
25. II.2.
26. II.8.
27. II.2.
28. II.27.
29. II.8.
30. II.6.
31. II.8.
32. II.14.
33. II.8; II.11; II.16.
34. II.2.
35. II.8.
36. II.7.
37. II.24.
38. II.16.
39. II.27.
40. II.8.
41. II.2.
42. II.13.
43. II.5; II.6; II.12; II.14.
44. II.14.

References without Citation

Aretinus,[45] Petrus
Alting[46]
Alvares de Auxil.[47]
Amama[48]
Ambrosius[49]
Amesius[50]
Anselmus[51]
Aquinas[52]
Augustinus[53]
Athanasius[54]
Balduinus, Franscis.[55]
Basil[56]
Bellarminus[57]
Biel, Gabriel[58]
Boetius[59]
Buxtorf[60]
Burmannus[61]
Capellus, Ludov[62].
Cloppenburg[63]
Cyrillus[64], Alexandrinus
Damascenus[65]
Descartes or Cartesius[66]
Dionysius[67]
Drexelius[68]
Drusius[69]
Eusebius[70]
Epiphan[71]
Episcopius[72]

Ficinus, Marsilius[73]
Forber[74]
Fullerus[75]
Galatinus[76]
Gattaker[77]
Gellius[78]
Gerhard[79]
Hoornbeeck[80]
Isidorus[81]
Ireneus[82]
Justinus[83]
Cajetanus[84]
Klaubert[85]
Lactantius[86]
Laertius[87]
Lorinus[88]
Luther[89]
Ludovicus[90]
Mastricht, Petrus van[91]
Maimonides[92]
Meisn. (unknown)[93]
Mercerus[94]
Molinæus[95]
Mornæus[96]
Nazianzenus, Gregorius[97]
Niceponus[98]
Origenes[99]

45. II.2.
46. II.26.
47. II.14.
48. II.4.
49. II.8.
50. II.1; II.14; II.26.
51. II.16.
52. II.19; II.24.
53. II.7; II.8 (4x); II.16; II.24 (2x).
54. II.8.
55. II.6.
56. II.8.
57. II.19.
58. II.24.
59. II.19.
60. II.4.
61. II.14.
62. II.4.
63. II.27.
64. II.24.
65. II.4; II.8; II.21.
66. II.20 (2x)
67. II.4.
68. II.12; II.15.
69. II.4; II.5.
70. II.4; II.7; II.24 (2x); II.26.
71. II.7; II.8 (2x).
72. II.26.

73. II.24.
74. II.7.
75. II.4 (2x).
76. II.4.
77. II.4.
78. II.2.
79. II.24.
80. II.27.
81. II.17.
82. II.5; II.26.
83. II.4; II.24.
84. II.19.
85. II.24.
86. II.8. (2x); II.24.
87. II.24.
88. II.24.
89. II.17.
90. II.24.
91. II.2 (3x); II.3 (2x); II.6; II.10 (2x); II.11; II.12; II.13; II.14,II.20 (2x); II.24.
92. II.4; II.17.
93. II.24.
94. II.2.
95. II.14.
96. II.2; II.24.
97. II.8.
98. II.24.
99. II.8; II.24.

Petavius (Jesuit)[100]
Philo[101]
Plotinus[102]
Pruknerus[103]
Rhetorfortes[104]
Richardus (of St. Victor)[105]
Sabande, [106] Raimundus de
Scaliger[107]
Schevicavimus, [108] Gysb.
Scotus[109]
Seldenus[110]
Seneca[111]
Siculus, Diodorus[112]

Smalcius[113]
Socinius[114]
Spicelius[115]
Sylvius, Franscisc. [116]
Tertullianus[117]
eusTheodort. [118]
Theophilus. [119]
Twissus[120]
Videlius[121]
Voetius[122]
Vorstius[123]
Wittichus[124]
Zanchius[125]

100. II.8.
101. II.4; II.5.
102. II.24.
103. II.6.
104. II.13.
105. II.24.
106. II.24.
107. II.24.
108. II.24.
109. II.24.
110. II.19.
111. II.10.
112. II.8; II.24.

113. II.27.
114. II.6; II.10; II.13.
115. II.2 (2x).
116. II.1.
117. II.5; II.6; II.8.
118. II.8.
119. II.21.
120. II.13.
121. II.21.
122. II.24 (2x).
123. II.6; II.11; II.21.
124. I.14; II.5; II.11; II.12; II.13.
125. II.4.

Names Only

Aristotle[126]
Arius[127]
Arminius[128]
Athanasius[129]
Aquinas[130]
Aquila[131]
Augustinus[132]
Balduinus[133]
Basilius[134]
Bellarminus[135]
Beza[136]
Bidellus[137]
Calvinus[138]
Calixtus[139]
Carpocratus[140]
Cerintus[141]
Chemnitus[142]
Chrysostomus[143]
Cloppenburg[144]
Cocceius[145]
Comes,[146] Marcellius
Damascenus[147]
Danæus[148]
Descartes[149]
Diodatus[150]
Drusius[151]
Epicurus[152]
Euthymius[153]

Fagius, Paulus[154]
Fonseca, Petrus[155]
Frank[156]
Genebrardus[157]
Grotius[158]
Hakkadosch[159] (Rabbi)
Hieronymus[160]
Heraclitus[161]
Huberus, Samuel[162]
Jarchi, Salomon (Rabbi)[163]
Joris, David[164]
Junius[165]
Kimchi, David (Rabbi)[166]
Ludovicus[167]
Lucullus[168]
Maimonides[169]
Macidonius[170]
Maresius[171]
Markrobius[172]
Martyr[173]
Menzerus[174]
Mercerus[175]
Mohammed[176]
Molina, Ludovicus[177]
Nacham[178] (Rabbi)
Noetus[179]
Origenes[180]
Owen[181]

126. II.11.
127. II.24; II.26.
128. II.26.
129. II.13.
130. II.24.
131. II.21.
132. II.5; II.16.
133. II.6.
134. II.27.
135. II.2; II.26.
136. II.13; II.16; II.26.
137. II.27.
138. II.4; II.16; II.26.
139. II.10.
140. II.26.
141. II.26.
142. II.20.
143. II.14; II.16.
144. II.27.
145. II.17.
146. II.7.
147. II.14; II.27.
148. II.4.
149. II.2 (2x); II.3 (3x); II.14.
150. II.16.
151. II.4.
152. II.23.
153. II.16.

154. II.17.
155. II.13.
156. II.27.
157. II.26.
158. II.17; II.26.
159. II.4.
160. II.5.
161. II.26.
162. II.14; II.17 (2x).
163. II.4.
164. II.27.
165. II.2; II.4 (2x).
166. II.4; II.19.
167. II.2.
168. II.2.
169. II.4.
170. II.24.
171. II.11.
172. II.16.
173. II.4.
174. II.20.
175. II.4.
176. II.23; II.26.
177. II.13.
178. II.4.
179. II.7.
180. II.14; II.16; II.17.
181. II.2.

Paracelsus, Theophratus[182]
Perkins[183]
Piscator[184]
Philoponus, Joh. [185]
Plato[186]
Ponthinus[187]
Puccius, Franscisc.("a Italian Socinian")[188]
Sabelius[189]
Scotus, John.[190]
Smalcius[191]
Spinoza, Joh[192]
Soctrates[193]
Somasatenus, Paul[194]
Spinoza, Bened[195]
Swenkfeldius[196]
Symmachus[197]
Tertullianus[198]
Theodoretus[199]
Theophylactus[200]
Thyssius[201]

Tullius[202]
Twissus[203]
Vaninus, Ceasar[204]Caesar[204]
Veronius, Arnoldus[205]
Vives[206]
Vorstius, Conrad[207]
Vossius[208]
Walaeus[209]
Wiegelius[210]
Zanchius[211]

182. II.24.
183. II.14.
184. II.16.
185. II.24.
186. II.12.
187. II.24; II.26.
188. II.14; II.17 (2x).
189. II.7.
190. II.3; II.24.
191. II.26.
192. II.2.
193. II.12.
194. II.26.
195. II.2.
196. II.27.
197. II.21.
198. II.5; II.6 (2x).
199. II.16.
200. II.27.
201. II.17 (2x).

202. II.2; II.12.
203. II.14.
204. II.2 (2x).
205. II.20.
206. II.2.
207. II.3; II.6 (2x); II.7; II.10 (3x); II.11 (3x); II.12 (2x); II.13; II.20 (2x).
208. II.2.
209. II.14.
210. II.20; II.27.
211. II.4.

Appendix IV.2.1 Structure of Chapter *De Spiritualitate et Simplicitate Dei*

John 4:24, πνεῦμα ὁ θεός, καὶ τοὺς προσκυνοῦντας αὐτὸν ἐν πνεύματι καὶ ἀληθείᾳ δεῖ προσκυνεῖν

I.   Introduction - explains relationship with preceding chapters.

Exegetical

II.   The words of the text provide an answer for the essence of God
   A.   Description of God
       1.   Descriptor, the subject of the sentence, ὁ θεός
       2.   Description, πνεῦμα
   B.   Practical consequence
       1.   The ministers, τοὺς προσκυνοῦντας
       2.   The worship, or adoration
            (a)   In spirit
            (b)   In truth
       3.   The necessity, δει

[The remainder of the chapter is summarized on the next page for comparison purposes]

Doctrinal· Spirituality

III.   That God is a Spirit is testified: Old and New Testament, Origines, Augustine.

IV.   With reason: God is the first Being, independent, simple, infinite, immutable.

V.   In what sense God is a Spirit.

VI.   What belongs to the spiritual essence.

VII.   What affections have a spiritual nature

Elenctic

VIII.   Question 1: Is God really a Spirit? Tertullian, Socinians, Vorstius, Cartesian theologians. Question is answered and followed by objections, which are replied to.[1]

IX.   Question 2: Is God corporeal? Audians, Tertullian, Anthropomorphists.

X.   Question3: Is God's corporeality not thin?

XI.   Question 4: Should God be represented by images? Lutherans, Roman Catholics.

XII.   Question 5: Is it permissible to pray to God, imagining Him as an (old) man?

Practical

XIII.   Application 1: How one should pray and think about God.

XIV.   Application 2: Warning to hypocrites.

XV.   Application 3: Examine one's worship of God.

XVI.   Application 4: Exhortation to devote ourselves to God.

XVII.   Application 5: Exhortation to have a purified spirit.
     (1)   Of what uncleanness one must be purified from
     (2)   For what reason
     (3)   By what means

XVIII.   Application 6: What is spiritual worship? And what is the reason for it?

XIX.   Application 7: Exhortation for spiritual prayers

Doctrinal – Simplicity

XX.   Simplicity is consequence of Spirituality and is testified in Scriptures

XXI.   With reason : God is the first Being, independent, immutable, infinite, eternal, perfect.

XXII.   In what sense Simplicity

Elenctic

XXIII.   Question 1: Is God real Simple? Heathens, Anthropomorphists, Tertullian, Socinians. Answer to question is followed by objections, which are replied to.

XXIV.   Question 2: Does Scripture teach Simplicity? Anthropomorphists, Audians, Socinius.

Practical

XXV.   Application 1: God's Simplicity is the foundation of one's imperfection and divine perfection

XXVI.   Application 2: Exhortation to rest in simplicity to God's will.

XXVII.   Application 3: Exhortation to serve, worship God in simplicity
     (1)   In what sense
     (2)   Why one ought to do this
     (3)   Means

XXVIII.   Application 4: Exhortation to live in simplicity and uprightness with neighbor

XXIX.   Application 5: Exhortation to be satisfied with one's lot, even when it is simple

---

[1] This is found in all questions stated in II.6

Appendix IV.2.a Structure of the Chapters on the Holy Trinity.

	Exegesis	Doctrinal	Exegesis	Doctrinal	Practical

1.	Son (II.24.ii.1)
	Benefit – grace...redemption
	Benefactor
	• Lord
	  o General
	  o Person
	  o Mediator
			Son (II.26.ii)	Redemption (II.26.vi)	

		Mediator (II.24.xii) • Surety • Goël • Redeemer	Mediator (II.26.ii)	Mediator (II.26.xiii) Surety Goël Redeemer Explainer Judge Head	Mediator (II.26.xxii) Surety (II.26.xxi) Redeemer Explainer Judge Head
	• Jesus – redeemer. • Christ – mediator.				
2.	Father (II.24.ii.2) Benefit – love Benefactor • Lord • Creator • Lawgiver • Father	(II.24.xii, xiv) Lord Creator Lawgiver Father	(II.25.ii) Ruler/Lord Lawgiver Judge Prosecutor	(II.25.vii) Lord Creator Lawgiver Prosecutor Father	(II.25.xiii-xviii) love Lord Creator Lawgiver/Prosecutor Father

3.	Holy Spirit (II.24.ii.3)
	Benefit – communion
	Benefactor
	
	• Spirit
	• Holy
		communion (II.24.x)
		
		Spirit (II.24.xii)
		Holy (II.24.xiv)
			(II.27.ii)
			
			Benefactor
			  Comforter
			  Spirit
			  Holy
			
			Mission
			
			Benefit
			  Teaching
			  Reminder
				
				Comforter (II.27.xiv)
				
				Holy (II.27.xiii)
				
				Mission (II.27.xi)
				
				Teaching (II.27.xii)
					
					Communion (II.27.xxii)
					
					Holy (II.27.xxiv)
					
					Teaching (II.27.xxiv)

Chapter 24 – Holy Trinity
Chapter 25 – Father
Chapter 26 – Son
Chapter 27 – Holy Spirit

Appendix IV.2.b Structure of the Doctrinal Sections

Chapter	24	25	26	27
Paragraph				
VII Communion of Three Persons:				
Heavenly economy		III	III	III
VIII-X Distinction between (Essence and) Persons:				
Divinity		IV	VIII	VII
Personality		V	V	V
Distinct of other Persons		VI	VI	VI
XI Economy of Three Persons:				
XII Offices		VII	XIII	XI
XIV Attributes		VIII	XIV	XV

Bibliography

Primary Sources

Alting, Jacobi. *Opera omnia theologica, analytica, exegetica, practica, problematica & philologica.* 5 vols. Amsterdam: Gerardus Borstius, 1687.

Ames, William. *Marrow of Sacred Divinity.* London: Edward Griffin, 1642.

Aquinas, Thomas. *Summa Theologica.* Translated by the Fathers of the English Dominican Province. Benziger Bros. edition, 1947.

Augustine, "The Trinity." *Fathers of the Church,* vol. 45. Translated by Stephen McKenna. Washington, D. C: Catholic University Press, 1963.

Bekker, Baltasar. *Naakte uitbeeldinge van alle de vier boeken der Betoverde weereld, vertonende het oogmerk van den schryver tot wechneeminge van vooroordeelen en een kort begryp des ganschen werx.* Amsterdam: Daniel van den Dalen, 1693.

. Benthem, Hechinri L. *Holländischer Kirchen- und Schulen-Staat.* Frankfurt an der Oder: Förster, 1698.

Bijbel, dat is de gansche Heilige Schrift...met niewe bijgevoegde verklaringen op de duistere plaatsen. Amsterdam: Wed. G. De Groot, 1738.

Brakel, Wilhelmus à. *ΛΟΓΙΚΗ ΛΑΤΡΕΙΑ, dat is Redelyke Godtsdienst, in welken de Goddelijke Waerheden des Genade-Verbondts worden verklaert, tegen partyen beschermt, en tot de practyke aengedrongen.* 2 vols. Rotterdam: Reynier van Doesburgh, 1700.

Braunius, Johannes. *Leere der Verbonden.* 3d ed. Amsterdam: Isaac Stokmans, 1723.

Brown, John. *A Compendious view of natural and revelead religion.* Edinburgh: W. Anderson, 1782. Reprinted as *The Systematic Theology.* Introduced by Joel R. Beeke, and Randall J. Pederson. Grand Rapids: Reformation Heritage Books, 2002.

Buddeus, J. F. *Isagoge Historico-Theologica ad Theologiam universiam.* Lipsea: Thomas Fritschi, 1730).

Burmannus, Franciscus. *Synopsis Theologiæ & speciatim Oeconomiæ Foederum Dei.* Utrecht: Cornelius Jacobi Noenardus, 1671.

_____. *Synopsis, dat is Kort Begryp der Heilige God-geleertheit, en insonderheit van de Huishouding der Verbonden Gods.* Translated by Dirk Smout. 2 vols. Utrecht: Franscois Halma, 1688.

Burman, Caspar. *Trajectum eruditum, virorum doctrina inlustrium, qui in urbe Trajecto et regione Trajectensi nati sunt sive ibi habitarunt, vitas, fata et scripta exhibens.* Utrecht: Padenburg, 1738.

Calmet, Augustin. *Commentaire litteral sur tous Les Livres de l'ancient et du nouveau Testament.* 8 vols. Paris: Augustins, 1724.

Calvin, John. *Calvin's Commentaries.* 22 vols. 1844-55. Reprint, Grand Rapids: Baker Books, 1984.

Cloppenburgh, Johannis. *Theologica Opera Omnia.* Amsterdam: Gerardus Borstius, 1684.

Cocceius, Johannes. *Opera Omnia Theologica.* 10 vols. Amsterdam: P&J Blaev, 1701.

_____. *Opera Anekdota Theologica et Philologica.* 2 vols. Amsterdam: Jansonio-Waesbergios, Boom & Goethals, 1706.

Cocquius, A. *Theologiæ praxis, de ware practycque der godt-geleertheit.* Utrecht: Simon de Vries, 1658.

Comrie, Alexander, and Nicolaas Holtius. *Examen van het ontwerp van tolerantie, om de leere in de Dordrechtse Synode Anno 1619 vastgesteld met de veroordeelde leere der Remonstranten te verenigen: voorgesteld in eenige samenspraken, door een genootschap van voorstanders der Nederlandse formulieren van eenigheid/geschreven, tot versterking van de liefhebbers der waarheid.* Amsterdam: Nicolaas Bijl, 1753-1759.

D'Outrein, Johannes. *De Droefheid die naar God is, werkende een Onberouwelijke Bekeeringe tot Zaligheid. Mitsgaders de ware Selfs-Verloochening.* Amsterdam: Jacobus Borstius, 1710.

De Benedictis, Giovanni B. *Difesa della terza lettera apologetica di Benedetto Aletino, divisa in tre discussioni, una teologica, l'altra filosofica della filosofia cartesiana, la terza critica,* Rome: Antonio DeRossi, 1705.

Dinant, Petrus. *De Brief van de H. Apostel Paulus aan die van Efeze.* 3 vols. 2d ed. Rotterdam: Jan Daniel Beman, 1726.

Edwards, Jonathan. *The Works of Jonathan Edwards.* 22 vols. New Haven, London: Yale University Press, 1998.

Erskine, Ralph. *Faith no fancy, or, A treatise of mental images: discovering the vain philosophy and vile divinity of a late pamphlet entitled [sic] Mr. Robe's fourth letter to Mr. Fisher, and showing that an imaginary idea of Christ as man (when supposed to belong to saving faith, whether in its act or object), imports nothing but ignorance, atheism, idolatry, great falsehood, and gross delusion.* Philadelphia: William M'Culloch, 1805.

Essenius, Andreas. *Compendium theologiæ dogmaticum: ubi præter explicationes theticas, & assertiones scripturarias, in controversiis vera sententia passim confirmatur argumentis, ad certas & paucas classes revocatis: præcipuæ adversariorum exceptiones atque objectiones clare proponuntur, & solvuntur: usus autem practici suis locis etiam adscribuntur.* Utrecht: Meinardus à Dreunen, 1669.

Fisher, Edward. *The Marrow of Modern Divinity,* with notes by Thomas Boston. Reprint, Seoul, New York: Westminster Publishing House, 1645.

Foertstius, Michael. *Selectorum theologorum breviarum, id est discussio principalium punctorum theologicorum nostro tempore maxime controversorum.* Jena: Lager, 1708.

Fruytier, Jacobus. *Sion's Worstelingen of historische samenspraken over de verscheide en zeer bittere wederwaardigheden van Christus Kerke, met openbare en verborgene vyanden: in de reformatie, ten tyde der Remonstranten, in deze onze dagen.* Rotterdam: Johan van Doesburg, 1715.

Glaserus, Hermannus. *Catechesis theoretico-practica. Dat is een eenvoudige verklaringe van de voornaamste hoofd-stukken onses catechismus.* Amsterdam: H. Burgers, 1729.

Gomarus, Franciscus. *Opera theologia omnia.* Amsterdam: Johannes Jansonius, 1664.

Goodwin, Thomas. *Opera, ofte alle de theologische werken: meest betreffende de practyke der godzaligheid en den wandel van een christen in de plichten nevens God en zyne even-naasten.* Trans. Jacobus Koelman. 3d ed. Amsterdam: Adrianus Douci, 1749.

Hagen, Petrus van der. *Verborgenheyt der Godsaligheit.* Amsterdam: Johannes van Someren, 1677.

Heidanus, Abraham. *Corpus theologiæ christianæ in quindecim locos.* 2 vols. Leiden: Johannes de Vivie & Jordanus Luchtmans, 1686.

Heidegger, Johann Heinrich. *Corpus theologiæ christianæ.* 2 vols. Zürich: David Gessner, 1700.

Henry, Matthew. *An Exposition of the Old and New Testaments: Wherein Each Chapter is Summed Up as to Its Contents...with Practical Remarks and Observations.* London: Patridge and Oakey, 1706.

Hooker, Thomas. *De ware zielsvernedring en heilzame wanhoop.* Trans. J. Koelman. Amsterdam: J. Wasteliers, 1678.

Hoornbeeck, Johannes. *De esu sanguinis et suffocati ad Act. XV, resp.* Van Maestricht. Utrecht: Henricus Versteeg, 1650.

———. *Disputatio theologica practica, de devotione, resp.* Daniel Radaeus. Leiden: Elsevier, 1659.

———. *Disputatio theologica, practica, de mundo, resp.* Jacobus Corf. Leiden: Elsevier, 1659.

———. *Summa controversiarum religionis cum infidelibus, hæreticis, schismaticis: id. Est, Gentilibus, Judæis, Muhammedanis; Papistis, Anabaptistis.* Utrecht: J. à Waesberge, 1658.

———. *Theologia practica.* 2 vols. Utrecht: Henricus Versteegh, 1663-1666.

Hopkins, Samuel. *The system of doctrines: contained in divine revelation, explained and defended: showing their consistence and connection with each other: to which is added, A treatise on the millennium.* Boston: Isaiah Thomas and Ebenezer T. Andrews, 1793.

Hugenpoth, Johann Hermann. *Dissertatio Theologica Continens Aliquot Positiones De Actione Dei Circa Indurationem Cordis Human, resp.* Joannes Theodor Helmius. Duisburg: Franc. Sas, 1670.

Koelman, Jacobus. *De Pointen van Nodige Reformatie.* Rotterdam: de Wilde, 1678.

_____. *Reformatie Nodigh omtrent de Feest-dagen, Naaktelijk vertoont ende bewezen.* Rotterdam: H.Goddaeus, 1665.

_____. *Eenige originele brieven geschreven aan Do Balthasar Bekker, over sijn boek de Betoverde werelt.* Amsterdam: Daniel van den Dalen, 1692.

_____. *Het vergift van de Cartesiaansche philosophie: grondig ontdekt en meest historischer wijze, uit de schriften van des Cartes zelfs, en van andere schrijvers, zo voor als tegen hem, getrouwelijk aangeweezen.* Amsterdam: Johannes Boekholt, 1692.

Kok, Jacobus. *Vaderlandsch woordenboek.* Amsterdam: Johannes Allart, 1785-1799.

Le Long, Isaac. *Hondert-Jaarige Jubel-Gedachtenisse der Academie van Utrecht.* Utrecht: M. Visch, 1736.

Love, Christopher. *Theologia practica, dat is: Alle de theologische wercken.* Trans. C. van Diemerbroeck. Utrecht: Hermannus Ribbius, 1657.

Maccovius, Johannes. *Loci communes theologici.* Franeker: Joannes Arcerius, 1650.

Marck, Johannes à. *Opera Omnia.* 27 vols. Amsterdam: Gerardus Borstius, 1699-1706.

_____. *Compendium Theologiæ Christianæ didactico-elencticum.* Amsterdam: R. & G. Wetstenios, 1722.

Maresius, Samuel. *Collegium Theologicum sive Systema Breve Universæ Theologiæ.* Groningen: Franciscus Bronchorstus, 1656.

Mastricht, Petrus van. See Appendix I.1.1 Works of Petrus van Mastricht

Mather, Cotton. *Manuductio Ad Ministerium, Directions for a Candidate of the Ministry.* Boston: Thomas H. -eck, 1726.

Moor, Bernardus de. *Commentarius perpetuus in Johannis Marckii Compendium Theologiæ Christianæ didactico-elencticum.* 6 vols. Leiden: Johannes Hasebroek, 1761.

Oomius, Simon. *Dissertatie van de Onderwijsingen in de Practycke der Godgeleerdheid.* Bolsward: Samuel van Haringhouk, 1672.

_____. *Institutiones theologiæ practicæ, ofte onderwysingen in de practycke der godtgeleertheydt: eerste tractæt des tweeden boeck's van het eerste deel, vervattende de verhandelinge der theologia didactica.* Bolsward: Wed. Van Samuel Haringhouk, 1676.

_____. *Cierlijke Kroon des Grysen Ouderdoms.* Leiden: Daniel van den Dalen, 1707

Owen, John. *The Works of John Owen.* London: Johnstone and Hunter, 1850-1855.

_____. *Theologoumena pantodapa: sive, De natura, ortu, progressu, et studio veræ theologiæ, libri sex: quibus etiam origines & processus veri & falsi cultus religiosi, casus & instaurationes ecclesiæ illustiores ab ipsis rerum primordiis, enarrantur.* Oxford: Hen. Hall, 1661.

Paquot, Jean Noël. *Mémoires pour servir à l'histoire littéraire des dix-sept provinces des Pays-Bas, de la principauté de Liége, et de quelques contrées voisines.* Louvain: de l'Imprimerie académique, 1765.

Pearson, J. *Een Uitlegging van het Geloof*. Transl. M. Neef. Utrecht: Johannes Ribbius, 1681.

Perkins, W. *A Commentary on Galatians*. Ed. G. T. Sheppard, with introductory essays by B. S. Childs, G. T. Sheppard, and J. H. Augustine. Pilgrim Classic Commentaries. New York: Pilgrim, 1989.

Perkins, William. *The Workes of Mr. William Perkins, A Golden Chaine*. Cambridge: John Legatt, 1612.

Petri, Wolfgang. *Die Reformierten Klevischen Synoden im 17. Jahrhundert*. Rheinlag-Verlag: Cologne, 1981.

Polyander, Johannes, Andreas Rivetus, Antonius Walæus, and Antonius Thysius. *Synopsis purioris theologiæ*. 6th ed. Ed. H. Bavinck. Leiden: D. Donner, 1881.

Pontanus, Henricus. *Laudatio Funebris In excessum Doctissimi Et Sanctissimi Senis, Petri van Mastrigt, S. S. Theol. Doctoris & Professoris: Quam jussu amplissimi Senatus Academici D. XXIV. Februarii / postridie sepulturæ dixit Henricus Pontanus*. Rotterdam: Van Veen, 1706.

Poole, Matthew. *Synopsis Criticorum aliorumque S. Scripturæ interpretum*. 5 vols. London: E. Flesher, 1669-76.

Ramus, Petrus. *Commentariorum de Religione Christiana*. Frankfurt: Wechel, 1594.

Ridderus, Franciscus. *Sevenvoudige Oeffeningen over de Catechismus zijnde, ziel-bereydende, wærheydt-bevestigende, geloofs-bevorderende, dwalingh-stuttende, practyck-lievende, gemoet-onderrichtende*. Rotterdam: Joannes Borstius, 1671.

Shepard, Thomas. *De Gezonde Geloovige*. Amsterdam: Joannes Boekholt, 1686.

Spanheim, Friedrich. *Opera*. Leiden: Johannem du Vivié, Isaaco Severino, 1701-1703.

Stoddard, Salomo. *Een leidsman tot Christus*. Leiden: Buurman & De Kler, undated.

Turretin, Franciscus. *Institutio theologiæ elencticæ*. 3 vols. Geneva: Samuel de Tournes, 1679-1685.

Undereyck, Theodor. *Der Närrische Atheist/ Entdeckt und seiner Thorheit überzeuget/ In Zwey Theilen In dem Ersten/ Als ein solcher/ der da wissentlich willens und vorsetzlich/ ihme selbst und anderen/ die Gedancken/ welche sie von Gott haben/ nehmen wil. In dem Zweyten/ Als ein solcher/ der da unwissend und ungemerckt/ auch unter dem Schein des wahren Christenthums/ ohne Gott in der Welt lebet*. Bremen: Herman Brauer 1689.

———. *Hallelujah, dat is, Godt in den sondaar verheerlijkt, ofte verhandelinge van het Grote Genadenwerk Godes in Christo*. Trans. Wilhelm Vos. Amsterdam: Jan Bouman, 1694.

———. *De dwaase atheist: ontdekt en van sijn dwaasheyd overtuygd*. Trans. Jodocus Fridericus Rappardus. Amsterdam: Jan Groenwoud, 1702.

Voetius, Gisbertus. *De praxi fidei*, in *Disputationes Selectæ*. Utrecht, 1642.

_____. "*Reedenvoeringe van de Nuttigheit der Akademien en Schoolen, mitsgaders der Wetenschappen en Konsten.*" Isaac le Long, *Hondert-Jaarige Jubel-Gedachtenisse der Academie van Utrecht.* Utrecht: M. Visch, 1736.

_____. *TA ΑΣΚΗΤΙΚΑ sive exercitia pietatis in usum juventutis academicæ nunc edita; addita est, ob materiæ affinitatem, Oratio de pietate cum scientia conjungenda, habita anno 1634.* Gorichem: Paul Vink, 1664.

Voetius, Gisbertus, and Johannes Hoornbeeck, *Disputaty van geestelicke verlatingen.* Dordrecht: Symon onder de Linde, 1667.

Witsius, Herman. *Twist des Heeren met sijn wyngaerdt.* Leeuwarden: Jacob Pieters Hagenær, 1669.

_____. *Excercitationes Sacræ in Symbolum quod Apostolorum dicitur.* Franeker: Johannes Gyselaar, 1689.

_____. *Miscellaneorum sacrorum libri IV.* Utrecht: Franciscus Halma, 1692.

_____. *Oefeningen over de Grondstukken van het Algemeyne Christelyke Geloove en het Gebed des Heeren.* Rotterdam: Daniel Beman, 1699.

_____. *De oeconomia Foederum Dei cum hominibus.* Herborn, Nassau: Johannes Nicolai Andreas, 1712.

_____. *Practicale godgeleertheid, of algemeene pligten der christenen ten opzigte van Godt, van Christus, van zich zelven en zyn naasten.* Trans. uit Latin. 2d. ed. Rotterdam: Nicolaas Topyn, 1732.

_____. *Theologiæ practicæ: quo veri ac interioris christianismi genuinum exercitium.* Groningen: Jacobus Sipkes, 1729.

_____. *The Apostles' Creed.* Translated from the Latin and followed with notes, critical and explanatory by Donald Fraser. 1823. Reprint, Escondido: The den Dulk Christian Foundation, 1993

Witte, Petrus de. *Wederlegginge der Socianiaensche Dwalingen.* 2 vols. Amsterdam: Arent van den Heuvel en Baltes Boeckholt, 1662.

Wittich, Christoph. *Dispvtatio Theologica de Stylo Scripturæ Quem adhibet cum de rebus naturalibus sermonem instituit.* Duisburg: Ravins, 1655.

_____. *Annotationes ad Renati Descartes Meditationes.* Dordrecht: Casparus, 1685.

Secondary Sources

Aa, Abraham Jacob van der. *Biographisch woordenboek: bevattend levensbeschrijvingen van zoodanige personen, die zich op eenigerlei wijze in ons vaderland hebben vermaard gemaakt.* 1852-1878. Reprint, Amsterdam: Israël, 1969.

Achelis, E. Chr. *Die Homiletik und die Katechetik des Andreas Hyperius.* Berlin, 1901.

Album Studiosorum Academiæ Rheno-Trajectinæ 1636-1886. Utrecht: Beijers en Van Boekhoven, 1886.

Althaus, P. *Die Prinzipien der deutschen reformierten Dogmatik im Zeitalter der aristotelischen Scholastik*. Leipzig: A. Deichertsche Verlagsbuchhandlung Werner Scholl, 1914.

Ames, William. *The Marrow of Theology*. Ed. John D. Eusden. Grand Rapids: Baker Books, 1997.

Armstrong, Brian G. *Calvinism and the Amyraut Heresy: Protestant Scholasticism and Humanism in Seventeenth-century France*. Madison: University of Wisconsin Press, 1969.

Arrenberg, Reinier. [1788]. *Naamregister van de Bekendste en Meest in Gebruik Zynde Nederduitsche Boeken*. Reprint, with an introduction by F. A. van Lieburg. Rotterdam: Lindenberg Boeken and Muziek B.V., 1999.

Asselt, Willem. J. van. *Amicitia Dei, een onderzoek naar de structuur van de theologie van Johannes Coccejus (1603-1669)*. Ede: Grafische vormgeving ADC, 1988.

_____. "Hebraica Veritas: zeventiende-eeuwse motieven voor de bestudering van het Hebreeuws door predikanten." *Kerk en Theologie* 46 (1995): 309-324.

_____. "Herwaardering van de gereformeerde scholastiek." *Kerktijd* 7 (1995): 1-12.

_____. E. Dekker, eds. *De Scholastieke Voetius, een luisteroefening aan de hand van Voetius' Disputationes Selectæ*. Zoetermeer: Boekencentrum, 1995.

_____. *Johannes Coccejus, Portret van een zeventiende-eeuws theoloog op oude en nieuwe wegen*. Heerenveen: Groen, 1997.

_____. P. L. Rouwendal, eds. *Inleiding in de Gereformeerde Scholastiek*. Zoetermeer: Boekencentrum, 1998.

_____. E. Dekker, eds. *Reformation and Scholasticism: An Ecumenical Enterprise, Texts and Studies in Reformation & Post-Reformation Thought*. Grand Rapids: Baker Academic, 2001.

_____. "Petrus van Mastricht." *Biographisch Lexicon voor de geschiedenis van het Nederlands Protestantisme*, ed. O. J. De Jong, F. J. R. Knetsch, D. Nauta, G. H. M. Posthumus Meyjes, and J. Trapman. Kampen: Kok, 2001.

_____. "Protestant Scholasticism: Some Methodological Considerations in the Study of its Development," *Nederlands Archief voor Kerkgeschiedenis*, 81, no. 3 (2001).

_____. "Puritanism Revisited: Een Poging tot Evaluatie." *Theologia Reformata* 44:3 (September, 2001): 221-232.

_____. *The Federal Theology of Johannes Cocceius*. Leiden-New York: Brill, 2001.

_____. "The Fundamental meaning of Theology: Archetypal and Ectypal Theology in Seventeenth-century Reformed Thought." *Westminster Theological Journal* 64 (2002): 322.

_____."Christus Sponsor. Een bijdrage tot de geschiedenis van het coccejanisme." *Kerk en Theologie*, 53 (2002), 108-124.

_____. "Natuurlijke theologie als uitleg van openbaring? Ectypische versus archetypische theologie in de zeventiende-eeuwse gereformeerde dogmatiek." *Nederland Theologisch Tijdschrift* 57 (April, 2003).

Backus, Irena D., and F. M Higman. *Théorie et practique de l'exégèse: Actes du troisieme Colloqui international sur l'histoire de l'exégèse biblique au XVIe siècle.* Geneve: Droz, 1990.

Backus, Irena, ed. *The Reception of the Church Fathers in the West.* 2 vols. Leiden: E. J. Brill, 1997.

Bakker, Nico T. *Miskende Gratie van Calvijn tot Witsius.* Kampen: J.H. Kok, 1991.

Barth, Karl. *Die Kirchliche Dogmatik.* Zürich: EVZ-Verlag, 1970.

Bavinck, Herman. *De Zekerheid des Geloofs.* Kampen: J. H. Kok, 1918.

_____. *Gereformeerde Dogmatik.* 4 vols. Kampen: Kok, 1921.

Beeke, Joel R. *Personal Assurance of Faith: English Puritanism and the Dutch "Nadere Reformatie": from Westminster to Alexander Comrie (1640-1760).* Ph.D. diss., Westminster Theological Seminary, 1988.

_____. *Assurance of Faith, Calvin, English Puritanism and the Dutch Second Reformation.* New York: Peter Lang, 1991.

_____. "The Dutch Second Reformation," *Calvin Theological Journal,* 28, no. 2 (1993): 298-327.

_____. "Gisbertus Voetius: Toward a Reformed Marriage of Knowledge and Piety." *Protestant Scholasticism, Essays in Reassessment,* ed. Carl R. Trueman and R. S. Clark. Carlisle: Paternoster Press, 1999.

_____. *Practical Puritanism.* Grand Rapids: RHB Publishers, 2004.

Bell, Michæl D. *Propter potestatem, scientiam, ac beneplacitum Dei: The Doctrine of the Object of Predestination in the Theology of Johannes Maccovius.* Th.D. diss., Westminster Theological Seminary, 1986.

Berg, J. v. d. "De Puriteinen en de Prediking." *Homiletica* 17e jrg., no. 3 (1958): 27-32.

Berkhof, L. *Principles of Biblical Interpretation.* Grand Rapids: Baker Books, 1950.

_____. *Systematic Theology,* with a new preface by Richard A. Muller. Grand Rapids: Eerdmans, 1996.

Biografisch lexicon voor de geschiedenis van het Nederlandse Protestantisme. 5 vols. Kampen: J. H. Kok, 1978-2001.

Bizer, Ernst. "Die reformierte Orthodoxie und der Cartesianismus," *Zeitschrift für Theologie und Kirche,* 3 (55)1958.

_____. *Reformed Orthodoxy and Cartesianism, Translating Theology into the Modern Age*, Ed. Rudolf Boltman *et al.*; translated by C. MacCormick. New York: Harper Torchbooks, 1960.

_____. *Frühorthodoxie und Rationalismus*. Zürich: EVZ Verlag, 1963.

Bland, Kalman P. "Issues ub Sixteenth-Century Jewish Exegesis." *The Bible in the Sixteenth Century*, Ed. David C. Steinmetz. Durham: Duke University Press, 1990.

Böhl, Eduard. *Von der Rechtfertigung durch den Glauben: ein Beitrag zur Rettung des protestantischen Cardinaldogmas*. Leipzig: K. Gustorff; Amsterdam: Scheffer, 1890.

_____. *The Reformed Doctrine of Jusification*. Transated by C. H. Riedesel. Grand Rapids: Wm. B. Eerdmans Publ. Co., 1946.

Boer, C. *Hofpredikers van Prins Willem van Oranje: Jean Taffin en Pierre Loyseleur de Villiers*. Den Haag: Historische Studie, 1951.

Bogue, Carl W. *Jonathan Edwards and the Covenant of Grace*. Cherry Hill, NJ: Mack Publishing Co., 1975.

Boot, I. *De allegorische uitlegging van het Hooglied*. Woerden: Zuiderduijn, 1971.

Born, Gernot, and Frank Kopatschek. *Die Alte Universität Duisburg 1655-1818*. Duisburg: Mercator Verlag, 1992.

Bösken, Walter. *Geschichte der Evangelischen Kirchengemeinde*. Magdeburg: Heinrichshofen, 1900.

Bray, Gerald. *Biblical Iinterpretation Past & Present*. Downers Grove: InterVarsity Press, 1996.

Bray, John S. *Theodor Beza's Doctrine of Predestination*. Nieuwkoop: B. De Graaf, 1975.

Brecht, Martin. "Pietismus." *Theologische Realenenzyklopädie*, ed. Gerhard Müller *et al.* Berlin/New York: Walter de Gruyter, 1996.

Bredt, Joh. Victor. *Die Verfassung der reformierten Kirche in Cleve-Jülich-Berg-Mark*. Ansbach: C. Brügel, 1938.

Brienen, T. *De Prediking van de Nadere Reformatie*. Amsterdam: T. Bolland, 1981.

_____. L. F. Groenendijk, W. J. op 't Hof, and C. J. Meeuse. "Nadere Reformatie, een poging tot begripsbepaling," *Documentatieblad Nadere Reformatie* VII (1983): 109-16.

_____. K. Exalto, J. van Genderen, C. Graafland, W. van 't Spijker, eds. *De Nadere Reformatie. Beschrijving van haar voornaamste vertegenwoordigers*. Zoetermeer: Boekencentrum, 1986.

_____. K. Exalto, J. van Genderen, C. Graafland, W. van 't Spijker, eds. *De Nadere Reformatie en het Gereformeerd Piëtisme*. Zoetermeer: Boekencentrum, 1989.

_____. K. Exalto, C. Graafland, B. Loonstra, W. van 't Spijker, eds. *Theologische aspecten van de Nadere Reformatie*. Zoetermeer: Boekencentrum, 1993.

_____. "Nadere Reformatie: opnieuw een poging tot begripsbepaling." *Documentatieblad Nadere Reformatie*, XXI (1995): 110-117.

Brink, G. van den, and M. Sarot, eds. *Hoe is Uw Naam? opstellen over de eigenschappen van God*. Kampen: Kok, 1995.

_____. *Understanding the Attributes of God* (New York: Peter Lang Publishing, 1999).

Broek, Roelof van den. *Hy leeret ende beschuttet: over het wapen en de zinspreuk van de Universiteit Utrecht*. Diesrede Utrecht, 1995.

Brummer, Vincent. *Over een persoolijke God gesproken*. Kampen: Kok, 1988.

Brunner, Emil. *Dogmatics*. London: Lutterworth Press, 1949.

Bullock, K. O'Dell. "Post-Reformation Protestant Hermeneutics." *Biblical Hermeneutics: A Comprehensive Introduction to Interpreting Scripture*, ed. Bruce Corley, Steve Lemke, and Grant Lovejoy. 2d ed. Nashville: Broadman & Holman Publishers, 2002.

Burnett, S. G. *The Christian Hebraism of Johann Buxtorf (1564-1629)*. Ph.D. diss., University of Wisconsin, 1990.

Burnett, Stephen G. *From Christian Hebraism to Jewish Studies Johannes Buxtorf (1564-1629) and Hebrew Learning in the Seventeenth Century*. Leiden: E. J. Brill, 1996.

Campen, M. van. "Het verbond en Israel bij Calvijn en de *Nadere Reformatie*." *Het joodse volk en het verbond*, ed. C. Boer. 's-Gravanhage: Boekencentrum, 1988).

Cramer, J. A. *De Theologische Faculteit te Utrecht ten tijde van Voetius*. Utrecht: Kemink en Zoon, 1932.

_____. *De Theologische Faculteit te Utrecht in de 18e en het begin der 19e Eeuw*. Utrecht: Broekhof, 1936.

Cremer, H. "Die christliche Leher von den Eigenschaften Gottes." *Beiträge zur Förderung christlicher Theologie*, ed. H. Cremer. Gütersloh Verlagshaus G. Mohn, 1897.

Danaher, Willam J. *The Trinitarian Ethics of Jonathan Edwards*. Ph.D. diss., Yale University, 2002.

Davies, Brian. "Classical Theism and the Doctrine of Divine Simplicity." *Language, Meaning and God: Essays in Honor of Herbert McCabe, OP*, ed. Brian Davies. London: Cassell, 1987.

Dibon, Paul. *La philosphie Néerlandaise au siècle d'or. Tome I: L'Enseignement philosophique dans les Universités néerlandaises à l'époque précartesienne (1575-1650)*. Amsterdam: Elsevier, 1954.

Diestel, L. *Studien zur Föderaltheologie, Jahrbücher für deutsche Theologie*, 10 (1865): 209-76.

Dijk, K. *Het Rijk der Duizend Jaren*. Kampen: J. H. Kok, 1933.

_____. *Om 't Eeuwig Welbehagen, De Leer der Praedestinatie*. Amsterdam: De Standaard, tweede druk, 1925.

Dodds, Elisabeth D. *Marriage to a Difficult Man. The Uncommon Union of Jonathan and Sarah Edwards.* Philadelphia: Westminster Press, 1971; reprint, Laurel: Audobon Press, 2003.

Duker, A. C. *Gisbertus Voetius.* 3 vols. Leiden: Brill, 1897-1915.

Eekhof, A. *Het Gereformeerde Protestantisme.* 's-Gravenhage: Nijhoff, 1915.

Elshout, Bartel. *The Pastoral and Practical Theology of Wilhelmus à Brakel.* Grand Rapids: Reformation Heritage Books, 1997.

Elwood, Douglas J. *The Philosophical Theology of Jonathan Edwards.* New York, Columbia University Press, 1960.

End, G. van den. *Guiljelmus Saldenus, een praktisch en irenisch theoloog uit de Nadere Reformatie.* Leiden: Groen en Zoon, 1991.

Evenhuis, R. B. *Ook dat was Amsterdam.* 5 vols. Amsterdam: Ten Have, 1971.

Fatio, O. *Méthod et Théologie. Lambert Daneau et les débuts de la scolastique réformée.* Geneva: University Press, 1976.

Faulenbach, H. "Die Anfänge der Pietismus bei den Reformierten in Deutschland." *Pietismus und Neuzeit: ein Jahrbuch zur Geschichte des neueren Protestantismus.* Göttingen: Vandenhoeck & Ruprecht, 1979.

_____. "Johannes Coccejus." *Orthodoxie und Pietismus,* ed. Martin Greschat. Stuttgart: W. Kohlhammer, 1982.

Feingold, Mordechai., ed. *The Influence of Petrus Ramus: Studies in Sixteenth and Seventeenth Century Philosophy and Sciences.* Basel: Schwabe, 2001.

Fesko, John V. *Diversity within the Reformed Tradition: Supra- and Infralapsarianism in Calvin, Dort, and Westminster.* Ph.D. diss., University of Aberdeen, 1999.

Feyl, O. "Die Viandrina und das östliche Europa." *Die Oder-Universität Frankfurt: Beiträge zu ihrer Geschichte,* ed. M. Knäbke, R. Kusch, and R. R. Targiel. Weimar: Hermann Böhlaus Nachfolge, 1983.

Fiering, Norman S. "Will and Intellect in the New England Mind." *The William and Mary Quarterly,* vol. xxxix, no. 4 (1972).

Frame, John M. *The Doctrine of God. A Theology of Lordship.* Phillipsburg: P&R Publishing, 2002.

Gawthrop, Richard L. *Pietism and the Making of Eighteenth-century Prussia.* Cambridge, UK: Cambridge University Press, 1993.

Geesink, W. *De Ethiek in de Gereformeerde Theologie.* Amsterdam: W. Kirchner, 1897.

Genderen, J. van. *Herman Witsius, bijdrage tot de kennis der Gereformeerde theologie.* 's-Gravenhage: Guido de Bres, 1953.

Gilmore, G. William, ed. *New Schaff-Herzog Encyclopedia of Religious Knowledge.* Grand Rapids: Baker Books, 1954.

Glasius, B. *Godgeleerd Nederland, Biographisch Woordenboek van Nederlandsche Godgeleerden.* Vol. 2. s-Hertogenbosch: Gebr. Muller, 1853.

Goebel, Max. *Geschichte des Christlichen Lebens in der Rheinisch-westphaelischen evangelischen Kirche.* Koblenz: Bädeker, 1849.

Goeters, Johann F. G. "Der reformierte Pietismus in Bremen und am Niederrhein im 18. Jahrhundert." *Der Pietismus im achtzehnten Jahrhundert,* ed. M.Brecht and K. Depperman. Göttingen: Vandenhoeck & Rupricht, 1995.

Goeters, W. *Die Vorbereitung des Pietismus.* Leipzig: J. C. Hinrichs'sche Buchhandlung, 1911.

Goudriaan, Aza. *Philosophische Gotteserkenntnis bei Suárez und Descartes, im Zusammenhang mit der niederlandischen reformierten Theologie und Philosophie des 17. Jahrhunderts.* Leiden-Boston-Koln: Brill, 1999.

_____. "Petrus van Mastrigt." *The Dictionary of Seventeenth and Eighteenth-Century Dutch Philosophers.* Bristol: Thoemmes Continuum, 2003.

Graafland, C. *De zekerheid van het geloof.* Wageningen: Veenman, 1961.

_____. "Jodocus van Lodenstein (1620-1676)." *De Nadere Reformatie, beschrijving van haar voornaamste vertegenwoordigers,* ed. T. Brienen, et al. Zoetermeer: Boekencentrum, 1986.

_____. "Gereformeerde Scholastiek VI, De invloed van de Scholastiek op de Nadere Reformatie," *Theologia Reformata,* XXX, no. 4 (1987).

_____. *Van Calvijn tot Barth, oorsprong en ontwikkeling van de leer der verkiezing in het Gereformeerd Protestantisme.* 's-Gravenhage: Boekencentrum, 1987.

_____. *Van Calvijn tot Comrie, oorspong en ontwikkeling van de leer van het verbond in het Gereformeerd Protestantisme.* Zoetermeer: Boekencentrum, 1996.

_____. *Bijbels en daarom Gereformeerd.* Kampen: Groot Gouderiaan, 2001.

Grandia, J. J. *Immutabilitas, necessitas et contingentia: speurtocht naar de structuur in de theologie van de vermaarde, godzalige, hoogh-geleerde heer, d'hr. Melchior Leydecker, S.S. Theol. Doctor en Professor tot Utrecht.* Master Thesis: Faculty of Theology of University of Utrecht, 1990.

Gravemeijer, E. C. *Leesboek over de Gereformeerde Geloofsleer.* Utrecht: H. Ten Hove, 1896.

Greijdanus, S. *Schrifbeginselen ter Schrifverklaring en Historisch overzicht over theorieën en wijzen van Schriftuitleggingen.* Kampen: Kok, 1946.

Gritisch, Eric W. *A History of Lutheranism.* Minneapolis: Fortress Press, 2002.

Groot, Aart de. "Jean de Labadie." *Orthodoxie und Pietismus.* Martin Greschat, ed. Stuttgart: W. Kohlhammer, 1982.

_____. Otto J. de Jong, eds. *Vier eeuwen Theologie in Utrecht.* Zoetermeer: Meinema, 2001.

Guelzo, Allen C. *Edwards on the Will*. Middletown, Conn.: Wesleyan University Press, 1989.

Haar, J. van der. ed. *Het Blijvende Woord 1*. Dordrecht: Gereformeerde Bijbelstichting, 1985.

_____. ed. *Het Blijvende Woord 2*. Leerdam: Gereformeerde Bijbelstichting, 1991.

Harinck, C. *De Schotse Verbondsleer, van Robert Rollock tot Thomas Boston*. Utrecht: De Banier, 1986.

Heinrich, Gerd. "Frankfurt an der Oder." *Theologische Realenzyklopadie*, ed. Gerhard Muller. Berlin, New York: de Gruyter, 1977, 1988.

Heppe, Heinrich. *Geschichte des Pietismus und der Mystik in der reformirten Kirche, namentlich der Niederlande*. Leiden: Brill, 1879.

_____. *Reformed Dogmatics*. Trans. G. T. Thomson. London: Allen & Unwin, 1950.

Hirsching, F. C. G., ed., *Historisch-literarisches Handbuch berühmter und denkwürdiger Personen, welche in dem 18. Jahrhundert gestorben sind*. Leipzig: 1794-1815.

Hoeksema, Herman. *Reformed Dogmatics*. Grand Rapids: Reformed Free Publishing Association, 1966.

Hoekstra, H. *Bijdrage tot de kennis en de beoordeling van het Chiliasme*. Kampen: Kok, 1903.

Hoekstra, T. *Gereformeerde Homiletiek*. Wageningen, 1935.

Hof, W. J. op 't. *Engelse piëtistische geschriften in het Nederlands, 1598-1622*. Rotterdam: Lindenberg, 1987.

Hofmeyr, J. W. *Johannes Hoornbeeck as Polemikus*. Kampen: J. H. Kok, 1975.

_____. Gerald J. Pillay, eds. *A History of Christianity in South Africa*, vol. 1. Pretoia: Haum, 1994.

Hog, James. *Wet en Evangelie*. Trans. E. Kuyk. Amsterdam: Kuyk, 1947.

Huisman, F. W. *Bibliografie van het gereformeerd Pietisme in Nederland to 1800*. Woudenberg: Uitgeverij Op Hoope, 2001.

Immink, F. G. *Divine Simplicity*. Kampen: J. H. Kok, 1987.

Israel, Jonathan I. *Radical Enlightenment, Philosophy and the Making of Modernity 1650-1750*. Oxford: Oxford University Press, 2001.

_____. *The Dutch Republic, Its Rise, Greatness, and Fall 1466-1806*. Oxford: Oxford University Press, 1998.

Itterzon, G. P. van. Het gereformeerde leerboek der 17^e eeuw "Synopsis Purioris Theolgiæ." 's-Gravenhage, 1931.

Jöcher, Christian Gottlieb, ed. *Allgemeines Gelehrten-Lexicon: Darinne die Gelehrte aller Stände*. 1750-1751. Reprint, Hildesheim: Olms, 1960.

Jou, Do-Hong. *Theodor Undereyck und die Anfänge des reformierten Pietismus.* Diss., Bochum, 1993.

Kaajan, H. "Mastricht (Petrus van)." *Christelijke Encyclopædie voor het Nederlansche volk,* ed. F. W. Grosheide and G. P. van Itterzon. 2d rev. ed. Kampen: Kok, 1959.

Kamin, Sarah. *Rashi's Exegetical Categorization: In respect to the distinction between Peshat and Derash.* Jerusalem: Arts, 1986.

Katchen, Aaron L. *Christian Hebraist and Dutch Rabbis. Seventeenth Century Apologetics and the Study of Maimonides' Mishneh Torah.* Cambridge, Mass.: Harvard University Press, 1984.

Kennedy, James C. *Jonathan Edwards in a Dutch context: History and Prophecy in 17th Century Holland.* Unpublished article, 1988.

Kennedy, John. *The Days of the Fathers in Ross-shire.* Inverness: Christian Focus Publications, 1979.

Kernkamp, G. W. *De Utrechtsche Universiteit 1637-1936.* 2 vols. Utrecht: A. Oosterhoek's Uitgevers Maatschappij, 1936.

Kersten, Hendrik. *De Gereformeerde Dogmatiek.* Utrecht: De Banier, 1988.

Kim, Jinyong. *Exegetical Method and Message of Peter Martyr Vermigili's Commentary on Judges.* Ph.D. diss., Southern Baptist Theological Seminary, 2002.

Klauber, Martin I. "Continuity and Discontinuity in post-Reformation Reformed Theology: An Evaluation of the Muller Thesis," *Journal of the Evangelical Theological Society* 33 (1990).

Knapp, Henry M. *Understanding the Mind of God: John Owen and Seventeenth-Century Exegetical Methodology.* Ph.D. diss., Calvin Theological Seminary, 2002.

Kneale, W. M., and J. Kneale. *The Development of Logic.* Oxford: Clarendon, 1962.

Knipscheer, H. "Mastricht." *Christelijke Encyclopedie,* ed. F. W. Grosheide and G. P. van Itterzon. J. Kok: Kampen, 1959.

Koning, Frederic J. *The Doctrine of Predestination in Scholastic Calvinism: an Evaluation of the Muller Thesis.* Th.M. thesis, Regent College, 1999.

Kristeller, Paul Oskar. *Renaissance Thought, The Classic, Scholastic and Humanist Strains.* Harper & Row: New York, 1961

_____. *Renaissance Thought and Its Sources.* New York: Columbia University Press, 1979.

Krull, A. F. *Jacobus Koelman.* Amsterdam: Ton Bolland, 1972.

Lachman, David C. *The Marrow Controversy.* Edinburgh: Rutherford House, 1988.

Lee, B. J. *Cocceius's Exegesis of the Epistle of the Hebrews.* Ph.D diss., Calvin Theological Seminary, 2002.

Lieburg, F. A. van. *De Nadere Reformatie in Utrecht ten tijde van Voetius. Sporen in de gereformeerde kerkeraadsacta.* Rotterdam: Lindenberg, 1989.

Linde, S. van der. "De betekenis van de Nadere Reformatie voor Kerk en Theologie." *Kerk en Theologie* 5 (1) (1954): 215-25.

_____. "De antropologie der Nadere Reformatie." *Waarheid, wijsheid en leven.* Kampen: Kok, 1956.

_____. "Mastricht, Petrus van." *Christelijke Encyclopaedie voor het Nederlansche volk,* ed. F. W. Grosheide. Vol. 4. Kampen: Kok, 1956.

_____. "Mystiek en bevinding in het Gereformeerd Protestantisme." *Mystiek en bevinding,* ed. G. Quispel *et al.* Kok: Kampen, 1976.

_____. *Opgang en Voortgang der Reformatie.* Amsterdam: Ton Bolland, 1976.

Lindroth, Sten. *A History of Uppsala University, 1477-1977.* Stockholm: Almqvist & Wiksell international, 1976.

Löhr, Rudolf, and Jan Pieter van Doorn, *Protokolle der Niederländisch-Reformierten Gemeinde in Köln von 1651-1803.* Köln: Rheinland Verlag Düsseldorf, 1971.

Loncq, G. J. *Historische schets der Utrechtsche Hoogeschool tot hare verheffing in 1815.* Utrecht: Beijers en Van Boekhoven, 1886.

Loonstra, B. *Verkiezing, verzoening, verbond : beschrijving en beoordeling van de leer van het "pactum salutis" in de gereformeerde theologie.* 's-Gravenhage : Boekencentrum, 1990.

Los, F. J. *Wilhelmus à Brakel,* introduced by W. van 't Spijker. Leiden: Groen en Zoon, 1991.

Lovelace, Richard F. *The American Pietism of Cotton Mather: Origins of American Evangelism.* Grand Rapids: Christian University Press, 1979.

Lubac, Henry de. *Exégèse médiévale: Les quatre sens de l'écriture.* 4 vols. Paris: Aubier, 1959-1964.

Maclean, Ian S. "The First Pietist: Jodocus van Lodensteyn." American Society of Church History, 2002.

Macleod, John. *Scottish Theology. In relation to Church History.* Edinburgh: Knox Press, 1974.

McDermott, Gerald R. *One Holy and Happy Society, the Public Theology of Jonathan Edwards.* University Park: Pennsylvania State University Press, 1992.

McGahagen, Thomas A. *Cartesianism in the Netherlands, 1639-1676; The New Science and the Calvinistic Counter-Reformation.* Ph.D. diss., University of Pennsylvania, 1976.

McKim Donald K. *Ramism in William Perkins' Theology.* New York: Lang, 1987.

_____. ed. *Encyclopedia of the Reformed Faith.* Louisville: Westminster, John Knox Press, 1992.

Miller, Perry. *The New England Mind, The Seventeenth Century.* Cambridge, Mass: Harvard Univeristy Press, 1982.

Milz, Joseph. *Die Universität Duisburg 1655-1818.* Duisburg: Buschmann, 1980.

Miskotte, K. H. *De praktische zin van de eenvoud Gods.* Amsterdam: Uitgeversmaatschappij Holland, 1945.

Moltmann, Jürgen. *Pradestination und Perseveranz: Geschichte und Bedeutung der reformierten Lehre* "de perseverantia sanctorum. "Neukirchen: Kreis Moers, Neukirchener Verlag, 1961.

_____."Zur Bedeutung des Petrus Ramus für Philosophie und Theologie im Calvinusmus." *Zeitschrift für Kirchengeschichte,* LXVII (1957).

Morimoto, Anri. *Jonathan Edwards and the Catholic Vision of Salvation.* University Park, Penn: Pennsylvania State University Press, 1995.

Morris, William S. *The Young Jonathan Edwards.* Brooklyn: Carlson Publishing, 1991.

Mueller, J. T. *La Doctrine Chrétienne.* La Petite Pierre: Éditions "Le Luthérien" Église Évangélique Luthérienne, 1956.

Mühlpfordt, G. "Die Oder-Universität 1506-1811." *Die Oder-Universität Frankfurt: Beiträge zu ihrer Geschichte,* eds. M. Knäbke, R. Kusch and R. R. Targiel. Weimar: Hermann Böhlaus Nachfolge, 1983.

Muller, Richard A. "*Duplex cognition dei* in the Theology of Early Reformed Orthodoxy." *Sixteenth Century Journal,* x. 2 (1979): 60.

_____. "Giving Direction to Theology: The Scholastic Dimension." *Journal of Evangelical Theological Studies,* 28/2 (1985): 183-193.

_____. *Dictionary of Latin and Greek Theological Terms, Drawn Principally from Protestant Scholastic Theology.* Grand Rapids: Baker Books, 1985.

_____. *Christ and the Decree.* Durham, NC: The Labyrinth Press, 1986.

_____. *Post-Reformation Reformed Dogmatics.* Vol. 1. Grand Rapids: Baker Books, 1987.

_____. *God, Creation, and Providence in the Thought of Jacobus Arminius. Sources and Directions of Scholastic Protestantism in the Era of Early Orthodoxy.* Grand Rapids: Baker Books, 1991.

_____. *The Study of Theology: From Biblical Interpretation to Contemporary Formulation.* Foundations of Contemporary Interpretation 7. Grand Rapids: Zondervan, 1991.

_____. *Post-Reformation Reformed Dogmatics.* Vol. 2. Grand Rapids: Baker Bookhouse, 1993.

_____. "The Covenant of Works and the Stability of Divine Law in Seventeenth-Century Reformed Orthodoxy: A Study in the Theology of Herman Witsius and Wilhelmus à Brakel." *Calvin Theological Journal,* 29, no. 1 (1994).

_____. "Calvin and the Calvinists: Assessing Continuities and Discontinuities between Reformation and Orthodoxy," parts 1 and 2. *Calvin Theological Journal* 30 (1995); 31 (1996).

_____. "Biblical Interpretations in the 16ᵗʰ & 17ᵗʰ Centuries." *Historical Handbook of Major Biblical Interpretations*, ed. Donald K. McKim. Downers Grove: InterVarsity Press, 1998.

_____. *The Unaccommodated Calvin*. Oxford, New York: Oxford University Press, 2000.

_____. "The Problem of Protestant Scholasticism—A Review and Definition." *Reformation and Scholasticism: An Ecumenical Enterprise, Texts and Studies in Reformation & Post-Reformation Thought*, eds. W. J. van Asselt and E. Dekker. Grand Rapids: Baker Academic, 2001.

_____. *After Calvin. Studies in the Development of a Theological Tradition*. Oxford: Oxford University Press, 2003.

_____. *Post-Reformation Reformed Dogmatics*. 4 vols. Grand Rapids: Baker Academic, 2003.

_____. John L. Thompson, eds. *Biblical Interpretation in the Era of Reformation, Essays Presented to David C. Steinmetz in Honor of His Sixtieth Birthday*. Grand Rapids: William B. Eerdmans Publishing Company, 1996.

Nebe, A. *Homiletische Portretten. Eene bijdrage tot de geschiedenis der predikunde en der evvangeliepredeking*. Utrecht, 1881.

Neele, Adriaan C. *A Study of Divine Spirituality, Simplicity, and Immutability in Petrus van Mastricht's Doctrine of God*. Th.M. thesis, Calvin Theological Seminary, 2002.

Niet, C. A de. *Gisbertus Voetius De Praktijk der Godzaligheid*. Utrecht: De Banier, 1996.

Nischan, Bodo. *Prince, People, and Confession: The Second Reformation in Brandenburg*. Philadelphia: University of Pennsylvania Press, 1994.

Oberman, H. A. *The Dawn of the Reformation*. Edinburgh: T & T Clark, 1986.

_____. *The Impact of the Reformation*. Grand Rapids: W. B. Eerdmans, 1994.

_____. ed. *Gregor von Rimini. Werk und Wirking bis zur Reformation*. Berlin, New York: Schuster, 1981.

Ong, W. J. *Ramus. Method and Decay of Dialogue: From the Art of Discourse to the Art of Reason*. Cambridge, Mass: Harvard University Press, 1958.

Oort, J. van. *De onbekende Voetius*. J. Van Oort, C. Graafland, A. De Groot, O.J. de Jong, eds. Kok:Kampen, 1989.

Otten, W. "Medieval Scholasticism: Past, Present and Future." *Nederlands Archief voor Kerkgeschiedenis*, no. 3 (2001): 81.

Pannenberg, Wolfhart. "The Appropriation of the Philosophical Concept of God as a Dogmatic Problem of Early Christian Theology." *Basic Questions in Theology: Collected Essays*. Trans. George H. Kehm. Philadelphia: Fortress Press, 1971.

Peare, C. Owens. *William Penn: A Biography*. Philadelphia: J. B. Lippincott Co., 1957.

Pieper, J. *Scholastik Gestalten und Probleme der mittelalterlichen Philosophie*. München: Kösel, 1960.

Pillay, G.J. J.W. Hofmeyr, eds. *Perspectives on Church History. An Introduction for South African Readers*. Pretoria: De Jager-Haum Publishers, 1991.

Plagge, Andreas. "YVON, Pierre." *Bautz Biographisch-Bibliographischen Kirchenlexikons*, Band XXII (2003).

Plantinga, Alvin. *Does God Have a Nature?* Milwaukee: Marquette University Press, 1980.

Plantinga Pauw, Amy. *The Supreme Harmony of All. The Trinitarian Theology of Jonathan Edwards*. Grand Rapids: William B. Eerdmans Publ. Co., 2002.

Poole, David N. J. *The History of the Covenant Concept from the Bible to Johannes Cloppenburgh: De foedere Dei*. San Francisco: Mellen Research University Press, 1992.

Post, S. D. *Pieter Boddært en Rutger Schutte, Pietistische dichters in de achttiende eeuw*. Houten: Den Hertog, 1995.

Preetz, Martin. *Die Deutsche Hugenottenkolonien: Ein Experiment des Merkantilismus*. Ph.D diss., Jena 1930.

Preus, Robert D. *The Theology of Post-Reformation Lutheranism*. St. Louis: CPH, 1972.

Prins, W. *Het Geweten. Een Exegetisch-Historisch-Dogmatisch Onderzoek*. Delft: W. D. Meinema, 1937.

Proost, P. *J. van Lodenstein*. Amsterdam: Brandt, 1880.

Rasmussen, Karl. *Glückstadt im Wandel der Zeiten*. Glückstadt: Augustin, 1966.

Ratschow, C. H. *Lutherische Dogmatik zwischen Reformation und Aufklärung*. 2 vol. Gütersloher Verlaghaus: Gütersloher, 1964-66.

Raup, W. *Biographisch-Bibliographisch Kirchenlexikon*. Bremen: Bautz, 2000.

Reuter, K. *Wilhelm Amesius, der führende Theologe des erwachenden reformierten Pietismus*. C. Brugle: Ansbach, 1940.

Reuver, A. de. "Wat is het eigene van de Nadere Reformatie?" *Documentieblad Nadere Reformatie*, XVIII (1994): 149-53.

_____. *Bedelen bij de Bron. Kohlbrugge's geloofsopvatting vergeleken met Reformatie en Nadere Reformatie*. Zoetermeer: Boekencentrum, 1992.

_____. *Verborgen omgang, Sporen van Spiritualiteit in Middeleeuwen en Nadere Reformatie*. Zoetermeer: Boekencentrum, 2002.

Rijk, L. M. de. *Middeleeuwse wijsbegeerte, Traditie en vernieuwing*. Assen/Amsterdam: Van Gorcum, 1977.

Ring, W. *Geschichte der Universität Duisburg*. Duisburg: Stadtarchiv, 1920.

Ritschl, A. *Geschichte des Pietismus*. Bonn : Marcus, 1880-1886.

Roden, Günter von. *Die Universität Duisburg*. Duisburg: Walter Braun Verlag, 1968.

Roessingh, P. H. *Jacobus Alting, een Bijbelsch Godgeleerde uit het midden der 17e eeuw.* Groningen: van Zweeden, 1864.

Rooden, P. T. van. *Theology, Biblical Scholarship and Rabbinical Studies in the Seventeenth Century: Constantijn L'Empereur (1591-1648) Professor of Hebrew and theology at Leiden.* Leiden: E. J. Brill, 1989.

_____. "Nut en nadeel van de biografie." *Tijdschrift voor Sociale Geschiedenis* 15 (1989): 66-73.

Rossouw, H. W. *Klaarheid en Interpretasie. Enkele probleemhistorische gesigtpunten in verband met die leer van die duidelikheid van die Heilige Skrif.* Amsterdam: Van Campen, 1963.

Ruler, A. A. van. "De bevinding in de prediking." *Theologisch Werk*, ed. A. A. Van Ruler. Nijkerk: Callenbach, 1971.

Rullmann, J. C. ed. *Kerk en Maatschappij in verleden en heden.* Amsterdam: N. V. Uitgevers-Maatschappij Enum, 1934.

Rutgers, William H. *Premillennialism in America.* Goes: Oosterbaan & Le Cointre, 1930.

Ryken, P. G. "Scottish Reformed Scholasticism." *Protestant Scholasticism, Essays in Reassessment*, ed. Carl R. Trueman, and R. Scott Clark. Carlisle: Paternoster, 1999.

Sarot, Marcel. *God, Passibility and Corporeality.* Kampen: Kok, 1992.

Saxby, T. S. *The Quest for the New Jerusalem, Jean de Labadie and the Labadists, 1610-1744.* Dordrecht, Boston: M. Nijhoff Publishers, 1987.

Schneppen, H. *Niederländische Universitäten und Deutsches Geistesleben von der Gründung der Universität Leiden bis ins späte 18. Jahrhundert.* Münster: Aschendorfsche Verlagsbuchhandlung, 1960.

Schrenk, G. *Gottesreich und Bund im Älteren Protestantismus vornehmlich bei Johannes Coccejus.* 1923. Reprint, Darmstadt: Wissenschaftliche Buchgesellschaft, 1967.

Schuringa, Gregory D. *Embracing* Leer *and* Leven: *The Theology of Simon Oomius in the context of the* Nadere Reformatie *Orthodoxy.* Ph.D. diss., Calvin Theological Seminary, 2003.

Seeberg, Reinhold. *Lehrbuch der Dogmengeschichte.* Leipzig: Erlangen, 1923.

Sepp, C. *Het Godgeleerd Onderwijs in Nederland gedurende de 16e en 17e eeuw.* Leiden: De Breuk en Smits, 1873-1874.

Sesboüé, Bernard, and Joseph Wolinski. *Histoire des Dogmes: Le Dieu du Salut.* Paris: Desclée, 1994.

Shim, Jai-Sung. *Biblical Hermeneutics and Hebraism in the Early Seventeenth Century as Reflected in the Work of John Weemse.* Ph.D. diss., Calvin Theological Seminary, 1998.

Skalnik, James V. *Ramus and Reform: University and Church at the End of the Renaissance.* Kirksville, Mo.: Truman State Univ. Press, 2002.

Sluis, Jacob van. "De Cartesiaanse Theologie van Herman Alexander Roëll." *Vier Eeuwen Theologie in Utrecht*, eds. A. De Groot and O. J. de Jong. Zoetermeer: Meinema, 2001.

_____. *Herman Alexander Röell*. Leeuwarden: Fryske Akademy, 1988.

Spijker, W. van 't. "Teellincks opvatting van de meschelijke wil." *Theologia Reformata* VII, no. 3 (1964).

Sprunger, Keith L. "Ames, Ramus, and the Method of Puritan Theology." *Harvard Theological Review*, 59 (Apr., 1966): 148-51.

_____. *Dutch Puritanism: A History of English and Scottish Churches of the Netherlands in the Sixteenth and Seventeenth Centuries*. Leiden: E. J. Brill, 1982.

_____. *The Learned Doctor William Ames*. Chicago: University of Illinois Press, 1972.

Strengholt, L. *Bloemen in Gethsemane, Verzamelde studies over de dichter Revius*. T. Bolland: Amsterdam, 1976.

Steenblok, C. *Voetius en de Sabbat*. Gouda: Gereformeerde Pers, 1975.

Steinmetz, David C. "The Superiority of Pre-Critical Exegesis." *TTs* 37 (1980): 27-38. Reprinted in *A Guide to Contemporary Hermeneutics*, ed. Donald K. McKim. Grand Rapids: Wm. Eerdmans, 1986: 65-77.

Stephens, Bruce M. *God's Last metaphor: The Doctrine of the Trinity in New England Theology*. Chico: Scholars Press, 1981.

Stoeffler, F. Ernest. *The Rise of Evangelical Pietism*. Leiden: Brill, 1971.

Story, Robert H., ed. *The Church of Scotland, past and present: its history, its relation to the law and the state, its doctrine, ritual, discipline, and patrimony*. London: William Mackenzie, 1890.

Symongton, Andrew. *Introductory Lecture on the Principles of the Second Reformation*. Glasgow: Henderson, 1841.

Tanis, James. *Dutch Calvinistic Pietism in the Middle Colonies, A Study in the Life and Theology of Theodorus Jacobus Frelinghuysen*. The Hague: M. Nijhoff, 1967.

Targiel, R. R. "Nachbetrachtung einer Austellung." *Die Oder-Universität Frankfurt: Beiträge zu ihrer Geschichte, ed.* M. Knäbke, R. Kusch, and R. R. Targiel. Weimar: Hermann Böhlaus Nachfolge, 1983.

Tellingen, A. E. van. *Het leven en enige aspecten uit de theologie van Petrus van Mastricht (1630-1706)*. Master Thesis: Faculty of Theology of University of Utrecht, 2003.

Tholuck, A. *Das akademische Leben des siebzehnten Jahrhunderts mit besondere Beziehung auf die protestantisch-theologischen Fakultäten Deutschlands*. Halle: E. Anton, 1854.

_____. *Geschichte des Rationalismus: Erste Abteilung, Geschichte des Pietismus und des ersten Stadium der Aufklärung*. Berlin: E. Anton, 1865.

_____. *Vorgeschichte des Rationalismus*. Berlin: E. Anton, 1861.

Traas, C. *Het leven en werk van Abraham Boekholt (1664-1709). Boekenverkoper te Amsterdam.* Amsterdam: VU, 1987.

Trueman, Carl R. *The Claims of Truth: John Owen's Trinitarian Theology.* Carlisle: Paternoster Press, 1998.

Trueman, Carl R., and R. Scott Clark, eds. *Protestant Scholasticism: Essays in Reassessment.* Carlisle: Paternoster, 1999.

Valen, L. J. van. *Gelijk de Dauw van Hermon.* Zwijndrecht: Het Anker, tweede druk, 1982.

Verbeek, Th. H. M. "Descartes and the problem of atheism: the Utrecht Crisis." *Nederlands archief voor kerkgeschiedenis,* 71 (1991): 211-223.

_____. "J. Koelman en de filosofie zijner dagen." *Documentatieblad Nadere Reformatie,* 20 (1996), 62-71.

_____. *Descartes and the Dutch.* Carbondale, Ill.: Southern Illinois University Press, 1992.

Verboom, W. *De catechese van de Reformatie en de Nadere Reformatie.* Amsterdam: Buijten & Schipperheijn, 1986.

Verkruijsse, J. "Holland 'gedecideerd'. Boekopdrachetn in Holland in de 17e eeuw." *Holland regional-historisch tijschrift,* 23 (1991): 225-42.

Vermeij, Rienk. *The Calvinist Copernicans. The reception of the new astronomy in the Dutch Republic 1575-1750.* Amsterdam: KNAW, 2002.

Vermigili, Peter Martyr. *Commentary on the Lamentations.* Trans. and ed. with introduction notes by Daniel Shute. Kirksville, Mo.: Sixteenth-Century Essays and Studies, 2002.

Visscher, H. *Guilielmus Amesius.* Haarlem: J. M. Stap, 1894.

Visser, Derk. "Van Mastricht, Petrus (1630-1706)." *Encyclopedia of the Reformed Faith,* ed. Donald K. McKim. Louisville: Westminster/John Knox Press, 1992.

Vlastuin, W. van. *De Geest van Opwekking, Een onderzoek naar de leer van de Heilige Geest in de opwekkingstheologie van Jonathan Edwards (1703-1758).* Heerenveen: Groen, 2001.

Vliet, Jan van. *William Ames: Marrow of the Theology and Piety of the Reformed Tradition.* Ph.D. diss., Westminster Theological Seminary, 2002.

Vos, A. "Voetius als reformatorisch wijsgeer." *De onbekende Voetius,* ed. J. van Oort Kampen: Kok, 1989.

_____. *Kennis en Noodzakelijheid.* Kampen: Kok, 1981.

Vrijer, M. J. A. de. *Ds. Bernardus Smytegelt en zijn "Gekrookte Riet."* Vianen: De Banier, 1968.

_____. *Henricus Regius, een 'Cartesiaansch' hoogleeraar aan de Utrechtsche Hoogeschool.* 's-Gravenhage: M. Nijhoff, 1917.

Wallace, Dewey D. *Puritans and Predestination: Grace in English Protestant Theology, 1525-1695*. Chapel Hill: University of North Carolina Press, 1982.

Wallmann, Johannes. *Der Pietismus*. Göttingen: Vandehoeck & Ruprecht, 1990.

Weber, H. E. *Reformation, Orthodoxie und Rationalismus*. 3 vols. Gütersloh: Bertelsmann, 1937-1951.

Williams, James E. Jr. *An evaluation of William Perkins' Docrtine of Predestination in the Light of John Calvin's Writings*. Th.M. thesis, Dallas Theolgical Seminary, 1986.

Woude, C. van der. *Op de Grens van Reformatie en Scholastiek*. Kampen: Kok, 1964.

Ypey, A. *Algemeene Kerkelijke Geschiedenis*. Haarlem: F.Bohn, 1816.

_____. I. J. Dermout. *Geschiedenis der Nederlandsche Hervormde Kerk*. 2 vols. Breda: W. van Bergen en Co., 1819, 1822.

Zee, G. van der. *Vaderlandse Kerkgeschiedenis van de Hervormding tot heden*. J. H. Kok: Kampen, 1930.

Index

Curriculum Vitae

De schrijver van deze studie werd geboren op 14 Oktober 1960 te Rotterdam. Na de middelbare school studeerde hij biochemie. Vervolgens was hij internationaal werkzaam in de pharmaceutische en biotechnologische industrie als onderzoeker en bestuurder. In 1989 is hij overgestapt naar de informatie-technologie industrie, waar hij werkzaam was als bestuurder in Noord- en Zuid-Amerika, woonachtig in de Verenigde Staten van Amerika. In 1999 begon hij met zijn theologische studie, die hij afrondde met een Master of Theological Studies (2001) en *cum laude* Theological Master (historische-theologie) (2002) aan Calvin Theological Seminary, Grand Rapids, USA. Na zijn positie als decaan en theologisch hoogleraar aan het Farel Reformed Theological Seminary te Montréal, Canada en als deeltijd-predikant van de l'Église Reformée du Québec, is hij thans deeltijd-predikant van de Nederduitsch Hervormde Kerk van Afrika, Pretoria (Eben Haëzer gemeente) en als wetenschappelijk medewerker voor 'na-reformatorisch onderzoek' verbonden aan de Universiteit van Pretoria, Zuid Afrika. Tevens is hij betrokken bij de ontwikkeling van internet-gebaseerd (theologisch) onderwijs. De schrijver is gehuwd met Kornelia Klop; zij hebben zes kinderen, Ruth, Matthew, Hadassah, Deborah, Joël and Salóme.

The writer of this study was born October 14, 1960 at Rotterdam and studied biochemistry. Subsequently, he worked internationally in the pharmaceutical and biotechnology industry as researcher and manager. In 1989 he joined the information-technology industry in a management function and worked in North and South America while residing in the United Stated of America. In 1999 he begun with the study of theology, which he completed with a Master of Theological Studies (2001) and *cum laude* Theological Master (historical-theology) (2002) of Calvin Theological Seminary, Grand Rapids, USA. Following a position as dean and professor of theology at Farel Reformed Theological Seminary, Montréal, Canada and part-time minister of l'Église Reformée du Québec, he serves currently as part-time pastor the Eben-Haëzer congregation of the Nederduitsch Hervormde Kerk of Africa, Pretoria and as scholar for Post-reformation Reformed studies at the University of Pretoria, South Africa. In addition, he is involved in a project for web-based (theological) education. The writer is married with Kornelia Klop; they have six children, Ruth, Matthew, Hadassah, Deborah, Joël and Salóme.